M000004194

"This is a book that no *cheekako* or longtime Alaskan planning a fishing trip here should be without."

—*Alaska Magazine*

"It is hard to imagine a more comprehensive treatise on the opportunities awaiting anglers in the 49th state."

—*Travel Weekly*

"Have you often caught yourself salivating over those behemoths in Alaska fishing brochures? Drool no further. Pick up a copy of **Alaska Fishing: The Complete Guide** and start planning the complete trip.

"This book has it all, from tips on guides and lodging to breakouts covering ranges, life history, fishing techniques (freshwater and brine), and hot spots for 13 popular sport fish.

"The bulk of the book—and where it really shines—is its region-by-region synopses, each highlighting dozens of lakes, rivers, bays, straights, or entire water systems."

"Our rating: ☆☆☆☆"

—*L.A. Daily News*

"Now one comprehensive volume gives you all the information you'll need to catch five species of Pacific salmon, plus rainbow and cutthroat trout, grayling, steelhead, halibut, lake trout, pike, sheefish, and charr. A must for Alaska-bound anglers."

—*Sports Afield*

Text copyright © 1997 by René Limeres and Gunnar Pedersen
Maps copyright © 1997 by Foghorn Press
All rights reserved by Foghorn Press

This book may not be reproduced in full or in part without the written permission of the publisher, except for use by a reviewer in the context of a review. Inquiries and excerpt requests should be addressed to:

Foghorn Press
Rights Department
340 Bodega Avenue
Petaluma, CA 94952
foghorn@well.com

To order individual books, visit the Foghorn Press Web site at www.foghorn.com, or call 1-800-FOGHORN (364-4676) or (707) 773-4260. Foghorn Press titles are distributed to the book trade by Publishers Group West, based in Emeryville, California. To contact your local sales representative, call 1-800-788-3123.

Although the authors and publisher have made every effort to ensure that the information in this book was correct at press time, the authors and publisher do not assume and hereby disclaim any liability to any party for any loss, damage, or potential travel disruption caused by errors or omissions, whether such errors or omissions result from negligence, accident, or any other cause.

Library of Congress ISSN Data:
August 1997
Alaska Fishing
The Complete Guide to Hundreds of Prime Fishing Spots on Rivers, Lakes, and the Coast
Second Edition
ISSN: 1079-6916

Leave No Trace, Inc., is a program dedicated to maintaining the integrity of outdoor recreation areas through education and public awareness. Foghorn Press is a proud supporter of this program and its ethics.

The Foghorn Press Commitment

Foghorn Press is committed to the preservation of the environment. We promote Leave No Trace principles in our guidebooks.

Printed in the United States of America

ALASKA FISHING

René Limeres and
Gunnar Pedersen

with contributions by
Kenneth T. Alt, Thomas Cappiello, Gary Souza, Steve Wottlin

Foghorn Press

BOOKS BUILDING COMMUNITY™

52095

9 780935 701517

Editor in Chief   *Donna Leverenz*

Editor   *Howard Rabinowitz*

Production Coordinator   *Kyle Morgan*

Production Assistant   *Mark Aver*

Cover Photo   *René Limeres*

Illustrations: *Thomas Cappiello, William Hickman, René Limeres, Mark Whitfield*

Interior photographs:
Page 11—Gunnar Pederson
Page 166—Paul Allred
Page 202—René Limeres

Preface

This book joins quite a few others on the subject, written over the years by authors of varying backgrounds. Each has attempted, in his or her own way, to describe the remarkable and vast sportfishing opportunities in the state of Alaska. More subcontinent than state, with diverse terrain, extreme weather, and a bewildering variety of fish species, the Last Frontier places very real limitations on any one writer's experience and resources, a fact which must be taken into account when reading most of the guides currently available.

The idea for this project began a while back with a dream of creating a complete reference on Alaska fishing, written collaboratively by a diverse group of guides, outdoor writers, biologists, and hard-core sport anglers. Our goal was to compile a comprehensive, insightful, and (hopefully) flavorful guide that can be of use to readers of all backgrounds.

Like others before us, we gathered our baseline information from the research data and experiences of personnel within the Alaska Department of Fish and Game and other agencies, both state and federal. However, we also sought out the expert input of many guides, outfitters, air taxi operators, and lodge owners, for, as fellow members of this profession, most of us know well (and cherish) the unique and abundant opportunities for "hands on" experience that our work allows. In the course of a typical summer season, we witness hundreds of angling encounters, under every condition imaginable, in a dozen or more watersheds, and for a whole gamut of species. This experience—along with that of biologists, local fishers, river runners, and others in the field—represents a significant component of knowledge on the subject.

In developing this book, we departed somewhat from the standard approach to the subject. We begin with a rundown of the important Alaska sport species—including their distributions, life histories and habits, popular fishing methods, and the best sportfishing spots. Then we focus on Alaska's six major geographical regions and their sport angling highlights, with specific information for more than 250 of the state's best rivers, lakes, and marine areas. With regional analyses of conditions, highlights, weather, access, and available services, along with appendices and a fully cross-referenced index, this guidebook, to our knowledge, is the first of its kind to attempt a thorough and integrated account of Alaska and its remarkable fishing. We hope you find it enjoyable and useful.

—René Limeres and
Gunnar Pedersen

Alaska Fishing
The Complete Guide to Hundreds of Prime Fishing
Spots on Rivers, Lakes, and the Coast

Contents

Alaska Overview Map

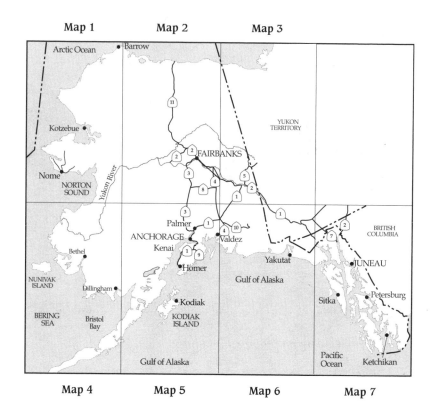

Map 1   Map 2   Map 3

Map 4   Map 5   Map 6   Map 7

How to Use This Book

This book is a comprehensive guide for anyone seeking greater knowledge on angling in Alaska, regardless of previous fishing experience. The book's organization allows you to access detailed information on the state's six major fishing regions, plus comprehensive chapters on the major Alaskan sport species and how to fish them. You can locate your ideal Alaskan fishing spot in three ways:

1. If you know the name of the area you'd like to fish (bay, inlet, lake, river system, etc.), use the index beginning on page 421 to find the corresponding page.

2. If you'd like to travel to a particular part of Alaska and want to find out what fishing is available there, turn to the regional chapters to read about your area.

The state is divided into six separate areas, more or less following the standard physiographic "provinces" recognized by the state's geographers, according to terrain, climate, and conditions:

- **Arctic:** The north slope of the Brooks Range to the Arctic Ocean, from Point Hope to the Canadian border, pages 167–180.

- **Northwest:** Norton Sound drainages, including the lower Koyukuk and western Brooks Range lakes (southern slope), pages 181–202.

- **Interior:** The central part of the state between the Alaska and Brooks Ranges, bounded by the Middle Fork of the Koyukuk River on the west, pages 203–224.

- **Southwest:** The Alaska Peninsula and Aleutians, Bristol Bay, and lower Kuskokwim and Yukon River drainages, pages 225–264.

- **Southcentral:** Gulf Coast drainages from Cape Saint Elias and Shelikof Strait, including the Kenai Peninsula and Kodiak and Afognak Islands, pages 265–324.

- **Southeast:** The Panhandle from Dixon Entrance to Icy Bay (and coastal streams to Cape Suckling), pages 325–390.

3. If you're interested in a specific type of sportfishing and want to find out which geographic regions provide good fishing for a particular species, turn to the chapter on the Alaskan species you want to fish. Major sportfishing locations are listed in the final pages of each chapter.

In the Alaskan Species section of the book, we emphasize the 14 major species of importance to anglers, and have omitted or only casually referred to other fish of lesser interest, including burbot, whitefish, and lingcod. This does not imply that you'll find no opportunities to fish these species in Alaska. Readers who want more information on any of the minor sport species available in Alaska should contact the Alaska Department of Fish and Game (see the Resources appendix on page 409 for the address and phone number).

The species chapters can be an invaluable resource for trip planning. They feature tips on the best locations and months for fishing certain species, as well as many other helpful details. For each species, we provide a list of top trophy specimens and the locations they were captured; this information is compiled from over 30 years of records gathered by the Alaska Department of Fish and Game under their annual Trophy Fish Awards program. A "quick reference" section on the major sport fish species and descriptions of important Alaskan fly patterns is provided at the end of the book for further reference.

- **Maps:** Overview maps are provided at the beginning of each regional section, along with locations of the areas detailed. In addition, the U.S. Geological Survey map references (topographic contour 1:63,360 or 1:250,000 maps) are given for each listing; addresses for purchasing USGS maps are given on page 409 in the Resources appendix.

- **Highlights:** We describe the fishing at each destination from fair to excellent, using a variety of adjectives, such as "outstanding," "superb," "great," "decent," and "good" that hopefully will be meaningful and not too subjective for most folks. Keep in mind that this is Alaska, where even "fair" fishing can far surpass anything most people are used to in home waters.

- **Species:** In our destination descriptions, we list the major species of interest that occur in fishable numbers. Species that are listed in italics are found only infrequently.

- **Contacts:** Each listing contains local contacts for information and services. Included are lodging, air taxi services, guides and outfitters, and state and government organizations. When planning your trip, please consult these contacts for the latest conditions and up-to-date information.

About River Running

In our descriptions of rivers, we frequently give information pertaining to their suitability for floating by raft, canoe, or kayak, using the following international scale for rating degree of difficulty:

- **Class I:** Moving water with some riffles and waves, but few or no obstructions. Beginning river runners can negotiate it, usually with no problem.

- **Class II:** Small rapids with standing waves up to three feet high; clear channels can be negotiated without

scouting, with some maneuvering required. It is recommended that boaters have some river experience.

- **Class III:** Rapids with high waves, some irregular, capable of swamping a canoe or other open craft. Some passages may require scouting or difficult maneuvering. Intermediate white-water skills are required for safe passage.

- **Class IV:** Long, difficult rapids and turbulent waters. Passage may be severely restricted and complex maneuvers are required. Scouting and "lining" boats from shore is commonly required. Safe passage by canoe or small open boat is generally not possible. This water is for boaters with a high level of white-water experience only.

- **Class V:** Extremely difficult and hazardous white-water, with long and/or violent rapids, chutes and difficult passages, requiring complex maneuvers, scouting, "lining," and even portages. There are significant hazards to life in the event of a mishap, with difficult rescue conditions. Expert white-water skills are required.

- **Class VI:** Extreme white water encountered usually only in floodwater conditions and rare locations. Dangerous and life threatening, this water is for top-notch experts only.

The above scale is a very general rating applied to rivers during normal water levels. Conditions can change dramatically and swiftly on most Alaskan rivers, so caution is the rule for safety.

Alaskan Fishing Ethics

Familiarize yourself with current Alaska fishing regulations and obey all bag limits and restrictions. Report all violators: call 1-800-478-3377.

Respect the rights of property owners along rivers, streams, and lakes by contacting them, if possible, before you trespass on their lands. Some of their addresses are given in the destination descriptions.

Keep only the fish you intend to eat or take for mounting; practice proper catch-and-release techniques whenever possible. See the appendix detailing catch-and-release fishing methods on page 413.

Be courteous to other anglers and respect their right to privacy.

Tread lightly—use minimum impact camping techniques and please don't litter!

Use the information given for locations only as a general guide for trip planning. Conditions vary from year to year, even from month to month, on many of Alaska's waters. Consult with local sources before making any final trip arrangements.

Check with the Alaska Department of Fish and Game for the latest regulation information and any new restrictions that may apply.

Magnificent scenery, productive streams, and easy access are the highlights of many Alaska fishing locations.

Introduction

Alaska has been a challenge and source of wonder to generations of adventurous people. Every school kid knows that the 49th state is more than twice the size of Texas, and has America's tallest mountains, deepest wilderness, largest animals, and most frightening extremes of weather. It also has a coastline longer than that of all the other states combined, along with some of the wettest, iciest, and snowiest places on the continent. But what's most important—to anglers, anyway—is the abundant water that all this snow, ice, and rain give rise to: Countless rivers, streams, creeks, lakes, and ponds drain the state's prodigious runoff, in an amount that yearly equals or surpasses the combined annual surface water flow of all the states east of the Mississippi!

Much of this water is glacially silted, too swift or shallow, or otherwise inhospitable to fish. But enough of it is perfectly suited, by its location, size, purity, and the grace of Nature, to support an abundance and diversity of cold-water game fish species that exists nowhere else on Earth. Five species of Pacific salmon—king, sockeye, chum, silver, and pink—along with rainbow, cutthroat, and steelhead trout, charr, arctic grayling, northern pike, and sheefish, all await the angler in unheard-of numbers.

This staggering amount and variety of water, and the amazing sportfishing it holds, is the essence of *Alaska Fishing*. For the angler contemplating a vacation in Alaska, knowing what species are available and when, where, and how they may best be encountered, not to mention the logistics involved, has always been the most daunting aspect of the planning process, even for longtime Alaska anglers. This book can help readers sort through the confusing claims, blatant hype, and gray areas that exist in the popular literature and tourist publications.

As a fishing destination, Alaska stands apart from all others. It's still very wild, with most of its better waters free from the intrusion of hatcheries. The occurrence of species here follows the broad, uniform pattern of Nature, instead of the random and artificial distributions seen most elsewhere. This guide should help you develop an understanding of this natural distribution so that you can better plan and enjoy your fishing.

Keeping in mind that a fishing vacation in the Last Frontier encompasses much more than just catching fish, we hope readers will use this guide as a starting point, an invitation to explore the most awesome destination that exists for sport anglers. A timeless land, where the frantic pace and contrived needs of the human world are lost in vast distances and magnificent, untouched landscapes, Alaska is a refreshing antidote to modern civilization. And once you've experienced the breadth and beauty of the land and its fantastic sportfishing, life will never seem the same. Another trip and another river always beckons. May it always be so.

Getting Ready To Go

Alaska Trip Planning

In today's busy world, with time and money at a premium, folks are demanding the very best in service and value from the travel industry, and Alaska's sportfishing business is no exception (just ask any guide or lodge owner). Yet, despite the best intentions of everyone involved in the planning and delivery of the great Alaska adventure—the visitor information people, travel agents, lodge owners, guides and outfitters, air taxi services, not to mention the folks footing the bill—every summer brings its share of disappointment and frustration, when fishing trips somehow don't measure up to expectations.

A certain measure of blame lies with the industry itself, which sometimes fuels unreal expectations with hyped-up literature, glossy brochures, or big talk over the phone. Alaskan tourism is a competitive business, and many in the industry are pressed to "make the sale," even if they have to bend the truth a little. But misrepresenting services (and fishing potential) just to snare peoples' business is plain fraud, not much different than the shams of the proverbial snake-oil salesman. Fortunately, the overwhelming majority of people involved in Alaska tourism are sincere, dedicated professionals who would just as soon poke themselves in the eye than sell you a trip or service you won't be satisfied with.

As a consumer, however, the ultimate responsibility for getting the kind of Alaskan fishing vacation you deserve is yours alone. No one can read your mind or know your heart to deliver the arrangements and the fishing that are right for you. Like shopping for a car or a home, planning a successful Alaska fishing vacation is a process that begins with identifying what you want, surveying the available market, asking some serious questions, "kicking some tires," and then bargaining hard with a few prospective businesses. The end result is a signed contract and two satisfied parties—hopefully. What follows are some fundamental points to keep in mind that can make the whole process more efficient and ultimately more satisfying.

Knowledge Is Power

The fact that you've got this book in your hands shows that you recognize the importance of educating yourself before planning your fishing vacation in a place as diverse and immense as Alaska. Read this book (and any other similar publications you can find) and pore through the sporting literature for material on Alaska's fishing. Libraries, bookstores, sport shops, fishing clubs, and the Internet are obvious sources for information. Consult the public agencies listed in this book for trip planning materials they may have to offer (see the Resources appendix on page 409). You should also try to talk to folks who have fished Alaska before, and make a point of attending one of the winter trade shows in the major cities to meet and chat with lodge owners, guides, air taxi services, and outfitters. You may even find some worthy television shows on your local channels or cable. The more general background you have on Alaska and its fishing opportunities, the better you can decide exactly what you want to do, how and where you want to do it, and with whom. Knowledge is the ultimate trip insurance.

Seek and Find

Once you have a fairly good idea of the what, when, and where of the fishing you're after, you can begin to narrow your choices and save tons of time, instead of shooting in the dark. There are services and facilities that cater to every whim and desire imaginable as far as fishing in Alaska goes, and usually you can eliminate quickly the ones that don't have what you're after with preliminary contact by phone, mail, or in person. Magazines, vacation planners, travel agencies, sportfishing organizations, trade shows, and word-of-mouth are the standard avenues for finding organizations that specialize in the kind of Alaskan sportfishing you want to experience.

Ask Questions

It's critical to ask the questions that need to be answered in your selection process. Make a list of the important things you want from your vacation—species and type of fishing desired, preferred accommodations, meal requirements, budget constraints, etc.—and work through each and every item as you consider possibilities. When talking to lodge owners, guides, air taxi services, and outfitters, don't be shy. Get satisfactory answers to all your questions and don't consider doing business with anyone who hesitates to give you the facts or tries to intimidate you. Most reputable people in the business enjoy talking with someone who knows enough to ask intelligent questions, and is not put off by inquisitiveness or meticulousness with details. Remember these pointers when you deal with people in the industry:

• Are you talking with an owner, manager, guide, booking agent, or someone else? It's important to deal directly, whenever possible, with the people who will be personally responsible for your arrangements, as they are best capable of answering any questions or concerns you may have, and will be most committed to seeing that you get what you've bargained for.

• Make sure you discuss exactly what is to be provided in the way of transportation, accommodations, meals, guide service, equipment, licenses, and gratuities. Don't assume anything. If you're considering a stay at a fishing lodge, will you be fishing locally or making trips by boat or plane to various locations? A lodge that does daily fly outs charges considerably more but isn't necessarily a better value, particularly if it's located in an area noted for bum weather where you can't fly for two or three days each week. (Be sure and inquire about the kind of fishing you can expect around the lodge!) Ask about the liability insurance provided, particularly if you're going to be engaged in hazardous activities like daily flights in small planes or white-water rafting. And if you're planning a trip with some of your fishing buddies, see if a group discount is offered.

• Be certain to explain exactly what kind of fishing you're after and the services, accommodations and prices you had in mind. See how closely what they have to offer matches what you want. Be prepared to compromise somewhat.

• Listen and learn from each and every person you contact along the way about local fishing conditions, available services, and accommodations. Be open to suggestions and advice about your trip planning from those who are in the know.

Get References

As part of the narrowing down process, be sure to ask your prospective guide, outfitter, or lodge owner for a list of former clients to contact for references. Any operator who balks at this request should be dismissed immediately from consideration. Some of the questions to ask former clients are:

• Did you receive the services you were promised?

- Did the accommodations, fishing, and services match your expectations? What about the weather?
- How many times have you done business with the operator, and will you do business with him in the future?

Naturally, any ambiguous or negative response to any of the above should be cause for concern and doubt as to whether this is the person or organization with whom to do business.

Get an Agreement in Writing

When it comes time to narrow it down and lay your hard-earned money on a particular lodge, outfitter, or guide, be sure to get a contractual written agreement for all services, equipment, and/ or arrangements to be provided and the fees to be charged. Read the contract over carefully before signing and discuss any discrepancies or unclear wording. This is most important, as the written agreement is the legally binding document that holds the provider to deliver everything specified. It's your guarantee of getting what you've bargained for.

Trust Your Guide

Once you've committed to a services contract with a guide or lodge, it's time to give them your absolute trust and attention in following their recommendations for your travel arrangements, equipment, and any other trip preparations. Don't show up without any of the gear they recommend and don't bring anything not specified unless you clear it beforehand with your trip mentors. Remember, these folks are professionals who know local conditions and fishing like nobody's business, so heed their instructions carefully.

Timing Considerations

Despite what some of the travel literature suggests, Alaska's fishing is not a continuous "fish in the bucket" cornucopia of angling, at least not in any one location. Even in Alaska, the fishing has its ups and downs, with some very distinct advantages to each part of the season, from early spring to late fall, some of which have little direct impact on the fishing itself, but which can affect your vacation significantly in other ways.

The big question, of course, is one of fish availability and how it fits in with your schedule and desires. If you've never been to Alaska, it's probably wise to plan a trip for early summer (late May to early July) to enjoy the best of the chinook salmon fishing. If you could care less about the king of salmon, you might be happier stalking spring rainbows or even fall coho salmon for your first Alaskan angling experience. Seasoned Alaskan anglers can fine-tune their timing to partake of the best trophy fishing or peak period for a particular species (early October for Alaska's biggest rainbows, for example). The choices are many, and certainly not easy to make, but here's a summary of the best times to fish the major species throughout Alaska:

- **Rainbow Trout:** late April to June and August to early October
- **Steelhead Trout:** late April to June and late September to November
- **Arctic Grayling:** mid-May to mid-September
- **Northern Pike:** late May to early October

- **Cutthroat Trout:** May to June and August to October
- **Arctic Charr/Dolly Varden:** April to June and August through September
- **King (Chinook) Salmon:** late May to early July
- **Red (Sockeye) Salmon:** mid-June to late July
- **Chum (Dog) Salmon:** early July to early September
- **Pink (Humpback) Salmon:** mid-July to mid-August
- **Silver (Coho) Salmon:** early August to early October
- **Pacific Halibut:** late May to early September
- **Sheefish:** May to October
- **Lake Trout:** May to early July and late August to early September

Bear in mind that wide variations in run timing exist from region to region, even among certain streams within an area, so it's best to inquire with reputable sources, like the local Alaska Department of Fish and Game, guides, or air taxi services, for timely information. Many anglers plan their trips to fall on the cusp between different runs or peak periods, such as late July or late August, in hopes of sampling good angling for several species. Though it certainly can be done, especially with broadly overlapping species like pinks, silvers, rainbows, and charr, don't expect to stretch it to include all the salmon that run during Alaska's fishing season (the notorious "grand slam" for the five Pacific salmon). The condition of stragglers from the end of the king and sockeye runs, not to mention the availability of early fish a week or two before the main silver and pink runs, make it neither desirable nor predictable from an angler's standpoint.

Other Considerations

Other factors can affect your fishing vacation, some of which aren't mentioned in the brochures or the splashy color magazine layouts for fear of turning people off—bugs and bum weather, for instance. Alaska certainly has its share of both. But did you know that there is a "peak period" for each? The notorious Alaskan mosquito and its allies come out in greatest force during the warmest time of year, in the weeks surrounding Summer Solstice (from June until mid-July). A fishing trip in August or early September, while offering some of the best fishing of the season, also has the advantage of being virtually free of many of the swarming hordes that plague folks earlier in the season.

Weather, always a factor in Alaska, tends to be more benign (drier and calmer) in the spring and early summer throughout most of the state, deteriorating through late summer and fall, although the pattern can vary dramatically from year to year. If you're planning a trip to the Arctic or Northwest region, keep in mind that the fishing season is effectively finished there by mid-September or even earlier in some years.

If you're planning a camping or float-fishing trip, remember that the amount of daylight varies throughout the season. A trip in June or early July can offer exhilaratingly long hours of daylight, for almost nonstop fishing and leisurely camping, while the same outing in late September will have 12 hours of legitimate darkness, making for a much different pace. These great fluctuations of light and dark are even more pronounced in the Northwest and Arctic regions.

Guides and Outfitters

Alaska's guides and outfitters have often been cast as a maverick lot, reputedly drinking and swearing too much, lying outrageously, and otherwise not presenting very high standards of professionalism. While this may have been more true years ago, today's Alaskan guides and outfitters are astute businessfolk, dedicated pros in an industry that demands much in the way of time and personal commitment.

For the most part, you'll find them to be an extremely diverse and likable bunch, eager to share their knowledge and love of Alaska's incomparable fishing. The many different services they provide cover the full range of visitor activities related to fishing, but can be summarized briefly as follows:

Short-Trip Guides

Far and away the greatest number of guides currently operating in Alaska offer services that cater to the shorter, flexible itineraries of today's visitor. Usually hanging a shingle in the more populous regions, like Southcentral's Kenai Peninsula or the larger communities of the Southeast region, these guides offer a variety of short-trip options ranging from a half day to several days fishing, using boats or small planes. Accommodations, if provided, are simple, often at small cabins, bed-and-breakfasts, hotels, tent camps, or on-board vessels. Some meals and gear are usually provided. This group includes the many charter boat captains, river fishing guides, and small air taxi operators across Alaska, many offering unguided outfitting as well. Advance reservations are preferred, but walk-ins and last-minute inquiries are often welcome. Prices range from $75 per person for a half-day trip to $250 per person for a full day, depending on the location and the services provided.

Wilderness Guides

The real thing—the hard-core, seasoned cadre of the Alaskan guiding profession, wilderness guides represent the highest level of training, education, and commitment in the industry. Many have a college education, wilderness emergency medical training, and other qualifications. Most of them operate out of the major hubs—such as Anchorage, Fairbanks, Dillingham, Nome, Kotzebue, and Bettles—and offer trips that range in length from three to 14 days (or more). They handle everything from float trips to spike camps, usually offering unguided outfitting as well. Reservations generally must be made at least two months in advance, although, if room allows, they can sometimes fit folks in at the last minute. The better operations can provide some of Alaska's finest wilderness fishing experiences, with personalized service, outstanding professionalism, and itineraries that include some of the state's best fishing water in places like Katmai, Iliamna, Bristol Bay, and the lower Kuskokwim. Prices vary from $250 to $400 per day per person, usually all-inclusive (covering transportation, meals, guided fishing, and anything else from the point of departure).

Outfitters

Today's Alaska outfitters provide a full spectrum of possibilities for exciting, less expensive vacations for the "do-it-yourselfer." Anglers can arrange for rentals of rafts, boats, cabins, tent camps, and even camping gear and fishing tackle from many of the major hubs, on a daily or weekly basis. Most of the more established guide, lodge, and air taxi businesses still outfit to customers as part of their business, so check when inquiring about their services. (See the "Contacts" section in individual destination listings and the Resources appendix on page 409 for the names and addresses of local and statewide outfitters.) Rates vary from region to region, but you can expect to pay $75 to $100 per day for a full-size boat or raft, with a slight discount for weekly rental. Keep in mind that with high-air cargo rates, it may be more prudent to pay higher rates on-site with air taxi or local outfitters than ship rentals from one of the major hubs.

Lodges

Rustic fly-in fishing lodges are a celebrated part of that potent Alaska fishing mystique. While the best of them can certainly deliver an experience that is hard to duplicate any other way, you'll find a wide variety of services and accommodations to suit the different needs and budgets of anglers of all persuasions. If you're considering a lodge stay, it's helpful to know the main types of facilities available, what they offer, and their price ranges.

Deluxe Lodges

These are the cream of Alaska's lodging and service facilities, usually located in remote stream or lakeside locations in the best parts of Bristol Bay and Southeast and Southcentral Alaska, with awesome fishing out the door or not too far away. These custom operations often feature plush accommodations, daily fly-outs to Alaska's best fishing spots, knowledgeable guides, gourmet food, and some rather exclusive clientele to rub shoulders with. Some even provide on-site fly-fishing seminars or personal instruction, European chefs, in-house tackle shops and fly-tying benches, an open bar, and more. Itineraries and schedules are usually fixed, with regular hours for fishing and dining. Expect to pay for all the luxury and service, however, from $2,800 to $4,500 per week per person.

Family-Style Lodges

These lodges are a step down in luxury from the big glamour establishments, but they still offer outstanding service and accommodations, without all the frills. Some of the better ones pride themselves—and rightfully so—on delivering more real fishing time than any custom lodge. Located in remote or semiremote areas, many in Southcentral and Southeast, these less costly facilities usually offer fly-outs or boat fishing packages, bunk-style or small, shared cabin accommodations, and informal, family-style dining with plenty of good, home-cooked food. Fishing can be outstanding, depending on the location, time of year, quality of the guides, and other factors. Research and referrals are the best ways to find a good operation. Costs range from $1,800 to $3,000 per week per person.

Fishing Camps/Tent Lodges

You say you're a hard-core angler who wants a basic bunk near a great stream or lake? These camps offer accommodations that range from a bunkhouse to small cabins, heated tents, and even large boats or barges right on the water. Fishing is usually done from banks, by wading, or from skiffs. The rustic fish camp ambience is enhanced by plentiful, home-cooked food, and lots of fishing opportunities (24 hours a day if desired) in some of the best fishing locations in Alaska. Some of these operations are truly unique, set in areas far off the beaten path and run by remarkable individuals, locals usually, who can deliver more than your money's worth in abundant fishing. Many also offer unguided packages as outfitters, providing camps already set up in choice locations. As with the family-style lodges, the best way to locate a reputable operation is by word of mouth and research. Prices vary from $1,500 to $2,400 per week per person.

U.S. Forest Service Cabins

A very viable alternative to Alaska's lodges, tent camps, and hotels are cabins administered by the U.S. Forest Service. Distributed throughout much of Southcentral and Southeast Alaska, they're primarily set within Chugach and Tongass National Forests and serve as perfect hubs in reaching many prime angling destinations. Most of the cabins sit next to or near lakes, streams, and bays in picturesque wilderness settings.

Accessible by floatplane, wheelplane, boat, trail, and even road, these are natural A-frame, log-style cabins made of plywood. Inside you get wooden bunks for four people or more, a table, an oil or wood stove (or both), and benches. Many cabins, particularly those situated by lakes, have small, nonmotorized skiffs available for use by fishers and hunters who want to explore the area in more depth. Other equipment, such as splitting mauls, saws, and brooms, are commonly available. However, electricity, bedding, drinking water, and cooking utensils are not provided. It's very wise to pack along a gas or propane cook stove, insect repellent, and an air mattress or pad just in case.

Very reasonably priced, U.S. Forest Service cabins cost $25 per night per party. Reservations are recommended up to a year in advance for some of the more popular sites. Local charter services access most Forest Service cabins; consult the "Contacts" section of individual listings for names and phone numbers of trransportation companies.

Bush Pilots and Air Taxis

If you had to pick the most romantic figure in all of Alaska's wilderness fishing scene, it surely must be the intrepid soul who braves Alaska's skies to shuttle the people and supplies that make it all happen: the bush pilot. Steadfast and reliable through thick and thin, he keeps everyone on schedule during the busy summer season, which is not an easy job in a place so vast and primitive and subject to wild weather. Your average Alaska bush pilot also knows the local fishing locations like no one else you'll meet, so it's definitely to your advantage to get on his good side and cultivate a working relationship with him, especially if you plan on returning for more adventure.

Most air taxis bill by the hour, which can vary from $125 to over $600, depending on the size of plane used (fees usually include return flight time). A variety of interesting craft is in service all across Alaska, but the real workhorses are the single-engine Cessnas, Pipers, and DeHavillands, which have proven their versatility and reliability over the years in the most challenging conditions. Since most of Alaska's better stream and lake locations involve some flying to reach them, air transportation is usually a significant part of total trip costs. If you are planning a do-it-yourself excursion, some of the ways you can keep air taxi costs down are:

- **Travel with a small group.** Usually two to four people is an ideal group size for lowering per-person costs and achieving higher efficiency, not to mention the time saved in spreading the work load. You'll also have much more fun if you go with a group of buddies with similar interests.
- **Use scheduled commercial flights whenever possible.** You can buy a ticket to just about any village or town in even the most remote parts of Alaska on the regular scheduled flights offered by the major air carriers (shipping your gear as cargo), then contract with local flight services for arrangements to and from nearby fishing locations. Careful planning and research are required, but this can save you a bundle over chartering small planes from major hubs like Anchorage or Fairbanks.
- **Shop around.** Have a definite idea of the number in your party, the kind of trip you have in mind, and the rivers, lakes, or bays you wish to fish before you contact anyone for preliminary arrangements. If possible, get quotes from at least two other services. Air taxis have different planes and rates vary; some can even save you money on the "back haul" if they've got flights already going to the area you're interested in.
- **Go light.** The number one mistake seen among tourists, and the bane of every bush pilot, is the excessive amount of gear most people bring for an expedition. Limit yourself to 40 pounds of personal gear—clothes, sleeping bag, camera, fishing rods—and streamline your equipment list to a bare minimum. (If you're traveling with a group, coordinate your planning to avoid duplication of gear.) You'll save money (cargo costs these days average 50 cents per pound one-way from Anchorage to the state's better fishing areas), and enjoy your trip more with less gear to lug around.

Helicopter Fishing

by Robert Farmer

All across Alaska, virgin streams await discovery. The most exclusive of these lie along the coast, from Kotzebue Sound south to Unimak Island, then east along the Pacific to the Southeast archipelago. The upland reaches of these coastal areas, mostly inaccessible, hold immeasurable beauty, along with untouched fish populations and some of Alaska's last great wilderness fishing, and they are now open for serious exploration by helicopter.

"Heli-fishing," still quite new to Alaska, is limited to three lodges currently offering this unique experience. Crystal Creek Lodge in Southwest fishes upland streams in the Nushagak drainage,

Talaheim Lodge on the Talachulitna River in Southcentral fishes the upper stretches of this famous trout and salmon run on the west side of Cook Inlet, and Deshka River Lodge near Mount McKinley in Southcentral offers an ambitious heli-fishing program that covers an area from Katmai National Park in Southwest to Wrangell/St. Elias near the eastern border of the mainland.

The advantages of heli-fishing go beyond the obvious opening of formerly inaccessible fishing sanctuaries. Because of high costs, the experience is exclusive and limited, especially suited to fly-fishing and catch-and-release fishing. Those with physical limitations can reach prime waters with little or no arduous hiking or demanding boat rides. Perhaps most importantly for the future, the exclusivity of heli-fishing virtually eliminates exploitative angling whose primary measure of success is "price per pound." The few reputable lodges who operate helicopters in Alaska only select environmentally conscious anglers who appreciate this international treasure. Rates are steep, however, and openings are limited. Costs average $700 per day to $4,600 per week. Crystal Creek Lodge is limited to 20 guests per week, Talaheim takes only two guests per week, and Deshka River Lodge can handle 12. The experience is rated quite high by all who have had the opportunity to fish this way. It promises to be more popular in the future as more accessible waters become visited more often and anglers seek the peak experiences that only truly wild waters can provide.

Float Trips

Perhaps the most exhilarating way to experience Alaska's wild rivers and their incomparable fishing is to float down from headwaters in lightweight rafts. While certainly not an option for everyone, float trips offer some distinct advantages over fly-ins, camps, and lodges. For one, the float trip offers an intimate river experience, traveling through remote headwater sections that few can access by any other means. The entire length of the river can be fished, and schedules and streamside camps allow for convenient, 24-hour-a-day access to prime areas like salmon-spawning redds, where the rainbow trout, charr, and grayling are abundant and hungry. Variety and catch rates on float trips are unequaled.

Since neither motors nor mechanized equipment is used, the entire trip is one of peaceful immersion in the sounds and sights of the wilderness, with wildlife frequently sighted during the downstream journey. The downside to the float-trip experience can be the weather, with particularly foul stretches hampering comfort. High-quality equipment, including tents, rain gear, and footwear are essential, as are maps, bear protection, and wilderness survival and boating skills. The services of an experienced guide are highly recommended, and fees range from $250 to $400 per day per person, all inclusive. The location usually determines the price, as some trips require extensive travel by small plane. The best rivers for float-fishing in Alaska are in the Bristol and lower Kuskokwim Bays of the Southwest region.

Species

Chapter 1
Chinook: The King of Salmon

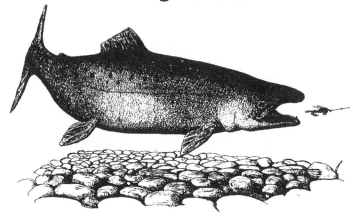

Someday, in your wildest fish dream come true, you may find yourself on the wind-whipped tundra of the Bering Sea coast, at one of a handful of small native villages that lie at the mouths of the great rivers there. A kindly old man with sparkling eyes and a face like shoe leather greets you warmly, then listens intently to your strange request. With a nod and a toothless grin, he motions to his youngest son to fetch the skiff and run you upriver. The boy quickly takes you around a few bends to a big fork in the river, where he deposits you and your gear on the gravel and is gone in a flash. For the next few days and sleepless nights (there are no nights dark enough for sleeping this far north in June), you are caught up in the magic of one of the greatest miracles to yearly befall these desolate coasts—the stirring arrival of the first and most awesome of the Pacific's five salmon of summer. It's a fish prized through the ages for its size, gaminess, and good eating: the one they call chinook, the king of salmon.

Not given to recklessness like his cousin the coho, and certainly not the same class of fighter as the exalted steelhead,

the chinook supremely outclasses all of his peers, in sheer size and strength alone. Husky from summers out in the rich North Pacific, he'll tip the scales at 40 or 50 pounds or more—a formidable adversary, especially when fresh from the sea. When an ocean-bright 30-pounder slams your fly and rips into half your backing with lightning speed, you'll swear you've snagged a whale. The ensuing grudge match can last hours, during which the brawny lord of all salmon will test you and your gear to the limit. (A few years back, a Minnesota man made the news by fighting a monster Kenai River king for a day and a half!) But if you're tough—and lucky—enough to slug it out with him to the end, you'll stagger ashore with a prize definitely worth the trip to these waters. For the only thing more impressive than the fight of a big king salmon is the magnificent sight of one up close: immense, full-bodied, with sides of buffed platinum tinged with purple, and muscular, tapered flanks; his countenance suggests both power and grace— the ultimate sea-roaming, river-running, fish-eating machine.

Introduction

More than an angler's prize, the great chinook (*Oncorhynchus tshawytscha*) has been an integral part of Pacific Northwest culture for centuries. The fish was first encountered by white men over 250 years ago on the epic voyages of Vitus Bering. Explorers Lewis and Clark and Alexander Mackenzie wrote about the chinook and the elaborate rituals the native coastal tribes performed for its annual return. (In the mythology of these people, the great salmon embodied the spirits of supernatural beings from the sea, who ascended the rivers to sacrifice themselves for the survival of their captors.) The chinook has managed to survive the ravages of man, and today, in Alaska at least, he retains a measure of his former glory.

Here in the Last Frontier, the mighty king salmon has become almost a pop icon. We have made him our state fish and used his name and image shamelessly in countless business promotions, names of streets and subdivisions, and works of art. As the focal point of a multi-million dollar sportfishing industry (and prized commercial and subsistence species), the chinook's significance and stature is elevated beyond any measure. Hooking and landing a big king salmon has been and probably always will be the quintessential Alaska angling experience for the thousands of folks who travel from the four corners of the world to fish here.

Description

Chinook salmon are the largest of the five species of Pacific salmon, regularly reaching weights of 30 pounds or more, although their average weight in Alaska is around 18 pounds. The International Game Fish Association (IGFA) sport-caught world record is a king of 97.25 pounds from the Kenai River in 1985, although fish of well over 100 pounds are caught now and then in commercial fishing nets. (A 126-pound giant was taken in a fish trap near Petersburg in 1949, and fish up to 135 pounds have been reported from Southcentral's Cook Inlet.) Their length at maturity is usually 30 inches or more.

A mature chinook fresh from the sea is full-bodied, with sides of bright silver, a deep blue-black back, and large, irregular cross-markings across the upper sides and fins. Its belly is white; its tail is broad and moderately forked, with spots on both lobes. (This, along with a black gum line on the lower jaw, helps distinguish smaller king salmon from the similar coho salmon, *O. kisutch*.) Teeth on mature chinooks are well developed, especially in breeding males.

Spawning fish undergo moderate changes in physical appearance. Both sexes turn dusky red to copper or brown (sometimes with blackish or purple shading), while males develop hooked jaws, ridged backs, and more dramatic coloration. Juvenile king salmon are hard to distinguish from other small salmon, trout, or charr, but normally have wider parr marks, tinted edges on the adipose fins, and moderately forked tails.

The flesh of a king salmon is usually a deep red color, but it can vary to pink or white in some locations, depending on diet and other factors. Its meat is prized for eating, as it is rich and flavorful—perfect grilled, smoked, or canned. King salmon ranks along with the red or sockeye salmon as one of the North Pacific's most valued food fishes.

Range, Abundance, and Status

King salmon were originally distributed coastally from Hokkaido, Japan, to the Anadyr River in Asia and from Kotzebue Sound to central California in America.

The least abundant of the Pacific salmon, they have historically been most concentrated in larger river systems (the San Joaquin—Sacramento River system of California and Washington's mighty Columbia each supported runs in excess of a million fish at one time). Today, king salmon are found in greatest numbers from British Columbia north to the Yukon River. In Alaska, chinook runs occur along most of the southern and western coasts, from Dixon Entrance in Southeast Alaska to Point Hope in Northwest Alaska, with the most significant populations found in the state's great rivers—the Yukon, Kuskokwim, Nushagak, Susitna, and Copper.

Though the chinook has not fared well by man throughout much of its range (the Columbia and other once-great salmon rivers of the Pacific Northwest have runs so decimated that they are now under protection by the Endangered Species Act), the chinook's status in Alaska remains remarkably stable. Commercial catches have been above 600,000 fish in recent years, while sport anglers annually harvest more than 120,000. The greatest threat to the future of Alaska's wild chinook seems to be the proliferation of hatcheries and creation of "mixed stock" fisheries that fuel an insatiable and unrealistic public demand for more angling opportunity. (Hatchery releases of kings now contribute to a significant percentage of the commercial and sport harvests in certain areas of Southeast and Southcentral Alaska—up to 50 percent or more.)

Life History and Habits

Chinook are in many ways the most ecologically diverse of the Pacific salmon. They are the longest lived, and can return sexually mature at anywhere from two to nine years of age, which allows them to attain the greatest size of any

salmon (up to 100 pounds or more). In Alaska, they generally spend a year or two in freshwater as fry, then three to five years at sea before returning in early summer (May through July) to their rivers of origin. Their wanderings are potentially among the most extensive of any fish species, involving forays into the far reaches of the North Pacific and river migrations of more than 1,500 miles in the Yukon River.

Spawning occurs during July and August in larger streams and rivers, preferably over gravel or pebble bottom structure. Eggs hatch usually in late winter or early spring, with the alevins remaining in the protection of the gravel for two to three weeks until the yolk sac is absorbed and they emerge as fry. Newly emerged fry feed on insects, plankton, and crustaceans. They school in pool edges, under cutbanks, and around aquatic vegetation and logjams for protection from predators and strong currents. In the spring of their second year of life (or occasionally their third year), Alaska chinook "smolt up" and proceed en masse to the sea. Remaining close to shore, these adolescent, estuarine chinook feed on small fish, crustaceans, and mollusks, rapidly increasing in size until they're large enough to venture into the open sea. Some stocks, particularly those found in Southeast Alaska, may spend their entire lives in protected inshore waters, providing the basis for year-round local fisheries. These are called "feeder kings." Others make extensive migrations into the North Pacific and Bering Sea during their third year of life.

While in the open sea, chinooks feed almost exclusively on other fish—herring, sand lance, eulachon, pilchards, pollack, smelts, and anchovies—with seasonal binges on squid, crab larvae, euphausiids, and amphipods rounding out their diets. Chinook salmon have been found in a great range of depths, from just below the surface to over 250 feet, depending on the season. They're subject to the same predators as the other members of the Pacific salmon clan. Fry get eaten by charr, rainbow trout, coho, terns, and mink, among others. Older fish in the sea are at risk from larger pelagic fish, marine mammals (seals, whales, and sea lions), and, of course, man.

A king's final year in the ocean brings a substantial size increase, and for Alaska fish this can occur anywhere from two to seven years of age or more. Precocious returning two-year-old fish, called "jacks," are a well-known phenomenon in many river systems. In Alaska, however, most fish return at four to six years. Mature Alaska kings begin showing up in freshwater in May, with peak periods of river migration occurring in June and early July. Generally, fish that show earliest complete the longest migrations; this trip may be considerable in systems such as the Yukon, where a significant number of chinook travel the entire river length to spawn in Canada (a journey of more than 2,000 miles). Actual spawning takes place during July and August, and, as with the other Pacific salmon species, is instigated by the female's digging of the redd. Nest location is influenced by a variety of factors, but kings seem better able to utilize the larger substrate and greater stream flows of main channels, probably because of their size.

Kings have some interesting habits that should be noted by anglers. Like other salmon, they'll frequently show themselves in tidal waters and in lower river sections, making it easy to pinpoint their location. They can hold in bays and off the mouths of rivers for days, even weeks sometimes, until conditions (water flow, temperature, and wind direction) are just right to make their in-migrations, at times even making extensive movements into freshwater and back out to sea. (Some fish tagged far up certain rivers have been recovered in ocean nets miles away!) Because of their size, they are inclined to move and hold deeper than other salmon, preferring the main channels of rivers, although at times they use side channels and sloughs. In freshwater, chinook are very sensitive to light; they prefer the low light of late or early hours and cloudy or windy days for most of their activity.

Fishing Alaska's King Salmon

Sportfishing for the king of salmon has become serious business in Alaska. On Southcentral's Kenai River, the state's most popular fishery, visitors are often shocked to find a scene more reminiscent of New Jersey than the Last Frontier. On a typical day in June or July, a mad army of anglers swarms the river, engaging in aggressive, no-holds-barred combat for the Kenai's world famous run of giant kings (up to 80 pounds or more). Farther west and north, the action is generally more subdued, but it's still a far cry from peaceful wilderness. Only in the far reaches of Southwest and in isolated bays of Southeast can one enjoy any measure of real solitude along with abundant fishing.

In Southeast, nearly all chinook angling effort occurs as a saltwater intercept fishery, targeting returning salmon bound for Canada, the Pacific Northwest states, and parts of Alaska. Major spawning only occurs in a handful of large river systems in Southeast—the Taku, Alsek, and Stikine, with a dozen or so lesser rivers supporting small runs of several thousand fish or less. Hatcheries and enhancement efforts have augmented the fishery considerably in some areas. Most chinook fishing is done by trolling or mooching from boats, with either bait or lures, with some jigging (see page 36 for details). Non-breeding, immature king salmon, called "feeders," can be caught year-round.

Farther north into Southcentral you'll find the state's most popular and intensively managed king salmon stream fisheries—the fabulous Kenai and the clear-water tributaries of the Susitna and Copper Rivers. There, most effort is spent drift fishing or back trolling from boats, with a significant amount of bank fishing in some areas. Saltwater angling for kings occurs in lower Cook Inlet, Kachemak, and Resurrection Bays, and to a lesser extent, Kodiak Island and Prince William Sound. The remote, clear-flowing streams of Southwest's Bristol Bay and lower Kuskokwim River hold Alaska's most abundant opportunities for shore casting and stalking the mighty king on a fly rod, although a significant amount of boat fishing occurs on the larger rivers (Nushagak, Alagnak, Naknek, Togiak, and others).

Freshwater Methods and Gear

From northern Southeast to Norton Sound, most of the fishing effort for Alaska's chinook salmon involves drifting, trolling, or casting lures or bait in freshwater. In the big rivers, this is most effectively done from boats, but significant innovations in gear and increased access to prime waters have made shore casting (with spinning, bait-casting, and fly-fishing gear) more popular than ever. Here's a rundown of the more popular techniques used:

Drifting and Trolling

Alaska's most deadly chinook lure is nothing more than a bright, buoyant plastic whirligig, commonly called a drift bobber. Rigged off a swivel on a 24-inch section of 25- to 40-pound leader, with a lead dropper (three-quarters to three ounces lead), and drifted along the bottom, the bobber is deadly for all salmon, as well as trout and charr. Spin-N-Glo and Cheaters are the two most popular brands, the larger sizes (0 to 4 and Super Spin-N-Glo) and brighter fluorescent colors (red, orange, chartreuse, and yellow) being the standard for kings on all major Alaska chinook rivers from the Gulkana to the Unalakleet. The addition of flashy hook skirts, colored yarn, drops of fish scent, or cured salmon roe (attached with an egg loop hook snell) considerably enhances their appeal.

You can fish the Spin-N-Glo or Cheater from shore with a "quartering" cast upstream and a steady retrieve to reel in slack as the rig bounces downriver along bottom; you can prolong the drift considerably by walking downstream as you reel, if conditions allow. Or you can use a side planer (see illustration on page 29). But most anglers fish bobbers from a skiff, drifting or trolling with 25 to 75 feet of line, depending on water depth. Since the drift bobber is buoy-

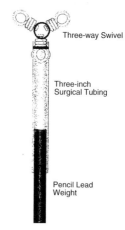

Three-way Swivel

Three-inch Surgical Tubing

Pencil Lead Weight

Alternate rigging for dropper weight

Chinook: The King of Salmon

Drift Setup

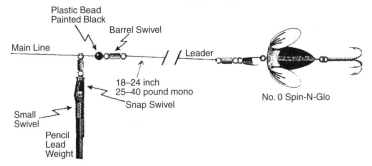

ant, it's nearly impossible to foul on the bottom, and it's effective fished slowly or fast. The important thing is to have enough lead rigged to keep it on or near bottom. You'll see the rod tip twitch with each bounce if it's properly weighted. You also need razor-sharp hooks, as chinooks have super-hard mouths. Anglers generally wait on the strike until the fish takes the rod down hard, especially when fishing with bait.

Next to drift bobbers, plugs are the most commonly used trolling lures on Alaska's king rivers, and you'll see great boxes crammed full of them in guides' boats along the Kenai, Naknek,

Gulkana, and other popular big rivers. Big diving plugs like Magnum Tadpollys, Wiggle Warts, and Hot Shots, or the Flatfish (T-55) or Kwikfish (K14-16) in blue/silver, chartreuse/silver, fire red-orange, metallic red or green, and chartreuse seem to be the most used.

Back trolling is a very efficient and frequently used technique. For this, you point your skiff upriver. Use the motor to slow the drift considerably, so that the lure is essentially working in the current with little or no actual upstream movement. The idea is to probe the bottom slowly and intercept kings holding around underwater structure or moving

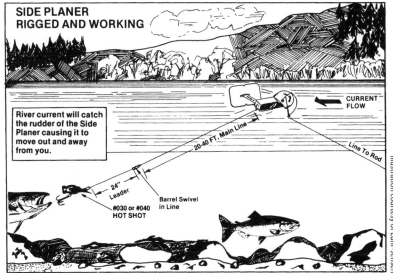

Illustration courtesy of Luhr-Jensen

Chinook: The King of Salmon

Diving Planer

Drift Bobber

Bead

Eggs

3 to 4 feet of 20–40-pound mono

To Rod

Illustration courtesy of Luhr-Jensen

Jet Diver™

up deep channels. Drift bobbers, plugs, and spinners are the lures most commonly used. They're usually rigged off a diving planer, which is a fan-shaped, flat plastic device that planes downward in the current when pulled behind the boat (see illustration above). Plugs with deep diving lips, like the Model 25 and 35 Hot Shots, Magnum Wiggle Warts, and Tadpollys, can usually be fished alone. For rigging, use three to four feet of heavy mono line, 20- to 40-pound test, run off the back of the planer with a clip swivel for the terminal end and a clip for attaching to the planer. Then let out the whole thing gradually at speed until it's about 30 to 75 feet behind the boat, depending on the depth of the river. You can sit and wait for the fish or drift slowly backwards and probe bottom; depending on how many kings are in the river, either method will produce strikes. Note that since kings have a tendency to "slap" the lure two or three times prior to the actual take, most anglers wait for the fish to bury the rod tip before setting the hook. Planers will pull a lure or bait down to about 20 feet, and can even be rigged alone as lures, as they're available in a variety of bright colors.

If you back troll with plugs, always check the action of your rig in shallow water before using it to ensure that your lure is swimming upright in a straight line. You may have to "tune" the action with a pair of pliers, especially if you're using a plug and bait combination. To do this, bend the eye on the nose of the plug to compensate for the direction of

lean so that the lure swims upright. Adjustments can also be made on the belly eye or eyes, holding the hook, if the plug is really out of balance. It's important to check the lure's action at fast speed, too.

Back Bouncing

Like back trolling, back bouncing is an intensive technique that can be very effective in deep holes or eddies. The boat is faced upstream and motored or anchored against the current. The lures are fished off the back, but by hand, like jigging—raising and lowering off bottom and playing more line out as the lure is worked farther downstream from the skiff. The rigging is virtually the same as is used for drifting, although you may want to shorten the leader somewhat, with a sliding sinker setup being slightly more efficient than swivel rigging; you should usually use more weight (up to six ounces). The boat can be slipped backwards in a strong current to help keep the lure on bottom. Spin-N-Glos, plugs, and eggs are most commonly used. Like jigging, most fish taken by back bouncing will be hooked on the upstroke, so a quick and powerful motion is required and hooks must be kept razor sharp by frequent honing.

Spin Fishing and Spinners

Spin fishermen have traditionally relied on large "flasher" spinners like the Jensen Tee-Spoon (sizes 5 and 6) or Skagit Special (sizes 6 to 8) in hammered nickel, brass, fire red, chartreuse, or rainbow blades as their standard

Alaska chinook drift lure, rigged like a drift bobber with a lead dropper and 24-inch leader off a three-way swivel. The spinner can be used alone or with bait like salmon roe. Dragging it behind a boat requires more attention than with a bobber, however, as the big spinner will hang on bottom if worked too slowly. For casting, these big spinners are too clumsy and unbalanced, especially in heavy wind. Spin-casters instead should opt for the 1.25-ounce Mepps Giant Killers (in silver, gold, prism, or fluorescent red or orange blades, dressed in bright bucktail) or the superbly balanced, seven-eighths-ounce no. 6 Super Vibrax Series spinners (silver, black, or gold blades with a fluorescent orange, yellow, or green bell, or the new "Firetiger" finish). Big spoons like the seven-eighths-ounce Pixee (green or pink insert) are also extremely effective. The trick is to fish slowly and deeply, allowing the lure to sink properly after the cast, and using a retrieve just fast enough to keep it off the bottom. Depending on the current and depth, additional weight may be required—use a half-ounce rubbercore sinker attached above the lure or rig a dropper and swivel as you would for drifting. For more efficient and enjoyable casting, if conditions allow (such as in bigger, slower water), you might want to try dropping down a notch in tackle, say to 12- to 15-pound test and a medium-weight salmon rod. You'll be making obvious sacrifices in your ability to handle big fish, but you'll be able to cast the big spinners farther without adding extra weight.

Bait Fishing

In glacial, extremely deep, or turbid waters where the use of bait is still allowed, its effectiveness on kings is unmatchable, either alone or as an attractant on lures. Most anglers use salmon roe, herring, sardines, and even shrimp. Spin-N-Glos and cured salmon roe have perhaps taken more Alaska kings than any other lure and bait combination, but big spinners and even plugs benefit immensely from the addition of a "natural sweetener." A short strip of herring or sardine, wound flesh-side-out with fine thread to the bottom of a plug, is a standard enticement used by many Southcentral river guides. Remember that you'll definitely need to "tune" the plug before fishing it in this manner. Some anglers even add fish oils and other scents to their baits or lures.

Gearing for Freshwater King Salmon

Most anglers with little or no experience on Northwest rivers have difficulty imagining just how strong a big chinook can be. No matter how well your rod handles lunkers back home, it can snap like a twig and your biggest reel can become a smoldering piece of useless scrap metal under the awesome strain of an Alaska king salmon in strong current. To give yourself half a chance with these giants, start with a heavyweight, medium-action, spinning or back-bounce casting rod; match it with a tournament-quality, heavy freshwater or light saltwater reel (Ambassadeur 6500 to 7000 series, Shimano AX, or Spheros) capable of holding 200 yards of 20-pound test mono. Use only the highest quality line (17- to 30-pound test mono or braided) and terminal tackle (swivels, snaps, hooks, etc.), and check frequently for wear.

Fly-fishing Kings

There comes a time in your evolution as a sport angler when you should forsake the fancy, high-tech ease of modern gear and boats and stalk the king of salmon on more even terms: in waders, armed with no more than a long, limber rod,

Shallow, moderately fast holding water is ideal for fly-fishing king salmon in lower rivers.

braided line, and some bright feather- and tinsel-adorned hooks. Ideally, you should seek a productive salmon river with clear water, not too deep or far from the sea, where you can sight fish, as it usually takes fairly precise presentation (within a few feet, depending on conditions) to prompt chinooks to strike a fly. The closer to salt water, the brighter and more aggressive they'll be. The best areas are river channels, mouths, confluences, tailouts, edges of sloughs, ledge pools, and behind boulders and islands. Keep in mind that kings usually don't have any problem moving up through the main channel, so don't overlook any possible main-stem lies. Fish deep, with a light strip, always working the fly directly in front of holding or moving salmon. If you must fish blindly, look for signs of fish before you commit to extensive casting, lest your efforts be wasted on empty water. The take of a king in freshwater is usually not vigorous, although they can hit hard at times, especially when on the move. For this reason, keep your hooks razor sharp, your line taut, and your rod ready for the slightest response. Fishing late and early hours, overcast or windy days, and after high tides will be the most productive times in lower river areas.

Gear and Flies

You'll need stout, high-quality gear: a super strong 10- or 11-weight, slow action fly rod, with a matching high-performance, heavy freshwater or light saltwater reel (capable of holding 150 yards of backing), and a variety of lines for the conditions you'll encounter. This includes saltwater or steelhead taper floating, five- and 10-foot sink-tip, full sink, and even high-density sink or shooting tapers. Super-long, two-handed Spey rods to 13 feet (or more) are used on some of the big rivers, for efficient long casting of the big flies in the all-too-frequent winds, but they're difficult and tiring to use. Some of the new generation light, powerful, moderately long rods (to 11 feet) might prove a better alternative (other than fishing from a boat or from locations where you can cast downwind).

King salmon flies should be big, gaudy creations of mylar, tinsel, marabou, bunny hair, or bucktail, tied on sharp, forged hooks (size 2 to 5/0) like the Mustad AC3406 or AC36890, Tiemco TMC 800S, or Gamakatsu Aberdeen, in colors of silver, red, orange, pink, purple, yellow, or chartreuse. Some of the more popular commercially tied patterns for

Alaskabou Streamer

kings are the Alaskabou, Outrageous, Wiggletail, and Fat Freddie. Oversized versions of popular Alaska salmon and trout patterns like the Polar Shrimp, Bunny Bug, Woolly Bugger, Maraflash, and Egg-Sucking Leech are also very effective, as are saltwater patterns—Clouser Minnow, Deceiver, Tarpon Fly, Herring Fly, and Shrimp—and big tube flies. Leaders and tippets should be short for sinking line presentations, no more than four feet (15- to 20-pound test).

Guides' Tips for Freshwater King Salmon

- **Fish 'em early, fish 'em late:** Kings are more active in freshwater during the low-light, quiet hours. Plan your serious fishing for 9 P.M. to 1 A.M. and 5 A.M. to 8 A.M. (Remember: There is no real darkness in June or July.)

- **Watch the tides:** If you're within 15 miles of the sea, you'll do better if you consult a tide book and fish intervals after the high tides or during incoming tides at or near river mouths.

- **Bad weather, good fishing:** Cloudy, rainy days may be miserable, but fishing is always better then than on bright, sunny days.

- **Hot colors:** Bring an assortment of the most vibrant fluorescent colors (orange, red, chartreuse, pink, etc.) you can find in flies, plugs, spoons, spin-

ners, and drift bobbers, and change frequently until you find what's hot. Don't get stuck in a rut with what worked on yesterday's river or yesterday's conditions. Experiment!

- **Single and sharp:** If you haven't already done so, replace all treble hooks with super-sharp, single or bait hooks (nos. 1/0 to 5/0). Check and sharpen your hooks frequently out in the field.

- **Get 'em while they're fresh:** Try to fish kings no more than 50 miles from salt water if possible; they'll be brighter and more aggressive, and they'll give a totally undiminished account of themselves on the end of a line.

- **Keep it short:** Use shorter leader/tippet lengths of four feet for all your sinking presentations on a fly rod.

Saltwater Methods and Gear

In the salt, king salmon can be taken year-round in the form of immature fish called "feeders," which spend part, if not all, of their adult lives in inshore waters. Along with the larger, mature, pre-spawning chinook available in late spring, these fish are taken throughout Southeast and parts of Southcentral with rigging and methods similar to those used farther south. Most of the strategies used to take them exploit the chinooks' powerful feeding drives; trolling and mooching bait and lures from boats are far and away the most popular ways of working the water. A very limited amount of shore fishing takes place in certain locations, and fly-casting is even rarer. Area and seasonal variations exist in the methods and gear used, so it's wise to get some local input before you gear up for any serious Alaska saltwater king salmon pursuits. However, an understanding of the basic techniques and rigging will serve you well,

Trolling Rig

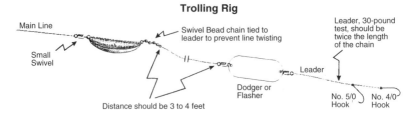

Main Line

Small Swivel

Swivel Bead chain tied to leader to prevent line twisting

Leader, 30-pound test, should be twice the length of the chain

Distance should be 3 to 4 feet

Dodger or Flasher

Leader

No. 5/0 Hook

No. 4/0 Hook

A diving/trolling sinker such as the Pink Lady or Deep Six (both by Luhr-Jensen) is most often substituted for the keel sinker weight. When using downriggers, run the main line directly to the dodger/flasher.

no matter where, when, or how you decide to challenge the king of salmon in the ocean environment.

Trolling

As the most efficient method of taking kings over a wide range of conditions, saltwater sport trolling borrows considerably from decades of experience hard-won by commercial salmon trollers throughout Southeast and elsewhere, who have refined the art of attracting and hooking salmon to a high level of efficiency.

Dodgers and Flashers

For years, the use of metal fish attractors has been a standard practice for saltwater salmon. The most commonly used types are "flashers" and "dodgers"— long, thin rectangular blades that spin or sway when trolled, adding considerable strike-inducing stimuli (flash, sound, and erratic action) to trailed baits or lures. Dodgers are usually four to 10 inches long, with a slightly concave shape to develop a side-to-side motion

best suited to complement the action of spoons, plugs, and live bait at a slow to medium trolling speed. Flashers are generally larger (up to 14 inches or more) and spin completely around in 360-degree rotations. They're generally used with lures like hoochies and flies that have no action of their own, and in deep water trolling situations where maximum attractor stimuli is desired. Both kinds come in a variety of sizes, colors, and finishes; chrome, chrome/silver scale, green, pearl pink, white, and orange are some of the most popular used in Alaska.

For sport trolling kings, usually two to (rarely) six lines are employed off the back and sides of the boat, using downriggers, diving sinkers (i.e., Pink Lady), or keel weights to pull the terminal rigging (particularly large spinners) down to the desired depth. In Alaska, dodgers or flashers in combination with herring (whole, plug-cut, or strips), hoochies, plugs, spoons, or streamer flies are most often used. For best action, the attractor is generally rigged a minimum of three to four feet behind the sinker or diver, and at least six feet (or more) from a downrigger. A stout leader (30-pound test) about twice as long as the flasher or dodger connects to the terminal end. Trolling depth and speed vary, but kings generally are found deeper than coho (60 to 120 feet

Pink Lady diving/trolling sinker

Illustration courtesy of Luhr-Jensen

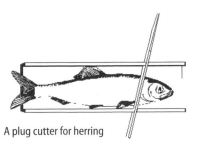

A plug cutter for herring

Rigged, "plug-cut" herring

for feeders, less for prespawners) and take a slower trolled lure or bait.

Bait Fishing

Most serious Alaska saltwater king salmon anglers prefer bait over all other enticements, as a properly handled and rigged herring will usually outfish anything else over a broad range of conditions. A four- to seven-inch, fresh or flash-frozen, whole, plug-cut, or harness-rigged herring (using a "Herring Aid") is preferred by most experienced sport trollers. The idea, similar to when fishing coho, is to rig the bait to impart the lifelike spin of a stunned or maimed bait fish when pulled through the water. "Hoochies," plastic-skirted squid imitations (in colors of pink, green, or blue), are frequently added above the herring for more appeal.

Mooching

Mooching is a popular and very effective saltwater technique for fishing bait in the sheltered, tidally influenced waters of bays, estuaries, and river mouths—anywhere fish tend to be deeper or concentrated by currents or structure. You'll see it done more fre-

quently by recreational anglers than by high-powered charter boat operators, since it's a more laid-back and personal technique that puts the action in the hands of the individual fisherman, not the man at the throttle. Because the bait can move through the water column, it is also a more efficient and intensive way of working water when fish aren't actively feeding near the surface.

For mooching, the herring is generally rigged the same as for trolling: either cut or whole, to spin when pulled through the water. Attractors are not used, with the leader running straight off the banana lead (one to six ounces) four to five feet or more to the bait. Fishing with the tides, line is stripped or slowly free-spooled from the reel until the rig hits the desired depth (usually above bottom). The bait is then worked by the action of the drift, by retrieving line, or with a slight troll (motor mooching). The most efficient way is determined by the tides, concentration of fish, prevailing winds, and

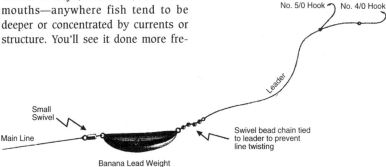

No. 5/0 Hook   No. 4/0 Hook

Leader

Small Swivel

Main Line

Swivel bead chain tied to leader to prevent line twisting

Banana Lead Weight

Teezer™

personal preference. A certain amount of finesse and skill is required. For instance, setting the hook is delayed on fish that hit the bait on the upswing until the rod loads, while salmon that pick up the bait while on its descent will create slack line, which should be reeled in quickly to set the hook.

Jigging

An intensive technique related to mooching, jigging employs long, weighted metal bait fish imitations (jigs) fished vertically from a drifting or anchored boat. It can be extremely effective under the right conditions—sometimes more effective than any other technique—and has caught on with many serious salmon anglers throughout Southeast. Line is free-spooled to the desired depth, then the jigs are raised and lowered quickly, giving them a tantalizing, fluttering action through the water column. Jigging works best in tight fish concentrations, such as around bait balls, and is usually done with a fish finder.

Finding the Fish

Saltwater king salmon fishing in Alaska, as elsewhere, targets feeder or prespawning kings, each with its own behavior, movements, and locations that at times will demand separate strategies. Some of the best locations for mature, prespawning chinook are the well-known commercial trolling drags (such as the Breadline out of Juneau, Biorka Island out of Sitka, and the west side of Gravina Island out of Ketchikan) where anglers traditionally intercept returning salmon at shallow depths. Feeder chinook will be found in areas of great-

est food concentration, usually, but not always, deeper than prespawners. Locating bait patches or conditions favorable to feeding is the name of the game. Other than obvious visual signs like seabird flocks or other boats, the most common way to do this is with fish finders, depth sounders, and nautical charts, concentrating on areas like channels, points, straits, bays, rip zones, and reefs. Fishing the tides (especially about an hour or so before and after the change), or during the low-light times of day can be much more important when fishing chinook, as they're less energetic and more light-sensitive than coho.

These are just some of the basics of Alaska saltwater king salmon angling. A more complete knowledge of the habits of chinook and how tides, currents, time of day, and other factors affect fishing conditions is, of course, best acquired firsthand, in the company of others more experienced, like charter boat skippers, commercial trollers, or seasoned saltwater sport anglers.

For beginners, the best advice is to go out a few times with people in the know, observe carefully, and ask plenty of questions. (For some recommended saltwater guides in Southcentral and Southeast, see the regional listings on pages 265 and 325.)

Gearing for Saltwater King Salmon

For saltwater trolling, most Alaska anglers use a stiff, heavy-weight trolling or downrigger rod, usually seven to eight-and-a-half feet long, with medium-fast action, to handle the increased

Alaska's Top 10 Trophy King Salmon

97 pounds, 4 ounces	Kenai River (Southcentral)	1985
Les Anderson (state and world record)		
95 pounds, 10 ounces	Kenai River (Southcentral)	1990
93 pounds, 0 ounces	Kelp Bay (Southeast)	1977
92 pounds, 4 ounces	Kenai River (Southcentral)	1985
91 pounds, 10 ounces	Kenai River (Southcentral)	1988
91 pounds, 4 ounces	Kenai River (Southcentral)	1987
91 pounds, 0 ounces	Kenai River (Southcentral)	1995
89 pounds, 3 ounces	Kenai River (Southcentral)	1989
89 pounds, 0 ounces	Kenai River (Southcentral)	1994
88 pounds, 11 ounces	Kenai River (Southcentral)	1980

resistance from weights, flashers, and planers. A high-quality, levelwind inshore reel (such as a Shimano TLD, Daiwa Sealine, or Ambassadeur 7000 series) capable of holding at least 250 yards of 25-pound test is used. Lighter gear can be employed when fishing from downriggers.

Mooching rods for Alaska are generally longer, more limber, and with faster action, and are usually mated with sturdy bait casters or special mooching reels capable of holding 200 yards of 20-pound test. Jigging rods are generally short (six to seven feet) and stout, with a fast, cue-stick taper for working lures vertically and producing a strong hookset. Reels are generally the same size as those used for trolling or mooching, with strong drags and spooled with 25- to 40-pound mono.

Alaska's Major King Salmon Locations

Southeast

Sportfishing effort here is mostly a saltwater intercept fishery. Feeder kings are available year-round in many locations, with mature, streambound fish taken from mid-April to mid-July. A few scattered shoreline fisheries exist, mostly for returning hatchery fish. In the many straits, sounds, and bays of the region, you'll find a number of concentration points for feeding and migrating king salmon. Southeast's only significant freshwater king fishery is in the Situk River, near Yakutat, with more limited activity at Akwe River.

- **Yakutat:** Yakutat Bay; Situk, Akwe Rivers

- **Haines:** Chilkat, Chilkoot Inlets

- **Skagway:** Taiya Inlet

- **Juneau:** Lynn Canal, Favorite, Saginaw Channels; Stephens Passage; Cross Sound; Icy, Chatham Straits

- **Sitka:** Whale Bay; Sitka, Salisbury Sounds

- **Petersburg:** Frederick Sound, Wrangell Narrows, Duncan Canal

- **Wrangell:** Eastern Passage; Stikine, Zimovia, Sumner Straits; Ernest Sound

- **Ketchikan:** Behm Canal, Gravina Island, Clarence Strait, Revillagigedo Channel

- **Klawock (Prince of Wales):** Bucareli Bay, Gulf of Esquibel

Southcentral

Angling for chinook in Southcentral is predominantly freshwater fishing, and includes the state's most heavily targeted, world famous trophy fisheries of Kenai River and surrounding Cook Inlet. Ninety-nine percent of all Alaska trophy fish over 70 pounds come from these waters. Feeder kings are available year-round in lower Cook Inlet, Kachemak Bay, outer Resurrection Bay, Prince William Sound, and along most of the Gulf Coast (Kodiak to Cordova). Mature streambound fish are available from late April to late July. Some shoreline opportunities exist, primarily for hatchery fish. The run timing for freshwater king salmon fisheries is usually from late May to early August, peaking between early June and early July (later in some rivers).

- **Wrangell Mountains**: Klutina, Gulkana, Tonsina, Tazlina River systems

- **Kenai**: Lower Cook Inlet salt water (Whiskey Gulch, Deep Creek, etc.); Kachemak Bay (Homer Spit, Halibut Cove, etc.); Kenai, Moose Rivers; Anchor, Ninilchik, Kasilof, Deep Creeks

- **Lower Cook Inlet**: Chakachatna, McArthur River systems

- **Susitna**: Talachulitna, Talkeetna Rivers; Lake, Montana, Willow, Little Willow, Sheep, Peters, Alexander Creeks; clear-water sloughs and stream mouths along main stem Susitna

- **Upper Cook Inlet**: Little Susitna, Chuitna, Lewis, Ivan, Theodore Rivers; Beluga River tributaries

- **Kodiak**: Karluk, Red (Ayakulik) Rivers; Chiniak Bay salt water

- **Chugach**: Resurrection Bay, Passage Canal, Valdez Arm, Orca Inlet

Southwest

Although Southwest has no saltwater fishing for chinook, it does have the state's most abundant, highest-quality stream fishing, with unmatched opportunities for fly-fishing. The run timing is from the beginning of June through July; the peaks are mid-June to early July.

- **Bristol Bay**: Alagnak, Naknek, Wood, Togiak, Nushagak River systems

- **Alaska Peninsula**: King Salmon (Ugashik), Chignik, Meshik, Sandy Rivers; Nelson Lagoon system

- **Kuskokwim**: Goodnews, Arolik, Kanektok, Aniak, Holitna River systems

- **Lower Yukon**: Andreafsky, Anvik Rivers

Northwest

Most drainages from Yukon to Kotzebue Sound support some spawning populations; only a few (in Norton Sound) are noteworthy. The run timing is mid-June to mid-July, peaking in late June or early July.

- **Norton Sound**: Unalakleet, Shaktoolik, Inglutalik, Tubutulik, Kwiniuk Rivers

Interior

Most fish have traveled extensively in freshwater to reach locations in Interior and are in less than prime condition, but good fishing can be found in and below nearly every clear-water confluence and slough of the Yukon River (for fish migrating to spawning sites on the upper Yukon and in Canada). The run timing is from late June to early August; the peak occurs in mid-July.

- **Tanana**: Salcha, Chena, Chatanika Rivers; Nenana River clear-water tributaries

Chapter 2
Silvers: The August Salmon

It is the height of the short northern summer, and fireweed stands tall as corn next to old Charlie Wassilie's gear shed. From this vantage point high above the Kuskokwim, he scans a landscape little changed since his ancestors arrived eons ago, then offers me a chunk of smoked salmon and some of his thoughts.

"Fishing should pick up, soon . . . Freddie's caught some out in the Bay already . . . but with the river so low, I don't know. I remember when I was a boy, one summer we didn't get any until September."

Charlie's been busy these last few weeks, using this special lull time—when the rivers ebb with the last of the runoff and the big runs of king and chum subside—to fix gear, smoke fish, and work on boats. He has faith that soon enough Alaska's late summer rains will flood the rivers, and on the crest will come frantic hordes of salmon, pumping new life into the land. For Charlie and his people, the arrival of these last salmon of summer means the completion of crucial food stores necessary to carry them through the long winter. But for *gussuks*, or white men like me, these fish have a significance that goes far beyond their food value. Silvers or coho salmon are the punchiest fighters of the entire Pacific salmon clan.

Nothing gets the adrenaline flowing like the thought of bright, rambunctious coho, and the sweet torture they can inflict on a fly and an eight-weight rod. The show of these August salmon marks the end of Alaska's glorious summer— a bittersweet but exhilarating time for Alaska anglers—and a call to embrace some of the best and last fishing of the season.

Introduction

The aggressive and acrobatic silver or coho salmon (*Oncorhynchus kisutch*) gets high marks from Pacific anglers, who pursue them with a passion perhaps second only to that shown for the mighty chinook. Found in great numbers along the coast of Alaska from the Southeast region to Norton Sound, the silver has traditionally been an important commercial and subsistence species, as well as the cornerstone of Alaska's fabulous late summer sportfishery. The arrival of these fish along the coast in late July kicks off a wave of excitement, as dozens of fish derbies get under way and countless sport anglers prepare for what many consider the high point of Alaska's fishing season.

A reckless and voracious predatory nature—important to his success as a species—is what sets the silver apart as a world-class game fish. No other salmon takes a lure as vigorously or predictably, even long after it has stopped feeding in freshwater. And once hooked, the August salmon fights spectacularly, with long, hard runs and vigorous leaping. With big fish of 12 to 15 pounds or more on a fly rod or light- to medium-weight spinning tackle, the battle can be one of freshwater angling's most challenging.

Description

The Alaska silver is a powerful, medium-sized salmon. When fresh from the sea, it has a steel blue or green back, chrome sides, and a whitish belly, with a sprinkling of moderate-sized, irregular black markings along the top sides. You can easily mistake it for a small chinook, although a silver's tail is usually less forked, smaller, and spotted only on the upper lobe, and the silver does not have the dark gum line of a king salmon. Like other Pacific salmon, spawning silvers undergo dramatic changes in appearance, particularly males. A deepening of the body, with dark red hues developing along the sides, greenish-black shading on the back and head, and enlarged jaws and teeth are some of the more recognizable transformations that occur after the silver enters freshwater.

The third largest of the Pacific salmon, Alaska silvers can reach weights of up to 20 pounds or more, although they average six to nine pounds (more in certain areas of the state). For many years, the world's largest silver salmon came from Southeast Alaska and the coast of British Columbia (up to 30 pounds), but recently transplanted stocks in the Great Lakes have surpassed the largest specimens caught from the species' natural range. The current International Game Fish Association (IGFA) world record is a whopping 33-pounder caught in Pulaski, New York, in 1989, while the biggest sport fish caught in Alaska's waters was a 26-pound silver taken from Icy Strait in 1976.

Besides providing some of the greatest sport to be had on rod and reel, silver salmon also make for some of the finest eating of any fish in the North Pacific. Their flesh is orange-red, firm and flavorful, not as rich or as prized as that of the sockeye or chinook, but in many ways more suited for grilling, frying, smoking, or canning.

Range, Abundance, and Status

Silver salmon have a potential range that encompasses most of the North Pacific basin, from Hokkaido, Japan, (and scattered points farther south) north to the Anadyr River, across the Bering Sea and south along the North American coast to Monterey Bay, California. Comprising only a small portion of the total Pacific salmon population—less than 10 percent—they're much more abundant along our coast than in Asia, and have had their range extended considerably through extensive propagation efforts.

In Alaska, silvers are found continuously from Dixon Entrance below Ketchikan to Norton Sound, then sporadically to Point Hope (68 degrees north latitude), with their greatest numbers concentrated from Kuskokwim Bay south. The Kuskokwim River is the state's largest producer, with runs reaching up to a million fish in peak years.

This midsized salmon has a noted preference for short, coastal streams, and you'll find him at his best in the steep, well-watered terrain of Kodiak Island, the North Gulf Coast, and Southeast Alaska. (There are more than 2,000 known silver salmon streams there alone.) Silvers in these waters routinely reach weights of 12 pounds or more, with 20-pounders not uncommon. Via the immense Yukon and Kuskokwim Rivers, the silver salmon is able to penetrate the state's vast interior and utilize the abundant glacial gravels of the Alaska Range, spawning inland as far as tributaries of the upper Tanana River. Through intensive stocking and propagation efforts by the Alaska Department of Fish and Game, numerous landlocked, enhanced, and "terminal" (nonbreeding) populations of silver salmon thrive today, providing increased opportunities, particularly for urban anglers.

Many areas of Alaska, like Southeast, are currently enjoying record harvest levels, and even though enhanced runs comprise a significant part of the total catch, overall the status of Alaska's silver salmon is as good as it's ever been, which means that anglers can expect to encounter some of the world's most productive fishing for the species for years to come, on thousands of rivers, lakes, and bays.

Life History and Habits

Silvers, like the rest of the salmon, have interesting life histories and habits. After emigrating from the sea in late summer and fall (late July through September in most of Alaska), they seek out river headwaters and side channels to spawn, mating and depositing fertilized eggs much as other salmon species do. The breeding act peaks during October and November and is usually completed by January, although it may extend into April in certain locations.

Hatching sometime in midwinter, young coho quickly move into stream margins, side channels, and small pools to feed on small insects and plankton. Territorial and voracious, they display the same aggressive tendencies that will distinguish them as great sport fish later in life. (The small fry that congregate under cutbanks and chase and nip passing objects are usually coho.) Minnows, smolt, and even their own kind are subject to their depredations, and they can inflict serious damage on other important species like sockeye salmon and rainbow trout.

From the data available, it seems that Alaska's silvers spend a year or two (rarely three) in freshwater, before smolting and heading to the ocean in spring or early summer (May to July). While at sea, they feed heavily and grow rapidly on steady diets of fish (herring, sand lance, smelt, and other small salmon) and invertebrates (crab larvae and shrimp), tending to prefer the top of the water column to 100 feet down.

Spending their entire ocean existence near shore or in circular wanderings far out into the Gulf of Alaska, Alaska silvers mostly return to spawn at the end of their second summer at sea, at three or four years of age. A significant percentage of oddball age classes—precocious, two-year-old fish called "jacks," or five- or even six-year-old fish—can occur at times in some systems. Timing and duration of runs varies, as the fish seek optimum stream flow and water temperatures before entering freshwater, but silvers can usually be found in the mouths of rivers anywhere from late July and early August in the north to September and October in the south.

More social than chinook, but not as gregarious as sockeye or pink salmon, prespawning silvers congregate extensively in bays, river mouths, lake outlets, pools, and sloughs, and show themselves frequently, making easy targets for sport anglers. But it is their temperament and feeding behavior more than anything that is their undoing in encounters with the sport angler. Born bullies, young coho in small, enclosed areas kill each other in their drive for food and territory (unlike chinook and other salmon). Their legendary gluttony inflicts serious depredation on young sockeye salmon, trout, and charr in rivers. Out at sea, silvers commonly drive schools of frantic bait fish up to the surface in tightly packed balls, and with chomping jaws gorge to the bursting point.

Freshwater Methods and Gear

Spin Casting and Bait Casting

The vast majority of coho caught in the state's rivers and tidewaters are taken on spinning gear and hardware. A medium-weight, medium-action salmon rod (seven to eight-and-a-half feet long), matched with a high-quality, open-faced reel and eight- to 17-pound test, along with an assortment of popular spinners, plugs, and spoons is the preferred armament, from northern Southeast to Norton Sound.

More than any other salmon, silvers strike at flash, which explains why the Super Vibrax spinner and Pixee spoon (both made by Blue Fox of Cambridge, Minnesota) are the most popular salmon lures in Alaska. Silver and gold, with orange, pink, yellow, or chartreuse attractors, seem to be the most productive color combinations, in sizes 4 to 6 for the spinners and half ounce and seven-eighths ounce for the spoons. Other popular silver salmon lures for spin casting are the larger-sized Mepps Aglia, Panther Martin, and Rooster Tail spinners, and the Krocodile, Hot Rod, and Kastmaster spoons (half ounce or larger) in nickel/chrome, brass, fire red, red prism, yellow, or chartreuse combinations.

Because of their innate aggressiveness, silvers quite often pursue lures through the water, even rising to the surface on occasion, especially in tidal water or in the lower sections of rivers. Once in freshwater, however, they tend to avoid extravagant expenditures of energy, so careful casts and slower retrieves produce the most strikes. Fish main stem lies as you would for kings, but give special attention to sloughs, cutbanks, eddies, tailouts of pools, and feeder confluences, as silvers group in these areas to rest and engage in prespawning behavior, making for concentrated fishing opportunities. In clear streams, locating and targeting silvers in these holding zones is greatly simplified, but in turbid or very deep water, the angler must look for showing fish or choose the most likely holding locations.

From an upstream position, cast ahead of the lie. In very clear or shallow water, use caution when approaching silvers, as they can spook easily. With a steady but slow retrieve, work the lure so that it passes through at fish eye level. Work the lie several times, varying the placement, retrieve speed, and depth; then move on (no matter how good the water looks), because there are almost always plenty of eager silvers to be had elsewhere. If you are sight-fishing a salmon group, work the lure deep along the upstream or downstream edge of the school, watching carefully for a response of any kind. Quite often, a "taker" (usually an aggressive male) will burst from the ranks and nab or pursue the lure. If you don't hook him immediately, you can usually get him on subsequent casts.

At times silvers may refuse to bite the normal enticements, such as in bright and sunny conditions, in extremely turbid or clear water, or when they are on the move or have been in freshwater too long. You may see them cruising sloughs, holding in tailouts, showing themselves and generally doing the

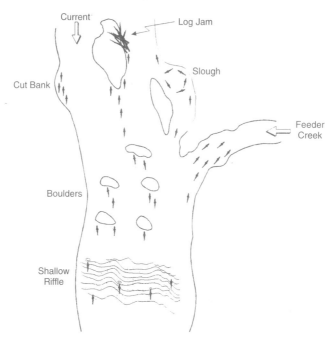

Typical silver salmon river lies.

same things they normally do, but refusing to hit the standard spinners, spoons, or plugs. This is to be expected every now and then, but you can sometimes force these non-biters to hit with different tactics. For one, if you're sight-fishing, tighten up your casts and retrieves to work the lure right in front of their noses, repeatedly, until you anger them into striking. Another trick is to change lure size and color. Go oversize and brighter (orange, red, yellow) for turbid waters, and smaller and more subdued (black, purple, brown) for bright, clear waters. If that doesn't work, try a different action or retrieve. Some anglers are able to induce strikes with erratic, jerky retrieves of their spinners and spoons, while others have done the same by switching to plugs and crank baits. The idea here is to incite a response with stimuli that go beyond what the silver normally encounters under these conditions.

Bait Fishing

One traditional, surefire way of loosening the jaws of even the most finicky August salmon is to drift some salmon roe through their lies. This is still an immensely popular technique on many silver streams (although it's illegal in some areas). Under most conditions, a ball of roe on a single egg hook drifted along bottom will outfish any other method, especially when fishing glacial or run-off water. Most egg anglers use the conventional "egg loop" snell on a no. 1/0 egg or steelhead hook, fished with a lead dropper or rubber core sinker. You can dress things up with a piece of colored yarn, or even more deadly, a drift bobber, like a no. 4 Spin-N-Glo. The bait is fished on a drift, keeping a taut line as the rig bounces along bottom. Silvers tend to pick up roe gently and mouth it a bit before either spitting it out or running with it, so you need to be ready and watchful of the slightest hesitation or disturbance in your line.

Drift/Troll Fishing

On larger rivers like the Kenai, Naknek, and Alagnak, trolling and drifting plugs, drift bobbers, and spinners from boats are standard practice for silver salmon. Spin-N-Glos, Tee-Spoons, Hot Shots, and Okie Drifters are the lures of choice, usually sweetened with bait (salmon roe). Rigging and techniques are almost identical to those used for king salmon (including drifting, trolling, back trolling, back bouncing—see the chinook chapter on page 24 for details), except that the gear is lighter and smaller. A medium-weight, fast-action steelhead or salmon casting rod (seven to eight-and-a-half feet) works fine, mated to a high-quality casting reel loaded with 200 yards of 10- to 17-pound line.

Fly-fishing

In many ways, silver salmon are the Pacific Coast's perfect game fish for fly-fishing. More abundant and widespread than either the chinook or steelhead, they are quick on the take, very sporting, and spectacular jumpers. In the quality and variety of angling they can provide over a wide range of conditions, they are certainly without peer.

You don't need expensive, sophisticated gear or techniques to enjoy Alaska's matchless fishing for the species. A stout seven- or eight-weight rod, matching reel, some floating or sink-tip line, 1X to 3X (8- to 12-pound) tippet, and some basic patterns, work fine for most conditions. For big fish in heavy current, you may want to bump up to a nine-weight rod. The basic streamer and wet fly presentations used for trout and the other salmon will be equally effective on Alaska's silvers most of the time, with long casts, long leaders, and fancy pre-sentations being neither necessary nor desirable.

As with the other salmon, the closer to salt water you can intercept the Alaska silver, the better. Bays and estuaries, river mouths, and lower stream sections right above tidewater are ideal. Farther into freshwater, the silvers' behavior, appearance, and gaminess begins to change. The basic approach should be similar to that used for chinooks: deep drift presentations and "short strip" streamer swings through main stem lies and holding water, such as channels, sloughs, pools, confluences, eddies, and current seams—anywhere silvers might be resting or moving through. (Keep in mind that silvers usually move less through main channels than kings do.) Sight-fishing in clear water, with the more precise casting it allows, is best. The take of a silver is usually much more noticeable and abrupt than that of a chinook, and quite often it will hook itself and begin running and jumping immediately. During the peak of the runs in average streams, coho congregate by the dozens in good holding water, so you can have all the action your arms can handle once you find a good location.

Coho fly

A whole genre of Alaska salmon flies has evolved to capitalize on the silver's fondness for bright, gaudy patterns (not to mention the average fly fisher's fetish for colorful, artsy creations). Flash Flies, Sparklers, Maraflash Flies, Krystal Bullets, Flashabous, Silver Comets, and the like vie for your attention and dollars at the local fly shop. They're all very effective on Alaska's August salmon, as are the more traditional Northwest patterns like the Skykomish Sunrise, Polar Shrimp, Leech, and Woolly Bugger (in sizes 2 to 6). What's more, these flies are all easy to make on your own, with a vise, some thread, hooks, and an assortment of colored tinsel, feathers, and yarn. With very little imagination and some practice, you can come up with your own creations that are just as effective, more durable, and less expensive than commercial flies.

Under certain conditions, silver salmon can even be lured up to the surface with dry flies, a fact anglers often discover by accident when skating streamers at the beginning of a backcast or the end of a drift. Generally, it works best to have shallow, clear water (four feet or less), with good floaters like the Irresistible, Bomber, Wulff, Elk Hair Caddis, or Double Humpy in sizes 4 to 10. Some anglers even do well with shrew or mouse imitations and other topwater specialty patterns like the Pollywog. Unlike fly-fishing for trout, for silvers you'll want to use short, fast strips across the current, to make surface commotion and noise. (Remember, these fish are not feeding.) Techniques and patterns used for summer steelheading (such as skating flies and riffle hitches) can also raise Alaskan silver salmon.

- **Top Flies for Alaska Silver Salmon:** Flash Fly, Coho Fly, Polar Shrimp, Egg-Sucking Leech, Purple Woolly Bugger, Maraflash, Krystal Bullet, Alaskabou, Comet, and Everglow.

Pink Pollywog

Saltwater Methods and Gear

Like any salmon, silvers are at their fighting best in salt water, and a good number of the state's sport anglers wouldn't have them any other way. From Kodiak to Ketchikan, an almost unlimited amount of inshore opportunity beckons, with the excitement of abundant fishing and the incomparable beauty of Alaska's magnificent coast. The basics of saltwater silver fishing are within easy grasp of most anglers and include more or less the following:

Bait Fishing

Despite all of the advances in gear and lures, trolling (or "mooching") herring remains far and away the most productive method for taking saltwater silver salmon, if you believe the fishing derby records and salty charter boat captains. Using fresh if possible (or frozen if not), small- to medium-sized fish (three to five inches), whole or "plug cut" according to preference, you rig the bait to impart a tantalizing spin when dragged or drifted behind the boat (see the saltwater section in the chinook chapter on page 33 for more details on trolling and mooching). The bait is usually rigged behind an attractor (flasher or dodger), with downriggers, weights, or diving planers used to reach the proper depth. The addition of bait harnesses ("Herring Aid" or "Salmon Killer"), plastic jig skirts (hoochies), and fish oils are popular ways of enhancing the bait's appeal.

Regardless of how you cut (or don't cut) the bait, the trick is to imitate the action of a stunned or wounded bait fish, with the herring rolling in tight, fast circles or big lazy spirals. The action should be determined by the speed of the troll, drift, or retrieve and the way the fish are rigged (or cut). The two types of movement are both effective for salmon under a wide range of conditions, but most coho anglers prefer the tighter, faster action. Fishing 25 to 75 feet behind the boat, most work the herring along the edge of bait patches and in other areas likely to hold salmon, varying their speed and course to work the water most efficiently.

Lures

Spoons, spinners, plugs, and jigs can also be very effective, at times even more so than bait. Over the years, commercial trollers have caught scads of salmon by fishing only simple spoons and plastic squid-like jig skirts called "hoochies." And some of the best saltwater sport anglers in Southeast Alaska can catch more fish on hardware, if the conditions are right, than an army of bait anglers could. When coho are concentrated and actively feeding, trolling, casting, or jigging lures is the most exciting and enjoyable way to fish. Some of the more popular lures used for silvers in salt are medium-sized (half-ounce to one-ounce) Krocodile, Pixee, Reflecto, Hot Rod, and Crippled Herring spoons; medium to large (three-eighths-ounce to five-eighths-ounce) Super Vibrax, Mepps Aglia, Bolo, Skagit, and Shyster spinners; small to medium (one-eighth-ounce to $5/16$-ounce) J-Plugs, Flatfish, Hot Shot, Rapalas, and Kwikfish; and small (2.5-inch) jigs like the Buzz Bomb, Dart, Teezer, Chinook Special, and Stinger. The most effective colors seem to be combinations of green, white, silver, and blue (sometimes spiced with attractor red, orange, or yellow). Small keel sinkers (one to three ounces) can be used to get the lure down if needed. The best areas for fishing lures are usually along beaches, heads of bays, tide rips, jetties, kelp beds, and anywhere you spot bait fish concentrations or showing salmon. Shore fishing opportunities abound near almost every community along Alaska's southern coasts; check with locals for the best spots.

Finding the Fish

To freshwater anglers accustomed to stalking their quarry within the confines of riverbanks, the challenge of locating salmon in the wide-open sea can be daunting. But since silvers are predominantly top-water feeders (usually within the top 40 feet or so), finding fish in inshore waters can be as simple as spotting surface activity or locating bait patches. Flocking seabirds, jumping or rolling salmon, milling bait fish, even the presence of other boats are dead giveaways. Always bring binoculars for scouting water! If nothing obvious is

Pierce lead hook through side of mouth (do so with mouth closed), pushing shank completely through. Then the point of the hook should be pushed completely back through the side of the fish, just forward of the edge of the gill cover, as shown in illustration. The trailing hook can either be buried into the herring (as shown) or left trailing freely behind. This arrangement will give the head of the herring a slight bend that will force the fish to spin and roll as it is drawn through the water.

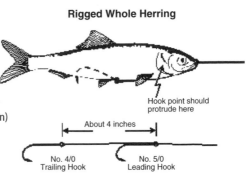

Rigged Whole Herring

Hook point should protrude here

About 4 inches

No. 4/0 Trailing Hook   No. 5/0 Leading Hook

Sea bird activity is a sure sign to look for when searching for feeding silvers.

Gearing for Saltwater Silver Salmon

For trolling with diving planers and weights, you'll need a medium-action, heavy salmon trolling rod, seven to eight-and-a-half feet long, mated with a high-quality levelwind reel capable of holding several hundred yards of 20- to 30-pound test mono or braided line. For fishing downriggers, lighter gear is often used: 10- to 20-pound line on a medium-weight salmon rod and matching reel. Mooching usually involves a longer, more limber rod (up to 10 feet) than that used for trolling, and a good levelwind reel loaded with at least several hundred yards of 12- to 20-pound test line. Jigging outfits are usually comprised of short, stout, fast-taper rods mated to a levelwind with a good drag and loaded with 15- to 25-pound test braided line. For spin casting, a medium-weight, fast-action salmon or steelhead rod, 7.5 to 8.5 feet long, with a matching spinning reel loaded with 200 yards of eight- to 12-pound test mono, is recommended.

present, carefully examine kelp beds, shorelines, tide rips, the back eddies of points and islands, the heads of bays with salmon streams, and around any kind of underwater structure (such as drop-offs, shoals, or reefs). You can expect to encounter silver salmon at anywhere from 60 feet to the surface in these locations. Depending on how hungry they are, the availability and concentration of bait fish, their prespawning condition, the tides, and many other factors, you should do well with trolling, mooching, casting, or jigging lures and bait.

Fish locators and depth sounders, marine charts, and downriggers, in addition to a knowledge of the waters, go a long way toward ensuring success in the challenging marine environment. The services of a licensed charter boat operator or friend with a boat, gear, and local experience are highly recommended for someone new to saltwater angling for silvers.

Herring fly

Saltwater Fly-fishing

Fly-fishing silvers in Alaska's inshore waters isn't nearly as prevalent or popular as you might imagine. Most of it is done in the sheltered inside waters of Southeast, where conditions are more conducive to fly-casting. The basic challenge is finding salmon near the surface and then matching the size and color of local forage fish. Anglers work bait patches, kelp beds, creek mouths, tide rips, shorelines, and the like with long, fishhair or bucktail bait fish imitation streamers (three to five inches

Alaska's Top 10 Trophy Silvers

26 pounds, 0 ounces (state record)	Icy Strait, Juneau (Southeast)	1976
25 pounds, 4 ounces	St. Nicholas Creek, Prince of Wales Island (Southeast)	1991
24 pounds, 0 ounces	Grant Cove, Ketchikan (Southeast)	1986
23 pounds, 8 ounces	Yakutat (Southeast)	1981
23 pounds, 2 ounces	North Shelter Island, Juneau (Southeast)	1974
23 pounds, 0 ounces	Italio River (Southeast)	1981
23 pounds, 0 ounces	Handtrollers Cove, Juneau (Southeast)	1982
22 pounds, 14 ounces	Pasagshak River, Kodiak (Southcentral)	1993
22 pounds, 11 ounces	North Pass, Juneau (Southeast)	1987
22 pounds, 9 ounces	Lynn Canal, Juneau (Southeast)	1976

long), tube flies, or standard saltwater patterns like the Tarpon Fly, Deceiver, and Clouser Minnow (size 2 to 3/0). The most productive colors seem to be combinations of white, yellow, green, pink, blue, purple, and orange. A long, seven-, eight-, or even nine-weight rod is preferred, with matching reel, a long sink-tip, full sink line, or shooting taper, and short leader/tippet of eight- to 12-pound test.

Trolling flies with downriggers or "bucktailing" along the surface, a common practice in British Columbia and waters farther south, is done only infrequently in Alaska. It requires a big fly reel spooled with mono (15- to 20-pound test); large, bushy, single or tandem hook streamer flies; and weights up to three ounces if fishing without downriggers. Anglers usually fish more than one rod (except in Alaska, where only one rod is allowed by law), with different weights and lengths of line, to work the flies at various depths and increase the chances of a strike.

Alaska's Top Trophy Silver Salmon Locations

• **Yakutat:** Situk, Italio, Lost, Kiklukh Rivers (Southeast)

• **Juneau:** Shelter Island, Handtrollers Cove, Stephens Passage (Southeast)

• **Kodiak:** Pasagshak, Karluk, Uganik, Saltery Rivers (Southcentral)

• **Kenai River** (Southcentral)

Alaska's Major Silver Salmon Locations

Alaska anglers catch over one-half million silver salmon each year, predominantly by saltwater trolling and freshwater spin casting, with most effort concentrated in Southeast (Ketchikan, Juneau, and Yakutat) and Southcentral (Kenai Peninsula and Susitna River). A smaller but significant amount of silver fishing occurs on clear-flowing drainages of the North Gulf Coast (east of Cordova) and the more remote rivers of Southwest (northern Alaska Peninsula to the lower Kuskokwim) and Norton Sound. Popular stocked, landlocked coho fisheries also exist in and around the Anchorage area, the Kenai Peninsula, and the Interior region.

Southeast

Angling for silvers here is predominantly marine trolling. The Haines/Skagway, Prince of Wales, and Yakutat areas receive most of the freshwater sport effort. Runs last from July to November, peaking in September and October.

- **Yakutat:** Yakutat Bay; Situk, Italio, Lost, East Alsek, Akwe, Doame, Kiklukh, Tsiu, Kaliakh, Tawah Rivers
- **Haines/Skagway:** Chilkoot, Chilkat Rivers; Lutak Inlet
- **Juneau:** Upper Lynn Canal, Favorite/ Saginaw Channels, Northern Stephens Passage, Chatham/Icy Strait, Cross Sound; Montana, Cowee Creeks; Surge, Klag Bay, Mitchell Bay, Youngs (Admiralty Creek), Sweetwater Lake systems
- **Sitka/Petersburg:** Ernest, Sitka, Frederick Sounds; Wrangell Narrows/ Duncan Canal, Lower Stephens Passage, Eastern Passage; Stikine, Zimovia, Upper Clarence, Sumner Straits; Duncan Saltchuck, Blind Slough; Petersburg, Kadake, Thoms, Ohmer, Anan, Aaron, Sitkoh Creeks; Salmon Bay, Eva, Redoubt, Petersburg, Red Lake systems; Kah Sheets, Harding, Kadashan, Plotnikof, Castle Rivers; Stikine River system; Port Banks, Katlian River/Bay, Starrigavan Creek/Bay
- **Ketchikan/Prince of Wales:** Gulf of Esquibel, Bucareli Bay, Clarence Strait, Behm Canal (Yes Bay, Bell Island, Clover Pass), Revillagigedo Channel, Gravina Island; Staney, Wolverine, Ward, Ketchikan Creeks; Sarkar, McDonald, Salmon Bay, Saltchuck Lakes; Klawock, Thorne, Karta, Wilson, Blossom, Naha, Kegan River systems

Southcentral

The Southcentral region has Alaska's most fished silver salmon streams, many offering outstanding fishing. The run timing is from late July into November, with a peak in August and September.

- **Chugach/Prince William Sound:** Katalla, Bering River systems; Alaganik Slough, Martin River systems; Thirtynine Mile, Ibek, Clear Creeks; Controller Bay Stream; Eyak, Johnson Bay, Nellie Martin/Patton, Beach, Robe, San Juan Rivers; Valdez Arm, Wells Passage, Knight Island/ Passage, Montague Strait, Hinchinbrook Entrance, Orca Bay, Resurrection Bay, Passage Canal
- **Wrangell Mountains:** Tonsina River system (Landlocked: Strelna, Lou's Lakes)
- **Kenai Peninsula:** Kenai, Moose, Russian, Anchor, Swanson, Kasilof, Ninilchik Rivers; Deep, Crooked Creeks; Kachemak Bay, English Bay, Rocky River (Landlocked: Engineer, Upper Jean, Portage, Scout, Union, Island, Stormy, Arc, Centennial, Encelewski Lakes)
- **Upper Cook Inlet:** Little Susitna River; Cottonwood, Wasilla, Fish, Jim Creeks; Lewis, Theodore Rivers
- **Lower Cook Inlet:** Kamishak, Chakachatna-McArthur, Crescent, Kustatan, Beluga, Chuitna, Amakdedori Rivers; Polly, Silver Salmon Creeks
- **Mat-Su Valley:** (Landlocked: Matanuska, Echo, Victor, Wolf, Finger, Lucille, Memory, Loon, Christiansen Lakes)
- **Susitna River:** Chulitna, Deshka, Talachulitna, Talkeetna, upper Susitna (tributaries) Rivers; Alexander, Lake, Willow, Montana, Sunshine, Peters, Caswell, Greys, Sheep Creeks
- **Anchorage/Turnagain:** Ship, Campbell, Bird Creeks; Twentymile, Placer River systems
- **Kodiak/Afognak/Shuyak Islands:** Shuyak, Chiniak, Ugak, Big, Neketa Bays; Carry Inlet; Portage, Danger,

Deadman, Akalura, Roslyn, Salonie Creek systems; Pauls Creek/Bay system; Karluk, Afognak, Red (Ayakulik), Saltery, Uganik, Dog Salmon, Terror, Zachar, Pasagshak, Spiridon Rivers; Chiniak Bay streams (Buskin, Sid, Olds, American Rivers); Olga, Malina, Miami, Little River Lake systems

• **Shelikof Strait (West):** Swikshak, Big Rivers

Southwest

Southwest has some of Alaska's finest freshwater silver salmon opportunities in terms of quality and abundance, with fly-fishing possibilities almost limitless. Many streams with strong runs (especially on the Alaska Peninsula) receive little or no pressure. The run timing is late July into early September, with the peak in August.

• **Bristol Bay:** Nushagak-Mulchatna, Wood, Togiak, Alagnak, Naknek River systems

• **North Alaska Peninsula:** Egegik, Ugashik River systems (including King Salmon River); Nelson Lagoon system; Port Heiden; Cinder, Chignik, Meshik, Ilnik Rivers; Swanson Lagoon

• **South Alaska Peninsula:** Russell Creek, Mortensen Lagoon, Thin Point Cove (Cold Bay), Lefthand Bay, Beaver River, Volcano River, Belkofski Bay

• **Kuskokwim:** Goodnews, Arolik, Kanektok, Kisaralik, Kwethluk, Kasigluk, Aniak, Holitna Rivers

• **Lower Yukon:** Andreafsky, Anvik Rivers

Northwest

Northwest's high-quality fishing opportunity is limited to eastern Norton Sound and a few Seward Peninsula drainages. The run timing is from August to mid-September, with a peak in August.

• **Norton Sound:** Unalakleet, Shaktoolik, Ungalik, Inglutalik, Kwiniuk, Tubutulik Rivers

• **Seward Peninsula:** Fish-Niukluk, Nome, Sinuk Rivers

Interior

There are a few outstanding opportunities for late fall-running silver salmon in Interior, primarily from late August into November, peaking during late September and October.

• **Upper Tanana:** Delta Clearwater River; Nenana-Clear Creek, Seventeenmile Slough

Chapter 3
Sockeye: The Shy Salmon

It is early July, and you are at hand to witness an amazing spectacle taking place on the rivers of Southwest Alaska. For days and weeks on end, waters that lie fallow most of the year seethe with hundreds of thousands of bright salmon, fresh from a journey across the open sea. En route to spawning areas miles upriver, these energetic hordes choke side channels and crowd the banks in numbers that must be seen to be believed, at times forming a shimmering blue wave of tails and fins that stretches for miles through these crystal waters.

The guide beaches the raft at the head of a set of rapids and you hop ashore, hastily assembled rod in trembling hands. A familiar lure flipped into the current tumbles through the surging ranks with no takers. Surprised, you cast again, this time with careful presentation and retrieve. Nothing. Still another cast brings not the slightest response, although these waters literally boil with salmon. How can this be? You try different lures and tactics, flailing the river with increasing frustration, as fish jump everywhere in mockery of your efforts. After 20 minutes of nary a nibble, you're about to give up and swear off fishing for good, when your guide steps in with a knowing smile.

Wielding a long, limber rod and a strange fly you've never seen before, he wades out and lays his line in a short arc upriver. It moves quickly downstream, then stops, as a chrome torpedo crashes through the foam and flips furiously along the surface. Like a skyrocket on a tether, the fish careens wildly. It reenters the river, rips out into the main channel at the speed of light, then somersaults into the boil of a big rapid. Levering its body against strong current, the enraged salmon strips into the backing. This is a fish out of control, and no one knows it better than your guide, who wisely lowers the rod, tightens up, and parts ways with this freedom-crazed fighter. Wasting no regret, your trusted companion quickly busies himself with raising another, while you scramble to do the same—if you can get ahold of one of those flies!

Introduction

In many ways, the sockeye or red salmon (*Oncorhynchus nerka*) is the most challenging and enigmatic of Alaska's five salmon for sport anglers. Prolific almost beyond measure in some parts of the state and extremely coveted for its flesh—the richest of all the salmon—the sockeye has long been the state's most valuable commercial species, contributing millions to Alaska's economy (up to $200 million a year for Bristol Bay alone). But because of its steadfast reluctance to take a lure, for the longest time it was not even considered a sport fish.

Since sockeyes spend most their lives grazing plankton, they're more predisposed to passive behavior than fly-shredding bouts of predatory aggression. But beneath that meek exterior and generic appearance lies an intensity and physical prowess that is truly astounding. Endowed with amazing energy—the strongest swimmers of the salmon, they can easily leap 15-foot waterfalls—sockeyes move up from the sea into the far reaches of rivers with remarkable speed. More than any other salmon, they are creatures of single-minded purpose, possessing a supreme will to let nothing short of instant death keep them from their destiny upriver.

Anglers who succeed in tempting this normally tight-lipped salmon are in for one of the world's wildest battles on light tackle. With explosive leaps, mad, reel-smoking dashes up and down river, and incredible stamina, they are, for their size, the strongest and most demanding of all game fish in Alaska, an assessment unanimously confirmed by all who have come away from their first sockeye encounter with bruises, broken gear, and battered nerves.

Description

Sockeyes display a remarkably uniform appearance throughout their range in Alaska. Millions of fish come in from the sea weighing around six pounds each, with large specimens tipping the scale at 10 to 12 pounds or more. (The state record sport fish is a 16-pounder from the Kenai River.) They average 24 inches in length, with streamlined bodies of metallic blue/gray/green on the back, silver sides, and silver-white bellies. Prominent markings on the top sides and tail fins of sockeyes are almost always absent; this, along with the presence of 30 to 40 fine, closely spaced and serrated rakers on the first gill arch, identifies the species. Sea-bright sockeye closely resemble chum salmon. As the sockeye is predominantly a plankton feeder, teeth on prespawning fish are usually less developed than those on other salmon.

Spawning sockeye salmon present one of Nature's most striking images. The males develop vivid red bodies, greenish-black heads, thick humps, and hooked jaws, while females tend to be more subdued in appearance. Color can vary in intensity and hue in different populations. Juvenile sockeye have short, dark oval parr marks usually ending at or just below the lateral line. Kokanee, the landlocked form of sockeye, are very similar in appearance, but much smaller, reaching about 10 inches in length and rarely exceeding a pound and a half in weight in Alaska.

Sockeye are the most prized of Alaskan salmon for eating, with rich, red flesh of unparalleled flavor, whether grilled, smoked, or canned. Their value as a food fish, uniformity in size, and relative abundance has made them the most desirable and economically significant component of Alaska's commercial, subsistence, and personal fisheries.

Range, Abundance, and Status

Originally, sockeye salmon ranged coastally from northern California and Oregon to Point Hope, Alaska, (with scattered sightings in the Arctic Ocean) and in Asia from Hokkaido, Japan, to the Anadyr River in northeastern Siberia. The third most abundant of the Pacific salmon, they are found now in greatest numbers from the Fraser River in British Columbia to Alaska's Bristol Bay (and in Asia, in the rivers of Kamchatka). In the immense, lake-river habitat of the Alaska Peninsula and Bristol Bay, sockeye runs can number in the millions, supporting valuable fisheries and rich, diverse food chains (see the chapters on charr and rainbow trout on pages 77 and 97).

Alaska's sockeye populations have fluctuated over the years, rebounding from depressed levels in the 1960s and 1970s to current record levels. (Commercial fishers caught 65 million and sport anglers caught well over a half million fish in 1993.) In terms of habitat, current runs, and changes in the world salmon market, things look very bright for the future of this amazing resource and the almost unlimited potential it holds for world-class sportfishing.

Life History and Habits

The remarkable success of sockeye salmon as a species stems from their ability to directly exploit the astounding productivity of the north Pacific, using its rich blooms of plankton as their main food source and the countless lakes found along the coast as their nurseries. Because of the economic importance of this fabulous fishery, Alaska's sockeyes have been the most extensively studied of the state's salmon, and quite a bit is known of their life history and movement patterns.

Mature prespawning sockeye salmon begin appearing in rivers across the state in early summer (usually from late May on), with peak migration periods from mid-June through early August. Their local abundance can be staggering, choking the larger river systems in the most productive parts of their range with numbers in the millions. As a general rule, sockeyes are found in rivers that are connected with lakes, but some sockeye are adapted to breeding entirely in rivers or, rarely, in estuaries. (Estuarine fish tend to go to sea the first summer after hatching.) Residuals—sea-run fish that for some reason spend their entire lives in freshwater—and true landlocked populations such as kokanee live in numerous lakes throughout the Southeast region and a few in Southcentral Alaska. Favored sockeye spawning locations are in stream outlets directly below lakes, in feeder creeks, and along gravelly lake shores, with peak activity occurring in late summer and fall (August through October).

Like the rest of the Pacific salmon, the female sockeye digs the gravel nest, then mates in several bouts of egg-laying that may involve the digging of more than one redd and fertilization by several males. Up to 4,000 or more eggs are deposited and incubate in anywhere from six weeks to five months, depending on water temperature. Breeding is terminal, though fish may linger for weeks after spawning, despite pronounced physical deterioration. Young sockeye fry emerge in early spring (April to May) and usually migrate to the nursery lake by summer. In lake shallows, they feed primarily on insects and crustaceans before moving in schools to deeper waters to consume plankton in the upper water column. Some fry migrate downriver to the sea after their first summer, but most Alaska sockeye spend two, and in some cases even three years in freshwater before smolting. Smolt out-migration occurs in the spring, usually from May to June.

Once in the ocean, young sockeye grow rapidly on diets of crustaceans, squid, zooplankton, and on rare occasion even small fish such as sand lance, eulachon, herring, and rockfish. Their deep ocean existence takes them considerable distances out into the North Pacific, where they usually complete two or three immense, counterclockwise circuits before returning to inshore areas to prepare for spawning. In open water, they tend to stay near the surface (less than 15 meters deep) most of the time. The ocean stay of Alaskan sockeyes varies, but usually lasts two or three years (rarely four); most sockeyes that return are four to six years old. Principal predators of sockeye in the ocean are whales, seals, and humans. In rivers and lakes, they are preyed on by charr, rainbow trout, coho salmon, seabirds, eagles, bears, and humans.

Sockeyes have some unique and interesting habits that can be exploited by anglers. Along with pinks, they're the most gregarious of salmon, grouping by the thousands for their upstream migrations, where they mill in estuaries, river mouths, lake outlets, sloughs, and pools to rest from their strenuous journey. They also have a tendency to hug shorelines and utilize side channels and sloughs. Both of these habits make them especially vulnerable to predation (by bears and anglers).

Like the other salmon, sockeyes show themselves quite frequently in freshwater—breaching and jumping as they engage in prespawning behavior. This is easily mistaken for aggression, and has led many an unknowing angler into futile bouts of casting. Their legendary aloofness is perhaps the most mysterious and exasperating aspect of their nature for anglers to comprehend. Under most conditions, standard hardware and conventional salmon/trout patterns, along with traditional techniques, can be totally ineffective. Until someone comes up with the magic "plankton fly" that somehow sparks a strike response from deep within the primitive sockeye

brain, sport angling for the shyest of salmon will continue to be Alaska's most iffy enterprise, involving a special set of conditions, techniques, and fly patterns.

Fishing Alaska's Sockeye Salmon

Almost all of the state's sport angling for sockeye salmon occurs in streams and rivers, concentrated in areas of greatest abundance from Southeast to Kuskokwim Bay, but especially Prince William Sound, the Kenai Peninsula, and Bristol Bay. A limited number are taken in salt water by salmon trollers, incidentally or with special lures, flies, and techniques developed farther south in the coastal waters of British Columbia and the Pacific Northwest states. Saltwater fly-fishing effort at present is slight or nonexistent. Nearly all of the consistent freshwater methods involve specialized techniques with streamer flies, with the exception of fishing for the landlocked kokanee populations, where special lures are used.

Freshwater Methods and Gear

Despite their nonaggressive nature, sockeye salmon can, under certain conditions, be coaxed to strike. Saltwater commercial trollers, especially in waters down south, have known for years that specially rigged spoons, hoochies (plastic-skirted jig streamers), streamers, and even bare, colored hooks will draw strikes from red salmon, albeit usually not in great numbers. In some areas of British Columbia and farther south, a thriving saltwater sportfishery has developed using streamers of a certain pattern and color. In Alaska, however, sockeyes are taken mostly in freshwater with a variety of enticements. On most rivers, sparsely tied flies of bucktail or colored yarn produce the best results, although in a few areas, spoons, spinners, bait, and even colored sponge balls seem to work at times. Though no one seems to have any rational explanation as to why sockeyes will hit certain lures in some areas and not in others, there seems to be a consensus, at least for freshwater, of the conditions that are most favorable for eliciting a strike response of some kind.

Favorable Conditions

Concentration

Dense fish concentration may be the sole factor common to all situations, both in salt and freshwater, where sockeyes routinely hit sport gear. For reasons obvious and obscure, sockeyes are more prone to strike when they're jammed up in great numbers, even though they lack a strong predator response. Since your lure passes in front of many mouths in these conditions, your chances of a take are obviously much greater. There's an undeniable stress factor at work that may prompt a sockeye strike response, whether it be feeding reflex, aggravation, or territoriality. Timing your efforts to coincide with the height of the run, the tides, or commercial fishing closures, or selecting more prolific locations, are all ways to maximize your chances of success. So, too, is an ability to read water and hone in on better areas. Shallow waters tend to concentrate fish, as do lake outlets and inlets, river mouths, confluences, and structures like waterfalls, channels, rapids, and islands.

Movement

Another important aspect common to most good Alaska sockeye water is fairly strong current. Despite what you may be inclined to believe, your chances of enticing sockeyes in calm water are very slim under most conditions. (At rare times, sockeyes hit on the edges of sloughs, in lake outlets, and river mouths.) Moving fish seem more apt to respond to strike stimuli, for various reasons (such as aggravation, oxygen stress, or reflexive feeding behavior); they mouth the fly more frequently in swift current, especially when in great concentrations.

Water Depth and Clarity

Because of the effect water depth has on fish concentration, visibility, and fly presentation, shallow waters of three feet or less are considered ideal for fishing sockeyes. Water clarity is also important. Clear streams and rivers are preferred, as they allow for sight-fishing and precise casting. Deep, turbid waters should be shunned by the sockeye angler.

Presentation

Direct observation of countless sockeyes during river migrations will reveal that under most conditions, it is a rare fish (usually one in a thousand) that breaks rank even slightly for a lure moving above or below it in the water column. Any lure worked at eye level has the most chance of a take, but only for the brief second when it passes in front of the fish's mouth, for sockeyes rarely if ever pursue a lure in freshwater. Unless you have no other options, blind casting for sockeyes should be avoided. Clear water and sight-fishing with tight presentations is the ticket for the best success.

The Comet

Fly-fishing for Sockeyes

Fly-fishing for Alaska sockeyes began in earnest during the 1960s and early 1970s on streams in Katmai and the Kenai Peninsula. The success of trollers working southern waters prompted river anglers to search for sporting ways of catching the feisty reds, which up to that point had been caught almost exclusively by snagging, a practice the Alaska Department of Fish and Game soon banned in freshwater. Experimenting anglers had initial luck in some rivers using sparsely tied streamer flies of select color and pattern, fished with a modified, tight wet fly swing. Over a period of time, some of these patterns—the Coho (Russian River) Fly, Comet, Sportsman Special, Kenai Fly, and others—developed reputations as surefire sockeye slammers, and a new, exciting sportfishery was born.

No two Alaska anglers can agree on which patterns and colors work best for sockeye salmon (and why), but if you observe the action on some of the state's more noted sockeye locales, you'll have to conclude that certain patterns seem to take a good share of the fish landed. A lot of this owes to familiarity and reputation—what the local shops and "experts" are pushing and/or what happens to be hot at the moment. The important thing to remember is the basic principles that seem to work: simply tied, sparse hackle, yarn, or bucktail wing flies in color combinations of yellow, red, chartreuse, orange, pink, and white (mostly in sizes 2 to 6). With a little experimenting, it's easy to create your own sockeye standards that outperform the old tried and trues.

Technique

Let's imagine the ideal freshwater sockeye salmon fishing location: a stream of gin-clear water, two to three feet deep, with moderately fast current. Thick schools of advancing sockeye salmon pass not far from shore. Here, spin fishers should rig up with a soft-core sinker, split shot, or pencil lead dropper with a short 18-inch leader, experimenting to find the correct amount of weight to keep the fly at the proper depth (eye level of the sockeyes) for its drift above bottom. Depending on conditions, fly fishers should use a sink-tip or floating line, as short a leader/tippet as possible (three feet is fine for sinking line), and possibly a split shot or even short section of lead core line for proper depth. Both types of angler should cast and retrieve in typical wet fly fashion, quartering upstream so that the fly swings by the noses of sockeyes directly in front or slightly downstream of position.

Once you've determined the right weight to get the fly to fish level and have the basic cast and retrieve down, concentrate on presentation. Keep a taut line at all times (fly fishers use a slight strip) with the fly always swinging past the salmon at eye level. Sockeyes usually don't spook easily, and you should be able to wade fairly close to them. Make your casts short—15 feet is fine—and work only the stretch of water that lies in the arc 45 degrees above and 45 degrees below your position. A "flipping" technique (borrowed from trout fishing) can be very effective: Use a short length of line and a circular whip of the rod (aided by a sharp downward pull of line through the guides as you begin lifting upward) to lob out for another drift in a fraction of the time it takes for an overhead or side cast. Practice this until it becomes automatic; it's much more efficient and less tiring than regular casting and reeling.

One of the hardest things for beginners to learn is the subtle nature of the sockeye take; it can be very similar to that of a finicky winter steelhead—barely perceptible. Keep a tight line at all times! Any variation in the drift that might signal a connection with a sockeye should be treated as such, with an instant snap of the rod (and downward pull of the line if you've got it in your other hand) to set the hook instantly. Keep your hooks "sticky sharp," using the new chemically sharpened, forged hooks (Gamakatsu Octopus, Mustad Accu-Point, or Tiemco saltwater stainless) for best results.

When you hang a sockeye, you'll know it, as they usually become airborne as soon as they feel the slightest resistance. Drive the steel home and hang on, keeping the rod up to slow the fish down. After some initial spectacular leaps, sockeyes will generally try a rod-ripping run into the main channel. Try to keep the fish out of the strongest currents if possible, and don't hesitate to break one off if it's foul-hooked or hopelessly downriver, as a prolonged battle that exhausts the fish (and your wrist) isn't sensible or desirable, with all the fish available this time of year.

Other Tactics

If you don't have any luck getting them to hit using the technique just outlined, check your depth and presentation carefully. Try different patterns or colors, smaller flies (to size 10), a faster retrieve, or even some hardware if all else fails. Sockeyes mysteriously go on and off the bite or change preferences for no apparent reason, so you must be flexible and prepared to try different things, even changing locations if necessary.

In some instances, bait (if legal) can be used with good results when all else fails. In the slower, lower sections of some rivers, sockeyes sometimes pick up balls of roe bounced along the bottom. A split shot about 18 inches in front of a super-sharp no. 1/0 egg or steelhead hook, and fresh roe if you can get it, works best. Be warned, however, that this is also a deadly method for hooking king and chum salmon, which run at the same time, so be ready for surprises.

Saltwater Methods and Gear

Only minimal saltwater sport angling for sockeyes has been attempted in Alaska, mostly by trollers in the Southeast region. Using flashers or dodgers rigged in front of small hoochies, spoons, plugs, streamers, and even bare, colored hooks, trollers are able to interest sockeyes into striking in some areas, although not with the consistency seen in waters off southern British Columbia. The most productive colors seem to be pink, fluorescent red/orange, blue, green, white, and purple. Downriggers, diving planers (Pink Lady), or salmon sinkers (four to eight ounces) are used to reach proper depth, which can vary considerably and is usually determined by experimentation or with fish locators. The best trolling speed is very slow, but varies. Inlets, bays, and straits that are associated with abundant sockeye streams are obviously the best areas to concentrate your efforts.

For saltwater fly-casting, sparse bucktail or bunny hair streamer flies, tied in sizes 2 to 2/0, in colors of pink, orange, green, or red, seem to work best. You'll need to locate schools of returning salmon holding in bays and estuaries, then work a streamer through with a light strip, using a saltwater taper, 15-foot sink-tip line, and short leader. As in freshwater sockeye fishing, you'll have the best success with heavy concentrations of fish and precise presentations of your fly. The most productive areas are Kachemak Bay, Kodiak, Prince William Sound, and southern Southeast Alaska.

Fishing Kokanee

In order to fish Alaska's diminutive, lake-dwelling kokanee, you'll need a boat, as most kokanee lakes are deep and fish populations are scattered during open water season. In Southeast, home to most of the state's good kokanee water, you can take these fish on a variety of flies, small spoons and spinners, jigs, and even bait. Kokanee rarely reach one pound in weight, so an ultralight spinning or lightweight fly rod works best. Most are caught incidentally, while angling for more desirable species like cutthroat trout.

As feeders on small aquatic organisms, kokanee school at various depths and locations through the season. Shorelines, bays, inlets/outlets, drop-offs, and islands are common areas to find this concentrated activity; the subdued light of early morning and late evening or cloudy, breezy days are most conducive to surface feeding. Once you locate schools of kokanee, try working a small spoon or spinner (like the Luhr-Jensen no. 0 Kokanee Special Needlefish, no. 1 Kokanee King, or $1/_{32}$-ounce Panther Martin) in their vicinity, fished right below the surface with an erratic retrieve. Experiment with different color combinations, lures, and retrieves until you connect with a fish. (Keep in mind that kokanee, unlike their saltwater brethren, have soft mouths, so set the hook gently.) Fly fishers should fish small (size 12 to 16) nymph, midge, shrimp, or scud patterns, in orange, pink, or brown.

If you encounter no obvious signs of feeding, the best strategy is to troll a spoon or spinner at various depths through likely areas until fish are located. Begin deep right above bottom and work your way up through the water column until you connect with a feeding kokanee, then stay with that depth and location as long as possible. A fish locator is obviously useful in these blind fishing situations. Like saltwater sockeye, kokanee can be extremely finicky and capricious, going off and on the bite without any warning or reason. (They'll sometimes hit only tiny bait shrimp, maggots, grubs, scuds, and the like.) Patience and experimentation are the keys to success.

Equipment

Spinning/Bait Casting

Anglers who want to use spin or bait casting gear for sockeyes should equip themselves with a medium-weight, seven- to eight-and-a-half-foot, medium-action salmon or steelhead rod and matching high-quality reel. Line used should be a minimum of 150 yards of tough, tournament quality monofilament, such as Trilene Big Game, Trilene XT, or Maxima, in 12- to 17-pound test.

Fly-fishing

Fly-fishers should use a stout seven- or eight-weight graphite rod (nine to 10 feet long), a matching heavy-duty reel with strong drag and sufficient capacity for at least 100 yards of backing, and floating or five-foot sink-tip line. Use a short leader/tippet three to four feet long for sinking presentations, of size 2X to 0X (with 10- to 14-pound test).

Top Flies for Alaska Sockeyes: Coho (Russian River) Fly, Comet (orange, pink, or chartreuse), Brassie, Sockeye Willie, Kenai Fly (red, pink, or chartreuse), San Juan Worm (red or chartreuse), Alaska Mary Ann, Green Butt Skunk, Sportsman Special, and Egg-Sucking Leech (all size 2 to 8 hooks).

Alaska's Top Trophy Sockeye
Salmon Locations
• **Brooks River** (Southwest)
• **Mulchatna River system**
  (Southwest)
• **Lake Iliamna–Kvichak River system**
  (Southwest)
• **Agulukpak River** (Southwest)
• **Kenai River system** (Southcentral)

Alaska's Major Sockeye Salmon Locations

Although sockeyes can be taken on sport gear nearly everywhere within their range under the right conditions, the most consistent fishing can be had on clear-flowing streams that receive great concentrations, from Southeast to Kuskokwim Bay. Far and away the best of these are the crystal waters of Bristol Bay and the Alaska Peninsula, where individual runs can number in the millions, and conditions are perfect for fly-fishing. The Kenai Peninsula, Kodiak Island, and, to a lesser extent, a few other areas in Southcentral are the state's most popular areas for freshwater sport angling.

Southeast

The region has scattered opportunities, mostly in southern Southeast (such as Petersburg, Prince of Wales, and Ketchikan), with quite a few kokanee lakes. The run timing is from mid-June to early September, with a peak in July.

• **Yakutat:** Situk, East Alsek, Kiklukh, Doame Rivers
• **Haines:** Chilkoot, Chilkat River systems
• **Juneau:** Auke, Taku Rivers (Kokanee: Hasselborg, Turner, Florence Lakes)
• **Sitka/Petersburg:** Petersburg, Thoms, Sitkoh, Anan Creeks; Kah Sheets, Stikine, Sarkar River systems; Sweetwater, Red Lake systems; Salmon, Mitchell, Klag Bay systems; Virginia Lake/Creek; Lake Eva (Kokanee: Marten Lake)
• **Ketchikan/Prince of Wales:** Kegan, Karta, Thorne, Naha River systems; Hatchery, Smuggler's, Salmon Bay, Ward Creeks; McDonald, Hugh Smith Lake systems; Yes Bay (Kokanee: Orchard, Manzanita, Wilson, Reflection Lakes)

Alaska's Top 10 Trophy Sockeyes

16 pounds, 0 ounces (state record)	Kenai River (Southcentral)	1974
15 pounds, 11 ounces	Kenai River (Southcentral)	1989
15 pounds, 3 ounces (world record)*	Kenai River (Southcentral)	1987
15 pounds, 2 ounces	Brooks River (Southwest)	1993
15 pounds, 0 ounces	Kijik Lake (Southwest)	1980
14 pounds, 12 ounces	Kenai River (Southcentral)	1979
14 pounds, 12 ounces	Koktuli River (Southwest)	1993
14 pounds, 8 ounces	Kenai River (Southcentral)	1973
14 pounds, 8 ounces	Lynn Canal (Southeast)	1974
14 pounds, 8 ounces	Stuyahok River (Southwest)	1978

First and second largest sockeye caught in Alaska were not properly registered with the IGFA to qualify for world-record status.

Southcentral

Alaska's most heavily utilized fisheries occur here on the Kenai River (and tributaries) and clear-water streams flowing into the Susitna and Copper Rivers. The run timing is from early June to early September, peaking in July.

- **Kenai Peninsula:** Kenai, Russian, Moose, Kasilof Rivers (Kokanee: Hidden Lake, Trapper Joe Lake)
- **Kachemak Bay:** China Poot Lagoon
- **Cook Inlet:** Susitna River (clearwater tributaries), Lake Creek, Talachulitna River, Talkeetna River (clear-flowing tributaries), Fish Creek (Big Lake), Jim Creek, Little Susitna River, Big River Lakes, Crescent River, Little Kamishak River
- **Copper River:** Gulkana River system; Klutina, Tonsina, Tazlina Rivers
- **Copper River Delta and Eastern Prince William Sound:** Eyak River, Alaganik Slough, McKinley Lake, Martin River, Clear Creek system (including Tokun Lake), Bering River system (clear-water tributaries)
- **Western Prince William Sound:** Eshamy Lagoon/Lake, Coghill River
- **Kodiak:** Dozens of good sockeye streams, with Southcentral's best flyfishing: Karluk, Buskin, Pasagshak, Saltery, Uganik, Fraser, Upper Station, Afognak, Kaflia, Litnik, Dog Salmon, Red Rivers; Portage, Pauls, Malina Creeks; Olga Lake system

Southwest

Southwest has the world's most abundant sockeye salmon runs, along with the most perfect conditions for flyfishing, with dozens of great locations. The run timing is from late June to early August, with a peak in July.

- **Bristol Bay:** Lake Iliamna–Kvichak (including Lake Clark and tributaries), Nushagak-Mulchatna (including lower Tikchik Lakes), Togiak, Igushik, Wood (including Wood River Lakes and tributaries), Alagnak River systems
- **Alaska Peninsula:** Many outstanding possibilities, most seldom fished due to remoteness and weather: Naknek (including all locations in Katmai), Egegik (including Becharof and tributaries), Ugashik, Meshik, Chignik, Nelson Lagoon, Sandy, Bear River systems
- **Kuskokwim:** Goodnews, Arolik, Kanektok River systems

Northwest

The Northwest's fishing opportunities for sockeye are extremely limited, with only scattered occurrences in Norton Sound, and even rarer sightings in Kotzebue Sound. The run timing is from late June to early August, with a peak in July.

- **Norton Sound:** Sinuk, Snake, Pilgrim River systems
- **Kotzebue Sound:** Kelly River (Kelly Lake) of lower Noatak River

Chapter 4
Chum Salmon: Bulldog Battlers

Late June on the lower Kanektok River in Southwest Alaska's Kuskokwim Bay is as good a place as any to sample some of the state's finest stream fishing for salmon. Here, in crystal waters perfect for the fly, you can witness an amazing procession of Pacific salmon in numbers that few rivers this size can match.

Most folks who travel to this world-famous destination this time of year aren't expecting to have their big rods yanked, tweaked, or even snapped by a species that some barely consider a sport fish: the chum salmon. But in Alaska, land of surprises, where the obscure, medium-sized salmon is regarded as mere dog food in many places, these coastal waters hold bright, aggressive chums so full of energy and stamina that they frequently outperform the mighty king of salmon, the chinook, much to the amazement of all. Schooled in sloughs along the lower river, these silvery, husky brutes frequently slam flies meant for the big salmon monarchs, and provide fast-paced, incredibly exciting fishing action that has changed more than one fisherman's attitude toward the "lowly" chum. Indeed, after witnessing firsthand the workout a rampaging chum salmon can put a nine- or even a 10-weight through, anglers are apt to

forget the great king and concentrate their efforts on the more numerous and sporting "bulldog battler."

Introduction

Many anglers get to know the humble ocean-fresh chum *(Oncorhynchus keta)* by mistake, and never suspect its true identity, thinking it instead to be a sockeye or silver salmon. The most underrated of all salmon species, chums are not highly regarded within the angling community for various reasons, none of which are based on truth. When hooked, a bright chum is capable of matching ounce for ounce any battle antics its near relative, the silver salmon, can dish out. They are strong, and when encountered in large numbers, tend to be very aggressive. Rarely performing the aerial ballet of a sockeye salmon, the chum instead will employ tactics more in line with that of a bulldog holding on to a bone—a tug-of-war equaled by none.

Description

At times ocean-bright chum salmon are difficult to distinguish from fresh red salmon, since both species have dark greenish-blue metallic backs, silvery sides, and similar body shape. However, the chum's belly, in addition to being white, often has an iridescent silvery shine. Also, some of the fins have whitish tips, and the pupil of the eye may appear larger. The wrist of the tail is typically narrower, proportionally, than on other salmon. Faint, black specks may be present on the dorsal and adipose fins and back of some specimens.

Spawning chum salmon are calico in color; the sides are marked with vertical stripes in flaming red, yellow, and black, while the head is greenish brown with a touch of golden yellow on the cheeks. Males develop a hooked jaw with a series of large, protruding teeth, which partially accounts for their nickname, "dog" salmon. Females have a dark horizontal band along the lateral line and are generally not as colorful. The pectoral, anal, and pelvic fins all feature whitish tips.

Chum salmon fresh from the sea have a flesh color of light orange, which in some populations may be closer to red. Like pink salmon, chums are not especially prized table fare, due to the rapid deterioration of the flesh as the fish close in on their spawning grounds. However, they are extremely important both as a commercial and subsistence species, and they are becoming increasingly popular as sport fish. The chum salmon's flesh is excellent eating on bright fish fresh from the sea.

Second largest of the Pacific salmon, chums have been known to reach weights of 30 to 40 pounds and lengths to three feet in certain locations. Averaging five to 10 pounds, occasionally more, any fish over 15 pounds is considered very large in most areas of Alaska, with the Southeast region consistently producing the heaviest specimens (20-plus pounds). Chum salmon of exceptional size are also reported from parts of the Northwest.

Range, Abundance, and Status

Of all species of Pacific salmon, the chum has the widest natural geographic distribution. It's found from South Korea and the island of Kyushu in the Sea of Japan up along the coast of Siberia and over into Alaska. It ranges south along the coast to Monterey, California. In the Arctic Ocean, chum salmon are present from the Lena River in Russia east to at least the Mackenzie River in Canada's Northwest Territories. Chums have also been planted in arctic Russia's White Sea, with reports of strays in the North Atlantic of northern Europe. Throughout its range in North America, chum salmon are rarely encountered in any abundance south of the Columbia River and are most plentiful in Alaska.

Within Alaska, the chum salmon is known to appear along the entire coastline, being especially abundant from Dixon Entrance below Ketchikan north to Point Hope above Kotzebue. Major populations occur in every region of the state except the Arctic. Even the Interior has large runs—the Yukon River produces numbers fluctuating between two and nine million, possibly more in some years. Major commercial and subsistence fisheries exist in areas of Southeast, Prince William Sound, Kodiak Island, Cook Inlet, Bristol Bay, the Kuskokwim and Yukon Rivers, and Kotzebue Sound.

Usually found within 50 miles of salt water, some populations commit extensive migrations: Chum salmon swim up the Yukon River through the entire state of Alaska into Canada to reach their spawning grounds near the Yukon–British Columbia border—an incredible distance of over 2,000 miles.

Of all the Pacific salmon in Alaska, chums have been the least utilized, except in certain areas of Northwest and Interior where they have traditionally been an important source of food. Though often viewed as nothing more than potential dog food by many users, chums are rapidly gaining recognition for their value as a commercial and sport species. Stocking programs to benefit commercial fishing fleets have become quite widespread in parts of Southcentral and Southeast.

Life History and Habits

Beginning in spring and continuing through summer into fall, mature chum salmon begin migrating through the clear, blue waters of the Pacific Ocean and Gulf of Alaska toward the rivers of their birth. Age of the returning fish varies between two and five years (the average is three), with some northern populations as old as six or seven years. Nearing inshore waters, the fish begin to congregate in schools or runs, according to which river they are bound for. The exact time of arrival is influenced by many factors, but is usually from midsummer to early fall, with older fish appearing earlier than younger fish.

Once near freshwater, chums begin a period of milling that may last from a few days (if spawning areas are far up inland rivers) to several weeks (when spawning occurs in intertidal stretches of streams or in the vicinity). The period of milling becomes shorter as the spawning season progresses. Entrance up chosen drainages concurs with high tides and often with rising water levels, such as after a heavy rain.

Runs peak from early July to early September in most of Alaska. The time of entrance, however, extends from early May to mid-December, depending greatly on geographic location (runs generally occur earlier to the north and progressively later to the south). Runs called "early" and "late" locally are usually the "summer" and "fall" runs described by biologists.

Reluctant to ford barriers of any significance, chums are predominantly found in shallow rivers and creeks, one to three feet deep, with clean gravel bottoms and moderate current flow. As a rule, glacial or heavily silted waters are not preferred for reproduction but commonly serve as migration corridors for fish bound for clear-water tributaries. There are exceptions to this rule, however. In Southeast, Southcentral, and Interior, a few populations of fall-run chums spawn in main stem glacial rivers late in the season as cooling temperatures halt the flow of silt from meltwater.

Early-run spawners use main stems of deep, fast-flowing rivers and streams where the colder temperatures require longer time for egg incubations and juvenile growth. Late-run chums commonly spawn in shallower, slower-flowing spring water that has more favorable temperatures through the winter and thus allows shorter incubation time and higher growth rates among offspring. There are also more subtle differences between the two races of fish, both physiological and behavioral.

Spawning peaks during periods of falling temperatures from August to October throughout most of the range, but may occur as early as July or as late as February in some locations. Similar to pink salmon, intertidal spawning of chums is widespread in many areas (mostly Southcentral and Southeast). Chum eggs tend to be larger than those of the other salmon, and an average female can carry between 2,000 and 4,000. Eggs hatch sometime in winter and early spring; soon after (April to June), the young fry migrate directly to sea, much like pink salmon. Feeding on a variety of small organisms like plankton, crustaceans, and crab larvae, young chums eventually switch to a mixed diet that includes small fish. Size increase is greatest during the first three years of ocean life, slowing after age four. Due to the genetic variability among stocks and habitat, chums from different areas differ in growth rate, age at maturity, and ultimate size.

Freshwater Methods and Gear

Myth has it that chum salmon seldom strike in freshwater, but don't believe it. Not only will these fish strike lures and flies, but they do so as readily as a king or silver under the right conditions. The trick is to find the right water.

The Right Water

The best water to consistently hook chum salmon is two to three feet deep, with moderate to fast current, and clear with perhaps just a slight tint of glacial green or turbidity. Lures and flies should be fished near or along bottom, and allowed to tumble or drift through pools, runs, and sloughs, or under cutbanks— any prime holding areas for migrating chum salmon. Although at times chums will strike under nearly any conditions, you should avoid extremely shallow and clear waters, or excessively turbid or glacial streams (except under special circumstances described below).

Many an angler who has fished for silver or red salmon during late summer and early fall is familiar with the chum in its splendid glory of calico colors. These spawners are usually quite aggressive, and can even be a nuisance when encountered in large numbers— especially when other, more desirable species (like coho or rainbows) are around. But few anglers who have fished around Alaska will argue that the chum, when fresh in on the tide,

chrome-flanked and full of sea lice, isn't every bit the equal in sport of his cousins that get all the attention. Surprisingly, many anglers claim never to have encountered a chum in this condition in freshwater. The fact is, they are fairly common in lower rivers, but are almost always misidentified as silver or red salmon.

The brightest fish and best action for the species occurs in early summer in the major coastal drainages, the closer to salt the better. As chums like the intertidal zone and lower reaches of rivers, you'll encounter aggressive hordes in holding areas there during the peak of immigration (usually late June through early August). Kodiak Island, Southcentral's Susitna River drainage, the Alaska Peninsula, Bristol and Kuskokwim Bays, and countless areas throughout Southeast all offer some of the best conditions possible for these feisty, early-run river chums. Changing into spawning colors quickly, these chums lose a little of their zip and aggressiveness farther up into freshwater, but they still can provide some abundant and exciting fishing in holding water, often in company with sockeye and king salmon.

Large, glacial watersheds can provide prime locations to intercept chums destined for clear headwater tributaries. Dime-bright fish can be taken out of the mouths of streams up to 40 or 50 miles or more from the sea, with a few populations staying reasonably fresh even after several hundred miles. These fish are genetically programmed to stay brighter longer than stocks spawning lower in the river!

The Right Lure

The best lures for river chums are large (half-ounce or bigger) spoons such as Pixees, Hot Rods, and Krocodiles in silver, brass, or gold with orange, green, or red highlights; large Vibrax or Mepps spinners (nos. 4 to 6) in silver, gold, "Firetiger," red, or orange blades (and/or bells); and medium large (no. 2) Spin-N-Glos and Cheaters in orange, red, yellow, or silver. A wide range of flies can be used under most conditions to successfully stimulate a strike response—flash flies, attractors, egg patterns, leeches, and specialty patterns like the Alaskabou and Outrageous, in sizes 1/0 to 6. Fish them deep, with short, erratic strips, for best results.

Quite often in glacial or turbid waters, the use of roe is common practice for fishing chums, either alone or as a sweetener on lures like Spin-N-Glos. Drifted along bottom, these scent-emitting enticements are deadly when all else fails.

Whereas kings and silvers, and to some degree pinks, will attack hardware out of a basic feeding and aggravation response, chums seem to hit more out of aggravation alone, and will frequently pursue lures for short distances, nabbing as they go. Spot casting can usually be both exciting and very rewarding, as fish can be prompted to strike with repeat casts. Chums rarely hit with the authority of a hungry trout or charr; usually the take is more of a bump than anything. Anglers must be on the alert and ready to respond with a powerful hook set, as these fish, like all salmon, have very hard jaws. Super-sharp hooks are a necessity. Once hooked, chums will react instantly with powerful bulldog runs and frequent leaps in a remarkable display of strength and will. Fish of full nuptial maturity are very prone to strike lures out of territorial aggression, and should be avoided for obvious reasons.

Gearing for Freshwater Chums

Spinning

A six- to 7.5-foot, medium-action, light- to medium-weight salmon rod, with a matching high-quality reel loaded with tournament-grade eight- to 12-pound test line is preferred for Alaska's chum salmon. For difficult stream conditions or salt water, use heavier gear (15- to 20-pound test). Because of the prominent, razor-sharp teeth that chums develop once in freshwater, a shock leader of at least 20-pound test is recommended, which should be inspected frequently for wear. Needlenose pliers or vice grips are definitely recommended for hook releases.

The best lures are medium-sized (half-ounce to seven-eighths-ounce) spoons or spinners in green, blue, and silver with bright orange, red, and yellow highlights: Pixee, Krocodile, Little Cleo, Dardevle, Hot Rod, Syclops, Mepps, Vibrax, Bang Tail, and Rooster Tail. Drift bobbers and plugs in colors of orange, red, yellow, and silver are also used.

Fly-fishing

We recommend a stout seven- or eight-weight rod, nine- to ten-and-a-half feet long, with complementary reel, and matching floating, sink-tip, or full sink lines, along with eight- to 12-pound test tippet. Heavier setups (nine-weight rod and 15-pound tippet) are required for strong current. Tippet/leader length should be short, about four feet for all sinking line presentations.

- **Top Fly Patterns for Freshwater:** Comet, Boss, Polar Shrimp, Flash Fly, Mickey Finn, Orange/White Wiggletail, Coho, Alaskabou, Outrageous, Egg-Sucking Leech, Alaska Mary Ann, Woolly Bugger, and Teeny Nymph.

- **Top Fly Patterns for Salt Water:** Herring Fly, Clouser Minnow, Deceiver, Candlefish, and Sandlance.

Saltwater Fishing for Chums

Chum and red salmon share a common trait when encountered at sea—both can be reluctant to strike anglers' offerings. Much of the popular literature describes the finicky nature of the "salty dog," giving little or no explanation for it, and even fewer suggestions for remedying the situation. (Some accounts offer "snagging" as the only legitimate harvest method!) But for an angler wishing to square off with these brutes in an honest, sporting way, there certainly are other options to consider.

Anglers trolling or mooching for king or silver salmon will hook into chums incidentally—that much is true—and a few will even have consistent success targeting the species using certain color hoochies (blue or green) or special lures. Rarer still are those who take chums on flies in inshore waters. What must be remembered is that, unlike silver and king salmon, the chum (and red) salmon is not a voracious fish predator and may feed at times on such items as squid, crabs, or even plankton, calling for a different strategy than pulling flashers, plug-cut herring, or big streamers through the water.

The key to successful saltwater chum fishing is concentration and natural presentation. Do not look for hot angling in wide-open, offshore areas. Chums out at sea have generally not schooled up yet; given their feeding habits, they are extremely hard to fish, unlike silvers or even feeder kings that can sometimes be found in tight concentrations working bait patches. Usually, you'll have the greatest success with the species inshore, around estuaries, off beaches, and in bays associated with major spawning streams. When fish are stacked up in dense masses, with some rolling or even jumping on the surface, conditions are ideal. All that is needed is the appropriate "jaw breaker."

Large, flashy spoons and spinners can trigger a response in these tidewater chums, particularly the large males. The best colors seem to be silver/blue prism, silver/green prism, gold/orange, and yellow/green. As some anglers have already discovered, these fish can also be worked with exciting results using flies resembling plankton or small bait fish, stripped through schools of fish in short, erratic bursts. Herring, candlefish, and smolt patterns in blue/green/silver/white have proven highly effective. A touch of attractor orange, pink, or red seems to liven the response.

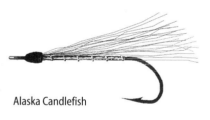

Alaska Candlefish

Still in its infancy, saltwater fishing for chums is wide open for exploration and discovery. Kodiak Island, Prince William Sound, and parts of the Southeast have almost infinite possibilities for inshore angling of chums, which are neglected for the pursuit of more glamorous fish like the coho or king. Prospective anglers should strive to know the chum's habits and responses in its natural environment—and go from there with experimentation and intuition.

Alaska's Top 10 Trophy Chum Salmon

32 pounds, 0 ounces (state and world record)	Caamano Point (Southeast)	1985
28 pounds, 2 ounces	Caamano Point (Southeast)	1985
28 pounds, 0 ounces	Boca de Quadra (Southeast)	1991
27 pounds, 9 ounces	Jackpot Bay Creek (Southeast)	1989
27 pounds, 8 ounces	Behm Canal (Southeast)	1990
27 pounds, 3 ounces	Behm Narrows (Southeast)	1977
25 pounds, 6 ounces	Island Point (Southeast)	1985
25 pounds, 0 ounces	Behm Narrows (Southeast)	1983
25 pounds, 0 ounces	Herring Cove (Southeast)	1982
25 pounds, 0 ounces	Caamano Point (Southeast)	1991

Alaska's Major Chum Salmon Locations

Southeast

Southeast has outstanding chum fishing (both salt- and freshwater), with some of Alaska's largest chums taken from select areas. The run timing is from July to October, peaking from late July to early August.

- **Yakutat:** East Alsek River
- **Juneau:** Cross Sound; Icy Strait; Stephens Passage; Chilkat River; Fish, Cowee Creeks
- **Sitka:** Sitka Sound, Mitchell Bay system, Katlian River
- **Petersburg/Wrangell:** Stephens Passage; Castle, Kah Sheets, Eagle, Harding Rivers; Kadake, Petersburg, Ohmer, Red Lake, Falls, Irish, North Arm, Thoms Creeks
- **Ketchikan/Prince of Wales Island:** Behm Canal, Gravina Island/Tongass Narrows; Sarkar, Unuk, Klawock, Karta Rivers; Fish Creek

Southcentral

You'll find some outstanding chum fishing in Southcentral, mostly on Kodiak, Prince William Sound, some Susitna tributaries, and upper Cook Inlet. The run timing is from early July to September, with a peak in mid-July through early August.

- **Susitna:** Little Susitna, Deshka, Talachulitna, Talkeetna Rivers; Alexander, Willow, Little Willow, Goose, Sheep, Caswell, Montana, Lake, Jim Creeks
- **Kenai:** Kachemak Bay; Chuitna River; Silver Salmon Creek
- **Kodiak:** American, Dog Salmon Rivers; Roslyn, Salonie, Russian Creeks
- **Chugach:** Resurrection Bay, Valdez Arm, Knight Island, Wells Passages

Southwest

Some of Alaska's most abundant stream fishing can be enjoyed in the Southwest region, with perfect conditions for sight fishing and fly-fishing. There are dozens of outstanding locations here, often with great concurrent action for king and sockeye salmon. The run timing is from late June through July, with a peak in the first two weeks of July.

- **Bristol Bay:** Nushagak (includes Mulchatna and Nuyakuk), Wood, Igushik, Togiak, Kvichak Rivers
- **Alaska Peninsula:** Ugashik Lake system; Egegik, Naknek, Alagnak Rivers; Izembek–Moffet Bay streams; Russell

Creek, Belkofski Bay River, Canoe Bay River, Stepovak Bay streams

- **Kuskokwim:** Goodnews, Kanektok, Aniak, Holitna Rivers
- **Lower Yukon:** Andreafsky, Anvik Rivers

Northwest

This region has some outstanding but little-fished sources, primarily in eastern Norton and Kotzebue Sounds. The run timing is July and August, with a peak in the first part of July.

- **Eastern Norton Sound:** Unalakleet, Shaktoolik, Ungalik, Inglutalik, Tubutulik Rivers
- **Seward Peninsula:** Fish-Niukluk, Fox, Kwiniuk Rivers
- **Kotzebue Sound:** Kobuk, Noatak, Wulik Rivers

Interior

Although Interior has abundant fish runs, the fish are in less than prime condition because of their great distance from the sea. The Yukon River is North America's prime producer. Many areas offer possibly good sportfishing, including all river mouths along the Yukon and Tanana Rivers. The run timing is from July to November, peaking in July (early run) and September (late run).

- **Yukon River:** Nulato, Nowitna, Chandalar Rivers
- **Tanana River:** Salcha, Chatanika, Delta Clearwater Rivers
- **Nenana River:** Julius, Clear Creeks
- **Koyukuk River:** Gisasa, Hogatza, South Fork, Dakli, Jim Rivers
- **Porcupine:** Sheenjek, Coleen, Black Rivers

Chapter 5
Pinks: The Humpback Salmon

If you visit any of Alaska's major coastal rivers in late summer for silver salmon and trout, you must be prepared to encounter another fish that can quite literally steal the show: a diminutive brawler that floods estuaries and lower rivers in some years and pounces without hesitation on nearly every offering flung into the water—the pink, or humpback, salmon.

Rather than curse him, as some anglers do, for his unceasing interference and often strange looks—a gnarled caricature of a salmon with a grotesque hump and pinched jaws—you may wisely decide to enjoy the abundant sport this spunky little fellow has to offer. Because they strike at partial to bright flies, small spoons, and spinners, these smallest of salmon can provide endless hours of diversion and highlights to Alaska's mixed bag of late-summer fishing excitement.

ing interest among anglers who have learned to recognize the fine qualities of these feisty little salmon.

Catch them in the prime of their life, at sea or intertidal areas of clear-water streams, and prepare to witness firsthand a fishery of magnitude and intensity never before imagined. A prolific member of the Pacific salmon clan, pinks quite often outnumber their larger brethren. When encountered by the tens of thousands, the water seems to boil with activity, in an experience that can trigger mixed emotions—awe and humility. Surrounded by countless dime-bright, three- to five-pound fish swarming in a seething mass of heads, tails, and fins, one can only begin to comprehend the importance of this species within the ecosystems of coastal Alaska. Angling for these playful fish brings you close to the essence of Alaska.

Introduction

One of the most delightful light-tackle game fish found in Alaska's coastal waters is the pink salmon (*Oncorhynchus gorbuscha*). Although hampered by persistent rumors concerning their sporting abilities as well as edibility (or lack thereof), pinks have nonetheless stood the test of time and today enjoy a grow-

Description

When encountered fresh from the sea, the pink salmon is a sleek and slender fish displaying a dark blue or green back, silvery sides, and a white belly. Faint oval-shaped spots cover the back and both lobes of the tail fin. Due to their size, bright pinks are sometimes misidentified as jack king salmon.

Spawning fish appear dirty brown with sides of mottled, yellowish green. Males develop a distinctive humped back (hence their popular name) and an elongated, hooked snout. Females generally retain their seagoing shape. Large, black oval markings dot the back and are especially prominent on both tail lobes. The belly and lower jaw is creamy white to yellowish white.

The flesh of bright, sea-run pink salmon is an orange to a slight pink hue and of moderately soft texture. It's not much pursued by most anglers, since pinks have a tendency to change from the ocean phase to spawning phase during a short period of time, often even before entering freshwater. But when caught fresh and bright from the sea, the pink makes good table fare. Pink salmon are an important species within the commercial fishing industry and comprise the bulk of Alaska's canned salmon.

The smallest members of the Pacific salmon family, the pinks' size range varies little from one watershed to another. Typically averaging only three to five pounds in weight (20 to 25 inches in length), the pink salmon seldom exceeds seven or eight pounds throughout its range. However, a few rivers and streams produce larger specimens that may approach 10 or 12 pounds or more. Throughout the state, odd-year pinks tend to be slightly heavier than even-year fish, except for on the Alaska Peninsula. You can usually take trophy pinks from certain areas of Southeast and Southcentral.

Range, Abundance, and Status

The pink salmon is without a doubt the most abundant of all salmon species (comprising 60 percent in numbers and 40 percent in weight of the commercial catch in the North Pacific) and ranges from Sacramento, California, north to the Bering Strait and along the coast of Siberia as far south as northern Japan and North Korea. Transplant projects involving pink salmon have brought the species to such remote locations as northern Europe and Russia, parts of South America, and the east coast of the United States and Canada.

In Alaska, pink salmon are plentiful from Dixon Entrance below Ketchikan north to Point Hope above Kotzebue, with sporadic occurrences around Point Barrow in the Arctic Ocean to the Mackenzie River delta in the Northwest Territories.

Major pink salmon populations are found in the multitude of island streams in Southeast and Prince William Sound, coastal Blying Sound, Kodiak Island, Cook Inlet, Bristol Bay, the lower Yukon and Kuskokwim Rivers, and Norton Sound. Seldom do pinks move far upriver, and they usually spawn within 50 miles of the coast. However, they're occasionally found as far inland as Ruby on the Yukon River (about 350 miles from the sea), with unconfirmed reports of fish in Fairbanks area streams.

Intense stocking efforts by various private hatcheries have created "terminal" fisheries in many parts of the state, mostly to benefit commercial interests.

Life History and Habits

Coastal offshore areas begin to see pinks returning from Gulf of Alaska feeding grounds in late spring. Runs are typically strong by midsummer in inshore waters and continue to arrive until early fall, concentrating in huge schools according to which spawning stream they belong. During the final homeward migration, the fish feed heavily and significantly increase in growth and distance traveled.

Unlike other Pacific salmon, pinks have a fixed life span of 18 months. One- or three-year-olds are rarely found. Fish planted in lakes as landlocked stocks have demonstrated higher deviance in age variation than sea-run populations. Thus, even-year and odd-year fish do not mix and are considered two quite distinct genetic stocks.

Nearing freshwater, a period of "milling" commences which may last up to several weeks until full maturity, in some instances, if spawning beds are situated in intertidal areas or near salt water. However, this milling period may be no longer than a few days if the fish are committed to an extensive migration through a major river to reach headwater streams where they will reproduce. There is no milling after pinks have attained full maturity. Sharp increases or decreases in stream volume or temperature regulate migration into freshwater.

Pink salmon runs typically appear in midsummer to late summer to spawn in fast-flowing coastal rivers and streams. Runs tend to peak during July and August throughout most of the range, but bright pinks may be present in freshwater anytime between early June and late October, depending on location, area, and region. As with other salmon species, runs with varying peaks are distributed by geographic zones associated with different temperature regimes. Males tend to appear earlier than females, and when pinks are large, run timing is earlier.

Many regions of the state have stronger runs of pinks on even-numbered years, with smaller returns on odd-numbered years. However, the trend may be reversed in some areas, and even nonexistent in others. Also, the resilience of pink populations can be demonstrated by weak runs rebounding to strong runs in only one or two generations.

Not adept at leaping waterfalls or negotiating even short stretches of high-velocity current flow, these small salmon are much more prone to spawn in lower areas of rivers and creeks. During abnormally strong runs with high spawner density, pinks tend to migrate further upstream than in normal years. "Straying" is particularly common among artificial runs of pink salmon, but is otherwise relatively low to almost nonexistent in natural populations.

Spawning typically peaks in August and September throughout Alaska, with a few populations beginning as early as July or as late as November. One reason why these salmon are so abundant almost everywhere they're found is that they can spawn in almost any conditions, from mere trickles of water up to large rivers. However, their general preference is for shallow (five inches to three feet deep), moderate-flowing, clear-water streams with clean gravel substrate. Waters with mud-covered bottoms, slow or no current, and deep, quiet pools are avoided. The low-light hours see the most active spawning, with size of males and females defining an assortative mating hierarchy. Up to five males may spawn with one female, and males with more than one female.

Pinks commonly use intertidal areas for reproduction, especially in parts of Southcentral and Southeast, since pink eggs can withstand a high degree of salinity. In some coastal streams, as much as 75 percent or more of spawning takes place in tidal areas, with spawners returning to their redds after the tide recedes and current resumes.

A female pink may deposit anywhere between 1,100 and 2,300 eggs in several nests, guarding the area from 10 days up to three weeks. Approximately 50 percent of the eggs are lost during spawning due to predators or, when spawning density is very high, suffocation. The eggs hatch in late winter and, after a brief stay in freshwater, the juvenile salmon move out into the sea during April and May. For the first couple of months, the pink fry remain within a few miles of the stream mouth and are preyed upon heavily by other fishes, including silver salmon smolts. The growing pinks feed on a variety of small organisms, such as larval fishes, plankton, and occasionally insects, eventually switching to a diet of small fishes as size increases. High seas pinks are suspended at a depth between 30 and 120 feet, may travel vast expanses during their stay (3,000 to 4,000 miles), and suffer a marine mortality of nearly 97 percent, most of which occur during the first few months of life.

Fishing Alaska's Pink Salmon

Saltwater Fishing for Pinks

Sometimes it seems that pink salmon will hit anything that moves through the water. At other times they appear to be shy and very reluctant to strike at any lure. One might say that such is the way of the salmon, but a closer look at the habits of these fish can help reveal effective methods for fishing them under certain conditions.

It's fairly common to hook pink salmon during the summer and fall months while trolling or mooching for other species like silvers. These small salmon, when encountered in heavy concentrations, can sometimes be a nuisance because of their aggressiveness; yet there are moments when the bite is off and every lure in the tackle box won't get as much as a single strike. The type of water sometimes plays a huge role in saltwater pink fishing, and knowing exactly what kind of lure to use under various conditions is the trick. And, of course, concentration is another very important factor.

The typical diet of an adult, sea-run pink usually consists of small bait fish and plankton. A medium-sized, flashy spoon is an all-time favorite lure among anglers in coastal regions. Needless to say, they don't always work, but then again, what does? Quite recently, a few anglers began experimenting with alternative lures, imitating the food of pink salmon. They came up with great results, proving that herring, sculpin, and smolt pattern flies (Black-Nosed Dace and Blue Smolt) in green or blue are effective in clear or semiclear waters wherever large concentrations of pinks can be found.

Due to their often staggering numbers, it's possible to find good action for pinks in most coastal areas. The most consistent pink fishing, however, can be had in bays and coves with clear-water spawning streams in the immediate vicinity. These fish have a habit of "milling" around in big schools near freshwater outlets and are commonly spotted porpoising not far from shore. Incoming and high tides are generally the best times to try surf casting, as the movement of ocean currents puts the fish in a migrational mode and forces them closer to shore. At low tide, look for pinks further offshore where they are primarily reached by boat.

In crystal-clear waters, salmon sometimes have a tendency to spook, and with pinks it is no different. Small spoons, spinners, and flies in silver with a touch of dark, neutral colors such as blue and green work well under such conditions. Avoid very large, flashy lures in fluorescent orange, chartreuse, and red. Although such spectacular high-visibility lures may produce fish at times, they are much more useful in glacially influenced waters. A cut piece of herring suspended beneath a bobber is a trick many anglers enjoy and fishes well in clear and semiclear coastal waters.

Freshwater Fishing for Pinks

The world of angling does not have much to equal the fast and frenzied light tackle action possible when fishing freshwater pinks. In many parts of the range, their abundance can be truly awesome; a fish on every cast is not at all unusual. Coastal streams in particular receive heavy runs of beautiful pinks, and should definitely be the focus of attention for the highest quality fishing.

Like chum salmon, pinks or "humpies" are very underrated by the majority of anglers. It's certainly not because of a lack of fish or their finicky feeding habits. At times they are so plentiful and aggressive one would be hard put not to catch them. The main impediment to their acceptance is probably the grotesque appearance they develop when in full spawning phase, especially males with their gnarly jaws and humped backs. Few anglers would recognize a sleek and slender dime-bright pink full of spunk straight out of the blue Pacific Ocean. They're frequently mistaken for jack kings, small silvers, and even Dolly Varden.

Pinks are also thought to be poor sport fish that do not give anglers the exhilarating fight that other salmon species offer. Well, the majority of anglers with these opinions have not had the chance to hook into a sea-run pink on ultralight gear. Since these little salmon only average three to four pounds, who would expect them to perform like great sport fish on tackle intended for much larger reds or silvers? Gear down appropriately and get ready for an unforgettable showdown.

The best places to find chrome-bright pink salmon are in coastal rivers and streams. Pinks commonly spawn in the lower reaches of most drainages and within a week to 10 days reach full nuptial maturity. It's vital that anglers who are serious about catching quality fish head straight to intertidal areas and deep holes and runs immediately above them. Large glacial systems that force pinks to migrate extensive distances to reach spawning beds can yield silvery specimens at the mouth of tributaries some 40 or 50 miles from salt water. In contrast, small and shallow creeks may never see anything other than full-fledged spawners, as the fish usually mill around off the stream mouth until ripe and ready. Pick a location with at least a fair amount of volume in addition to a few feet of depth, with water preferably clear or semiclear, and a moderate current flow.

Look for fresh pinks in the early stages of a run. With few exceptions, when the number of fish present in a drainage peaks, it usually means that the best is already over. These salmon change into spawning mode quickly, often while still in salt water, and many, if not most, will arrive ripe during what would otherwise be the high point of the season. The period of availability for pinks is relatively short compared with kings, silvers, and reds. It lasts a total of about four to six weeks, with the second or third week producing the freshest fish.

Try to avoid using oversized lures for pinks. Although they may be very aggressive toward these lures at times when conditions are right, truly outstanding action can be had using smaller spoons and spinners in neutral colors (green, blue, silver, bronze) in waters with high visibility, and larger lures in bright, fluorescent colors (red, orange, chartreuse) in semiglacial, turbid, or low-light conditions. Medium-sized chartreuse and silver combination lures also work well in glacial waters. Much the same goes for flies as for hardware.

Pinks seem to be "on the bite" more often in rivers and creeks that have a fairly rapid flow and at least two to three feet of water. As with most salmon, all lures, including flies, should be fished near or right above bottom for best results. Holding areas such as deep holes, runs, and pools are great for finding schools of waiting pinks. Although one may spot a lot of fish in spawning condition in shallower areas, the brighter (and larger) specimens are usually caught from the deeper sections of a stream.

In very slow and still waters, pink salmon can be considerably more difficult to catch, especially under bright, clear conditions. Anglers trying small, dark lures and flies do best. A slow, erratic retrieve is warranted. Fly fishers should strip their flies in short bursts. However, if the water is a bit on the greenish glacial side, slightly larger lures may be necessary and the colors less neutral with more accent toward visibility. Fish tend to respond more readily to anglers' offerings in such drainages.

Spin Gear/Tackle

Ultralight six- to seven-and-a-half-foot rods, fast action, with matching reels and four- to six-pound test line are the preferred setups for the best sport with pink salmon, but heavier tackle is used in areas with strong current or when surf casting.

For lures, use small, flashy spoons and spinners in color combinations of silver, gold, green, blue, black, red, orange, and chartreuse (Pixee, Krocodile, Little Cleo, Syclops, Dardevle, Vibrax, Mepps, Rooster Tail, and Bang Tail).

Fly Gear/Tackle

Fly fishermen usually prefer a five- to six-weight rod (8.5 to 9.5 feet) for pinks, matched with a suitable reel and either floating or sink-tip line. Tippets are generally four- to eight-pound test, and are no more than four feet long for sinking presentations.

Fly Patterns for Pinks

The most effective flies for pink salmon have a bit of flash and/or attractor color: Comet, Boss, Polar Shrimp, Flash Fly, Kispioux Special, Thor, Alaskabou, Blue Smolt, Coho, Egg-Sucking Leech, and Black-Nosed Dace.

Alaska's Top 10 Trophy Pink Salmon

12 pounds, 9 ounces (state record)	Moose River (Southcentral)	1974
12 pounds, 4 ounces	Kenai River (Southcentral)	1974
11 pounds, 14 ounces	Shelter Island (Southeast)	1980
11 pounds, 8 ounces	Montana Creek (Southeast)	1973
11 pounds, 7 ounces	Chilkoot River (Southeast)	1983
11 pounds, 6 ounces	Coghill Lake (Southcentral)	1977
11 pounds, 6 ounces	Biorka Island (Southeast)	1969
11 pounds, 4 ounces	Chilkoot River (Southeast)	1981
11 pounds, 0 ounces	Kenai River (Southcentral)	1984
10 pounds, 8 ounces	Tongass Narrows (Southeast)	1977

Alaska's Major Pink Salmon Locations

It would be difficult to find a coastal stream that does not have a population of pink salmon, since this species has a habit of invading just about any type of water more than two or three feet wide and four or five inches deep. For the best fishing possible for the brightest fish, look for rivers and streams of at least moderate width and depth, near salt water.

Southeast

You'll find tremendous opportunities for pinks in this region, given the multitude of coastal clear-water streams. The saltwater action is almost unparalleled. The run timing is from July into September, peaking mid-July through mid-August.

- **Yakutat:** Situk River
- **Juneau:** Cross Sound, Icy Strait, Lynn Canal, Stephens Passage, Favorite/Saginaw Channels; Chilkat and Chilkoot Rivers; Montana, Turner, Auke, Cowee Creeks
- **Sitka:** Sitka Sound and Chatham and Peril Straits; Nakwasina, Katlian Rivers; Lake Eva, Sitkoh Creeks; Mitchell Bay system
- **Petersburg/Wrangell:** Wrangell Narrows/Duncan Canal; Stephens, Eastern Passages; Ernest, Frederick Sounds; Clarence, Sumner, Zimovia Straits; Kah Sheets, Eagle, Castle Rivers; Hamilton, Gunnuck, Bear (Big), Irish, Andrew, Aaron, Anan, Red Lake, Thoms, Petersburg, Ohmer, Falls, Pat, Fools, Ketili, Government, St. John, Oerns, Marten, North Arm, Snake, Kunk, Porcupine, Kadake Creeks
- **Ketchikan/Prince of Wales Island:** Behm Canal; Revillagigedo Channel; Gulf of Esquibel; Bucareli Bay; Gravina Island; Clarence Strait; Sarkar, Klawock, Harris, Thorne, Karta, Naha, Unuk, Kegan, Wilson, Blossom Rivers; Ward, Wolverine, Ketchikan, Whipple Creeks

Southcentral

Southcentral's Cook Inlet and Kodiak offer top freshwater angling for bright, sea-run pinks, while Prince William Sound enjoys some of the best ocean fisheries for the species statewide. The run timing is from July to September, peaking mid-July into mid-August.

- **Susitna:** Talkeetna, Deshka, Talachulitna, Little Susitna, Theodore Rivers; Willow, Little Willow, Sheep, Montana, Alexander, Goose, Caswell, Lake Creeks
- **Kenai-Cook Inlet:** Lower Cook Inlet and Kachemak Bay; Kenai, Anchor, Ninilchik, Chuitna, Seldovia, Windy Left, Windy Right, Bruin Bay, Kamishak, Amakdedori, Little Kamishak, Rocky Rivers; Deep, Stariski, Brown's Peak, Humpy, Port Dick, Bird, Sunday, Resurrection Creeks
- **Kodiak:** Shuyak Island; Uyak, Ugak, and Chiniak Bays; Karluk, Ayakulik, Pasagshak, Saltery, Afognak, Buskin, Uganik, Olds, American, Dog Salmon Rivers; Pauls, Portage, Salonie, Roslyn, Akalura, Malina, Olga, Russian Creeks
- **Chugach:** Resurrection Bay, Valdez Arm, Wells Passage Area, Orca Bay, Coghill River, Cow Pen Creek

Southwest

The abundant pink fisheries in Southwest are little utilized, because of their remoteness or the presence of other more prized species. The run timing is July and August, peaking in the first half of August.

- **Bristol Bay:** Nushagak River system (including Mulchatna, Nuyakuk, and lower Tikchik Lakes); Wood, Kvichak, Togiak Rivers

- **Northern Alaska Peninsula**: Naknek, Alagnak, Ugashik, Egegik River systems; Herendeen–Port Moller Bay streams
- **Southern Alaska Peninsula**: Abundant throughout, including Aleutian and Shumagin Island streams
- **Kuskokwim Bay**: Goodnews, Eek, Arolik, Kanektok Rivers
- **Lower Yukon**: Andreafsky, Nulato Rivers

Northwest

The pink salmon is one of the primary species (along with chum salmon) residing in Norton Sound, with plenty of excellent fishing opportunities that are seldom utilized because of the area's remote locations. Run strength fluctuates greatly from one year to the next, with general timing from July to August, and a peak from mid-July to early August.

- **Norton Sound**: Golsovia, Unalakleet, Shaktoolik, Inglutalik, Ungalik, Tubutulik Rivers
- **Seward Peninsula**: Kwiniuk, Eldorado, Nome, Snake, Fox, Sinuk, Niukluk, Pilgrim, Solomon, Kuzitrin Rivers; Safety Lagoon

Chapter 6
Charr: Fish of the Rainbow

Mike Spisak and his Supercub fishing buddies have taken the concept of reading water to new, unheard-of heights in remote Northwest Alaska. As pilots based out of Kotzebue, they survey the fishing potential of hundreds of miles of crystal streams from a thousand feet up, and then, with small, maneuverable planes that can set down on gravel bars no bigger than a driveway, they tap an untouched treasure of trophy angling on those big, braided Arctic streams.

As you can imagine, Mike's got quite a reputation for making fish dreams come true, especially for giant charr, a fish he's especially interested in (judging by the number of trophies that cover his office walls). If you're persistent enough, as I was a few years back, he might even take you to some of his choice spots, like the upper Kelly River, a dazzling clear tributary of the Noatak that has produced a string of record fish in recent years, including the largest charr ever taken on rod and reel in Alaska, a whopper of nearly 20 pounds. I was lucky enough to go on charr safari with Mike scant weeks after this record fish was taken, during an exceptionally mild and beautiful fall for that part of the world. Because of the dry weather, the Kelly was flowing low and very clear, with crystal blue pools strung out like

beads to the horizon. Even more tantalizing were the fish swimming within those waters—hundreds of them crowding the larger pools and runs.

"Are they really charr?" I shouted, astounded by the sight of so many salmon-sized fish holding position in water that seemed more appropriate for small grayling.

"Yeah, they're charr, all right. But wait till you see the big ones . . ." teased Mike, like a true bush pilot. We continued up the valley and then I saw he wasn't kidding: In a set of deep pools hemmed in by steep rock walls were some of the largest charr I'd set eyes on. Either I was dreaming, or some of these fish would go 20 pounds or more. Mike assured me there were no king salmon in the Kelly, so this was the real thing— a trophy charr bonanza!

The next four days were a magical blend of sun-kissed afternoons, frosty, aurora-filled nights, and some of the most incredible fishing I've ever experienced. I caught scores of charr, many of them big enough to grace the walls of a man's castle, and a few that might have even placed in the record book, easily pushing the 16-pound mark. But for someone who had spent the best part of his youth getting cranked up over bright,

10-inch brookies from beaver ponds, the excitement of stalking these big brutes in the full lusty bloom of their spawning colors was almost more than I could handle.

It would be difficult to imagine a creature of more exquisite beauty than a fall charr. *Akalukpik* to the Eskimo, they are the "fish of the rainbow." Said to have descended from the sky ages ago, they retain all of the colors of the Heavens, in an artistry so sublime it can inspire visions of taxidermy in the most confirmed catch-and-release angler. (A 13-pound buck with scarlet spots the size of silver dollars and a belly as fiery as the most awesome northern sunset prompted me, a longtime devotee of no-kill fishing, to take a trophy for my den wall.)

On my last evening on the Kelly, I finally hooked one of the monsters we'd seen from the air. He had a tail as big as a shovel, and although I didn't see too much of him before he snapped my nine-weight in a mad dash downriver, I know he was probably the biggest charr I'll ever lose in my days roaming and fishing this great world of ours. When Mike came to get me the next morning, he laughed when I showed him the rod and told me he'd seen a couple of 30-pounders on his way upriver.

Introduction

Perhaps more than any other fish, the charr is associated with the mystique of our wildest places and most pristine waters. Its delicate beauty has inspired poetic admiration from generations of anglers. Part of a worldwide northern fish group (genus *Salvelinus*), charrs in North America include some of our most well-known and widespread sport species: the brook trout of eastern streams; the Dolly Varden and bull trout of the west; and lake trout and Arctic charr of the north.

In Alaska, they're found in a variety of forms, from the creeks and sheltered tidewaters of Southeast to the vast, naked rivers of the Arctic, in numbers that can be truly astounding. In preliminary investigations done in Alaska during the late 1800s, the U.S. Fish Commission encountered thick hordes of the feisty "salmon trout" in nearly every stream and bay surveyed. Later, intense efforts by the salmon industry to control their numbers during the 1920s and 1930s barely affected their abundance, despite the eradication of millions annually. For the most part, this remarkable fishery remains undiminished to this day—a good thing, as the Alaska charr is a fine, underrated game fish, certainly the equal of the more glamorous species that share its waters. It's capable of providing exciting fishing action 12 months of the year, in nearly every fishable body of water from Ketchikan to Kotzebue and beyond.

Alaska's different varieties of charr may be an endless delight to anglers, but they're a headache for biologists, who are still struggling to make sense of their complex life histories and develop a universal classification for the species. Major problems arise in differentiating the various forms of Dolly Varden *(Salvelinus malma)*, the western brook charr, from the arctic charr *(Salvelinus alpinus)*, as their ranges overlap in western and Arctic Alaska, and outward appearance can be almost identical at times. It would simplify matters greatly for sport anglers, guides, and outdoors writers (perhaps scientists as well) if we could begin to think of the various forms of this species complex as simply "charr." With this in mind, we'll use "charr" throughout this book to mean Dolly Varden and/or arctic charr, although we may be more specific when dealing with areas like Southeast or

Southcentral, where almost all of the fish are Dolly Varden. Lake charr, or lake trout as we have come to know them, have long been recognized as a distinct, stable species (*Salvelinus namaycush*), so we'll treat them separately (see page 89).

Description

Charr are built along the same classic lines as trout, with powerful, streamlined bodies, slightly forked tails, large mouths, small scales, and attractive coloration. What distinguishes them from true trout is their more minute scales (100 to 150 along the lateral line), lack of teeth on the upper middle jaw shaft, and different marking scheme (lighter spots on a dark background, as opposed to the trouts' darker spots on a light background).

Coloration and markings on Alaska's Dolly Varden/arctic charr vary considerably, according to location, age, life history, and sexual ripeness. Back and upper sides on sea-run fish are generally steel blue to silver or gray, varying to brown or green in river and lake resident charr. Sides are usually silver-blue or gray in sea-runs, or brown, orange-brown, dusky green, and even gold in lake and river forms; bellies are usually whitish. Markings consist of small to medium-sized concentric red, pink, cream, or orange spots across the back and sides, not always distinct in bright sea-run fish. Lower fins are dusky yellow, orange, or carmine, with prominent white leading edges; tails are slightly forked. Worm-like markings on the back and dorsal fins, found on the eastern brook charr (*S. fontinalis*), are usually absent on Alaska fish.

A sexually mature charr is among Nature's most striking creations, developing intense coloration and physical changes. Beginning in late summer, the bellies and lower sides of fish preparing to spawn are imbued with flaming red-orange (the word "charr" has Gaelic or French roots for blood or blood-red colored), backs turn emerald green or brown, and spotting becomes a brilliant scarlet. Males develop ridged backs and hooked jaws tinged with black and orange.

Charr is also one of the finest eating fish in the world, with firm pink or orange flesh more delicately flavored than salmon. Its fat content is perfect for all methods of cooking, whether deep fried, baked, sautéed, broiled, or smoked. Lightly seasoned, grilled steaks of charr or tender fillets, dipped in spicy batter and deep fried, rank as some of the finest treats from Nature's kitchen.

Range, Abundance, and Status

Alaska's charr are part of a northern species complex that dominates the waters of northern Europe, Siberia, Alaska, Canada, and some of our northern states. They're found in nearly all of Alaska's coastal drainages, in a continuous band from the Beaufort Sea down to the tip of the Southeast Panhandle (including the Aleutian Islands), occurring mostly as resident and sea-run river forms, with isolated populations of lake dwelling and even dwarf stream charr found throughout Arctic, Interior, Kodiak Island, and the Kenai Peninsula.

As the state's most widespread and abundant sport species, Dolly Varden/arctic charr have shown no measurable decline in numbers or distribution, despite a long history of exploitation. Now recognized as a legitimate and desirable game fish, the future of charr in Alaska has never looked so good; hopefully, the state will continue to offer what is undoubtedly some of the world's most prolific and varied angling for the species.

Life History and Habits

Alaska's charr have interesting and, in many ways, little-understood life histories. Sea-run forms begin their lives in much the same way as salmon, spending their initial development in freshwater lakes and streams, feeding on minute aquatic life. At anywhere from one to seven years of age (usually four to six) they smolt, heading seaward in the spring of the year. Unlike salmon, however, they usually remain close to shore for the duration of their ocean stay (usually less than 120 days), wandering in nearby bays or, in some instances, traveling as far as several hundred miles along the coast. Almost all charr overwinter in freshwater. Sea-run fish begin their in-migration sometime in late summer or fall (late July through September), although not necessarily to their natal streams. Charr have been found wintering in rivers hundreds of miles from home; recently, several tagged fish from Northwestern Alaska were found in a river along the coast of Siberia.

Resident or freshwater charr in Alaska can have complicated and varied movement patterns, with some fish spending their entire lives in streams (stream-resident charr), some overwintering in lakes and moving into streams to feed and spawn (lake-resident charr), and others, like the dwarf charr (the "old man fish" of the Inuit), living out their entire existence in small creeks, springs, or headwaters. The presence of different forms of resident and anadromous charr in the same system may be exasperating to biologists, but anglers need only concern themselves with the general habits of the species, which are similar for all forms.

Charr are opportunistic and voracious predators, using any available food sources—insects, leeches, snails, small fish, salmon spawn (and flesh), and even rodents and small birds. Growth rate and potential size are variable, but Alaska's Dolly Varden/arctic charr tend to grow slowly and live for up to 20 years, with the most northern fish reaching maximum size and age for the species. Canada's Northwest Territories have produced some of the largest charr in the world (25 pounds or more, with the current International Game Fish Association world record of 32 pounds, nine ounces from the Tree River in 1981), and there are reports of even bigger fish from eastern Siberia. In Alaska, the largest charr (up to 15 pounds or more) come from the Kotzebue Sound area, in the northwest corner of the state. The current state record, a 19-pound, 12.5-ounce fish, was caught there from a tributary of the Noatak River in 1991. Stream-resident forms are much smaller and grow more slowly than lake-resident or oceangoing fish, and in some systems, residual or dwarf forms might only reach 10 to 12 inches in length.

Alaska's charr reach sexual maturity at anywhere from four to seven years of age (up to nine in the extreme Arctic) and spawn in late summer and fall (July through November), with most systems receiving major spawning activity in September and October (some rivers have a separate summer and fall run). Their spawning behavior closely mimics that of the Pacific salmon, except that they do not necessarily die after breeding and can return to repeat the mating ritual two or even three times in rare cases. In some areas, overwintering sea-run charr remain in freshwater during their spawning years, feeding and competing with resident fish before heading upriver in late summer (late July to August) to breed.

The northern charr's gluttony and lack

of feeding sophistication is legendary; stories of monster 20- and 30-pound fish hanging around shore-side canneries feeding on fish waste or of anglers limiting out on bare hooks are not hard to believe if you've fished much around the state. One of my own early encounters with the delicate feeding habits of the species involved a 12-pound Dolly Varden that tried to swim away with a stringer of rainbows I had tied to a riverbank. Similar stories abound. The charrs' well-known fondness for salmon smolt and spawn led at one time to a territorial bounty for their eradication, though later studies proved their appetite no more destructive than that of the rapacious rainbow trout or coho.

Fishing Alaska's Charr

Anglers in Alaska catch almost one-half million charr each year, close to 10 percent of the state's total sport fish catch. Most of these fish come from northern Southeast, the Kenai Peninsula, Kodiak, and Bristol Bay, with smaller but significant numbers from the Kuskokwim, Northwest, Arctic, and Prince William Sound. Many anglers take Alaska's charr incidentally, while trolling for king and coho salmon or fly-fishing for rainbows, but a growing number of anglers target charr specifically, particularly during spring and fall, or in areas such as Northwest, Arctic, or Southwest that are known for outstanding trophy potential.

Spring

Although Alaska's charr can be caught any time of year, they're best fished in spring and late summer through fall, when the great seasonal changes and movements of salmon bring concentrated feeding patterns. After ice-out, all charr become extremely active, leaving overwintering areas and feeding heavily on emerging food sources (such as fish, insect larvae, and crustaceans). They gather in river mouths, estuaries, confluences, inlets and outlets of lakes, and along shorelines, as these are the first waters to stir with life as winter loosens its grip. Studies have shown charr to feed extensively and at times exclusively on salmon fry, smolt, and alevins when available; it's the presence and movement of great numbers of these young salmon, more than anything else, that makes Alaska's spring charr fishing so extraordinary.

On any of the hundreds of salmon-rich streams and lakes across Alaska (particularly those of Bristol Bay, Kodiak, the Alaska Peninsula, and Southeast), during peak periods of young salmon emergence in the spring, waters can actually churn with the frenzy of feeding charr as they slash through schools of fry, smolt, or alevins. If you time it right, you can get in on some of the most exciting, fast-paced fishing action imaginable, using spinners, spoons, flies, or jigs to easily provoke these ravenous hordes.

The trick is to locate feeding fish or concentrations of young salmon, not always a simple task in Alaska's immense waters and erratic conditions. Timing and location are essential. May and June are the peak months for spring juvenile salmon movement across most of Alaska, with the most prolific waters—such as Katmai, Kodiak, and Iliamna—obvious choices for the best fishing. Target lake outlets and inlets, bays, shorelines with deep drop-offs, river mouths and confluences, pool eddies, and cutbanks—anywhere that young salmon might be concentrated and/or provide efficient ambush sites for charr. Studies have shown the low-light, extreme late evening and early morning hours (10 P.M. to 2 A.M.) to be most conducive to juvenile salmon movement, so time your efforts to fish as close to those hours as humanly possible. (Cloudy, windy, and rainy days are also best.) Look for obvious signs of feeding or shoaling activity—surface disturbances, "shimmering" in the water, or flocks of wheeling and diving seabirds (gulls and terns).

Many guides and lodges nowadays spot charr from the air, hopping from one locale to the next until they find a sizable group. But if you don't own a plane, you'll have to rely on the whims of Nature and your own fish sense to connect with these hungry spring feeders. You may have to fish blind, casting to likely holding water or trolling from a boat, using spoons and plugs as the best first choices (try one-quarter- to half-ounce Krocodiles, Pixees, Crippled Herrings, or Hot Rod spoons in nickel, chrome/neon blue, chrome/silver prism, chrome/fire stripe, or gold/orange; or one-eighth- to half-ounce Wiggle Warts, Hot Shots, Tad Pollys, and Shad Raps, in silver, blue-silver, and gold scale finish). Vary your retrieve, depth, and location until you locate feeding fish, much as you would for lake trout. Spinners are also excellent choices for spring charr, especially in inlet and outlet waters or streams. Try nos. 0 to 3 Mepps silver or gold, long-bladed Aglias, or the Super Vibrax no. 1 to 3 in nickel and gold blades.

If you're fly-fishing, start with a generic smolt or fry imitation streamer—perhaps a no. 2 to 4 Coronation or Supervisor— as a "searching" pattern, fishing a light strip (inches, not feet) through likely holding areas. A floating line or sink-tip works best, depending on the strength of the current and depth of the water. On flowing water, make cross-current, downstream sweeps, just as you would for spring trout down south. Use the line drag and a little rod tip action, if necessary, to imitate the nervous pulses of movement these little fish display as they dart through the water. Some other patterns to include in your spring charr arsenal are Marabou and Silver Muddlers, Matukas, Woolly Buggers, Leeches, and an assortment of smolt/fry variations (even alevin patterns) and attractor patterns (such as Polar Shrimp, Skykomish Sunrise, and Mickey Finn), in sizes 2 to 8 (the larger hooks sink better). Don't be afraid to experiment; some of the biggest charr you'll ever see are taken on the most unlikely fly creations.

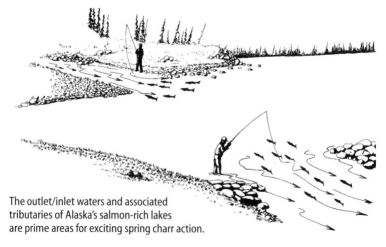

The outlet/inlet waters and associated tributaries of Alaska's salmon-rich lakes are prime areas for exciting spring charr action.

Sea-Run Charr

Surprisingly, most overwintering sea-run charr do not linger long in freshwater during the spring dispersal, but instead move quickly down into river mouths. Studies conducted in western and Arctic Alaska show a great proportion (50 percent or more) of fish captured during out-migration to have empty stomachs. Once they reach the mouths and estuaries, however, they begin feeding heavily like their freshwater counterparts, with diets that consist almost exclusively of fish and crustaceans. They're caught quite freely at these times (usually in late March, April, or early May, depending on the location) by anglers casting from shore or boats—working tide rips, saltchucks, spits, jetties, beaches, bays, and river mouths. Southcentral (especially Kodiak, Homer, Seward, and Prince William Sound) and northern Southeast are traditionally the most popular areas for this spring saltwater charr fishing.

Long, silver, Norwegian-style casting spoons and jigs (three-eighths to three-quarter ounce) are deadly on these sea-roving spring charr, as they imitate very closely the sand lance, herring, and young salmon on which they feed. Spinners, diving minnow plugs, crank baits, and flutter spoons in silver, gold, green, white, and blue combinations can be worked effectively as well at times. If conditions are right, you can even find success fly-fishing—working river mouths, spits, beaches, and other likely areas with bait fish imitation streamers (such as smolt, candle fish, sand lance, and herring patterns).

Look for signs of surface activity just as you would in freshwater, but be aware that saltwater charr quite often feeds deep or off bottom. If you're fishing from a boat, a fish locator or depth sounder can save a lot of time in putting you where the action is. Most anglers working the salt this time of year have the best luck fishing the tides (two hours before and after high tide), although you can find good charr fishing around the clock in the more productive zones.

Early Summer

From June on, Alaska's coastal waters jam up with mind-boggling numbers of salmon. In the major systems, thousands, even millions of fish, swim up from the sea into rivers, lakes, and streams, creating abundant angling for salmon and the countless charr and trout (rainbow and cutthroat) that gather in anticipation of the feast to come. Most of these egg pirates are primed and anxious, and can be easily provoked into striking.

These fish are keyed into slightly different stimuli than during their spring smolt bash, with attractor colors the spice that really grabs them. Spinners, spoons, and plugs in silver or gold with fluorescent red, orange, pink, or chartreuse seem to work best. Fly fishermen have the best results with patterns like the Polar Shrimp, Egg-Sucking Leech, Mickey Finn, Alaska Mary Ann, and Purple Woolly Bugger, along with proven standby forage imitations like the Silver Muddler Minnow, Matukka, and Smolt. Fish with a sink-tip line, short leader, and short strip, for best results.

The trick now is to fish deep and not too fast, as charr become less inclined to energetically pursue prey once the salmon arrive. Work river mouths, confluences, pools, and inlet/outlet waters, paying special attention to any areas where you find salmon (cast around and behind them). This is where the quick, agile charr (and rainbow and cutthroat trout) hold, as they shadow their larger cousins' movements. If you're working deep lake or river water from a boat or raft, you might want to try a drift rig (pencil lead or walking sinker off a three-way swivel) with a plug (three-eighths to five-eighths ounce) or fluorescent Spin-N-Glo (size 4 to 10). I've witnessed outstanding results with these in the big waters of Southwest in conditions where spinners or spoons weren't really efficient.

Late Summer

Just when you think Alaska's fishing can't get any better, August rolls around and the action peaks. By now, most charr and trout are concentrated in the gravelly middle and upper main stems of rivers and in feeders, where salmon spawning is under way. First king salmon, then sockeye and chum, and finally silvers and pinks glut these areas with their profuse spawn and carcasses—and spur hosts of resident species like charr, rainbow trout, cutthroat trout, grayling, and even whitefish into a frantic free-for-all.

In late summer (usually mid-July to early August) in most coastal systems, the great influx of sea-run charr peaks. They form mass congregations in river mouths and lower holding areas before moving upriver to join their fellow egg pirates on the spawning gravels. These sea-run charr are in peak condition—firm, fat, and full of energy—and with their great abundance and voracious hunger can provide some of the best sport Alaska has to offer.

During this period, Alaska's river scene is a high-energy, mixed bag of fishing excitement. Gangs of charr, along with squads of zippy rainbows (or cutthroat trout in Southeast) and even bold grayling compete for a piece of the action, while waves of fresh salmon arrive daily. You can take different species on consecutive casts and haul amazing numbers of fish from the better holes. This is the premier time for egg patterns, flesh flies, and bright attractors: familiar Alaskan standards like the Glo Bug, Two-Egg Marabou, Polar Shrimp, Bunny Bug, and Egg-Sucking Leech. Depending on how much these fish have had to eat and other factors, you can expect good to excellent results drifting any of the above through holding water—pools, riffles, cutbanks, sloughs, or confluences—anywhere salmon might congregate or spawn. Cast to the periphery of any holding salmon you can locate (avoid disturbing or provoking them when on their redds) and fish a dead drift or light strip above bottom. Just as you would for spring charr, don't use a leader longer than four feet, as these fish aren't the least bit leader-shy under most conditions.

Spinners can be deadly at this time of year. Thousands of August charr have succumbed to the potent appeal of a no.1 to 5 Mepps—Black Furies, fluorescent Aglias and Comets; or pink, red, or chartreuse Rooster Tails (three-eighths ounce to three-quarter ounce); or the eminently popular Blue Fox Super Vibrax series spinners (nos. 2 to 6) with gold, brass, silver, or "Firetiger" blades and fluorescent orange, red, or yellow bells. Fish them deep and with slow retrieve for best results.

During late summer, certain conditions can arise, such as high, turbid flows from heavy rains or an overabundance of salmon spawn during peak run years (especially for sockeyes or pinks), during which the standby patterns and techniques may not produce as they should. This is when you need some extra oomph on the end of your line. For fly fishers, an assortment of specialty Alaskan patterns has evolved for these situations—gaudy, overstated streamers like the Outrageous, Pink Sparkler, Baker Buster, Orange Wiggletail, and

Alaskabou—that clobber a fish with maximum doses of color and flash. They're a little bit much to cast, but these flies can produce when nothing else seems to work, so be sure to include some in your late summer charr arsenal. Adding bright yarn, dropper flies, spinner-fly combinations, super-bright or oversize lures, erratic retrieves, and even fish oils (where legal) are some other tactics anglers use for added punch under these difficult conditions.

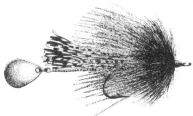

"The Almighty One," a.k.a. "The Gay Blade," a specialty spinner-fly tied by Matt Potter, is deadly on late summer charr and rainbow trout.

Fall

From August to October across much of coastal Alaska, vast numbers of charr crowd rivers and streams to spawn and/or overwinter, providing unique fishing opportunities. Some of the year's best trophy angling can be had in the fall, with an abundance of fish in prime condition, many in striking spawning colors. At this time, charr are overly aggressive, and readily hit spoons, spinners, plugs, and flies in bright attractor colors. (Spawners may become picky as they begin breeding, but they should be left alone anyway.) The big waters of Bristol Bay and the Alaska Peninsula, Southcentral's Kenai River, the lower Kuskokwim tributaries, and the fabulous fisheries of Northwest and Arctic Alaska are some of the best areas for fall charr fishing, particularly for magnificent trophy specimens (to 10 pounds or even more). Late August through

September is the best time for fall charr safaris, as the weather is still not too extreme. (The Arctic region is an exception, as winter can set in beginning in early September.)

Native Alaskans have harvested great numbers of charr during these fall migrations. For centuries, at traditional sites along the Arctic coast, they herded charr into stone weirs and speared them by the thousands. A great deal of fall subsistence harvesting still occurs in the coastal Northwest region, where villagers net fat charr by the thousands in river mouths and estuaries.

Winter

Because charr are one of the few fish that can be taken readily through the ice all winter long, they sustain an important fishery through Alaska's long dark, cold season. The Inuit used carved ivory jigs, spears, and fur-adorned bone hooks in the old days, but now most charr are taken through the ice with small jigs, spoons, and bait. Most of the ice fishing for charr occurs in certain lakes in Southcentral's Kenai Peninsula and Mat-Su Valley, parts of Bristol Bay, a few lakes in Interior (for stocked fish), and waters along Kotzebue Sound.

Gearing for Charr

Ultralight or lightweight, medium-action, five- to seven-foot graphite rods, with matching reels and four- to eight-pound test line are the most popular spinning outfit sizes for fishing Alaska's charr. On bigger water or for trophy fishing, anglers usually upgrade to a light- to medium-weight, slightly longer (to eight feet), stiffer rod and eight- to 12-pound line, or use a light to light/medium, fast-action casting rod (six to seven-and-a-half feet) with eight- to 12-pound line.

For fly-fishing, a six- to eight-weight, eight- to nine-foot, fast-action graphite rod with matching reel and floating

Alaska's Top 10 Trophy Charr

19 pounds, 12.5 ounces Ken Ubben (state record)	Noatak River (Northwest)	1991
18 pounds, 15 ounces	Wulik River (Northwest)	1994
17 pounds, 9.5 ounces	Wulik River (Northwest)	1995
17 pounds, 8 ounces	Wulik River (Northwest)	1968
16 pounds, 14 ounces	Lake Iliamna (Southwest)	1973
16 pounds, 8 ounces	Wulik River (Northwest)	1988
16 pounds, 4 ounces	Noatak River (Northwest)	1994
16 pounds, 0 ounces	Wulik River (Northwest)	1967
15 pounds, 6 ounces	Wulik River (Northwest)	1992
15 pounds, 3 ounces	Noatak River (Northwest)	1992

or sink-tip line is the preferred setup. Keep your leader tippets short on the sinking line presentations; four feet is plenty. Larger hooks (to size 1/0), high-density sinking lines, and weights can be used to help achieve proper depth in extreme water conditions.

Where to Go

So many areas in Alaska offer outstanding fishing for charr that it's difficult to rate any above the others. You can narrow the choices, however, depending on what you're after. For saltwater angling, the waters around Kodiak Island, Prince William Sound, and northern Southeast are probably the most popular. For spring charr, I would certainly rate the big lakes and rivers of Iliamna, Katmai, the Tikchik Lakes area, and the Alaska Peninsula as tops, while for late summer charr action, I would add the streams of the lower Kuskokwim, and the Togiak, Nushagak, and Wood River systems to the above. Where to go for the best trophy charr angling? The big lakes of the northern Alaska Peninsula (Becharof, Ugashik, Naknek), Iliamna, the Kenai River, the North Slope, and the incredible drainages of Kotzebue Sound all provide world-class charr angling.

Alaska's Top Trophy Charr Locations

- **Wulik River** (Northwest)
- **Noatak River** (Northwest)
- **Iliamna Lake and River** (Southwest)
- **Ugashik Lake** (Southwest)
- **Naknek Lake** (Southwest)
- **Kenai River** (Southcentral)

Alaska's Major Charr Locations

Southeast

The Southeast region has some of the state's most abundant Dolly Varden charr, found in nearly every stream that supports fish. Saltwater angling options abound. Nearly three-quarters of the fish are taken in northern Southeast (Yakutat, Haines, and Juneau areas).

- **Yakutat:** Situk, Italio, Akwe, Lost, Kiklukh, Tsiu, Kaliakh, Alsek River systems
- **Juneau:** Chilkat, Chilkoot, and Lutak Inlets; Northern Stephens Passage; Icy Strait; Cross Sound; Gastineau Channel; Auke, Goulding, Kathleen, Turner, Dewey, Windfall Lakes; Cowee, Montana, Admiralty, Peterson Creeks; Taiya, Chilkat, Chilkoot Rivers; Mitchell Bay system

- **Sitka/Petersburg:** Lower Stephens Passage; Salisbury, Ernest, Frederick, Nakawasina, Sitka Sounds; Peril, Upper Clarence, Zimovia, Chatham Straits; Wrangell Narrows/Duncan Canal, Bradfield Canal; Blind Slough; Wilson Beach; Falls, Bear, Exchange, Aaron, Thoms, Anan, Kadake, Andrew, Pat, Sweetwater, Hamilton, Petersburg, Ohmer, Starrigavan, Saltchuck Creeks; Castle, Eagle, Harding, Indian, Nakawasina, Kah Sheets Rivers; Salmon, Eva, Surge, Klag Bay Lake systems
- **Ketchikan/Prince of Wales Island:** Clarence Strait; Behm Canal; Gravina Island; Revillagigedo Channel; San Alberto Bay; Carroll, Wilson, Blossom, Harris Rivers; Thorne, Kegan, Karta, Naha River systems; Humpback, Hugh Smith, Essowah, McDonald, Ward Cove, Orchard Lakes

Southcentral

Almost 70 percent of the state's sport-caught charr are taken here, mostly from the Kenai Peninsula.

- **Kenai Peninsula:** Kenai, Kasilof, Anchor, Russian, Ninilchik Rivers; Deep, Stariski Creeks; Grouse, Summit, Jerome, Swanson River Lakes; Rocky River; Kachemak, Resurrection Bays
- **Copper River and Eastern Prince William Sound:** Cordova and Valdez Arm; Eyak, Klutina, Bering, Katalla, Tonsina River systems; Power, Clear Creeks; Alaganik Slough; Martin, Tsaina, McKinley Lake/River systems
- **Prince William Sound:** Jackpot Bay; Eshamy Lagoon; Coghill, Beach, Nellie Martin/Patton, San Juan Rivers; Boswell, Markarka Creeks
- **Knik Arm:** Big Lake, Little Susitna River, Wasilla Creek, Nancy Lakes
- **Susitna River:** Talkeetna River system; Willow, Lake, Alexander Creeks

- **Upper Cook Inlet:** Chuitna, Theodore Rivers; Crescent Lake system
- **Lower Cook Inlet:** Kamishak River
- **Kodiak:** All bays in vicinity of salmon streams, especially Uyak, Ugak, Chiniak, Mill, Monashka, Perenosa, Seal Bays; Shuyak Island. All salmon-producing streams, especially Karluk, Buskin, Pasagshak, Saltery, Olds, Thumb, Uganik, Ayakulik, American, Spiridon, Dog Salmon, Zachar, Little Rivers; Portage, Pauls, Akalura, Roslyn, Salonie, Malina Creeks; Barabara Lakes

Southwest

Southwest has some of Alaska's finest freshwater charr angling in terms of abundance and size (with some fish up to 10 pounds). Saltwater fishing occurs only on Kodiak Island.

- **Alaska Peninsula:** Nearly all streams and lakes, down to and including the Aleutian Islands; those with heavy salmon runs generally offer the most outstanding fishing: Naknek Lake/River system (including Brooks Rivers, American Creek, Idavain Creek/Lake, and other associated streams and lakes); Becharof Lake; Egegik River system; Ugashik Lakes/River system; Chignik River system; Aniakchak, Meshik, Bear Rivers; Nelson Lagoon system
- **Bristol Bay:** All major salmon systems also have prolific charr populations, especially: Iliamna-Kvichak system (mostly Iliamna, Kvichak, Newhalen Rivers, and Lake Iliamna); Nushagak system (mostly Mulchatna, Nuyakuk, upper Nushagak main stem); Wood River–Tikchik Lakes (mostly outlet/inlet streams: Agulukpak, Agulowak, Wood River, Peace River, Lynx Creek, Little Togiak, etc.); Togiak River system; Igushik River; Kulukak River

- **Kuskokwim:** Outstanding fishing for sea-run and resident charr from Kuskokwim Bay to Holitna: Goodnews, Arolik, Kanektok, Eek, Kwethluk, Tuluksak, Kisaralik, Kasigluk, Aniak, Holitna River systems
- **Nunivak Island:** Some huge, trophy sea-run specimens have been taken from streams here.
- **Lower Yukon:** Andreafsky, Anvik Rivers

Northwest

Thirty percent of the state's largest trophy charr have been taken from this region.

- **Eastern Norton Sound:** Unalakleet, Shaktoolik, Inglutalik, Ungalik, Tubutulik, Kwiniuk Rivers
- **Seward Peninsula:** All salmon streams, especially Fish-Niukluk, Nome, Pilgrim Rivers; Salmon Lake; Snake, Sinuk, Solomon, Kuzitrin, Agiapuk, Bonanza, Eldorado, Buckland Rivers

- **Kotzebue Sound:** Lower Noatak River and tributaries (Kelly, Kugururok, Nimiuktuk Rivers); Kobuk River drainage (including Walker, Selby Lakes); Wulik, Kivalina Rivers

Arctic

The Arctic region has outstanding, barely explored fishing possibilities for big charr.

- Colville River system (especially Anaktuvuk, Chandler, Killik Rivers); Sagavanirktok, Canning, Kongakut, Hulahula Rivers; Chandler, Karupa-Cascade, Galbraith, Elusive, Schrader-Peters Lakes

Interior

Only small, stream resident charr occur naturally in streams here, but some stocked fishing is available in lakes near Fairbanks.

- Tanana, Nenana Rivers (clear-water tributaries); Quartz, Harding, Coal Mine Road, Chena Lakes

Chapter 7
Lake Trout: Old Man of the Lakes

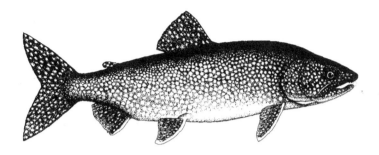

The Inupiat of Northwest Alaska tell the legend of a giant fish called *idluk*, which is found in the deepest, most remote lakes of the Brooks Range. Said to be as old as the hills, this finny will-o'-the-wisp is reputed to reach sizes large enough to swallow a man whole. Fabulous tales like this are easy to dismiss as nothing more than folklore, having no basis in the reality that surrounds most of our lives. But perhaps they're more than legend.

Some years back, two men were fishing the headwaters of the Kobuk River at Walker Lake in the central Brooks Range. It was early summer, and they were putzing around in a small raft, enjoying the exquisite weather and 24-hour daylight that time of year brings to Northern Alaska. The hour was late, but they had a notion to troll some big plugs before they called it a night. Fishing with heavy lines and stout bait casters, they watched in amazement when one of the beefy rods doubled and its reel screamed, only seconds after they had let their lures out. Now these fellows were experienced Alaska anglers and men of the wilderness, with years of time in some of Alaska's most remote backcountry. But to this day, they swear that whatever it was on the end of their line that night was no ordinary fish. Clamping down on the drag and pumping the big rod for all he was worth, one of them barely brought the beast under control. As it gyrated and spun the light boat around and around, they realized they didn't have a ghost of a chance with the thing. But what really got them was that when the behemoth headed for the lake's far shore, some 15 miles away, it was only slightly fazed by the raft it was dragging behind. The way they tell it, after 20 minutes in tow, with no indication of the fish tiring and a strong offshore breeze kicking up, they agreed it was best to cut loose, and so they parted ways with this lake monster.

Introduction

The lake trout (*Salvelinus namaycush*) is one of our better-known northern fish denizens. Originally found in deep, clear, cold waters from New England to the Arctic, the big, native trout of the northern lakes is actually a charr, closely allied with the familiar eastern brook trout and western Dolly Varden. It has the distinction of being our continent's largest and longest-lived freshwater salmonid, reaching weights of 100 pounds and living more than 50 years.

In Alaska, the lake trout is widely distributed and thriving, with fishing potential in many waters comparable to some of the better fisheries in Northern Canada. But because anglers in Alaska have a variety of world-class fisheries at hand, few areas in the state receive the intense, systematic effort seen in lake trout waters elsewhere. Many of the state's good lake trout waters remain underutilized, a bonanza of exciting angling yet to be discovered.

Not a spectacular game fish by any stretch of the imagination, the laker's reputation is nonetheless secure. He's the fish of the primitive northern wilderness, inhabiting the crystal depths of the loneliest watersheds, even where no other species thrive. Draw a map of Alaska, pick out any lake of size, depth, and elevation, and it's a safe bet you'll find some testy, spotted, gray charr waiting to pick a fight with you there.

Description

Built like a true trout, with a large mouth and protruding belly, the lake trout looks every bit the predator that he is. His basic color scheme involves a darker background of silver gray to brown (sometimes greenish) with a profusion of white, yellow, or gold oval spots and vermiculations across the back and sides. Bellies are usually cream-colored, with lower fins of trademark charr coloration: clear, milky, yellow, or orangish, with narrow white borders. Tail fins on lake trout are usually deeply forked, with red or pink spots absent from the sides—two distinctive character differences that distinguish them from the other charrs.

The average size of Alaska's lake trout varies, but is usually from three to five pounds in most waters that are not overfished. The state's largest lake trout generally come from deep, large lakes with abundant food sources, with fish of 20 pounds or more considered trophy specimens for Alaska (the state record is a 47-pound fish from a lake in the central Alaska Range). In recent years overfishing has left a predominance of smaller fish in many of the more popular lakes. New, stringent harvest regulations and more active management policies (a departure from the liberal days of early statehood) should restore the high quality of some of Alaska's more accessible waters.

The lake trout's appeal is enhanced by its excellent eating qualities. Its firm, white, pink, or orange flesh has a delicate flavor and is superb fried, baked, or smoked. Don't count your outdoor career complete until you've sat on some gravelly shore and indulged your hearty appetite with succulent lake trout fillets, lightly seasoned and grilled over a smoky fire.

Range, Abundance, and Status

Interestingly enough, lake trout occur only in North America, originally in a wide swath of lakes stretching from New England to the Great Lakes, across most of Canada, down into the Rockies, and up into Alaska (a range that coincides with the limits of the last major period of glaciation).

In Alaska, lake trout are common in the alpine lakes of the Alaska Range, Bristol Bay, the Kenai and Alaska Peninsulas, the Brooks Range, and the central and eastern Arctic coastal plain. They're absent from Kodiak, the Seward Peninsula, low-lying lakes of the Yukon and Kuskokwim basins, the northwest Arctic coast, and the Alaska Peninsula south of Ugashik Lake. Even though they're almost always associated with lake systems, some stream-dwelling populations occur in the Sagavanirktok, Colville, and Canning Rivers of the Arctic.

Very little has been done to adequately assess the status of any but the most accessible of the state's lake trout stocks. All indications, however, point to a healthy fishery, though many of the state's more heavily fished locations are showing the effects of overharvesting, with a decline in average size and number of trophy specimens. More conservative management and a growing trend toward catch-and-release fishing hopefully mean a brighter future for the quality of angling.

Life History and Habits

Extensive studies conducted throughout Canada have taught us much about the general life history and habits of lake charr. Lake trout research in Alaska has been limited, focusing mostly on the more accessible lakes of the Alaska Range. We know that, like all charr, lake trout are voracious, opportunistic predators that spawn in the fall (not necessarily every year), and have movement and feeding patterns that change with the season. There are some key differences, however, between lake trout and their charr cousins that are noteworthy for anglers.

The most obvious characteristic unique to the species is their preference for lake habitat for rearing, feeding, and spawning. Almost all of the lake trout you'll encounter in Alaska will be associated with some lake body (except for the distinct river-dwelling populations mentioned above). The need for cold, highly oxygenated water determines their movements and feeding patterns to a great extent. With the arrival of spring breakup, lakers move into shallows to feed, consuming small fish, mollusks, crustaceans, insect larvae, and even rodents. When available, fish are the preferred prey of larger lake trout. As water temperatures rise, lake trout go deep, preferring to remain within the thermally stratified sections of water closest to 50 degrees. Studies have shown that even in lakes with abundant food supplies, many lake trout will forgo a meal for an empty stomach if it means they have to leave their preferred band of cooler water for any length of time.

With the arrival of cooler temperatures in Alaska (in late August and September in most of the state), lake trout begin to congregate for spawning in offshore areas of shallow to moderate depth (less than 40 feet), with gravel or rocky bottoms free of sand or mud. Ideal spawning areas are far enough from shore to escape the pounding of wind-induced wave action, but shallow enough to resist sedimentation. Spawning at night, lake trout do not use a nest, unlike salmon. Instead, they scatter their eggs and allow them to settle into the cracks and crevices of the substrate, where they slowly develop and hatch in late winter.

Alaska's lake trout are slow growing, late maturing, and long-lived; fish older than 25 years are not uncommon, with some specimens from the Arctic exceeding 50 years. (Arctic populations tend to mature later and live longer.) Because of their slow growth rates, long lives, and rather low fecundity, trophy lake trout populations are surprisingly easy to overfish, a fact that many fish managers (and lodge owners) have begun to realize only recently, hopefully in time to save the trophy potential of the more hard-hit locales that have already had most of the worthy specimens gleaned by overharvesting. Nowadays, many of the better trophy lake trout fisheries in northern Canada have strict catch-and-release policies, a trend that may soon catch on in some of Alaska's more urban-accessible waters.

Fishing Alaska's Lake Trout

Because of the similarities in life cycle and feeding habits across their range at high latitudes, many fishing strategies for Alaska's lakers will be similar to those used in lakes of northern Canada, with some notable differences.

Spring

In spring, as the returning sun frees fish from their icy prisons and winter stupor, charr become very active and begin feeding extensively. Lake trout cruise shallows and feed near the surface, aggressively pursuing anything that remotely resembles food, especially small fish, crustaceans, and mollusks. In Alaskan waters, their spring recklessness may be heightened by the presence of competitor species or a richer, more varied forage (such as juvenile salmon or charr).

Rambunctious feeding and spring conditions make for some of the easiest fishing of the year. Almost any properly presented lure or fly has an even chance with spring lakers, and in shallow crystal lake waters, there's no trick to locating them. Timing, weather, and location are the key factors in your success at this time of year. Although many of these lakes don't get fished until they're open enough to allow for floatplane or boat access, if you can get

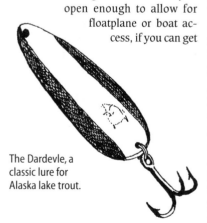

The Dardevle, a classic lure for Alaska lake trout.

to them just as the leads are opening up—especially around outlet waters—you can enjoy amazing action. Some fish-crazed pilots even land ski planes on the rotten ice of remote lakes in late spring and toss spoons or jigs into the slush water surrounding the edges, with awesome results.

No matter how soon after ice-out you get to fish these trout lakes, the idea is still the same: Work the open water as it becomes available, which generally occurs sooner around outlet and inlet streams, bays, and shorelines that lie on the windward side. Sunny weather really can bring lakers out into these open areas. Bright spoons, jigs, or spinners (such as a Krocodile, Dardevle, Super Vibrax, or Mr. Twister) tossed into these pocket waters usually do the trick.

Spring is one of the few times you can do well with flies, as lakers tend to scatter and go deeper later in the season. Smolt, leech, sculpin, and attractor patterns, size 1/0 to 6, work exceedingly well for Alaskan spring lakers, with nymphs and even dry flies eliciting strikes under the right conditions. Look for signs of fish in the shallows of small bays, outlet/inlet waters, and beaches with drop-offs, in the early morning or late evening hours, when they're prone to prowl. One of the greatest thrills of fishing wild lake trout waters is to be gently stirred from sleep by the slurping of big fish in the shallows, only yards from your lakeside camp.

After the ice completely disappears and lakes start to warm, fish may not be so easy to find. Work any obvious shallow feeding locations, just as you would for charr this time of year (in many of Alaska's lake systems the two freely mingle with each other during spring feeding). If you don't have any luck, you'll need to probe deeper water, from shore, boat, or raft. A big, heavy, bright spoon (such as the Krocodile, Dardevle, or Pixee) is a time-tested favorite for this kind of fishing, as is a diving plug (Wiggle Wort, Tadpolly, Rapala, or Flatfish). Both should be worked deep and with a slow retrieve or troll. Quite often between late spring and early summer, lakers can be found moderately deep, to 15 feet or so, in off-shore areas like shoals or bays that have concentrations of bait fish. A small boat and fish locator or depth sounder can help in these conditions, especially on the big water lakes.

Summer

Much has been written about the lake trout's preference for cooler, oxygen-rich waters and bottom structure. As northern waters warm from the advancing sun and nonstop daylight, lakes tend to stratify into more or less defined layers of temperature and oxygen saturation. Although this is especially true in the big, deep lakes of southern Canada, it may not always be the case in Alaska's high-latitude waters, where the thermocline isn't so pronounced due to cooler yearly temperatures and lake sizes and depths.

As summer advances, lake trout tend to scatter from their spring haunts to deeper water, but not necessarily to the deepest parts of the lake. Depending on factors like the availability of food, bottom structure, weather, and time of day, you can expect to encounter them in water 10 to 40 feet deep in most Alaska lakes during summer (July and August). Many smaller lakers (two to eight pounds) stay fairly close to shore near lake outlets and inlets, islands, bays with cover, and beaches with fast drop-offs, even during the hottest part of summer. The low-light hours and cloudy or windy days are the best times to encounter these shallow holding summer lakers, with spinners, small spoons, or bait fish and attractor patterns the most popular and effective enticements.

No matter what kind of stratification or structure a lake has, the summer feeding habits and movements of Alaska's lake charr can be greatly influenced by the wide range of food sources available. This is particularly true in the salmon-rich Southwest lake systems of Katmai, Iliamna, the Tikchiks, and Kuskokwim Bay, and to a lesser extent, in certain locations on the Arctic slope, where it is not uncommon to encounter lakers feeding heavily in streams, miles from lake sources. Even though these fish rarely push the 10-pound mark, they are quite often abundant, fat, and feisty—a welcome surprise when angling the standard river fare.

For trophy fishing the big water lakes, July and August are the prime times for deep-water trolling. This usually means stout rods, downriggers, fish locators, thermistors (temperature reading devices), and flashers, if you're a serious sport angler or guide on the more popular big water fisheries. Most folks use large (four-inch plus) trolling spoons like the Canadian Wonder, Diamond King, Tom Mack, and Apex along with long plugs (up to nine inches) like the Kwikfish, Flatfish, Magnum Rapala, and Jensen Minnow, in colors of silver, gold, silver/blue, silver/green, green/yellow, or white pearl. Slow but varied trolling speeds at depths of 15 to 60 feet through areas of structure (such as shoals, reefs, islands, and shelves) seem to produce the most fish. A good knowledge of the lake's bottom structure, thermocline, forage, and areas of fish concentration (along with fish locators or depth sounders) can spell success with trophy lakers in these waters. For this reason, it makes good sense to seek the services of a reputable guide, especially if you're new to an area or have limited experience with lake trout.

Fall

Even though the fall season can be quite short in Alaska, it's another favored time for fishing lake trout. From late August well into September, lakers begin their prespawning movements. During this phase, they're more concentrated near gravelly or rocky beaches, shoals, small bays, and other areas conducive to spawning, in water up to 15 feet deep. If you time it right and know where to go, you can get into some of the year's best fishing. The company of a knowledgeable guide or local angler can save a lot of guess work and wasted time in searching out these areas. Bright spinners, spoons, jigs, and bait fish/attractor pattern streamers (such as Yellow Marabou, Mickey Finn, Smolt, Gray Ghost, Marabou Muddler, and Leech) work well on these excitable, concentrated fall lakers. Since many Alaska anglers are busy with hunting activities during this time of year, some truly outstanding and accessible fall fisheries remain underutilized (see Where to Go on page 95).

Winter

Lake trout are one of the few Alaska sport species that can provide consistent angling through the long winter season. Most ice fishing for lake trout occurs in the more urban-accessible waters of the upper Susitna, Tanana, and Copper Rivers and the Kenai Peninsula, where anglers can take lakers along with other winter species, such as burbot, charr, whitefish, and pike. Jigs, spoons, and bait are the most commonly used enticements.

Gearing for Alaska's Lake Trout

Spin and Casting Gear

For spin fishing Alaska's lake trout under most conditions, rig up with a light/medium or medium-weight, six- to medium or medium-weight, six- to eight-and-a-half-foot, medium-action, freshwater spinning rod, matched with a high-quality, open-faced reel capable of holding at least 175 yards of eight- to 12-pound test nylon monofilament line. Casting gear anglers want a medium-weight, fast-action seven- to eight-and-a-half-foot rod, with a matching reel that holds 200 yards of 12-pound test.

For deep-water trolling, a medium-weight, downrigger or backbounce rod, seven-and-a-half to eight feet, is recommended, matched with a sturdy reel (such as Ambassadeur 6500 or 7000 series, Penn 9M, or Daiwa Sealine LD30) and at least 200 yards of 15- to 30-pound test mono or braided line (depending on whether you're fishing downriggers).

Fly-fishing Gear

For most fishing (depending on water depth, length of casts, wind, and other factors), you'll probably want to rig up with a long (nine to 10 foot) seven- or eight-weight rod, matched with an appropriate reel, and an assortment of lines—floating, short and long sink-tips, and full sinks—to handle the variety of conditions. Keep leaders short (four feet or less) for all but the rare surface presentations, and use a tippet of around (2X) 10-pound test for best results.

Fishing Bait

The use of live bait, a deadly, effective, and time-honored tradition elsewhere, is restricted in Alaska by a statewide ban to prevent introduction of non-native species. Though you can't rig a squirming, six-inch grayling to tantalize the big ones like they do in Canada, you can do quite well at certain times trolling a rigged whitefish or a spoon with a four- to five-inch whitefish, grayling, or herring strip added for extra pizzazz. Some anglers have even had good results drifting chunks of whitefish, shrimp, and even salmon eggs through weedy bays, channels, and outlet and inlet waters. Keep this in mind if conditions aren't favorable to the more standard approaches.

Where to Go

With all the attention lavished on Alaska's world famous salmon and rainbow fisheries, the state's outstanding lake trout potential is easily overlooked. Well-known, popular locations like Lake Louise–Susitna, Paxson–Summit, Crosswind, Hidden, and Harding continue to produce some amazing trophy fish (20- to 30-pounders) year after year, despite mounting pressure. More remote, higher quality fishing can be had with short hikes in to the mountain lakes off the Denali Highway (such as Landmark Gap, Glacier, Sevenmile, and Butte Lakes) or the more remote Dalton Highway, Alaska's only road to the Arctic (see descriptions on page 176 in the Arctic chapter).

The best lake trout fishing in the Last Frontier can't be reached by car or foot, of course. You'll need to climb in a small plane and fly beyond the fringes of civilization to the state's more isolated waters. Some of these are not too far or expensive to access. The majestic Wrangell and Talkeetna Mountain Ranges, north and east of Anchorage, contain numerous lakes with great fishing that can be reached with relatively short, inexpensive flights from the nearby hub towns of Palmer, Talkeetna, and Glennallen. The fabulous Southwest region likewise contains many headwater lakes that are seldom sampled, but have some of the state's best wild lake trout angling. And for those lucky souls blessed with time and resources to explore Alaska's ultimate wilderness watersheds, there are the remote lakes of the Brooks Range and Arctic North Slope, where one can encounter the "old man of the lakes" in his most primeval surroundings.

Alaska's Top Trophy Lake Trout Waters

- **Lake Louise** (Southcentral)
- **Lake Clark** (Southwest)
- **Harding Lake** (Interior)
- **Paxson Lake** (Southcentral)
- **Crosswind Lake** (Southcentral)

Alaska's Major Lake Trout Locations

Southcentral

The Southcentral region holds some of Alaska's most heavily fished but pro-

Alaska's Top 10 Trophy Lake Trout

47 pounds, 0 ounces (state record)	Clarence Lake (Southcentral)	1970
33 pounds, 8 ounces	Lake Clark (Southwest)	1980
33 pounds, 4 ounces	Harding Lake (Interior)	1993
32 pounds, 4 ounces	Lake Clark (Southwest)	1983
30 pounds, 15 ounces	Lake Louise (Southcentral)	1973
29 pounds, 8 ounces	Skilak Lake (Southcentral)	1985
29 pounds, 2 ounces	Old John Lake (Interior)	1981
28 pounds, 6 ounces	Lake Clark (Southwest)	1982
28 pounds, 5 ounces	Harding Lake (Interior)	1994
28 pounds, 4 ounces	Lake Clark (Southwest)	1983

ductive lake trout waters, including some outstanding trophy locations.

- **Susitna Drainage:** Susitna, Tyone, Louise, Clarence, Watana, Crater, Big, Deadman, Chelatna, Stephan, Shell, Butte Lakes
- **Copper Drainage:** Paxson, Summit, Crosswind, Fish, Deep, Shell, Fielding, Tangle (Upper and Landlocked), Klutina, Tonsina, Tazlina, Tanada, Tebay, Hanagita Lakes
- **White River Drainage:** Rock, Ptarmigan, Beaver Lakes
- **Kenai Peninsula:** Hidden Lake; Kenai River system (including Skilak and Kenai Lakes); Swan, Juneau, Trail Lakes; Trail River, Tustumena Lake–Kasilof River
- **Cook Inlet:** Beluga, Chakachamna, Crescent Lakes
- **Prince William Sound:** Tokun Lake

Southwest

Southwest has some of the state's best lake trout waters in terms of abundance, though few trophy (20-pound-plus) fish are taken, perhaps because these lakes receive so little focused fishing effort.

- **Kvichak Drainage:** Lakes Clark, Iliamna; Kokhanok Lakes; Gibraltar, Lachbuna, Kontrashibuna, Kijik Lakes
- **Katmai:** Lakes Naknek, Brooks, Kulik, Nonvianuk, Kukaklek, Coville-Grosvenor
- **Alaska Peninsula:** Ugashik, Becharof Lakes
- **Nushagak Drainage:** Tikchik Lakes; Twin, Fishtrap, Snipe, Turquoise Lakes
- **Togiak Drainage:** Nenevok Lake
- **Upper Kuskokwim River:** Whitefish (Hoholitna), Telaquana, Two Lakes
- **Lower Kuskokwim River:** Aniak, Kisaralik, Heart, Kanektok River Lakes (Kagati-Pegati, Kanuktik, Klak, Ohnlik, etc.); Goodnews River Lakes (Goodnews, North, South, Middle Fork, Kukatlim, Canyon, etc.); Arolik Lakes

Interior

Alaska's Interior region includes some of the state's most popular fisheries in the Tanana drainage and some excellent remote lakes.

- **Eastern Brooks Range:** Upper Chandalar River: Ackerman, Squaw, Chandalar Lakes; Upper Koyukuk River: Big, Twin Lakes; Sheenjek River drainage; Old John Lake
- **Tanana:** Tangle Lakes; Fielding, Boulder, Glacier, 16.8 Mile, Sevenmile, Harding, Landmark Gap, Monte, Tetlin, Two-Bit Lakes

Northwest

The Northwest has many outstanding possibilities in numerous remote Brooks Range mountain lakes. A few of the more well-known ones are listed below:

- **Kobuk River Valley:** Walker, Minakokosa, Selby-Narvak, Norutak Lakes
- **Noatak River Valley:** Feniak, Matcharak, Desperation Lakes; Kiingyak, Kikitaliorak Lakes; other Howard Pass lakes
- **Koyukuk River:** Wild, Iniakuk, Helpmejack, Agiak Lakes

Arctic

Arctic has the state's wildest lake trout waters, many receiving little, if any, fishing pressure. Their potential for high-quality fishing is tops.

- **Colville River:** Etivluk River Lakes (Betty, Etivluk, Nigu, Tukuto, etc.); Karupa, Cascade Lakes; Chandler, Amiloyak Lakes; Anaktuvuk River Lakes (Irgnyivik, Shainin, Tulugak, Lower Anayak, etc.); Itkillik Lake
- **Central Plain Lakes:** Teshekpuk and other lakes east of the Ikpikpuk River
- **Dalton Highway Lakes:** Galbraith, Elusive, Toolik, Itagaknit, Kuparuk, Campsite Lakes
- **Eastern Slope:** Porcupine, Schrader, Peters Lakes

Chapter 8
Rainbow Trout: Fish with a Heart

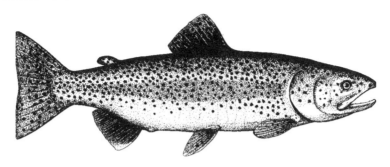

An Alaska guide's job might seem a dreamy, fun-filled adventure to some folks. The reality, however, is one of long hours of difficult, demanding work dealing with the vagaries of Alaska's weather, wild rivers, and unpredictable fishing. But it does have its special moments.

Billie, a young wrangler from Montana up for a summer of guiding, isn't quite sure he likes this game. It's been a most trying trip so far—nasty weather, very poor fishing conditions, and some difficult guests who are relentless in hounding the new guide for his lack of experience. At one of our stops to make lunch and a much needed fire, he grabs one of the spinning outfits off the back of the boat, and in his only attempt at fishing the entire trip, sends a no. 6 Vibrax spinner hurtling across river with an angry heave. I watch it make an enormous arc and plunk down behind an island, and then it happens: As if on cue, a bright, muscular missile as long as my arm launches from the same spot, straight up, clearing the water by an easy four feet. It's a rainbow trout, by God, with a spinner dangling from its mouth!

There's only one problem—Billie's got a quarter mile of line billowing in the wind, and from the looks of things, this wild 30-incher will have him stripped before he's even got his bail flipped. The berserk rainbow jumps six or seven times, furious at an easy meal gone bad. By now, every eye on shore is riveted to this spectacle. The husky mossback re-enters his watery realm and holds in the strong current, allowing Billie precious seconds to regain line—but only for an instant, for the fish shoots off in a blinding run that cruelly strips all the hard-won gains from the reel. I can see there isn't a prayer of holding this fish, but that doesn't really matter. In these brief, crazy moments, the whole trip is turning around.

The giant rainbow—by now beyond all hope of landing—launches into a frenzy of cartwheels that seems to defy gravity. The inevitable is close at hand, and I sense a shared feeling of relief when the line finally parts with a loud twang and the incredible fish goes free. In the strange hush that follows, Billie, acting like he does this sort of thing all the time, calmly walks back to the boat, puts the rod down and, hiding a grin that says it all, mutters, "Yeah, I guess they're out there." (The next day, I can't help but notice, guests are thronging to him for fishing advice.)

Introduction

The rainbow trout (*Oncorhynchus mykiss*) needs no introduction to American anglers. Perhaps the most prized of all our cold-water game fishes, the colorful, native trout of the Pacific Coast has been dazzling us for decades with its high-spirited antics. This glamorous fighter reaches its finest expression in the icy, vast waters of Alaska, where a challenging but rich environment has honed him to a robustness seldom seen elsewhere. Alaska rainbows are indeed big, and in the deep, strong currents they inhabit, they rank as one of the premier challenges in the world of light tackle angling.

The state's immense, wild rainbow territory—from Southeast to Kuskokwim Bay—encompasses hundreds of rivers and lakes, in what is undoubtedly the last significant stronghold for the species. For serious trout anglers the world over, visiting this rainbow mecca is the dream of a lifetime. In terms of dollars and effort anglers put forth to pursue good fishing, no other Alaska species, except perhaps the great king salmon, elicits the same kind of fanatical esteem from anglers of all persuasions.

Description

More streamlined and graceful in form than any salmon, Alaska's rainbow trout presents an unmistakable but varied appearance. The back is generally an olive green or gray, the sides are silver (silver-gray), and the belly whitish. A broad pink, lilac, or scarlet stripe along the midline is the salient identifying feature, from which the fish also derives it name. It also has a liberal sprinkling of small to medium black spots over the upper body and entire tail fin, which is usually less forked than in the salmon or charrs. Belly fins are pinkish to pearly white. Appearance can vary with time of year, diet, maturity, and location. Each watershed seems to produce its own color variation. Fish from the big lakes, such as Iliamna, Naknek, and Kenai, are bright silver and sparsely marked, like steelhead, while rainbows from small tributary systems can be exquisitely hued (lilac, rose, or crimson) with pronounced markings (the leopard rainbows of Bristol Bay, for example). Spawning in spring brings coloration and physical changes, but not as dramatic as in salmon.

Size is similarly varied, with the largest rainbows coming from the state's big lake and river systems (Naknek, Iliamna, Wood-Tikchik, and Kenai). Fish of four to seven pounds or more are caught there with regularity, with rainbows of more than 10 pounds not uncommon. On most Alaska rainbow streams, however, you can expect fish that average about two to three pounds, with the occasional five-pounder or bigger. (The largest sport-caught rainbow ever taken in Alaska was an International Game Fish Association world record steelhead, a few ounces over 42 pounds, but freshwater resident fish of more than 20 pounds are rare these days. See the steelhead chapter beginning on page 108 for more details on Alaska's sea-run rainbows.) The isolation of most of the state's waters, the short fishing season, and the growing predominance of catch-and-release no doubt contribute to the hefty average size of most of Alaska's wild rainbows.

Range, Abundance, and Status

Rainbow trout were historically distributed along most of the Pacific slope, from northern Mexico to Kamchatka. In Alaska, they occur naturally from streams and lakes in Southeast to tributaries of the lower Kuskokwim River in

Southwest, but not continuously along this range, as they are conspicuously absent from areas such as the Northern Gulf Coast, Prince William Sound, and most of the Alaska Peninsula. Steelhead, the sea-run form of the rainbow trout, have a more extensive but sporadic Alaska distribution. Through propagation and transplanting, numerous new lake fisheries for rainbows now exist in parts of Alaska, such as Southcentral and Interior.

The status of the wild rainbow in Alaska seems remarkably secure, bolstered by the new ethics in sport angling, and its call for catch-and-release, single barbless hooks, the phasing out of bait, and more conservative management. Though many an old-timer may wistfully recall the bygone days of truly stupendous rainbow fishing, Alaska still has far and away the world's best fishing for the species, in terms of abundance, variety, and trophy potential.

Life History and Habits

The key to success in stalking the wild, big, and beautiful Alaska rainbow lies in a thorough understanding of its life cycle and feeding habits and associated movement patterns. Rainbow trout begin their lives in much the same manner as their larger cousins the salmon, hatching from eggs laid and fertilized in a gravel streambed (spawning usually occurs in late April, May, or June in Alaska). Young fry develop quickly, feeding on insect and crustacean life almost exclusively in their first year of life, but opportunistically taking any food source that's available, especially as they grow older.

Larger rainbows feed extensively—and at times exclusively—on minnows (sticklebacks, sculpins, and juvenile salmon). When available, they also prey heavily on leeches, freshwater shrimp, snails, and even small rodents (voles, mice, and shrews). Insect life (nymphs and emerging) is also utilized to a varying extent. During summer and fall, practically every rainbow trout in Alaska becomes associated at some time or another with spawning salmon for a chance at their abundant, rich roe, a choice food source for achieving the prime condition necessary to survive Alaska's long, lean winters. At times, they may even pick flesh off dead salmon. In major systems that see annual returns of millions of salmon, the significance of this roe (and flesh) to resident populations of rainbow, charr, and other fish species is substantial and crucial, for it allows large populations of these species to survive in waters that are otherwise quite unproductive.

The Alaska rainbow usually reaches sexual maturity in three to five years, and can live to well over 10 years, with habitat and available food resources playing a big part in life span and ultimate size. Growth is slow, and occurs mostly during the four to five warm months of the year, when food is most plentiful. A 10-pound rainbow may well be 12 years old. Despite the apparent abundance of large fish, most of Alaska's waters are deceptively low in productivity, which is all the more reason to practice a strict catch-and-release policy when fishing these beauties in their last wild strongholds.

Knowing what the main food sources are for Alaska's rainbows (and how to imitate and present them) can be the easy part of the angling equation. The real trick is locating fish, for like Alaska's charr, rainbows can have immense and complicated movement patterns, shifting locations throughout the season to exploit all food sources as they become available. In smaller lakes and other closed systems, the Alaskan rainbow's movements are more local and predictable. An understanding of these important feeding movements—when, where, and how they occur, and the appropriate angling strategies—is essential for success.

Fishing Alaska's Rainbow Trout

Spring

As the ice leaves Alaska's lakes and rivers in April and May, rainbow trout become more active, feeding heavily, as mature fish prepare for spawning. Like charr, they opportunistically seize any available insects, crustaceans, and small fish, especially young salmon. In most of the large lake and river systems that contain rainbows (such as Kenai, Iliamna, Naknek, and Wood-Tikchik), alevins, fry, and out-migrating smolt are a primary food source for rainbow trout and charr, making fishing strategies similar for both. (See the charr chapter beginning on page 77 for additional details on spring charr fishing techniques.) The best springtime fishing locations are the lake outlets and inlets, river mouths, confluences, and pools of these major salmon systems, with the most effective lures usually those that mimic young salmon or other forage species: small spinners and spoons, plugs, smolt- and fry-patterned streamers, sculpin, and leech patterns. Cloudy days and the darker hours of early morning and late evening offer the most productive fishing.

The potent appeal and ease of fishing spinners makes them hard to beat for Alaska spring rainbows, with the most popular being the Super Vibrax, Mepps Aglia (long), Rooster Tail, and Panther Martin, in silver, gold, or copper, sizes 0 to 3 or $1/_{32}$ to one-sixth ounce. In deep water near lake outlets or in big rivers,

spoons can be more effective, and many Alaska anglers use the smaller (one-eighth- to three-eighths- ounce) Pixees, Krocodiles, Kastmasters, and Hot Rods with good results. Under most spring conditions, you'll do best fishing with a steady, not too fast retrieve, working areas of likely fish concentration or any water where you see feeding activity.

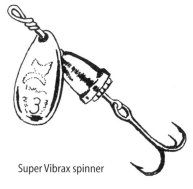

Super Vibrax spinner

In smaller lakes and rivers, rainbows rely more on insect larvae, crustaceans, leeches, and fish like sculpins or sticklebacks. Nymph patterns and Muddler, Leech, and Woolly Bugger streamers—along with small spoons, spinners, and jigs—can all be equally effective under these conditions. In deep lakes with no outlet, good locations to target for fishing effort are shorelines and around prominent structure (islands, reefs, and drop-offs), if no signs of feeding are present. Early morning and late evenings are the most active times. Here, a boat and an electronic fish finder can improve your chances of success tenfold, but don't underestimate the effectiveness of skillful shore angling on these usually hungry and plentiful lake rainbows. Some of the better locales for this kind of spring fishing are the dozens of small lakes scattered throughout the Kenai Peninsula, Mat-Su Valley, Kodiak, Interior, and Southeast.

Summer

As spring shifts into summer, Alaska's incredible salmon runs pump life into most of the state's waters, and rainbow trout, like charr and other resident species, shift their activities to key into the movements of their larger spawning cousins. In river mouths, lake outlets, sloughs, confluences, and deep pools—anywhere salmon congregate—you can expect attendant hordes of excitable rainbows shadowing the salmon that will later provide vital sustenance through their rich roe and flesh.

The outlets and inlets of the big lakes in Southwest, when the huge sockeye migrations hit in early July, provide the best of Alaska's early summer rainbow fishing. If you time it right in these waters, you can have some incredible action with the big, excitable fish that gather there. Egg-pattern flies, bright attractors, and silver, gold, or fluorescent spinners, spoons, plugs, and even drift bobbers all seem to work well on these easily provoked trout. The techniques used for charr at this time of year are equally effective on rainbows, including fishing the periphery of salmon lies, using deeper presentations, and attractor colors. (See the charr chapter beginning on page 77 for details.)

When spinner fishing these early summer rainbows, colors like fluorescent red, orange, pink, and chartreuse are most effective, especially when used in combination with the standard silver or gold. Stick-on reflective tape or a piece of colored yarn works well to dress up unadorned lures, and allows for creative experimentation with a variety of colors and combinations. The most popular spinners for early summer are the same as used earlier in the spring—Vibrax, Mepps, Rooster Tail, Panther Martin—with sizes up to no. 5 or $^{7}/_{16}$ ounce used. Locate groups of salmon, if possible, and cast directly behind or to either side of them, fishing deep with a steady retrieve. In turbid flows or other situations where salmon can't be located, work deep pools, sloughs, confluences, cutbanks, river mouths, and lake outlets, wherever salmon might be.

Rainbow Trout: Fish with a Heart 101

Once the salmon reach their home gravels and begin their passion play, Alaska's rainbow fishing kicks into high gear. A favorite time of year for many anglers is late August and September, as the bugs generally have diminished and the sporting silver salmon arrive to spice up the action. In just about every lesser tributary stream or gravelly middle to upper main stem of the hundreds of salmon systems spread along the coast, thousands of salmon will be busily engaged in the mating ritual, some of them already occupying their shallow, scooped-out nests on bottom. These are the areas where late summer rainbows (and charr) can be found in greatest concentration.

The big salmon get so caught up in their ardor, they almost seem oblivious to the egg-stealing onslaughts of trout, charr, and grayling. Anything that comes drifting through these areas remotely resembling salmon roe (of pink, red, orange, or white color)—be it an egg-pattern fly, a fluorescent-bladed spinner, a drift bobber, or even a yarn-wrapped hook—usually draws immediate response from the hungry hordes that get quite rambunctious under these competitive conditions. In many ways, this is Alaska rainbow fishing at its best, as you can do things that would astound most conventional trout angler and still catch dozens of fish.

Some of the more popular spinning lures for late summer rainbow fishing are nos. 2 to 5 Super Vibrax ("Firetiger" finish or silver or gold blade with fluorescent orange bell), nos. 2 to 5 Mepps Black Fury or Aglia (fluorescent red, orange, or yellow blade), one-quarter- to half-ounce Rooster Tail (fluorescent red, pink or chartreuse), half-ounce Pixee with red or pink insert, and the three-eighths- and half-ounce Hot Rod (in nickel or brass with a fire stripe).

Fall

From September until freeze-up, cooling temperatures, diminishing daylight, and tightening food supplies spark a desperate hunger and wanton recklessness among Alaska's rainbow population. With the wane of the salmon runs, they leave the upper sections of rivers and tributaries and move down into the main stems, feeding heavily along the way. In the large lake and river systems, big rainbows move into the shallows of tributary streams and rivers, scouring the bottom for lingering salmon roe, even stripping the flesh off carcasses to bolster reserves against the long, dark siege ahead. It's prime time for the trophy angler. Bristol Bay's Lake Iliamna–Kvichak River system, Naknek Lake and River system of Katmai, Southcentral's Kenai River, and other locations are world famous for their late fall, big rainbow trout fisheries. If you haven't already done so, make at least one fall outing to fish these waters. With any luck, you can have the kind of trout fishing most folks only dream about. (See the location descriptions on pages 251, 256, 257, 292, and 293 for more details about fishing these areas.) Egg patterns, flesh flies, attractors, plugs, spoons, and bright drift bobbers fished deep are most effective. Late September and October are the traditional peak periods for this special trophy season.

Winter

Once hard winter starts in Alaska (usually in November), rainbows seek the sanctuary of deep pools, river main stems, and lakes, slowing down to conserve energy with the cold and diminished light. Feeding is limited and consists of the occasional minnow, crustacean, or larvae. Not as exciting to catch this time of year, these winter trout still put up a tussle and provide a significant amount of angling opportunity through the ice in areas like Southcentral's Mat-Su Valley and Kenai Peninsula, and around Fairbanks, Delta, and Glennallen.

Fly-fishing

There's something about a big trout on a fly that no other fishing experience can match, especially when it's a wild, husky Alaskan rainbow. Seasoned anglers who've fished around are often disappointed, however, when they discover that these Alaskan fish are not wily, selective trout requiring fancy casts and artful presentations. For the most part, Alaska's trout ask little in the way of technique or finesse from fly anglers. The challenge instead is one of determining those "here today, gone tomorrow" rainbow whereabouts and dealing with the varied and often demanding conditions encountered on most of the state's waters. Here's a rundown of the basics:

Spring

In spring, conditions on most Alaskan waters are similar to those encountered in many western rivers at this time—high, turbid flows, marginal weather, and feeding activity concentrated on forage fish, crustaceans, and nymphs. The challenge for the fly anglers remains the same: to locate feeding fish, then determine and present the proper prey imitation in a manner most like the real thing. You'll use most of the same techniques here as you would stateside for streamer fishing this time of year—floating lines or sink-tips, quarter casts, and downstream, cross-current swings of the fly. Since minnows are the predominant prey, you'll be fishing mostly smolt, fry, leech, and sculpin patterns (sizes 2 to 6), in addition to perennial rainbow favorites (in the same sizes) like purple,

black, or brown Matukas, Woolly Buggers, Muddler Minnows, and attractors like Polar Shrimp, Mickey Finn, and Skykomish Sunrise. Small alevin and nymph patterns (sizes 8 to 12) can also be quite effective early in the season. Short, fast strips and jigging rod twitches to impart lifelike, strike-provoking action seem the most productive retrieve tactics for these heavily feeding spring rainbows.

River mouths, lake outlets and inlets, confluences, pools, and tailouts—anywhere rainbows might advantageously locate themselves to ambush prey—are the areas where you should concentrate your efforts. In smaller, closed lakes with no signs of surface feeding, you may have better success with nymphs, shrimp, or scud patterns (nos. 6 to 10), so experiment a little if you don't have any luck with streamers. And since Alaskan rainbows are not leader-shy, all of your subsurface presentations will be much easier and more effective with tippets shortened to three to four feet.

Summer

Summer brings the great influx of salmon and rainbows that are keyed almost exclusively into feeding on roe. This means egg-pattern flies and drift presentations for most waters. The simplest, most popular Alaskan egg fly is, of course, the Glo Bug—a puff of orange, pink, or red chenille on a size 2 to 12 egg hook. It's extremely effective fished on a dead drift, right above bottom, especially in the vicinity of holding or spawning salmon. Other popular egg patterns include the Babine Special, Two-Egg Marabou, Egg-Sucking Leech, and Spawn Sac.

The use of "bead eggs," a novel and extremely effective variation of the egg pattern fly, has become increasingly popular for Alaska's late summer trout

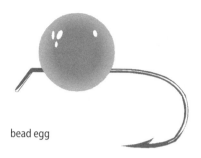

bead egg

and charr. Originally developed by Katmai guides, the bead egg is nothing more than a bright, translucent orange, pink, or red plastic bead (5 mm to 8 mm) and small egg hook (nos. 6 to 10), fished on a dead drift (using floating line), usually below a small split shot (about a foot above the bead). The bead can ride on the line above the hook or be pressed onto the shank using heat. Use a smaller, reddish bead for sockeye salmon waters and a larger orange bead for streams where chum salmon predominate. (Some guides even paint the beads with pearlescent nail polish to achieve a more lifelike color.) Pale, opaque shades of pink and orange seem to work well also, especially in late summer and fall, so it's best to bring along an assortment.

When fishing beads (or Glo Bugs), strike indicators, attached to the end of the leader or fly line terminus, are most useful. For most situations, a short leader (two feet or so) and tippet (four to six feet) will suffice. The bead egg is most deadly drifted through holding water and salmon spawning areas, where egg-lusting rainbows and charr congregate. Pay close attention to your mend as the take is often lightning fast and brief. The beauty of fishing beads is their economy (only pennies per setup), efficiency, and minimum impact on trout, as you usually only hook the lip, for a quick release with the small, barbless egg hooks you'll be using.

Situations and conditions may arise during summer when a simple egg or attractor pattern might not bring the results you expect. Here, you may need more precise casting and presentation (if you can sight-fish), or some oversized, gaudy attractor and egg flies like the Pink Sparkler, Wiggle Tail, Outrageous, Alaskabou, or other specialty patterns (see the appendix on page 403) developed to tantalize rainbows with maximum color and flash. Purists may shudder at the thought of even considering such creations for fly-fishing, but no one can argue their effectiveness.

Fall

Fall fly-fishing for Alaska's rainbows is usually the most exciting and productive of the year, as fish are in prime condition and actively feeding on all available food sources. Egg, Flesh Fly, Attractor, and, to a limited extent, bait imitations like Leeches, Muddlers, and Sculpins all take fish at this time of year. If you're lucky enough to make your way to the big waters of Katmai, Kenai, or Iliamna for the fabulous late fall fishery, bring some heavy trout or steelhead gear along: long, stout eight- or even nine-weight rods, beefy lines (floating, five- and 10-foot sink-tips, and high-density sink) and some of your biggest flies, such as Bunny Bugs, Woolly Buggers, Matukas, Two-Egg Marabous, Spawn Sacs, and Polar Shrimp. Quite often, you'll be fishing big, deep, fast water, and the stout gear will make casting easier and give you a fighting chance with the steelhead-sized rainbows you'll encounter.

Dry Fly–Fishing and Patterns

Not too much is said about dry flies for Alaska's rainbows, for the simple reason that wet presentations produce so fabulously well in most waters throughout the year. Great opportunities for ex-

The Mouse—Alaska's most famous "dry fly."

citing surface fishing go underutilized during late spring and summer all across Alaska's rainbow country, but you can get in on some of this abundant action if you know what to look for and come prepared with the proper gear and fly selection.

Emerging insect activity in Alaska's waters occurs mostly during the warmest days of June and July, although skillful anglers can raise fish any month of the year under the right conditions. The Alaskan rainbow doesn't seem very discriminating in its surface feeding behavior, with numerous patterns producing good results: Elk Hair Caddis, Humpy, Wulff, Adams, Cahill, and even the Gnats or Mosquito, in sizes 8 through 14. Standard floating line presentations seem to work fine for these northern trout, and you can probably shorten your leaders somewhat under most conditions without any noticeable effect. Your best chances for hooking a trout on a dry fly this time of year is during warm, sunny spells, in water that is less than six feet deep, of moderate to fast current—in tail-outs, riffles, lake outlets, and shallow runs.

- **Alaska's 10 Deadliest Rainbow Patterns:** Polar Shrimp, Woolly Bugger, Glo Bug Smolt, Egg-Sucking Leech, Marabou Muddler, Babine Special, Mouse, Flesh Fly, Elk Hair Caddis.

Gearing Up for Rainbow Trout

Hard-core Alaska fly fishers can amass an amazing arsenal of gear for the wide range of situations they fish rainbows in, but one can get by quite nicely with just the basics. For most of Alaska, we're talking about a six- to eight-weight, eight- to nine-and-a-half-foot, medium-action graphite rod, matching reel, and an assortment of lines (floating, sink-tips, full-sink, high-density, etc.). Hook sizes most commonly used vary from nos. 2 to 12, while tippets for Alaska's rainbows are usually in the four- to 12-pound range.

You must either have gear to match the water or find the water to match the gear, as the saying goes. Nowhere will this be more true than in Alaska's rainbow country, where you'll find an amazing range of conditions from mile to mile, making for difficult, if not impossible, fishing at times. The trick is to have a system that's versatile and easy to use. Many folks bring along two, three, or more complete outfits to handle the changing water conditions normally encountered during the course of a trip (for instance, a six- or seven-weight and floating line for fishing dry flies in shallow water, and a seven- or eight-weight with sinking-tip line for fishing the deeper pools and runs). "Sinking heads," short, looped sections of high-density lead core fly line, are a versatile, less expensive alternative to bringing a boatload of spare spools and full length lines, and are readily available in a variety of weights.

Spinning

The majority of Alaska's spin anglers gear up for rainbows with ultralight or light- to medium-weight graphite rods (six- to seven-and-a-half feet), medium- to fast-action, matched with monofilament line of four- to 10-pound test, on high-quality, open-faced reels. For big water trophy fishing, a light to medium steelhead or heavy trout rod (seven- to eight-and-a-half feet) with fast action, and a matching high-quality reel with line weights of eight- to 15-pound test is most popular.

Bait Casting

For drift fishing and trolling the big lakes and rivers (Kenai, Naknek, Kvichak, Wood-Tikchik, and others), bait casters are the equipment of choice. You'll generally work these waters by boat, pulling plugs, spoons, or specially rigged drift bobbers—such as Spin-N-Glos, Tee-Spoons, Okie Drifters, Hot Shots, and Tadpollys—right above bottom, through deep, swirling blue pools for giant, silvery rainbows. For these conditions, eight- to nine-foot, medium- to fast-action steelhead rods are hard to beat, matched to 10- to 15-pound mono on high-quality reels like Ambassadeur, Daiwa, and Shimano.

Alaska's Top Trophy Rainbow Trout Waters

- **Naknek River and Lake** (Southwest)
- **Kenai River** (Southcentral)
- **Lake Iliamna–Kvichak River system** (Southwest)
- **Nushagak River system** (Southwest)

Alaska's Major Rainbow Trout Locations

Anglers in Alaska catch well over one-half million rainbow trout a year. Most of this angling effort takes place in the populous Southcentral region and concentrates on the Kenai and Susitna River systems and lakes in and around Anchorage. A considerable amount of rainbow fishing also occurs in the immense, clear river and lake systems of Bristol Bay, which offer the state's finest trout fishing experiences. Some promising but underutilized rainbow fishing exists in scattered lakes and streams throughout Southeast, the Kenai Peninsula, Susitna and Copper River valleys, and Kodiak Island.

Southeast

Most of Southeast's waters have steelhead, which in their younger forms are commonly mistaken for resident rainbows, but there are dozens of lakes containing stocked and native, non-anadromous rainbow populations.

- **Yakutat:** Situk Lake
- **Juneau/Skagway:** Dewey, Hoktaheen,Surge, Peterson Lakes
- **Sitka/Petersburg/Wrangell:** Red, Thoms, Anan, Boulder, Reflection, Avoss, Rezanof, Plotnikof, Davidof, Salmon, Politofsky, Sukoi, Grebe, Swan, Goat, Eagle, Khvostof, Gar, Betty, Jetty, Marten, Petersburg, Blue, Sitkoh Lakes
- **Ketchikan/Prince of Wales Island:** Naha River/Lake system; Karta and Thorne Rivers; Harriet Hunt, Connell, Ketchikan, Nakat, Filmore, McDonald, Rainbow, Hugh Smith, Sarkar, Sweetwater, Kegan Lakes

Alaska's Top 10 Trophy Rainbows

23 pounds, 0 ounces	Naknek Lake (Southwest)	1991
22 pounds, 7 ounces	Kenai River (Southcentral)	1982
20 pounds, 1 ounce	Kenai River (Southcentral)	1985
20 pounds, 0 ounces	Kenai River (Southcentral)	1992
19 pounds, 12 ounces	Kvichak River (Southwest)	1981
19 pounds, 8 ounces	Naknek Lake (Southwest)	1981
19 pounds, 6 ounces	Naknek Lake (Southwest)	1979
18 pounds, 8 ounces	Naknek River (Southwest)	1969
18 pounds, 8 ounces	Kvichak River (Southwest)	1980
18 pounds, 4 ounces	Kenai River (Southcentral)	1987

Southcentral

- **Kenai:** Kenai River; Russian River; upper Deep Creek; Anchor River; upper Moose River and associated lakes; Swanson, Longmere, Dolly Varden, Vagt, Grant, Upper/Lower Russian, Upper/Lower Ohmer, Jean, Kelly, Peterson, Egumen, Watson, Mosquito, Forest, Rainbow, Paddle, Longmere, Douglas, Cabin, Chugach Estates, Wik, Daniels, Barbara, Cecille, Stormy, Johnson, Quintin, Encelewski Lakes
- **Anchorage:** Campbell Creek, Otter Lake
- **Mat-Su Valley:** Matanuska, Echo, Kepler/Bradley, Irene, Long, Ravine, Knik, Reed, Kalmbach, Seymour, Dawn, Marion, Nancy, Lynne, Honeybee, Crystal, Florence Lakes
- **Susitna:** Deshka, Talachulitna, upper Talkeetna, East Fork Chulitna, upper Susitna (Indian River, Portage, Prairie Creeks) River systems; upper Kashwitna, Montana, Little Willow, Peters (Kahiltna River), Lake, Sheep, Byers Creeks
- **Cook Inlet:** Chuitna, Theodore, Beluga Rivers
- **Wrangell:** Upper Gulkana, Tebay River systems; Crater, Tex Smith, Tolsona, Van, Silver, Sculpin Lakes
- **Chugach:** Blueberry, Worthington Lakes
- **Kodiak:** Reports of rainbow trout populations in lakes and rivers quite often turn out to be immature steelhead trout. Some natural, though small, populations of true rainbow trout occur in the following drainages: Saltery, Buskin, Uganik, Olga Lakes, and Ayakulik River. Stocked rainbow trout are found in a few lakes along the Kodiak road system, like Woody and Long Lakes.

Southwest

The Southwest is Alaska's ultimate region for abundant, wild rainbow trout. Hundreds of rivers, streams, and lakes offer some of the world's best fly-in fishing, with many trophy opportunities awaiting rainbow anglers.

- **Bristol Bay:** Lake Iliamna–Kvichak River system (Kvichak, Newhalen, Copper, Gibraltar, Tazimina Rivers; Talarik, Dream, Belinda Creeks); Nushagak-Mulchatna River system (Chilikadrotna, Mulchatna, Little Mulchatna, Koktuli, Stuyahok, Nuyakuk, upper Nushagak Rivers); Wood River lakes and associated tributaries (Wood, Agulowak, Agulukpak, and Peace Rivers; Lynx, Grant, Little Togiak Lakes, etc.); Tikchik and Nuyakuk Lakes; lower Tikchik River; lower Togiak River system
- **Alaska Peninsula:** Naknek Lake/River system (Brooks River; Grosvenor, Coville Lakes; American, Idavain Creeks, etc.); Alagnak River system (Nonvianuk-Kukaklek, Kulik, Battle Lakes; Funnel, Moraine Creeks, etc.); Egegik River system (clear-water tributaries of King Salmon River)
- **Kuskokwim River:** Goodnews, Kanektok, Arolik, Kwethluk, Kasigluk, Kisaralik, Aniak Rivers

Interior

Interior does not have naturally occurring populations of rainbows, but it has numerous stocked lakes with good fishing possibilities: Quartz, Birch, Harding, Little Harding, Johnson, Robertson, Donna, Little Donna, Koole, Rainbow, Dune, Jan, Lisa, Lost, Craig, Coal Mine Road, Fort Greely Lakes; Piledriver Slough.

Chapter 9
Steelhead: Prince of Sport Fish

by Gary Souza

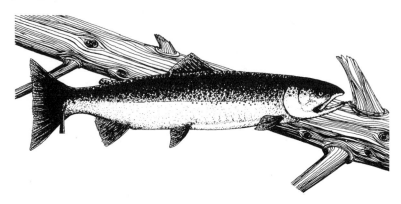

The early morning fog hangs like a heavy curtain at water's edge and the mercury hasn't yet crested the magic 40-degree mark, but it's time to don waders and leave the warmth of the 48-footer anchored in the inlet and head into shore on the ebb tide.

Once ashore, a 1.5-mile hike takes us through alder, spruce, hemlock, cedar, and a despised thorny shrub that grows everywhere along these coasts and lives up to its name—Devil's club. We arrive near several promising-looking runs below a 12-foot falls. The tannic water here is the color of weak tea, but looks fishy nonetheless. We waste no time breaking the rods out and getting our lines in the water.

"Fish on!" yells Larry. I turn and see a dark fish of about 12 pounds tear downstream, jumping all the while. After 30 seconds the line suddenly slacks. Fish off, Larry. Our little group fishes out the remainder of the day and manages to hook 16 steelhead and several Dollies, cutthroats, and rainbows. Not bad numbers for a day's fishing, although the majority are dark fall fish.

The weather on the second day is similar to the first: drizzly and cold. The fishing is about the same. Thirteen hooked, but most of them dark fish. The troller rocks and rolls all that night, as the southeast wind gusts to 60 miles per hour. Forced to "lay on the hook" instead of attempting the trip back across Clarence Strait, the skipper fights a grin as he informs his guests, "Guess we'll just have to stay here and make the best of the situation."

A late start the next morning puts us on the river at 11 A.M. It's risen a foot and a half, yet still appears very fishable. I begin at one of my favorite holes about a mile up from salt water and quickly hook a hot, bright hen. They're unmistakable when hooked, as half their fight is in the air. Bright males are great, too, but they usually jump less and fight more in bull-dog fashion, shouldering down in a prolonged tug of war. I admire her gunmetal blue back and silvery flanks, noticing several sea lice above her anal fin. "New fish!" I slide her back to her freedom.

After hooking three more bright steelhead, I move upstream to join my companions. We are the only ones on the river that day, and we're thankful for it. Another bright hen leaps for the sky four times and runs off 50 feet of line in a single burst. When the fish is brought in, she turns and streaks like a lightning bolt 75 yards downstream into a logjam, where the line parts with a twang and the steelhead goes free.

Rain and the Southeast wind have given us a special bonus day of fishing. We paddle back to the *Julie Ann*, our floating hotel, with 19 steelhead hooked.

Introduction

The steelhead trout (*Oncorhynchus mykiss*), the sea-roving form of the rainbow, is perhaps the most pursued and prized of the north Pacific's many fine game fish. An elite band of anglers from the all over the world diligently pursues them with a passion that borders on the fanatical, braving all manner of stream conditions, weather, and logistics (not to mention expense) to enjoy some high-quality fishing.

And while some may find the mystique of "steelheading" hard to grasp, its appeal is infectious and easily understood after only a single bout with the supercharged saltwater rainbow. They fight spectacularly, with the same high energy and astounding leaps of their riverbound brothers—only more so, because of their size and the vigor imparted by their life in the sea. As iron is to steel, the rainbow trout's noble qualities of spirit, beauty, and grace are refined and tempered in the steelhead, prince of sport fish.

Steelheading in Alaska has been described in many ways. Of all that has been written and said, however, perhaps the most significant and attractive feature is the opportunity to angle for wild fish in wild environs, a luxury in these days of put-and-take fisheries. Alaska, too, is changing. Unfortunately some places aren't as wild as they once were and some runs have been depleted. Yet, overall, the state still offers some of the world's best chances left to experience a little of "how it used to be" everywhere for this magnificent species.

"Explosive fish are the steelhead and salmon that stalk our memories and dreams," wrote Ernest Schwiebert. We pursue steelhead in Alaska not because of their size or numbers, but because of the experience afforded. Through these experiences, one welcomes the stalkers of our memories and dreams.

Description

The steelhead is discernible from salmon species by the eight to 12 rays in the anal fin (most salmon have 12 to 17). Usually more streamlined and slender than resident rainbow trout, the steelhead in its ocean phase exhibits a bright silvery sheen that is essential to survival. The top sides are a shiny, gunmetal blue, contrasted with silver-white below the lateral line. It has black, regularly spaced spots on the back and sides, as well as on both lobes of the tail.

In preparation for spawning, the steelhead's colors become more similar to resident rainbow trout. The gunmetal blue dorsum changes to an olive black. A distinct reddish color develops on the flanks above and below the lateral line, and the shiny white undersides become a dusky gray. Upon completion of spawning, the steelhead's colors gradually revert to their ocean phase.

Steelhead in Alaska aren't noted for their size relative to races elsewhere, such as the outsized fish of the Skeena River drainage in northern British Columbia. Steelhead in the Southeast region average eight to nine pounds. The fish of other regions are slightly smaller, usually averaging seven to eight pounds (the steelhead from Kodiak's famous Karluk River fall into this size class). Stories of 20-pound-plus fish run rampant, but most of these accounts are just that—good fish stories. Of all the hooked steelhead logged in my fishing diary, the largest remains a 38-inch buck that probably weighed slightly less than 20 pounds. I have personally witnessed two fish weighing more than 20 pounds landed and released. Will Jones, owner of Prince of Wales Lodge for many years, has seen only five hooked steelhead that reached or exceeded 20 pounds. Quite a few outsized fish have been taken from the Situk River of Yakutat during certain years.

Range, Abundance, and Status

The native range of the steelhead closely follows that of the resident river rainbow along the north Pacific rim: from the mountains of northwest Mexico to the rocky coast of the Kamchatka Peninsula. In Alaska, they're distributed from Dixon Entrance to the vicinity of Cold Bay on the Alaska Peninsula. They are found most continuously from the southern Southeast region to the North Gulf Coast, with sporadic distribution west into Cook Inlet, Kodiak, and both sides of the Alaska Peninsula. Though numerous isolated occurrences suggest otherwise, no documented spawning populations exist north of Chignik on the Alaska Peninsula, or in Bristol Bay or upper Cook Inlet. The state's most isolated northern run occurs in the upper Copper River north of Cordova.

There are 331 streams in Southeast now known to receive steelhead. The majority of these, totaling 276, occur from south of Frederick Sound to Dixon Entrance. Comprehensive data on the great majority of Alaska steelhead systems is, unfortunately, not available at present.

Runs of steelhead in Southeast are relatively small compared to steelhead streams in many other places. The largest runs total only 500 or more fish annually. Far more streams receive 200 to 300 fish annually, and the greatest number of streams are estimated to receive runs of 100 fish or slightly more. These numbers are obviously quite low relative to the size of salmon runs in Alaska, and to many steelhead runs elsewhere. The largest estimated run in southern Southeast returns to the Karta River on Prince of Wales Island and exceeds 1,000 fish annually. The Anchor River on the Kenai Peninsula and the Karluk River on Kodiak Island historically receive larger numbers than average. The fabulous Situk River near Yakutat in its heyday had runs of more than 5,000, although in recent years that number has dwindled.

With regard to Southeast streams, one can only guess why run numbers are less than those of streams elsewhere. The Alaska Department of Fish and Game's Southeast sportfish biologists believe that it may be due in part to low insect diversity and lower nutrient recruitment. (The streams of Southeast tend to exhibit a shortage of minerals and other factors critical to a productive stream's ecology.) Most, if not all, Alaskan steelhead streams are strongly influenced by the presence of salmon, and without the addition of spent fish to the nutrient cycle, would most likely be almost sterile.

Life History and Habits

Steelhead are large anadromous rainbow trout that rear in freshwater streams. Most Alaskan fish spend three years in freshwater before they journey to the ocean as six- to seven-inch smolts. During this time, they attain their large size relative to most resident rainbow trout.

They return to freshwater as sexually mature adults after two or three years. Most runs of spring steelhead are comprised of a significant portion of repeat spawners. (Research has shown that repeat spawners can account for as high as 45 percent of a given run, although the average percentage is usually lower.) These repeat spawners usually account for the fish that exceed 30 inches.

Steelhead return to streams in the Southwest region, the Kenai Peninsula, and Kodiak Island primarily in the fall. Southeast receives runs in three seasons. There are only a few known runs of summer steelhead (notably on Baranof Island). Fall-run fish begin returning to Southeast in September and October and continue through December and early January, depending upon the system's timing and weather conditions. Fall-run fish are limited in their habitat requirements compared to spring-run fish. The majority of fall runs return to river systems with lakes. The exceptions are large streams with enough deep pools to allow overwintering survival (in lieu of lakes). Most fall-run fish exhibit habits similar to spring-run steelhead. They hold in the same water, and can be found in the same type of spawning habitat. All races spawn in the spring regardless of when they enter freshwater.

There are some key exceptions to the many common traits among fall- and spring-run fish: Fall fish return sexually immature. At times, fall fish also tend to be more aggressive toward the anglers' offerings than spring fish. This is due in part to warmer water temperatures and true feeding tendencies. I've personally landed many early fall fish that were gorged with pink salmon spawn—with small, pale pink eggs dropping from their jaws as I released them. Some of these fish will hold in the upper reaches of holes and runs in order to opportunistically pick off drifting eggs. Fish under these conditions are easy prey to egg imitations drifted through their lie.

Spring-run steelhead are by far the most widespread race in Southeast. Many streams with low flows are host to spawning steelhead during the spring months. These fish begin returning in March, with April and May being the peak arrival periods. Research has determined that female spring fish also spend less time in freshwater than males. On occasion I've landed chrome-bright hen fish with sea lice, which had already spawned just a short distance from tidewater. These short appearances in freshwater are especially common in smaller streams during low water periods, and can present a frustrating challenge to the angler.

My fishing log (and similar records of other Southeast steelhead fanatics) reveals steelhead hooked in 10 calendar months, a relatively long season for Alaska. However, the peak and best fishing times can be quite short.

Fishing Alaska's Steelhead

Drift Fishing

Under most water conditions and in all seasons, drift fishing is the most effective way of hooking steelhead. When all other methods fail, steelhead can usually be hooked in deep water with drift fishing. In Alaska, as elsewhere in the Pacific Northwest, most (but not all) drift fishing is done with an eight- to nine-foot graphite, medium-action rod, in tandem with a level wind bait casting reel. The rod should have a sensitive tip to detect when fish "mouth" bait, and a stout butt section for solid hook-setting and fighting capabilities. Most accomplished drift anglers agree that the bait caster affords advantages for drift fishing that the spinning reel does not. Mounted on top, the bait caster allows "more feel," as the angler has greater contact with the stream bottom through the line and because his thumb is on the spool. Hook setting is done quickly, with the thumb firmly on the spool while briskly lifting the rod. Although most spinning reels lack a drag overriding feature and often slip during the hook set, this technique prevents slippage while setting the hook. Also, the level wind reel, because of its design, is inherently stronger and has a superior drag. Lamiglass and G. Loomis produce good graphite drift rods, and several manufacturers (including Daiwa, Shimano, and Ambassadeur) make high-quality reels.

The single most important element to drift fishing is the dynamics of the terminal end of the line during the drift. (This ought to be obvious, but surprisingly isn't.) Regardless of what type, color, or size of attractor the angler is using, its correct action during the drift is paramount to the angler's success. (Here, "attractor" is used in a much broader sense than elsewhere in this book.) Simply stated, the attractor must drift with a natural appearance. It must not hang on the bottom, and should not even "skip" with the weight as some have proposed. Rather, it should drift with as near a neutral buoyancy as possible. The closer you can come to attaining a natural drift, the better your chances are of getting steelhead to pick up the bait. When attempting to choose the amount of weight to attach above the attractor, you should remember that too little weight is always better than too much as a general rule. Numerous lures are used effectively for drift fishing, the best for Alaska being Li'l Corkies, Spin-N-Glos, Glo Glos, and other egg-simulating attractors.

Jig Fishing

Fishing jigs has become increasingly popular in recent years, because of its ease and efficiency over a wide range of conditions. It's a particularly effective method in slow currents, for the "tanks" and "frog water" encountered on many streams.

An eight- to nine-foot, medium-weight spinning rod and matching reel (with eight- to 15-pound test mono) is the preferred setup for jig fishing, as the spinning reel is ideally suited to pay out line freely during the downstream portion of the drift. Terminal tackle consists of small feathered jigs ranging in weight from $1/16$ to one-quarter ounce, with the one-eighth-ounce jig most popular in Southeast waters. The hottest colors are pink, pink/white, pink/purple, black/pink, black/white, orange, and red/yellow.

Fish the jigs below a large, two-inch-diameter plastic bobber, varying leader length with water depth to ensure a drift right above bottom. Cast the bobber and jig setup upstream and drift it through potential holding water, keeping an eye on the bobber for the slightest bump or sway to indicate a take by a fish.

An angler who has become adept at drift fishing before graduating to fly-fishing usually becomes a more effective fly fisher, with greater insight into the steelhead's habits of holding in various lies, and how they "take" or "mouth" the attractor.

Spin Fishing

Spinners can be very effective for fishing steelhead. However, you must remember that steelhead in very cold water generally don't move well to take spinners, but more readily mouth an attractor drifted directly to them. Many anglers work around this by using ultralight gear and smaller spinners for cold-water conditions, working the blade ever so slightly as the lure tumbles through steelhead lies and into close striking range of lethargic fish. With the smaller, more sensitive gear, the often subtle take is more easily felt. These setups can also be very effective in extreme shallow or bright conditions, when steelhead spook. Some of the more popular spinners used for steelhead are the Mepps Aglia, Vibrax, and Rooster Tail, in sizes 1 to 5 and colors of silver, gold, fluorescent red, black, chartreuse/yellow, pink, and green. Many of the techniques used in fishing spinners for Alaska steelhead are similar to those used for rainbow. (See the chapter on rainbow trout that begins on page 97.)

Fly-fishing Alaska's Steelhead

The experience of stalking and hooking a steelhead in its wild environs using fly gear is arguably the most sporting and satisfying in all of angling, and certainly among the most exciting to be had in Alaska. Under most conditions, the fly fisher knowingly sacrifices many potential hook-ups when choosing fly equipment over drift gear. The exceptions are during low-water conditions or in extremely shallow parts of a stream, like riffles, tailouts, and some pocket water.

Green Butt Skunk

Although most hardcore steelheaders have amassed a large arsenal of tackle, a modest amount of main tackle can suffice. A nine- to nine-and-a-half-foot, eight-weight rod is the main stick used. Some choose seven-weights followed by the less used nine-weight for extreme conditions. In choosing main tackle, it's more practical to invest money in good rods, rather than reels with expensive disc drag systems. Most streams are small compared to the large streams of the Pacific Northwest. Thus, quality rods are always a necessity for casting, line mending, and fighting. For much of Alaska, expensive disc drag reels are often overkill, as fish don't make the long runs they would in big water down south. In terms of brands of rods, Sage, Loomis, Winston, Scott, and Lamiglas all make very popular, high-quality rods known for their casting and mending performance. Most importantly, they're aesthetically pleasing and easy to use. The choice of reels should be made based upon one's own fishing needs and budget, as you can choose from a myriad of high-quality models.

In selecting fly lines for Alaska, several lines should be carried astream. The same general rules apply as when fishing the state's rainbow water—a full-floating line, a sink-tip or two, and a full-sink, with a high-density sink or shooting taper for extreme conditions. Some anglers carry short sections of these super high-density lines instead, to attach when conditions warrant. (For more information on fly lines for steelhead, see the chapter on rainbow trout that begins on page 97.)

Of all folklore circulated among the steelheading fraternity, the greatest lore surrounds fly patterns. Far too much is said and has been written about the subtle nuances of fly patterns for steelhead. Most likely this stems from the real need for hundreds of trout patterns to suit the many great variables involved in fishing the variety of species and conditions encountered. Although one may respect the rich tradition behind the many local patterns and beliefs, it is possible for anglers to isolate some general principles.

Lani Waller simplified the discussion in his 3M videos when he classed flies as bright, drab, and dark patterns. The bright patterns include flies of loud color, such as orange, pink, and chartreuse. These are most effective on bright fish under normal and high-water conditions. Flies such as the burlap and muddler are examples of drab patterns, which are especially effective during low-water periods and for fish that have been worked over by other anglers. Dark patterns describe such well-known standbys as the Skunk, Silver Hilton, and Black Bunny Leech. These patterns work in a broad range of conditions and situations; on some systems in the Skeena drainage in British Columbia, they're the main patterns used. They tend to be more effective on long river systems where fish have already journeyed quite a distance from salt water.

When a fly fisher exclaims, "This is the fly for this system," one can only presume that he or she understands the special conditions on that stream or, more often, that the angler is trying to apply trout fly pattern methodology to steelheading. I'll never forget the horrified looks of guides on New Brunswick's Miramichi as they watched me release Atlantic salmon that were hooked on traditional steelhead and Alaska coho patterns. The fish struck the given pattern because it was right for the situation with regard to size, general color, silhouette, and drifting dynamics—not because it contained or lacked a small tuft of some obscure feather or material. Unfortunately, with far too many fly patterns, it seems that a certain amount of ego can be wrapped in with the feathers, fur, and tinsel, making it impossible to assess their true worth.

Anglers determined to represent something found naturally in streams with their fly might try using Glo Bugs. As the accomplished fly fisherman André Puyans has often commented, "Why be a snob about it? After all, it is matching the hatch." It's ironic that the pattern that does "match the hatch" is scorned by some as not being a real fly pattern. However you feel about them, Glo Bugs are highly effective and can outproduce all other flies in some situations. Carry a wide variety of colors and sizes in your vest.

Techniques

Two methods are of particular interest when fly-fishing steelhead. The first is the traditional across- and down-current technique called the "wet fly swing." This involves a cast across or quartered upstream, followed by a series of line mends (repositioning the trailing line with a flip of the rod, which alters the amount of drag on the fly) to slow down, speed up, or sink the fly. The second, less popular method used in creeks and smaller systems is the use of strike indicators. This technique is well known by accomplished trout nymph anglers. The indicator, made of a Li'l Corkie, a piece of styrofoam, or a tuft of synthetic fabric, is placed at a point between the floating fly line and the fly. After casting upstream, the angler makes a series of mends in order to sink the fly en route to attaining a true drag-free dead drift. The fly may be weighted, or the angler may add a microshot a short distance above the fly. Although some in the steelheading community reject this method, it has been accepted for years among trout anglers.

Reading the Water

Steelhead are usually found in holding water that has a depth of four feet or more. They opt for moderate current instead of slack water, where some Pacific salmon hold, or fast white water. They prefer currents moving at a rate of a few miles per hour, and are especially fond of secondary currents or seams on the edge of the main current. Anglers should look for these flow characteristics and any obstructions that may cause them, such as boulders and logs. If a fish is hooked in a given spot, chances are good fish may be there again under similar conditions, provided there are no major changes in the streambed composition.

Most steelhead streams in Alaska are fairly short, small, and brushy, compared with the huge and wide mainland streams of the Pacific Northwest states and British Columbia. The structure of the streambeds remains more constant in these smaller Alaskan streams, and they hardly ever "go out" in the sense of being too muddy to fish, although occasionally they may be too high and of less than ideal clarity. The large mainland streams usually experience a great disparity in flow range due to the large areas they drain.

Ethics for Alaskan Steelheaders

Preserve Wild Steelhead

Any discussion of ethics has to begin with the importance of preserving wild steelhead stocks. Only a handful of Alaska's streams have been enhanced by hatchery smolts. In the long run, the mixing of gene pools that results from these mixed stock fisheries is detrimental to the sustained health of the wild stock. It's also expensive and fosters the angling public's fall hope that hatchery enhancement will fix serious problems caused by overfishing, habitat destruction, and poor management. Alaska's greatest resource is the health and integrity of her wild fisheries. Learn why it is truly important to keep the wild fish runs as they are, and join the cause.

Practice Catch-and-Release Fishing

When a wild stock is lost or mixed, it's lost permanently, never to be restored again. If this is so obvious, why aren't more folks practicing catch-and-release fishing in Alaska? Perhaps it is because of a lack of knowledge about the fragility of the resource. If most of Southeast's runs are comprised of approximately 100 fish, can there be any harvesting without damage? The answer is probably no for quite a few of these small systems. Numerous runs have already shown signs of depletion. Learn the correct techniques for playing and releasing a fish with minimal impact. These include using barbless hooks and gearing up with the proper line and rod weight so as not to overstress the fish. (See the appendix on page 413 for more information on catch-and-release techniques.)

Don't Use Bait

The use of bait is a poor practice for this day and age. Bright steelhead—indeed all trout and salmon—are suckers for good-looking roe. Even very inexperienced anglers soon learn this. Unfortunately, few anglers respond with a hook set in a timely enough manner when the fish mouths the bait, resulting in a deeply hooked fish, leading inevitably to serious harm or death. Most streams in Alaska restrict the use of bait while fishing for steelhead.

Leave Spawning Fish Alone

Steelhead that are observed holding for any length of time in tailouts, small riffles, or other shallow stream locations in April and May are probably nearing spawning. Many of these fish can be spotted digging out redds, swimming in mating rituals, guarding nests, and acting in ways that normal fish do not. To try for these fish, especially when there are other steelhead in normal holding water, is unsporting. Why harass fish that are doing the very thing that sportfishers should want them to be doing—producing more wild steelhead?

Respect the Privacy of Others

With the exception of several streams accessible by roads and near towns, most Alaskan steelhead streams are still uncrowded. When you encounter other anglers working a run or hole, you should proceed to another unfished area. Only join another angler on a given hole after receiving permission. (This differs from the practice in many northern British Columbia rivers where fly fishers follow anglers through fish-holding runs.)

Get Involved

Join your local chapter of Trout Unlimited and get involved with issues of conservation, no matter how small or insignificant they may seem. The skills and knowledge you gain will be helpful in understanding some of the broader more complex issues that are affecting the health of the entire north Pacific fishery. Educate yourself, inform others, and set an example with your personal responsibility, on and off the river.

Alaska's Major Steelhead Locations

Southeast

Most of Alaska's steelhead streams are located in Southeast. There are several hundred documented systems, with small runs (200 fish or less) the general rule. Spring steelhead dominate, with peaks in May, but some significant late winter and late fall fishing can be had also.

- **Ketchikan:** Fish, Ketchikan, Ward Creeks; Naha River; McDonald Lake system
- **Prince of Wales:** Harris, Karta, Klawock, Kegan, Thorne Rivers; Staney, Salmon Bay Creeks
- **Wrangell:** Anan, Aaron, Eagle, Thoms Creeks
- **Petersburg:** Petersburg, Hamilton, Kadake, Ohmer, Falls, Kah Sheets, Duncan Saltchuck Creeks; Castle River
- **Sitka:** Sitkoh, Hasselborg, Eva Creeks; Plotnikof, Port Banks Rivers
- **Juneau:** Peterson Creek, Taku River
- **Yakutat and Gulf Coast:** Situk, Italio, Tsiu Rivers

Alaska's Top 10 Trophy Steelhead

42 pounds, 3 ounces (state and world record)	Bell Island, Behm Canal (Southeast)	1970
26 pounds, 0 ounces	Douglas Island (Southeast)	1980
26 pounds, 0 ounces	Situk River, Yakutat (Southeast)	1988
24 pounds, 8 ounces	Waterfall Resort, Prince of Wales (Southeast)	1990
23 pounds, 9 ounces	Situk River, Yakutat (Southeast)	1987
23 pounds, 8 ounces	Situk River, Yakutat (Southeast)	1982
23 pounds, 0 ounces	Situk River, Yakutat (Southeast)	1985
22 pounds, 0 ounces	Situk River, Yakutat (Southeast)	1987
21 pounds, 14 ounces	Situk River, Yakutat (Southeast)	1974
21 pounds, 8 ounces	Situk River, Yakutat (Southeast)	1986

Southcentral

The Southcentral region has some of the state's most heavily fished steelhead streams on the Kenai Peninsula, with considerable high-quality opportunities on Kodiak Island (17 known steelhead systems). These are mostly all fall and winter run fish, with peaks in late September through October.

- **Kenai:** Anchor, Ninilchik, Kasilof Rivers; Deep, Stariski Creeks
- **Chugach:** Copper River tributaries: Tebay (including Hanagita River), Tazlina, upper Middle Fork Gulkana Rivers (Dickey, Twelvemile, Hungry Hollow Creeks)
- **Kodiak:** Karluk, Ayakulik, Afognak, Uganik Rivers; Pauls, Akalura, Malina, Saltery Creeks

Southwest

Southwest Alaska has a handful of documented spawning streams that are scattered along the Alaska Peninsula to Cold Bay, with rumors of many more. All indications are that these are fall-run fish, September through October being their peak run. This is definitely the unexplored frontier of steelheading in North America.

- **Port Moller:** Bear, Sandy Rivers
- **Nelson Lagoon:** Sapsuk, Nelson Rivers
- **Cold Bay:** Russell, Trout Creeks

Chapter 10
Cutthroat: The Noble Trout
by Thomas Cappiello

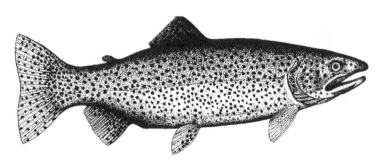

It was the end of my junior year in college, and my '62 VW van was packed for a summer of fly-fishing the West, when I received a fateful call from the U.S. Forest Service. They were looking for help on a remote project in Prince William Sound, Alaska, and I listened intently to details of the job offer, over piles of maps, insect hatch charts, and astounding estimates of Montana's 2,000 fish per mile. I found the lure of blue ribbon western trout streams hard to resist, but Alaska—land of salmon, the ultimate wilderness—was the chance of a lifetime.

Six weeks later I found myself in Cordova, loading my gear into a 1955 DeHavilland Beaver. An awesome, hour-long flight through a forested maze of bays and islands, and a 45-minute hike straight up a mountain, brought me to base camp (and a realization of what "remote" in Alaska means). My supervisor and campmates, a seasoned bunch, lost no time briefing me, a total greenhorn, on the finer points of Alaska fishing. They spoke of run timing, spinning gear, barn-door halibut, salmon by the thousands, and Pixee lures. But I had my designs at the moment on some

slightly different rewards—casting a fly into some of those delectable ponds and streams I'd passed earlier on the trail.

A light breeze from the ocean spilled over a hill and rippled the surface of the most perfect little lake you could imagine. Lily pads lined the edges, and near the small outlet, a rise and some tiny grayish bugs swarming above water hinted of action to come. Nervously, I tied a no. 16 Mosquito on and promptly hung my first two casts in the bushes nearby. A good-sized fish swirled not six feet in front of me—I was such a wreck I could barely tie a knot! I finally rolled a fly out, letting it drift in the weak current and twitching it ever so slightly. It vanished in a flash as a bright little package of muscle took off for the sky. Not more than a foot long, this feisty little warrior was everywhere at once in his valiant struggle for freedom, and threw me off guard when I saw blood streaming from under his gills. Horrified, I drew him in and realized I'd been had, by a fish that was no stranger to me. This beautiful trout, heavily spotted, with a luster like a newly minted gold coin, had two brilliant scarlet slash marks on his throat—the definitive brand of a cutthroat trout, a fish I knew well from my youth on the coastal streams and rivers of northern California.

As if looks weren't enough, these fish were abundant and eager, and I was soon hooking them on practically every cast. I stayed until sunset, then stumbled back to camp, where the guys were finishing a game of cards in the kitchen tent. It was midnight, and I'd been fishing for six hours.

As I lay collapsed on my bunk, drifting off to sleep to the haunting lullabies of loons in the distance, thoughts of new and wonderful fishing experiences filled my head. I pondered on how many lovely cutthroats had never seen a fly in the countless ponds and streams of this coastal paradise. The Madison River would have to wait.

Introduction

The cutthroat trout (*Oncorhynchus clarkii*) was the first true trout to be documented in the United States of America. Described in accounts of exploration dating as far back as the 1500s, specimens sent to England in 1833 from a river in Washington were officially recorded and the species named in honor of Captain William Clark of the famed Lewis and Clark expedition.

Cutthroats are the native trout of the Rocky Mountains—the abundant and at times gullible fish found in small foothill creeks, rivers, and mountain lakes from New Mexico to Alberta. They occur in a coastal form as well; as "harvest trout" or "bluebacks," they're well known and sought after in the tidal waters of the Pacific Northwest states and British Columbia. In Alaska, these fish are the jewels of the coastal wilderness: small, brightly colored trout that liven the fishing and enhance the ecology of countless small streams, bogs, and lakes from Prince William Sound to

Ketchikan. And though they take a back seat to the state's other sport species when it comes to prestige and glamour, cutthroats have a definite mystique and noble character, that, like the small brook trout of the East, endears them to a dedicated following of anglers.

Description

Two red slash marks under the lower jaw make the cutthroat trout of the Pacific Northwest easily identifiable and give the fish their name. An upper jaw line that extends well beyond the eye, heavy spotting on the body and fins, and the presence of small teeth behind the tongue are other recognizable features to look for, although they may not always be present, making the fish sometimes difficult to distinguish from the rainbow trout. (Rainbows and cutthroats sometimes hybridize, which can further complicate identification.) Markings are often indistinct or nonexistent on sea-run fish. Color can vary from a dark olive-green back, gold or bronze sides, and pale-white belly to a deep metallic blue back and bright silver sides.

Most of the cutthroats caught in Alaska are four and five years old and average eight to 10 inches long. The larger, trophy size (three pounds plus) resident fish are at least nine and up to 15 years old. Moving between salt and freshwater places additional stress on sea-run fish, so they rarely live longer than eight years and grow more than 20 inches.

Range, Abundance, and Status

Coastal cutthroat trout range from the Eel River in northern California to Prince William Sound in Alaska, and thrive in many watersheds within the coastal temperate rain forests. Both resident and sea-run (anadromous) forms occur in Alaska. Sea-run cutthroat normally do not travel more than 20 to 50 miles from the mouth of their home stream. Populations of resident forms rarely exceed 4,000 fish, and most anadromous populations are several hundred to a thousand (2,000 is large). Resident fish are typically small and stunted, although in some Southeast lakes they grow as large as eight pounds. Despite being few in number within a single drainage, more than 50,000 cutthroats are caught yearly by anglers from hundreds of lakes and streams in Alaska. Populations are fragile and highly susceptible to overfishing and habitat destruction. Even the enhancement of other desirable species such as coho salmon can have a negative impact on cutthroat abundance. In the past 10 years, sport harvests in Alaska have declined while effort has increased dramatically. This has prompted the Department of Fish and Game and other agencies to take a much more aggressive management approach to expand knowledge of cutthroat ecology and enact more conservative regulations in many areas.

Life History and Habits

Two forms of coastal cutthroat thrive in Alaska: anadromous and resident. Anadromous, or sea-run, cutthroats have a life history similar to that of sea-run Dolly Varden. They usually go to sea in the spring (late April to early June) at two or three years of age, but as early as age one or as late as age six. Little is known of their lives in the ocean, but tagging studies have shown most fish venture no more than 20 miles from their home stream, many staying within estuaries or the mouths of rivers. They return to freshwater in late summer through fall, and by October, most of Alaska's "cuts" are in their overwintering streams and lakes. After overwintering, mature fish move into spawning tributaries, immature fish head out to sea, and juveniles remain in freshwater. This usually occurs during April or May. Cutthroats can display the same complexity of movement as charr, spawning in different streams than they overwinter in, even traveling through salt water from overwintering lakes to reach spawning areas. After spawning, adults begin seaward migrations, sometimes lingering in freshwater or estuaries to feed on smolts. Time at sea is usually short, lasting anywhere from six weeks to three months.

Resident Alaska cutthroats spend their entire lives in the freshwater of lakes, streams, sloughs, and small bog ponds. With the exception of seaward migrations, their life history closely parallels that of anadromous cuts. They mature at four to six years of age and spawn primarily in tributaries of small to moderate size, with gentle gradients. The number of eggs per female depends on size and condition of fish and can be as few as 200 to as many as 4,000, but the average is between 1,100 and 1,700. Eggs are buried in redds, similar to other members of the salmon-trout-charr family. Preferred gravel is pea-sized or slightly larger and fairly clean of sand and fines. Spawning usually takes place in the spring from late March to early June, depending on latitude and local climate. Hatching occurs in six to seven weeks and fry emerge one to two weeks later (usually during June). Fry grow quickly, usually to three to four inches long by the first fall and five to six inches long by the end of their second growing season.

Whether resident and anadromous forms are genetically different is not clear, but the two forms can occur in the same system. Little research has focused on why certain stocks are anadromous and others are not, beyond situations where physical barriers, such as waterfalls, prevent migration.

Diet

Knowing what cutthroats feed on is certainly important to anglers. Small trout will heavily utilize terrestrial and aquatic insects, especially midge and mosquito larvae. As opportunists, however, their diet varies with location and time of year. As they get older, cuts still pursue midges, mosquitoes, caddis flies, mayflies, and stone flies, but prey more heavily on fish, such as sticklebacks, kokanee, juvenile salmon, and sculpins. Leeches also make up a small portion of the cutthroat's diet. In salt water, cuts feed on small shrimp (euphausiids), juvenile herring, capelin, and salmon smolts. Salmon spawn is an extremely important food source to all cutthroat trout, as it allows for the rapid weight gain that is essential for winter survival. Availability of salmon eggs may be one of the primary motivations for sea-run cutthroats to return to freshwater. Resident cutthroats often don't have the luxurious and diverse food sources the sea-runs enjoy, yet the largest cutthroats taken in Alaska (more than five pounds) have been from lakes without anadromous salmon. The key to the size of these landlocked forms is the availability of kokanee or landlocked sockeye for forage in many Southeast lakes.

Fishing Alaska's Cutthroat Trout

Since cutthroat trout are notoriously voracious and will respond to just about any enticement—such as bait, flies, spinners, spoons, and jigs—locating fish is the key challenge for the Alaska cutthroat angler. Throughout most of their range, they are few in number and have dynamic and at times elusive behavior, so understanding their life history and

migratory patterns is essential. Cuts prefer slow to moderate water velocity and often hunker near bottom or around structures. In streams, they linger in pools, under cutbanks, in confluences and tailouts, and behind logs and boulders. In lakes, they usually stay near outlet and inlet streams, shorelines with lily pads, islands, and drop-offs. Southeast lakes can stratify dramatically in the summer—especially tea-colored bog waters that act as solar energy collectors and attain unbearable surface water temperatures—so fish may avoid the shallower feeding locations, seeking deeper, cooler waters.

Spring

Access to cutthroats in early spring (April and May) can be difficult with rotting snow and ice conditions, and some areas are closed to protect spawning populations. But the opportunities for exciting early spring fishing are many and worth going for. Best areas for spring cuts are the mouths of inlet and outlet streams in lakes, river mouths, estuaries, and the main stems and confluences of rivers with spawning populations. After ice-out, anglers can fly in to some of the better Southeast lakes (see locations at end of this chapter on page 125) and enjoy some of Alaska's best fishing—Humpback, Turner, Jims, Wilson, and other lakes have all produced trophy cutthroat during the month of May.

After spawning, cutthroat in or near salmon systems congregate in strategic locations for intercepting out-migrating smolt, such as lake outlets, stream pools, river mouths, and estuaries. Salmon smolt out-migrations occur sporadically throughout the day but peak between 10 P.M. and 2 A.M., so fishing during evening hours can be extremely productive. When fishing lower rivers, I like to fish around a moderate high tide, the best time being about two to three hours before and after flood. I look for smolts scattering and fleeing, seabird activity, or surface disturbances of any kind that might signal concentrations of cutthroat. This can be exciting fishing for short periods of times and the angler must be ready to make quick, accurate casts when a feeding binge is in progress. Because Dolly Varden charr are more numerous in Alaska's coastal systems, you'll probably catch much more of them than cutthroat, as well as other surprises. (I've caught greenling, juvenile Pacific cod, and starry flounder while fishing tidal zones for cutthroats.)

Imitating forage fish with lure and fly is, of course, "most killing" at this time. Small, bright spinners like the matchless Super Vibrax series in sizes 0 to 2, or one-eighth- to one-quarter-ounce Rooster Tail, are hard to beat, as are one-eighth-ounce Pixee, Kastmaster, or Crippled Herring spoons. Streamer fishing with smolt and other bait-fish patterns (Coho fly, Muddler) and bright attractors can be equally effective, using the standard "wet fly swing" through likely holding water.

Summer

Anadromous: Sea-run cutthroat can be extremely difficult to locate once out in the ocean, and few anglers have consistent success catching them after the smolt runs are over and they move seaward. (Cutthroats that spend the entire summer in estuaries are the exception.) Sea-run cuts begin reentering freshwater along with salmon in some systems during early to mid-July. This inward migration can take place rapidly within a week or spread out through the summer, depending on location. Most cutthroat runs occur with either the first pink salmon runs in July or the later coho runs of August and September. The first places to try are estuaries, river mouths, tidal pools, and any holding water in lower rivers and streams, fishing the incoming tides for best results.

If you've done your research and picked a stream with a healthy run of sea-run cuts, you can expect an exciting, mixed bag of fishing in and around tidewater, especially during the height of the salmon invasions. Pink or silver salmon jump and surface everywhere, difficult to avoid in their prespawning testiness. Dollies, too, can be thick. Interspersed among this rowdy bunch should be some incredibly aggressive cutthroat trout. A deep, slow retrieve of a small spinner or streamer in bright, attractor colors is usually all it takes to bring them in.

Resident: Resident cutthroats spend considerable time surface feeding during the warm summer months, and usually can be easily targeted for some excellent dry fly–fishing. Look for them along lake shorelines, in outlets and inlets, pools, and riffles, much the same as you would in streams and mountain lakes further south this time of year. A small boat or float tube will allow you greater access to prime areas. Lily pads can offer some challenging fishing (use heavier tippets of eight- to 10-pound test line to minimize break-offs in these snag-filled waters). They attract damselfly nymphs and adults, amphipods (freshwater shrimp), snails, and other prey. Cutthroats cruise the borders and employ the "ambush predator" strategy of pike on unsuspecting prey. My favorite flies for these conditions are a Hare's Ear Nymph (sizes 10, 12), olive or brown Leech (sizes 8 to 10) and a no. 12 Haystack. (A deer hair wing, no hackle, with muskrat-dubbed body is highly visible to the angler, floats well, and holds up to numerous takes, especially if the dubbed body is reinforced with gold or copper wire.) In the evenings in some lakes, a small (nos. 12 to 14) Black Caddis danced along the shoreline works well to antagonize cutthroats and juvenile coho. I've also had some success with adult damselfly imitations.

Hardware tends to target larger, more aggressive fish this time of year. I like to use 1/12- to 1/8-ounce red and yellow Rooster Tail spinners, 1/8-ounce Pixee, and 1/12- to 3/16-ounce silver or gold Kastmaster spoons. Lead head (bright yellow, pink, or black) jigs work well, too, and are less susceptible to snags. Fish the same holding areas you would target for spring fishing, along with any spots that show signs of feeding activity, below or on the surface, and vary the depth and speed of the retrieve until you connect with a fish. Spinning gear allows fast coverage of water and often quick results.

In systems with sticklebacks, gold lures or flies tend to work very well. In lakes where kokanee are the dominant forage species, silver smolt imitations can be very effective. Solid black leech patterns don't seem to work quite as well as olive or brown. I've also had good success with a small Woolly Bugger–type pattern tied with peacock herl body, marabou, or ostrich tail, and palmered with dark brown or black hackle. During salmon runs, Glo Bugs, other egg patterns, and flesh flies are the ticket to "match the hatch." During heavy pink salmon invasions, when fish tend to be glutted with spawn, I've had good luck fishing Egg-Sucking Leeches and weighted white Marabou Muddlers (both no. 8), perhaps because they imitate other prey species making off with something good.

Fishing streams, bogs, and sloughs: The islands in Prince William Sound and Southeast are full of small, unnamed lakes and muskeg bog ponds, many receiving little, if any, angling pressure. From waters as small as a quarter acre,

with little more than a trench connecting to a lower-order stream, I've yanked dozens of colorful, feisty cuts. The presence of juvenile coho is a good sign to look for when prospecting for cutthroat trout in likely areas, as the two occur together frequently. Taking a minute or two to search for surface activity is another way to spot the fish.

Fall

The fall season is a popular time to fish for cutthroat trout, both resident and sea-run, because fish are in prime condition and extremely voracious. Some of the best fishing for sea-run cutthroats can be had in small lakes with overwintering populations or the inlet and outlet waters of larger lakes. The cooling temperatures and shortening days prompt fish into reckless feeding binges that can make for some electrifying action. My most memorable experiences with cutthroat have taken place in September and October, when coho are busying streams and lake tributaries with spawning activity. In some places I've seen hundreds of fat sea-run cuts concentrated near outlets, in deep pools or river mouths, ravenous for anything that comes their way. Attractor patterns, egg and flesh flies, forage imitation streamers (sculpins, muddlers, leeches), bright spinners, spoons, and even jigs all work well for these hungry fall cuts.

Winter

It's common knowledge that cutthroats can be caught through the ice, but because of fluctuating winter conditions, few anglers are willing to risk the potentially dangerous ice on Southeast lakes during most winters, regardless of how good fishing could be. Unlike streams in Washington and Oregon, no migrations of cutthroats have been documented in Alaska in the winter, although there are persistent rumors of bright sea-runs being caught in estuaries in February and March.

Gearing Up for Cutthroat

Tackle

Use an ultralight spinning rod, five to six feet, medium-action, with 150 yards four- to eight-pound test mono on a high-quality, ultralight spinning reel. Or use a five- to six-weight, seven- to nine-foot fly rod with matching, floating, or sink-tip line and 2X to 4X tippet. Use leader of seven to nine feet. For deep-water trophy fishing, use a light- to medium-weight spinning or steelhead casting rod, seven to eight-and-a-half feet, medium-action, with 150 yards of 10- to 15-pound line on a high-quality spinning or casting reel.

Lures

Many lures work well for cutthroat. The list includes: Vibrax spinners sizes 0, 1, and 2 in silver or gold blades/body and fluorescent orange bell; Rooster Tail spinners sizes 0, 1, and 2 in red and yellow; one-eighth-ounce Pixees with red or pink inserts; Kastmasters in $1/_{12}$-, one-eighth-, and one-quarter-ounce sizes in silver or gold (or with blue or red); and lead head jigs (Foxee Jigs) in $1/_{32}$-, $1/_{16}$-, and one-eighth-ounce sizes and natural colors such as amber, black, and chartreuse.

Also effective are wet flies (sizes 6 to 12) including Glo Bug, Polar Shrimp, Spruce, and Scud (in orange, pink, or brown), Hare's Ear Nymph (sizes 10 and 12) and Fall Favorite; Dry Flies (sizes 10 to 14) including Haystack, Dark Blue Damsel, Mosquito, Black Gnat, Irresistible, and Elk Hair Caddis; Streamers (sizes 6 to 8) including Muddler Minnow, Woolly Bugger, Sculpin, Bunny Bug, Smolt, Olive Leech, Brown Leech, Black Leech, Egg-Sucking Leech, and White Marabou Muddler.

Catching Trophy Cutthroat

If catching a trophy in one of the Southeast Panhandle's premier lakes is your goal, a boat is almost a necessity to fish the better water. The U.S. Forest Service provides small boats for the fortunate souls able to obtain cabin reservations at some of the more popular locations (check beforehand for availability and condition of craft). If you're not so lucky, a canoe or inflatable raft might be the way to go. A portable fish finder and bathymetric lake map, if available, will greatly improve your chances of locating fish.

Trophy resident cutthroat trout can be taken shallow during spring near inlet waters, but disperse and go deep during the summer. The most effective way of catching them is by trolling. Conventional trolling gear—lead weights or planer on 10- to 15-pound test, with a small flasher or "cowbell" attractor and medium-sized spoons (Luhr-Jensen Crippled Herring, Nordic, and Diamond King, or Blue Fox Trixee)—trolled slowly, moderately deep (15 to 30 feet), works best. Also try deep diving plugs like Normark's Rapala and the Luhr-Jensen Power Dive Minnow. Downriggers can also be employed, but remember that one line per person is all that's allowed in Alaska's cutthroat lakes. Keep in mind that the immensely popular and effective method of trolling bait such as herring or shrimp is now illegal in these lakes.

If you're fishing without electronic aids, concentrate your trolling effort along shorelines with steep drop-offs, in deep waters surrounding islands or rocks, bays with inlets and any other areas that might appeal to larger, lazier trout in search of a fish dinner. The lower-light periods of the day have proven most productive for catching the big ones, so time your efforts accordingly.

Alaska's Top 10 Trophy Cutthroats

8 pounds, 6 ounces Robert Denison (state record)	Wilson Lake (Southeast)	1977
7 pounds, 8 ounces	Wilson Lake (Southeast)	1981
7 pounds, 6.5 ounces	Turner Lake (Southeast)	1991
6 pounds, 5 ounces	Wilson Lake (Southeast)	1973
6 pounds, 14 ounces	Reflection Lake (Southeast)	1977
6 pounds, 12 ounces	Orchard Lake (Southeast)	1973
6 pounds, 7 ounces	Turner Lake (Southeast)	1980
6 pounds, 3 ounces	Ella Lake (Southeast)	1982
6 pounds, 2 ounces	Humpback Lake (Southeast)	1969
6 pounds, 0 ounces	Patching Lake (Southeast)	1980

Alaska's Major Cutthroat Locations

So many water systems are known to contain cutthroat in Alaska (and many more yet to be cataloged) that it is impossible to list all the best areas. Some locations, like Hasselborg and Turner Lakes, are so noteworthy and popular that they barely need mentioning, while others may be local spots known to only a few anglers. Local Fish and Game or Forest Service offices, guides, air taxis, and regional publications can provide invaluable help in finding the better cutthroat trout locations. Most lakes have resident fish, but some also support sea-run cutthroats as well, while certain lakes and stream have only sea-run fish. Remember that timing is crucial for anadromous fishing, but not a critical consideration for resident populations.

Southeast Panhandle

Ketchikan: More cutthroat are caught in this region than in any other. This area includes Revillagigedo (locals call it simply "Revilla") Island and the mainland, which includes Misty Fjords National Monument. The U.S. Forest Service has cabins and shelters on some of the prime cutthroat locations. Lakes and streams on the road system can also provide good fishing for cutthroat and other species, including steelhead. Small rowboats that can handle two- to nine-horsepower motors are available at some of the cabin locations, but check with the Forest Service for the latest conditions before finalizing your plans.

For trophy fish, try Humpback, Ella, Wilson, Reflection, Manzanita, Orchard, and Patching Lakes, For good sea-run cutthroat, try Ward Cove Creek, Naha River, and Manzanita Bay.

Juneau: This area encompasses Admiralty Island, but includes part of the mainland. Not much is available along the road system in Juneau, except at Twin Lakes. In some years, anglers have caught more than 2,000 cutthroats there. The most popular cutthroat trout lakes are accessed by plane.

For roadside fishing, try Twin Lakes and Auke Lake.

For trophy fish, try Hasselborg and surrounding lakes, Turner Lake, and Jims Lake.

Other good spots include Florence Lake (excellent fishing, but logging in the area detracts from the experience); Young and Salmon Lakes; Sitkoh Lake and Stream; Baranof Lake and Stream (no other species are available here); Eva Lake and Stream.

Petersburg/Wrangell: Eagle, Kah Sheets, Pats, Virginia Lakes; Castle River; Thomas Creek and Lake; Petersburg Creek and Lake; Blind Slough.

Haines/Skagway: Chilkat Lake and River, Mosquito Lake, Chilkoot Lake.

North Gulf Coast: This entire area is an unexplored paradise of streams and small lakes, including Bering River tributaries; Katalla, Akwe, Situk, and Kiklukh Rivers; and the Kaliakh River system.

Prince William Sound: Many named and unnamed ponds and lakes have feisty populations of small resident cutthroats. Try Stump Lake (Montague Island), Green Island Lake (Green Island), Eshamy Lake, and Cowpen Lake.

Cordova and vicinity: For roadside fishing, try Alaganik Slough, McKinley Lake, Eyak Lake and River, Southern Orca Inlet; also Hawkins Island Cutoff (this is saltwater fishing, so a boat is necessary).

For remote fishing in the Cordova area, try Junction/Hidden Lake (Canoe Passage, Hawkins Island) and Marten Lake and River (East Copper River Delta).

Chapter 11
Arctic Grayling: The Sailfin

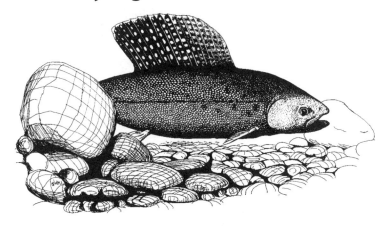

During midsummer in Alaska, the fishing wanes as the great salmon runs subside, and some anglers have a hard time drumming up action that can compare in any way with the electrifying excitement of June. Things might slow to a complete crawl were it not for an amazing fishery that comes into its own this time of year. In headwaters, lake outlets, and countless swift, rocky streams across this immense state, abundant insect hatches brought on by the warmest, sunniest days of the year spark a frenzy of feeding activity among resident populations of one of the northland's most charming fighters—the arctic grayling. In some of the more prolific areas, such as the lakes of the northern Alaska Peninsula, the headwaters of Bristol Bay, and the rambling, clear streams of Northwest, you'll find vast armies of "sailfins" dimpling the surface of rivers and lakes like raindrops as they feed voraciously on emerging insect life.

It can be a simple matter of laying a dry fly on these waters to produce some nonstop fishing fun, reminiscent of youthful days and plucky panfish. These grayling, usually not the least bit shy, will rise to the occasion instantly and fight vigorously, running in tight circles and using their broad shape to great advantage. This is Alaska's best and only real dry fly–fishing of the season, and folks here wouldn't consider the summer complete if they didn't break out light, whippy rods at least once and enjoy some of this delightful diversion at least once.

Introduction

The arctic grayling (*Thymallus arcticus*) is a most interesting and exotic resident of northern waters. Found in the clear, swift stretches of nearly every river and stream throughout the northland, including Alaska, the grayling is a valued sport species, abundant and eager to the fly as is no other fish in the high latitudes.

With his unfurling banner decorated in royal colors of purple, crimson, and gold, the grayling has a striking, aristocratic appearance that distinguishes it from all other northern fish. A valiant and spirited fighter, he'll surprise you with his top-water antics and subsurface rolls, outmaneuvering other species many times his size. Pursued by a dedicated following of anglers, the grayling is an essential part of the Alaska fishing experience, not to be missed in the rush to sample the state's other fabulous species.

Description

The general appearance of the grayling is of a sleek and slender dark whitefish, with a characteristically large dorsal fin that may extend as far as the adipose fin on some mature males, but is slightly smaller and rounder in females. The mouth is small, with numerous fine teeth on both jaws. Coloration varies considerably between watersheds and ranges, from silvery gray to dirty brown to almost black; spawning individuals generally are darker. Black vermiculations decorate forward sides and scales are large. The dorsal and pelvic fins are especially noteworthy for their unusual color variety—pink to blue dots and stripes, their leading edges being white to pink, increasing in brilliance during spawning. The belly is yellowish white, but may appear gray in some populations.

The flesh is white and flaky and of delicate taste when eaten fresh. Due to its fragile nature, grayling meat has no commercial value. However, the fish is regarded with high esteem for its food value within the angling community and often seen as a significant supplement for subsistence users in remote areas.

Not particularly known for size, Alaska grayling average about eight to 12 inches in length, with some populations producing good numbers of fish in the 15- to 18-inch range. Maximum weight is four to five pounds and 22 to 23 inches, given the right growing conditions, but rarely exceeding three pounds and 20 inches. Most trophy-sized grayling are taken from parts of Southwest and Northwest, but a few specimens from isolated stocks in Southcentral and Interior can also reach significant proportions.

Range, Abundance, and Status

A widespread species, the arctic grayling can be found in varying degrees of abundance from Hudson Bay in Canada westward to the Ob River in Russia and south along the Asian continent to the Yalu River. It's present from central Alberta and the headwaters of the Missouri River in Montana north to Alaska, being most abundant in northern Canada and Alaska. A near relative of the arctic grayling is present in northern Scandinavia, Finland, and western Russia. Introductions of the species have extended its range into mountainous regions of Colorado, Utah, and Vermont.

In Alaska, grayling are most numerous in cold, clear waters of the subarctic from the Alaska Peninsula north to the Seward Peninsula in inland rivers, streams, and lakes, and east through the vast Yukon River watershed into Interior and in clear-water drainages of the Copper River. The grayling is abundant in all remote waters of Alaska—particularly Southwest, Northwest, Interior, and Southcentral—with minor populations in large, glacial mainland rivers in Southeast. Successful stockings of this prolific sport fish have been made into several lakes on the Kenai Peninsula, the Anchorage area, Kodiak Island, and parts of Southeast.

Life History and Habits

Starting in March or April in lowland areas to the south, but not until June in mountainous regions to the north, arctic grayling congregate at the mouths of spawning streams. As soon as the ice breaks, the fish move on up, usually in numbers that may range in the hundreds to thousands or more depending on drainage size. The urge to spawn is so intense at times that some fish proceed upstream through channels cut in the ice by overflow. Most grayling spawn in fairly small bog or marshland streams with sandy gravel substrate, although this is not a strict preference. They avoid spring-fed creeks, however.

Grayling commit quite extensive migrations, up to 100 miles or more in some areas and regions. This is particularly true for populations overwintering in deep channels of large, glacial watersheds with spawning streams at the headwaters. The journey may last from a few days to one or two weeks. The fish usually mill around the immediate area for some time, waiting for rising temperatures which trigger a major upstream movement.

Peak reproductive activity takes place anytime between mid-May and mid-June. There is no redd constructed, but a slight depression is often created during the mating rituals. Females deposit from 3,000 to 9,000 eggs, which are adhesive, attaching to bottom structure. The eggs hatch in 11 to 30 days, depending on water temperature.

The young, which some describe as "two eyeballs on a thread," begin feeding on minute aquatic organisms on the third or fourth day, and do so vigorously after the eighth day. Growth accelerates each year from birth up to age five, at which time it slows down, the length of the fish being about eight to 15 inches. After age 10, growth (if any) is minimal. As is common in many resident fish populations, growth rates are higher in regions to the south due to longer open water season and optimal feeding conditions. In the southern part of the range in Alaska, maturity is reached as early as age two or three, but mostly not until age four or five. Maturity is later in the Arctic and colder mountainous regions, usually commencing at age five but sometimes not until age eight. (Seward Peninsula fish have been aged at up to 20 years, which accounts for their larger than average size.)

After spawning has been completed, the adult grayling, depending on stream habitat, either moves to upstream areas within the same drainage or leaves it altogether for another watershed more suitable for feeding. It's very common for grayling to use streams full of spring meltwater for spawning and, after the water levels recede in early summer and become too shallow, to move back into lakes or larger rivers and creeks until freeze-up.

Summer feeding grounds are often located at the headwaters of large river systems in small, clear-water streams or springs with plenty of riffles and deep pools and undercut banks. In landlocked lakes, the fish are distributed throughout specific areas with cooler temperature regimes, but tend to avoid deep water, seeking cool, upwelling springs instead. Showing a low tolerance towards warm water, these fish thrive best in cold drainages (35 to 50 degrees Fahrenheit) where they actively feed on insects, both aquatic and terrestrial, in addition to small numbers of fish. Night feeding is common.

As temperatures drop in autumn, arctic grayling begin to prepare for winter by going into a feeding frenzy. Night feeding halts, shifting to midday, and insects are no longer the sole diet. In areas with heavy runs of spawning salmon, grayling will prey heavily on salmon eggs and even flesh from carcasses. Toward the end of September into October, just prior to freeze-up, the fish begin a rapid downstream movement to overwintering areas. By November very few grayling remain in upstream areas, with most spending the winter in the lower stream sections where the water is deep enough to survive.

During the cold winter months, grayling are suspended in lakes and deep holes and pools of large rivers until the following spring. They're lethargic at this period of time, moving about relatively little, and feeding is minimal.

Fishing Alaska's Grayling

The arctic grayling is indeed one of the more pleasant sportfish species to angle in Alaska. Despite its somewhat diminutive size compared to most salmon, trout, and charr, it's a delight on ultralight tackle or a light fly rod, attacking flies as well as hardware with abandon. Not too picky about anything, grayling can be caught throughout the open water season, unlike salmon and other species. Excellent fishing can be had on any day from spring through fall, given proper knowledge of the habits of this fine gamester.

Spring

One of the best times of the year to get in on nonstop action for grayling is during the spring spawning runs (April and May). Even before the ice breaks up on tributary streams draining into large lakes and glacial rivers, these sporty fish gather in masses at the mouths waiting for the right moment. Anglers lucky enough to find such a school can expect literally a fish on every cast using small spinners and flies. Salmon smolt and parr streamers in sizes 8 and 10 are particularly effective, as are smaller dry flies (such as Humpy, Elk Hair Caddis, and Black Gnat) in sizes 12 to 18. However, care should be exercised on small creeks not to deplete the population by overharvesting, as they can be easily "caught out" by a few anglers in a very short period of time. Catch-and-release is a good

idea. As the spawning streams break up, the fish swarm up by the thousands in many areas and provide boundless opportunities for two to three weeks before dropping back into main stem rivers or moving on to other streams for the rest of the summer to feed.

Summer

Although some locations may see a lull in activity during the short summer months (June to August), superb angling can still be found in many areas. Avoid lowland waters in the southern range and concentrate efforts on clear mountain lakes and streams or inland areas to the north. Grayling do not take the summer heat well. They get sluggish in warm water and migrate in large numbers to cooler locations to feed. Anglers should seek out cold and shallow creeks for best results. In true grayling country it's hard to find a trickle of water deeper than a few inches that does not at least have a few fish present. Lakes can be very productive, especially in the early mornings or late evenings along the shorelines, but also at the inlets, outlets, and springs where cooler water temperatures prevail. A good, steady rainfall is often great for fish-on-every-cast action, and makes larger specimens a possibility. Summer means dry fly–fishing at its best, with spinners also producing exceptional results.

Fall

From September to October is probably the best time of year to tangle with grayling. After the long summer days and abundant feed, the fish are now in prime shape, strong and chunky and full of fight, and, with falling temperatures, very aggressive towards most anything that moves through the water. Nymph and wet flies tend to yield fast-paced action, and egg imitations work like a charm in waters where spawning salmon are present. Traditionally, the week or so before freeze-up is tops for large grayling; the lower sections of clear-water streams are best bets. Sculpin pattern flies and spinners buzzed through deep holes and runs are deadly, and have tricked many a trophy-sized fish. Dry flies, although they may work at times, aren't always very effective.

Winter

Without a doubt, this is the most challenging time of year to catch grayling. From November to March, most streams are frozen over, and ice fishing on lakes has never been truly consistent. The fish are less active, quite deep, and don't show much interest in the way of artificial lures. Occasionally a few specimens may be taken incidentally when fishing for other species such as rainbow trout and landlocked salmon. They seem to prefer small baits above anything else. Cocktail shrimp, worms, and maggots do make connections, but action is best described as fair. In other parts of the grayling's range (northern Europe), anglers have experienced good results using tiny jigs called Mormyshka, but these have not yet been tried to any extent in Alaskan waters.

Techniques for More and Bigger Grayling

Arctic grayling are primarily visual feeders, and anglers must do their best to present their offerings in a way that seem both natural and desirable to the fish. Learning how to read the water is important, as is a complete and thorough understanding of the fish's habits and behavior under various climatic conditions.

During the warmer summer months when insect activity is peaking, feeding primarily occurs at or near the surface and mid-depth. During this time, flies, both wet and dry, produce outstanding fishing. The ones that most closely resemble insects are preferred, particularly light, neutral, and dark patterns in sizes 10 to 20. For waters with fast current, use the larger sizes; smaller ones work best for quiet or flat waters such as lakes. Rooster Tail–type spinners are also highly productive in sizes 0 to 3.

In many areas, fish is an important dietary supplement, and sculpin and salmon smolt patterns in size 2 or smaller work well for producing vicious strikes. Larger grayling are often fooled by the larger sizes. If salmon are present, salmon egg imitations can be unbeatable. Of all the options, spinners are the best fish imitators since they have the correct combination of flash, vibration, and motion. Sizes 0 to 3 are most popular; many a trophy grayling has fallen for the irresistible buzzing and whirling of those flashy blades.

Anybody can catch a grayling out of a hole, but to consistently hook larger fish is the trick. A curious fact is that these arctic gamesters almost always display a form of hierarchy whenever present in pools and deep holes and runs. The largest and most dominant fish are found at the head of the flock, so to speak, with fish size decreasing throughout the holding area until only the smallest are left. The "leaders" are in an ideal position to have the first choice of food, intercepting particles as they drift by. Knowing this, anglers should place casts in the riffles just above the holding area and allow their offerings to tumble or drift downstream precisely on line to where the lineup begins and the big fish lurk. Remember, the larger-sized grayling tend to hug the bottom while the youngsters are found in the middle water column—so fish at the right depth. In fall, however, the hierarchical order begins to break down as the grayling hastily leave smaller streams to overwinter in lakes or larger rivers.

During the summer months when arctic grayling are actively feeding, avoid still or quiet water in stream areas and prospect for pools or runs with moderate to strong current flow, since calm stretches lack the amounts of forage drifting by. The fish prefer the faster water, which has a constant flow of nutrients important to sustaining energy and growth. Unlike other resident freshwater sport fish, grayling are much more pliable in their habits and commonly chase dragging flies several yards. They will move upward in the water column more frequently to intercept items floating on the surface.

In lakes, look for concentrations of fish at the inlets and outlets and areas that have a mud- and sand-covered bottom. Bottom structure is important because only certain types attract forage that grayling are dependent on. Rock and gravel structures are less ideal and will probably not hold many fish. On sunny days it pays to fish the deeper water columns around vegetation mats using shiny spinners and flies with some flash. In early morning and late evening, darker lures are more effective in the shallows at the mouth of tributary streams or along the shoreline.

Grayling feel most at home in clear drainages, but significant populations also exist in lakes, ponds, and streams with murky, muskeg-type water. The standard fishing techniques apply, but lures and flies should be a bit more on the colorful or flashy side since grayling are very visible feeders. This is particularly true in flooding streams, tinted brown due to heavy rain activity. During periods of turbid water, grayling seek out areas with less current and will of-ten hold near the bottom. Under such conditions, larger spoons and spinners outfish flies due to their mass, sonic vibrations, and flash.

A most curious behavior tied into the feeding pattern of grayling is excitement and agitation. Anglers that have fished for them quite extensively know that there are times when a large school of grayling holding in a pool will show no interest in any type of lure presented to them. However, at a certain point, one fish may dash out and mouth an offering out of irritation. Oddly enough, this commotion can stir up the school considerably, triggering an aggressive response, and more fish will follow the first.

Spin Tackle and Gear

Ultralight gear (six- to seven-and-a-half-foot, fast-action rod) with two- to four-pound test line is preferred, but a slightly heavier outfit may be advisable in waters where larger species such as salmon, trout, and charr are present.

For lures, use small spoons and spinners, and plugs. Dark, natural colors are best, such as black, brown, blue, green, and copper, but silver and gold with a touch of red and yellow work very well also. Popular brand-name spinners include Mepps, Vibrax, Panther Martin, and Rooster Tail.

Fly Tackle and Gear

For fly-fishing the Alaska grayling, most folks use a four-, five-, or six-weight rod (eight to nine feet in length), but under the right conditions anglers may want to gear down and use a six- to seven-foot, two- or three-weight rod. Single action reels are fine as long as they match the rod. Floating line and a short sink-tip are all that's usually needed in the way of fly lines. When floating dries for grayling, leaders and tippets should be shorter (four to six feet) than those used for dry fly presentations for trout as grayling are not leader-shy. Shorten up to four feet for sinking presentations. Tippets most commonly used are two- to four-pound test.

Fly Patterns

Most any pattern dry fly will work: Black Gnat, Mosquito, Light Cahill, Elk Hair Caddis, Humpy, Wulff, and Adams, in size 10 or smaller. Egg imitation or attractor patterns are also very effective, with Orange Woolly Buggers, Two-Egg Marabou, Glo Bugs, Iliamna Pinkie, and Polar Shrimp among the top producers. Forage imitations like the Woolly Worm, Black Ant, Muddler Minnow, Hare's Ear Alevin, and Nymph and Stonefly patterns are also good.

Alaska's Top Trophy Grayling Locations

- **Becharof Lake** (Southwest)
- **Sinuk River** (Northwest)
- **Pilgrim River** (Northwest)
- **Goodnews River** (Southwest)
- **Boston Creek** (Northwest)
- **Ugashik Lakes** (Southwest)

Alaska's Major Grayling Locations

Arctic grayling are not tolerant of polluted environments, and thrive best in clean, clear lakes and streams in remote areas.

Southeast

Scattered opportunities exist from stockings done years ago.

- **Sitka:** Beaver Lake
- **Juneau:** Antler Lake
- **Petersburg/Wrangell:** Tyee Lake
- **Ketchikan/Prince of Wales Island:** Naha River system; Manzoni, Marge, Summit Lakes; Big Goat, Shinaku Creeks

Southcentral

The region offers some fairly good grayling fishing, but much of the more accessible locations have been well worked over for larger fish; for truly exceptional action, the best bet is to hike or fly in to remote headwater tributaries.

- **Matanuska/Susitna:** Bonnie, Harriet, Long, Seventeenmile Lakes; Clear, Lake, Coal, Alexander Creeks; Deshka, Talachulitna, Talkeetna, upper Susitna Rivers
- **Kenai:** Crescent, Grayling, Fuller, Twin, Bench, Paradise Lakes; Crescent Creek
- **Kodiak:** Abercombie, Aurel, Cascade, Cicely, Long Lakes
- **Chugach Mountains:** Long Island Lakes

Alaska's Top 10 Trophy Grayling

4 pounds, 13 ounces	Ugashik Narrows (Southwest)	1981
4 pounds, 4 ounces	Ugashik River (Southwest)	1975
4 pounds, 3 ounces	Ugashik Lake (Southwest)	1973
4 pounds, 3 ounces	Ugashik River (Southwest)	1976
4 pounds, 2 ounces	Ugashik Lake (Southwest)	1972
4 pounds, 2 ounces	Sundial Lake (Southwest)	1977
4 pounds, 0 ounces	Ugashik Lake (Southwest)	1972
4 pounds, 0 ounces	Ugashik Lake (Southwest)	1978
4 pounds, 0 ounces	Ugashik Narrows (Southwest)	1979
4 pounds, 0 ounces	Sinuk River (Northwest)	1984

- **Wrangell Mountains:** Gulkana, Little Tonsina, Tyone Rivers; Mendeltna, Cache, Tolsona, Moose, Gunn, Sourdough, Haggard, Poplar Grove Creeks; Mae West, George, Little Junction, Louise, Connor, Susitna, Gillespie, Tyone, Dick, Kay, Tolsona, Arizona, Twin, Paxson, Summit, Tanada Lakes

Southwest

Southwest has some of Alaska's best fishing in terms of abundance and average size, with trophy potential possible in many watersheds, particularly those with headwater lakes. Fly-fishing conditions are the best in Alaska.

- **Bristol Bay:** Kvichak River/Lake Iliamna/Lake Clark system; Wood-Tikchik Lakes; Nushagak, Igushik, Togiak River systems
- **Alaska Peninsula:** Alagnak, Naknek, Becharof, Ugashik Lake systems
- **Lower Kuskokwim:** Goodnews, Arolik, Kanektok, Kwethluk, Kisaralik, Aniak, Holitna Rivers
- **Lower Yukon:** Andreafsky, Anvik Rivers

Northwest

Some of the largest trophy grayling come from this area (Seward Peninsula streams).

- **Norton Sound:** Unalakleet, Shaktoolik, Ungalik Rivers
- **Seward Peninsula:** Fish-Niukluk, Sinuk, Snake, Nome, Kuzitrin, Tubutulik, American-Agiapuk, Pilgrim River systems
- **Kotzebue Sound:** Noatak, Kobuk, Wulik Rivers
- **Arctic:** Kuparuk, Sagavanirktok, Kongakut, Canning Rivers

Interior

- **Tanana:** Goodpaster, Salcha, Chatanika, Chena, Chitanana, Cosna, Zitziana, Tangle Rivers; Kantishna, Nenana River systems; Clearwater, Rock, Fish, Crooked Creeks; Big Swede, Landmark Gap, Glacier, Boulder, Tangle Lakes
- **Yukon:** Nowitna, Ray, Dall, Hadweenzic, Melozitna, Tozitna, Charley, Black, Kandik, Nation, Seventymile, Hodzana Rivers; Birch, Beaver Creeks
- **Brooks Range:** Jim River

Chapter 12
Northern Pike: The Water Wolf

A small floatplane skims with diminishing speed along the surface of a giant lake in the heart of Bristol Bay. It slows and drifts into a quiet lagoon near a major inlet stream. A group of East Coast anglers, looking like they stepped from the pages of a catalog, clamber ashore, loudly proclaiming to the pilot that they intend to catch every big rainbow trout occupying these vast waters, by day's end and their scheduled return. The pilot smiles; he's heard this kind of talk before. He shoves his plane off and taxis to the far side of the lake, then quickly lifts off into the wind and the expansive horizon.

The members of our group busy themselves with the matter at hand. There are dozens of trout lurking here, surely, and giant grayling and charr as well, for these are Bristol Bay's prime waters—nirvana for the elite of cold water's finest fighters. None of this bunch is quite prepared, however, for the surprise that Nature has in store for them this August morning. As one East Coast gentleman strips a big fly through the deep crystal waters, an ominous, crocodile-like form emerges from the shallows. Hesitating at first, then with lightning speed, it streaks in a greenish blur toward the center of the lake, in a line that intersects the angler's retrieve. With little warning, the man's rod is wrenched vio-

lently from his grasp. The limber stick offers little resistance and quickly vanishes in the lake's waters, with an astonished angler in vain pursuit.

Introduction

The northern pike (*Esox lucius*), a.k.a. the water wolf, jackfish, snake, or devilfish, is the familiar and notorious toothy glutton of northern waters, renowned for its supreme savagery when feeding. Lean and mean, with a giant maw and rakish jaws like the barracuda, the pike is the ultimate "lie in wait" ambush predator, with body plan and demeanor designed to wreak havoc on a variety of prey—fish, rodents, even waterfowl—with lightning-swift speed. No other fish attacks a lure with the resolve and vigor of a hungry northern pike.

The pike's wantonness lends well to fantastic legends among Alaska's indigenous people. The Athapaskans speak of giant pike that dwell in large lakes and sloughs along the great waterways of the Interior, where, should a man be foolish enough to stray near these "devil waters," he can be consumed in a single gulp. Similarly, the Eskimo tell of forbidden waters, wherein lurk evil spirits incarnate in the form of monster northerns the size of trees. White folks, too, speak of the northern's incredible boldness. One old trapper I knew swore a six-footer had gone after him one spring when he fell into a slough in a remote part of the Kuskokwim country.

Legends and spirits aside, the northern pike is a tremendously underrated and underutilized sport species in Alaska. Perhaps due to the presence of so many other more notable game fish, and the prejudice many folks feel toward this maligned fighter, little focused effort occurs for pike in many areas that offer outstanding fishing. But the fact remains—Alaska's better pike potential is every bit the equal of anything that Canada has to offer, with the added appeal of almost no angling competition on most waters.

Description

An adult northern pike is not easily confused with other fish. Its body is elongated and somewhat compressed, the dorsal fin riding far back toward the tail. The head is large and dark green above, and light or pale below; the snout is flattened, and some 700 very sharp teeth decorate the pike's powerful jaws. The back and sides are dark green, brown, or grayish green, with the sides showing numerous elliptical yellowish spots arranged in irregular longitudinal rows. The scales are moderately small and may have a touch of gold to the edges. The belly and lower jaw is creamy white. Dorsal, anal, and caudal fins are typically greenish yellow, in some populations even appearing almost orange or red with dark blotches. A color variant known as silver pike is also found in Alaska, as well as in the Lower 48.

Pike meat is white and flaky and considered quite flavorful, but it's also very bony, which may contribute to its false reputation of not being a good food fish. However, after mastering how to cut boneless fillets, most folks agree that pike are no less than scrumptious.

Officially, northern pike in Alaska are not known to achieve the same dimensions as fish in central and northern Europe (65 to 90 pounds), but specimens up to 50 pounds or more are believed to thrive in many vast, remote watersheds of the state. Here they typically average between three and 10 pounds, but many areas yield trophy pike up to 20 pounds. Fish of 45 pounds or more are reputed to have been taken from drainages on the Yukon River, parts of Bristol Bay, and isolated waters of the Northwest.

Range, Abundance, and Status

Northern pike enjoy a circumpolar distribution. They range from northern Italy and Spain to the Scandinavian countries, and from the British Isles to the Pacific coast of Siberia. In North America, pike are found from New England, Missouri, and Nebraska to the Arctic coast of Alaska. They are particularly abundant in Alaska, northern Canada, and Russia and on the Scandinavian peninsula.

Within Alaska, pike are most numerous in sloughs and slow-flowing clearwater drainages of Interior and Southwest, particularly the Yukon and Tanana River systems, but are also very common in lakes and streams of Northwest and Southcentral. Southeast is the only region in Alaska that does not have populations of northern pike, aside from a small remnant stock from the last Ice Age present in the Ahrnklin River system in the Yakutat area. Illegal transplants of this species have extended its range to include the Susitna River drainage, waters in and around Anchorage, and lakes connected to the Kenai River in Southcentral.

Although the pike's popularity as a sport fish is beginning to spread from Interior to other parts of the state, there are still untold numbers of ideal pike waters yet to be discovered and fully recognized. Few locations have been tapped to their maximum potential, and many more outstanding pike fisheries are discovered each year.

Life History and Habits

Each and every spring, mature northern pike leave the cold depths of over-wintering areas to seek out shallow, marshy areas to spawn. This significant movement commences right after break-up, usually sometime in May or even June, depending largely on geographic location. Lake populations commonly use shoreline areas, channels, and sloughs with suitable bottom structure, but may at times leave the lake environment and migrate to slow-moving streams. River populations commit similar migrations, preferring sloughs and lower reaches of tributary rivers and creeks for reproduction. However, spawning migrations are seldom extensive and generally no more than a few miles.

The most important factors in choice of spawning habitat are shallow and quiet water with emergent vegetation and mud bottoms with vegetation mats. Actual spawning occurs only during daylight in areas no deeper than one or two feet, and ceases at night or during periods of heavy cloud cover, rain, and, in some instances, cold air temperatures. Like other sportfish species, pike may return to spawn in the same exact location every year.

Northern pike are neither very territorial nor monogamous and frequently spawn with several members of the opposite gender. The spawning act is repeated often (every few minutes for up to several hours), as only relatively few eggs are released at a time. Depending on the size and age of the mature female, eggs number anywhere between 2,000 and 600,000. A ready-to-spawn female contains both large, ripe eggs and immature eggs that will ripen the following year.

After expulsion, the eggs settle anywhere along bottom, where they remain until hatched, a period of time that may range from four or five days up to a month, depending largely on water temperature. After hatching, the young feed off the yolk sacks until they are old enough to consume zooplankton, later switching to a diet consisting of insect larvae and nymphs. Mortality from egg to fry is very high (99.9 percent), primarily caused by predation from fish species and birds, competition for food, and even cannibalism by larger pike. Before long, juvenile pike begin to forage on small fish, at which time growth increases dramatically. Rate of growth is fast the first few years, then slows. Also, the growth rate appears to be more rapid in the southern range, progressively slower to the north, and largely tied in with water temperature. Maturity is attained as early as age two, but for the most part not until age three or four. Pike in more northern latitudes live longer.

After spawning, the spent adult pikes stay on or near the spawning beds anywhere from one and a half months up to four months. At this time, they're engaged in a feeding frenzy and are particularly vulnerable to anglers. Fish makes up the greater part of a big northern's diet and in some areas may be its exclusive food. They're not picky at all about what kinds of fish are consumed, however, devouring whatever is available. Burbot, grayling, whitefish, suckers, and even smaller pike are among the favored species, but they prey upon juvenile and adult salmon as well. Pike also consume frogs, mice, shrews, and large insects without hesitation, and are serious predators of young waterfowl in some areas. To sum it up: northern pike will eat anything they can catch and swallow.

Northern pike have long been both despised and admired for their uncanny ability to infiltrate new drainages, using rivers as well as tiny trickles of water to spread their range. Their hardiness is of prehistoric proportion. Reports of pike in brackish water have been confirmed, with one such specimen caught in a set net in upper Cook Inlet. The fish was purple in color due to its reaction to salt water; more than likely, it was scouting for new watersheds to inhabit. But usually, pike strictly reside in freshwater.

Fishing Alaska's Northern Pike

For many years, the pike had a reputation as a trash fish with no apparent purpose whatsoever except to prey upon valuable young salmon and trout. However, after decades of disregard (including massive extermination attempts), the northern pike has finally received the respect it deserves, and is today regarded as a legitimate sport species throughout the northern hemisphere. They're plentiful, aggressive toward artificial lures, and popular as a food item.

Spring

Some of the fastest and most rewarding action for large trophy pike occurs in the spring. Starting in mid-May and continuing through June, big spawners take up their positions in the shallows around weed beds near shore in lakes, ponds, sloughs, and streams. Just prior to and after reproduction, fishing can be excellent. (Approach weed beds carefully so as not to spook any fish.) In many loca-

tions, it's possible to spot the pike suspended right beneath the surface, still and motionless, like driftwood or logs—until a lure is thrown out.

The Dardevle: the classic lure for northern pike

Flashy spoons and plugs retrieved with an erratic action through promising water almost always produce smashing strikes, but few things can match the excitement of watching a 20-pound-plus toothy monster attack a top-water lure or fly from below. It's a thrill not soon forgotten. However, these days anglers should be selective about the number and gender of the fish they retain. Since the majority of large pike are female and crucial to the well being of the local stock, and the total number of fish present on the spawning beds represent a good portion of the adult population, catch-and-release is encouraged. If fly-fishing, do not use a dead-drift—it will most likely be ignored. Instead, use short, fast strips—enough to leave a good wake on surface presentations. If there are pike nearby, the fly will not make it back unassaulted.

Summer

Come summer, top-water lures cease to be most effective and many anglers switch to traditional hardware such as spoons, plugs, and spinners. At this time, most of the fish have left the shallows for slightly deeper water, but the action is still good. Generally, pike don't migrate far from the spawning grounds, and will linger on the edge of deep water and heavy vegetation in sloughs, rivers, and lakes until freeze-up. Boaters fare best on lakes, although angling from shore is productive in some rivers and streams. On lakes with minimal vegetation, pike tend to migrate more in search of food and rely more on smell than any other sense to catch a prey. Oily baits are very effective (herring, hooligan, and whitefish), either rigged alone or used as attractors with jigs, spoons, or plugs.

Some of the better locations to find pike in summer and fall are in backwater sloughs and the mouths of slow-flowing streams where they empty into silty rivers. The glacial-green mix is a favorite hangout for big northerns, and many of these succumb to properly presented spoons and plugs and even bait. But, as always, avoid open water and concentrate efforts near vegetation and structure.

Winter

In winter, ice fishing for pike can be exciting and fascinating. In the early part of the season (November to January), pike are generally found in relatively deep water between 15 and 30 feet, but can certainly be encountered throughout all layers at times. Ice houses come in handy on lakes as they provide anglers with shelter, and the darkness inside accents the little light emanating from the water. Decoys have traditionally been used for decades, both in Alaska and abroad, to lure fish in close enough for spearing, but lures such as big spoons and jigs and bait (fish chunks and animal parts) are equally popular and productive. Be prepared for big fish and drill a hole at least one foot in diameter.

Spin/Bait Casting Gear

For spinning or bait casting, a six- to eight-foot medium-heavy freshwater, medium-action rod with matching high-quality reel and eight- to 20-pound test line is the preferred setup. Wire or super-heavy mono shock leaders are requisite for preventing break-offs from the northern's abundant, sharp teeth. Hooks and other terminal tackle should be super strong and of the highest quality. Trophy fish and/or bigger waters will require heavier gear.

Effective pike lures include a wide assortment of large spoons, plugs, spinners, and crankbaits in silver, gold, yellow, green, orange, brown, and black. Wobbling, darting, and diving actions and skirts, legs, and tails mimicking the action and likeness of forage species (fish, frogs, voles, rats, etc.) seem to be the key. Some of the more popular commercial lures include the Pixee, Krocodile, Dardevle, Red Eye, Wigglerspoon, Doctor, and Silver Minnow spoons; the Rapala, Flatfish, Jitterbug, and Tadpolly plugs; no. 6 Super Vibrax and Mepps Giant Killer spinners; and Moss Boss, Jaw Breaker, Hulapopper, Sputterbug, Mouse, and Frog top-water lures.

Fly-fishing Gear

Fly fishers wanting to do battle with pike need at least a long, eight-weight rod (nine weight or even more is recommended for casting some of the large, bulky pike flies) with stout backbone and matching reel with a strong drag. Lines used are generally WF floating or sink-tip, mated to a 12- to 20-pound leader/tippet with the last 12 inches wire or super-heavy mono. Braided alloy leader material and commercially prepared pike leaders are promising new developments worth experimenting with.

Waterdog diving "fly" for pike

Fly Patterns for Alaska Pike

Large attractors and forage species imitations work best, such as Flash Fly, Alaska Mary Ann, Outrageous, Alaskabou, Sculpin, Bunny Bug, and Bunny Leech. Also excellent are tube flies and saltwater patterns like the Clouser Minnow, Deceiver, and Tarpon Fly. Large top-water "flies" like the rabbit fur Lemming, deer hair Frog, Mouse, or diving "Pollywog" creations, and even poppers, can be exciting and productive, but expensive, and seldom survive more than four or five vicious strikes before disintegrating. You can keep it simple and cheap if you tie your own. Aim for flies with a certain amount of bulk since they help grip pike's teeth. Super sharp, sizes 3/0 to 4 hooks are recommended.

Alaska's Top Trophy Pike Waters

- **Innoko River** (Southwest)
- **Alexander Lake** (Southcentral)
- **East Twin Lake** (Interior)
- **Nowitna River** (Interior)
- **Trapper Lake** (Southcentral)

Alaska's Major Pike Locations

The most abundant northern pike populations are found in parts of Interior, Southwest, Southcentral, and Northwest, with the best fishing found in low-lying river, slough, and lake habitat (such as the Yukon, Tanana, and Kanuti Flats, and lower Innoko, Selawik, Noatak Rivers, among others). Southwest, Northwest, and Interior boast the larger fish, but respectable specimens are now being caught in certain locations in Southcentral.

Top 10 Trophy Northern Pike

Interior has long represented Alaska as the leading producer of trophy and record northern pike, but angling interest is shifting to little-fished drainages of Southwest and Southcentral; both are developing reputations for large pike that may exceed 30 pounds and perhaps nudge the 40-pound mark.

Weight	Location	Year
38 pounds, 8 ounces (state record)	Innoko River (Southwest)	1991
38 pounds, 0 ounces	Fish Creek (Interior)	1978
31 pounds, 2 ounces	Donkey Lake (Southcentral)	1992
30 pounds, 4 ounces	Innoko River (Southwest)	1995
29 pounds, 11 ounces	East Twin Lake (Interior)	1988
29 pounds, 0 ounces	Innoko River (Southwest)	1990
28 pounds, 6 ounces	Innoko River (Southwest)	1991
28 pounds, 2 ounces	Wilson Lake (Interior)	1971
28 pounds, 0 ounces	Lake Clark (Southwest)	1982
27 pounds, 8 ounces	Alexander Lake (Southcentral)	1992

Southeast
- **Yakutat:** Antlen River Lakes

Southcentral
- **Susitna:** Chelatna, Bulchitna, Red Shirt, Lynx, Vern, Flathorn, Sucker, Alexander, Hewitt, Whiskey, Trapper Lakes
- **Kenai:** Cisca Lake, Mackey Lakes system

Southwest
- **Bristol Bay:** Nushagak River system; Wood River–Tikchik, Clark, Telaquana, Chulitna, Long, Whitefish, Pike Lakes
- **Alaska Peninsula:** Portions of Naknek Lake system
- **Kuskokwim:** Lower Aniak, Holitna Rivers
- **Lower Yukon:** Lower Andreafsky, Anvik, Innoko Rivers

Northwest
- **Norton Sound:** Unalakleet, Shaktoolik, Ungalik, Kwiniuk Rivers
- **Seward Peninsula:** Fish, Kuzitrin, and Pilgrim Rivers; Imuruk Basin; Buckland River
- **Kotzebue Sound:** Lower Kobuk, Selawik, Noatak Rivers
- **Lower Koyukuk River:** Main stem and tributaries: Gisasa, Dulbi, Huslia, Dakli, Hogatza, Kateel Rivers

Interior
- **Tanana:** Chisana, Nabesna River systems; Chatanika, Tolovana, lower Tatalina, Cosna, Chitanana, Chena, Zitziana Rivers; Swan Neck Slough; Fish, Gardiner, Moose, lower Goldstream Creeks; Jatahmund, Wellesley, Dog, Island, Wien, Wolf, East Twin, West Twin, Deadman, Mucha, Volkmar, Tetlin, Minchumina, Mansfield, George, Bear Lakes
- **Middle Yukon:** Melozitna, Tozitna, Nowitna, Hodzana, Hadweenzic, Chandalar, Christian, Sheenjek, Ray, Dall, lower Charley, lower Nation, Kandik, Porcupine, Black Rivers; lower Hess, Birch, Beaver Creeks

Chapter 13
Sheefish: Tarpon of the North
by Kenneth T. Alt

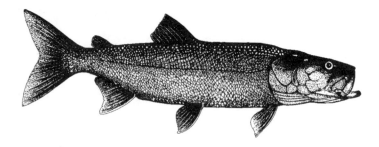

Many times I'd heard the Eskimos tell of the early summer spawning run of smelt in the lower Kobuk and of the ravenously hungry sheefish that congregated there. But I fished the river for many years before I had the good fortune of being at the right place and time to actually witness this amazing spectacle. It was during the second week of June one year, when I was stirred from sleep by a commotion in the river, scant yards from my tent door. Just as my native friends had said, the water churned with untold thousands of silvery smelt, driven into a mad frenzy by the savage onslaught of big sheefish that seemed to be everywhere. A lure tossed into the fray was instantly pounced upon by fish weighing anywhere from three to 30 pounds, supercharged with an energy and jumping ability that I'd never seen before. My fishing partner brought out his fly rod and, with a white streamer, hung one big shee after another in exhilarating battles that were every bit as spectacular as fishing for tarpon. The action continued as the smelt made their way upriver, but after an hour or two of nonstop arm-yanking excitement, we were too bushed to pursue them any further.

Introduction

The sheefish (*Stenodus leucichthys*), also called "inconnu" and "Eskimo tarpon," is a large, predatory whitefish related to the salmon and trout. Its long, slender body shape, extended lower jaw (similar to the pike), silvery color, and size distinguish it from the more common whitefish species. The world's largest and only whitefish consistently caught on hook and line, the sheefish tends to dwell in freshwater rivers, although in the Kuskokwim, lower Yukon, and Selawik-Kobuk Rivers, some populations may spend part of their life cycle in the estuarine portions of river mouths. They spawn in the upper reaches of clear-water rivers and are highly migratory, with some sea-run populations traveling a total of 2,000 miles to and from spawning sites. Fish of the more local populations may only undertake migrations of 200 miles or less. They do not die after spawning, as do salmon, and may return to spawn repeatedly.

Sheefish in Alaska and elsewhere have long served as a subsistence food for rural residents and their dogs. A few small, highly regulated commercial fisheries exist on the more abundant populations. Called *inconnu* ("unknown fish") by early French-Canadian fur traders, the Alaskan shee today remains an obscure sport fish, mostly because of its remote and limited distribution, seasonal availability, and the presence of more glamorous and desirable sport fish species. Only in recent years has the International Game Fish Association recognized it as a trophy fish for record-keeping purposes. Many are taken incidentally by anglers fishing for pike, who are surprised by a long, silvery torpedo of a fish exploding from the water.

Despite its lack of notoriety, the sheefish has tremendous sport fish potential, as it readily takes a variety of lures and flies, reaches respectable size, and has outstanding fighting and eating qualities. Its tail-walking, top-water acrobatics have earned it the respectful name of "Eskimo tarpon" or "Tarpon of the North," as it compares favorably with the silvery, leaping giant of tropical waters.

Description

Sheefish from all stocks show little variation in shape and color throughout life. They have narrow, tapered bodies, with long heads and pike-like mouths that can open wide like a tarpon. Their color is silvery, with backs of light blue or pale brown, and whitish bellies. Markings are usually absent. Sheefish inhabiting darker-colored waters in Interior Alaska are slightly darker than fish coming up from the sea. The sheefish body is deepest behind the pectoral fins, with a fleshy adipose fin in front of the tail. Eyes are large; scales are silvery and come off easily. During spawning, males maintain their torpedo-like body shape, while the belly of a female becomes flaccid and the vent area enlarges.

Juveniles as small as six inches have the same recognizable pike-like mouth and head as adults. Occasionally they're found with a metallic green sheen on the upper body, which turns to blue or brown as the fish grows. In all populations in Alaska, a sheefish-whitefish hybrid can be encountered. This fish is a bit browner in color than a sheefish and has a terminal (trout-like) mouth rather than the extended lower jaw of sheefish. The hybrid fights more like a whitefish, rapidly wiggling its head during capture. It seldom exceeds five pounds in weight.

Most Alaskan shees reach a weight of five pounds at 26 inches and 10 pounds at 30 inches. At 30 pounds, a sheefish might be 34 to 38 inches. There is much variation in size, with sheefish of local populations in the Minto Flats, Nowitna, Porcupine, and upper Yukon River areas seldom exceeding 12 pounds and 32 inches in length while Kuskokwim and Yukon River anadromous populations reach 25 pounds and 39 inches. Only in the Kobuk-Selawik drainages are fish of 50 pounds or more found. (The current Alaska and world record sport-caught fish is a 53-pounder from this area.) Females grow larger than males.

Sheefish flesh is white in all cases. The small-sized fish are quite bland in taste, while larger-sized fish contain more fat and are very tasty. Sheefish are excellent baked, fried, barbecued, or smoked. Raw frozen sheefish, eaten with seal oil, is an Eskimo delicacy. As with other fish, sheefish lose body fat during the spawning process and eating value diminishes.

Range, Abundance, and Status

In Alaska, sheefish have a limited distribution from the Kuskokwim River to the Kobuk-Selawik drainages in Northwest. Except for feeding and overwintering fish that appear in Selawik Lake and Hotham Inlet, sheefish are not normally found in lakes. (Small numbers have been stocked in landlocked lakes in Interior, however.) In the Kuskokwim River, they're found from tidewater upstream to the vicinity of Telida. In the Yukon River, they reside throughout the entire drainage, from the mouth upstream to the Laird and Bell Rivers (Porcupine drainage) in Canada. You won't encounter sheefish in smaller rivers that empty directly into the ocean, with the possible exception of a small population in the Koyuk River. They're not found on the Seward Peninsula or on Alaska's North Slope. They also inhabit all of the great north-flowing rivers of central and eastern Siberia, including the Ob, Irtysh, Lena, Yenesei, and Kolyma. They are absent on North Slope Alaska rivers, but are found east in Canada's Mackenzie River system as well as in the Anderson River.

Sheefish reach their greatest abundance in Alaska's larger, slower-moving waters. They enter first-order tributaries of the Kuskokwim and Yukon Rivers, but on the Kobuk and Selawik Rivers they're confined to the main stem and associated sloughs in the lower reaches. Anadromous populations are larger both in numbers and in individual size; the lower Yukon River or Kobuk-Selawik populations might contain 10,000 spawners, while the nonanadromous local populations in the Minto Flats and the Nowitna, Porcupine, Black, and upper Yukon Rivers may have only a few hundred fish each at most.

Sheefish stocks in Alaska are not as closely monitored as salmon, but all indications show stable, healthy populations, with some natural fluctuations due to climatic conditions and other variables. Since sea-run populations don't venture far out into the ocean, they're safe from most marine predators and gill nets. Presently there is little development threatening overwintering, spawning, and rearing habitat, and in Alaska at least, their migrations are not impeded by dams as occurs elsewhere in parts of their range. The small, nonanadromous populations are most easily affected by overfishing and habitat alteration. Because of scant biological data available, sheefish management has always been rather conservative. Subsistence fishing harvests declined during the 1970s and 1980s as snow machines replaced dog teams, while commercial harvests have remained stable and sport-take only slightly increased. As more anglers become familiar with the fabulous "Eskimo Tarpon," fishing pressure can only rise; hopefully, this will be offset by the growing catch-and-release ethic taking hold among anglers everywhere.

Life History and Habits

A most important aspect of sheefish behavior in terms of sportfishing is their migratory nature. Since sheefish do not die after spawning, they undertake both upstream and downstream migrations to prime areas for feeding and overwintering. In the major rivers, the upstream spawning movements begin at ice breakup, generally preceding the salmon in-migration. These migrations slow considerably as fish linger at mouths of tributary streams to feed. For instance, in the Kuskokwim River, sheefish reach Aniak by early June, Sleetmute by late June, and the McGrath area by late July. In the Yukon River, the spawning run is spread throughout the lower and middle river in June and July, but the peak reaches the Tanana area by mid-August and the Rampart area by early September. In the Kobuk and Selawik Rivers, the run hits the lower rivers in late spring, then proceeds upriver as summer progresses; it reaches the Kiana and

Selawik areas in late June, the Ambler area in mid-July, and the upper Kobuk River area in August and early September. A portion of the lower Yukon River stock continues up the Koyukuk River to spawn near Hughes and Allakaket, while the majority of the population spawn in the main Yukon between Beaver and Fort Yukon.

Total distance traveled can be quite impressive. Fish tagged on the Alatna River and in the main stem Yukon near Fort Yukon have been recovered at the mouth of the Yukon River three to four months after spawning, for a round-trip migration of 2,000 miles. Migrations of freshwater populations may range from less than 100 miles for fish in the Koyuk River to more than 400 miles for Porcupine River shees. Sheefish are quite old before their first spawning, with females from the Kobuk-Selawik population spawning at age 12 to 14. Males spawn three to four years earlier. Fish of the faster growing Minto Flats population spawn at younger ages and have a shorter life span.

The sheefish is an Arctic spawner, as is evidenced by major populations on the Kobuk, Selawik, Koyukuk, Alatna, Porcupine, and Black Rivers breeding within a few miles of the Arctic Circle. For egg laying, they require a combination of six to eight feet of water, moderate to fast current, and a bottom of small to medium gravel—a condition found only in upper sections of certain rivers within their range, usually quite remote. Spawning occurs in late September and early October, with fish in the main stem Yukon spawning as late as October 18, when water temperatures are near freezing and the river runs with ice. Shees cease feeding for three to four months before spawning (their large reserves of body fat sustain them during migration, spawning, and overwintering), but can

still be enticed to take a lure or fly. Spawning itself takes place only during late afternoon and early evening, and frequently occurs on or near the surface, with eggs often shot into the air. Fertilized eggs sink to the bottom where they slowly develop in the near-freezing water; young hatch out in April or May. Fry are carried downstream by spring floods to suitable slow-moving habitats for rearing.

In the rearing and feeding portions of their life history, shees are found in association with pike, burbot, suckers, lampreys, and five species of whitefish. They grow rapidly and usually weigh three to four pounds at five years of age, feeding on plankton and insects initially but turning to fish predation by age one. Suckers, lampreys, small pike, and whitefish are the most important forage species. Sheefish must swallow their prey whole since they have no teeth for gripping; consequently food items tend to be less than eight inches in length. Concentrations of shees in Selawik Lake and Hotham Inlet feed actively throughout the winter, as it is believed all sheefish in Alaska do.

Sheefish continue to grow throughout their life. The impressive size of the Kobuk and Selawik River fish is due to the fact that they live so much longer than other Alaska sheefish. (A 40-pound trophy there might be 19 to 21 years old, whereas age 13 for Yukon River and 11 for Minto Flats sheefish is the maximum.) They have no significant predators other than man, although adult pike, burbot, and even their own kind prey on the young.

The incredible abundance of sheefish one day and their total absence in the same area the next can be extremely frustrating for anglers. Being a schooling species, they're prone to move en masse from areas, for reasons related to food availability, water clarity, depth, and temperature. They exhibit these same schooling tendencies under the ice, while feeding, and during migrations. Except for the later stages of the spawning migration, when they no longer feed (but can be enticed with attractor flies and lures), sheefish of all sizes are found in schooling aggregations.

Shees are not considered strong swimmers. They often utilize large eddies, sloughs, and stream mouths for resting, hugging the shore, and staying close to bottom in strong current. In these situations they're vulnerable to a well-placed lure or fly and subsistence gill nets. Their upstream migrations are easily blocked by falls or other impasses that pose no problem for salmon or trout.

Sheefish feeding habits vary. Quite often they feed deep or off bottom (on lampreys, for instance), but under certain conditions (when bait fish are present) they can be active near or on the surface. The frenzy of sheefish smashing bait on top of the water presents, of course, classic conditions for the most exciting angling, as this is when they're at their most reckless and prone to wild leaping.

Unfortunately not all sheefish fight like the tarpon they resemble and, like any other species, at times they may be as challenging as the proverbial log—especially prespawners or fish in the warm water habitats of interior Alaska. Fish taken off bottom tend to not fight as spectacularly as those from the upper water column. Unlike salmon or trout, shees generally do not make long runs and tend to be more acrobatic the larger they get.

Fishing Alaska's Sheefish

Sheefish sport angling in Alaska is still in its infancy; recreational fishing pressure has increased only slightly over the past 10 years, unlike the phenomenal growth seen in other sport fisheries in Interior and Arctic Alaska. The estimated 1993 catch was 6,666 fish (1,619 harvested). The majority (almost two-thirds) comes from Northwest Alaska's Kobuk and Selawik Rivers, while the Kuskokwim River, Yukon River, and Tanana River drainage follow. A sizable number of shees harvested in Northwest Alaska are taken through the ice in the slightly brackish waters of Hotham Inlet and Selawik Lake.

Methods

For successful sheefish angling, locating your migratory quarry is the primary goal. Once you've found the general area containing fish, you need to determine the depth they are holding or feeding in. Surface-feeding shees are easy to spot. They often jump completely out of the water pursuing their prey, or drive "boils" of bait fish to the surface—which often draws gulls and terns to the melee, making their presence even more obvious. In these situations, a fly or lure fished in the upper three feet of the water column usually produces bone-jarring strikes. The annual out-migration of chum, king, and silver salmon smolt in northern Alaska rivers during June and early July provides a short but rich feeding bonanza for sheefish and excellent opportunities for the sport angler, if he or she can locate feeding concentrations, especially at the mouths of clear tributary streams.

Occasionally sheefish in a spawning aggregation can be observed rolling on the surface, especially in early evening. These fish are not feeding but may be trying to break the eggs loose in the egg skein prior to spawning. They can be enticed to strike a slowly retrieved lure or fly in the upper water column.

Anglers should pay special consideration to sheefish that spend the entire summer feeding at the mouths of virtually all clear-water streams and sloughs of Interior and northern Alaska rivers. A lure or fly cast into the interface of the muddy and clear water usually gets results, as sheefish often feed or rest throughout the entire water column in this zone. The fish in these groups generally are smaller, but quite often they bite more readily than spawners. In the Yukon River, there are anadromous sheefish which do not migrate annually to sea, in addition to a number of freshwater local populations; these fish can provide steady angling from breakup to freeze-up.

When sheefish are feeding or holding on bottom, it is imperative to get your lure or fly down deep, as close to the fish as possible. Quarter casts with heavy lures, slow retrieves, high-density fly lines, and sinkers are the ticket in these conditions, but keep in mind that the strike from these fish is much more subtle than from surface feeders. Most of the fishing for sheefish in Alaska is done from a boat, anchoring near feeding or holding areas, then using short casts with lure or fly. Bait fishing is generally not employed to catch the species.

While sheefish and pike often coexist in the same area of a river, their specific habitat requirements are different. Sheefish are hardly ever found in shallow water, close to willows and brush, or in grassy sloughs. Instead, they prefer the open water of deep holes and sloughs or tributary mouths. If the angler is catching more pike than sheefish, the water he is fishing is probably too shallow. If he is catching charr, salmon, or grayling, he is probably in the wrong habitat. Sheefish have a hard mouth, and the angler must strike with sufficient force to drive the hook home.

Those fish that jump will become airborne as soon as they feel the hook and, as with tarpon, present a special challenge to hold, especially with energetic fish in the 20- to 40-pound range.

In ice fishing, locating the school of sheefish is 90 percent of the battle. In rivers, deep holes located during open water are the best locations to try, but on Selawik Lake, Hotham Inlet, and certain other locations, random testing of a large number of holes by groups of anglers on snow machines is the preferred technique. Once a school is found, a large number of holes are drilled in the vicinity and excellent fishing is usually enjoyed, sometimes for days before the school leaves in their search for food. Most anglers use a stout jigging stick with 15 to 25 feet of 75- to 100-pound Dacron line. A three- to four-inch lure is tied directly to the line and jigged two to four feet under the surface with an erratic, slow motion. As you can imagine, hauling a big 30- or 40-pound fighting shee up through the ice can be quite a job, not unlike trying to contain a bucking horse on a short rope.

Gear

Medium- or medium/heavyweight freshwater spinning or casting rods, matched to high-quality reels with good drags and 200 yards of 10- to 15-pound line are the gear of most successful sheefish outings in Alaska. When fishing for smaller shees in Interior and the upper Yukon River, lighter tackle (down to six- to eight-pound line) is sufficient and can provide better action. Best lures include Dardevles, Krocodiles, Hot Rods, and Pixees in weights from three-eighths to one ounce. Traditional red and white, bright orange, and silver seem the best colors. (In some locales, such as the upper Kobuk River, only bronze-colored lures work.) Fish the heavier sizes to get down in deeper, swifter water. Diving plugs and rattling crank baits (like Wiggle Warts, Shad Raps, Hot Shots, Rat-L-Traps) can also be worked effectively. For ice fishing, large (three-inch) Doktor lures in silver and bronze are dynamite, but other bright spoons and jigs can be used, with good results at times.

Fly rods should be seven- to nine-weight with plenty of backbone to coax large fish from the currents. In slower water or for smaller fish, you can get by with lighter gear, down to a five-weight in some instances. Flies used for feeding sheefish should resemble prey items—white Woolly Buggers, Smolt patterns, Leeches (including Egg-Sucking Leech), in sizes 4 to 1/0. Large (up to size 3/0), attractor streamer flies work well for fish that aren't feeding, with colorful patterns utilizing some of the newer materials such as Krystal Flash and Flashabou most popular.

It is most essential to get the fly as close to the fish as possible for best results. Use short leaders and tippets of eight to 12 pounds, depending on conditions and the size of fish pursued. Flies should be weighted even when sheefish are feeding on the surface. Floating and sinking-tip lines are adequate for feed-ing fish, but for fish holding in deep water or nonfeeding prespawners, a weighted line such as the Teeny Nymph works better. A shock leader or wire leader is not really necessary because sheefish do not have teeth, but sharp hooks are a definite plus for penetrat-ing their hard bony mouths.

Alaska's Major Sheefish Locations

Kuskokwim River: Most sheefish taken in the Kuskokwim River are fish feeding during the summer upstream migration. Since the Kuskokwim is muddy, prime angling locations are always at the mouths and lower reaches of clear-water tributaries. Sheefish are found in early June in streams between Bethel and Aniak, while in July they appear in the Holitna, Tatlawiksuk, and clear-water streams between Sleetmute and McGrath. Upstream of McGrath, the spawning mi-gration spreads out and fish are found in the Takotna River, Middle Fork, Big River, North Fork, and in the Telida area. A few nonspawning fish are present all summer in Kuskokwim streams. Since most sheefish in the Kuskokwim over-winter below Bethel, little ice fishing for them occurs.

Alaska's Top 10 Trophy Sheefish

53 pounds, 0 ounces (state and world record)	Pah River (Northwest)	1986
52 pounds, 8 ounces	Kobuk River (Northwest)	1968
49 pounds, 0 ounces	Kobuk River (Northwest)	1995
43 pounds, 0 ounces	Kobuk River (Northwest)	1993
42 pounds, 4 ounces	Kobuk River (Northwest)	1994
39 pounds, 8 ounces	Kobuk River (Northwest)	1967
38 pounds, 12 ounces	Kobuk River (Northwest)	1987
38 pounds, 0 ounces	Kobuk River (Northwest)	1979
37 pounds, 11 ounces	George River (Northwest)	1971
37 pounds, 4 ounces	Kobuk River (Northwest)	1978

Yukon River: In the lower Yukon River, sheefish stop at the mouths of tributary rivers to feed while migrating upstream during early summer. Often the water is too muddy early on, but as tributaries clear, sheefish can be taken. The lower Innoko River in the Shageluk and Holikachuk areas is a major feeding zone. In the Ruby area, sheefish are present in the Yuki, Melozitna, and Nowitna Rivers from late June to mid-July. During July and August, they can be found in the lower reaches of Ray, Dall, Hodzana, and Chandalar Rivers, and Hess, Birch, and Beaver Creeks. They are present in the streams between Circle and Eagle such as the Charley, Kandik, Nation, Seventymile, and Tatonduk Rivers and Eagle Creek. The huge migration of spawners reaching the vicinity of the Dalton Highway bridge in early September remain in the muddy water and thus are inaccessible to anglers.

After these sheefish have migrated back to the lower Yukon River area for over-wintering, there is an active ice fishery during November, March, and April in the villages from Holy Cross downstream to the mouth of the Yukon. The Koyukuk River has its own spawning migration and, although fish pass through lower Koyukuk River villages during August, little sportfishing occurs until the run reaches Hughes in late August and September. The main Koyukuk River from Hughes to Allakaket and the lower 40 miles of the Alatna River provide good sportfishing during September and early October. The Porcupine contains two populations of sheefish, but their small numbers and small size has little appeal to anglers. Sheefish are found in the Porcupine during summer in all sloughs and rivers that enter the Porcupine from the mouth at Fort Yukon to the Canadian border. They are found up the Black River beyond Chalkytsik area and up the Sheenjek River to the mouth of the Koness River.

Tanana River: In the Tanana River, most sheefish are found in the Minto Flats, although they can be taken in clear-water streams from the mouth at Tanana upstream to Fairbanks. The Tolovana, Tatalina, and Chatanika Rivers and Goldstream Creek in the Minto Flats contain sheefish in the deeper holes from breakup to early August. They are found throughout most of the Chatanika River to milepost 30 on the Steese Highway and in the Tolovana River upstream of Minto village. Other locations where sheefish are found in the lower Tanana River include Fish and Baker Creek and the Chitanana, Zitziana, and Kantishna River systems, while closer to Fairbanks a few are taken at the mouths of clear-water streams such as Rosie and Nelson Clearwater Creeks and the Chena River. Most of the Chena River fish are taken soon after breakup near the mouth, while smaller numbers are taken throughout summer in the lower 20 miles of the Chena.

Kobuk and Selawik Rivers: Major sheefish fishing areas include the entire Kobuk River upstream to the Reed River, the Selawik River upstream for about 125 miles, and the extensive lake, stream, and slough system of Hotham Inlet and Selawik Lake. In the Selawik area, sheefish are found in the Tuklomarak and Fox Rivers, Inland Lake and its tributaries, and the man-made channel connecting Inland Lake to the Selawik River. Once sheefish begin moving up the Kobuk and Selawik Rivers, they remain in the main river except for resting stops at mouths of sloughs and tributary streams. Don't expect to find sheefish very far up the tributaries of these two rivers.

As summer progresses, good fishing locations in the Selawik River are the deep holes upstream of Selawik village. In the Kobuk River, prime early summer (June) fishing grounds include all the channels making up the mouth of the Kobuk River, Hotham Inlet, and deep holes and sloughs upstream to Kiana. This run reaches the Ambler area by mid-July. During mid- to late summer, the run spreads out, but prime fishing spots include deep holes in the main river, sloughs, and tributary mouths from Ambler upstream to Kobuk village.

The spawning run of fish can be intercepted at various points from Kobuk upstream to the Reed River until the last week of September, when the fish complete spawning and migrate rapidly downstream to feeding and overwintering areas.

Winter ice fishing locations are essentially all of Hotham Inlet and Selawik Lake, as the fish form huge schools and migrate throughout both bodies of water during the winter months.

Chapter 14
Pacific Halibut: Denizens of the Deep
by Peter Hardy

Floatplanes are used to access many prime halibut waters.

A taste of the excitement that sportfishing for halibut can provide came on a picture-perfect day one early August in Southcentral. A three-hour run on calm seas south from the port of Homer took the charter boat *Sourdough* past sea otters, puffins, and porpoises to the rugged Barren Islands of lower Cook Inlet. Shirtsleeve weather, no wind, and a minuscule three-foot tide change promised pleasant sun tanning, if nothing else.

Hopes were high when I lowered a whole herring 150 feet to the bottom. It undulated slowly as I gently raised and lowered the 20-ounce sinker, occasionally tapping bottom to keep the bait in the prime strike zone. Soon the easy tugs of a characteristic halibut bite gave way to a solid pull as a large one inhaled the bait. A 10-minute fight brought the 146-pounder on deck. Impressed with such early success, I opted to help as the other anglers fought bending rods to land impressive prizes of their own. By early afternoon the stern was awash with the white undersides of big halibut. With only a half hour left to fish, I rebaited and immediately hooked another big one. Weighing in at 102 pounds back at the dock, it bookended my first double 100-pounder day and pushed the boat's total to 11 fish of more than 100 pounds for the trip. What a fantastic rack of fish from a glorious day on the water!

Introduction

The Pacific halibut (*Hippoglossus stenolepis*) is renowned as a premium eating fish, but has only recently come into its own as a sport fish with the development of light, strong gear and techniques to match. Although halibut are available as far north as Norton Sound in the Bering Sea, present sport effort is concentrated along the Gulf of Alaska from Ketchikan through Southcentral's Prince William Sound, Cook Inlet, and the Kodiak Islands. From there, it ranges out to virgin territory near Dutch Harbor/ Unalaska in the Aleutian Islands. With a charter fleet of more than 100 boats, Homer in Southcentral is justifiably proud of its ranking as the world capital of halibut fishing. The high-volume commercial port of Dutch Harbor/Unalaska is the rising star of halibut sportfishing with the pending International Game Fish Association (IGFA) world record of 459 pounds taken in June 1996. A 439-pounder in 1995 hinted at what was to come, as did commercial catches of big ones weighing more than 500 pounds in recent years.

Fishing halibut is enjoyable on many levels. The marine environment entices with seals, whales, and myriad sea birds to watch. The big flatfish species share waters with other edible species such as rockfish, lingcod, and salmon, all of which take baits meant for halibut. It's a fish that almost any angler with patience who can tolerate a day on the ocean has a chance to hook, and with care, has a good chance to boat. Noted outdoorsman Jay Massey likens halibut fishing to big game hunting in that a trophy may appear at any time, often when least expected.

A halibut's bite is only rarely like a freight train's plummet out of nowhere. Usually it's just nibbles and tugs that eventually culminate in a rod-yanking pull. The pull is your clue to drive home the hook with a short, sharp strike. Depending on its size, the fish may make a determined run, struggle vainly close to the boat, or just lay there. The first and last actions indicate good size. The battle may go back and forth for five minutes to two hours as the angler tries to pump the fish to the boat. Bigger fish may come up with little fuss, only to see the surface and dive all the way back to the bottom.

Immediately after the hook-up and often during the fight, a good size halibut gives a characteristic head shake as it attempts to shed the hook. The strength of that shake and the sheer mass against which the angler pulls can be enough to give goose bumps of anticipation until the behemoth finally materializes out of the depths. Then the cry "I've got color!" as the fish sideslips, flashing its white belly, triggers rapid action to prepare gaff, harpoon, and firearm to safely subdue and land the beast. The best finally comes once the chef is done in the kitchen and serves this delectable white fish for dinner.

Description

As a member of the right eye flounder family and the largest flatfish of the Pacific Coast, the halibut can reach immense proportions. Commercial catches to 550 pounds and 9.5 feet in length have been recorded. Fish in excess of 100 pounds are commonplace in many areas of the state, particularly in offshore locations that receive little or no fishing pressure. However, the average halibut caught by most sport anglers is much more modest and falls in the 10- to 40-pound category, with the yearly heaviest 'but weighing in at 400 pounds or so. It's interesting to note that all very large halibut are females; males rarely exceed 50 pounds. And, a blessing to anglers, females far outnumber the males of the species.

Aside from their occasional "barn door" size, halibut are fairly easily recognized. The body shape is more elongated than other species of flounders, the width being approximately one-third the length. Scales are small and smooth with the lateral line forming a high arc over the pectoral fin. The mouth is quite small, not extending past the middle of the lower eye, and contains well-developed teeth on both sides of the jaw. Coloration tends to vary according to the bottom environment of its habitat, but it's usually dark brown or green to gray on the top side, with the bottom side uniformly white. This allows halibut to avoid detection by both prey and predator.

Range, Abundance, and Status

Pacific halibut can be found from Cape Muzon in Southeast along the coast in varying degrees of abundance through Southcentral and the Gulf of Alaska into the Bering Sea, and on to Point Hope along the Arctic. Its range in the North Pacific runs from central California to northern Japan, with the most important fisheries occurring in British Columbia, Southeast and Southcentral Alaska, and the Bering Sea.

For centuries, halibut has been a key source of subsistence for indigenous Pacific Coast peoples. Much of their folklore mythologizes the fish. Native Americans carved immaculate designs on their ivory fishhooks to ensure good luck and large fish. Today, anglers of all backgrounds hunt this white-fleshed monster, with the majority of sport effort originating in major coastal ports such as Ketchikan, Sitka, Petersburg, and Juneau in the Southeast region, and Valdez, Seward, Homer, and Kodiak in Southcentral Alaska. More than 65 percent of the statewide harvest comes from Southcentral (primarily lower Cook Inlet and Kodiak Island) and the Southeast archipelago (where halibut are second only to king salmon). The annual sport harvest is about 1.5 million pounds. Due to halibut's popularity, this number increases yearly, despite the fact that current state regulations allow only two fish of any size to be kept per day.

Life History and Habits

Male halibut become sexually mature at age seven or eight, females slightly later at eight to 12 years. Concentrations of spawning fish are found in deep water along the continental shelf during the winter months (November through March) with peak activity occurring from December to February. Females may produce between two and three million eggs, which hatch after two weeks and become free-floating larvae, drifting hundreds of miles with ocean currents. After six months, the larvae's fish-like form begins to flatten and its left eye migrates to its right side. Juvenile halibut spend their first few years on the bottom of shallow, inshore waters (the

Bering Sea is a major nursery ground for growing flatties). Young halibut move to deeper water at around age five and eventually commit extensive migrations that may range 2,000 miles or more, moving in a clockwise direction east and south throughout the Gulf of Alaska.

Occupying depths of between 60 and 3,600 feet, halibut thrive on flat-bottomed structure such as sand, fine gravel, mud, and clay. Adult diet consists of fish (mainly cod, turbot, and pollock, but also sand lance and herring), squid, crab, shrimp, clams, and marine worms. Females grow faster, reach greater weight, and live longer (up to 45 years) than males. The growth rate depends largely on location, food availability, and other factors. For example, in recent years fish in Cook Inlet have declined in their weight-to-age ratio while those in the Aleutians seem particularly fat.

Fishing Alaska's Halibut

Since halibut are highly migratory and move inshore and offshore according to the seasons, anglers do best in late spring, summer, and fall when fish feed in fairly shallow coastal areas. In winter, the fish are situated too deep and far from shore to be accessible to anglers. However, in some trenches near the Gulf, anglers can catch smaller fish fairly regularly throughout the cold months.

Tidal-influenced depressions, major channels, tidal rips, reefs, and shelves bordering steep dropoffs are prime areas since these attract bait fish and, subsequently, voracious halibut. Also, stream mouths can be productive since 'buts often gather there in late summer and fall in anticipation of salmon carcasses washing out to sea. The best catches are made in 30 to 60 feet of water, with some locations producing good catches down to 300 feet—especially early and late in the season as the fish are in transition between offshore spawning and inshore feeding grounds. In summer, mid-depths of 100 to 250 feet can produce decent catches. Many successful anglers, and especially guides, use sonar recorders and hydrographic charts in identifying likely areas.

Gearing Up for Pacific Halibut

Hooks

The standard hook for years was the O'Shaughnessy in sizes 10/0 or 12/0. It's been replaced in recent years by the circle hook in size 16/0. The O'Shaughnessy is also called the "J" hook for its traditional design. Available in plain or stainless steel, the plain steel is easier to sharpen but requires more care (freshwater rinsing and air drying) after each use than the stainless one does. This style is used to make lead head jigs (see the Lure section on page **XX** of this chapter).

12/0 O'Shaughnessy "J" Hook

Only light line anglers who want the easy hook setting that a needle sharp, open design model provides should use the O'Shaughnessy. Its defects are major. One is that the angler must maintain constant pressure while reeling up a fish in order to prevent the hook from working free. The second flaw is that it is a killing hook. Fish swallow it easily, hooking themselves in the gills or in the throat where unhooking leads to serious bleeding. With a daily limit of only two halibut, the urge to release smaller, uninjured fish in order to continue legal fishing for a larger fish creates an ethical dilemma for the conscientious angler. Fortunately, it needn't reach that point, thanks to a second option: the circle hook.

Modern circle hooks were developed by the Japanese commercial fishing industry from an ancient Polynesian design. Long liners needed a self-acting hook that was difficult for fish to dislodge since their gear often lay on the bottom for a day or longer. Its shape is like a capital G. The shank is half the length of the J hook's, reducing the fish's leverage to pry it loose. Also, the tip is longer and is bent at a right angle toward the shank, creating the effect of a second barb. It firmly hooks most fish in the lip or in the corner of the mouth. Any pressure imbeds the point deeper, much like the action of a simple corkscrew. In field tests, commercial fishers caught 35 percent more halibut with this type of hook, yet left fish largely unharmed. Sport fishers eager to practice catch-and-release fishing have taken note and the hook is "catching on" in popularity.

The Mustad model 39965 in size 16/0 is readily available, as is a similar model from Eagle Claw. VMC produces the excellent model 9788 PS in size 3, which has an anodized finish and a round point that is sharp out of the box. Gamakatsu makes an expensive ($7) forged hook in sizes 45 or 50 that is very sharp and is known for its ability to hook solidly. They all work, especially with the angler's attention to keeping sharp points and tying good knots.

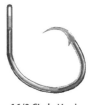

16/0 Circle Hook

Standard Leader

2/0 - 4/0
Rosco Bargel Swivel

18-inch to 24-inch Hard Braid Nylon Leader (Evergreen
or White) "Gangion Line" 200 - 400 lb. Test

16/0 Circle Hook

Leaders

Sportfishing leaders are usually 18 to 24 inches long. Green, braided nylon leader line (such as Neptune by Sunset) of 150- to 300-pound test makes superb leaders. Commercial fishing supply stores carry half-pound spools for under $15, which can make more than 100 leaders. Only a cutting tool is required to start, and a flame to singe each end once the tying is done. New leaders can be made on a moment's notice and they're easy on the hand when grabbed to control or boat a fish. This material resists abrasion and stays strong after many uses. You'll find countless other uses for this line on a boat, not least of which is to truss a halibut so that it can't thrash. The standard leader has a hook on one end and a large swivel on the other. My improved version adds 12 to 24 inches of leader on which I thread a large snap swivel and then tie another swivel. This creates a leader to which only bait and a sinker need be added. It allows light biting fish to take line a short distance before they feel the sinker's weight. It handles even the biggest sinkers with minimal wear and it makes deck hands happy since they don't have to risk line cuts when hauling aboard small halibut for release.

Pre-tied nylon monofilament leaders are available in 200- to 400-pound test. A casual angler can last an entire season with a half dozen unless he fishes in gear-stealing territory. Serious bait and jig fishers should plan to spend at least $100 for crimps, a crimping tool, and leader material to make their own. Practice is important in order to make uniform crimps that won't slip and won't cut or weaken the leader. Once fishing, check mono leaders often for nicks and plan on replacing them after landing big fish. Reuse the hook and swivel later. Most anglers in Alaska don't use wire leaders.

Many leader makers add plastic squid imitations (hoochies) and/or five to 10 inches of glow-in-the-dark surgical tubing above the hook. These serve to attract fish, help hold scent, and act as a sheath to protect the mono from damage. When used over braided nylon, the tubing acts as a stiffener to help the angler keep the bait from tangling his main line when lowering it to the bottom.

Swivels

Use the best that you can afford. That means quality ball bearing swivels and coast-lock or cross-lock style snaps. If using Crane or Rosco swivels, use no. 3/0 (approximately 300-pound test) or larger. I tend to stay away from three-way swivels after an offshore brand

Improved Leader

12 inch leader

2/0 - 4/0
Swivels

no. 55 or 56
Duolock Snap
for Sinker

Three-Way Swivel

came apart on one of the biggest halibut catches of my life. A captain showed me that the heaviest American-made ones can take trophy fish. For those who still have doubts, there's a 600-pound test-rated three-way barrel swivel. Add a snap to the non in-line lobe of the swivel to attach the sinker.

Sinkers

Bank sinker

Halibut fishers will be interested in four types of sinkers. The cheapest and easiest to obtain is the bank variety. All lead, it's cast in an elongated figure eight shape and is usually available in two- to 20-ounce sizes. It has flattened sides that help prevent it from rolling.

Cannonball sinkers are round with a brass wire loop or an imbedded swivel for attachment to the terminal gear. Their compact shape makes them excellent for bottom bouncing, although they do roll easily on deck. Slightly more expensive than bank sinkers, they're made in sizes to four pounds.

Cannonball sinker

Bar sinkers (charter boat specials) are rectangular, like a sash weight with a wire loop; sometimes they have a rounded bottom. They come in whole sizes from one to five pounds and they don't roll.

Charter Special

The fourth type is a pyramid sinker, which is designed to dig into the bottom. Surf casters developed it to anchor their bait as far out from shore as it could be cast. Shore-bound halibut anglers may find it useful, but it's rarely suitable for boat fishing.

Plastic sliders are available that work fine for sinkers to 20 ounces. Heavier sinkers may break the slide, which limits their use in some waters. Thread the main line through the slide and tie to the leader swivel. The snap on the slider lets the angler increase or decrease the size of the sinker in order to stay on the bottom with minimum weight as the tide rises or falls.

Line

For years the standard line was braided Dacron in 80-pound test. Its virtues include high strength, limited stretch, low memory, freedom from rot, abrasion resistance, and ease of knotting and handling. Its disadvantage is that its relatively large diameter causes it to balloon when pushed by strong currents, which necessitates heavy sinkers to hold the baited hook on the bottom. In areas with smaller tide changes, 50-pound Dacron can be used by light tackle anglers.

Hard finish, low stretch monofilament in 40- to 60-pound test has proven itself capable of handling big fish in

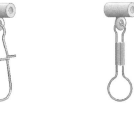

Nylon Sinker Slides

Sinker Snap Duolock no. 55 or 56
(replaces existing snap)

depths of less than 150 feet and light tide changes using bait or with jigs of two to 12 ounces. Brands such as Ande, Maxima, Berkley Big Game, or Stren High Impact are suitable for this fishing. Mono's inherent stretch gives a shock absorber effect to help beat the biggest fish. The usual injunction to constantly check your line for wear doubly applies here.

New lines made of Spectra fibers solve most of these problems. Incredibly thin, yet strong, 80-pound Spectra is the diameter of 30-pound Dacron, and 130-pound Spectra is the size of 50-pound Dacron. Its slick finish combines with the smaller diameter to allow very little water resistance. Anglers can fish at greater depths with less lead than ever before. Abrasion resistance is a problem, and I've had break-offs that would never have occurred with Dacron. The lowest stretch of any line means that there is little forgiveness, even with the most limber rods. I've learned to watch for damage even more than with my monofilament. As the product is new, you may encounter production quality problems.

A coating on Tuf-line Plus Spectra line is designed to help prevent abrasion. It seems to work. You must learn special knots using doubled line to keep the line

from cutting itself. Use Super Glue to reinforce and protect your knots. This new technology isn't cheap. Plan to spend 12 to 16 cents per yard for Spectra lines versus four to six cents per yard for braided Dacron. Use care when handling it under pressure since it can act like a wire cheese slicer and cut a finger quickly. Lay the line on your reel in a crisscross pattern so that it won't dig into itself, causing the drag to work in a jerky manner that might lose a fish. These caveats notwithstanding, Spectra is a great step forward in line technology if used properly.

Reels

Your reel must be sturdy and saltwater resistant with a good drag system. The latest reels feature technological advances such as graphite components for lightness and strength, improved drag washers for smoothness, and a viable level wind capability. Lever drags with pre-set strike settings and larger drag surfaces than the old style star drags give instant, smooth control of line release that makes light line fishing a practical reality.

In the days of Dacron lines, a no. 4/0 reel was the smallest that an angler could use to hold the minimum of 200 yards of 80-pound test line required in

Pacific Halibut: Denizens of the Deep 157

most waters. Now, with the advent of the thinner Spectra fiber lines, that's the large end of the spectrum. Penn, Shimano, Fenwick, and Daiwa all make quality products, most of which require using your thumb to level the line on the spool when retrieving. However, Penn has introduced the 345GTI, a graphite level wind that works fine for the angler who uses 50- or 80-pound Dacron. Novices and children like it as it eliminates the sometimes vexing task of manually leveling the line while trying to fight a fish. It's not recommended for the daily rigors of charter boat fishing, nor can I recommend it for the Spectra lines since it can't cross-lay the line.

A gear ratio of 3:1 or higher is critical for fishing the depths that halibut demand. Otherwise it feels as though you're stuck in low gear when reeling fish or checking bait since little line is retrieved with each turn of the handle on models with lower gear ratios. Some expensive reels have two-speed gearing with a low gear for big fish.

Rods

Thanks to new materials, rods are shorter and lighter, yet stronger, than ever. Gone are the days of the 6.5-foot, solid fiberglass, "pool cue" action trolling rod. It's been replaced by a 5.5-foot, fast taper, high-strength fiberglass or graphite composite stand-up rod. Metal guides have competition from high-tech metallic oxide guides that reduce friction and dissipate heat while resisting line wear. Long foam fore grips and foot-long butt sections allow anglers to tuck rods closely to their bodies, giving leverage for battling big fish while standing at a boat rail. Gimbal fittings keep rods from rolling laterally as fish are fought to the surface.

Light to medium line test-rated rods are 30 to 80 pounds or 40/50 to 100

pounds. Heavy rods rate at 80 to 130 pounds. These are highly arbitrary designations determined by each manufacturer. Bend the tip and test the action for yourself. The heaviest rods handle large sinkers when tides run high, such as in Cook Inlet's 26-footers.

Many rods are equipped with a roller tip, which acts like a pulley to ease taking in line under stress. Look for ones with close tolerances since the thinner lines can wedge between the roller and the frame, causing fraying and breakage. Also, the rod must be kept upright so that the tip is perpendicular to the horizon for the roller to work properly. Many rod builders avoid this problem by using complete sets of metallic oxide guides. With full circle eyelets, the rod can even be fished upside down if necessary! These rods work well in a holder or in the hands of any easily distractable anglers. They're nice for jigging, too.

An excellent all-around rod length is 5.5 feet. Those fishing exclusively with bait might enjoy a five-footer, where a jigger would appreciate a six-foot model. Those in small boats fishing close to the water should use shorter rods to make hook setting easier. In general, use shorter rods for greater lifting power and ease of handling. Light tips increase sensitivity and the enjoyment of fighting smaller fish, yet sturdy butt sections give the backbone needed to control and land big ones.

Regarding materials, uniform diameter, solid fiberglass blanks have given way to hollow, high-strength fiberglass (S or E glass) which is lighter, more flexible, and more sensitive. However, Penn has led a resurgence in solid fiberglass by offering tapered blanks which approximate the feel of hollow glass, but which are much more durable under rough handling at lowest cost. G. Loomis offers Hybrid rods that blend graphite and fiberglass. You'll find many quality hollow glass rods of standard guide configuration. A radical product from Daiwa is almost guideless since the line runs through the blank. Early handling tests gave good results with ongoing line wear studies pending. Who can imagine what technological advances will be next?

Lures

Jigs are plain chromed metal or metal with paint schemes that resemble bait fish. Another variety is the lead head jig; either plain or painted (sometimes in luminescent off-white) which has a rubber sea worm or shrimp tail (scampi). Many colors are available, but white or "glow" have proven effective for visibility at the greatest depths (200 feet or more). Add a piece of bait such as an octopus tentacle, a herring strip, or a squid to enhance chances of attracting a bite.

Jigs as light as four to six ounces can catch big fish when tide and currents permit, though eight- to 24-ouncers are more the norm. They often induce strikes when bait won't. Jigs are attractive to bottomfish and even to salmon. Since motion is essential, continuous jigging while prospecting for fish can become tiring, but once you hit a concentration of fish, they work wonderfully. Where bites on bait are usually tentative, there's no doubt when a fish hits a jig. It's an exciting way to fish and, unless the tail gets chewed off, you know that you still have a viable lure even if the fish strikes but misses getting hooked. Drop it back and hook the fish the second time it tries, since halibut are aggressive and rarely hook shy.

Examples of metal jigs are the Vi-Ke, a Norwegian-style cod jig; the Teezer, a needlefish imitator; and the Metzlar Mooch-A-Jig, which resembles a herring. The painted Yo HoHo represents any bait fish, while the lead heads with

their tails and skirts resemble fish, crab, or octopus, depending on how they're dressed and fished. Metal jigs benefit from the addition of color, scale finish decals, or tape.

Accessories

Fighting belts are a worthwhile investment since they protect the abdomen from bruising whenever the rod is rested against the angler's body. The simplest are leather or plastic triangles with a molded cup for the rod butt and a sturdy belt strap to circle the waist. Fancier models have a metal bar designed to lock into the matching gimbal fitting on rod butts. This keeps the rod from rolling with the torque created by cranking the reel. Larger models rest on the tops of the thighs or completely encircle the hips with two neoprene padded arms. These are extremely comfortable to wear and effectively distribute the force of a fighting fish. Shoulder harnesses, vests, or kidney belts with two quick-release snaps for attachment to the reel take stress off the arms and the hands. This is particularly important in an extended battle, since the angler is standing rather than using a fighting chair.

Bait

Halibut are voracious feeders on other fish and shellfish. I once caught a 50-pounder that had 14 half-dollar-size king crab in its stomach. Herring, salmon, needlefish, eulachon (hooligan), sculpins, octopus, and crab comprise much of their diet. Herring is a popular bait because it's readily available and gives off an excellent scent. Fresh or fresh frozen is best. A whole fish is particularly good, given the "bigger bait, bigger catch" theory. Charters use a half or a third of a large herring, but this isn't a problem since they have six to 16 baits in the water creating a scent trail.

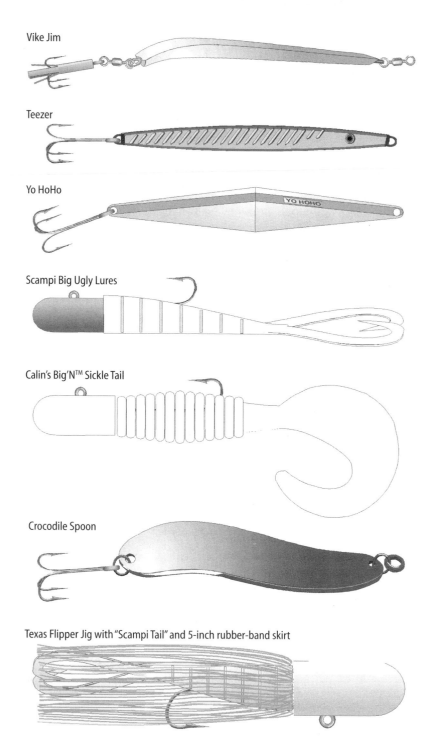

Vike Jim

Teezer

Yo HoHo

Scampi Big Ugly Lures

Calin's Big'N™ Sickle Tail

Crocodile Spoon

Texas Flipper Jig with "Scampi Tail" and 5-inch rubber-band skirt

Pacific Halibut: Denizens of the Deep

One of the halibut's favorite foods, octopus, is a superb bait because it's durable. Squid is similar, but it has only a fraction of the durability of octopus. It's found in most supermarkets as well as in bait shops. Either may be used with herring on the same hook. Put a two- or three-inch-diameter chunk of octopus on the hook, sliding it past the eye and onto the leader knot, or ribbon fold and hook a squid in the same way. Then impale a half herring below it as usual. The combination is deadly, because even if the herring is stolen, the mollusk remains. The deeper the angler is fishing, the more he or she appreciates that quality.

Fresh gray cod, cut in steaks or in fillets, is a tough, toothsome bait. Salmon heads or strips work well. Whole, frozen pinks or chums are reasonable to use even at grocery store prices. A 2-by-10-inch strip of salmon split six inches from one end and hooked at the other makes a superb bait. Even when tattered by numerous strikes, it retains its appeal. Leave it on when adding a new one and spice the bait with a piece of herring. Scents such as herring, shrimp oil, or even a garlic spray can help attract fish.

Techniques

When using bait, free spool the sinker to the bottom with a thumb-controlled fall. This prevents leader/line tangles and a backlash on the reel when the weight stops. Also, occasional stops during the fall reduce the belly in the line, especially in a strong current. Engage the gear mechanism and crank two or three turns. Set the drag at two-thirds tension so that line will barely release. Hold the rod horizontally and gently undulate the bait by raising and lowering the rod tip. Keep the bait within three feet of the ocean floor. During slack tide big fish can be caught five to15 feet up (or higher), and sometimes they can be at any depth in the water column (visible on your fish finder or depth sounder).

Remember that most bites start as gentle tugs or nibbles. Give slack line by dropping the rod tip to a 45-degree down angle. Wait a count of 10. If the fish puts immediate heavy pressure or runs with

Metzler Mooch-A-Jig 12

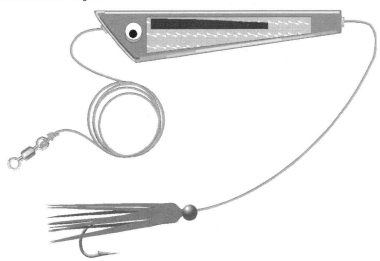

the bait, you needn't wait the full count. If the fish doesn't tighten the line, lift the rod gently with your thumb locked against the reel spool until you feel solid weight and/or a head shake. Set the hook with a short, hard strike. Don't lift the rod past 45 degrees up on the set or while pumping the fish. As soon as the fish is hooked, remove your thumb pressure or risk getting it burned.

Hang on! The fish may run. If it does, lower the rod tip and lighten the drag so that the line doesn't break while still maintaining pressure on the fish. Sometimes the captain may have to maneuver the boat to follow the fish. Only when the fish stops should you retighten the drag and begin to bring it in with a pumping action. Lift the rod without reeling, then drop the tip and crank on the way down. Use your thumb to level the line while reeling it in. Take your time to enjoy the fish. It's less wear on you and on your gear, making it easier to boat the fish when it's tired.

Two main fishing techniques are used with jigs. With lead heads, allow the jig to hit bottom. Raise the rod to lift the lure two to four feet, then allow it to drop while keeping constant line tension since bites usually come on the fall. Grand, sweeping lifts are not necessary. Gentle lifts and drops, punctuated by an occasional dramatic upsweep, are more effective and less tiring. If your boat is anchored and the bottom is smooth, rest the jig on it for a minute, then snap it up. This can produce a savage strike. Otherwise, maintain intermittent contact with the bottom until you strike a fish. The upturned hook design of lead heads snags the ocean floor less than other styles.

Jigs with single or treble hooks at the bottom end require a modified technique. Once the lure touches bottom, reel two or three turns before beginning to jig.

Both methods demand keeping constant tension on the line once a fish is hooked in order to prevent the counter-weighted hook from working free (and releasing the fish). Some serious anglers slip a second hook (sizes 10/0 to 12/0 O'Shaughnessy) over the point of the jig's hook after installing the rubber tail. This stinger hook settles to the bottom of the jig hook's bend, where it nabs short striking fish.

Let the crew know as soon as you see the fish. Do not lift its head out of the water as that usually will send it diving back to the bottom. Loosen the drag and hold the fish suspended with your thumb on the reel spool. On the crew's order lift the fish the rest of the way to the top, making every effort to have it lay flat. Then it can be harpooned or gaffed. It may be shot and/or it may be bled with a cut to the gills. When the fish is pulled over the railing, it's your job to grab and hold the sinker, releasing it only after the fish is pacified and unhooked. This saves the crew from injury by a flying sinker caused by a thrashing fish. Have the line, leader, and hook checked for damage before baiting again.

Drifting is used to prospect for fish concentrations, to fish when tides and currents are too strong for safe anchoring, or to fish well-known holes where it's important to be able to stay with a big fish (and keep it from taking all of your line). This method is tough on gear because of snags. It requires a deft touch to keep that from happening. Hooks require more frequent sharpening.

Anchoring can be a very productive waiting game. Anglers' baits alone establish a scent trail that leads fish to your hook, but a scent bag of ground fish and oils tied on the anchor chain can draw fish even better. Also, while on anchor you soon learn the contour of the bottom under your boat, preventing the loss of gear.

Fly-fishing for Halibut

It's possible to catch halibut on flies, and these days experts are busy developing techniques for this infant sport. Apparently, the best times to fish are in the spring when the fish first come into shallow water to feed and then again in late summer when they return to creek mouths to dine on washed-out salmon carcasses. It's critical to fish in clear waters, such as those of Southeast, Prince William Sound, or the Aleutians since the fly purist depends on a sight-feeding response from his quarry. Casting from a boat anchored in 25 feet of water over a salmon migration route or a school of spawning herring, with a scent bag hanging, should offer one successful approach.

Rods, reels, and lines suitable for king salmon, tarpon, or bill fish should be suitable for halibut. An 11- or 12-weight rod, a saltwater drag reel with 200 yards of 30-pound test Dacron backing, and a cannonball sink-tip line would do the trick. One- or two-hook herring or needlefish pattern flies on needle-sharp saltwater hooks are good options, with an extra large flesh fly a possibility for the late summer and fall salmon feeding frenzy. The spring phenomenon of halibut feeding actively in three- to six-foot depths on schools of out-migrating salmon smolts offers an ideal opportunity for the fly angler fortunate enough to be there at the right time.

Guides' Tips

1. Use the best gear you can afford and then take care of it. Don't scrimp on terminal tackle—it doesn't take a big fish long to expose the weakness of any swivel, leader, or hook.

2. Use a tide table when planning any halibut trip in order to maximize your chances of success. Avoid the big minus or plus tides when water movement will limit your time to fish. A midmorning and a midafternoon change would be ideal.

3. Learn good knots. Practice and use them, particularly for the new Spectra fiber lines.

4. Keep your bait or lure near the bottom.

5. Be patient. Give the fish time to take the bait well into its mouth before striking. Big baits for big fish demand even more time.

6. Respect the power of the fish. Kill it cleanly, then immobilize it in case it thrashes reflexively. An easy way to do this is to tie a rope around the tail and then run it through the gills and mouth before cinching it tight like a bowstring.

7. Respect the meat (worth up to $8 per pound retail). Bleed the fish, keep its dark side down, and keep it cool. Do not put it back in the water. Once dead, a fish loses its ability to keep external water from penetrating its skin, causing the flesh to soften. Use ice or dampened cloth such as burlap to cool it.

8. Match your gear to the situation. If taking your own rod and reel on a charter where the boat uses 130-pound test line, don't take your 50- or 80-pounder. Don't use Dacron if the boat has Spectra. Try to match the style of their leaders and their sinker weights. Single hook rigs are quicker, easier, and safer for the crew to unhook when you want to release a fish. The place for fancy rigs and light lines is on a private boat or charter where your actions won't negatively impact others by reducing their fishing time.

Alaska's Major Halibut Locations

Southeast

- **Revillagigedo Channel:** Foggy Bay, White Reef, Snail Rock, Point Alava
- **East Behm Canal:** Alava, Princess Bays; Short Pass
- **Clarence Strait:** Doctor, Clover Points; Twenty-Fathom Bank; Grindall Passage; Vallenar, Kasaan Bays
- **Bucareli Bay:** Ports Caldera, Saint Nicholas, Estrella; San Alberto Bay; Baker, Cabras, San Juan Bautista, San Fernando Islands; San Cristobal Channel; Point Providence
- **West Behm Canal:** Behm Narrows; Helm Bay; Betton, Back Islands
- **Gulf of Esquibel:** Maurelle, St. Joseph, Noyes Islands; Warm Chuck Inlet; San Cristoval Channel
- **Sumner Strait:** Point Baker; Port Protection; the Eye Opener; McArthur Reef; Kah Sheets Bay; Vank, Sokolof, Greys, Rynda, Liesnoi, Kadin Islands; lower Duncan Canal
- **Upper Clarence Strait:** Blashke, Rose Islands; Seal Rock; Key Reef; upper Kashevarof Passage
- **Ernest Sound:** Point Warde; Blake Island
- **Zimovia Strait:** Young Rock; Woronkofski Island
- **Frederick Sound:** Thomas, Portage, Pybus Bays; Sukoi Islets; Frederick, Boulder, West Points; upper Wrangell Narrows; Pinta Rocks; Turnabout Island; Cape Fanshaw
- **Chatham Strait:** Tebenkof, Sitkoh, Florence, Funter Bays; North Passage Point; Gedney Harbor; Tenaker Inlet; Hanus Reef
- **Sitka Sound:** Vitskari Rocks; St. Lazaria Island; Starrigavan Bay; Olga, Hayward Straits; Nakwasina Sound/Passage
- **Lower Stephens Passage:** Pybus, Gambier, Holkham Bays; Midway, Whitney Islands
- **Upper Stephens Passage:** Taku Harbor; Grand, Colt, Horse, Shelter Islands; Gastineau, Saginaw, Favorite Channels; Young, Auke Bays; Outer, Middle, Inner Points
- **Lynn Canal:** Vanderbilt Reef; St. James Bay; Poundstone Rock
- **Icy Strait:** Point Couverden; Couverden, Spasski, Hoonah, Pleasant, Lemesurier Islands; the Sisters; Port Frederick; Halibut Rock; Icy, South Passages; Mud Bay; outer Idaho Inlet

Alaska's Top 10 Trophy Halibut

459 pounds, 0 ounces (state record)	Unalaska Bay (Southwest)	1996
450 pounds, 0 ounces	Cook Inlet (Southcentral)	1995
440 pounds, 0 ounces	Point Adolphus (Southeast)	1978
439 pounds, 0 ounces	Dutch Harbor (Southwest)	1995
422 pounds, 0 ounces	Ugak Bay (Southcentral)	1992
404 pounds, 9 ounces	Icy Strait (Southeast)	1981
379 pounds, 0 ounces	Cook Inlet (Southcentral)	1996
376 pounds, 0 ounces	Lutak Inlet (Southeast)	1992
374 pounds, 0 ounces	Kachemak Bay (Southcentral)	1985
372 pounds, 0 ounces	Cook Inlet (Southcentral)	1985

Southcentral

- **Resurrection Bay/Blying Sound:** Capes Junken, Fairfield, Cleare; Latouche Passage; Chiswell Islands; Nootka Bay
- **Cook Inlet:** Ninilchik; Deep Creek; Happy Valley; Anchor Point; Compass Rose; Point Pogibishi; Flat, Elizabeth, Barren Islands; the Sand Waves; Magic Mountain; the Deep
- **Kodiak:** Williams Reef, Buoy Four, Long Island, Whale Pass, Chiniak Bay, Humpback Point
- **Prince William Sound:** Jack, Galena, Anderson Bays; Potato Point; Naked, Montague Islands

Southwest

- **Unalaska/Dutch Harbor:** Hog Island; Devilfish Point; Unalga Pass; Capes Cheerful, Wislow

Adventure, solitude, and some outstanding fishing can be had on Alaska's remote Arctic lakes and rivers.

Chapter 1

Arctic Fishing

Arctic Alaska

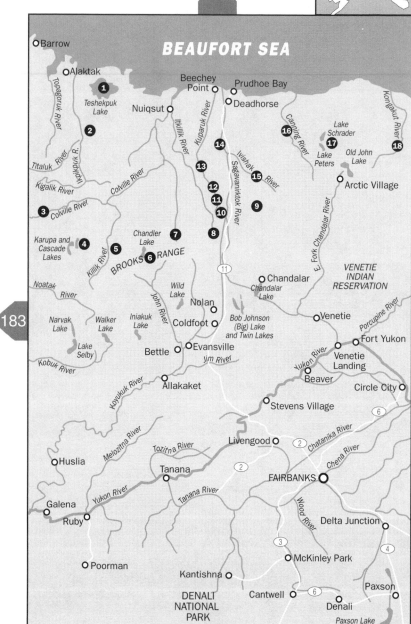

BEAUFORT SEA

Barrow

Alaktak

Topagoruk River

1 Teshekpuk Lake

Beechey Point

Prudhoe Bay

Deadhorse

Kongakut River

Nuiqsut

Kuparuk River

2

Ikkllik River

16

Canning River

Lake Schrader

17

18

Titaluk River

Ikpikpuk R.

14

Lake Peters

Old John Lake

Kigalik River

13

Ivishak River

Colville River

15

12

Sagavanirktok River

Arctic Village

3 Colville River

11

10

9

Karupa and Cascade Lakes

4

5

Chandler Lake

7

8

Killik River

BROOKS 6 RANGE

11

VENETIE INDIAN RESERVATION

Noatak River

John River

Wild Lake

Chandalar

Chandalar Lake

E. Fork Chandalar River

Porcupine River

Narvak Lake

Walker Lake

Iniakuk Lake

Nolan

Bob Johnson (Big) Lake and Twin Lakes

Venetie

183

Lake Selby

Coldfoot

Fort Yukon

204

Kobuk River

Bettle

Evansville

Jim River

Venetie Landing

Koyukuk River

Allakaket

Yukon River

Beaver

Circle City

Stevens Village

6

Huslia

Melozitna River

Tozitna River

Livengood

2

Chatanika River

Chena River

Tanana

2

FAIRBANKS

Galena

Yukon River

Tanana River

Wood River

Delta Junction

Ruby

4

3

Poorman

McKinley Park

Kantishna

Cantwell

6

Paxson

DENALI NATIONAL PARK

Denali

Paxson Lake

Arctic Hot Spots

Arctic

Like a great wall, the 720-mile arc of the Brooks Range divides waters flowing west and south to the Yukon and Kotzebue Sound from those flowing north to the Arctic Ocean. The Brooks Range also seals off the northernmost part of the state from the climate, vegetation, and human development to the south. This area, from the crest of the Brooks Range north to the Beaufort and Chukchi Seas, is called the Arctic or North Slope, or simply the "Slope." It is Alaska's true Arctic, the state's most remote, inhospitable, and least visited region. Offering limited fishing variety and a short open-water season, and with expensive access and notoriously difficult weather, the Slope certainly can't compete solely as an angling destination with Alaska's gentler and better endowed regions. But it does have some unique fishing opportunities, in addition to some of the last true wilderness—the Arctic National Wildlife Refuge (ANWR)—and most pristine rivers in North America. Adventurers willing to take on the Slope will find rich rewards on the rivers, lakes, tundra, and mountains of Alaska's Arctic.

Country, Climate, and Conditions

The broad, flat, treeless coastal plain is the feature that most people associate with the Slope. Underlain by permanently frozen ground with poor drainage, much of this area is covered with small, shallow "thaw" lakes, most of which are barren of fish populations (Teshekpuk and some central coastal plain lakes are the exceptions—see description on page 171 for details). The rivers, almost all north-flowing, rapid-runoff streams, originate in the foothills and mountains of the Brooks Range to the south. The more outstanding ones, clear flowing and spring fed, along with a handful of scattered, deep mountain lakes, provide most of the region's better fishing opportunities.

The extreme climate is the major factor limiting the area's fishing potential. For much of the year, the Arctic Slope suffers a cruel regime of darkness, bitter cold (temperatures running minus 30 to minus 50 degrees Fahrenheit), and near constant winds, alleviated only by the return of the spring sun in April. Ice can reach a thickness of seven feet and persist into July in some areas, with many rivers and shallow lakes freezing solid by winter's end. The surprisingly scant precipitation—eight inches or less for most of the region—creates rapidly fluctuating and turbid water conditions in most of the streams, many of which can practically dry up after the spring thaw. All of this doesn't sound very appealing to fish, and species like salmon are at their very limits of environmental tolerance here. Chum and pinks are found only sporadically, while other types of salmon are practically nonexistent. The charrs—arctic, Dolly Varden, and lake trout—and grayling are the only sport fish that really thrive here, providing most of the Slope's fishing opportunities. A few northern pike, along with whitefish and some burbot, round out the Slope's species.

Beyond curtailing fishing options, the climate also impedes exploration and enjoyment of this area. Ice breakup generally comes in late May or early June, but can be delayed into July in the high-elevation lakes and in some areas along the coast, while freeze-up can begin as early as mid-September. From late May through August, you can expect sunny and reasonably temperate weather here, with temperatures in the 40s to 70s (degrees Fahrenheit), even climbing to the 80s in the foothills. Come prepared for damp, cold winds, extended foggy periods, and even snow at any time during summer. This is true especially along the coast, where the advancing and retreating ice pack greatly affects the weather. Swarms of mosquitoes and other biting insects infest the inland tundra during the warmer months of June and July, making head nets, bug jackets, and repellent mandatory.

If all of this has put you off from even considering this region, be assured that it's not as bad as it sounds, but you must come well prepared. Few places on Earth can be so unforgiving, and nowhere in Alaska will you be so isolated. Only highly experienced wilderness trekkers, with the finest quality gear and a meticulously planned expedition, should attempt this region without the assistance of a veteran guide.

Arctic Fishing Highlights

While the Arctic's sportfishing certainly won't win any awards for diversity, most of its streams and lakes get little or no pressure—only from occasional hunters or native subsistence users—so they offer potentially very high quality wild fishing, particularly for lake trout, big sea-run charr, and grayling. Countless lakes and streams beckon with the promise of virgin angling, but the price of getting in and out is high, and the window of opportunity for good weather and open water very narrow.

Access, Services, and Costs

Except for a few scattered villages and some oil industry facilities, the Arctic Slope is totally uninhabited. Access is almost exclusively by plane (from Bettles or Fairbanks), except along the North Slope Haul Road (also known as the Dalton Highway), which bisects the region from Prudhoe Bay to Atigun Pass (see the descriptions of the Dalton Highway locations on page 176). Distances are great; services and facilities are extremely limited and expensive. Air taxi from the major hubs (Deadhorse, Umiat, Kaktovik, and Barrow) to and from area fishing locations typically can cost up to $1,000 or more for a party of two.

Arctic Run Timing

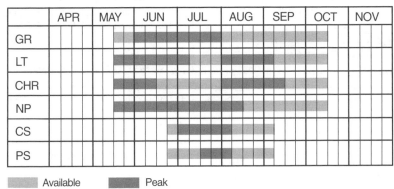

	APR	MAY	JUN	JUL	AUG	SEP	OCT	NOV
GR								
LT								
CHR								
NP								
CS								
PS								

Available   Peak

GR=Grayling, LT=Lake Trout, CHR=Charr, NP=Northern Pike, CS=Chum Salmon, PS=Pink Salmon

Note: Time periods shown are for bright fish, in the case of salmon entering rivers, or for general availability for resident species. Salmon are present in many systems long after the periods shown, but are usually in spawning/postspawning condition. Peak sportfishing periods for each species are highlighted. Run timing can vary somewhat from drainage to drainage and generally follows a later trend in waters to the west and north in Alaska. Check with local contacts listed for area run-timing specifics.

Western Central Slope

The barren coastal plain predominates (to 115 miles inland) in the western and central Arctic Slope regions, with expansive wet tundra, winding rivers, and thousands of shallow lakes. Significant sportfishing possibilities are limited to the giant Colville River system and certain lakes (many unnamed) near the coast, between the Colville and Ikpikpuk Rivers. Because of the isolation and difficulty of access, these waters see little visitation at present, but have noteworthy potential for high-quality wild fishing (for lake trout, grayling, and some salmon). Access is from Umiat, Prudhoe Bay, or Barrow.

❶ Teshekpuk Lake

Location: On the central Arctic coastal plain, 75 miles southeast of Barrow, 430 miles northwest of Fairbanks; see map page 168.

USGS maps: Teshekpuk B-1, B-2, C-1, C-2; Harrison Bay C-5.

How to get there: By floatplane or helicopter from Barrow, Umiat, or Deadhorse (via scheduled or chartered flights from Fairbanks).

Highlights: One of the Arctic's least visited but most promising lake trout fisheries.

Species: Grayling, lake trout.

Regulations: Open year-round, all species.

Facilities: No developed public facilities.

Contact: For an air taxi, contact Umiat Air Service, P.O. Box 60569, Fairbanks, AK 99706; (907) 488-2366.

Fishing Teshekpuk Lake: The largest body of water on Alaska's North Slope, Teshekpuk Lake runs 25 miles across and covers 315 square miles. Located on the coast 12 miles west of Harrison Bay, it's an anomaly (along with other nearby lakes east of the lower Ikpikpuk River) among the thousands of shallow, coastal plain thaw lakes. Teshekpuk's abundant fish populations include substantial numbers of grayling and hefty lake trout (which are larger than average, judging from samples taken by locals and the Alaska Department of Fish and Game). For anyone seeking largely untouched, concentrated lake trout opportunities, with the potential for large fish, Teshekpuk Lake, and the neighboring Ikpikpuk Lakes, are worth a visit.

❷ Central Coastal Plain Lakes

Location: On the central Arctic coastal plain, 75 miles southeast of Barrow, 415 miles northwest of Fairbanks; see map page 168.

USGS maps: Teshekpuk A-1, A-2, A-3, B-1, B-2, B-3; Harrison Bay A-4, A-5, B-4, B-5; Umiat C-5, D-5.

How to get there: By floatplane or helicopter from Barrow, Umiat, or Deadhorse (all serviced by regularly scheduled flights from Fairbanks).

Highlights: An unexplored frontier of wild lake trout fishing.

Species: Grayling, lake trout.

Regulations: Open year-round, all species.

Facilities: No developed public facilities.

Contact: For an air taxi, contact Umiat Air Service, P.O. Box 60569, Fairbanks, AK 99706; (907) 488-2366.

Fishing the Central Coastal Plain Lakes: The Ikpikpuk River flows from the foothills of the Brooks Range onto the coastal plain and into Smith Bay, west of Teshekpuk Lake. It is sluggish and shallow, with tea-colored water, and only an occasional grayling or northern pike to tempt anglers. Of greater interest here are the dozens of small, unnamed lakes lying east of the river in the central coastal plain, south of Teshekpuk and west of the Colville River (see next listing). All of the lakes are relatively shallow, but the deeper ones (depths greater than 20 feet) support fish populations. Like Teshekpuk, many of these lakes contain abundant grayling and good-sized lake trout. These are remote and expensive waters to access, but they're virtually unexplored and offer exciting fishing possibilities.

❸ Colville River

Location: On the western Arctic coastal plain, 335 miles northwest of Fairbanks; see map page 168.

USGS maps: Misheguk Mountain C-2, C-3, D-2, D-3; Utukok River A-1, A-2; Lookout Ridge A-4, A-5; Howard Pass D-1, D-2, D-3, D-4; Killik River D-5; Ikpikpuk River A-1, A-2, A-3, A-4, A-5; Umiat A-5, B-3, B-4, B-5, C-3, D-3; Harrison Bay A-2, A-3, B-1, B-2.

How to get there: By floatplane or wheelplane from Umiat, Kaktovik, Fairbanks, Bettles, or Deadhorse to points along the river, or by boat access from Umiat to the lower river and tributaries.

Highlights: The Arctic Slope's major river system, with good fishing potential for big sea-run charr, grayling, lake trout, and some salmon (chum and pink) in its main stem and tributaries.

Species: Charr, grayling, *chum salmon, lake trout, pink salmon.*

Regulations: Open year-round, all species.

Facilities: The town of Umiat, located along the lower river, has limited services and facilities; otherwise, there are no developed public facilities.

Contact: For guided or unguided float trips down Colville headwaters, contact Sourdough Outfitters, P.O. Box 90, Bettles, AK 99726, (907) 692-5252; or ABEC's Alaska Adventures, 1550 Alpine Vista Court, Fairbanks, AK 99712, (907) 457-8907. For an air taxi, contact Umiat Air Service, P.O. Box 60569, Fairbanks, AK 99706; (907) 488-2366.

Fishing the Colville River: The Colville is the longest river on the Arctic Slope, running over 420 miles (the seventh longest river in Alaska) with many meandering tributaries. It supports a remarkable diversity and abundance of fish for a river this far north (16 species total), with charr, chum and pink salmon, grayling, lake trout, whitefish, and others found in its vast reaches. Fish are most abundant in the main stem (from the Itkillik River to the town of Umiat), and mouths and lower sections of the tributaries. Killik, Anaktuvuk, Chandler, and Itkillik Rivers have the best stream fishing.

Not much real sportfishing occurs on the Colville, except by locals and occasionally hunters and kayakers. It's a big river with deep, long pools—not easy to fish unless you know your way around. The best solution is to contact Umiat Air Service, which can provide boat or plane transportation to the local hot spots. Because of its length, the river is seldom floated in its entirety from its headwaters, but a few of the tributaries can be run by kayak or raft, usually in early summer when the water is high. (For details on floating the Colville, contact ABEC's Alaska Adventures or Sourdough Outfitters at the address and phone number listed above.)

North Slope Foothill and Mountain Lakes

Considering the major ice-scouring the Brooks Range received during the last periods of glaciation, surprisingly few glacial lakes of any size exist in the mountains and foothills north of the divide. Most of the North Slope foothill and mountain lakes that support fish populations are small, deep-catch basins, lying at the headwaters of tributary streams of large rivers, like the vast Colville River system. Almost all of these basins have abundant lake trout, grayling, and charr, and can provide outstanding fishing adventures, especially when combined with raft or kayak floats down the rivers they are associated with. The open-water season is short, however; the elevation and latitude of most of these lakes generally results in ice cover from early October (if not before) until late June.

④ Karupa and Cascade Lakes

Location: On the central North Slope, 515 miles northwest of Anchorage; see map page 168.

USGS map: Killik River B-3.

How to get there: By plane to Bettles or Umiat via Fairbanks, then by floatplane to the lakes.

Highlights: Two of the North Slope's prettiest mountain lakes, with excellent fishing for lake trout, landlocked charr, and grayling.

Species: Charr, grayling, lake trout.

Regulations: Open year-round, all species.

Facilities: No developed public facilities.

Contact: For an air taxi, contact Bettles Air Service, P.O. Box 27, Bettles, AK 99726, (800) 770-5111.

Fishing Karupa and Cascade Lakes: Twin headwaters for the Karupa River, lovely Karupa and Cascade Lakes lie in the high mountains of Gates of the Arctic National Park, about 15 miles west of the upper Killik River. They're small but very deep—more than 120 feet, making them two of the deepest lakes in the Brooks Range. The lakes' milky turquoise waters provide good to excellent fishing for lake trout and landlocked charr, with abundant grayling in the inlet and outlet streams. Traditional sites for Eskimo hunters intercepting migrating caribou, these lakes aren't visited much by anglers because of their isolation and elevation (3,000 feet), but they're among the more outstanding small mountain lakes on the North Slope.

Cascade Lake lies on the other side of a high ridge, about a mile northeast of Karupa, and is connected to it by a short gorge at its southern end. Cascade is smaller (about two miles long), but higher in elevation by 500 feet than its twin, Karupa. Cascade usually has more abundant fishing and clearer water than Karupa. The outlet stream is noted for its fine grayling fishing. With nice beaches for camping, Cascade is certainly worth the hike over from Karupa if you're planning a trip there.

⑤ Killik River Lakes

Location: On the central North Slope, 490 miles northwest of Anchorage; see map page 168.

USGS maps: Killik River A-2, A-3, B-2, C-2, D-1; Ikpikpuk River A-2.

How to get there: By plane to Bettles or Umiat via Fairbanks, then by wheelplane or floatplane to the lakes or gravel bars along the upper river. It is possible to float by kayak or raft to the Colville River and the outpost of Umiat, or to plane-accessible points downriver.

Highlights: One of more popular North Slope drainages for recreation, with good fishing potential for grayling, charr, lake trout, and rare northern pike in its many headwater lakes.

Species: Charr, grayling, lake trout, northern pike, *chum salmon, pink salmon.*

Regulations: Open year-round, all species.

Facilities: No developed public facilities.

Contact: For guide services, contact Sourdough Outfitters, P.O. Box 90, Bettles, AK 99726; (907) 692-5252. For an air taxi, contact Umiat Air Service, P.O. Box 60569, Fairbanks, AK 99706; (907) 488-2366.

Fishing Killik River Lakes: The Killik is one of the better known North Slope rivers, with a reputation for outstanding float trip possibilities. The river begins in the Brooks Range in Gates of the Arctic National Park, then flows 105 miles north to the Colville River. As it emerges from the mountains, the upper river area encompasses quite a few small, clustered lakes (Udrivik, Imiaknikpak, Kaniksrak, and Tululik) that are moderately deep and hold lake trout and charr, along with some of the Slope's few opportunities for northern pike. Wildlife viewing and hiking along the river are quite outstanding. Below the lakes, the Killik picks up steam, with canyons, rapids (some rated Class II and Class III), and heavily braided sections. From here, the trip down to the Colville by raft or kayak can be a real adventure.

❻ Chandler Lakes

Location: On the central North Slope, 274 miles northwest of Fairbanks; see map page 168.

USGS maps: Chandler Lake A-5, B-5.

How to get there: By plane to Bettles or Umiat via Fairbanks, then by floatplane to the lakes.

Highlights: A more popular North Slope fly-in lake with good to excellent fishing for land-locked charr, lake trout, and grayling.

Species: Charr, grayling, lake trout.

Regulations: Open year-round, all species.

Facilities: No developed public facilities.

Contact: For information, contact Gates of the Arctic National Park and Preserve, P.O. Box 74680, Fairbanks, AK 99707; (907) 456-0281. For an air taxi, contact Bettles Air Service, P.O. Box 27, Bettles, AK 99726, (800) 770-5111.

Fishing Chandler Lakes: On the edge of Gates of the Arctic National Park, 26 miles west of Anaktuvuk Pass, lies lovely Chandler Lake. In a beautiful setting at nearly 3,000 feet elevation, it is the largest mountain lake on the North Slope (five miles long). Along with several other good fishing lakes (Little Chandler, White, and Amiloyak Lakes), it forms the headwaters of the Chandler River. Chandler Lake is known for its lake trout and landlocked charr fishing, with larger fish (including lakers up to 30 pounds) more common than in most other mountain lakes of the region. Grayling are also abundant in the inlet and outlet streams.

Amiloyak is the uppermost lake in the Chandler chain, situated in a valley near the Continental Divide, about seven miles southwest of Chandler Lake. It's small, less than two miles long, but has excellent fishing for lake trout (up to 20 pounds) and landlocked charr (up to six pounds), with some grayling in several tributary creeks. You can also hike to fish nearby Agiak Lake, two miles on the other side of the divide. Little Chandler lies to the north, adjacent to and a tributary of the big lake, connected by a short outlet. It, too, has decent fishing. White Lake lies in a bowl off the river, a few miles northwest of Big Chandler. It also has good lake trout and charr populations. However, being situated at a 3,000-foot elevation this far north, these waters are only ice free for a short time each year, from mid-June to early September.

❼ Anaktuvuk River Lakes

Location: In the central Brooks Range, 260 miles northwest of Fairbanks; see map page 168.

USGS maps: Chandler Lake A-3, B-3, C-2, C-3, D-2, D-3.

How to get there: By plane to Bettles via Fairbanks, then by floatplane or wheelplane to the headwaters. Raft or kayak trips are possible on the river to points below the headwaters, with wheelplane pickup.

Highlights: An important North Slope river, with good fishing potential for grayling, lake trout, and big charr.

Species: Charr, grayling, lake trout.

Regulations: Open year-round, all species.

Facilities: No developed public facilities.

Contact: For guide services, contact Sourdough Outfitters, P.O. Box 90, Bettles, AK 99726; (907) 692-5252. For an air taxi, contact Umiat Air Service, P.O. Box 60569, Fairbanks, AK 99706, (907) 488-2366; or Bettles Air Service, P.O. Box 27, Bettles, AK 99726, (800) 770-5111.

Fishing Anaktuvuk River Lakes: Long associated with the central Brooks Range Eskimo culture, the Anaktuvuk is one of the more significant North Slope rivers. For thousands of years, the indigenous Nunamuit peoples have hunted caribou along the river's banks and fished its waters for sea-run charr, grayling, and lake trout. The river rises in the Endicott Mountains (on the edge of Gates of the Arctic National Park), and flows 135 miles to the Colville. Numerous small and moderately deep lakes (such as Tulugak, Irgnyivik, and Natvakruak), nearly all with good lake trout and grayling fishing, lie along the upper river. The swift and braided Anaktuvuk River, known for abundant, big grayling and charr, can be floated during higher water down to the Colville. It's a rewarding trip, and July is generally the best month to undertake it; check with air taxi services for the latest conditions.

Shainin or Willow Lake is located 22 miles northeast of Anaktuvuk Pass, at the head of the Kanayut River, a major tributary of the Anaktuvuk River. It's a small but pretty alpine lake (elevation 2,700 feet), with milky blue, deep water and abundant grayling and lake trout, even some charr. It doesn't get fished much, except by a few Eskimo hunters, but it's worth considering if you're planning a trip to the Anaktuvuk area. Folks who have fished it report outstanding catches from August through early September.

⑧ Itkillik Lake

Location: In the central Brooks Range, 270 miles northwest of Fairbanks; see map page 168.

USGS map: Philip Smith Mountains B-5.

How to get there: By plane to Bettles or Umiat via Fairbanks, then by floatplane to the lake. A winter trail is accessible from the Dalton Highway at Galbraith Lake.

Highlights: A well-known Brooks Range lake with good fishing for lake trout and grayling.

Species: Charr, grayling, lake trout.

Regulations: Open year-round, all species.

Facilities: No developed public facilities.

Contact: For an air taxi, contact Bettles Air Service, P.O. Box 27, Bettles, AK 99726; (800) 770-5111.

Fishing Itkillik Lake: Thanks to its proximity to the Dalton Highway (just 15 miles west of Pump Station no. 4) and good fishing, Itkillik Lake has been one of the more popular foothill lakes. Slightly smaller than Shainin Lake (see previous listing), Itkillik is located within Gates of the Arctic National Park, where it heads a river by the same name that drains into the Colville River, 220 miles south. Fishing has always been good for lake trout and grayling, but it has been hit more in recent years by folks who access the highway lakes north of Atigun Pass.

⑨ Elusive Lake

Location: In the central Brooks Range, 12 miles east of the Dalton Highway, 260 miles north of Fairbanks; see map page 168.

USGS map: Philip Smith Mountains C-3.

How to get there: By small wheelplane or floatplane from Arctic Village, Bettles, or Umiat. There is also winter trail access by snowmachine from the Dalton Highway.

Highlights: Good lake trout fishing with relatively easy access.

Species: Grayling, lake trout.

Regulations: Open year-round, all species.

Facilities: No developed public facilities.

Contact: For an air taxi, contact Umiat Air Service, P.O. Box 60569, Fairbanks, AK 99706, (907) 488-2366; or Bettles Air Service, P.O. Box 27, Bettles, AK 99726, (800) 770-5111.

Fishing Elusive Lake: Located in the Ribdon River Valley, 12 miles east of the Dalton Highway, Elusive Lake can be accessed by wheelplane (there's a gravel strip on the east end of the lake) and floatplane, or by a snowmachine trail during the winter from a highway maintenance camp on the Dalton. It's one of the more popular foothill lakes for ice fishing (lake trout), especially in late winter and early spring.

Dalton Highway

The 414-mile Dalton Highway, or North Slope Haul Road, was built in 1974 by the Alyeska Pipeline Service Company to facilitate construction and maintenance of the Trans-Alaska Pipeline. Originally reserved for support services and oil field personnel, the Dalton south of Disaster Creek (Dietrich Camp, milepost 211) first opened to the general public in June 1981, with travel restrictions along the remainder lifted in 1995. Sportfishing for all species, except salmon, is now allowed along the road corridor (five miles on each side).

The Dalton north of Atigun Pass provides limited access to a number of North Slope lakes and rivers, including the Toolik, Galbraith, and Campsite Lake areas and the Kuparuk, Toolik, and Sagavanirktok Rivers. Fishing opportunities for lake trout, charr, and grayling are plentiful in most of these waters, especially for folks who take the initiative to explore beyond the immediate reaches of the road. For instance, dozens of small, fish-filled lakes lie within hiking distance of the highway between Pump Stations nos. 3 and 4. You can reach the Sagavanirktok River, a prime drainage for large sea-run charr, from certain points north of Pump Station no. 3. With an inflatable raft or canoe, the possibilities are almost limitless. Adventurous anglers planning on traveling this primitive road should come prepared, however, for a shortage of services (there are none north of Coldfoot), hazardous driving with dust, flying rocks, and barreling 18-wheelers, and few pullouts to stop at along the way. The most popular time to travel the Dalton for fishing is from July through mid-September, with late spring (April) ice-fishing safaris by snowmachine a tantalizing option.

⑩ Galbraith Lakes

Location: In the central Brooks Range, 250 miles north of Fairbanks, adjacent to the Dalton Highway; see map page 168.

USGS map: Philip Smith Mountains B-5.

How to get there: By wheelplane to an airstrip 1.5 miles west of Galbraith Lakes, or by hiking from the Dalton Highway near Pump Station no. 4 (mileposts 270 and 276).

Highlights: Easily accessible lakes with good seasonal fishing for lake trout, charr, and grayling.

Species: Charr, grayling, lake trout.

Regulations: Open year-round, all species except salmon.

Facilities: No developed public facilities.

Contact: For an air taxi, contact Umiat Air Service, P.O. Box 60569, Fairbanks, AK 99706, (907) 488-2366; or Bettles Air Service, P.O. Box 27, Bettles, AK 99726, (800) 770-5111. For the latest road conditions, contact the Department of Transportation at (907) 456-7623.

Fishing Galbraith Lakes: Galbraith, Tee, and Atigun Lakes lie in the lower Atigun River Valley, adjacent to the west side of the Dalton Highway near Pump Station no. 4. Situated at a 2,600-foot elevation, these are mountain lakes, with beautiful scenery and fairly abundant fishing, but with a limited season of open water. Galbraith has always been the most productive and popular of these waters, with good seasonal catches of lake trout and landlocked charr. The other two lakes, the largest of a group of lakes along the upper Atigun River, contain good fishing as well, and may be reached from milepost 270, near the access road to Pump Station no. 4. The best time to fish these waters is from late June through early July and August.

⑪ Campsite Lakes

Location: Five miles south of the Dalton Highway, 12 miles east of Toolik Lake; see map page 168.

USGS map: Philip Smith Mountains C-4.

How to get there: By hike-in trail from the Dalton Highway.

Highlights: Easy hike-in lakes off the Dalton Highway, with fairly abundant lake trout and charr fishing.

Species: Charr, grayling, lake trout.

Regulations: Open year-round, all species.

Facilities: No developed public facilities.

Contact: For an air taxi, contact Umiat Air Service, P.O. Box 60569, Fairbanks, AK 99706, (907) 488-2366; or Bettles Air Service, P.O. Box 27, Bettles, AK 99726, (800) 770-5111. For the latest road conditions, contact the Department of Transportation at (907) 456-7623.

Fishing Campsite Lakes: The Campsite Lakes area includes about a dozen or more small, fairly deep lakes clustered along upper Oksrukuyik Creek, a tributary of the Sagavanirktok. Nearly all have fish in them—abundant lake trout, landlocked charr, even burbot. Campsite Lake is the largest and most popular of the group. All of them can be reached by trail from the Dalton Highway (milepost 295), and along with Toolik and Galbraith Lakes, offer the area's best chances for some really fine, road-accessible lake trout and charr fishing.

⑫ Toolik and Itagaknit Lakes

Location: Approximately 257 miles north of Fairbanks in the upper Kuparuk River drainage, adjacent to the Dalton Highway; see map page 168.

USGS map: Philip Smith Mountains C-5.

How to get there: By plane or car. A marked access road leads one mile west of the Dalton (milepost 284) to Toolik Lake.

Highlights: A very popular Dalton Highway lake area, with good seasonal fishing for lake trout and grayling.

Species: Charr, grayling, lake trout.

Regulations: Open year-round, all species except salmon. For details, consult the current Alaska Department of Fish and Game regulations or contact the ADF&G Fairbanks office, (907) 456-4359.

Facilities: No developed public facilities.

Contact: For an air taxi, contact Umiat Air Service, P.O. Box 60569, Fairbanks, AK 99706, (907) 488-2366; or Bettles Air Service, P.O. Box 27, Bettles, AK 99726, (800) 770-5111. For the latest road conditions, contact the Department of Transportation at (907) 456-7623.

Fishing Toolik and Itagaknit Lakes: Toolik and Itagaknit are the largest of a group of clustered lakes along the upper Kuparuk River drainage, just a short distance west of the Dalton Highway (the nearest lake can be reached by access road or a nearby airstrip). Small but deep (up to 100 feet), the lakes and their numerous connecting streams have good populations of grayling, and small- to medium-sized lake trout and charr. With a little hiking and exploring in the spring or fall, you can find some less fished, more productive waters.

⑬ Kuparuk River

Location: West of the Sagavanirktok River, flowing north, crossed by the Dalton Highway; see map page 168.

USGS map: Philip Smith Mountains C-4.

How to get there: By foot trail from the Dalton Highway, which it crosses (milepost 290) approximately five miles east of Toolik Lake.

Highlights: One of the North Slope's best grayling rivers, with excellent fly-fishing.

Species: Grayling, lake trout.

Regulations: Open year-round, all species.

Facilities: No developed public facilities.

Contact: For an air taxi, contact Umiat Air Service, P.O. Box 60569, Fairbanks, AK 99706, (907) 488-2366; or Bettles Air Service, P.O. Box 27, Bettles, AK 99726, (800) 770-5111. For the latest road conditions, contact the Department of Transportation at (907) 456-7623.

Fishing the Kuparuk River: The most popular grayling fishery on the North Slope, the Kuparuk flows west of the Sagavanirktok River and can be accessed easily along its upper east fork from the Dalton Highway, about five miles beyond Toolik Lake Road, at milepost 290. Kuparuk has great fly-fishing along its upper reaches; by North Slope standards, the grayling are plentiful and big. Farther upstream lies a small headwater lake of the same name, which has abundant lake trout.

⑭ Sagavanirktok River

Location: On the central Arctic Slope, 300 miles north of Fairbanks; see map page 168.

USGS maps: Philip Smith Mountains A-4, B-4, B-5, C-3, C-4, D-3, D-4; Sagavanirktok A-3, A-4, B-3, C-3, D-3; Beechey Point A-2, A-3, B-2, B-3.

How to get there: By small plane to the upper river (Atigun River or upper main stem) from Umiat, Deadhorse, Fairbanks, or Bettles. It's possible to float by kayak or raft with takeout along the lower river (Franklin Bluffs or Deadhorse). You can also access the river from the Dalton Highway at several points.

Highlights: An accessible North Slope river with outstanding fishing potential for large charr and some grayling.

Species: Charr, grayling, *chum salmon, lake trout, pink salmon.*

Regulations: Open year-round, all species except salmon. For details, consult the current Alaska Department of Fish and Game regulations or contact the ADF&G Fairbanks office, (907) 456-4359.

Facilities: No developed public facilities.

Contact: For guide services, contact Sourdough Outfitters, P.O. Box 90, Bettles, AK 99726; (907) 692-5252. For an air taxi, contact Umiat Air Service, P.O. Box 60569, Fairbanks, AK 99706, (907) 488-2366; or Wright Air Service, P.O. Box 60142, Fairbanks, AK 99706, (907) 474-0502.

Fishing the Sagavanirktok River: The "Sag" is one North Slope river that most folks have heard of, since it's closely associated with Prudhoe Bay and the Dalton Highway, which parallels the river for 100 miles. It also has a reputation as an exciting white-water float. As the North Slope's most significant drainage for sea-run charr, with major habitat in its deep pools and miles of spring-fed tributaries, the Sag has great potential as a trophy fishery (with average size three to five pounds, and fish up to 10 pounds or more not uncommon), especially given its relatively easy access.

The Sag is wide and swift (Class I mostly, with some Class II and Class III stretches), with extensive braids for most of its length. It heads into the Philip Smith Mountains of the Arctic National Wildlife Refuge, flowing south for 175 miles before emptying into the Beaufort Sea east of Prudhoe. It has 20 tributaries, some with exceptional qualities like the Ivishak River, including substantial sportfishing potential. The best thing about the Sag is its easy access. You can fly into the headwaters, float down and be picked up by plane, or access the river from the

Dalton Highway at several locations where the road passes nearby (north of Pump Station no. 3, milepost 325, and in Happy Valley). Oil field workers commonly fish channels and sloughs on the lower river, with excellent results. The charr begin their fall spawning migrations sometime in early August; the best time to fish the river is from mid-August to early September. The Sagavanirktok also offers some fine grayling action, especially during the fall months when fish on every cast is possible along the middle and upper river.

Eastern Arctic Slope

From the Canning River east to the Canadian border, the land becomes significantly more varied in form and character than the rest of the Arctic Slope. The highest peaks of the Brooks Range, running north to east, crowd out the coastal plain to a narrow strip of rolling tundra (less than 10 miles wide near the border) and give rise to some of Arctic's most significant rivers. This area, perhaps best known for its wilderness (the 19-million-acre Arctic National Wildlife Refuge, including eight million acres of designated wilderness) and wildlife (caribou, musk ox, polar bear, and wolves), also has quite a few outstanding sportfishing possibilities for trophy-sized charr, grayling, and lake trout. Access is from Arctic Village, Fort Yukon Kaktovik, or Prudhoe Bay.

⑮ Ivishak River

Location: On the central Arctic coastal plain, 320 miles north of Fairbanks; see map page 168.

USGS maps: Arctic C-5, D-5; Sagavanirktok A-1, A-2, B-2, B-3; Philip Smith Mountains C-1, D-1.

How to get there: By small floatplane to Porcupine Lake or wheelplane to gravel bars along the upper river; you can float from the headwaters to takeout points below or continue down to the Sagavanirktok River.

Highlights: A National Wild and Scenic River and outstanding North Slope float trip, with excellent fishing for trophy-sized charr and good grayling prospects.

Species: Charr, grayling, *chum salmon, lake trout, pink salmon.*

Regulations: Open year-round, all species.

Facilities: No developed public facilities.

Contact: For guide services, contact Sourdough Outfitters, P.O. Box 90, Bettles, AK 99726, (907) 692-5252; or ABEC's Alaska Adventures, 1550 Alpine Vista Court, Fairbanks, AK 99712, (907) 457-8907. For an air taxi, contact Umiat Air Service, P.O. Box 60569, Fairbanks, AK 99706, (907) 488-2366; or Wright Air Service, P.O. Box 60142, Fairbanks, AK 99706, (907) 474-0502.

Fishing the Ivishak River: This Wild and Scenic River is one of the North Slope's premier floats, making for an outstanding wilderness trip that can be finished on the Sagavanirktok River. The Ivishak is also the Sagavanirktok's most significant tributary for big sea-run charr, with abundant spawning and wintering populations and excellent sportfishing potential.

You can fly into Porcupine Lake at the headwaters and enjoy some good lake trout fishing, then float down through a beautiful canyon to the foothills and the flat coastal plain. (Some dragging of the boats will be necessary right below the lake in low water conditions.) There's a strip near the confluence of the Echooka River where you can take out, or you can continue down to the Sagavanirktok (approximately 92 miles below the lake) for a five- to seven-day trip. Scenery, hiking, and wildlife-viewing opportunities are excellent on the upper river, as is the fishing, making this one of the best all-around trips on the North Slope. The best time to fish the Ivishak for big charr is in August, but like all Slope rivers, you should check with local air taxi services for conditions before making final arrangements.

16 Canning River

Location: On the eastern Arctic coastal plain, 350 miles north of Fairbanks; see map page 168.

USGS maps: Arctic C-4, C-5, D-3, D-4; Mt. Michelson A-3, A-4, B-4, C-4, D-4; Flaxman Island A-4, A-5.

How to get there: By wheelplane from Kaktovik, Deadhorse, Fairbanks, or Arctic Village to numerous gravel bar locations along headwaters, then floating down by raft or kayak (five to seven days), with wheelplane pickup on the lower river anywhere above the delta.

Highlights: Along with the Sagavanirktok River, one of the North Slope's most significant sea-run charr rivers, with exciting float possibilities and good grayling fishing.

Species: Charr, grayling, *chum salmon, lake trout, pink salmon.*

Regulations: Open year-round, all species.

Facilities: No developed public facilities.

Contact: For guided float trips, contact ABEC's Alaska Adventures, 1550 Alpine Vista Court, Fairbanks, AK 99712; (907) 457-8907. For an air taxi, contact Wright Air Service, P.O. Box 60142, Fairbanks, AK 99706, (907) 474-0502; or Alaska Flyers, 398 Eagle Ridge, Fairbanks, AK 99712, (907) 479-7750.

Fishing the Canning River: The Canning certainly deserves mention among the North Slope's better options for sportfishing, as it supports an abundant sea-run charr population with numerous headwater springs for overwintering survival. It begins in the steep recesses of the Philip Smith Mountains of the Arctic National Wildlife Refuge, flowing north 120 miles to Camden Bay, west of Kaktovik. It's a fairly easy white-water river (Class I and Class II) that's heavily braided and silty along most of its main stem below the mountains. Your best bet would be to put in somewhere along the upper Marsh Fork where the water is clear, then float, fish, and camp down to the confluence, leaving your pickup somewhere below in the river's middle or lower section.

Fishing is good for big charr and grayling all along the upper river in late summer, and it's a pretty float with awesome mountain scenery and lots of wildlife, well worth the time and expense of getting in and out. This trip is a great way to combine the wonders of the Arctic National Wildlife Refuge with some superb angling.

17 Lakes Schrader and Peters

Location: In Arctic National Wildlife Refuge, Sadlerochit River drainage, 325 miles northeast of Fairbanks; see map page 168.

USGS map: Mount Michelson B-2.

How to get there: By small plane from Kaktovik, Deadhorse, Fairbanks, or Arctic Village.

Highlights: The Arctic National Wildlife Refuge's only major lake system, with excellent fishing possibilities for lake trout and land-locked charr.

Species: Charr, grayling, lake trout.

Regulations: Open year-round, all species.

Facilities: No developed public facilities.

Contact: For an air taxi, contact Alaska Flyers, 398 Eagle Ridge, Fairbanks, AK 99712; (907) 479-7750.

Fishing Lakes Schrader and Peters: These deep and lovely twin lakes are well off the beaten path, even for the remote Arctic Slope. Seldom visited except by locals (mostly from Kaktovik), the lakes lie at the headwaters of the Sadlerochit River in the Arctic National Wildlife Refuge. They're reputed to have some of the best trophy lake trout and landlocked charr fishing on the Slope. Fish in the 20- to 30-pound range are possible, especially in the spring.

Access is expensive, with a small plane fly-in usually from Umiat, Deadhorse, or Kaktovik, landing at a small gravel strip or on the lakes (with floats). Kaktovik residents visit the lakes mostly in late spring, by snowmachine. The ice doesn't melt until late June, so the open-water season is quite short.

⑱ Kongakut River

Location: On the eastern Arctic coastal plain in the Arctic National Wildlife Refuge, 335 miles northeast of Fairbanks; see map page 168.

USGS maps: Table Mountain D-2, D-3, D-4; Demarcation Point A-1, A-2, B-1, B-2, C-2, D-2.

How to get there: By wheelplane (from Kaktovik, Fairbanks, or Deadhorse) to gravel bars along the headwaters. It is possible to float down by raft or kayak (eight to 10 days), with wheelplane pickup on the lower river.

Highlights: The Arctic National Wildlife Refuge's most popular river, with outstanding sea-run charr and grayling fishing.

Species: Charr, grayling, *chum salmon, lake trout, pink salmon.*

Regulations: Open year-round, all species.

Facilities: No developed public facilities.

Contact: For guided float trips, contact ABEC's Alaska Adventures, 1550 Alpine Vista Court, Fairbanks, AK 99712; (907) 457-8907. For more information, contact Arctic National Wildlife Refuge (ANWR), P.O. Box 20, 101 12th Street, Fairbanks, AK 99701; (907) 456-0250. For an air taxi, contact Alaska Flyers, 398 Eagle Ridge, Fairbanks, AK 99712, (907) 479-7750; or Wright Air Service, P.O. Box 60142, Fairbanks, AK 99706, (907) 474-0502.

Fishing the Kongakut River: It would be remiss not to list the Kongakut among the North Slope's better fishing rivers, even though this drainage certainly needs no more attention of late. Hidden in Alaska's most remote northeast corner, the "Kong" was somehow unofficially chosen as the showcase river for all the wild, delicate values of the Arctic coastal plain threatened by the oil exploration proposals of the late 1980s. It has perhaps seen more visitation in the last few years than in all the time since the Ice Age.

The Kong is, without a doubt, an extraordinary river. It flows strong and clear through the rugged heart of some of Alaska's most remote wildernesses, where, with any luck, you can catch glimpses of caribou, wolves, and even musk ox, while you float through "a pristine mountain setting of great aesthetic value" (according to the U.S. Fish and Wildlife Service). The fishing is very good; everyone who floats this river is impressed, rating the charr and grayling fishery of exceptional quality (the average Kongakut charr is larger in size than those encountered in any other North Slope river). Sounds exciting, right? But remember, floating the Kongakut is an expensive, serious trip, certainly not for casual, unprepared, or unassisted wilderness trekkers. The time to float for the best fishing, weather, and stream conditions is from early July through early August.

Chapter 2

Northwest Fishing

Northwest Alaska

Alaska State Map .... *page* 8

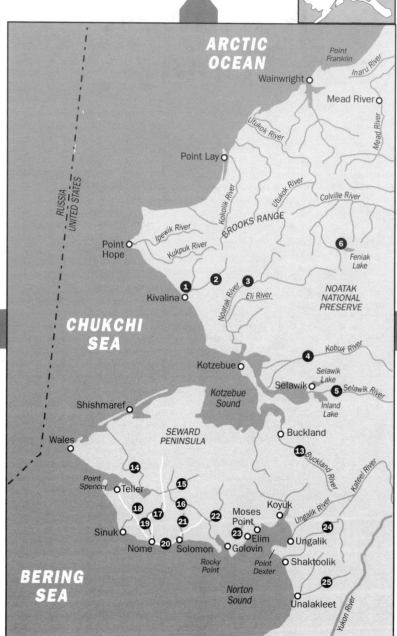

ARCTIC OCEAN

Point Franklin

Wainwright

Mead River

Inaru River

Mead River

Utukok River

Point Lay

Utukok River

Kokolik River

Colville River

BROOKS RANGE

Ipewik River

Point Hope

Kukpuk River

6

Feniak Lake

NOATAK NATIONAL PRESERVE

1   **2**   **3**

Noatak River

Eli River

Kivalina

CHUKCHI SEA

183

4   Kobuk River

Kotzebue

Selawik Lake

Selawik

5   Selawik River

Inland Lake

Kotzebue Sound

Shishmaref

SEWARD PENINSULA

Buckland

13   Buckland River

Kateel River

Wales

14

Point Spencer   Teller

15

18   **17**   **16**

Koyuk

Ungalik River

19

21   **22**

Moses Point

Sinuk

Nome   **20**   Solomon

23   Elim

Golovin

Ungalik   **24**

BERING SEA

Rocky Point

Point Dexter

Shaktoolik

Norton Sound

25

Unalakleet

Yukon River

182

226

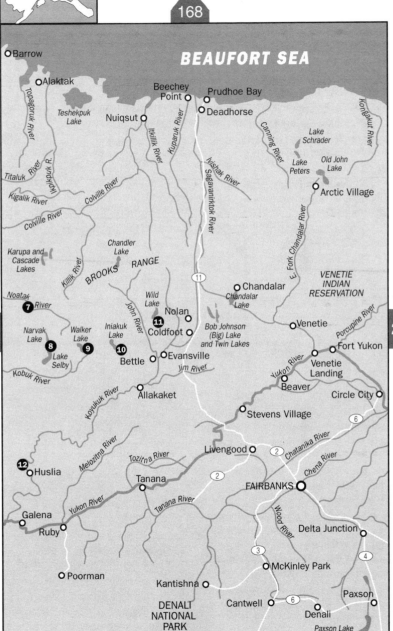

BEAUFORT SEA

○ Barrow

○ Alaktak

Teshekpuk Lake

Topagoruk River

Titaluk River

Kigalik River

Coville River

Ikpikpuk R.

Colville River

Nuiqsut ○

Ikillik River

Beechey Point ○

Prudhoe Bay
Deadhorse ○

Kuparuk River

Canning River

Ivishak River

Sagavanirktok River

Lake Schrader

Lake Peters

Old John Lake

Arctic Village ●

Kongakut River

E. Fork Chandalar River

Karupa and Cascade Lakes

Chandler Lake

BROOKS   RANGE

Killik River

John River

Wild Lake

Noatak River

7

Narvak Lake

8

Walker Lake

9

Iniakuk Lake

10

Lake Selby

Kobuk River

Nolan

11 Coldfoot ○

Bettle ○

Evansville ○

Jim River

Chandalar ○
Chandalar Lake

Bob Johnson (Big) Lake and Twin Lakes

VENETIE INDIAN RESERVATION

Venetie ○

Porcupine River

Fort Yukon ○

Venetie Landing ○

Yukon River

Beaver ○

Circle City ○

11

Koyukuk River

Allakaket ○

Stevens Village ○

6

Huslia ○

12

Melozitna River

Tozitna River

Tanana ○

Livengood ○

2

Chatanika River

Chena River

Galena ○

Ruby ○

Yukon River

Tanana River

FAIRBANKS ○

Wood River

Delta Junction ○

2

4

Poorman ○

Kantishna ○

DENALI NATIONAL PARK

Cantwell ○

McKinley Park ○

3

6

Denali ○

Paxson ○

Paxson Lake

182

204

Northwest Hot Spots

Northwest

Mike Spisak is a dangerous man. Give him five minutes on the phone and he'll get you to toss aside all worldly concerns and hop the next plane to Kotzebue. You see, Mike's a pilot with his own air taxi service, and he gets to do what most of us mortals can only dream about: He spends his working hours flying around in some of God's most awesome country, with long lunch breaks sampling some of the greatest fishing this side of Heaven. Of all the lies you'll hear in Alaska, his fish stories rank among the best. A conversation with Spisak in early April is all that's needed to get the juices flowing after a long Alaska winter. It goes something like this:

"Yep, just 20 miles across the Sound—Kobuk Lake. They're taking the big shees through the ice."

"How big?"

"Thirty, forty pounds all the time. You're not gonna believe this, but I saw an old guy draggin' what I thought was a seal behind his four-wheeler, and when I got closer, it was a sheefish. Must have been 70 pounds!"

"Mike, the world record is only 53."

"You're kidding me!"

"No. Was the fish certified anywhere?"

"Hell no, he chopped it up and fed his family and dogs with it!"

I should have ended the conversation right there. Instead, I let him go on about four-foot lake trout, pike as big as logs, 30-pound charr, and sheefish so big it takes three grown men to pull them in. Not that I'm a sucker for a story. It's just that, having been on Supercub safari with him and seen some of those tall tales come alive in the most amazing ways,

I'm not so quick to debunk any of his fantastic yarns any more. I know now, from all I've heard and seen, that the area Mike calls home, Northwest Alaska, is, without a doubt, one of the last true frontiers of fishing adventure. It's one of the world's few places where charr, sheefish, grayling, and pike reach giant sizes and succumb to old age or native stew pots long before their first encounter with a sport angler's lure. Land of the Inupiat Eskimo, big caribou herds, and Nanook the polar bear, this wilderness, with its amazing sport fish potential, promises to be the next area to open up to the inevitable wave of anglers pushing north and west for new thrills.

Country, Climate, and Conditions

Alaska's Northwest lies above the lower Yukon and includes Norton Sound, the Seward Peninsula, Kotzebue Sound, and the western Brooks Range. (For our purposes, we're including all north-flowing Arctic Ocean drainages in the Arctic chapter—see page 167.) Northwest encompasses a diverse and vast terrain, from the marshy Yukon flatlands and slight uplands along the coast to the expansive valleys and massive peaks of the Brooks Range. The land shows the transition from the more moderate taiga to the extreme tundra regime of the Arctic. Here, you'll find weird, frost-heaved polygonal sections of tundra, hundreds of shallow thaw lakes and scraggly stands of trees strung along river valleys, as the land and vegetation give way to the cold.

Northwest fishing is a mixed bag. Pacific salmon extend into the limits of their natural range here, with king and coho thinning out as you move up the coast (fishable runs are found only as far as Norton Sound) and sockeye occurring only sporadically north of the Yukon. That leaves chum and pink salmon as the predominant species for most drainages. Too far north to support rainbow trout, Northwest's waters still support surprising numbers of sea-run charr, grayling, lake trout, northern pike, and sheefish.

Fortunately the strong maritime influence of the nearby Bering and Chukchi Seas somewhat moderates the extreme harshness of the subarctic climate, especially along the coast. Summer days are usually cool, often overcast or foggy, with temperatures averaging in the low 50s, though they can be much warmer—into the 80s—and drier farther inland. Winters are long and cold, frequently with terrifying windchill, but generally without the absolute extremes of temperature seen in the interior regions. Annual precipitation is surprisingly sparse, 15 inches or less for much of the region, with most of it falling during the warm months. Ice breakup usually occurs in late May or early June, with freeze-up sometime in October.

Northwest Fishing Highlights

Of the many outstanding attractions awaiting sport anglers here, perhaps the best known are the trophy grayling and charr opportunities on the Seward Peninsula and rivers of Kotzebue Sound, where the two species generally run larger than anywhere else in the state. Trophy sheefish are another unique possibility, with waters of the Kobuk-Selawik area routinely yielding fish that far outclass specimens from other Alaska locations. Similarly, the remote and pristine lakes of the upper Noatak, Kobuk, and Koyukuk Valleys can offer quality wild lake trout fishing that is hard to match anywhere else.

Access, Services, and Costs

Beyond a few short roads linking Nome to surrounding towns on the Seward

Peninsula, travel in Alaska's Northwest region is totally restricted to airplanes and boats. Regular commercial airline service runs from Anchorage to Nome, Kotzebue, and Unalakleet; from these outposts, air taxi services provide connections to more remote areas.

Anglers will find more limited services and facilities than in other, more accessible parts of the state. There are few full-service lodges or outfitters (see listings on the Seward Peninsula and other areas in this chapter). Some lodging and guides are available in scattered villages along the coast and rivers. Air taxis are expensive, with typical fly-in costs (from the major hubs) to the better locations ranging from $600 to well over $1,000.

Northwest Run Timing

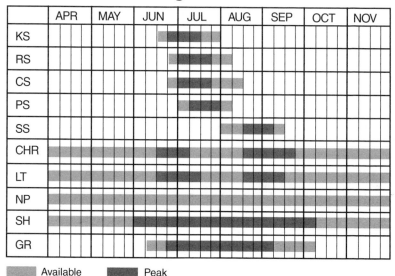

	APR	MAY	JUN	JUL	AUG	SEP	OCT	NOV
KS			Peak					
RS				Peak				
CS				Peak				
PS				Peak				
SS					Peak			
CHR	Available	Available	Peak/Available	Available	Available	Available	Available	Available
LT	Available	Available	Peak/Available	Available	Available	Available	Available	Available
NP	Available	Available	Available	Available	Available	Available	Available	Available
SH	Available	Available	Peak	Peak	Peak	Peak/Available	Available	Available
GR			Available	Peak	Peak	Peak	Available	

Legend: Available | Peak

KS=King Salmon, RS=Red Salmon, CS=Chum Salmon, PS=Pink Salmon, SS=Silver Salmon, CHR=Charr, LT=Lake Trout, NP=Northern Pike, SH=Sheefish, GR=Grayling

Note: Time periods shown are for bright fish, in the case of salmon entering rivers, or for general availability for resident species. Salmon are present in many systems long after the periods shown, but are usually in spawning/postspawning condition. Peak sportfishing periods for each species are highlighted. Run timing can vary somewhat from drainage to drainage and generally follows a later trend in waters to the west and north in Alaska. Check with local contacts listed for area run-timing specifics.

Kotzebue Sound

Within a space of 150 miles, some of the most significant sportfishing drainages in all of western Alaska empty their waters into Kotzebue Sound, north of the Arctic Circle. These include the Kobuk, Selawik, Noatak, Wulik, and Kivalina Rivers, which are known the world over for their abundant trophy charr and sheefish. Very pristine and highly regarded recreational waters, the largest and most fish-endowed of these drainages—the Noatak and Kobuk—are considered Alaska's premier rivers for wilderness adventure. Area angling highlights also include excellent grayling fishing and some fabulous, but virtually unexploited, northern pike opportunities.

❶ Kivalina River

Location: On the Chukchi Sea coast, 90 miles north of Kotzebue, 600 miles northwest of Anchorage; see map page 182.

USGS maps: Noatak D-5, D-6; De Long Mountains A-3, A-4, B-3.

How to get there: By small wheelplane from Kotzebue to gravel bars along the river, or scheduled wheelplane to Kivalina village, then boat transport upriver. It can be floated by raft or kayak.

Highlights: One of Alaska's best trophy charr fisheries.

Species: Charr, chum salmon, grayling, northern pike, pink salmon, *king salmon, silver salmon*.

Regulations: Open year-round, all species.

Facilities: No developed public facilities. Some limited supplies and rental boats are available in Kivalina village.

Contact: For an air taxi to the Kivalina River, contact Mike Spisak, Ram Aviation, P.O. Box 1167, Kotzebue, AK 99752, (907) 442-3205; or Cape Smythe Air, P.O. Box 810, Kotzebue, AK 99752, (907) 442-3020. For boat transportation along the Kivalina, contact Caleb Wesley, P.O. Box 48, Kivalina, AK 99750; (907) 645-2150.

Fishing the Kivalina River: The Kivalina is the less-known sister river of the fabulous Wulik, Northwest Alaska's best trophy charr stream. Of similar origins, size, and character, the clear-flowing, 64-mile Kivalina is also blessed with abundant runs of big sea-run charr that over-winter and spawn in its spring-fed tributaries and main stem. Slightly more remote and difficult to fish than the Wulik, the Kivalina doesn't quite receive the attention it deserves, considering the quality of fishing it offers.

The river has three main forks that converge about 27 miles above the mouth. Most of the sportfishing for fall charr and salmon takes place from there down to the lagoon. The lower sections of Grayling Creek (East Fork) and the Middle Fork of the Kivalina are important upper river spawning areas. The best time to fish here is mid-August through early September. Spring charr are fished heavily by natives in the lower river and lagoon in early June.

You can access the Kivalina from Kotzebue by wheelplane, putting down on gravel bars upriver or at the strip in the village near the mouth. (Rental boats and a guide can be had there as well.) The river can be floated by raft or kayak to its mouth at Kivalina Lagoon, with a return via scheduled or chartered wheelplane to Kotzebue. See the charr chapter on page 77 for details on fishing techniques and equipment.

❷ Wulik River

Location: On the Seward Peninsula, 600 miles northwest of Anchorage; see map page 182.

USGS maps: Noatak C-5, D-3, D-4, D-5; De Long Mountains A-2, A-3, B-2.

How to get there: By small wheelplane from Kotzebue to gravel bars along river. Raft or kayak travel is possible to spots downriver, with wheelplane pickup. You can boat along the lower river from the village of Kivalina.

Highlights: Alaska's most famous location for trophy charr.

Species: Charr, chum salmon, grayling, pink salmon, *king salmon, silver salmon*.

Regulations: Open year-round, all species.

Facilities: No developed public facilities. A private lodge is located on the river.

Contact: For guided or unguided lodge-based fishing on the Wulik, contact Midnight Sun Adventures, 1306 East 26th Avenue, Anchorage, AK

99508; (907) 277-8829. For an air taxi, contact Ram Aviation, P.O. Box 1167, Kotzebue, AK 99752, (907) 442-3205; or Cape Smythe Air, P.O. Box 810, Kotzebue, AK 99752, (907) 442-3020.

Fishing the Wulik River: For many years, the Wulik has had the reputation as the best place for trophy charr in Alaska. It's accessible from Kotzebue and easy to fish. In an average year, the Wulik receives tens of thousands of robust (on average five to seven pounds and up to 15 pounds or more), sea-run Dolly Varden that enter the river in late summer through fall to spawn and overwinter. A good portion of all of Alaska's record fish for the species have come from the Wulik.

Draining the westernmost slopes of the Brooks Range (the De Long Mountains) and emptying into the Chukchi Sea, for much of its length the 89-mile Wulik is perfect for wade-and-cast fishing: clear, gravel-bottomed, with pools, runs, and braided sections interspersed with plenty of bars for camping. Most of the fishing on the Wulik takes place from above Kivalina Lagoon to where the river branches into East and West Forks (42 miles above the mouth), with the greatest concentration of fall charr located above and below Ikalukrok Creek. Other popular areas for fishing are the channels above Kivalina Lagoon (chum salmon), the West Fork below the falls and 16 miles up from the East-West confluence (charr), Sheep Creek (big charr), Ikalukrok Creek (charr and salmon), and upper Tutak Creek (big grayling and charr).

For a fall trophy charr safari (from mid-August through mid-September), the Wulik is hard to beat. There's also exciting fishing during the spring out-migration in June and in late July for an early run of spawners. Besides charr, the Wulik also offers abundant grayling and chum salmon, along with some rare coho. Animal encounters—bears, caribou, wolves, and moose—are possible, and extreme weather, especially in September, is highly likely.

❸ Noatak River

Location: On Kotzebue Sound, 550 miles northwest of Anchorage; see map page 182.

USGS maps: Survey Pass C-5, C-6; Ambler River C-1, D-1, D-2, D-3, D-4, D-5, D-6; Howard Pass A-5; Misheguk Mountain A-1, A-2; Baird Mountains D-3, D-4, D-5, D-6; Noatak A-1, A-2, B-2, B-3, C-2, C-3, D-1, D-2.

How to get there: By small plane from Bettles or Kotzebue to headwater lakes (Matcharak and Pingo) or gravel bars along river. You can float fish in a raft or kayak, taking out at the village of Noatak (a one- to three-week trip, depending on put in) or gravel bars along way. Boat travel is possible along the lower river.

Highlights: Alaska's premier wild river, world famous for its trophy charr fishing.

Species: Charr, chum salmon, grayling, lake trout, northern pike, pink salmon, *king salmon, red salmon, silver salmon*.

Regulations: Open year-round, all species.

Facilities: No developed public facilities.

Contact: For rafting or float-fishing expeditions on the Noatak, contact Sourdough Outfitters, c/o Gary Bensen, P.O. Box 90, Bettles, AK 99726, (907) 692-5252; or ABEC's Alaska Adventures, 1550 Alpine Vista Court, Fairbanks, AK 99712, (907) 457-8907. For general information, contact the Noatak National Preserve, P.O. Box 1029, Kotzebue, AK 99752; (907) 442-3890. For an air taxi, contact Mike Spisak, Ram Aviation, P.O. Box 1167, Kotzebue, AK 99752; (907) 442-3205.

Fishing the Noatak River: By anyone's estimation, the 425-mile giant Noatak is Alaska's best backcountry river. (It was designated a UNESCO World Heritage Site in 1976, and later incorporated into Noatak National Preserve as a Wild and Scenic River in 1978.) Along with several other Kotzebue Sound drainages (such as the Wulik, Kobuk, and Kivalina Rivers), it has a world reputation for abundant, trophy sea-run charr (up to 15 pounds and more). Thousands of these robust fish jam the main stem and tributaries from late summer through fall (from August through September), to prepare for spawning and overwintering.

Set above the Arctic Circle, the Noatak rises on the slopes of the Schwatka Mountains in the western Brooks Range and flows southwest to Kotzebue Sound. Clear and fast for most of its length, with only minor rapids (Class I and Class II at most), the Noatak presents no major technical obstacles for floating, other than its size and remoteness; a trip down its entire length is a major, three-week undertaking that should not be taken lightly by anyone. Since the best angling is on the lower and middle sections of the river, a far better option for anglers is to put in on gravel bars or small tributary lakes at midriver (the Aniuk or Cutler Rivers are popular put ins). This cuts travel time considerably and allows more enjoyment of the lower river's abundant fishing. Most of the Noatak's big, chunky charr are intercepted at the mouths of the Kelly, Kugururok, Kugrak, Kaluktavik, and Nimiuktuk Rivers, although they do occur throughout most of the drainage. The Kelly produced the current Alaska state-record charr in 1991. (See the charr chapter on page 77.)

A popular option for anglers is to fly from Kotzebue in a small wheelplane, land on gravel bars on the lower Noatak or tributaries mentioned above, then camp and fish, even float down the river to the village of Noatak, or to pick-up points along the way. In addition to the river's great charr fishing, grayling and big chum salmon are very abundant. Fishing the Noatak for ravenous spring charr and grayling right after breakup (June) is also an exciting possibility. Countless unnamed lakes and sloughs in the Noatak Flats (between the Eli and Agashashok Rivers) are reputed to have pike of legendary proportions.

❹ Kobuk River

Location: On Kotzebue Sound, 475 miles northwest of Anchorage; see map page 182.

USGS maps: Survey Pass A-3; Hughes D-3, D-4, D-5, D-6; Shungnak D-1, D-2, D-3, D-4; Ambler River A-4, A-5, A-6; Baird Mountains A-1, A-2; Selawik C-5, C-6, D-3, D-4, D-5, D-6.

How to get there: By floatplane to headwater lakes via Bettles. Float-fishing is a popular option by raft or kayak down to the villages of Kobuk, Ambler, or Kiana, with wheelplane pickup and return to Kotzebue. Boat travel is possible to points along the lower river from the villages.

Highlights: A giant among Alaska's wild rivers with superb fishing for trophy sheefish; also charr, pike, lake trout, and grayling.

Species: Charr, chum salmon, grayling, lake trout, northern pike, pink salmon, sheefish.

Regulations: Open year-round, all species.

Facilities: No developed public facilities.

Contact: For guided and unguided rafting and float-fishing trips along the Kobuk River system, contact Sourdough Outfitters, c/o Gary Bensen, P.O. Box 90, Bettles, AK 99726, (907) 692-5252; or Peace of Selby, 90 Polar Road, P.O. Box 86, Manley Hot Springs, AK 99756, (907) 672-3206. For guided fishing along the lower river, contact Kiana Lodge, P.O. Box 89, Kiana, AK, 99749; (907) 475-2149. For an air taxi, contact Bettles Air Service, P.O. Box 27, Bettles, AK 99726; (800) 770-5111.

Fishing the Kobuk River: Like the Noatak, the Kobuk flows west to Kotzebue Sound, through the heart of some of the finest wild country in Alaska. Almost 350 miles long—one of Alaska's largest clear rivers—the Kobuk's size and features make it suited for a variety of high-quality wilderness fishing adventures, particularly float trips. This area has so much to offer that, like the Noatak, it's impossible to see it all in one trip. Many folks begin with an exploration of the upper river, flying in to one of several, beautiful headwater lakes (such as Walker, Selby, and Nutuvukti), camping and fishing for lake trout, charr, pike, and grayling. After a few days, they continue down the river by raft or kayak. There are two stretches of major rapids (Class III and Class IV) in the canyons of the upper river below Walker Lake that should be scouted beforehand. Other than that, the Kobuk is a fairly serene float as it winds its way through immense, scenic valleys, where caribou, bear, wolves, moose, and countless birds can be seen.

The trip downriver to the village of Kobuk takes at least eight days (more or less), and will take you through some astounding grayling and salmon holes, especially the mouths of the countless tributary creeks that empty into this 125-mile stretch of river. If you're interested in the Kobuk's famous, giant sheefish, the best time to fish is perhaps August or early September, when the big shees make their way upriver to spawn. Some of the more noteworthy fishing for these silvery brutes occurs near the junction of the notorious Pah River, where fish of 30 pounds or more can be taken.

Most people pull out at Kobuk, but farther

downriver you'll find some unique attractions. Some of the river's best salmon and charr fishing can be had during late summer in the north adjoining tributaries, from Ambler down to Kiana, while the biggest northern pike cruise the lower river's slow-moving pools and sloughs. There are some amazing sights as well, like the incredible Kobuk Sand Dunes and Onion Portage—the timeless caribou crossing halfway down the river and the site of numerous archeological digs. The float to Kiana will add an additional six days minimum to the overall trip time; kayaks or motor-assisted rafts are highly recommended, as the wide lower sections of river can slow to a crawl in headwinds. It's certainly possible to put in at Kobuk and float down, if you don't have two weeks to burn.

You'll discover many other options, of course. The Kobuk has several tributaries that make outstanding float trips on their own, sparkling clear, pristine mountain streams like the Salmon, Ambler, or Squirrel Rivers, with superb fishing for grayling, charr, and chum salmon. The numerous lakes in the upper Kobuk Valley are among the loveliest in all of the Brooks Range, nearly all holding lake trout, grayling, and pike. Local outfitters offer a variety of trips—tent camps, canoe floats, and hiking expeditions— that allow for exciting exploration and fishing.

❺ Selawik River

Location: On Kotzebue Sound, 475 miles northwest of Anchorage; see map page 182.

USGS maps: Shungnak B-2, B-3, B-4, B-5, B-6, C-3, C-5; Selawik B-2, B-3, B-4, B-5, C-1, C-2, C-3, C-4, C-5.

How to get there: By small plane to headwater lakes (in the Shiniliaok Creek vicinity) or gravel bars, with float options down to the village; or wheelplane to the village of Selawik, with foot or boat access to points along the river.

Highlights: One of Northwest Alaska's most potentially significant trophy sheefish rivers, which also holds outstanding northern pike fishing.

Species: Charr, grayling, northern pike, sheefish, *chum salmon, pink salmon*.

Regulations: Open year-round, all species.

Facilities: No developed public facilities. Limited supplies and services are available in Selawik.

Contact: For air taxi service to the Selawik, contact Ambler Air Service, P.O. Box 7, Ambler, AK 99786; (907) 445-2121. For guided fishing on the Selawik, contact Ralph Ramoth Sr., Selawik River Transport, P.O. Box 12, Selawik, AK 99770; (907) 484-2102.

Fishing the Selawik River: In early spring, some of Northwest Alaska's most exciting fishing action takes place on the ice of the large, freshwater estuary formed at the mouths of the Kobuk and Selawik Rivers, southeast of Kotzebue. Here locals, using bright jigs and spoons, stir the giant sheefish of Kotzebue Sound from their winter lethargy, with electrifying results. These semianadromous stocks attain the largest size of any sheefish in Alaska, with catches of 20- to 30-pound fish not uncommon. As breakup proceeds in May, the action shifts inland, following the sheefish as they gorge on whitefish and spring smolt. In summer, many of these same fish can be found upriver, feeding heavily and preparing for their fall spawning.

The Selawik takes it name from the Inupiat for "place where sheefish spawn." Along with the Kobuk River, it shares a reputation for Alaska's finest trophy angling for the species. The majority of visiting anglers come in summer and fall (June through September). Most fish upriver from the village of Selawik, targeting the mouths of the tributary creeks and main stem river up to about 20 miles beyond Ingruksukruk Creek. The countless sloughs and lakes in the immense flatlands surrounding the lower Selawik also make perfect habitat for monster northern pike, so don't miss the opportunity for some outstanding trophy fishing for "Mr. Gator Jaws" if you plan on visiting this drainage.

Northwest Mountain Lakes

In the upper Kobuk, Noatak, and Koyukuk Valleys lie scattered dozens of small, deep glacial lakes, many unnamed and seldom visited. Some of the more outstanding, listed below, are among

Alaska's most pristine mountain lakes, offering solitude, impressive scenery, and fine fishing for lake trout, grayling, pike, and even landlocked charr. Access is from Kotzebue or Bettles, with early summer (from June through early July) or fall (from mid-August through early September) the best times for fishing. Check with local air taxi services for the latest conditions.

❻ Feniak Lake (Noatak Drainage)

Location: In upper Noatak Valley, 550 miles northwest of Anchorage; see map page 182.

USGS maps: Howard Pass A-4, B-4.

How to get there: By commercial flight to Kotzebue or Bettles, then floatplane or wheelplane to the lake.

Highlights: One of the prettiest lakes in the western Brooks Range, with excellent fishing for lake trout and grayling.

Species: Grayling, lake trout.

Regulations: Open year-round, all species.

Facilities: No developed public facilities.

Contact: For an air taxi, contact Mike Spisak, Ram Aviation, P.O. Box 1167, Kotzebue, AK 99752, (907) 442-3205; or Ambler Air Service, P.O. Box 7, Ambler, AK 99786, (907) 445-2121.

Fishing Feniak Lake: Perhaps the finest of the many glacial lakes in the upper Noatak Valley, Feniak Lake is set in beautiful mountain country, its deep (75 feet) blue waters holding some superb lake trout fishing. Abundant catches and large fish (15 pounds or more) are common. There is a major inlet stream on the north side, while the outlet, Makpik Creek, exits from the south. Both streams offer good angling for grayling. Access is by float or wheelplane (there is a gravel strip nearby). Try Feniak in the spring or early summer (from June through July) for the most exciting fishing.

❼ Matcharak and Isiak Lakes (Noatak Drainage)

Location: In upper Noatak Valley, 475 miles northwest of Anchorage; see map page 183.

USGS maps: Ambler River C-1, D-1.

How to get there: By small plane from Kotzebue or Bettles.

Highlights: Beautiful, remote mountain lakes, with good fishing for lake trout and grayling.

Species: Charr, lake trout, northern pike, grayling.

Regulations: Open year-round, all species.

Facilities: No developed public facilities.

Contact: For an air taxi, contact Mike Spisak, Ram Aviation, P.O. Box 1167, Kotzebue, AK 99752; (907) 442-3205.

Fishing Matcharak and Isiak Lakes: Scenic Matcharak is one of many small but fairly deep lakes situated along the upper Noatak River. It's commonly used as a floatplane put in for float trips on the Noatak (with a small portage). Matcharak is known for its good lake trout and grayling fishing, with a few pike thrown in. Still, it can be inconsistent. Late spring and early summer are the best times to try.

Less than two miles from Matcharak, Isiak Lake lies on a small plateau above the Noatak. A gravel strip next to the lake provides access. A lovely little lake, it, too, provides some angling for lake trout, grayling, and pike. Isiak makes for a pleasant side trip when you put in at Matcharak to float the Noatak.

❽ Selby-Narvak and Minakokosa Lakes (Kobuk Drainage)

Location: In upper Kobuk Valley, 435 miles northwest of Anchorage; see map page 183.

USGS maps: Hughes D-5, D-6.

How to get there: By floatplane from Bettles.

Highlights: Good lake trout, grayling, pike, and landlocked charr fishing in a pristine and highly scenic setting.

Species: Charr, lake trout, northern pike, grayling.

Regulations: Open year-round, all species.

Facilities: A private lodge, cabins, and campgrounds are available.

Contact: For lodge or outpost camp fishing, contact Peace of Selby, 90 Polar Road, P.O. Box 86, Manley Hot Springs, AK 99756; (907) 672-

3206. For air taxi and outpost camp information, contact Bettles Air Service, P.O. Box 27, Bettles, AK 99726, (800) 770-5111.

Fishing Selby-Narvak and Minakokosa Lakes: Located only about 40 miles southwest of Walker Lake, these two beautiful, connected lakes are worth a visit by themselves, but especially if you're making a trip to the Kobuk or Pah Rivers, as the Selby-Narvak Lakes lie just a short distance off the river, midway down. (Fish the lakes for a few days, then float down the outlet stream to join with the Kobuk right above the Pah.) Angling is very good for lake trout, pike, and grayling in a lovely, secluded setting.

Minakokosa lies in between Selby and Walker Lakes. It's small, but very pretty and private, with decent lake trout fishing. Like the Selby-Narvak Lakes, it connects to the Kobuk, so you can include it in an extended float trip. Nearby Nutuvukti Lake also offers decent lake trout and pike fishing in a very remote setting. Tent camps, cabins, and boat and raft rentals are available from the local lodge; air taxis are recommended for outpost-based fishing adventures of the highest order.

❾ Walker Lake (Kobuk Drainage)

Location: In upper Kobuk Valley, 425 miles northwest of Anchorage; see map page 183.

USGS maps: Survey Pass A-3, A-4.

How to get there: By floatplane from Bettles.

Highlights: The most significant lake in the Kobuk Valley and one of the most outstanding western Brooks Range lakes, with excellent fishing for lake trout, grayling, pike, and landlocked charr.

Species: Charr, lake trout, northern pike, grayling.

Regulations: Open year-round, all species.

Facilities: No developed public facilities.

Contact: For air taxi service to Walker Lake, contact Bettles Air Service, P.O. Box 27, Bettles, AK 99726, (800) 770-5111; or Ambler Air Service, P.O. Box 7, Ambler, AK 99786, (907) 445-2121.

Fishing Walker Lake: This is one of the most popular fly-in destinations in the Brooks Range. Located about 45 minutes by small plane west

of Bettles at the head of the Kobuk River (in Gates of the Arctic National Park), this scenic, narrow 14-mile body of water is a popular put-in spot for floaters setting out for the long haul down the Kobuk River. It offers some of northern Alaska's finest fishing for lake trout (up to 30 pounds) and landlocked charr (up to 15 pounds), with good grayling opportunities in the outlet and mouths of tributary creeks and even some pike to be had. Late spring and early summer (from June through early July) are probably the most productive times to fish, but the lake is fairly consistent throughout the season, especially to anglers who have use of boats or rafts.

❿ Iniakuk Lake (Koyukuk Drainage)

Location: In upper Koyukuk Valley, central Brooks Range, 60 miles above the Arctic Circle, 45 miles west of Bettles, 425 miles northwest of Anchorage; see map page 183.

USGS map: Survey Pass A-1.

How to get there: By floatplane from Bettles.

Highlights: An easily accessed Brooks Range lake, with good fishing for northern pike, grayling, and lake trout.

Species: Grayling, lake trout, northern pike.

Regulations: Open year-round, all species.

Facilities: No developed public facilities. A private lodge is located on north end of the lake.

Contact: For lodge-based fishing, contact Patricia Gaedeke, Iniakuk Lake Lodge, P.O. Box 80424, Fairbanks, AK 99708; (907) 479-6354. For guided and unguided rafting and float-fishing down from the lake and along the Alatna, contact Sourdough Outfitters, c/o Gary Bensen, P.O. Box 90, Bettles, AK 99726, (907) 692-5252. For an air taxi to the lake, contact Bettles Air Service, P.O. Box 27, Bettles, AK 99726, (800) 770-5111.

Fishing Iniakuk Lake: A short flight northwest from Bettles takes you to lovely Iniakuk Lake in the Alatna drainage. Small (five miles long and only one mile wide), clear, and very deep (200 feet), Iniakuk lies in a spectacular setting, flanked by steep mountains on its west and east sides. Fishing is good for lake trout, grayling, and pike, especially in the spring after ice-out. There's a lodge on the north end of the lake. A short stay there, with a float down the outlet (Malemute Fork) to the Alatna, a Wild and Scenic River, is highly recommended. (Note: Water levels vary through the summer. Check with the folks at the lodge or Bettles Air Service for the latest river conditions before attempting a float down to the Alatna drainage.)

⑪ Wild Lake (Koyukuk Drainage)

Location: In the central Brooks Range, 40 miles north of Bettles, 435 miles northwest of Anchorage; see map page 183.

USGS maps: Wiseman B-4, C-4.

How to get there: By floatplane from Bettles.

Highlights: An easily accessed, popular Brooks Range lake destination, with outstanding scenery and good fishing for lake trout, pike, and grayling.

Species: Grayling, lake trout, northern pike.

Regulations: Open year-round, all species.

Facilities: No developed public facilities.

Contact: For guided and unguided fishing on the lake and associated river, contact Sourdough Outfitters, c/o Gary Bensen, P.O. Box 90, Bettles, AK 99726; (907) 692-5252. For an air taxi, contact Bettles Air Service, P.O. Box 27, Bettles, AK 99726, (800) 770-5111.

Fishing Wild Lake: Set at the head of its namesake river in a beautiful mountain setting, Wild Lake is only a short distance north of Bettles. One of the deepest lakes of its size (up to 250 feet) in the Brooks Range, the five-mile-long Wild offers good seasonal fishing for lake trout, pike, and grayling (especially around the inlet and outlet waters). It's best right after breakup in early June or in the fall (from late August through early September). A raft or other inflatable craft will greatly improve your chances of success on these deep waters. You may be able to combine a stay at the lake with a short, four-day float down the Wild River (if water levels permit), ending your trip at Bettles, for a fairly inexpensive, but outstanding, Brooks Range adventure. Because of its easy accessibility and private land development around the lake, however, at times Wild Lake offers a much tamer experience than its name suggests. Check with local outfitters for the latest river conditions before planning a trip.

⑫ Lower Koyukuk River

Location: A middle Yukon River tributary, 370 miles northwest of Anchorage; see map page 183.

USGS maps: Kateel River Quadrangle; Nulato D-4, D-6; Melozitna D-3; Hughes A-3, B-1, B-2, B-3; Bettles B-6, C-5, C-6, D-5, D-6.

How to get there: By floatplane or boat. The main boat access points are from Galena, Huslia, and Hughes.

Highlights: An unexplored fishing frontier, with high potential for trophy pike; also sheefish and grayling.

Species: Chum salmon, grayling , northern pike, sheefish, *charr, king salmon.*

Regulations: Open year-round, all species.

Facilities: Limited services, supplies, and lodging are available in the nearby villages of Hughes and Huslia.

Contact: For information on lodging and guided fishing on the lower Koyukuk, contact Athabasca Cultural Journeys, P.O. Box 10, Huslia, AK 99746, (800) 423-0094.

Fishing the Lower Koyukuk River: The 320-mile Koyukuk River, one the Yukon's largest tributaries, dominates north-central Alaska with its vast network of sprawling streams, which provide major habitat for a wide variety of fish species. In the extensive flatlands downstream of Hughes, the Koyukuk usually runs turbid from sediment and tannic water, but still has considerable sport fish potential for large pike (up to 48 inches) and sheefish in its countless, meandering sloughs, tributary lakes, and adjoining streams. Grayling (some of trophy size) and some salmon (chums, mostly, and occasionally kings) can be taken from the clearer waters of the Gisasa, Kateel, Dulbi, Dakli, and Indian Rivers, with some Dolly Varden charr reported in the Gisasa. Aside from locals, these areas receive very little fishing pressure. They're definitely worth investigating by the angler with time, resources, and a yen for a truly wild fishing adventure.

Seward Peninsula

The Seward Peninsula almost touches Siberia, nearly separating the icy Bering Sea from the even colder Chukchi. A remote expanse of rolling hills, tundra, sparse forests, and windswept coast, with an impressive array of wildlife, the Seward Peninsula boasts some fabulous history and unique fisheries. Remnants of its Gold Rush glory days are found everywhere. Even the names of some of its better rivers—spread along the southern half from Teller to Koyuk—speak of a colorful past: the Bonanza, Eldorado, Pilgrim, Snake, Fish, Solomon, and Nome. These streams still hold a treasure of fine angling for salmon, pike, charr, and trophy grayling. (A good portion of Alaska's record grayling have come from Seward Peninsula streams.) What's more, road access via three gravel highways links many of these great waters with Nome, making it possible to sample some of the area's best fishing by car. Check with the Department of Transportation in Nome, (907) 443-3444, for the latest road conditions.

⓭ Buckland River

Location: On the Seward Peninsula, 160 miles northeast of Nome, 485 miles northwest of Anchorage; see map page 182.

USGS maps: Selawik A-2, A-5; Candle B-2, B-3, B-4, C-1, C-2, C-3, C-4, D-2, D-3, D-4, D-5.

How to get there: By boat or small plane. Take a scheduled flight to Buckland from Kotzebue, then travel upriver by boat. Small planes can land on gravel strips or river bars along the upper river. The river can be floated.

Highlights: A significant, untapped river of lower Kotzebue Sound, with many sportfishing possibilities.

Species: Charr, chum salmon, grayling, northern pike, pink salmon, sheefish, silver salmon, *king salmon*.

Regulations: For the latest updates on closures or restrictions, contact the Alaska Department of Fish and Game's Nome office, (907) 443-5796.

Facilities: Boat rentals, sporting goods, groceries, licenses, and fuel are available in Buckland.

Contact: For information on guided fishing, contact Buckland's mayor, Lester Hadley, P.O. Box 24, Buckland, AK 99727; (907) 494-2107. For an air taxi to Buckland or the upper river, contact Olson Air Service, P.O. Box 142, Nome, AK 99762, (907) 443-2229 or (800) 478-5600; or Bering Air, P.O. Box 1650, Nome, AK 99762, (907) 443-5464.

Fishing the Buckland River: A pristine, multiforked river, the Buckland drains the Selawik and Nulato Hills at the base of the Seward Peninsula. Little known and seldom visited by any other than locals, it has potential for some high-quality fishing adventures, as it has significant salmon runs (all species except sockeye) and grayling, charr, pike, and even sheefish populations.

There are two major forks on the 125-mile Buckland, the South and West Forks, which merge about 44 miles up from the mouth. Most of the fishing is done from this point down to the village, but there are some outstanding possibilities (for salmon, grayling, and charr) on the clear-flowing West and North Forks and the Fish River. Numerous oxbow lakes and sloughs along the lower river provide outstanding pike fishing and good chances for sheefish.

Locals access the Buckland almost exclusively by jet boat, traveling upriver to camp, fish, hunt, or pick berries. The upper river can also be accessed in spots by small wheelplane, landing on gravel strips or suitable river bars, making headwater float trips a possibility. According to locals, this area is "very pretty, with nice hills for hiking, plenty of animals, no people, and lots of fish." The folks in the village are friendly and eager to show visitors how special their river is, with boats and guides available. (Buckland's mayor, Lester Hadley, is the contact for local services, and even guides trips himself.) Before you go, contact the Northeast Arctic Native Association, Regional Corporation, P.O. Box 49, Kotzebue, AK 99752, (907) 442-3301, for information on camping on native lands along the Buckland.

⓮ American-Agiapuk Rivers

Location: On the Seward Peninsula, Imuruk Basin drainage, 65 miles northwest of Nome,

560 miles northwest of Anchorage; see map page 182.

USGS maps: Teller A-2, B-2, B-3, C-2, D-2.

How to get there: By small plane or boat. There is boat access from Teller (serviced by flights from Kotzebue or accessed via the Nome-Teller Road) or the Kuzitrin River (accessed from Kougarok Road); small planes can land along strips or gravel bars on the Agiapuk or American.

Highlights: A fairly inaccessible Seward Peninsula location with outstanding sportfishing potential.

Species: Charr, chum salmon, grayling, northern pike, pink salmon, silver salmon, *king salmon*.

Regulations: For the latest updates on closures or restrictions, contact the Alaska Department of Fish and Game's Nome office, (907) 443-5796.

Facilities: No developed public facilities.

Contact: For an air taxi to the American-Agiapuk, contact Olson Air Service, P.O. Box 142, Nome, AK 99762, (907) 443-2229 or (800) 478-5600.

Fishing the American-Agiapuk Rivers: The Agiapuk is one of the more outstanding prospects for anyone looking for an out-of-the-way, high-quality Seward Peninsula fishing experience. Only a few residents of Nome and Teller visit the river, along with its tributary, the American, to hunt, fish, and camp along its remote stretches. It has abundant grayling and charr, and is a major spawning stream for chum, pink, and silver salmon.

Access is from either Teller, the Kuzitrin River, or Nome. Many people put in by small wheelplane on gravel strips along the upper American and spend their entire vacations here; some even float down. The Agiapuk is most frequently accessed by jet boat from Teller or from the Kuzitrin via the Kougarok Road. According to locals, this is a very pretty area, and the fishing is totally unexploited.

⑮ Kuzitrin-Kougarok Rivers

Location: On the Seward Peninsula, 525 miles northwest of Anchorage; see map page 182.

USGS maps: Teller A-1; Bendeleben A-6, B-3, B-4, B-5, B-6, C-6.

How to get there: By plane to Nome via Anchorage, then north on the Nome-Taylor Road to the Kuzitrin bridge crossing at Mile 68. The road parallels the Kougarok River beyond the bridge; boat travel is possible along both rivers.

Highlights: A fine, abundant grayling fishery, with significant pike opportunities.

Species: Charr, chum salmon, grayling, northern pike, pink salmon, silver salmon, *king salmon*.

Regulations: For closures or restrictions, contact the Alaska Department of Fish and Game's Nome office, (907) 443-5796.

Facilities: No developed public facilities.

Contact: For guided fishing adventures along the Kuzitrin, contact Nome Discovery Tours, P.O. Box 2024, Nome, AK 99672, (907) 443-2814. For transportation, contact Stampede Rent a Car, P.O. Box 633, Nome, AK 99762; (907) 443-3838.

Fishing the Kuzitrin-Kougarok Rivers: Adjacent to the Pilgrim, the Kuzitrin River is the largest drainage along the Nome-Taylor Road. It has outstanding fishing potential. Grayling, in particular, are super abundant, but generally run smaller than those on other area streams. You can also take northern pike, chum, pink, and some coho salmon.

The Kougarok is a major tributary that joins the Kuzitrin about 25 miles up from the mouth. Access is by a rough four-wheel-drive road leading past the Kuzutrin bridge crossing at Mile 68. Anglers fish it mostly for grayling and charr. Both of these rivers are best worked from a boat.

⑯ Pilgrim River

Location: On the Seward Peninsula, 540 miles northwest of Anchorage; see map page 182.

USGS maps: Nome D-1; Solomon D-6; Bendeleben A-6; Teller A-1.

How to get there: By commercial flight to Nome via Anchorage, then north on the Nome-Taylor Road to Salmon Lake or river points above. It can also be reached by boat from Teller via the Imuruk Basin.

Highlights: A very famous Seward Peninsula drainage, best known for its trophy grayling and pike fishing.

Species: Charr, chum salmon, grayling, northern pike, pink salmon, silver salmon, *king salmon, red salmon*.

Regulations: Salmon Lake and tributaries (including 300 feet of outlet) are closed to salmon fishing. For the latest updates on closures or restrictions, contact the Alaska Department of Fish and Game's Nome office, (907) 443-5796.

Facilities: A public Bureau of Land Management campground is available at the Salmon Lake outlet. There is no fee. Camping is first come, first served.

Contact: For guided fishing adventures along the Pilgrim, contact Nome Discovery Tours, P.O. Box 2024, Nome, AK 99672, (907) 443-2814. For camping information, contact the Bureau of Land Management, Nome Field Station, P.O. Box 952, Nome, AK 99672; (907) 443-2177. For transportation, contact Stampede Rent a Car, P.O. Box 633, Nome, AK 99762; (907) 443-3838.

Fishing the Pilgrim River: Perhaps the best known of the Seward Peninsula's famous trophy grayling fisheries, the Pilgrim has a reputation for large sailfins (two to three pounds) that few rivers its size can match. Originating at the outlet of Salmon Lake north of Nome, it flows northeast then northwest for some 71 miles before joining the Kuzitrin River at New Igloo above Imuruk Basin.

Nineteen miles down from the lake, the bridge for the Nome-Taylor Road (Mile 65) provides the most popular put in for boats to fish the productive middle and lower stretches of river. Anglers target big grayling, salmon, and charr in the next 15-mile stretch down to Historic Pilgrim Hot Springs, and from there to the mouth—30 miles of slower-moving, slough-filled water—most of the river's pike (up to 20 pounds) are taken. Salmon Lake and its main tributary, the Grand Central River, are important spawning areas for a rare run of sockeye salmon, but you can't fish them or any other salmon there. Instead, anglers target the lake's grayling and charr. Chums and pinks are the Pilgrim's main salmon species, with a few coho taken. The most popular areas to fish on the Pilgrim system are the lake outlet, the section of river below the bridge, and Iron Creek. The best time to angle is in July and August.

⑰ Nome River

Location: On the Seward Peninsula, 515 miles northwest of Anchorage; see map page 182.

USGS maps: Nome B-1, C-1, D-1.

How to get there: By commercial flight to Nome via Anchorage, then four miles east on Main Street to the river mouth. Follow the Nome-Taylor Road to upriver access points.

Highlights: The Seward Peninsula's most popular, easily accessed river with good salmon and charr fishing.

Species: Charr, chum salmon, grayling, king salmon, pink salmon, silver salmon.

Regulations: Open year-round, all species except grayling and chum salmon. For the latest updates on closures or restrictions, contact the Alaska Department of Fish and Game's Nome office, (907) 443-5796.

Facilities: No developed public facilities.

Contact: For guided fishing adventures along the Nome River, contact Nome Discovery Tours, P.O. Box 2024, Nome, AK 99672, (907) 443-2814. For transportation, contact Stampede Rent a Car, P.O. Box 633, Nome, AK 99762, (907) 443-3838; or Checker Cab, (907) 443-5136.

Fishing the Nome River: Thanks to its proximity to the Seward Peninsula's main hub, the Nome has always been an extremely popular and heavily fished drainage, especially since all 44 miles of its length can be easily accessed by road. Fished for years by locals for its salmon (pink, chum, and silver), grayling, and charr, it's worth a visit if you're planning a trip to Nome, even though the fishing in recent years is not what it used to be.

With headwaters in the Kigluaik Mountains, the river flows swiftly south through tundra and empties into Norton Sound about 3.5 miles east of Nome. It has numerous tributaries, all of them swift and clear runoff streams like the Nome itself. The most popular areas to fish are the mouth and the section between Mile 8 and the bridge at Mile 13 of the Nome-Taylor Road. You can usually fish the river for charr in late May and June down at the mouth, and in August and September from the Mile 13 bridge down. Pink and chum have been the Nome's main salmon highlights (usually from July through September), though in recent years depressed runs have forced closures on chum salmon fishing. Some silvers are also taken (from late August through September). Grayling, not as abundant in the Nome as in other prime Seward Peninsula streams, have been overfished in recent years; in 1992, the river was closed to grayling fishing.

Since the Nome lies just a stone's throw from town, you can inquire at the Nome office of the Alaska Department of Fish and Game at (907) 443-5796 for the latest sport fish updates. If conditions warrant, hit the river on the way to the Seward Peninsula's more glamorous fishing locales.

⑱ Sinuk River

Location: On the Seward Peninsula, 30 miles west of Nome, 560 miles northwest of Anchorage; see map page 182.

USGS maps: Nome C-2, C-3, D-2.

How to get there: By plane to Nome via Anchorage, then head 26 miles west on Teller Road to the lower river.

Highlights: One of the Seward Peninsula's best road-accessible fishing streams, with outstanding trophy grayling potential.

Species: Charr, chum salmon, grayling, pink salmon, silver salmon, *king salmon, red salmon.*

Regulations: The river is closed to chum salmon fishing. For additional closures or restrictions, contact the Alaska Department of Fish and Game's Nome office, (907) 443-5796.

Facilities: No developed public facilities.

Contact: For guided fishing adventures along the Sinuk, contact Nome Discovery Tours, P.O. Box 2024, Nome, AK 99672, (907) 443-2814. For transportation, contact Stampede Rent a Car, P.O. Box 633, Nome, AK 99762, (907) 443-3838; or Checker Cab, (907) 443-5136.

Fishing the Sinuk River: The Sinuk is the largest and best fishing river along the Nome-Teller Road, with outstanding potential for large grayling. (More than half of all record Seward Peninsula grayling were taken on the Sinuk.) Its headwaters lie in the Kigluaik Mountains and Glacial Lake, northwest of Nome. The river can be reached by a short drive west from town to a bridge crossing at Mile 26.7. From there, further access is possible by foot trails or jet boat. The Sinuk offers good fishing for charr and pink and silver salmon. It also has one of the Seward Peninsula's only significant spawning populations of red salmon, though few anglers have figured out how to get them to bite.

⑲ Snake River

Location: On the Seward Peninsula, eight miles west of Nome, 550 miles northwest of Anchorage; see map page 182.

USGS maps: Nome C-1, C-2, D-1.

How to get there: By commercial flight to Nome via Anchorage, then head eight miles west on Teller Road to a bridge. The upper river is accessible from Glacier Creek Road, and boat travel is possible upriver from the bridge or the mouth.

Highlights: One of the Seward Peninsula's more popular and productive fishing streams, noted for good grayling, silver salmon, and charr.

Species: Charr, chum salmon, grayling, pink salmon, silver salmon, *king salmon.*

Regulations: The river is closed to chum salmon fishing. For additional closures or restrictions, contact the Alaska Department of Fish and Game's Nome office, (907) 443-5796.

Facilities: No developed public facilities.

Contact: For guided fishing adventures along the Snake, contact Nome Discovery Tours, P.O. Box 2024, Nome, AK 99672, (907) 443-2814. For transportation, contact Stampede Rent a Car, P.O. Box 633, Nome, AK 99762, (907) 443-3838; or Checker Cab, (907) 443-5136.

Fishing the Snake River: The Snake is a popular road fishery located only eight miles west of Nome via the Nome-Teller Road. Best known for its good grayling fishing, the river also provides considerable opportunities for salmon (silvers and pink mostly) and charr in season.

Most people fish the Snake by foot, working the river from trails that lead from the bridge or Glacier Creek Road. Boat access is also possible along the lower river via the launch at the Nome Port. Fish it in July and August for salmon and grayling, or in June or late August through September for charr.

⑳ Safety Sound

Location: On the Seward Peninsula, 30 miles east of Nome, 500 miles northwest of Anchorage; see map page 182.

USGS maps: Solomon B-6, C-5, C-6.

How to get there: By commercial flight to Nome via Anchorage, then east on the Nome-Council Road to Mile 22, where the road crosses the lagoon outlet, then continues 11 miles along spit. Boat access is possible.

Highlights: Some potentially good, road-accessible beach fishing.

Species: Charr, chum salmon, pink salmon, silver salmon, *king salmon*.

Regulations: The sound is closed to chum salmon fishing. For additional closures or restrictions, contact the Alaska Department of Fish and Game's Nome office, (907) 443-5796.

Facilities: No developed public facilities.

Contact: For transportation, contact Checker Cab, (907) 443-5136.

Fishing Safety Sound: Traversed entirely by the Nome-Council Road, beginning at about Mile 17, Safety Sound is another location worth trying on the way out to Council. You can fish salmon (mostly pinks) and charr with some success at the lagoon outlet and along the inshore side of the spit. However, the action's much better on several notable fishing streams emptying into the other side (the Bonanza, Eldorado, and Flambeau Rivers). Access to these is by boat (or helicopter) only, and negotiating the tides and mudflats can be tricky. June and August are the best times to fish here.

㉑ Solomon River

Location: On the Seward Peninsula, 30 miles east of Nome, 500 miles northwest of Anchorage; see map page 182.

USGS map: Solomon C-5.

How to get there: By commercial flight to Nome via Anchorage, then east on Nome-Council Road to Miles 40 to 50, where the road parallels the east fork of the river.

Highlights: A popular fishing stream for charr and salmon, with plenty of access from the road to the Fish-Niukluk River.

Species: Charr, chum salmon, grayling, pink salmon, silver salmon, *king salmon*.

Regulations: The river is closed to grayling and chum salmon fishing. For additional closures or restrictions, contact the Alaska Department of Fish and Game's Nome office, (907) 443-5796.

Facilities: No developed public facilities.

Contact: For guided fishing adventures along the Solomon, contact Nome Discovery Tours, P.O. Box 2024, Nome, AK 99672, (907) 443-2814. For transportation, contact Stampede Rent a Car, P.O. Box 633, Nome, AK 99762, (907) 443-3838; or Checker Cab, (907) 443-5136.

Fishing the Solomon River: Thirty-two miles east of Nome, the Solomon enters Norton Sound near the old mining town of the same name. Accessed by the Nome-Council Road, which parallels the river for about 10 miles (between Miles 40 and 50), the Solomon is one of the more popular Seward Peninsula roadside streams. Anglers fish it mostly for charr and salmon. There are many good spots along the upper river where you can pull off the road and fish (or try the mouth), so it's certainly worth a stop or two on the way out to the more productive Fish-Niukluk River (see next listing).

㉒ Fish-Niukluk Rivers

Location: On the Seward Peninsula, 475 miles northwest of Anchorage, 60 miles east of Nome; see map page 182.

USGS maps: Solomon C-3, D-3, D-4; Bendeleben A-5.

How to get there: By commercial flight from Anchorage to Nome, wheelplane to Golovin or White Mountain, or 67-mile road access to the upper river at Council.

Highlights: The Seward Peninsula's premier fishing location, with excellent fishing for salmon, charr, and grayling.

Species: Charr, chum salmon, grayling, northern pike, pink salmon, silver salmon, *king salmon*.

Regulations: Open year-round, all species.

Facilities: Private lodges are located in the towns of Council and White Mountain.

Contact: For guided/unguided lodge and tent camp fishing, contact John Elmore, Camp

Bendeleben, P.O. Box 1045, Nome, AK 99762, (907) 443-2880 (winter address: 654 Highlander Circle, Anchorage, AK 99518); or White Mountain Lodge/Christina's Cache, P.O. Box 149, White Mountain, AK 99784, (907) 638-3431 or fax (907) 638-2042. For an air taxi to the river, contact Olson Air Service, P.O. Box 142, Nome, AK 99762, (907) 443-2229 or (800) 478-5600; or Bering Air, P.O. Box 1650, Nome, AK 99762, (907) 443-5464. For car rentals, contact Stampede Rent a Car, P.O. Box 633, Nome, AK 99762, (907) 443-3838; or Checker Cab, (907) 443-5136.

Fishing the Fish-Niukluk Rivers: The Seward Peninsula's Fish-Niukluk River system is one of the most popular and productive fisheries in Northwest Alaska. It's widely used by villagers from two communities along the river and by residents of Nome, who travel the 73-mile Nome-Council Road to make use of these waters for recreational and subsistence fishing. A local lodge and several outfitters service the growing number of visiting anglers drawn by the river's outstanding reputation.

Heading in the Darby and Bendeleben Mountains, the Fish and Niukluk Rivers (and tributaries) flow south toward Golovin Lagoon on Norton Sound. The rivers' character and fishing change from clear, gravelly upper stretches (both Fish and Niukluk), which harbor grayling, salmon, and charr, to slow, braided, dark water in the lower river (from Steamboat Slough down to the mouth—about 20 miles), where pike lurk.

The Fish-Niukluk system is noted for its fast-growing, big grayling (up to three pounds or more) and good silver salmon and charr fishing (also pink and chum salmon). It's also one of the few Seward Peninsula streams with a consistent spawning population of king salmon, and the lower river also has fairly abundant pike. Popular fishing areas include: the upper Fish River and its tributaries—Boston Creek (salmon, including king, and charr), the Rathlatulik River (big grayling), and the Etchepuk River (salmon, including king, and grayling); Steamboat Slough (pike); the Fox River (salmon and grayling—access from the adjacent Nome-Council Road); Ophir Creek (grayling); and the mouth of the Niukluk (all species in the river). Roads from Council provide access to many tributary creeks, and there are gravel

bars and a few scattered airstrips for small plane landings, allowing for float trips.

Eastern Norton Sound

The arc of eastern Norton Sound, from Stebbins to Cape Darby, includes several rivers with significant sportfishing potential and the last major runs of silver and king salmon along the coast. These are all runoff streams draining the highlands west of the lower Yukon, with water conditions that vary considerably through the season. Access is the limiting factor, as most of them can be reached safely only by boat or (sometimes) by small plane, and facilities and services are scarce to nonexistent.

㉓ Kwiniuk River

Location: On Norton Bay, Seward Peninsula, 445 miles northwest of Anchorage; see map page 182.

USGS maps: Solomon C-1, C-2, D-1.

How to get there: By scheduled or chartered wheelplane from Nome or Unalakleet to Moses Point or Elim. There is road access to the upper river or boat access to the mouth. It can be floated down to the mouth by raft or kayak from a put in at the hot springs 25 miles upriver.

Highlights: A very promising, out of the way Norton Sound drainage with abundant salmon, charr, and grayling.

Species: Charr, chum salmon, grayling, king salmon, pink salmon, silver salmon.

Regulations: Open year-round, all species.

Facilities: Limited services, supplies, and trip assistance are available in the villages of Moses Point and Elim.

Contact: For air taxi service to the village and river, contact Olson Air Service, P.O. Box 142, Nome, AK 99762, (907) 443-2229 or (800) 478-5600; Bering Air, P.O. Box 1650, Nome, AK 99762, (907) 443-5464; or Haagland Air, P.O. Box 207, Unalakleet, AK 99684, (907) 624-3595. For boat transportation, access to upper river, and guided fishing on the Kwiniuk and nearby Tubutulik River, contact John Jemewuk, P.O. Box 39046, Elim, AK 99739; (907) 890-3071.

Fishing the Kwiniuk River: The Kwiniuk is a short coastal stream that runs along upper Norton Bay, near the villages of Elim and Moses Point. Clear flowing and moderately fast, it's quite productive for its size, producing some of the last really strong runs of silver and king salmon this far north and west along the coast. According to locals and other sources, it has very promising sportfishing potential, with near-perfect stream conditions and relatively easy access.

The lower Kwiniuk can be reached by boat from Moses Point, while the upper river can be reached via a primitive road leading out from the village of Elim to a hot spring on the river, which is about 25 miles up from the mouth. From here, it is possible to float down by raft, canoe, or kayak, to a takeout at the mouth and village of Moses Point. The Elim–White Mountain area is perhaps the prettiest in all of Seward Peninsula, and nearby Tubutulik River is reputed to have impressive fishing as well (not to mention hot springs and some exciting white-water canyons). An exploratory trip to sample the country and some of its fishing possibilities is highly recommended.

㉔ Shaktoolik River

Location: On eastern Norton Sound, 410 miles northwest of Anchorage; see map page 182.

USGS maps: Norton Bay B-4, B-5, C-2, C-3.

How to get there: By scheduled or chartered wheelplane from Nome or Unalakleet to Shaktoolik Village, then by boat upriver. Limited small wheelplane access is also possible along gravel bars upriver, with float by raft or kayak down to the mouth.

Highlights: A remote Norton Sound drainage with high sport fish potential for salmon, charr, and grayling.

Species: Charr, chum salmon, grayling, king salmon, northern pike, pink salmon, silver salmon.

Regulations: Open year-round, all species.

Facilities: No developed public facilities.

Contact: For air taxi service to the village or river, contact Haagland Air, P.O. Box 207, Unalakleet, AK 99684; (907) 624-3595. For boat transportation upriver and guided fishing, contact Shaktoolik Native Corporation, P.O. Box 46, Shaktoolik, AK 99771; (907) 955-2341 or (907) 955-3241.

Fishing the Shaktoolik River: Along with the Unalakleet, the Shaktoolik is one of Norton Sound's most significant fish producers. With solid runs of salmon (all species except sockeye), plentiful charr and grayling, and excellent stream conditions, it has quite a bit of sportfishing potential that, up to now, has been underutilized because of its difficult access.

Like other promising rivers of the area, the Shaktoolik is a medium-sized, clear runoff stream that flows 100 miles or so to the coast from the uplands surrounding Norton Sound. Gravel bottomed, moderately fast (two to five feet per second, some rapids to Class II), with abundant pools, long runs, and shallow riffles, the river forks about 60 miles up from the mouth, at Kingmetolik Creek. Most of the fishing for salmon, grayling, and charr occurs in the stretch of river from this confluence down to the coastal flats 40 miles below.

Access is the trick. For starters, it's perhaps best to hop a flight from Unalakleet or Nome to Shaktoolik, run upriver by boat with someone from the village, then camp and fish (with a guide if you want). At times, it's also possible to land a small wheelplane on gravel bars in the foothills halfway up the river (check with the air taxi folks in Unalakleet first), then float down to the village in rafts (about three to four days). The fishing is quite good. In fact, there are some who rate the Shaktoolik among western Alaska's finest "undiscovered" streams for fly-fishing, with abundant, sea-run salmon (king and silver especially), charr, and big grayling. (Fish up to 20 inches are common.) It's definitely a river to add to the "dream list" of promising, unexplored Alaska fisheries. Early July or late August are the best times for a safari to these far-flung waters.

㉕ Unalakleet River

Location: On eastern Norton Sound, 375 miles northwest of Anchorage; see map page 182.

USGS maps: Norton Sound A-1, A-2; Unalakleet D-2, D-3, D-4.

How to get there: By plane from Anchorage to Unalakleet, then by boat to numerous sites along the river.

Highlights: One of western Alaska's most promising rivers for fishing king salmon (from late June through mid-July) and silver salmon (from late July through mid-September).

Species: Charr, chum salmon, grayling, king salmon, northern pike, pink salmon, silver salmon, *red salmon*.

Regulations: Open year-round, all species.

Facilities: There is a private lodge on the lower river and several outfitter tent camps. Otherwise, no developed public facilities are available.

Contact: For lodge-based guided fishing, contact the Unalakleet River Lodge, P.O. Box 99, Unalakleet, AK 99684, (907) 624-3031. For outpost camp fishing (guided and unguided), contact Vance Grishkowsky, P.O. Box 38, Unalakleet, AK 99684; (907) 624-3352.

Fishing the Unalakleet River: The most significant river in Norton Sound, the Unalakleet supports substantial commercial and subsistence fisheries with its consistent, strong runs of salmon (all species except sockeye). It's recognized as potentially one of the finest streams in all of western Alaska for sportfishing, although it receives only minimal angling attention at present due to its remoteness.

A Wild and Scenic River, the Unalakleet rises in the Nulato Hills and flows southwest approximately 105 miles through uplands and rolling tundra before emptying into Norton Sound below the village of Unalakleet. Access to the upper river is almost impossible by any means other than boat. Most anglers enlist the services of local guides or outfitters to fish the river's most productive water (the lower 15 miles of the main river and first five miles of the North River). You can raft the river down from the confluence of Old Woman River or Ten Mile Creek to the village in about five to seven days, with no major hazards except sweepers.

The clear-flowing Unalakleet has always been noted for its outstanding king and silver salmon fishing, but it also has staggering runs of chum and pink salmon, as well as numerous charr and grayling. There are plenty of deep pools and clear, gently flowing runs, so it's easy water to fish. Wildlife—moose, bear, some caribou, and numerous waterfowl—are commonly seen throughout the little-visited surrounding valley. All who have visited this remote drainage speak very highly of the experience. It's a prime trip to consider for a real out-of-the-way Alaska fishing adventure.

Fishing in the great Northwest.

Chapter 3

Interior Fishing

Interior Alaska

Alaska State Map ....*page* 8

183

326

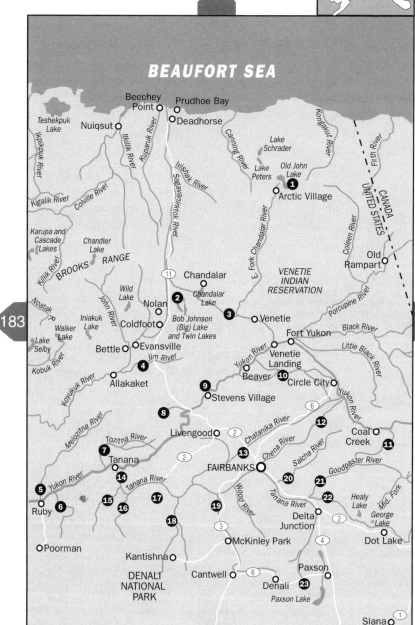

BEAUFORT SEA

Teshekpuk Lake
Ipkikpuk River
Nuiqsut
Ikilik River
Beechey Point
Prudhoe Bay
Deadhorse
Kuparuk River
Canning River
Lake Schrader
Lake Peters
Kongakut River
Firth River
CANADA
UNITED STATES

Kigalik River
Colville River
Ivishak River
Sagavanirktok River
Old John Lake
1 Arctic Village
Coleen River

Karupa and Cascade Lakes
Chandler Lake
Killik River
BROOKS RANGE
John River
Wild Lake
11 Chandalar
Chandalar Lake
E. Fork Chandalar River
VENETIE INDIAN RESERVATION
Old Rampart
Porcupine River

Noatak
Walker Lake
Lake Selby
Iniakuk Lake
Nolan
2 Coldfoot
Bob Johnson (Big) Lake and Twin Lakes
3 Venetie
Fort Yukon
Black River
Little Black River

Kobuk River
Koyukuk River
Bettle
Evansville
Jim River
4
Allakaket
Yukon River
Beaver
10 Circle City
Venetie Landing
Yukon River

Meloztna River
9 Stevens Village
8
6
12
Coal Creek
11

Tozitna River
Livengood
2
Chatanika River
Chena River
Salcha River
13 FAIRBANKS
Goodpaster River

7 Tanana
2
14
Tanana River
Wood River
20
21
Tanana River
22
Healy Lake
Mid. Fork
George Lake

5 Yukon River
Ruby
6
15
16
17
19
Delta Junction
2
Dot Lake

Poorman
18
3
McKinley Park
4

Kantishna
DENALI NATIONAL PARK
Cantwell
6
Denali
Paxson Lake
Paxson
23

Slana
1

Interior Hot Spots

Interior

Alaska's vast heartland, the Interior region, encompasses one-third of the state, in a gigantic area bound on the north and south by formidable mountains—the Alaska and Brooks Ranges—and on the east by the Canadian border. (For our purposes, the Middle Fork of the Koyukuk River forms the western boundary.) The immense Yukon River system, fifth largest on the continent, dominates the region, shaping the character of the land and its people. Along the great waterways here—the Yukon, Koyukuk, Porcupine, Tanana, and others—you can still catch a rare glimpse of the real Alaska, with its native villages and fish wheels, old trapper's cabins, birch forests, and country that, for the most part, remains the sparsely settled wilderness it always was.

Although it can't match the southern coastal regions' diversity of sportfishing, the Interior still has quite a bit to offer anglers, with thousands of miles of scenic, winding rivers, clear headwater streams, and countless lakes, ponds, and sloughs. Here you'll find some of Alaska's most abundant fishing opportunities for pike, sheefish, and grayling.

Country, Climate, and Conditions

Interior's varied terrain consists of extensive plateaus and moderate mountains, rolling hills, and immense lowland valleys created by the state's largest sprawling rivers. Great stands of paper birch, aspen, and spruce cover most of the lower elevations, with timberline at 2,300 to 3,000 feet in elevation. To the north and west, expanses of tundra take over, in country that resembles the terrain along the coast.

Interior's climate is strongly continental, with harsh seasonal extremes. Summer temperatures frequently climb into the 80s or even 90s (degrees Fahrenheit), while winter lows routinely plummet to minus 20 or minus 30 degrees, reaching minus 50 or less during intense cold snaps. Fort Yukon, in the center of the region, has recorded temperatures from 100 degrees to minus 75. Precipitation

Interior Map—page 204

is scant (12 inches or so annually), with the area having considerably more sunny, dry weather than coastal Alaska. Freeze-up generally occurs in October, earlier in elevated locations in the Brooks Range; breakup is usually from late April to early May. Because of the size of most of the rivers here, extreme and rapid changes in water conditions can occur during spring and summer, with heavy flooding always possible. As such, care should be taken when selecting campsites and planning itineraries.

Interior Fishing Highlights

The abundance of large main stem, lowland river terrain, with its preponderance of sloughs, lakes, and marshy ponds, is the perfect habitat for a variety of stillwater bait fish like whitefish, cisco, and suckers, which in turn provide ample forage for predatory game species like northern pike and sheefish. The Interior is well known for its outstanding fisheries for these two fighters (especially in the Tanana and Yukon Flats).

Because of the great distances from the coast, salmon here are fewer in number and species—mostly chum, with some kings and coho. High-quality fishing for these species is limited, occurring mostly in the mouths and lower sections of clear-water rivers, particularly those in the Tanana River drainage. (Alaska's most significant fall runs of chum salmon occur all along the middle Yukon River and its tributaries, but are used primarily for subsistence.) Grayling op-

portunities abound, however, in nearly every clear stream and headwater, with even some Dolly Varden found in scattered, swift streams (mostly in Tanana, Nenana, and Koyukuk River tributaries). Some outstanding opportunities for lake trout in the upper Tanana River drainage and Brooks Range round out the fishing highlights of the region.

Access, Services, and Costs

You can access Interior fishing locations by road, rail, plane, and boat. Fairbanks, the major hub, is serviced daily by jetliners from the outside world, with air taxi services providing access to numerous fly-in locations from there or to smaller hubs like Bettles and Fort Yukon. A highway network crisscrosses the region, linking the major communities to the rest of the state and Canada (via the Alaska Highway) and providing anglers with road access to quite a few good fishing areas. On the big waterways like the Tanana, Yukon, and Porcupine Rivers, boats are the best (and sometimes only) way to reach prime waters.

A variety of local services can help in planning an Interior fishing excursion. You'll find everything from half-day guided fishing tours to full-service wilderness lodges; prices range from fees comparable to those in Southcentral or Southeast Alaska, to considerably more for remote areas of the Brooks Range or upper Yukon (anywhere from $125 to $450 per day per person).

Interior Run Timing

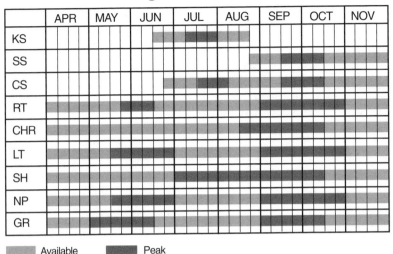

	APR	MAY	JUN	JUL	AUG	SEP	OCT	NOV
KS								
SS								
CS								
RT								
CHR								
LT								
SH								
NP								
GR								

■ Available　■ Peak

KS=King Salmon, SS=Silver Salmon, CS=Chum Salmon, RT=Rainbow Trout, CHR=Charr, LT=Lake Trout, SH=Sheefish, NP=Northern Pike, GR=Grayling

Note: Time periods shown are for bright fish, in the case of salmon entering rivers, or for general availability for resident species. Salmon are present in many systems long after the periods shown, but are usually in spawning/postspawning condition. Peak sportfishing periods for each species are highlighted. Run timing can vary somewhat from drainage to drainage and generally follows a later trend in waters to the west and north in Alaska. Check with local contacts listed for area run-timing specifics.

Eastern Brooks Range

This large area, from the Middle Fork of the Koyukuk River to the Canadian border, contains some very significant waters, such as the Chandalar River, the north tributaries of the vast Porcupine, and the South Fork of the Koyukuk. Principal highlights in this remote and seldom-visited area include untold miles of pristine grayling streams, virgin pike populations (especially the Chandalar River drainage), a few deep-water lakes with trophy lake trout potential, occasional sheefish, and even some rare opportunities for salmon (the lower Porcupine and Koyukuk drainages). Aside from some areas that can be reached from the Dalton Highway, access can be expensive, and services scarce—mostly locals operating from Bettles, Fort Yukon, Arctic Village, or Fairbanks. But the potential for high-quality wilderness adventure angling is certainly there.

❶ Old John Lake

Location: In the central Brooks Range (south side), Sheenjek drainage, 230 miles north of Fairbanks; see map page 204.

USGS map: Arctic A-2.

How to get there: By floatplane from Fairbanks or Fort Yukon. You can also reach the lake by four-wheeler trail from Arctic Village.

Highlights: A trophy lake trout water in the Brooks Range.

Species: Grayling, lake trout, northern pike.

Regulations: Open year-round, all species.

Facilities: Lodging, guide services, and limited supplies are available in Arctic Village.

Contact: For an air taxi, contact Wright Air Service, P.O. Box 60142, Fairbanks, AK 99706, (907) 474-0502. For lodging and guided fishing information, contact Arctic Village Tours, P.O. Box 82896, Fairbanks, AK 99708; (907) 479-4648.

Fishing Old John Lake: Set in the central Brooks Range, Old John Lake lies about 10 miles southeast of Arctic Village. A deep, mountain-basin lake of fairly good size (five miles long) draining into the upper Sheenjek River, Old John is one of the most well-known and beautifully situated of Alaska's Brooks Range lakes, significant as a centuries-old native hunting site for caribou and a consistent trophy lake trout water. (Two of the largest 10 lake trout caught in Alaska came from Old John.)

The lake is fished year-round by natives from Arctic Village, who access it by snowmachine or four-wheeler trail. Most visiting anglers fly in from Fairbanks or Fort Yukon in spring at breakup (late May) or in fall (September) for outstanding fishing. The lake and outlet stream also have an abundant grayling population, and some big northerns have come out of Old John and nearby lakes of the upper Sheenjek and East Fork Chandalar as well. The best bet here is to give the locals a call and arrange for a guided outing, as they have a lodge in town and are developing a tent camp facility on the lake for a variety of trip options. Rental boats are also available.

❷ Bob Johnson (Big) and Twin Lakes

Location: In the central Brooks Range, 195 miles north of Fairbanks; see map page 204.

USGS maps: Chandalar B-5, C-5.

How to get there: By small plane from Fairbanks, Bettles, or Fort Yukon. They can also be reached by trail from the Dalton Highway.

Highlights: Well-known, scenic lake destinations in the central Brooks Range, with good fishing for lake trout and grayling.

Species: Grayling, lake trout, northern pike.

Regulations: Open year-round, all species.

Facilities: No developed public facilities.

Contact: For an air taxi, contact Wright Air Service, P.O. Box 60142, Fairbanks, AK 99706, (907) 474-0502; or Bettles Air Service, 2453 Homestead, North Pole, AK 99705; (800) 770-5111.

Fishing Bob Johnson (Big) and Twin Lakes: No discussion of central Brooks Range fishing locations would be complete without mention of these two well-known, neighboring mountain lakes. Very scenic, deep-basin lakes that lie in the upper Koyukuk drainage east of Wiseman and just west of Chandalar Lake, Bob Johnson and Twin have long served as hunting camps as well as popular Brooks Range recreation spots for vacationers out of Fairbanks. Scattered cabins exist along the lakes and in the vicinity.

These clear lakes have good fishing for lake trout and grayling, with pike present in Bob Johnson. Twin is deeper and generally has bigger lake trout on average, although both lakes have seen a decline in larger fish over the years due to increasing angling pressure. The outlet and inlet streams (and connecting stream on Twin) right at breakup (late May usually) are probably the best bets for fishing these two.

❸ Upper Chandalar River

Location: In the north-central Brooks Range, Yukon drainage, 170 miles north of Fairbanks; see map page 204.

USGS maps: Chandalar A-1, A-2, A-3, A-4, A-5, B-1, B-2, B-3, B-4, C-1, C-2, C-3, C-4, D-1, D-2, D-3, D-4, D-5; Christian A-6, B-5, B-6, C-5, C-6, D-4, D-5, D-6; Fort Yukon C-4, C-5, D-5; Philip Smith Mountains A-2, A-3, A-4.

How to get there: By small plane from Fairbanks, Bettles, or Fort Yukon to headwater lakes, river bars, or gravel strips along the river.

Highlights: A remote river system with high wilderness recreation potential and good fishing possibilities for lake trout, northern pike, and grayling.

Species: Chum salmon, grayling, lake trout, northern pike, sheefish.

Regulations: Open year-round, all species.

Facilities: No developed public facilities.

Contact: For an air taxi, contact Wright Air Service, P.O. Box 60142, Fairbanks, AK 99706, (907) 474-0502; or Bettles Air Service, 2453 Homestead, North Pole, AK 99705, (800) 770-5111.

Fishing the Upper Chandalar River: The Chandalar River system drains a major portion of the central Brooks Range in its journey from mountain headwaters to the Yukon. (It joins the big river near the village of Venetie Landing.) An extensive, multiforked wilderness river known for exciting float adventures, the Chandalar also offers some notable angling possibilities.

Northern pike, sheefish, and even some salmon inhabit its lower reaches above Yukon Flats, but the upper river, with its many swift and pristine headwaters and numerous associated lakes, has the most exciting fishing. The larger headwater lakes of the Middle and North Forks—Chandalar, Squaw, and Ackerman—are scenic, deep mountain pools with solid lake trout populations. Chandalar has the best fishing, with definite trophy potential and the bonus of some good pike as well. All of the lakes have abundant grayling in their outlet and inlet streams. Late spring and fall are the best times—Chandalar and Squaw Lakes can get turbid from runoff and are best right at breakup and in the fall. The three main forks (especially the East Fork) of the Chandalar have a proliferation of foothill lakes in their upper reaches—many with untouched pike and grayling populations. All are very scenic and wild.

Though fly-ins to Chandalar, Ackerman, or Squaw Lakes in spring or fall (combined with hunting) are the most common way of fishing the system, a raft or kayak trip down from the headwaters is a tantalizing option that can combine exciting sport fish exploration with pristine white water, making an ideal wilderness float adventure.

❹ Jim River/ Prospect Creek

Location: In the central Brooks Range (south side), 165 miles north of Fairbanks; see map page 204.

USGS maps: Bettles D-1, D-2, D-3; Beaver D-6.

How to get there: By car via the Dalton Highway. Several bridges cross Prospect Creek and various branches of the Jim River (mileposts 135, 140, 141, and 144), the last being the most com-

monly used by anglers fishing the river. A winter road from Bettles provides additional access.

Highlights: A Haul Road location providing access to good fishing for grayling (from May through September) and other species.

Species: Chum salmon, grayling, northern pike, *king salmon.*

Regulations: Open year-round, all species.

Facilities: No developed public facilities. Undeveloped campsites are available at several spots along Bettles Winter Road.

Contact: For fishing information, contact the Alaska Department of Fish and Game, Sportfish Division, 1300 College Road, Fairbanks, AK 99701; (907) 456-8819.

Fishing the Jim River/Prospect Creek: If you're fishing the Haul Road, you'll probably want to stop at one of the Jim River or Prospect Creek crossings. They just look too good to pass by, and they're said to be two of the better fishing locations along the Dalton Highway. Tributaries of the South Fork Koyukuk, these clear, shallow streams, in their reaches beyond the immediate area of the highway, can provide decent grayling fishing, with some northern pike and a few salmon as added bonuses.

Most folks access and fish them at one of several bridge crossings, but it's best to float them by canoe or raft from the highway put ins, then take out at the Bettles Winter Road that crosses at several points below (either 10 miles down on the Jim River or a few miles farther on the Koyukuk). By floating farther in you'll get beyond the frequently fished stretches of river to more virgin water. Spring and early fall are the best times for grayling, while midsummer brings opportunities for catch-and-release salmon fishing.

Middle Yukon River

With its many sprawling tributaries and extensive, lake-dotted lowlands, the winding, wide Middle Yukon dominates the Interior region and provides major habitat for a variety of important sport species, including chum and king salmon, northern pike, sheefish, and grayling.

Silty in its main stem all the way up to the headwaters, the river's sport fish potential is concentrated in clearer tributary lakes, sloughs, and streams, with some well known for outstanding fishing—the Nowitna Flats, Tozitna, Ray, Dall, Hodzana, and Melozitna Rivers and others. Access is usually by riverboat from Fairbanks or major communities along the Yukon (Galena, Ruby, Tanana, and Manley).

The Yukon Flats, a vast wetland between Circle and Stevens Village, below the confluence of the Porcupine, is particularly noteworthy for its tens of thousands of lakes, marshy backwaters, and slow-moving streams—a paradise for big toothy pike and sheefish. Though this area, like the others, lies well off the beaten path, its potential shouldn't be overlooked. Access is by boat or small plane from Fort Yukon or Circle. Some of the better fishing locations within the Yukon Flats are the lower Hadweenzic, Christian, Chandalar, Sheenjek, Porcupine, and Black Rivers.

❺ Melozitna River System

Location: In the central Yukon River drainage, 230 miles west of Fairbanks, 305 miles northwest of Anchorage; see map page 204.

USGS maps: Melozitna A-4, A-5, B-4, C-1, C-2, C-3; Ruby D-5, D-6.

How to get there: By boat from Ruby to the mouth of the Melozitna and the lower river. Floatplanes arriving from Galena or Fairbanks can land on the main stem Yukon River near the confluence or on the middle river in straight sections of water. It is possible to raft/kayak from the middle of the river downstream to the mouth with three sets of rapids in Melozitna Canyon.

Highlights: A vast, remote drainage with good fishing potential for northern pike and grayling (from June through September).

Species: Arctic charr, chum salmon, grayling, northern pike, sheefish, *king salmon*.

Regulations: Open year-round, all species.

Facilities: No developed public facilities.

Contact: For fishing information, contact the Alaska Department of Fish and Game, Sportfish Division, 1300 College Road, Fairbanks, AK 99701; (907) 456-8819. For an air taxi, contact

Wright Air Service, P.O. Box 60142, Fairbanks, AK 99706; (907) 474-0502.

Fishing the Melozitna River System: The Melozitna originates in the Slokhenjikh Hills of the Ray Mountains in central Alaska and flows southwest to join the Yukon River near Ruby. It's a slow-moving river in the upper reaches, draining a significant area with many small ponds and muskeg swamps that greatly influence the color of the water. The river picks up speed as it moves through Melozitna Canyon (Class II and Class III) until the last few miles, where it slows down just prior to reaching the Yukon. Fairly remote but productive, the Melozitna offers good angling opportunities for several popular sport fish species.

Northern pike are abundant in the middle section of the Melozitna as this area is ideal habitat—slow, deep water with numerous sloughs. While the action can be fast and furious in spots, the fish are seldom very large. (A typical Melozitna pike weighs four to 10 pounds, but larger specimens are frequently taken.) The lower river section is generally too swift for pike, though a few fish may be taken at the confluence.

During the summer months, anglers whipping flies and tossing small spinners may connect with feisty arctic grayling up to 18 inches or more in any of the many clear tributaries from the headwaters to the mouth. Selecting swift, clear streams to feed in through the warmer months, the grayling move back into the main stem in fall when temperatures cool. Hot Springs Creek is one popular spot for great grayling fly-fishing.

Salmon are also present in the Melozitna. Chums are the most abundant, but you'll encounter a few kings spawning in some of the tributaries. In July, large numbers of summer-run chum ascend the river destined for suitable clear-water spawning areas, yet they do not support any extensive fishery and are only caught incidentally.

In midsummer, it's possible to hook sheefish in the four- to 12-pound range at the mouth, with fair action to be expected. These fish will be feeding and are intercepted here on their way upstream to fall spawning grounds. Charr are also taken now and then from the main stem river and a few tributaries.

Despite the fine fishing to be enjoyed throughout this extensive system, the Melozitna River doesn't receive a great amount of angling effort. It's mostly fished by folks from nearby Ruby and Galena, and occasionally Fairbanks, leaving many hot spots to be discovered in the area. If you're looking to explore a little-known river with great fishing possibilities, this is it.

❻ Nowitna River System

Location: In the central Yukon River drainage, 190 miles west of Fairbanks, 250 miles northwest of Anchorage; see map page 204.

USGS maps: Ruby A-1, A-2, A-3, A-4, B-1, B-2, B-3, C-2, C-3, C-4, D-3; Kantishna River A-6, B-6; Medfra B-6, C-4, C-5, C-6, D-4, D-5.

How to get there: By boat from the nearby town of Ruby to the mouth; by plane from Fairbanks or Galena, landing on the main stem Nowitna, sloughs, lakes, or the larger Yukon River. Rafting parties can put in near the headwaters and float to the mouth.

Highlights: A huge, remote clear-water Interior drainage with excellent fishing potential for northern pike (from June through September); also good fishing possibilities for sheefish (from June through October) and grayling (from June through September).

Species: Chum salmon, grayling, northern pike, sheefish, *silver salmon.*

Regulations: Open year-round, all species.

Facilities: No developed public facilities.

Contact: For guide services, contact Timberwolf Guiding Service, P.O. Box 70187, Tanana, AK 99777; (907) 366-7225. For fishing information, contact the Alaska Department of Fish and Game, Sportfish Division, 1300 College Road, Fairbanks, AK 99701; (907) 456-8819. For an air taxi, contact Wright Air Service, P.O. Box 60142, Fairbanks, AK 99706; (907) 474-0502. For more information, contact the Nowitna National Wildlife Refuge, P.O. Box 287, Galena, AK 99741; (907) 656-1231.

Fishing the Nowitna River System: Designated a Wild and Scenic River, the Nowitna begins on the northwest slopes of the Kuskokwim Mountains and flows 283 miles to its confluence with the Yukon. The entire drainage covers more than 7,000 square miles and is one of the larger, more productive clear-water systems in the Interior. There are more than 14,000 lakes and ponds within the Nowitna National Wildlife Refuge, a vast area that encompasses the lower and middle portions of Nowitna River, along with surrounding wetlands. This makes some remarkable sportfishing possible for slow-water species like pike and sheefish, which, up to now, have received very little attention from anglers.

Over the past few years, more and more interest has been directed toward the Nowitna's abundant and potentially large northern pike. Found throughout much of the river, these greedy water wolves reach weights of up to 32 pounds (sometimes larger), with specimens larger than 20 pounds not uncommon. Due to prime habitat, particularly on the middle and lower main stem and adjoining lakes, the fish are year-round residents, with phenomenal catch rates reported during the summer months. The lower portions of major tributaries also yield good numbers of pike, including the Sulatna, Little Mud, Lost, and Big Mud Rivers and Grand Creek.

Resident sheefish are found throughout most of the system with the greatest concentrations occurring in the middle and lower main stem Nowitna, sloughs, and lower portions of major tributaries. Lakes in this area only contain small numbers of sheefish. Good action can be expected along the Nowitna River in summer and fall, and the Sulatna River in September and October for large spawners typically weighing between six and 15 pounds. Arctic grayling are also found in fishable numbers in the main stem during spring and fall, while fairly swift headwater tributaries are generally better in summer.

You'll find other species like salmon and charr, but in lesser numbers. Both "summer" and "fall" runs of chum salmon ascend the Nowitna, spawning in various locations throughout the drainage. Silver salmon have also been reported but are far less numerous, while a small population of stunted, resident Dolly Varden are present in a few tributaries, such as California Creek and the Sulukna River.

The Nowitna is becoming increasingly popular for floating, which is a great way for anglers to discover the superb fishing and wildlife on one of the more remote rivers of Alaska's great Interior. Put in is via small plane at the Meadow Creek confluence, with takeout at the Yukon River, after about 250 miles of mostly Class I water.

❼ Tozitna River

Location: In the central Yukon River drainage, 140 miles west of Fairbanks, 290 miles north of Anchorage; see map page 204.

USGS maps: Tanana A-5, A-6, B-5, B-6, C-2, C-3, C-4, C-5, C-6, D-5.

How to get there: By boat and floatplane. From the town of Tanana, boaters can access the river mouth and upstream stretches for many miles. Visitors arriving by floatplane from Fairbanks, Galena, or other population centers usually land on the main stem Yukon River near the confluence with the Tozitna River.

Highlights: A largely remote and unexplored river system providing good fishing for sheefish (from June through August) and northern pike (June through September).

Species: Grayling, northern pike, sheefish, *chum salmon, king salmon.*

Regulations: Open year-round, all species.

Facilities: No developed public facilities.

Contact: For fishing information, contact the Alaska Department of Fish and Game, Sportfish Division, 1300 College Road, Fairbanks, AK 99701; (907) 456-8819. For an air taxi, contact Wright Air Service, P.O. Box 60142, Fairbanks, AK 99706; (907) 474-0502.

Fishing the Tozitna River: Draining the south slopes of the Ray Mountains, the tannic-stained Tozitna meanders southward to the Yukon River. Not quite as large as the nearby Melozitna and Nowitna Rivers, it is nonetheless a significant system consisting of numerous small lakes, ponds, and clear-water streams offering good sportfishing opportunities for those willing to explore this remote drainage.

Except for some of the creeks at the headwaters, the main stem Tozitna is slow flowing with many sloughs and oxbow lakes, particularly on the lower section near the mouth. The little angling pressure that does take place here occurs where the Tozitna empties into the silty waters of the Yukon. Fishing is decent overall, with

sheefish and northern pike being the more sought-after game fish. During the summer months, look for feeding sheefish right in the mouth where the two drainages mix. Flashy spoons tossed into the glacial Yukon and retrieved into the clear Tozitna often produce vicious strikes. Northern pike are spread throughout the lower and middle river. You'll find the best action in areas with characteristic pike habitat, such as sloughs, oxbow lakes, and outlets of tributaries, including the mouth of the Tozitna. There is plenty of prey in the river as evidenced by the huge numbers of whitefish in the system. Arctic grayling are sometimes taken in spring and fall during their migrations between the summer feeding grounds at the headwaters and the overwintering areas in the Yukon River.

Salmon are present in midsummer and may be caught incidentally when fishing for other species. Kings and chums both spawn in the river, but are usually quite dark when entering the fishery. However, you may hook the occasional semibright specimen at the mouth of the Tozitna.

Generally only subsistence fished by residents of Tanana, a small community located near the confluence of the Yukon and Tanana Rivers a few miles upstream, the Tozitna offers some sport angling during the summer months. It's worth a visit whenever in the area.

Note: The Alaska state record whitefish (nine pounds) came from the Tozitna.

❽ Ray River

Location: In the central Yukon River drainage, 90 miles northwest of Fairbanks, 335 miles north of Anchorage; see map page 204.

USGS maps: Livengood D-6; Tanana C-2, D-1, D-2; Bettles A-1.

How to get there: By boat from the Dalton Highway bridge where it crosses the Yukon River. It's a short ride, about 3.5 miles, to the mouth of the river. Another option is to use a floatplane from Fairbanks, landing on the main stem Yukon near the confluence.

Highlights: One of the more popular locations among boaters due to easy access and good fishing for northern pike (from June through September).

Species: Grayling, northern pike, sheefish.

Regulations: Open year-round, all species.

Facilities: There are no developed public facilities at the river, but a boat launch is located at the Dalton Highway bridge.

Contact: For fishing information, contact the Alaska Department of Fish and Game, Sportfish Division, 1300 College Road, Fairbanks, AK 99701; (907) 456-8819. For an air taxi, contact Wright Air Service, P.O. Box 60142, Fairbanks, AK 99706; (907) 474-0502.

Fishing the Ray River: For easy access and a decent shot at pike action on a semiremote river, the Ray is hard to beat. Smaller than many other drainages along the Yukon, the Ray River originates from the north slope of the Ray Mountains and meanders southward to the silty Yukon River. It's fairly wide from the mouth on upstream for perhaps a little less than a mile, but the Ray River is navigable to boaters for at least six to eight miles up the main stem. For many years, the Ray River has been a local hot spot and continues to produce great pike fishing even today.

Although a few incidental sheefish may be taken from the mouth of the Ray in the summer months, the main fishery here is for northern pike. Generally not known to produce very large fish (three to 10 pounds), the river does hold consistent action for these scrappy fighters, with occasional catches weighing into the teens. The last mile or so of the river is sometimes a hot spot, but pike may be encountered in significant numbers throughout much of the drainage, except around the headwaters. Deep, slow holes and pools often yield a few fish as do sloughs and still-water areas. Arctic grayling are present in fair numbers in the spring and fall months during their annual migrations to and from summer feeding grounds farther upstream. They may be effectively taken using flies and small spinners.

❾ Dall River System

Location: In the upper Yukon River drainage, 95 miles northwest of Fairbanks, 340 miles north of Anchorage; see map page 204.

USGS maps: Beaver A-5, A-6, B-6.

How to get there: By boat from the Dalton Highway bridge on the Yukon River via a launch by the bridge and a 20-mile ride up the Yukon to the mouth of the Dall River. Floatplanes can land on the main stem Yukon River near the confluence area.

Highlights: A noted local fishery with trophy potential for northern pike (from June through September); also good grayling fishing.

Species: Grayling, northern pike, sheefish.

Regulations: Open year-round, all species.

Facilities: No developed public facilities.

Contact: For fishing information, contact the Alaska Department of Fish and Game, Sportfish Division, 1300 College Road, Fairbanks, AK 99701; (907) 456-8819. For an air taxi, contact Wright Air Service, P.O. Box 60142, Fairbanks, AK 99706; (907) 474-0502.

Fishing the Dall River System: The main stem Dall originates just south of Dall Mountain near the Arctic Circle, while the West and East Forks flow out of the Yukon Flats within the Yukon Flats National Wildlife Refuge. It's an extensive drainage, comprising numerous clearwater streams, large and small lakes, and stillwater sloughs—the ideal habitat for pike, sheefish, and other slow-water species. The Dall is especially known for its hefty northerns. (A typical fish weighs anywhere between four and 12 pounds, with larger pike not uncommon— some old northerns up to 25 and 30 pounds have been taken.)

Most angling activity occurs at or near the confluence of the Dall and Yukon Rivers, but fishing is noteworthy in the lower sections of many adjoining streams and lakes, such as the area around East Fork. Although infrequently caught, sheefish there sometimes attack flashy spoons meant for pike. These silvery, aerial fighters are usually hooked where the clear waters of the Dall mix with the silty Yukon. Sometimes you'll encounter arctic grayling in good numbers on the lower river, especially in spring and fall, with the better action found during the brief summer months near the headwaters in small streams, lakes, and ponds. This river is one of the better bets for a do-it-yourself trip as access is fairly easy and the fish abundant and aggressive.

⑩ Birch–Beaver Creek Systems

Location: On the upper Yukon River drainage, 50 to 125 miles north of Fairbanks, 300 to 375 miles north of Anchorage; see map page 204.

USGS maps: Livengood B-1, B-2, C-1, C-2, D-1, D-2; Circle B-1, B-2, B-3, B-4, C-1, C-2, C-3, C-4, C-5, C-6, D-1, D-2, D-3, D-4, D-5, D-6; Fort Yukon A-2, A-3, A-4, A-5, A-6, B-3, B-4, B-5, B-6, C-5; Beaver A-1, A-2, B-1.

How to get there: By car and floatplane. The upper portions of Birch and Beaver Creeks are accessed by the Steese Highway from Fairbanks and often serve as starting points for extensive float trips. The mouths of these two drainages and surrounding lakes are more commonly reached by floatplane from Fairbanks or other towns in the region.

Highlights: A vast watershed with optimum angling opportunities; good fishing for northern pike and grayling (from June through September).

Species: Grayling, northern pike, *chum salmon, king salmon, sheefish, silver salmon.*

Regulations: Open year-round, all species.

Facilities: No developed public facilities.

Contact: For fishing information, contact the Alaska Department of Fish and Game, Sportfish Division, 1300 College Road, Fairbanks, AK 99701; (907) 456-8819. For an air taxi, contact Wright Air Service, P.O. Box 60142, Fairbanks, AK 99706; (907) 474-0502.

Fishing the Birch–Beaver Creek Systems: Birch Creek originates from within the Steese National Conservation Area on the east side of the White Mountains. It predominantly flows through areas with upland plateaus, forested valleys, and heavy marshland northward to the Yukon River. Beaver Creek begins in the White Mountains National Recreation Area and runs through rolling hills, jagged mountain peaks, and, finally, Yukon Flats marshes to the glacial Yukon River. Both systems are designated as Wild and Scenic Rivers and attract floaters who want to experience a remote yet accessible part of Alaska.

Birch and Beaver Creeks connect through a long channel towards the lower end of the drainages,

but in reality they are two separate systems. Both offer outstanding fishing, with northern pike and grayling being the dominant species. Pike are most abundant in the lower areas of the systems where ideal habitat can be found, such as sloughs, ponds, oxbow lakes, and a lot of deep, slow-flowing water. Although smaller pike may be found up near the headwaters, you'll find larger fish on the lower end. Due to their remoteness, the drainages aren't heavily fished, but anglers who venture here can snag trophy northerns that may weigh as much as 20 pounds or more.

Grayling thrive in the higher elevations, near the headwaters where the current is swifter and deep pools and riffles are present. Action can be very good at times using flies and spinners during the summer months. Feeding sheefish are taken incidentally, while pike fishing at the mouths of Birch and Beaver Creeks seldom ascends the systems for more than a few miles.

Floaters thoroughly enjoy prospecting the very scenic upper sections around the White Mountains along both creeks. If taking the Beaver Creek route, put in is off the Steese Highway on Nome Creek with a 127-mile Class I float down to the confluence with Victoria Creek. Take out here with a prearranged pickup by plane. For the Birch Creek route, access is also off Steese Highway at the headwaters of the stream. Put in there and float 126 miles to the Steese Highway bridge near the town of Circle. For the most part, Birch Creek has Class I water, except for a few Class III rapids that must be negotiated. Keep in mind that after long dry spell periods the water can be very low, making for difficult floating conditions. Kayaks and canoes are best suited for these trips.

⑪ Charley River

Location: On the upper Yukon River drainage, 125 miles east of Fairbanks, 330 miles northeast of Anchorage; see map page 204.

USGS maps: Charley River A-4, A-5, B-4; Eagle C-6, D-4, D-5, D-6.

How to get there: By plane and helicopter from Fairbanks, Tanacross, or other towns in the area. Wheelplanes and helicopters can use primitive landing strips just above Copper Creek and at Galvan near the headwaters, while floatplanes access the river mouth by landing on the Yukon River near the confluence.

Highlights: A National Wild and Scenic River with good to excellent fishing for grayling (from June through September).

Species: Grayling, northern pike, *chum salmon, king salmon, sheefish, silver salmon*.

Regulations: Open year-round, all species.

Facilities: No developed public facilities.

Contact: For fishing information, contact the Alaska Department of Fish and Game, Sportfish Division, 1300 College Road, Fairbanks, AK 99701; (907) 456-8819. For an air taxi, contact Wright Air Service, P.O. Box 60142, Fairbanks, AK 99706; (907) 474-0502. For more information, contact the Public Lands Information Center, 250 Cushman Street, Suite 1A, Fairbanks, AK 99701; (907) 451-7352.

Fishing the Charley River: Originating at 4,000 feet in the Mertie Mountains of the Yukon, within the Charley Rivers National Preserve, this beautiful, meandering river provides the chance for some great floating and good fishing.

The lower 16 miles or so of the drainage hold northern pike with the best chances for angling located near the confluence with the Yukon River. Expect fair action using flashy spoons and wobblers in sloughs and deep holes with slow-flowing current. Arctic grayling are considerably more abundant and usually encountered in the more mountainous regions of Charley and in clear-water tributaries near the headwaters. Anglers opting to float the Charley are in for some magnificent scenery, as well as a chance to match wits with both pike and grayling.

If you're spending some time at the mouth of the Charley where it meets the silty Yukon, you may hook sheefish in June and July. Don't be surprised to find a salmon on the end of the line. Small runs of king, silver, and chum salmon ascend the Charley River, starting in midsummer and continuing through fall.

The Charley River is rated Class II with some stretches of Class III and IV rapids. Usually running low and clear in summer, the river can rise several feet in mere hours after rainstorms, which may create a hazard for floaters. Put in is at Copper Creek with takeout at the river mouth, about a four-day trip. It's possible to extend the float an additional two days by continuing down the Yukon to the town of Circle, which can be accessed from the Steese Highway from Fairbanks.

Tanana River Valley

A major tributary of the Yukon, the Tanana originates primarily from meltwater draining off the immense Nabesna and Chisana Glaciers high in the Wrangell Mountains. The river flows more than 500 miles northwest before joining the mighty Yukon just west of the town of Manley. The most accessible and popular Interior watershed for recreation, the Tanana River drainage offers a wide variety of water and fishing, with abundant grayling, northern pike, lake trout, some sheefish, and the best of Interior's limited fishing for chinook and coho salmon. Since the Tanana is a braided, glacial river system, sportfishing potential is concentrated in clear, upland tributaries—the Salcha, Chena, Chatanika, and Delta Clearwater Rivers—and in sloughs, lakes, and slower streams along the Tanana Flats (the Minto, Tolvana, and Kantishna Rivers and Fish Creek).

⑫ Chena River System

Location: In the middle Tanana River drainage, in the Fairbanks area, 265 miles north of Anchorage; see map page 204.

USGS maps: Circle A-1, A-2, A-3, A-4, A-5, A-6; Livengood A-1; Big Delta C-4, C-5, C-6, D-4, D-5, D-6; Fairbanks D-1, D-2.

How to get there: By car from a series of city roads within Fairbanks; see a detailed city map. You can easily reach upper areas via Chena Hot Springs Road from the Steese Expressway.

Highlights: Easy access and great variety make up one of Interior's most popular fishing locations. Good fishing for king (in late July) and landlocked silver salmon (from November through April), rainbow trout (in June and from September through October), arctic charr (August through October), and grayling (June through September).

Species: Arctic charr, chum salmon, grayling, king salmon, northern pike, rainbow trout, sheefish, silver salmon.

Regulations: Closed to salmon upstream of the dam; other restrictions apply. For details, consult the current Alaska Department of Fish and Game regulations or contact the ADF&G Fairbanks office, (907) 456-4359.

Facilities: Hotel, commercial lodging, boat launching, sporting goods, groceries, water, gas and fuel, and guide services are available in Fairbanks.

Contact: For fishing information, contact the Alaska Department of Fish and Game, Sportfish Division, 1300 College Road, Fairbanks, AK 99701; (907) 456-8819. For hotel and lodging information, contact the Fairbanks Convention and Visitor's Bureau, 550 First Avenue, Fairbanks, AK 99701; (907) 456-5774 or (800) 327-5774.

Fishing the Chena River System: The Chena River originates from the mountains south of the Steese National Conservation Area. Many small tributaries enter the river along its course with at least one sizable lake annexed to the drainage. While the upper sections are fairly narrow and fast flowing, the lower Chena is wide and smooth with little current. Because of its proximity to Fairbanks, local angling interest is high.

Once a most productive arctic grayling fishery, the Chena River today is only beginning to re-cover from depressed populations caused by overharvesting. After a brief period of total clo-sure, the fishing is rebounding with catch rates increasing substantially the last few seasons. The upper river sections are delightful to fish as they have classic stream conditions—deep holes, pools, cutbanks, and shallow riffles and runs, perfect for enticing grayling with flies and small spinners. Badger Slough on the lower river also yields fish.

The lower Chena is a productive spot for salmon, with sporadic catches of sheefish and northern pike also reported. Summer runs of king and chum are present, with good catch-and-release fishing for kings possible in various holding ar-eas throughout the lower river (such as below the Flood Control Dam). A few "Tarpon of the North" sheefish are caught occasionally during the summer months when they come in to feed. Pike, however, are slightly more common; you'll have a fair chance of hooking one in sloughs and side channels (Badger Slough among others).

Chena Lake, located on Eielson Air Force Base and connected to the system via a small creek, is stocked with species that are not native to the area, such as landlocked silver salmon, rainbow trout, and arctic charr. It's a very popular and well-known Interior fishing location that pro-vides locals with fair to good action year-round.

If a visit to Fairbanks is on the itinerary, plan to spend a few pleasant hours checking out the Chena. Though the lower river is quite urban, the upper sections along Chena Hot Springs Road will surprise you with their solitude.

⓭ Chatanika River System

Location: In the lower Tanana River drainage, 20 miles northwest of Fairbanks, 265 miles north of Anchorage; see map page 204.

USGS maps: Circle A-6, B-4, B-5, B-6; Livengood A-1, A-2, A-3, A-4, A-5, B-2, B-3; Fairbanks D-2, D-3, D-4.

How to get there: By car from Fairbanks. The Elliott Highway crosses the middle section of the river, while the Steese Highway crosses and par-allels the upper sections with trails or side roads providing additional access. Small rafts or inflatables may be floated between the road access points. Canoes can be used on calmer sections of the middle and lower river.

Highlights: One of Interior's most popular rivers, offering good fishing for northern pike (from June through September), king salmon (in late July), and grayling (from June through September).

Species: Chum salmon, grayling, king salmon, northern pike, sheefish, *silver salmon.*

Regulations: Closed above the Elliott Highway bridge for king salmon fishing; other restrictions apply. For details, consult the current Alaska De-partment of Fish and Game regulations or con-tact the ADF&G Fairbanks office, (907) 456-4359.

Facilities: Campgrounds and boat launches are available at road crossings.

Contact: For camping information, contact the Public Lands Information Center, 250 Cushman

Street, Suite 1A, Fairbanks, AK 99701; (907) 451-7352. For an air taxi, contact Wright Air Service, P.O. Box 60142, Fairbanks, AK 99706, (907) 474-0502.

Fishing the Chatanika River System: The clear Chatanika River flows through a very scenic valley—surrounded by the Tanana Hills to the south and the White Mountains to the north and west—before joining the Tolovana River near Minto Flats State Game Refuge. The lower river meanders considerably, with deep holes and quiet sloughs, while the upper Chatanika is shallower and faster, with many riffles and runs. Situated so close to Fairbanks, the river serves as a recreational hub for many outdoor activities, including varied and abundant fishing.

Starting in late spring or early summer, a number of fine sport fish can be taken on the Chatanika. Arctic grayling invade the river, bound for summer feeding areas near headwaters, and voracious northern pike settle into slower sections on the middle and lower drainage. Later on, summer runs of king and chum salmon arrive and draw a fair amount of angling interest around the road crossings. (By the time they have gotten this far, they're usually well advanced into prespawning, so catch-and-release fishing is the general rule.) Towards fall, anglers can intercept migrating grayling and even some small spawning runs of sheefish (from September into October).

Major tributaries of the Chatanika, like Tatalina, Washington, and Goldstream Creeks, are all good for grayling during the summer months, while pike fishing is usually hot in the deeper holes and pools around confluence areas. Lower Goldstream Creek and Minto Lakes have both been long known as top pike locations in the Interior, with trophy specimens up to 20 pounds or more present. Other areas to try for big pike are the main stem Chatanika and the sloughs and holes of the nearby Tolovana River.

The middle and upper portions of the Chatanika River also offer unique opportunities for spearing whitefish in the fall, as large schools of these fish move through the shallows in September and October during spawning migrations. "Fishing" is usually done at night using lanterns, and some folks even take whitefish with bow and arrow.

Despite fairly high use over the years, the Chatanika River still holds up as a very productive drainage. It's well worth the time if you're planning a trip to the Fairbanks area.

⓮ Fish Creek System

Location: In the lower Tanana River drainage, 115 miles northwest of Fairbanks, 275 miles northwest of Anchorage; see map page 204.

USGS maps: Tanana A-3, A-4.

How to get there: By plane from Fairbanks. Experienced floatplane pilots can land on the main stem Tanana near the mouth of Fish Creek. Wheelplanes can use Fish Creek Island as a landing site, then anglers can canoe over to the fishing area.

Highlights: A small but famous stream known for its healthy pike population, with outstanding fishing possible (from June through September).

Species: Northern pike, *grayling*.

Regulations: Open year-round, all species.

Facilities: No developed public facilities.

Contact: For fishing information, contact the Alaska Department of Fish and Game, Sportfish Division, 1300 College Road, Fairbanks, AK 99701; (907) 456-8819. For an air taxi, contact Tundra Air, P.O. Box 87, Manley Hot Springs, AK 99756, (907) 672-3692; or Wright Air Service, P.O. Box 60142, Fairbanks, AK 99706, (907) 474-0502.

Fishing the Fish Creek System: Fish Creek is a small, meandering stream with a big reputation for northern pike. The old state record fish—a 38-pounder—was taken from the mouth back in 1978. The drainage continues to live up to its reputation for trophy specimens, with many fine pike still reported. The creek drains out of Fish Lake, a fair-sized body of water about 20 miles southeast of the town of Tanana. It's well known for its high productivity, so it receives a fair amount of angling pressure.

Considerably smaller in size and length than many other rivers along the Tanana, Fish Creek manages to hold its own because it has all the necessary ingredients for a healthy population of large northerns—plenty of sloughs, braided channels, ponds, and still backwaters, plus abundant forage in the form of whitefish and suckers. The water is tannic-stained from heavy bog and tundra infiltration. Most anglers concentrate their attention on the lower stream area and do very well there all through summer into fall, for pike in the four- to 10-pound class, with occasional catches up to 20 pounds or more. Spoons, top water plugs, and big, bushy flies are the ticket, according to locals, who insist the new state record is lurking somewhere within the area's deep, dark waters.

⑮ Chitanana River System

Location: In the lower Tanana River drainage, 115 miles west of Fairbanks, 265 miles north of Anchorage; see map page 204.

USGS maps: Kantishna River C-5, C-6, D-4, D-5.

How to get there: By plane from Fairbanks. Experienced floatplane pilots may land near the mouth of Chitanana on the main stem Tanana. Wheelplanes can land on the large gravel bar southeast of the confluence.

Highlights: A very remote, little-fished drainage with outstanding potential for northern pike (from June through September).

Species: Grayling, northern pike, sheefish.

Regulations: Open year-round, all species.

Facilities: No developed public facilities.

Contact: For fishing information, contact the Alaska Department of Fish and Game, Sportfish Division, 1300 College Road, Fairbanks, AK 99701; (907) 456-8819. For an air taxi, contact Wright Air Service, P.O. Box 60142, Fairbanks, AK 99706; (907) 474-0502.

Fishing the Chitanana River System: Also known as Redlands Creek, the Chitanana River begins in the northwestern slopes of Chitanatala Mountains west of the Kantishna drainage, where it flows north and east towards the glacial Tanana. Not a particularly broad river, it is nonetheless quite vast with considerable meandering, slow-moving water—perfect conditions for large numbers of toothy pike. Rarely fished, the Chitanana seldom disappoints the few anglers who make the effort to try its waters during the peak of pike season.

An abundance of fish in the four- to 10-pound range inhabit the tannic-stained river, and ample numbers much larger. This area of the Tanana is known for its monster pike up to 30 pounds and more. Casting flashy spoons for these greedy fish eaters can result in an occasional sheefish as well, especially when fishing near the confluence where the clear waters of the Chitanana mix with the silty Tanana. You can also expect fair numbers of arctic grayling during the spring and fall months.

Along with the Cosna River, the Chitanana has yet to be "discovered" and can offer some fabulous fishing.

⑯ Cosna River System

Location: In the lower Tanana River drainage, 110 miles west of Fairbanks, 250 miles north of Anchorage; see map page 204.

USGS maps: Kantishna B-4, B-5, C-4, C-5, D-3, D-4.

How to get there: By floatplane from Fairbanks or boat from Manley Hot Springs. Boaters can launch from Hot Springs Slough and access the mouth of the Cosna via the Tanana River. Experienced floatplane pilots can attempt to land on the Tanana near the confluence.

Highlights: A remote Interior river with great angling potential for northern pike (from June through September).

Species: Grayling, northern pike, sheefish.

Regulations: Open year-round, all species.

Facilities: No developed public facilities.

Contact: For fishing information, contact the Alaska Department of Fish and Game, Sportfish Division, 1300 College Road, Fairbanks, AK 99701; (907) 456-8819. For an air taxi, contact Wright Air Service, P.O. Box 60142, Fairbanks, AK 99706; (907) 474-0502.

Fishing the Cosna River System: Like the Zitziana River to the east, the Cosna originates in a highland region of the Kuskokwim Mountains in central Alaska. Meandering considerably during its northward course to a confluence with the glacial Tanana, the Cosna is a true wilderness drainage, with a reputation for good northern pike fishing.

Receiving very little angling effort, mostly at the mouth where its slightly tannic waters hit the silty Tanana, the Cosna drainage has miles of highly productive water, as it is an active feeding ground for hungry northerns and even a few sheefish. The summer and early fall months are the best times to hit its waters. Try the slow, deep stretches where pike between four and 10 pounds (and some even larger) have a habit of lurking for prey. Sheefish are less common and, for the most part, are only caught incidentally. You'll also find fair numbers of arctic grayling in the spring and fall.

⑰ Zitziana River System

Location: In the lower Tanana River drainage, 85 miles west of Fairbanks, 250 miles north of Anchorage; see map page 204.

USGS maps: Kantishna River B-3, C-2, C-3, D-1, D-2.

How to get there: By boat from Manley Hot Springs. Visitors can use the launch at the bridge crossing Hot Springs Slough to access the main stem Tanana River and the mouth of the Zitziana on the south side several miles upstream.

Highlights: A small, remote Interior river receiving little angling attention, but with good potential for sheefish (from June through August), northern pike (from June through September), and grayling (in May and September).

Species: Grayling, northern pike, sheefish.

Regulations: Open year-round, all species.

Facilities: No developed public facilities.

Contact: For fishing information, contact the Alaska Department of Fish and Game, Sportfish Division, 1300 College Road, Fairbanks, AK 99701; (907) 456-8819.

Fishing the Zitziana River System: The Zitziana is a small, meandering system that issues from the southwestern Kuskokwim Mountains about 75 miles west of Fairbanks. A fair amount of swamp and bog water contribute greatly to its brown, tannic-stained color. Its lower reaches, however, are ideal habitat for northern pike. Because of its remoteness, it receives very little angling pressure.

A local favorite among residents of Manley Hot Springs, the "Zit" has a history of producing good angling for at least three important species. You can take northern pike, the obvious favorite, at the Tanana confluence and upstream

for several miles. Typically weighing six to eight pounds, they are aggressive and plentiful, and best fished during summer and early fall. Sheefish are also present on the lower Zitziana and yield good catches where the off-colored water of the drainage mixes with the silty Tanana River. Although they're generally not very large (four to six pounds average, up to about 12 pounds), the Zitziana shees are quite numerous. Arctic grayling are also encountered in spring and fall during the annual migrations to and from summer feeding grounds in the headwaters.

The surrounding country is entirely wild, enhancing the experience for anyone wanting to partake of some serious pike fishing, with additional opportunities for sheefish and grayling.

⑱ Kantishna River System

Location: In the lower Tanana River drainage, 65 miles southwest of Fairbanks, 165 miles north of Anchorage; see map page 204.

USGS maps: Mount McKinley A-2, A-3, A-4, A-5, B-1, B-2, B-3, B-4, B-5, C-1, C-2, C-3, C-4, C-5, C-6, D-1, D-2, D-3, D-4, D-5; Healy B-6, C-6, D-6; Fairbanks A-6, B-6, C-6, D-6; Kantishna River A-1, A-2, A-3, A-4, B-1, B-2, B-3, C-1, C-2, D-1.

How to get there: By small plane from Fairbanks. Several lakes adjoining the system are used as landing sites for floatplanes, and some skilled pilots may also try oxbow lakes or quiet sloughs and straight stretches of the main river. Wheelplanes have access to a landing strip at Lake Minchumina.

Highlights: A very remote and scenic system with excellent fishing opportunities for northern pike (from June through September) and grayling (from May through September).

Species: Chum salmon, grayling, king salmon, northern pike, silver salmon, *sheefish*.

Regulations: There are seasonal closures on portions of the drainage for chum salmon. For details and further restrictions, consult the current Alaska Department of Fish and Game regulations or contact the ADF&G Fairbanks office, (907) 456-4359.

Facilities: Commercial lodging is available at Lake Minchumina.

Contact: For an air taxi, contact Wright Air Service, P.O. Box 60142, Fairbanks, AK 99706; (907) 474-0502. For lodging information, contact Denali West Lodge, P.O. Box 40, Lake Minchumina, AK 99757; (907) 674-3112.

Fishing the Kantishna River System: With headwaters in the Alaska Range, the Kantishna River system is extensive and remote. It features an amazing number of tributary streams, lakes, and sloughs, many of which are within Denali National Park. Some truly great fishing on this system is largely ignored, save for a few main lakes and other locations.

Northern pike and arctic grayling are the two main species of interest around the Kantishna drainage, with some of the finest pike opportunities in the state available here, particularly for trophy specimens. Lakes and sloughs of the Lake Minchumina area are particularly noteworthy, as are drainages farther down along the main stem. Mucha, Wein, West, and East Twin Lakes are relatively well-known spots for large northerns up to 30 pounds. Many smaller lakes, such as Alma, John Hansen, Sandless, and dozens of others with no names in the Bearpaw River area, offer abundant fishing. (These lakes are great ice fishing spots, too, and can be accessed by snowmachine via a trail from the Parks Highway.)

Arctic grayling are abundant in all clear-water streams, with the more alpine, faster, and clear-flowing sections being especially productive. Look for suitable locations near the headwaters of the Kantishna or clear tributaries of the glacial Toklat River.

The Kantishna River system also receives a number of salmon, including king, silver, and chum, during the summer and fall months. Some of the more concentrated areas are the mouths of clear-water streams and creeks that drain into the Toklat River. (A portion of the main stem Toklat is also home to a major run of fall chum salmon.)

The lower river has two small lakes, Geskakmina and Triangle, that have been stocked with fish. Geskakmina contains landlocked silvers and rainbow trout, while Triangle has some lake trout and grayling.

⑲ Nenana River System

Location: In the middle Tanana River drainage, 50 miles southwest of Fairbanks, 160 miles north of Anchorage; see map page 204.

USGS maps: Healy A-2, A-3, A-4, B-2, B-3, B-4, B-5, B-6, C-2, C-3, C-4, C-5, C-6, D-3, D-4, D-5, D-6; Fairbanks A-4, A-5, A-6, B-4, B-5, B-6, C-5.

How to get there: By car from Fairbanks or Anchorage. The George Parks Highway crosses the river and some of its tributaries at several spots and parallels the system for many miles. To reach the better fishing, however, a boat is necessary. The Denali Highway from Cantwell provides access to the upper drainage streams.

Highlights: A road-accessible Interior fishery with decent fishing opportunities for silver salmon (in late September) and grayling (from June through August); also king salmon (in late July), chum salmon (from mid-July through mid-September), and lake trout (from June through September).

Species: Chum salmon, Dolly Varden, grayling, king salmon, lake trout, silver salmon, *northern pike, sheefish*.

Regulations: Open year-round, all species.

Facilities: Campgrounds are available in several places along the highway. There is a boat launch in Nenana. Lodging and limited services and supplies are available in Nenana and McKinley Village.

Contact: For fishing information, contact the Alaska Department of Fish and Game, Sportfish Division, P.O. Box 605, Delta Junction, AK 99737; (907) 895-4632. For guide services, contact Arctic Grayling Adventures, P.O. Box 83707, Fairbanks, AK 99708; (907) 479-0479. For camping and lodging information, contact the Public Lands Information Center, 250 Cushman Street, Suite 1A, Fairbanks, AK 99701, (907) 451-7352; or Fairbanks Convention and Visitor's Bureau, 550 First Avenue, Fairbanks, AK 99701, (907) 456-5774 or (800) 327-5774.

Fishing the Nenana River System: The silty Nenana originates in Nenana Glacier, high in the Alaska Range east of Denali, and flows north to its confluence with the larger Tanana River near the town of Nenana. It's a fairly large system encompassing small lakes, numerous clear-water streams, and even glacial rivers like the Teklanika of Denali National Park. Roadside fishing spots produce action that ranges from poor to quite good, but some of the best fishing takes legwork or a boat ride to reach.

Arctic grayling are the most abundant sport species in the Nenana. They're available anytime between March and October, but are at a peak during the warmer months. Nearly all the clear tributary streams, from the headwaters above Cantwell down, offer some measure of fishing for them, but the more accessible locations have been worked over, with predictable effects on size and abundance. Some of the more out-of-the-way locations to try for bigger and better grayling are: streams along the Denali Highway (Upper Jack River, Monahan, and Brushkana Creeks); streams off the Stampede Trail north of Healy (Fish Creek, Eightmile Lake, Upper Savage, and Teklanika Rivers); clear tributaries of the Yanert (Moose and Revine Creeks); eastside tributary streams (Moose and Walker Creeks); and the less accessible sections of streams along the highway (Panguingue, Clear, and Julius Creeks). Spring and fall are the best times to fish, but the main stem has some exciting fishing as well in late winter, when the water clears. Open leads by the mouths of tributary streams and beaver ponds are good places to try with flies and small spinners, and you might even run into a few small Dolly Varden. (You also might encounter this increasingly rare species on some of the more remote clear-water creeks.) Use extreme caution on the river ice, however.

Broad Pass Lakes along the Parks Highway have populations of lake trout as well as grayling. Summit and Edes Lakes produced fish in the 10- to 15-pound range during their heyday, but now yield only smaller lakers. Lake trout are rumored to be in Slate Lake and other small lakes at the head of tributary streams.

In midsummer, runs of king and chum salmon make their way up the Nenana, followed by a much heavier showing of silvers in fall. Since most of these salmon are well into their prespawning changes, catch-and-release fishing is the only way to go. Several streams receive salmon, but the more outstanding ones are Seventeenmile Slough, the lower sections of Julius and Clear Creeks, June Creek, and an unnamed creek that used to be an old channel of the Nenana near Anderson. The best months for silvers are August and September.

⑳ Salcha River

Location: In the middle Tanana River drainage, 40 miles southeast of Fairbanks, 250 miles northeast of Anchorage; see map page 204.

USGS maps: Circle A-1, A-2; Big Delta B-5, B-6, C-2, C-3, C-4, C-5, C-6.

How to get there: By car from Fairbanks. The Richardson Highway crosses the lower river. To reach the mouth of the Salcha and its confluence with the Tanana River, follow the well-developed trail that begins at Munson Slough and head a half mile west to the area. Boats are frequently launched from the highway bridge to access upper sections of the river or the mouth.

Highlights: A unique, road-accessible catch-and-release fishery for king salmon (in mid-July); also good grayling fishing (from June through September).

Species: Chum salmon, grayling, king salmon, northern pike, silver salmon.

Regulations: Unbaited, artificial lures only; salmon fishing is prohibited upstream of the marker 2.5 miles above the Richardson Highway bridge. For additional restrictions, consult the current Alaska Department of Fish and Game regulations or contact the ADF&G Fairbanks office, (907) 456-4359.

Facilities: A boat launch and a campground are available near the highway crossing.

Contact: For camping information, contact the Public Lands Information Center, 250 Cushman Street, Suite 1A, Fairbanks, AK 99701; (907) 451-7352.

Fishing the Salcha River: One of the larger clear-water drainages of the Tanana accessible from the road system, the Salcha is wide and very deep in places, with a slow, steady current. Originating from the mountains near Fort Wainwright Military Reservation, the Salcha meanders west about 120 miles to join the glacial Tanana River near Aurora Lodge on the Richardson Highway. A very popular river for recreation among Interior residents, it receives a good amount of angling pressure during the midsummer salmon runs.

The Salcha River has one of the largest runs of king salmon in the Tanana Valley and offers good opportunities for catch-and-release fishing for chinook averaging 20 to 25 pounds, with lunkers to 45 pounds possible. The mouth of the river has the best fishing, with heavy concentrations of kings staging in the area in July, but deep holes and runs upstream can also yield good results. Fair numbers of summer-run chums are present in July as well, and come fall, some acrobatic coho show up. The silvers, bound for the Delta Clearwater River farther up the Tanana, are intercepted at the mouth of the Salcha in September and October, along with a few fall-run chums.

Although retention of salmon is legal, it is not recommended since the majority of fish will be very close to spawning and not prime table fare. Occasionally, however, a few semibright fish are taken in the early part of the run.

Arctic grayling are also available throughout summer and fall, with the best action on the middle and upper river, which can be accessed by boat only. Flies are the favored lure, but spinners work well here, too. Northern pike aren't abundant, but a few are landed now and then in sloughs or quiet stretches of the lower and middle river or at the mouth.

㉑ Goodpaster River System

Location: In the upper Tanana River drainage, Delta Junction area, 75 miles southeast of Fairbanks, 250 miles northeast of Anchorage; see map page 204.

USGS maps: Eagle B-6, C-6; Big Delta A-1, A-2, A-3, A-4, B-1, B-2, B-3, C-1, C-2.

How to get there: By boat, floatplane, and snowmachine. The river itself has traditionally been accessed by boat from Big Delta; launch at the Richardson Highway bridge where it crosses the Tanana River and run upstream to the confluence with the Goodpaster. Floatplanes are limited to Volkmar Lake, a tributary of the Goodpaster, which is located a few

miles southeast of the main river. In winter, snowmachines access Volkmar Lake by running up the frozen Tanana River, crossing over a wooded area to the lake.

Highlights: A traditional local hot spot with excellent fishing for northern pike (from June through September) and grayling (May through September).

Species: Grayling, northern pike, *king salmon*.

Regulations: Closed to salmon fishing; pike season runs from June 1 through March 31. For additional restrictions, consult the current Alaska Department of Fish and Game regulations or contact the ADF&G Fairbanks office, (907) 456-4359.

Facilities: No developed public facilities.

Contact: For fishing information, contact the Alaska Department of Fish and Game, Sportfish Division, 1300 College Road, Fairbanks, AK 99701; (907) 456-8819. For an air taxi, contact Wright Air Service, P.O. Box 60142, Fairbanks, AK 99706; (907) 474-0502.

Fishing the Goodpaster River System: Originating from Shawnee Peak and the Black Mountain area just north of Tanana Valley State Forest, the clear-flowing Goodpaster meanders through mountainous terrain and flatlands before reaching the glacial Tanana River. The drainage has a long history as one of the better sportfishing waters of the upper Tanana, with a fair amount of angling for pike and grayling from late spring into fall.

The lower river, around Goodpaster Flats, has plenty of slow-moving water with oxbow lakes and sloughs, creating a perfect habitat for large, hungry northerns. These toothy, aggressive fighters are abundant from the mouth upstream into the foothills beyond South Fork. In addition, Volkmar Lake, which connects to the river via a very small creek, also offers some consistent pike action, with the best occurring in early summer and fall. Although pike are generally not very large (ranging from three to 10 pounds), a few oldsters there may weigh as much as 25 pounds or even more.

The Goodpaster is also known for its superb fly-fishing for fat arctic grayling. These fine light-tackle scrappers are available throughout the system, from the mouth upstream to the headwaters, and are at their best from early summer into fall.

For a remote river experience within a reasonable distance from the road but far enough to escape the crowds, the Goodpaster River is highly recommended.

㉒ Delta Clearwater River

Location: In the upper Tanana River drainage, Delta Junction area, 85 miles southeast of Fairbanks, 245 miles northeast of Anchorage; see map page 204.

USGS maps: Mount Hayes D-3; Big Delta A-3, A-4.

How to get there: By car from the Alaska Highway via Clearwater and Remington Roads or from the Richardson Highway via Jack Warren and Remington Roads. To access the river mouth, most anglers use power boats or canoes launched at the campground near Clearwater Ranch. From there, it is a 10-mile run. However, some opt to launch at Clearwater Lake off Jack Warren Road, into the outlet stream, then continue up the Tanana River a few miles to the mouth of the Delta Clearwater.

Highlights: One of the best salmon streams in all of Interior Alaska. Excellent fishing for silver salmon (from late September through mid-October); good fishing for grayling (from July through September).

Species: Chum salmon, grayling, northern pike, silver salmon.

Regulations: For restrictions on salmon, consult the current Alaska Department of Fish and Game regulations or contact the ADF&G Delta Junction office, (907) 895-4632.

Facilities: A campground, a boat launch, and lodging are available in the Clearwater Ranch area.

Contact: For camping and lodging information, contact the Public Lands Information Center, 250 Cushman Street, Suite 1A, Fairbanks, AK 99701, (907) 451-7352; or the Delta Junction Visitor Information Center, P.O. Box 987, Delta Junction, AK 99737, (907) 895-9941 or (907) 895-5068.

Fishing the Delta Clearwater River: The Delta Clearwater originates on the slopes of Granite Mountain and from upwellings and seepages in the Tanana Valley just east of the Gerstle River. Its crystal clear waters are lined with dense vegetation as the stream meanders west to join the glacial Tanana River. With constant flow from its spring sources and abundant spawning habitat, it supports the Interior's largest runs of silver salmon, with outstanding sportfishing possible.

In some years, more than 20,000 coho invade the main stem Delta Clearwater River. Nearly all the fishing is catch-and-release, as the salmon are generally too far advanced in prespawning to eat. Still, the fishery is extremely popular with boat and shore anglers seeking a taste of some of the finest salmon action available in the Interior.

Usually beginning in early September, the run here is extended, lasting through the fall until the snow flies in November. Although fish are present in great numbers throughout the river, the lower section and confluence area is recommended for catching brighter, scrappier coho.

Another popular sport species you'll find here is the arctic grayling. These plucky, lightweight fighters are present in force from early summer through fall, and attack a variety of dry and wet flies and small spinners. Anglers targeting grayling usually do best in the upper sections of the Delta Clearwater around the forks where tributary streams join, but fishing can be productive in all parts of the river during certain times of the year, like the fall out-migration. Around the confluence with the Tanana, you can expect some northern pike encounters during the summer months and fair numbers of late-running chum salmon in September and October.

Even with temperatures sometimes falling to minus 40 degrees Fahrenheit, the Delta Clearwater remains partially ice free, though few anglers have the moxie to challenge the conditions beyond the normal season, from June through October.

㉓ Tangle Lakes System

Location: In the upper Tanana River drainage, 125 miles southeast of Fairbanks, 195 miles northeast of Anchorage; see map page 204.

USGS maps: Gulkana D-5; Mount Hayes A-4, A-5.

How to get there: By car from Anchorage or Fairbanks. The Denali Highway provides easy access to the entire lake system. Canoes or kayaks can be launched from areas near the road crossing and Tangle River to reach the most remote parts of the drainage. You can access some lakes in the system, such as Landmark Gap and Glacier Lakes, by trails from the Denali Highway.

Highlights: Outstanding angling opportunities for lake trout and Interior's best road fishing for grayling (from June through September), in an area of undisturbed scenic beauty.

Species: Grayling, lake trout.

Regulations: Open year-round, all species.

Facilities: Lodging, campgrounds, and canoe rentals are available.

Contact: For fishing information, contact the Alaska Department of Fish and Game, Sportfish Division, P.O. Box 605, Delta Junction, AK 99737; (907) 895-4632. For camping information, contact the Public Lands Information Center, 250 Cushman Street, Suite 1A, Fairbanks, AK 99701, (907) 451-7352; or Paxson Lodge, P.O. Box 3001, Paxson, AK 99737, (907) 822-3330.

Fishing the Tangle Lakes System: Situated in the Ampitheater Mountains on the south slope of the Alaska Range, near milepost 22.5 of the Denali Highway, the Tangle Lakes system consists of eight lakes and interconnecting streams that head the Delta River. The surrounding landscape is breathtaking. Here, rugged peaks rise to 6,000 feet, and abundant wildlife (including grizzly bear) roam the land beside this nationally designated Wild and Scenic River system. Its appeal is enhanced by the fact that this watershed has the best road-accessible grayling fishing in Interior Alaska, if not the entire state.

The system includes all waters upstream of the "Falls" on the upper Delta River. Generally crystal clear, this extensive drainage has major fish-producing lakes and streams that receive little angling pressure, except for those parts near the highway.

Starting in early summer and continuing through most of the fall, anglers have outstanding success fishing abundant sailfins with dry and wet flies and small spinners. They average eight to 15 inches, with occasional lunkers exceeding the magic 20-inch mark. Though the action can be very good in lakes and streams near the Denali Highway, the best of it certainly is found in locations only reached by trail or canoe. Inlet and outlet streams in the lakes and the shallow runs of the connecting streams and rivers are the hot spots to look for. The Delta River, from the outlet down to Eureka Creek, has excellent fishing and makes a great float trip from the lakes down to a takeout point adjacent to the Richardson Highway at milepost 212. (There are a series of falls and rapids two miles below Lower Tangle Lake, however.)

Lake trout are fairly abundant in the deep-water lakes of the system; try for them during late spring through early summer and in fall. Most of the fish taken are not very large as lakers go (averaging three to four pounds), but some reach trophy size (20 pounds). Landlocked Tangle, about four miles south of the highway, is probably the best to try. An inflatable craft is recommended for fishing the big ones.

The following are some of the better areas within the Tangle Lakes system for grayling, as well as lake trout where noted: Upper Tangle, Middle Tangle, Round Tangle (also lake trout), Landlocked Tangle (also lake trout), Long Tangle (also lake trout), Landmark Gap (also lake trout), and Glacier Lakes (also lake trout); and Rock Creek, Upper Delta, Upper Tangle, and Tangle Rivers.

Chapter 4

Southwest Fishing

Southwest Alaska

Alaska State Map .... *page 8*

Pastol Bay
Stebbins
Kotlik
Ophir
Takotna
Sterling Landing
Tonzona River
South Fork Kuskokwim
Skwentna R.
Windy Fork
Big River
Andreafsky River
East Fork Andreafsky
Anvik River
Yukon River
Innoko River
Bonasila River
Iditarod River
Takotna River
Kuskokwim River
Stony River

1 **2** **3** **4**

Yukon River
Kuskokwim River
Taksiesluk Lake
Bethel
Aniak River
Kisaralik River
Kwethluk River
Eek River
Holitna River
Whitefish Lake
Mulchatna River

5 **6** **11** **10** **12** **17** **18** **19**

Nuyakuk Lake
Lake Clark
Togiak Lake
Kanektok River
Kuskokwim Bay
Goodnews River
Togiak River
Nunavaugaluk Lake
Nushagak River
Lake Iliamna
Kamishak Bay
Lake Coville

7 **8** **9** **13** **14** **15** **16** **20** **21** **22** **23** **24** **25** **26** **27** **28** **29** **30** **31** **32** **33**

Goodnews
Togiak
Dillingham
Goodnews Bay
Togiak Bay
Nushagak Bay
Kvichak Bay
Naknek Lake
King Salmon River
Becharof Lake

34 **35**

HAGEMEISTER ISLAND

Bristol Bay

Ugashik Lake

36 **37**

KODIAK ISLAND

For fishing in the Kodiak Island area, please see map on page 267.

BERING SEA

Port Heiden

38

ALASKA PENINSULA

Black Lake
Chignik Lake

40

Port Moller
Bear Lake

39

GULF OF ALASKA

Southwest Hot Spots

Southwest

From the Alaska Peninsula west and north to the shores of Norton Sound lies an area almost the size of Montana, a region so rich and varied in resources and unspoiled beauty that it defies adequate description. Here are found the world's largest runs of Pacific salmon and the fabulous sportfishing locations of Bristol Bay, as well as the stark and scenic landscapes of Katmai (with its famous fishing brown bears) and the timeless Yupik Eskimo culture. A haven for wildlife, it contains unique marine mammal sanctuaries and one of the world's largest expanses of waterfowl habitat, which, along with other important wildlands in the area, have been set aside in some of the largest parks, refuges, and preserves in America.

Sport anglers will find special attraction in the thousands of miles of rivers and immense lakes found here. Unlike the glacial drainages that predominate elsewhere in Alaska, most of these waters run sparkling clear from abundant runoff sources and springs, providing perfect habitat for a profusion of salmon and an unrivaled variety of resident sport species—charr, grayling, rainbow trout, pike, lake trout, and even sheefish in some waters. No area better represents Alaska's extraordinary fishing opportunities than Southwest.

Devoid of any real roads, this is Alaska's definitive fly-in fishing country, with a world famous coterie of lodges, guides, and outfitters offering a range of exciting options for that ultimate fishing vacation. You can fly in to remote headwaters and spend days rafting a lonely river where fish have seldom seen a fly and brown bears stalk the shallows, or stay at a deluxe lodge and enjoy gourmet meals and plush accommodations after your daily excursions to world-class fishing locales. If your tastes run somewhere in between, you can even visit rustic "spike camps" on far-flung rivers with unpronounceable names, where you'll get a cot in a wall tent, three square meals a day, and all the fishing action your arms can handle. No matter how you decide to go, Southwest Alaska can consistently deliver a quality of angling that few areas in the world can match, a place where the serious can put their fishing passion to the ultimate test.

Country, Climate, and Conditions

Southwest Alaska is awesome country—wild and primitive, with unique and distinct features. There are more than 50 active volcanoes, remnant glaciers, ice-sculpted highlands and valleys, and immense rolling expanses of tundra, forests, and flat coastal plain. The intense glaciation during the last Ice Age created many deep bedrock basins that are of special significance. They cradle enormous lakes that have become the rearing grounds for the largest concentrations of salmon, trout, and charr in the world. Iliamna, Naknek, Nonvianuk, Becharof, Ugashik, and the interconnected Wood-Tikchiks all support phenomenal fisheries and provide in their outlets and associated river systems some of the greatest angling to be had anywhere.

Unlike the fishing, however, the raw maritime climate in Southwest Alaska is nothing to get excited about. The 1,600-mile arc of the Alaska Peninsula and Aleutian Islands effectively isolates the region from the moderating influences of the Gulf of Alaska; here the stormy Bering Sea and icy Bristol Bay are the dominant forces shaping the weather. Summers are typically cool, cloudy, and breezy, with brief sunny interludes (April through June is generally the sunniest part of the year) and temperatures ranging from the upper 40s to mid-70s (the average is in the 50s). Yearly rainfall is from 20 to 40 inches, with August through October the wettest months. Winters are long and cold, although not as extreme as those in Interior, with freeze-up occurring sometime in late October and breakup occurring in early May (later in some of the mountain lakes). At any time, strong low pressure systems can track up from the Bering Sea or Gulf of Alaska and bring prolonged periods of intense wind and precipitation. Travelers who venture into any part of this country during summer must come equipped with expedition-quality rain gear, tents, sleeping bags, undergarments, and footwear.

Southwest Fishing Highlights

A list of the area's outstanding angling locations reads like a roster of North America's dream waters, so blessed is this region with extraordinary fishing. In fact, there is so much good water that it makes for difficult, if not impossible, vacation choices for anglers (especially newcomers), as the fishing on any of these streams and lakes will easily eclipse the best angling most folks have experienced back home. If you've never been to Alaska and want a dazzling introduction to the smorgasbord of wild angling possible here, you can hardly lose in choosing any of the dozens of great Southwest locations. On the other hand, if you're a seasoned Alaska angler with a yen for something different than what you have experienced elsewhere in the state, you'll find major areas and locations with features that set them apart from other waters in Alaska (and the rest of the world).

Some of the region's more notable angling highlights are the fantastic stream fishing opportunities for salmon, particularly king, silver, and sockeye, as most of Alaska's major producing rivers for these species are located here (the Kvichak, Naknek, Egegik, Nushagak, Togiak, and Kuskokwim). Fly-fishing possibilities in the countless clear streams and lakes are almost infinite. So, too, are the numbers of feisty, fat charr and grayling you'll encounter in nearly every body of water, with trophy potential in some waters exceeded only by a few locations in Alaska's remote Northwest. And, of course, there are those fabulous rainbows. Can enough can be said of the peerless Southwest rivers and their armies of hungry, husky, wild Alaska rainbow trout? Nearly every drainage from Katmai to the Kuskokwim is amply endowed with them, with many waters holding trout of mythical proportions. The fly-fishing conditions couldn't be better, especially in spring and fall.

Access, Services, and Costs

With no connecting surface transportation, access to Southwest is generally by plane, through the hubs of Dillingham, King Salmon, Bethel, and Iliamna. All of these towns are serviced by regular scheduled commercial flights from Anchorage and have local air charters and connections available to make access possible to just about every village and fishing location within the region.

Southwest Run Timing

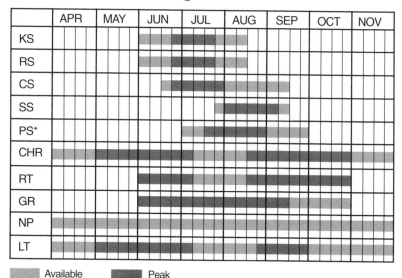

	APR	MAY	JUN	JUL	AUG	SEP	OCT	NOV
KS								
RS								
CS								
SS								
PS*								
CHR								
RT								
GR								
NP								
LT								

Available   Peak

KS=King Salmon, RS=Red Salmon, CS=Chum Salmon, SS=Silver Salmon, PS=Pink Salmon, CHR=Charr, RT=Rainbow Trout, GR=Grayling, NP=Northern Pike, LT=Lake Trout
*Available in even years

Note: Time periods shown are for bright fish, in the case of salmon entering rivers, or for general availability for resident species. Salmon are present in many systems long after the periods shown, but are usually in spawning/postspawning condition. Peak sportfishing periods for each species are highlighted. Run timing can vary somewhat from drainage to drainage and generally follows a later trend in waters to the west and north in Alaska. Check with local contacts listed for area run-timing specifics.

Lower Yukon

Alaska's two greatest rivers—the Yukon and Kuskokwim—spill their waters within 200 miles of each other in a broad, fan-shaped delta that is one of the world's great wetland habitats. Ideally suited for waterfowl, this area is too flat and marshy to support any high-quality sportfishing. However, the surrounding uplands give rise to a few notable drainages that receive little attention, even though they contain some abundant, even world-class angling opportunities. (See the listing for the Innoko River on page 232.) Access, difficult logistics, and lack of visitor services are the main obstacles for anyone looking to explore these more remote, but promising, rivers of the Southwest region.

❶ Andreafsky River

Location: Along the Lower Yukon River, 400 miles northwest of Anchorage; see map page 226.

USGS maps: Kwiguk A-2, A-3, B-1, B-2, C-1, C-2, D-1; St. Michael A-1; Unalakleet A-6; Holy Cross C-6, D-6.

How to get there: By plane from Anchorage to St. Marys via commercial flight, boat transport upriver, or small wheelplane to gravel bars at the headwaters; raft or kayak trips are possible down to the mouth and the village of St. Marys.

Highlights: A seldom-visited Wild and Scenic River, with good fishing for charr and king, silver, and chum salmon; outstanding float trip possibilities.

Species: Charr, chum salmon, grayling, king salmon, northern pike, pink salmon, silver salmon.

Regulations: Open year-round, all species.

Facilities: No developed public facilities. Guide services are available locally.

Contact: For air taxi service and information on guide services, contact Haagland Air, P.O. Box 195, St. Marys, AK 99658; (907) 438-2246. For guided float trips, contact Eruk's Wilderness Tours, 12720 Lupine Road, Anchorage, AK 99516, (907) 345-7678.

Fishing the Andreafsky River: The Wild and Scenic Andreafsky River of the lower Yukon features two parallel forks that flow southwest out of the Nulato Hills for 100 miles or so before joining on the coastal flatlands five miles north of the village of St. Marys. Although remote and difficult to access, this crystal mountain stream has great potential for high-quality wilderness fishing, with good salmon runs (kings, silvers, and chums), abundant pike, charr, and grayling, pleasant scenery and wildlife.

Getting up into the headwaters is difficult. You can contract through Haagland Air in St. Marys to run you upriver by boat (they offer guide service and tent camps). It's also possible to land on gravel bars (mostly on the upper North Fork) with small wheelplanes, depending on water levels. The river can be rafted in about a week; other than fast water, sweepers, and grizzly bears, there are no major hazards. Due to the cost and difficult logistics in getting here, not too many folks get to visit this lovely, pristine drainage, but everyone who has visited considers the experience well worth the extra effort and expense.

❷ Anvik River

Location: Along the Lower Yukon River, 375 miles northwest of Anchorage; see map page 226.

USGS maps: Holy Cross C-3, C-4, D-4; Unalakleet A-4.

How to get there: By plane from Anchorage or Aniak to Anvik via scheduled commercial flight, then boat to points upriver. Wheel and floatplane access are also possible to points along the river via St. Marys, Aniak, or Bethel.

Highlights: One of the Yukon River's major fish producers, with underutilized sportfishing potential for salmon, charr, and other species.

Species: Charr, chum salmon, grayling, king salmon, northern pike, pink salmon, sheefish, silver salmon.

Regulations: Open year-round, all species.

Facilities: No developed public facilities. A private lodge is located on the river, 60 miles above the mouth.

Contact: For an air taxi to Anvik River, contact Haagland Air, P.O. Box 207, St. Marys, AK 99684,

(907) 438-2246. For lodge-based fishing, contact Anvik River Lodge, P.O. Box 109, Bethel, AK 99559; (907) 543-5034 (winter) or (907) 663-6324 (summer).

Fishing the Anvik River: Not too many folks know of the Anvik River of western Alaska; fewer yet have fished it. But it's one of the most important fish producing tributaries of the entire Yukon—in fact, a million or more chum salmon spawn here in certain years. The Anvik can offer exciting angling adventure for a variety of species with virtually no fishing pressure.

The river heads in the Nulato Hills and flows south 120 miles or so before joining the Yukon at the village of Anvik, 318 miles up from the mouth. Like many Yukon and Kuskokwim drainages, it has a slow, wide, meandering lower section (with good pike and sheefish fishing). You'll find the best fishing conditions for salmon, charr, and grayling in the clearer, swifter upper sections (above the Yellow River confluence, 60 miles from the mouth).

Most people fish the Anvik by boat, but it can be floated from the headwaters, although access is difficult and generally limited to gravel bar landings with a small wheelplane. Anvik River Lodge, the area's only lodging, offers an array of fishing options. They access most of the river by jet boat, but also offer handmade cedar canoes for quiet, self-powered fishing. They do fly-outs to neighboring drainages like the Andreafsky and Innoko Rivers for salmon, sheefish, and monster pike (30 pounds plus) and can even provide raft, gear, and transport for float-fishing trips.

❸ Innoko River

Location: Along the Lower Yukon River tributary, 330 miles northwest of Anchorage; see map page 226.

USGS maps: Ophir A-4, A-5, A-6, B-5, C-1, C-2, C-3, C-4, C-5, A-1, A-2, B-2; Unalakleet A-1; Holy Cross A-2, B-2, C-2, D-1, D-2; Iditarod D-3.

How to get there: By scheduled or chartered wheelplane service (via McGrath, Bethel, or Aniak) to Holy Cross, Shageluk, Ophir, Cripple, or Takotna, then boat (or raft) along the river. Floatplane access is possible to numerous spots.

Highlights: An enormous, remote, meandering tributary of the lower Yukon, with tremendous potential for world-class trophy northern pike and abundant sheefish.

Species: Charr, chum salmon, grayling, king salmon, northern pike, sheefish, silver salmon.

Regulations: Open year-round, all species.

Facilities: No developed public facilities. Lodge-based fishing is available locally.

Contact: For wheelplane flights to villages and strips along river, contact Haagland Air, P.O. Box 211, Aniak, AK 99577; (907) 675-4272. For floatplane flights and guided fishing, contact Aniak Air Guides, P.O. Box 93, Aniak, AK 99557; (907) 675-4540. For lodge-based fly-outs to the Innoko, contact Anvik River Lodge, P.O. Box 1091, Bethel, AK 99559; (907) 543-5034 (winter) or (907) 663-6324 (summer). For outpost camp guided fishing on the Innoko, contact Bruce Werba, (907) 476-7121.

Fishing the Innoko River: Like a sleeping giant, the Innoko sprawls lazily across the Yukon flatlands west of McGrath, its vast potential unknown to most of the fishing world. Not the kind of river to excite trout and salmon anglers, much of it is big, slow water better suited for Alaska's "other" sport species—the wolfish northern pike and leaping sheefish. Fishing for these unsung fighters in the Innoko's abundant backwater is so good that word is spreading fast beyond the small circle of residents and local guides. This may soon become one of the hottest fishing spots in western Alaska.

This is an immense river system—the mainstem flows over 500 miles before emptying into the Yukon at Red Wind Slough, near the village of Holy Cross. (The Innoko's major tributary, the Iditarod, is more than 350 miles long.) For most of this length, it's a slow, wide, lowland river, with meandering and interconnected sloughs and lakes, especially in the lower section (downstream of the abandoned village of Holikachuk, about 90 miles). The water quality is turbid from the mud and swamp water. Only in the extreme upper reaches (above the North Fork) does the Innoko's character change noticeably toward that of a mountain stream, with swifter flows, gravel bottom, and clear water. This is really the only part of the river suited for salmon (coho, chum, and some king), grayling, and occasionally charr fishing, with several adjoining swift and clear mountain creeks (such as Beaver and Folger) offering some of the better angling options.

Access is by floatplane to points along the river, or by wheelplane to airstrips at Holy Cross, Shageluk, Cripple, or Ophir. The upper river can be floated by raft, with a put in by floatplane at Ophir (or further upriver, from a trail accessed from Takotna) and take out at Cripple or at points below.

The lower Innoko is an important feeding area for the migratory Yukon River sheefish population. (See the sheefish chapter on page 142.) In spring, it can offer some of Alaska's finest fishing for the species. Pike are especially plentiful, with the lower river's perfect habitat and abundant food sources (whitefish and cisco) producing some really big fish. Recent efforts over the past few years by local guides on the lower Innoko have produced dozens of northerns over 20 pounds, and even some 30-pounders (including the state record, at 38.5 pounds), capturing widespread attention and catapulting this sluggish behemoth of a river into public consciousness. The secret's out on Alaska's top water for monster pike and abundant sheefish!

Kuskokwim River

The 800-mile Kuskokwim is the second largest river in Alaska. With headwaters predominantly glacial (draining the western Alaska Range), the river's sportfishing is limited to its clear-flowing tributaries. The best of these empty into the lower river and Kuskokwim Bay, from headwaters in the highlands west of the Togiak River valley. These swift mountain streams are all similar in size and character, issuing from crystal headwater lakes over beds of rock and gravel. They support abundant runs of salmon and substantial populations of charr, grayling, and the state's westernmost rainbow trout. Some of these drainages are quite exceptional and are considered among the finest float-fishing rivers in Alaska, if not the world.

For public lands information on rivers of the lower Kuskokwim, contact: the Bureau of Land Management, Alaska State Office, 222 West Seventh Avenue, Suite 13, Anchorage, AK 99513, (907) 271-5960; Togiak National Wildlife Refuge, P.O. Box 270, Dillingham, AK 99576, (907) 842-1063; or Yukon Delta National Wildlife Refuge, P.O. Box 346, Bethel, AK 99559, (907) 543-3151.

❹ Holitna River

Location: Along the Middle Kuskokwim River, 225 miles southwest of Anchorage; see map page 226.

USGS maps: Taylor Mountains B-7, C-5, C-6, C-7, C-8, D-1, D-2, D-5, D-6, D-7; Sleetmute A-2, A-4, A-5, B-2, B-3, B-4, C-3, C-4; Lake Clark D-6, D-7, D-8.

How to get there: By floatplane (or in places small wheelplane) from Iliamna, Bethel, Aniak, or Lake Clark to the headwaters or the lower and middle river sections. Raft or kayak trips are possible down from headwaters (trips of one week to 12 days), with takeout on the lower river by floatplane or boat from the village of Sleetmute.

Highlights: A remote, seldom visited wilderness river system with good fishing for salmon, grayling, charr, pike, and seasonal sheefish.

Species: Charr, chum salmon, grayling, king salmon, lake trout, northern pike, pink salmon, sheefish, silver salmon, *rainbow trout*.

Regulations: Open year-round, all species.

Facilities: No developed public facilities. Lodge-based fishing and guide services are available.

Contact: For guided and unguided floats, contact Alaska Bush Adventures, P.O. Box 243861, Anchorage, AK 99524; (907) 522-1712. For lodge-based, fly-out fishing, contact Stony River Lodge, 13830 Jarvi Drive, Anchorage, AK 99708; (907) 345-2891. For an air taxi (wheelplane), contact Haagland Air, P.O. Box 211, Aniak, AK 99577, (907) 675-4272; (floatplane) Aniak Air Guides, P.O. Box 93, Aniak, AK 99557, (907) 675-4540; or (floatplane) Iliamna Air Taxi, P.O. Box 109, Iliamna, AK 99606, (907) 571-1248.

Fishing the Holitna River: The Holitna River system is comprised of fairly significant middle Kuskokwim tributaries that drain parts of the

Taylor Mountains and western Alaska Range before joining near the village of Sleetmute. These include the mainstem Holitna, Hoholitna, Kogrukluk, and Chukowan Rivers. Although they receive limited attention from sport anglers (mostly locals), collectively they support one of the most productive fisheries in the entire region, known for fair to good king, silver, chum, grayling, pike, and charr fishing. Sheefish are also taken in early summer on the lower river.

Access to the headwaters is limited; most folks put in either by floatplane or small wheelplane on the upper Holitna (from Kashegelok up) or at Whitefish Lake on the Hoholitna (for float trips). Fishing in the clearer, faster upper sections can be quite good for grayling, charr, and salmon, with abundant sheefish and pike taken seasonally in the sloughs and backwaters along the lower river. There are persistent rumors of rainbow trout being found in certain clear tributary streams. (Some are caught now and then from the river's mouth at Sleetmute.) The scenery and wildlife in the primitive backcountry of this system are outstanding, and accounts for the Holitna's popularity with hunters, who have traditionally been the river's only major visitors.

A few guides work the river, most of them locals, and some air taxis and lodges occasionally fly groups in to fish salmon, pike, or sheefish, but for the most part this system doesn't get nearly as much attention as it deserves. Like other similar drainages, the Holitna is greatly affected by runoff, with periods of even moderate rain raising river levels quickly and clouding the water, so fishing is very weather dependent. Other than that and the logistics involved in getting here, nothing should prevent this drainage from becoming the "next big thing" for adventure anglers in search of new, uncrowded water.

❺ Aniak River

Location: In the lower Kuskokwim River drainage, 300 miles west of Anchorage; see map page 226.

USGS maps: Bethel B-1, C-1, C-2, D-1, D-2; Russian Mission A-1, A-2, B-1, C-2.

How to get there: By plane from Anchorage to the village of Aniak via commercial flight, then wheelplane or floatplane to several headwater or midriver access points. It can be floated by raft or kayak from the headwaters (seven days or more to the lower river). Boat access to the lower river is possible from Aniak.

Highlights: One of Southwest Alaska's better mountain rivers for all-around fishing and high-quality wilderness float trips. Good to excellent rainbow trout, charr, grayling, and salmon (especially king, chum, and silver), with pretty scenery and some wildlife along the upper river. Angling pressure is relatively light.

Species: Charr, chum salmon, grayling, king salmon, lake trout, northern pike, pink salmon, rainbow trout, red salmon, sheefish, silver salmon.

Regulations: Open year-round; upstream of Doestock Creek, only unbaited, single-hook, artificial lures and catch-and-release on rainbows. For additional restrictions, consult the current Alaska Department of Fish and Game regulations or contact the ADF&G Dillingham office, (907) 842-2427.

Facilities: Several lodges and outpost camps operate along the lower river.

Contact: For lodge-based fishing, contact Alaska Dream Lodge, Route 1, Kuna, ID 83634; (208) 922-5648. For float-fishing trips, contact Eruk's Wilderness Tours, 12720 Lupine Road, Anchorage, AK 99516, (907) 345-7678. For an air taxi (wheelplane), contact Haagland Air, P.O. Box 211, Aniak, AK 99577, (907) 675-4272; or, for a floatplane, Aniak Air Guides, P.O. Box 93, Aniak, AK 99557, (907) 675-4540. To arrange a boat pickup along lower river, contact Golga Kalila, P.O. Box 37, Aniak, AK 99557; (907) 675-4287.

Fishing the Aniak River: The wild and remote Aniak is a three-pronged mountain river tributary of the lower Kuskokwim. In terms of its fishery, size, and recreation potential, it is perhaps the most significant river of the Kuskokwim drainage, and has only recently been discovered by sport anglers for its abundant salmon, charr, rainbow trout, and grayling possibilities.

Except for the lower section above the Kuskokwim, the Aniak flows clear and fast (with some white water in the upper tributaries) as it flows north off the western edge of the Kuskokwim Mountains in three main headwaters—Aniak Lake (and river) and the Kipchuk and Salmon Rivers. All three begin as swift, rocky alpine streams and have outstanding grayling and charr fishing (including lake trout in Aniak Lake), superb scenery, and quite a bit of wildlife (bears, moose, and caribou). The three forks become a maze of channels, sweepers, and log-jams before joining together in a major confluence 60 miles down from the lake. A nightmare to boaters (especially in high water), the substantial river debris and braids make great habitat for potbellied rainbows and throngs of charr and salmon. Fishing for these species is best from the confluence of the Kipchuk, Aniak, and Salmon Rivers down to about nine miles above the mouth at Doestock Creek, where the river becomes silty and mean-dering. The lower Aniak does have good pike fishing, and sheefish are even taken from the river's mouth in spring.

Several lodges and outpost camps lie scattered along the lower river and are accessible from the village of Aniak. For float trips, most folks put in on either the upper Salmon or Kipchuk Rivers by wheelplane (primitive airstrip access) via Aniak or Bethel. The trip down from Aniak Lake (floatplane access) is long, arduous, and poten-tially dangerous, best done by kayak, inflatable canoe, or a small, light raft, as heavy logjams, snags, sweepers, and vegetation make for diffi-cult passage. Abundant salmon spawning and healthy bear populations (both brown and black) make for frequent animal confrontations along this drainage, so take necessary precau-tions. The river can be floated in a week to 12 days, depending on where you put in.

The Aniak certainly has much to offer; its rain-bow and charr fishing in late summer can be quite superb, among the best available any-where in the region. The trick seems to be catch-ing good weather, as the river easily silts and spills out of its channel with disastrous results on the fishing and navigation. This is definitely not the river to try unassisted, unless you're an experienced wilderness voyager.

Guides' tip: Much of the Aniak is not easy to fish or float. Fast currents, logjams, and snag-infested, deep pools characterize most of the middle river. Bring plenty of terminal tackle and use heavier line or tippets to avoid excessive break-offs. Also, a large brush saw, ax, or small chainsaw is highly recommended to ensure safe passage if floating downriver by raft.

❻ Kasigluk River

Location: Along the lower Kuskokwim River, 360 miles southwest of Anchorage; see map page 226.

USGS maps: Bethel A-3, A-4, B-3, B-4, B-5, B-6, C-5, C-6, D-5.

How to get there: By plane from Anchorage to Bethel via commercial flight, then jet boat to the lower river.

Highlights: A popular local fishing spot, known for good salmon, charr, and rainbow trout.

Species: Charr, chum salmon, grayling, king salmon, pink salmon, rainbow trout, silver salmon, *northern pike, red salmon.*

Regulations: Open year-round, all species.

Facilities: No developed public facilities. Guide services are available.

Contact: For guided or unguided fishing on the Kasigluk River, contact KORV, Inc., P.O. Box 215, Akiak, AK 99552; (907) 765-7228. For boat transportation to and from the Kasigluk, con-tact Alaska River Runners, P.O. Box 7055, Bethel, AK 99559; (907) 543-3633.

Fishing the Kasigluk River: If you spend any time in the villages along the lower Kuskokwim River, you'll probably get an invita-tion to fish the Kasigluk. One of the best of the area's rivers that rise from the scenic Kilbuck Mountains, the Kasigluk flows north and west, clear and fast, before degenerating into a maze of muddy braids and sloughs in the flats along the big Kuskokwim.

Fishing is very good for king, silver, and chum salmon, as well as rainbow trout and charr, once you get above the silty, meandering lower sec-tion (usually the first 30 miles). The river can be accessed by boat from Bethel or one of the nearby villages (Kwethluk, Akiak, or Akiachak) and can be run quite a ways with a jet unit. Some people are even said to float down from the headwaters, although access would be difficult and naviga-tion hindered by the extensive braids and log-jams. A few local guides and outfitters currently work the river with outpost camps; they're the best bet for anyone wanting to sample this outstanding fishery off the beaten path.

❼ Kanektok River

Location: In Kuskokwim Bay, 350 miles southwest of Anchorage; see map page 226.

USGS maps: Goodnews Bay C-4, C-5, C-6, D-3, D-4, D-5, D-6, D-7, D-8.

How to get there: By plane from Anchorage to Dillingham or Bethel via commercial flight, then floatplane to Kagati Lake (or other headwater lakes) or wheelplane to the village of Quinhagak, with boat access to the lower river. A raft or kayak trip is possible from the lake to Quinhagak (five to seven days), with wheelplane pickup and return to Bethel.

Highlights: One of Alaska's most celebrated float-fishing rivers, with beautiful scenery and outstanding rainbow trout, sea-run charr, grayling, and king and silver salmon fishing. Perfect water for fly-fishing.

Species: Charr, chum salmon, grayling, king salmon, lake trout, pink salmon, rainbow trout, red salmon, silver salmon.

Regulations: Open year-round; on portions within Togiak National Wildlife Refuge, single-hook, unbaited, artificial lures only. For additional restrictions, consult the current Alaska Department of Fish and Game regulations or contact the ADF&G Dillingham office, (907) 842-2427.

Facilities: No developed public facilities. An outpost camp and guide and air taxi services are available locally.

Contact: For guided float trips, contact Ultimate Rivers, 5140 East 104th Avenue, Anchorage, AK 99516; (907) 346-2193. For guided and unguided spike camp fishing, contact Kanektok River Safaris, P.O. Box 9, Quinhagak, AK 99655, (907) 556-8211; or Bill Martin's Fish Alaska, Inc., P.O. Box 1887, Anchorage, AK 99510, (907) 346-2595. For air taxi service, contact Freshwater Adventures, Inc., P.O. Box 62, Dillingham, AK 99576, (907) 243-7676 (winter) or (907) 842-5060 (summer); or Yute Air, P.O. Box 947, Bethel, AK 99559, (907) 543-3003.

Special Note: The lower 17 miles of the river are owned by Quinhagak Village Corporation;

for information, contact Quanirtuuq Inc., P.O. Box 69, Quinhagak, AK 99655; (907) 556-8289. For information on public lands along the upper river, contact Togiak National Wildlife Refuge, P.O. Box 270, Dillingham, AK 99576; (907) 842-1063.

Fishing the Kanektok River: The Kanektok is one of several, sparkling blue tundra rivers that drain the fringe of mountains in the state's extreme southwest corner. Since the early 1980s, it has enjoyed worldwide notoriety for its exquisite stream fishing. Nearly perfect conditions and an abundance and variety of species—rainbow trout, sea-run charr, grayling, and king, red, and silver salmon—make it one of Alaska's finest rivers for float-fishing.

The river rambles for 90 miles from mountain sources at Kagati Lake to the flat coastal plain and silty waters of Kuskokwim Bay. Gravel bottomed, moderately swift (three to four miles per hour), with lots of shallow braids and pools containing amazing fish populations, the Kanektok is a fly fisher's dream. (At one time, it had some of the highest concentrations of catchable-size rainbow trout of any river studied by the U.S. Fish and Wildlife Service.)

The best way to fish it is from a raft, floating down from Kagati Lake. You won't meet any serious rapids, just fast water (occasional Class I stretches). The only hazards to speak of are the abundant sweepers, which can be dangerous in the numerous switchbacks and fast current. On the upper river, you'll find great scenic views and good grayling and charr fishing, while the best rainbow trout habitat seems to be the heavily braided middle and lower sections (from Klak Creek down) as the river emerges from the mountains. The lower 10 miles of river is the preferred location for intercepting the Kanektok's abundant runs of sea-bright silver and king salmon (some of the state's largest in average size) and sea-run charr.

One of the prettiest rivers you'll ever see, the Kanektok is blessed with some truly amazing fishing. While the rainbows aren't the giants you'll find in some of the big lake and river systems further east, they're abundant and very pretty, with deep crimson stripes and big, black spots (the leopard rainbow much hyped in the tourist literature). This river also has some of the best, late summer sea-run charr fishing south of Kotzebue, with lots of feisty, bright fish in the three to six pound range and an occasional eight-pounder. (The best time to catch them is from late July on.) You can stay at an outpost tent camp, if you're not into rafting, and several area lodges maintain spike camps on the middle and lower sections of the river, using jet boats for accessing the better holes. Ask anyone who has fished Alaska about the Kanektok, and you'll get a unanimous appraisal for its rank among the state's top fishing waters.

Guides' tip: The Kanektok is one of the rivers where the Alaska "deer hair mouse" earned its notorious reputation. In certain years, they can be very effective, so bring some along. Fish them under cutbanks and in shallows for explosive surface strikes from rainbow trout and charr.

❽ Arolik River

Location: In Kuskokwim Bay, 400 miles south-west of Anchorage; see map page 226.

USGS maps: Goodnews Bay B-6, C-7, C-8.

How to get there: By plane from Anchorage to Bethel or Dillingham via commercial flight, then floatplane to Arolik Lake or wheelplane to a primitive airstrip at Snow Gulch. From there, raft or kayak down to the lower river, with boat pickup from Quinhagak village. The lower river can also be accessed and fished by jet boat. Return to Bethel or Dillingham by wheelplane, then commercial flight back to Anchorage.

Highlights: Another superlative Kuskokwim Bay drainage, not as heavily fished as the Goodnews or Kanektok, but with the same abundant rainbow, sea-run charr, grayling, and salmon and nearly perfect stream conditions.

Species: Charr, chum salmon, grayling, king salmon, lake trout, pink salmon, rainbow trout, red salmon, silver salmon.

Regulations: Open year-round, all species.

Facilities: No developed public facilities. Guide services and boat transportation are available in the nearby village of Quinhagak.

Contact: For guided fishing, contact Kanektok River Safaris, P.O. Box 9, Quinhagak, AK 99655; (907) 556-8211. For an air taxi to the Arolik, con-

tact Freshwater Adventures, Inc., P.O. Box 62, Dillingham, AK 99576; (907) 243-7676 (winter) or (907) 842-5060 (summer).

Fishing the Arolik River: The Arolik receives just a fraction of the attention lavished on the more glamorous streams surrounding it, the Kanektok and Goodnews. Shorter than its neighbors, the Arolik flows north and west for about 45 miles from headwaters above the Goodnews, with two main forks and numerous smaller tributaries. It braids heavily and splits into separate mouths before emptying into Kuskokwim Bay about five miles south of the village of Quinhagak.

With abundant rainbows, charr, grayling, and salmon, fishing on the Arolik is every bit as good as that on the Kanektok or Goodnews; in fact, the trout fishing is even better because the river doesn't get hit as hard as the other two. Arolik Lake is noted for having some of the better lake trout fishing in the region. The catch is that the Arolik is not a cake walk river float like the others. The upper river is rocky and shallow in spots, especially below the lake, and during low-water times, floating may be difficult, if not impossible. You can float early in the season and take your chances, using a lightly equipped raft, inflatable canoe, or kayak. Or you can try to put in by wheelplane at an old mining strip on Snow Gulch, about 10 miles below the junction of the East and South Forks and skip those shallow stretches altogether. (Most of the better fishing is below there anyway.)

Ending your float trip on the Arolik won't be easy either. It would be ideal to have someone from Quinhagak run up in a skiff and meet you on the lower river, as the tidal influence makes rafting down into the mouth tricky and dangerous, not to mention trying a floatplane pickup there. The native village corporation, Quanirtuuq, Inc., owns lands along the lower river and is developing a rather exclusive sport fish operation there, with tent camps and guided and un-guided fishing from jet boats. Give them a call at (907) 555-8211 (ask for Joshua Cleveland) to make arrangements for a boat pickup or a short stay at their tent camp. They have regular week-long guided fishing packages, too, if you're not keen on rafting the river.

Note: The lands along the lower Arolik (below Snow Gulch) are owned by the Quinhagak Village Corporation. They charge a daily fee of $25 per person for use of their lands. Before embarking on a float expedition down the Arolik, contact them at: Quanirtuuq, Inc., P.O. Box 69, Quinhagak, AK 99655; (907) 556-8289.

⑨ Goodnews River

Location: In lower Kuskokwim Bay, 375 miles southwest of Anchorage; see map page 226.

USGS maps: Goodnews Bay A-6, A-7, B-4, B-5, B-6, B-7, C-4, C-5.

How to get there: By floatplane from Dillingham or Bethel to headwater lakes or the lower river. Four- to seven-day raft or kayak trips are possible from area lakes, with floatplane or boat pickup on the lower river or wheelplane pickup from the strip in the Goodnews Bay village.

Highlights: One of Alaska's premier float-fishing rivers, excellent for king and silver salmon, rainbow trout, grayling, and sea-run charr, with outstanding fly-fishing possibilities.

Species: Charr, chum salmon, grayling, king salmon, lake trout, pink salmon, rainbow trout, red salmon, silver salmon.

Regulations: Open year-round; on river sections within the Togiak National Wildlife Refuge, unbaited, single-hook, artificial lures only.

Facilities: No developed public facilities. A private outpost tent camp is located on the lower river.

Contact: For outpost camp fishing, contact Alaska River Safaris, 4909 Rollins Drive, Anchorage, AK 99508, (907) 333-2860. For guided float-fishing, contact Brightwater Alaska, P.O. Box 110796, Anchorage, AK 99511; (907) 344-1340. For floatplane charters to and from the river, contact Freshwater Adventures, Inc., P.O. Box 62, Dillingham, AK 99576; (907) 243-7676 (winter) or (907) 842-5060 (summer). For wheelplane flights to and from the village of Goodnews, contact Yute Air, P.O. Box 947, Bethel, AK 99559; (907) 543-3003.

Special note: Portions of the lower river are owned by the Goodnews Village Corporation; for information, contact Kuitsarak Inc., General Delivery, Goodnews Bay, AK 99589; (907) 967-8520. For public lands information, contact the Bureau of Land Management, Alaska State Office, 222 West Seventh Avenue, Suite 13, Anchorage, AK 99513, (907) 271-5960; or Togiak National Wildlife Refuge, P.O. Box 270, Dillingham, AK 99576, (907) 842-1063.

Fishing the Goodnews River: A world-renowned float-fishing destination, the Goodnews River system is one of the best known of the fabulously productive angling streams of Kuskokwim Bay. Like its sister drainage, the Kanektok, it has some of Southwest Alaska's finest stream fishing for salmon, trout, grayling, and sea-run charr.

Like other neighboring drainages, the Goodnews is a tundra river. Short (only 60 miles) and sparkling clear, it's comprised of three forks that drain the most southerly valley in Kuskokwim Bay. The Middle Fork and mainstem (North Fork) are the most commonly fished sections. Floatplane access is possible on numerous headwater lakes (including Goodnews, Canyon, Awayak, Nimgun, Middle Fork, and Kukatlim) and the lower river, which can also be accessed by boat. None of the forks contain any major hazards to boaters, except for swift water and some minor rapids between Canyon and Arayak Creeks in the upper mainstem. (Low-water conditions can slow things down to a drag in the shallow sections below the lakes, especially on the Middle Fork.) They can be floated in anywhere from four to seven days.

With its different forks, miles of tributaries, and numerous headwater lakes, the Goodnews offers a wealth of good fishing possibilities. It's noted for abundant, beautifully marked rainbow trout (the famous leopard rainbows, to 10 pounds), big grayling (to three pounds), sea-run charr (to eight pounds), and outstanding opportunities for salmon on a fly, particularly king and silvers. Nearly all of the deep, bedrock basin lakes contain abundant, underfished lake trout and charr.

Raft fishing is certainly the most exciting and productive way of experiencing rivers like the Goodnews, but you'll find drawbacks, among them the weather, which in Kuskokwim Bay can be notoriously bum. The river and surrounding terrain afford little cover, so come prepared with the finest quality rain gear, tents, and extra warm clothes. Also, given the brush and abundant salmon, bears can be a real hazard, so take necessary precautions. If all this sounds too serious for an expedition on your own, you might want to consider a stay in an outpost camp. (The Goodnews has one major spike camp operator on the lower river; see the Togiak River listing on page 242 in this chapter.) However you decide to do it, the Goodnews will reward you with stream fishing that is about as good as it gets anywhere in Alaska, especially if you fish during July and August.

Wood-Tikchik Lakes

Legend has it that a giant bear flattened the western end of the Alaska Range and carved the Tikchik Lakes with swoops of his great paws. Like long, deep gouges from colossal claws, the 12 lakes that make up the Wood River—Tikchik chain at the head of Bristol Bay run more or less parallel, varying in length from 15 to 45 miles and to depths of up to 900 feet. Hemmed in by steep, pinnacled slopes, they bear a striking resemblance to the deep blue fjords of northern Europe. Even more alluring is the fishing in the lakes and numerous streams and outlets; the abundant, pristine habitat supports major runs of salmon and a diverse assemblage of resident fighters—rainbow trout, charr, grayling, lake trout, and even big northern pike. With so much to offer, this area is one of the most coveted recreation destinations in all of Alaska.

To preserve the scenic wonder and diverse resources of this amazing area, in 1978 the state of Alaska designated 1.6 million acres of this region as Wood-Tikchik State Park. At 2,500 square miles, it is the largest state park in the nation, and is managed as a total wilderness.

⑩ Wood-Tikchik Lakes

Location: At the head of Bristol Bay, 325 miles southwest of Anchorage; see map page 226.

USGS maps: Bethel A-1, B-1; Dillingham A-8, B-7, B-8, C-7, C-8, D-6, D-7, D-8; Goodnews Bay B-1, C-1, D-1; Taylor Mountains A-7, A-8, B-8.

How to get there: By plane from Anchorage to Dillingham via commercial flight, then floatplane to the lake system. Kayak, canoe, raft, or boat travel is possible throughout the area. There is road access from Dillingham to the bottom lake (Aleknagik).

Highlights: America's largest state park, a wonderland of 12 scenic glacial lakes, with superlative possibilities for fishing adventure.

Species: Charr, chum salmon, grayling, king salmon, lake trout, northern pike, pink salmon, rainbow trout, red salmon, silver salmon.

Regulations: Open year-round, all species. On portions of the Agulowak River, single-hook, unbaited, artificial lures only; on the Agulukpak River, fly-fishing only during summer and catch-and-release rainbow trout from June 8 through October 31. For details and additional restrictions, consult the Alaska Department of Fish and Game regulations or contact the ADF&G Dillingham office, (907) 842-2427.

Facilities: No developed public facilities. Lodge-based fishing, guide services, and gear rental are available locally.

Contact: For park information, contact Wood-Tikchik State Park, P.O. Box 107001, Dillingham, AK 99576; (907) 842-2375 (summer) or (907) 345-5014 (winter). For lodge-based fishing, contact Bristol Bay Lodge, 2422 Hunter Road, Ellensburg, WA 98926; (509) 964-2094 (winter) or (907) 842-2500 (summer). For guide service throughout the Wood-Tikchik area, contact Ultimate Rivers, 5140 East 104th Avenue, Anchorage, AK 99516; (907) 346-2193. For air taxi to all points within the state park and gear rentals, contact Freshwater Adventures, Inc., P.O. Box 62, Dillingham, AK 99576; (907) 243-7676 (winter) or (907) 842-5060 (summer).

Fishing the Wood-Tikchik Lakes: Bristol Bay's fabulous lake country offers peerless possibilities for the adventure angler. Fly in to any one of the lakes and camp, fish, and explore—on land or water—for days, even weeks if you desire. Interconnected by short rivers, the lakes can be traversed almost entirely with a few short portages. Or take a raft or kayak down one of the swift outlet streams such as the Tikchik or Nuyakuk and enjoy superb fishing as you drift through magnificent wild country. On the tamer end of things, there are several world-class fishing lodges nestled here can provide all the comforts of home while you enjoy great fishing action out the front door. If your tastes run somewhere in between, the score of reputable guides and outfitters who service the area can accommodate just about any adventure whim.

Here you'll find some of Alaska's most abundant and exciting spring and late season fishing for rainbow trout and charr (including lake trout), which is concentrated in the major connecting streams and outlets. If you can make it to some of these waters at the right time (from June to early July and August to late September) with egg, attractor, or smolt patterns or flashy spoons and spinners, you'll find out what "wild" fishing is all about.

Some of the better Wood-Tikchik fishing spots are the Wood River outlet and the Agulowak River (Aleknagik Lake), Agulukpak River (Lakes Beverley-Nerka), the outlet of Little Togiak Lake (Lake Nerka), the Goldenhorn and Peace Rivers (Lake Beverley), the narrows connecting Tikchik and Nuyakuk Lakes, and the mouth of the Tikchik River and the outlet of the Nuyakuk River (Tikchik Lake).

⑪ Tikchik River

Location: In north-central Bristol Bay, 330 miles southwest of Anchorage; see map page 226.

USGS maps: Dillingham D-7; Taylor Mountains A-7, A-8, B-7, B-8.

How to get there: By plane from Anchorage to Dillingham via commercial flight, then floatplane to Nishlik and Tikchik Lakes. A raft or kayak trip is possible down from Nishlik Lake (six to eight days), with floatplane pickup at Tikchik and return to Dillingham.

Highlights: An outstanding wilderness float river with good fishing for grayling, charr, pike, rainbow trout, and some salmon (sockeye, chum, and pink).

Species: Charr, chum salmon, grayling, lake trout, northern pike, pink salmon, rainbow trout, red salmon.

Regulations: Open year-round, all species.

Facilities: Lodge-based fishing, guide services, and gear rental are available locally.

Contact: For guided float-fishing on the Tikchik River, contact Ultimate Rivers, 5140 East 104th Avenue, Anchorage, AK 99516, (907) 346-2193. For an air taxi and gear rental, contact Freshwater Adventures, Inc., P.O. Box 62, Dillingham, AK 99576; (907) 243-7676 (winter) or (907) 842-5060 (summer).

Fishing the Tikchik River: The Tikchik is one of Southwest Alaska's most outstanding wild rivers, with superb scenery, swift but not too challenging water, abundant wildlife, and good fishing. It drains Nishlik Lake, the uppermost lake of the Wood-Tikchik chain, emptying into Tikchik Lake some 65 miles or so below. Clear, fast, and gravelly, it makes an exciting wilderness float through some of Bristol Bay's more remote backcountry, with some good fishing for grayling, charr, salmon, and even some rainbows along the way.

The trip begins with an exciting plane ride through the heart of the Tikchik Lakes (an experience some say is worth the price of admission alone) to remote Nishlik Lake, where most folks put in. From there, it's a serene cruise (fast water, with some Class I) through lonely, mountain-ringed tundra valleys and canyons, where you can expect to see caribou, wolf, moose, ptarmigan, and waterfowl and enjoy outstanding fly-fishing for grayling and charr. Further down, the river gets braided and wider as it takes on more tributaries and enters lowland forest. (Watch for the sweepers!) The fishing gets more interesting, too, with some rainbows, brighter salmon, and more charr in the sections above Tikchik Lake. But be mindful of the bears, as there will be plenty along the river during salmon season.

Figure on at least a six- to seven-day trip to allow for leisurely floating and fishing. Allow plenty of time to enjoy Tikchik Lake. It makes a superb finale to the trip, with its scenic views and great fishing for charr, lake trout, rainbows, and even monster pike in the backwater sloughs.

If you want, you can continue down the Nuyakuk River for an additional four to five days, ending your trip at the village of Koliganek on the Nushagak River (see next listing). Whether or not you continue on the Nuyakuk, the Tikchik

River is one of the most highly recommended and enjoyable float-fishing trips in all of Southwest Alaska.

Guides' tip: August and early September are the best times to float the Tikchik for fishing (rainbows, charr, salmon). You can even combine a moose/caribou hunt with your float-fishing if you're so inclined. Don't forget some big spoons or big, flashy flies for the lake trout and pike in Tikchik Lake.

⑫ Nuyakuk River

Location: In north-central Bristol Bay, 300 miles southwest of Anchorage; see map page 226.

USGS maps: Dillingham D-4, D-5, D-6.

How to get there: By plane from Anchorage to Dillingham via commercial flight, then floatplane to Tikchik Lake or the upper river (below the falls). Raft or kayak trips are possible downriver to the town of Koliganek on the Nushagak River, with wheelplane pickup for a return to Dillingham. Boat access from Koliganek to the lower river is also possible.

Highlights: One of the Nushagak River's most outstanding tributaries, with excellent rainbow, grayling, and charr fishing, and good silver and sockeye salmon opportunities.

Species: Charr, chum salmon, grayling, king salmon, lake trout, northern pike, pink salmon, rainbow trout, red salmon, silver salmon.

Regulations: Open year-round, all species; on the upper river, single-hook, unbaited, artificial lures only. For additional restrictions, consult the Alaska Department of Fish and Game regulations or contact the ADF&G Dillingham office, (907) 842-2427.

Facilities: A private lodge is available on the upper river. An undeveloped campground is located near Nuyakuk Falls. Guide services and gear rentals are available locally.

Contact: For guided float-fishing, contact Ultimate Rivers, 5140 East 104th Avenue, Anchorage, AK 99516; (907) 346-2193. For lodge-based fishing on the Nuyakuk, contact Bill Martin's Fish Alaska, Inc., P.O. Box 1887, Anchorage, AK 99510; (907) 346-2595. For air taxi and gear rentals, contact Freshwater Adventures, Inc., P.O. Box 62,

Dillingham, AK 99576; (907) 243-7676 (winter) or (907) 842-5060 (summer).

Fishing the Nuyakuk River: In many ways, the Nuyakuk is the most exceptional tributary of the renowned Nushagak River system. Issuing crystal blue from Tikchik Lake north of Dillingham, it flows wide, swift, and deep for 45 miles to its juncture with the mainstem above the town of Koliganek. As the sole connection and fish pathway linking the Tikchik lakes with the Nushagak, it receives a sizable influx of migrating salmon and supports abundant populations of rainbow trout, charr, and grayling. Sportfishing, especially along the upper river, is among the best in all of Bristol Bay.

The Nuyakuk can be accessed by plane and boat along much of its length, but it's best fished by raft, floating down from the lake (a trip of four to six days). Considering the quality of the fishing and relatively easy access, surprisingly few folks have taken this outstanding trip. It might be the river's serious white water (two stretches of rapids, Class II to Class III, and one set of Class IV on the upper river) scares them off, but it shouldn't. With good gear, intermediate boat skills, and common sense, just about anyone can safely negotiate the upper Nuyakuk.

You should begin the trip at Tikchik Lake, as the fishing around the outlet and in the first few miles of river below is too good to miss, especially if you're keen on big rainbows, lake trout, and charr. The rapids right below the lake, however, are substantial and should be scouted beforehand from the ridge along the right side of the river. (The pilot who flies you in will generally know the current conditions and can advise you.) Don't miss fishing the deep holes right below the rapids, though; some of the biggest rainbows to come out of the Nushagak system are taken there.

If you're not up to a white knuckle challenge (or if your pilot advises that the river conditions are too hairy), you can put in five miles downriver, below Nuyakuk Falls, at one of the prettiest undeveloped campsites in all of Bristol Bay. For those running down from the lake, an unmistakable landing and portage trail on the right side of the river will allow safe passage. The fishing and camping at the falls is so good that you might not want to leave, but when you do, you'll find mostly smooth sailing (fast water and one stretch of Class I rapids) all the way down to the Nushagak, where you can end your trip at the town of Koliganek. You'll also find fine fishing for silver and sockeye salmon, which are best fished in the section of river below the falls.

The white water, scarcity of gravel bars for camping, and deep, fast flows are challenges that should only enhance your appreciation for the great fishing and other exquisite qualities found on this premier Southwest river.

Togiak River System

Between the world-renowned streams of lower Kuskokwim Bay and the Wood-Tikchik Lakes lies some noteworthy fishing water, mostly concentrated in the Togiak River system, a network of clear lakes and tributaries that drain the Ahklun and Wood River mountains northwest of Dillingham, in the heart of 4.7-million-acre Togiak National Wildlife Refuge. The mainstem from Togiak Lake down to the mouth has been a consistent and popular salmon fishing destination for years, while most of the headwaters (nine lakes and seven major tributaries) receive almost no pressure and offer tantalizing wild stream and lake fishing in awesome surroundings.

⑬ Togiak River

Location: In western Bristol Bay, 350 miles southwest of Anchorage; see map page 226.

USGS maps: Goodnews A-4, B-3, B-4, C-2, C-3, D-2.

How to get there: By plane from Anchorage to Dillingham via commercial flight, then floatplane to a headwater lake (usually Togiak or Upper Togiak) or points downriver. Four- to five-day float trips by raft or kayak are possible down to lower river, with floatplane pickup from Dillingham.

Highlights: A very scenic Southwest Alaska river with a history of good silver and king salmon runs and outstanding charr fishing.

Species: Charr, chum salmon, grayling, king salmon, pink salmon, rainbow trout, red salmon, silver salmon.

Regulations: Open year-round, all species.

Facilities: Lodge-based fishing and guide services are available in the area.

Contact: For public lands information on the Upper Togiak River, contact Togiak National Wildlife Refuge, P.O. Box 270, Dillingham, AK 99576; (907) 842-1063. For guided float-fishing on the Togiak, contact Ultimate Rivers, 5140 East 104th Avenue, Anchorage, AK 99516, (907) 346-2193. For lodge-based fly-out fishing, contact Bill Martin's Fish Alaska, Inc., P.O. Box 1887, Anchorage, AK 99510; (907) 346-2595. For an air taxi to all points along the river system, contact Freshwater Adventures, Inc., P.O. Box 62, Dillingham, AK 99576; (907) 243-7676 (winter) or (907) 842-5060 (summer).

Fishing the Togiak River: A 63-mile, crystal-clear waterway, the Togiak connects the Togiak Lakes with Bristol Bay, west of the Nushagak. A tundra river, it has been fished for years, at times offering outstanding silver and king salmon angling, in addition to rainbow trout, grayling, and superb charr, particularly the big, bright sea-run variety. The upper river flows through some of the most scenic mountain country in all of Southwest Alaska, home to abundant wildlife, including bear, moose, caribou, wolf, raptors, and migratory birds.

Fair-sized, deep, and wide, with considerable current but virtually no white water, the Togiak is an easy float, but it's difficult to fish with anything but spin and casting gear. Fly-fishing is essentially limited to the lakes, mouths of tributary streams, and occasional shallow riffle sections and sloughs. Most folks fly in to Togiak Lake and float down to the lower river (four to six days) by raft, putting out right below the Togiak Wilderness boundary at the mouth of Pungokepuk Creek. The tributaries (including the Gechiak, Ongivinuck, Kashaiak, Kemuk, and Pungokepuk Rivers) and headwater lakes are seldom visited, but are known to offer outstanding fishing for salmon, charr, and big rainbows.

Guides' tip: If you have the time, a put in on Upper Togiak Lake is highly recommended for its scenery and fishing. If you're planning a float trip, plan on adding three days to your trip time.

If possible, take a small "kicker" outboard along to make the lake crossing more enjoyable (it's 12 miles), if you plan on using a river raft.

Nushagak River System

West of Lake Iliamna, the heart of Bristol Bay is dominated by a river of immense size and importance—the Nushagak. Southwest Alaska's largest clear river system, it's a veritable giant of adventure fishing opportunity. With vast headwaters that stretch from the scenic Tikchik Lakes to the rugged highlands of Lake Clark country, the Nushagak and its hundreds of miles of pristine tributaries encompass a remarkable variety of terrain, enhanced by the presence of major runs of all five species of salmon and abundant populations of rainbow trout, charr (including lake trout), grayling, and northern pike. A river of rare character and uncommonly high potential, the Nushagak offers a diversity of fishing experiences that few rivers anywhere can match—alpine float trips, spike camps, custom lodges, and even big water trolling.

Some of the angling highlights of the mainstem and several of the more outstanding tributaries are detailed in the descriptions that follow (the Nuyakuk and Tikchik Rivers are covered in the region section beginning on page 239).

⑭ Nushagak River

Location: In central Bristol Bay, 275 miles southwest of Anchorage; see map page 226.

USGS maps: For the mainstem river: Dillingham A-5, B-4, B-5, C-3, C- 4, D-4; Taylor Mountains A-4, B-2, B-3, B-4, C-1, C-2, C-4, C-5. See additional listings for tributary map coordinates.

How to get there: By floatplane from Dillingham or Iliamna. Boat access is possible from Dillingham.

Highlights: Southwest Alaska's most significant river system, with unlimited fishing possibilities.

Species: Charr, chum salmon, grayling, king salmon, lake trout, northern pike, pink salmon, rainbow trout, red salmon, silver salmon.

Regulations: Most of the river is closed to king salmon from July 25 through December 31; otherwise open year-round, all species. Much of the upper river is restricted to unbaited, single-hook, artificial lures only, with portions catch-and-release only for rainbows. For details and additional restrictions, consult the Alaska Department of Fish and Game regulations or contact the ADF&G Dillingham office, (907) 842-2427.

Facilities: No developed public facilities. Guide services, lodging, and outpost camp fishing are available locally.

Contact: For outpost camp salmon fishing on the lower Nushagak or guided Nushagak float trips, contact Ultimate Rivers, 5140 East 104th Avenue, Anchorage, AK 99516; (907) 346-2193. For outpost camp fishing on the upper river, contact Western Alaska Sportfishing, P.O. Box 123 Aleknagik, AK 99555; (406) 665-3489 (winter) or (907) 842-5480 (summer). For outpost camp fishing on the Mulchatna River and tributaries, contact Dennis Harms, P.O. Box 670071, Chugiak, AK 99567; (907) 696-2484. For lodge-based fishing on Nushagak and tributaries, contact Bill Martin's Fish Alaska, P.O. Box 1887, Anchorage, AK 99510; (907) 346-2595 (winter) or (907) 842-2725 (summer). For an air taxi to all points along the Nushagak, contact Freshwater Adventures, Inc., P.O. Box 62, Dillingham, AK 99576, (907) 243-7676 (winter) or (907) 842-5060 (summer).

Fishing the Nushagak River: For those who like their fishing on the wild side, the Nushagak River has got it all. If you're hot on kings (and who isn't?), you can fly out to the lower river (the Portage Creek area) in early summer (late June and early July), stay at a spike camp, and experience some of Alaska's best stream fishing for the species, as tens of thousands of chrome-bright chinooks herd in fresh from the sea. The Nushagak has Alaska's third largest king run, with 75,000 to 100,000 fish returning in an average year. Its ample gravel bars, beaches, sloughs, and clear waters make for plentiful, but challenging, fly-fishing.

Later on in summer, the action shifts upriver for silver salmon, charr, and abundant rainbows and grayling, with spike camp fishing on the upper mainstem above Koliganek or at the mouths of the major tributaries (Koktuli, Stuyahok, or Mulchatna). If river rafting is your style, the Nushagak has world famous tributaries—two of them Wild and Scenic Rivers—that can provide some of Bristol Bay's best float-fishing. With nearly every lodge in Southwest Alaska visiting the river at some time during the season and dozens of area guides and outfitters providing a wide range of services, you should have no problem finding a Nushagak fishing adventure to suit your tastes and budget.

Special note: Most of the land along the middle and lower Nushagak is owned by native corporations. For the location of public easements and current land status, check with the Bureau of Land Management, 222 West Seventh Avenue, Suite 13, Anchorage, AK 99513, (907) 271-5960; or the Alaska Department of Natural Resources, Public Information Center, 3601 C Street, Suite 200, Anchorage, AK 99503; (907) 762-2261.

ⓕ Stuyahok River

Location: In northeast Bristol Bay, Nushagak drainage, 250 miles southwest of Anchorage; see map page 226.

USGS maps: Iliamna C-8, D-8; Dillingham C-1.

How to get there: By plane from Anchorage to Iliamna via commercial flight, then floatplane to lakes along the upper river or the Mulchatna confluence. Camp and fish, or raft and fish, to points downriver for floatplane pickup and return to Iliamna or Dillingham.

Highlights: A delightful headwater of the Nushagak and a well-known float trip, with good fishing for grayling, charr, rainbow trout, and king and silver salmon in season.

Species: Charr, chum salmon, grayling, king salmon, northern pike, pink salmon, rainbow trout, silver salmon.

Regulations: Open year-round, all species except king salmon, which is closed July 25 through December 31; single-hook, artificial lures only. For additional restrictions, consult the Alaska Department of Fish and Game regulations or contact the ADF&G Dillingham office, (907) 842-2427.

Facilities: No developed public facilities.

Contact: For air taxi service to the Stuyahok, contact Iliamna Air Taxi, P.O. Box 109, Iliamna, AK 99606; (907) 571-1248. For guided float-fishing down the Stuyahok, contact Ultimate Rivers, 5140 East 104th Avenue, Anchorage, AK 99516, (907) 346-2193.

Fishing the Stuyahok River: One of several small Nushagak tributaries that drain the highlands west of Lake Iliamna, the Stuyahok is short, only about 50 miles in length, and is fished mostly from rafts or from camps at its confluence with the Mulchatna. With no real white water, it's an easy, enjoyable float (a three- to five-day trip) for people of average wilderness boating skills. It offers pleasant scenery and good to excellent fishing for rainbow trout, charr, grayling, and king and silver salmon.

People usually access the upper river from Lake Iliamna by floatplane, using one of several pothole lakes for a put in. (Some may require short portages to reach the river.) Below this area, there is no floatplane access until the confluence. The upper Stu winds through pretty alpine foothills before entering the forested lowlands surrounding the Mulchatna. While it has no rapids to speak of, sweepers are abundant. You'll discover plenty of good fly-fishing water. The lower five miles or so of river, including the mouth, have the Stuyahok's best salmon fishing (and its most concentrated angling effort, too). All in all, the Stu makes for a sweet little fishing trip, highly recommended for newcomers as a great introduction to the fabulous streams of Bristol Bay.

ⓖ Koktuli River

Location: In northeast Bristol Bay, Nushagak drainage, 220 miles southwest of Anchorage; see map page 226.

USGS maps: Iliamna D-7, D-8; Dillingham D-1, D-2.

How to get there: By plane from Anchorage to Iliamna via commercial flight, then floatplane to lakes (along the upper river or in the Swan River–Koktuli area) or to the Koktuli-Mulchatna confluence. Raft or kayak trips are possible from the headwaters down to the Mulchatna confluence (four to six days), with floatplane pickup from Iliamna.

Highlights: One of the more popular upper Nushagak tributaries for sportfishing and an excellent float trip, known for its rainbow, grayling, king, silver, and sockeye salmon angling.

Species: Charr, chum salmon, grayling, king salmon, lake trout, northern pike, pink salmon, rainbow trout, red salmon, silver salmon.

Regulations: Open year-round, except for king salmon, which is closed from July 25 through December 31; unbaited, single-hook, artificial lures only. For additional restrictions, consult the Alaska Department of Fish and Game regulations or contact the ADF&G Dillingham office, (907) 842-2427.

Facilities: No developed public facilities.

Contact: For air taxi to the Koktuli River, contact Iliamna Air Taxi, P.O. Box 109, Iliamna, AK 99606; (907) 571-1248. For guided float-fishing, contact Ultimate Rivers, 5140 East 104th Avenue, Anchorage, AK 99516; (907) 346-2193.

Fishing the Koktuli River: Similar in size and character to the Stuyahok (see prior listing), the Koktuli River has been one of the more popular upper Nushagak tributaries for some time. Easily accessible by floatplane from nearby Lake Iliamna or Lake Clark, it's noted for its consistent salmon, grayling, and rainbow trout angling, with good fly-fishing in its clear waters. The majority of users are fly-in anglers working the mouth and lower river, but quite a few folks float it regularly.

Floatplanes can put in at the mouth or on lakes along the upper river or vicinity of the Swan River confluence. (Short portages are sometimes necessary.) From there, the river is an easy float (one to two days from the Swan River, four to six days from upper river), with no major hazards except sweepers and abundant logjams. Floaters can take out at the mouth or continue down the Mulchatna. Wildlife is abundant and includes bear, caribou, wolf, moose, and waterfowl.

⑰ Mulchatna River

Location: In northeast Bristol Bay, Nushagak drainage, 175 miles southwest of Anchorage; see map page 226.

USGS maps: Lake Clark B-7, B-8, C-6, C-7, C-8, D-3, D-4, D-5, D-6; Taylor Mountains A-1, A-2, B-1; Dillingham C-3, D-1, D-2, D-3.

How to get there: By floatplane to the upper river via Lake Clark or Lake Iliamna. Camp and fish, or raft or kayak, to points downriver, with floatplane pickup or takeout in villages along the Nushagak (with return to Dillingham via scheduled or chartered small plane flights). The lower and middle river are also accessible by boat from the Nushagak River.

Highlights: A Wild and Scenic River, and the largest and most heavily utilized tributary of the famed Nushagak, with good to excellent fishing for salmon, rainbow trout, grayling, and charr.

Species: Charr, chum salmon, grayling, king salmon, lake trout, northern pike, pink salmon, rainbow trout, red salmon, silver salmon.

Regulations: Open year-round, all species; on portions of the Mulchatna, unbaited, single-hook, artificial lures only. For details and additional restrictions, consult the Alaska Department of Fish and Game regulations or contact the ADF&G Dillingham office, (907) 842-2427.

Facilities: No developed public facilities.

Contact: For public lands information on Turquoise Lake and the upper river, contact Lake Clark National Park and Preserve, 4230 University Drive #311, Anchorage, AK 99508; (907) 271-3751. For guided spike camp fishing, contact Dennis Harms, P.O. Box 670071, Chugiak, AK 99567; (907) 696-2484. For guided float-fishing, contact Ultimate Rivers, 5140 East 104th Avenue, Anchorage, AK 99516, (907) 346-2193. For an air taxi to the upper river, contact Iliamna Air Taxi, P.O. Box 109, Iliamna, AK 99606, (907) 571-1248; or Air Adventures, P.O. Box 22, Kenai, AK 99611-0022, (907) 776-5444.

Fishing the Mulchatna River: As the main tributary of the immense, fish-rich Nushagak, the Mulchatna is one of Bristol Bay's most popular fly-in fishing destinations. A Wild and Scenic River with headwaters in the majestic Lake Clark country, the Mulchatna (and its main tributary, the Chilikadrotna) is also one of Southwest Alaska's most popular rivers for floating.

In its 250 miles, the Mulchatna changes character considerably, from a small, rocky alpine stream to a broad, braided river coursing through lowland forest. Along the way, it's joined by numerous tributaries, some of them well-known and popular fishing streams on their own, such as the Chilikadrotna, Stuyahok, and Koktuli. Access to the upper river is usually by floatplane from Lakes Clark or Iliamna, putting in at the Half Cabin Lakes area about 30 miles down from Turquoise Lake. (The headwaters at the lake are not commonly floated because of rocky, shallow conditions.) From there, it's an easy float, with fast water, some minor rapids (all Class I, one short Class II), but no major challenge to anyone possessing basic boating skills and a high-quality raft or kayak. (Be forewarned, however: There are abundant sweepers, especially below the Chilikadrotna confluence.) Most floaters end their trip somewhere below the Mulchatna-Chilchitna confluence (a five- to seven-day float), but longer trips are certainly possible.

Fishing on the Mulchatna is generally good to excellent, depending on water conditions and the time of year. (The river tends to muddy easily during heavy rains.) Traditionally, the mouths of the larger tributaries and mainstem up to the Koktuli have been some of Bristol Bay's most productive and popular fly-in areas for king and silver salmon, rainbow, grayling, and charr. Also, the river's abundant wildlife, particularly caribou and moose, attracts quite a bit of use from hunters each fall, who float in rafts or stay in commercial outpost camps and enjoy good fishing as a bonus. For folks wanting to sample some of Alaska's better spike camp fishing or an outstanding float-fishing trip, the Mulchatna is hard to beat.

⑱ Chilikadrotna River

Location: In northeast Bristol Bay, Nushagak drainage, 100 miles southwest of Anchorage; see map page 226.

USGS maps: Lake Clark C-2, C-3, C-4, C-5, C-6, C-7.

How to get there: By floatplane to the river headwaters via Clark or Iliamna Lakes. A raft or kayak trip is possible down to Mulchatna River, with floatplane pickup below the Mulchatna-Chilchitna confluence.

Highlights: A Wild and Scenic River, one of western Alaska's prettiest, and an exciting float-fishing trip, with good opportunities for grayling, rainbows, charr, and salmon.

Species: Charr, chum salmon, grayling, king

salmon, lake trout, northern pike, pink salmon, rainbow trout, red salmon, silver salmon.

Regulations: Open year-round, all species.

Facilities: No developed public facilities.

Contact: For public lands information on the upper river area, contact Lake Clark National Park and Preserve, 4230 University Drive #311, Anchorage, AK 99508; (907) 271-3751. For air taxi service, contact Iliamna Air Taxi, P.O. Box 109, Iliamna, AK 99606, (907) 571-1248; or Air Adventures, P.O. Box 22, Kenai, AK 99611-0022, (907) 776-5444. For guided float-fishing, contact Ultimate Rivers, 5140 East 104th Avenue, Anchorage, AK 99516; (907) 346-2193.

Fishing the Chilikadrotna River: The Chilikadrotna Wild and Scenic River is one of Southwest Alaska's premier float trips, with outstanding wilderness values and fine fishing. It begins in the rugged alpine reaches of the Alaska Range in Lake Clark National Park, 100 miles southwest of Anchorage. A white-water river, the 62-mile Chili is wide (100 to 200 feet), with swift, rocky flows, rapids (Class I to Class III), and plenty of sweepers—definitely not a river for inexperienced boaters.

Fishing is good from late June into September for charr, grayling, rainbows, and some salmon (mostly chum, silvers, and a few kings), with excellent conditions for fly-fishing along much of the river. The beautiful Twin Lakes at the headwaters have some very good lake trout populations, and some pike even roam in the sloughs along the river. Magnificent scenery, wildlife, and numerous hiking opportunities are a definite bonus along the way.

Most rafters put in at Twin Lakes or at several small lakes down below and take a seven-day journey down to the Mulchatna, putting out on long, flat stretches of river 12 to 13 miles below the confluence. You can easily arrange a longer voyage continuing down the Mulchatna; check with the air taxi service for details.

Lake Iliamna and Kvichak River System

Ocean-sized Iliamna, the largest lake in Alaska (more than 1,000 square miles), is the world's most productive sockeye salmon system. Along with the associated Lake Clark drainages, it supports runs of millions of returning fish. (In 1965, a staggering number of sockeyes—42 million—returned to spawn.) The vast, rich Lake Iliamna environs also produce bumper yields of some of the largest rainbow trout in the state. Studies done over the last 30 years show these fish to be a late-maturing, larger growing strain, with an average size around 20 inches, commonly reaching up to 15 pounds or more. Along with the fabulous locations of Katmai, Iliamna's immense, productive fisheries have long been synonymous with the finest trophy trout angling in Alaska, if not the world.

⑲ Lake Clark

Location: In Lake Clark National Park and Preserve, 180 miles southwest of Anchorage; see map page 226.

USGS maps: Lake Clark A-4, A-5, B-2, B-3, B-4.

How to get there: By wheelplane to Point Allsworth from Anchorage or Iliamna, then boat or floatplane to various points around the lake or associated tributaries. There is also direct floatplane access from Anchorage or Kenai.

Highlights: Alaska's most scenic lake area with good fishing for lake trout, grayling, pike, and sockeye salmon.

Species: Charr, grayling, lake trout, northern pike, red salmon.

Regulations: Open year-round for waters above Six Mile Lake; only unbaited, single-hook, artificial lures in Six Mile and tributaries. For additional restrictions, consult the current Alaska Department of Fish and Game regulations or contact the ADF&G Dillingham office, (907) 842-2427.

Facilities: Several private lodges are located on the lake, some offering daily guide service and boat rentals.

Contact: For information on the park, contact Lake Clark National Park and Preserve, 4230 University Drive #311, Anchorage, AK 99508; (907) 271-3751. For air taxi, guide services and tent camps within the Lake Clark area, contact Air Adventures, P.O. Box 22, Kenai, AK 99611-0022; (907) 776-5444. For a full-service lodge,

contact Alaska's Wilderness Lodge, 505 West Northern Lights Boulevard #220A, Anchorage, AK 99503; (800) 835-8032. For lodging and unguided fishing on Lake Clark and associated drainages, contact Marchant's, 6414 Tolhurst Court, Anchorage, AK 99504, (907) 337-0215 or (907) 781-2299.

Fishing Lake Clark: Beautiful, turquoise Lake Clark is the gateway attraction for a 3.6-million-acre national park and preserve, located west of the Chigmit Mountains, a short hop from Anchorage. Said by many to contain Alaska's most spectacular lakes and alpine scenery, this area also offers some noteworthy fishing, though the predominantly glacial waters and isolation from the coast limit its potential for salmon and trout.

Outstanding mountain lakes—including Clark, Twin, Telaquana, Tazimina, and Kijik—are the prime attraction here. These waters are perhaps best known for their superb lake trout (up to 30 pounds), charr, and sockeye salmon fishing, with some good grayling opportunities in the clearer tributary streams and northern pike in some of the shallower lakes, ponds, and sloughs. Rainbow trout are generally not found above the Six Mile Lake drainage. Because of its proximity to Anchorage and outstanding mountain scenery, the Lake Clark area sees more use every year and visitor services continue to expand as well. Plush lodges offer weekly stays with daily fly outs, or more modest, family-style lodges and inns provide boat excursions and guides to fish the lake and nearby streams. You can even contract the use of remote tent camps and cabins on the area's best fishing lakes and rivers.

For the true adventure angler, the park has two Wild and Scenic Rivers—the Mulchatna and Chilikadrotna—that can provide unforgettable float angling experiences. See the listing on the Nushagak River on page 243 for detailed descriptions.

⑳ Tazimina River

Location: In the Six Mile Lake drainage of Lake Iliamna, 180 miles southwest of Anchorage; see map page 226.

USGS maps: Lake Clark A-2, A-3, A-4; Iliamna D-5.

How to get there: By plane from Anchorage to Iliamna or Port Allsworth via commercial flight, then floatplane to the lakes or the lower river. Jet boat access is also possible to the mouth and lower river.

Highlights: One of the more popular Illiamna–Clark area stream locations, with excellent fishing for rainbow trout, sockeye salmon, and grayling; this is also a great short float trip.

Species: Charr, grayling, rainbow trout, red salmon.

Regulations: Spring closures (April 10 through June 7) for spawning trout; unbaited, single-hook, artificial lure fishing only. Catch-and-release only for rainbows in the lower river (one mile up from the mouth to the falls) during summer and fall. For additional restrictions, consult the current Alaska Department of Fish and Game regulations or contact the ADF&G Dillingham office, (907) 842-2427.

Facilities: No developed public facilities. Guide services are available.

Contact: For an air taxi, contact Iliamna Air Taxi, P.O. Box 109, Iliamna, AK 99606; (907) 571-1248. For guide services, contact Real Alaska, P.O. Box 242085, Anchorage, AK 99524-2085, (907) 243-2396.

Fishing the Tazimina River: For years the Lake Iliamna–Lake Clark lodge crowd has flocked to the Tazimina for its consistently superb rainbow trout, sockeye salmon, and grayling fishing. It's also one of the few fishing rivers in the area, along with the Gibraltar and Copper, that can be floated on a one- to four-day trip.

Located within Lake Clark National Park, the 54-mile, clear Tazimina drains a series of lakes of the same name before emptying into Six Mile Lake and the Newhalen River. Because of some waterfalls and portages (the most serious located nine miles from the mouth), most anglers usually access only the lower river (from the mouth to Alexcy Lake) via jet boat or floatplane. Rafters put in at either Lower Tazimina, Alexcy, or Hudson Lakes (with short portages) and vary the length of their float. Fly-fishing conditions on the Tazimina are excellent.

㉑ Newhalen River

Location: On the north shore Lake Iliamna, 200 miles southwest of Anchorage; see map page 226.

USGS maps: Iliamna C-6, D-5, D-6.

How to get there: By plane from Anchorage to Iliamna via commercial flight, then by car or foot to the river; boat transportation is available from the village of Newhalen.

Highlights: Some of Alaska's best, most easily accessed fishing for sockeye salmon and rainbow trout.

Species: Rainbow trout, charr, red salmon, grayling, lake trout.

Regulations: Spring closures (April 10 through June 7) to protect spawning rainbow trout; single-hook, unbaited, artificial lures only. For additional restrictions, consult the current Alaska Department of Fish and Game regulations or the ADF&G Dillingham office, (907) 842-2427.

Facilities: Lodging, guide services, and boat rentals are available in nearby Iliamna.

Contact: For lodging and boat rentals, contact Airport Hotel, P.O. Box 157, Iliamna, AK 99606; (907) 571-1501. For guided fishing, contact Real Alaska, P.O. Box 242085, Anchorage, AK 99524-2085; (907) 243-2396.

Fishing the Newhalen River: A short flight west from Anchorage to the village of Iliamna and a half-mile hike from the end of the airstrip takes you to one of Alaska's best fishing holes, the Falls on the Newhalen River. In early July, you'll find bright, frantic sockeye salmon stacked thick as cordwood here, and in the pools and rapids below the Falls (especially in spring and fall), maybe some of those famous, jumbo Iliamna rainbow trout. You might have to share these waters with some other folks, but it won't be anything like the mad scenes on the Kenai Peninsula and it's a whole 'nother class of fishing to boot.

A big, transparent-blue, white-water river, the 25-mile Newhalen connects Six Mile Lake and adjoining Lake Clark with immense Lake Iliamna. It's the major pathway for a mind-boggling migration of sockeye salmon that make their way up into the far reaches of this drainage in early summer. Most of the fishing effort for these salmon occurs right below a series of nearly impenetrable rapids (Class IV and Class V)—the Falls—on the lower river a couple of miles up from the mouth, but some productive water upriver can be accessed by road at a place called Upper Landing.

Below the Falls, you can fish for salmon until your arms go numb, then rent a boat (and a guide's services, if you want) and drift the stretch of river down to the lake for big rainbows (up to 12 pounds). However, the trout fishing doesn't really heat up until later on in the season—try September and October for the largest rainbows. Drifting egg, flesh, leech, and attractor fly patterns, or Spin-N-Glos and Li'l Corkies seems to be the ticket. (You can do quite well fishing from shore on this river.) The Newhalen is highly recommended for those who seek a relatively inexpensive alternative to the overrated and overcrowded fishing on most of the popular streams of Southcentral Alaska.

During the first three weeks in July, the Newhalen's famous run of sockeyes peaks, making easy targets for the skilled angler. Consult the chapter on sockeye salmon on page 51 for the best flies and techniques to use.

Special note: If you plan on a do-it-yourself excursion along the Newhalen, be aware that much of the land along the river is owned and managed by native corporations. For details on public easements and land ownership, contact the Bureau of Land Management, Alaska State Office, 222 West Seventh Avenue, P.O. Box 13, Anchorage, AK 99513 (907) 271-5960.

㉒ Talarik Creek

Location: On the northwest shore Lake Iliamna drainage, 220 miles southwest of Anchorage; see map page 226.

USGS map: Iliamna C-7.

How to get there: By plane from Anchorage to Iliamna via commercial flight, then a short floatplane flight west to the lagoon at the mouth of the river.

Highlights: The most famous Lake Iliamna fly-fishing stream; hard hit, but still worth a visit for its great rainbows.

Species: Charr, grayling, rainbow trout, red salmon.

Regulations: Spring closures (April 10 through June 7) for spawning trout; seasonal fly-fishing only and catch-and-release for rainbows (June 8 through October 31). For additional restrictions, consult the current Alaska Department of Fish and Game regulations or contact the ADF&G Dillingham office, (907) 842-2427.

Facilities: No developed public facilities. Guided fishing is available in nearby Iliamna.

Contact: For an air taxi, contact Iliamna Air Taxi, P.O. Box 109, Iliamna, AK 99606; (907) 571-1248. For guided fishing, contact Iliaska Lodge, 6160 Farpoint Drive, Anchorage, AK 99507; (907) 337-9844 (winter) or (907) 571-1221 (summer).

Fishing Talarik Creek: Most people are amazed, even disappointed, when they see Lower Talarik Creek for the first time. Entering Lake Iliamna from the north about 25 miles west of the Newhalen River, it's truly just a short dribble of water, dwarfed by most of the other drainages that empty into Lake Iliamna. The giant reputation this place carries is beyond all measure of its physical size. Still, this creek is amazingly productive, due to its location and perfect habitat for trout and salmon spawning. Since the '50s, Talarik's abundant, big rainbows and easy access have drawn anglers from near and far to sample its waters.

Talarik is also one of the most studied trout streams in Alaska. The Alaska Department of Fish and Game has sampled and tagged the creek's rainbows for the last 30 years or so, with some interesting findings. The majority of the rainbows here live the first few years of their lives in the creek, then migrate to the lake, where they grow rapidly, most reaching 18 inches or more by five years of age. They return to the creek (or other streams) yearly to spawn and/or feed on the abundant roe, smolt, and flesh of the sockeye salmon. The best time to fish Talarik is during these periods of in-migration, from June through early July, and September through October. For a river this small, the average size of Talarik's rainbows compares favorably with the best Lake Iliamna locations (the Kvichak and Newhalen Rivers), especially during late fall (October), when a large percentage of trophy fish are taken.

Most anglers land on the lagoon at the mouth, then hike upriver, fishing either fork for good results. You can also put in at one of the headwater lakes, then fish and wade down to Iliamna—a good tactic in the fall. Upper Talarik Creek also offers some good fishing at times, but it lacks the lower creek's convenient access and can be quite shallow in spots.

㉓ Copper River

Location: On the eastern Lake Iliamna drainage, 190 miles southwest of Anchorage; see map page 226.

USGS maps: Iliamna C-4, C-5.

How to get there: By plane from Anchorage to Iliamna via commercial flight. There is floatplane access to several headwater lakes (such as Copper, Meadows, and Pike) or the lower river. A one- to three-day (depending on the put-in location) float trip by raft or kayak is possible from the upper river.

Highlights: One of Lake Iliamna's most famous fly-fishing streams, with excellent angling for rainbow trout, sockeye salmon, and grayling.

Species: Charr, grayling, northern pike, rainbow trout, red salmon.

Regulations: Spring closures (April 10 through June 7) for spawning trout. Seasonal fly-fishing only and catch-and-release for rainbows (June 8 through October 31). For additional restrictions, consult the current Alaska Department of Fish and Game regulations or contact the ADF&G Dillingham office, (907) 842-2427.

Facilities: Lodge-based fishing is available locally.

Contact: For air taxi service to the Copper River, contact Iliamna Air Taxi, P.O. Box 109, Iliamna, AK 99606; (907) 571-1248. For lodge-based fishing on the river, contact Chris Goll, Rainbow River Lodge, 4127 Raspberry Road, Anchorage, AK 99502; (907) 243-7894.

Fishing the Copper River: Along with Talarik Creek, the Copper is perhaps the best known of Lake Iliamna's fabulous trout streams, and is particularly renowned for its superb fly-

fishing. In its glory days, just about every fly-out lodge in the area visited it routinely; for years, it was one of the lake's most floated streams.

The clear Copper originates in a series of lakes in the Chigmit Mountains east of Iliamna, flowing swiftly for some 15 miles before emptying into Intricate Bay. A 36-foot waterfall below Lower Copper Lake, 12 miles up from the mouth, serves as an effective barrier for most fish and fishermen; several lakes adjoining the river below the falls are the best points of access. (The river can be run from up above, as long as you take great care not to miss the short portage on the left side.)

The Copper's reputation comes from its nearly perfect fly-fishing conditions and ample supply of husky rainbows, which migrate in from the lake in spring and fall. Though the fish here aren't as large as those taken in the big water of the Kvichak or Katmai's Naknek River, the Copper is much better suited for the wade-and-cast stream angler. It's also a great river to fish dry flies for rainbows, perhaps one of Alaska's best in early season (June and July). The preferred method of fishing the Copper is to float down from below the falls in a raft (put in on Upper Pike Lake), fishing as you go, with a pickup at Lower Pike Lake (a one-day trip) or down below in the bay. A fancy lodge, Rainbow River, is set along the river for those who want to go in style. June, July, and September are the best times for rainbows on the Copper.

㉔ Gibraltar River

Location: On the southeast shore of the Lake Iliamna drainage, 215 miles southwest of Anchorage; see map page 226.

USGS maps: Iliamna B-5, B-6.

How to get there: By plane from Anchorage to Iliamna via commercial flight, then floatplane to Gibraltar Lake or (sometimes) the river mouth area. Floating down from the lake by raft is possible, with pickup by floatplane.

Highlights: A popular Lake Iliamna rainbow trout location.

Species: Charr, grayling, lake trout, rainbow trout, red salmon.

Regulations: Spring closures (April 10

through June 7) for spawning trout; seasonal fly-fishing only and catch-and-release for rainbows (June 8 through October 31). For additional restrictions, consult the current Alaska Department of Fish and Game regulations or the ADF&G Dillingham office, (907) 842-2427.

Facilities: No developed public facilities.

Contact: For an air taxi, contact Iliamna Air Taxi, P.O. Box 109, Iliamna, AK 99606; (907) 571-1248.

Fishing the Gibraltar River: One of the better known Iliamna fly-fishing streams, the Gibraltar offers its own lake access and fairly abundant fishing for rainbow trout and red salmon in season. Only about six miles long, the river drains Gibraltar Lake flowing north into Iliamna near Kakhonak Bay.

Most of the fishing on Gibraltar occurs near the lake outlet and on tributary streams like Dream and Southeast Creeks, both of which are outstanding trout locales on their own. The entire river offers good fishing, however, and is best worked by floating down from the lake in rafts (a one-day trip). A two-mile section of swift water in the middle section is the only possible hazard. Floatplanes may not be able to land by the mouth for a pickup if it's too windy; you may have to hike about three miles to the nearby village of Kakhonak for a plane ride back to Iliamna. The best times for rainbows are June and September, with the bigger fish more abundant in the fall.

㉕ Lake Iliamna

Location: In eastern Bristol Bay, 175 miles southwest of Anchorage; see map page 226.

USGS maps: Iliamna B-5, B-6, B-7, B-8, C-3, C-4, C-5, C-6, C-7, C-8, D-3, D-4, D-5.

How to get there: By plane via scheduled commercial flights from Anchorage, and floatplane or boat to various points along the lake.

Highlights: Alaska's most productive lake system, world famous for trophy rainbow trout and abundant sockeye salmon.

Species: Charr, grayling, lake trout, pink salmon, rainbow trout, red salmon, *chum salmon, northern pike, silver salmon.*

Regulations: Spring closures (April 10 through June 7) for rainbow trout; single-hook, artificial lures only. Certain lake drainages are fly-fishing only and seasonal catch-and-release. For details and additional restrictions, consult the current Alaska Department of Fish and Game regulations or contact the ADF&G Dillingham office, (907) 842-2427.

Facilities: No developed public facilities. The lake area is serviced by a score of reputable lodges, guides, outfitters, and air taxis.

Contact: For flights from Anchorage to Iliamna, contact ERA Aviation Inc., 6160 South Airport Drive, Anchorage, AK 99502; (800) 866-8394. For air taxi service within the Lake Iliamna area, contact Iliamna Air Taxi, P.O. Box 109, Iliamna, AK 99606; (907) 571-1248. For full-service lodges for the entire Iliamna area, contact Chris Goll, Rainbow River Lodge, 4127 Raspberry Road, Anchorage, AK 99502, (907) 243-7894; or Iliaska Lodge, 6160 Farpoint Drive, Anchorage, AK 99507, (907) 337-9844 (winter), (907) 571-1221 (summer). For daily lodging and boat rentals, contact Airport Hotel, P.O. Box 157, Iliamna, AK 99606; (907) 571-1501. For raft rentals and outfitting, contact Newhalen Rafts, Inc., P.O. Box 113, Iliamna, AK 99606, (907) 571-1374.

Fishing Lake Iliamna: With its mesmerizing blue vastness and infinite bays, islands, and gravel beaches, Lake Iliamna has a mystique all its own. One of the deepest lakes ever surveyed in Alaska (1,000 feet or more in spots), it has some rather unique fauna, such as freshwater seals, sturgeon, and even a mysterious giant creature that residents swear is Alaska's equivalent to Scotland's famous Loch Ness Monster.

The steelhead-sized rainbows are, of course, Iliamna's main attraction. Very little fishing is done in the lake itself, however; anglers instead target the numerous creeks and rivers emptying into this freshwater behemoth. Some of the more popular drainages have become legends on their own, places like the Talarik Creeks or the Copper, Gibraltar, Tazimina, or Kvichak Rivers, each with a history of remarkable fishing over the years. These streams are best hit in late spring (right after the opening in June) or fall (September and October) when the big trout cruise out of the lake for spawning or feeding activities. Most of the smaller water is fly-fished, with the larger, deeper rivers worked most efficiently by boat, drifting lures steelhead-style along the bottom. In early summer, some of Alaska's best opportunities for sockeye salmon also occur in the larger lake tributaries, including the Newhalen, Kvichak, Tazimina, and Iliamna Rivers.

Special note: Much of the land surrounding Lake Iliamna is privately owned by native corporations. There are no developed public facilities along the lake or tributaries. Before you attempt any unguided ventures in this watershed, check with the following agencies for information on the locations of public easements, restrictions, and fees: Iliamna Natives Ltd., P.O. Box 245, Iliamna, AK 99606, (907) 571-1256; or Bureau of Land Management, Alaska State Office, 222 West Seventh Avenue, P.O. Box 13, Anchorage, AK 99513, (907) 271-5960.

㉖ Kvichak River

Location: On the Lake Iliamna outlet, Bristol Bay, 250 miles southwest of Anchorage; see map page 226.

USGS maps: Iliamna B-8; Dillingham A-1, A-2, A-3, B-1; Naknek D-3.

How to get there: By plane. Access is from Anchorage to Iliamna via commercial flight, wheelplane flight to Igiugik at the mouth of the river, or floatplane directly to the river or outlet. Boat transport up and down the river is also possible.

Highlights: Perhaps Alaska's finest trophy rainbow trout fishery; also known for its phenomenal sockeye salmon.

Species: Charr, chum salmon, grayling, lake trout, northern pike, pink salmon, rainbow trout, red salmon, silver salmon, *king salmon*.

Regulations: Spring closures (April 10 through June 7) to protect spawning trout; unbaited, single-hook, artificial lures only. For additional restrictions, consult the current Alaska Department of Fish and Game regulations or the ADF&G Dillingham office, (907) 842-2427.

Facilities: Lodge-based fishing, guide services,

lodging, and boat rentals are available at the village of Igiugig.

Contact: For air taxi service to the river, contact Iliamna Air Taxi, P.O. Box 109, Iliamna, AK 99606, (907) 571-1248. For lodging, boat rentals, and guides, contact Dan Salmon, P.O. Box 4003, Igiugig, AK 99613; (907) 533-3219. For lodged-based fishing, contact Todd's Igiugik Lodge, P.O. Box 871395, Wasilla, AK 99687, (907) 376-2859.

Fishing the Kvichak River: As the primary outlet for giant Lake Iliamna, the state's largest, most productive body of freshwater, the Kvichak is arguably Alaska's foremost locale for jumbo rainbows (up to 15 pounds or more). In spring and fall, hordes of the big, lake-resident trout converge on the river to spawn and feed, providing some of Alaska's most exciting trophy fishing possibilities.

From its outlet at Igiugik, the Kvichak winds through flat, coastal tundra for 60 miles before spilling its jewel-like waters into muddy Kvichak Bay. It's a big river—wide, deep, and fast—not easy to fish from shore, except at the outlet and mouths of the tributary creeks (such as Peck's, Kaskanak, and Ole). Most anglers drift it from boats, from the outlet down through the extensive braided section (Kaskanak Flats) that begins five miles below the lake, using Spin-N-Glos, plugs, spoons, and Okie Drifters fished right above bottom. Fly-fishing is difficult and best done at the lake outlet, from the cutbanks of Kaskanak Flats, or in the mouths and lower sections of the tributaries. (Bright attractors, egg/flesh patterns, sculpins, leech, and smolt imitations work best.)

Weather and timing are crucial to your success in these big waters. Fall (late August to mid-October), the best time for trophy fish, also has notoriously foul weather that can quickly turn a fishing trip into a survival ordeal. Most of the big, lake rainbows are usually gone by the time the sockeyes return in late June, making the spring fishing period very short (these waters don't open for fishing until June 8). When it all comes together, though, the Kvichak shines as one of the world's finest big rainbow fisheries, with more large trout encounters possible in a day's fishing here than in a lifetime of effort most anywhere else.

Note: With its predictable runs of millions of sockeye salmon, the Kvichak also offers some of Alaska's best sportfishing for the species. Since there's lots of water to fish, it's best to enlist the services of a local guide if you're new to fishing the area.

Katmai

Few places in the world offer visitors such wonders as they'll find in magnificent Katmai National Park and Preserve. Set on the neck of the Alaska Peninsula, 300 miles southwest of Anchorage, Katmai has fascinating landscapes shaped by intense volcanic action, with unique wildlife (the famous fishing brown bears), glaciers, and scenic lakes and streams holding some of Alaska's best trout and salmon fishing.

It was Katmai's jumbo rainbow trout—some of Alaska's largest—that established the region as a world-class fishing destination in the 1950s. Although the park has been in existence since 1918, it wasn't until after World War II, when military personnel from the newly established Naknek Air Base at nearby King Salmon discovered the amazing trout fishing nearby, that word got out about the area's fabulous sport fish potential. Ray Peterson, a Bristol Bay bush pilot and entrepreneur, established some of the first sport fish camps to cater to the growing public demand for facilities here. These rustic camps—Brooks, Kulik, and Grosvenor—have changed little over the years, offering folks a chance to savor some of the world's best fishing and most breathtaking surroundings in the relaxed atmosphere of family-style lodging.

27 Alagnak River

Location: On eastern Bristol Bay, 250 miles southwest of Anchorage; see map page 226.

USGS maps: Iliamna A-7, A-8; Dillingham A-1, A-2, A-3.

How to get there: By plane from Anchorage to King Salmon via commercial flight, then floatplane to either headwater lake (Nonvianuk or Kukaklek) or points along the river. Floating by raft or kayak is possible to takeouts on the middle and lower river, with return to King Salmon via floatplane.

Highlights: One of Southwest Alaska's best trout and salmon rivers and most popular for float-fishing, with outstanding fly-fishing opportunities.

Species: Charr, chum salmon, grayling, king salmon, lake trout, pink salmon, rainbow trout, red salmon, silver salmon.

Regulations: Spring closures (April 10 through June 7) for rainbows; single-hook, unbaited, artificial lures only. Catch-and-release fishing only (June 8 through October 31) for rainbows at the Kukaklek outlet. For additional restrictions, consult the current Alaska Department of Fish and Game regulations or contact the ADF&G Dillingham office, (907) 842-2427.

Facilities: Private lodges and guide services are available along the river.

Contact: For lodge-based fishing, contact Alagnak Lodge, 4117 Hillcrest Way, Suite 1102, Sacramento, CA 95821; (800) 877-9903. For guided outpost camp and float-fishing on the Alagnak River system, contact Roger Denny, P.O. Box 770752, Eagle River, AK 99577; (800) 688-1032. For an air taxi to all points along the Alagnak River system, contact Branch River Air Service, 4540 Edinburgh Drive, Anchorage, AK 99515; (907) 248-3539 (winter) or (907) 246-3437 (summer).

Fishing the Alagnak River: For years, the Alagnak Wild and Scenic River has provided sport anglers some of Southwest Alaska's more accessible, world-class fishing for trout and salmon, along with abundant wildlife and pleasant scenery. With twin lake sources (Nonvianuk and Kukaklek) in fabulous Katmai country, the Alagnak (sometimes called the Branch River) spiritedly flows 70 miles or so before emptying into Kvichak Bay. Crystal clear, rocky, and swift, the upper sections of both branches offer perfect conditions for fly-fishing, particularly for abundant rainbow trout and prolific sockeye salmon in season. (The lake outlets, particularly Kukaklek, have been famous trophy rainbow locales since the late 1940s.) King and silver salmon fishing, usually quite good in most years, is best done in the slower, deeper lower river.

The best way to fish the Alagnak is by raft, putting in at either lake from King Salmon via floatplane. For a four- to six-day trip, you can float, fish, and camp along the river on your way to pickup points downstream. The best time is July for sockeyes and kings, and late August through September for silvers and rainbows. The Alagnak is also known for its abundant bear population (the famous bruins of Katmai National Park and Preserve); they can be especially prominent during the height of the sockeye run in July. Anglers are advised to use caution and common sense along the river corridor during this time of year. Caribou, moose, and wolves also roam here.

There are sections of white water (mostly Class I, some Class II, and one Class III rapid 12 miles below Kukaklek Lake), but for the most part the Alagnak presents no great technical challenge to floaters. It's a highly recommended trip for first-time anglers new to the wonders of Southwest Alaska.

Guides' tip: The upper Alagnak in early July has some of Alaska's finest fly-fishing for sockeye salmon. Consult the sockeye salmon chapter on page 51 for details on technique. If you go, bring along plenty of Sockeye Willies, Orange Comets, and Coho flies (orange/red/white and purple/yellow/white).

28 Nonvianuk and Kukaklek Lakes

Location: In Katmai National Park and Preserve, 250 miles southwest of Anchorage; see map page 226.

USGS maps: Iliamna A-6, A-7; Mt. Katmai D-3, D-4, D-5.

How to get there: By plane from Anchorage to King Salmon via commercial flight, then floatplane to lake locations.

Highlights: Very famous Katmai destinations for rainbow trout.

Species: Charr, grayling, lake trout, rainbow trout, red salmon, silver salmon, *northern pike.*

Regulations: Spring closures (April 10 through June 7) for seasonal spawning trout. Unbaited, single-hook artificial lures only; catch-and-release for rainbows in portions of both lake

drainages. For details and additional restrictions, consult the current Alaska Department of Fish and Game regulations or the ADF&G Dillingham office, (907) 842-2427.

Facilities: Private lodge and outpost camp facilities are available on Nonvianuk, Kukaklek, and Kulik Lakes.

Contact: For campground and general information, contact Katmai National Park and Preserve, P.O. Box 7, King Salmon, AK 99613; (907) 246-3305. For lodge-based fishing, contact Katmailand, Inc., 4550 Aircraft Drive #2, Anchorage, AK 99502; (800) 544-0551 or (907) 243-5448. For outpost camp fishing, contact Roger Denny, P.O. Box 770752, Eagle River, AK 99577; (800) 688-1032. For air taxi to points within the lake system, contact Branch River Air Service, 4540 Edinburgh Drive, Anchorage, AK 99515; (907) 248-3539 (winter) or (907) 246-3437 (summer).

Fishing Nonvianuk and Kukaklek Lakes: No list of the great fishing locations of Southwest Alaska would be complete without mention of the famous Nonvianuk and Kukaklek Lakes area. At the very edge of the chain of lakes that makes up the heart of Katmai, these two have been the focus of serious angling effort for decades, thanks to their relative proximity to Anchorage and abundant supply of big rainbows (routinely to 10 pounds or more). As headwaters of the renowned Alagnak River, they've also seen quite a bit of use by rafters who begin their trips here.

The most popular spots for fishing the lakes' rainbows are, of course, the outlets and the mouths of the tributary streams, with Kukaklek and Kulik Rivers and Moraine, Funnel, and Nanuktuk Creeks being especially noteworthy. Early June (right after season opening) and September through October are the prime times to encounter the big, bright, lake-dwelling trout. (The lakes and associated tributaries also have excellent lake trout, grayling, and charr fishing.)

As some of Katmai's most perfectly suited waters for wade-and-cast fishing are located here, quite a few lodges serve the area. Angler's Paradise Lodge on Kulik Lake (run by Katmailand) is perhaps the most famous of these. Their reputation has been built by the unmatchable quality of fly-fishing available right out their door on the Kulik River. Several outpost camps scattered throughout the area offer a more rustic and affordable option for folks wanting a modicum of comfort while enjoying some of Alaska's best trout fishing.

29 American Creek

Location: In Katmai National Park and Preserve, North Alaska Peninsula, 250 miles southwest of Anchorage; see map page 226.

USGS maps: Mount Katmai D-4, D-5, D-6.

How to get there: By plane from Anchorage to King Salmon via commercial flight, then floatplane to the headwaters at Hammersly Lake or the mouth at Coville Lake. Jet boat access is possible along the lower creek.

Highlights: One of Katmai's more famous and productive rainbow trout and charr locations, particularly in spring and fall.

Species: Charr, grayling, lake trout, rainbow trout, red salmon, *northern pike*.

Regulations: Open year-round. Single-hook, unbaited, artificial lures only (March 1 through November 14); catch-and-release only for rainbows (June 8 through October 31). For additional restrictions, consult the current Alaska Department of Fish and Game regulations or contact the ADF&G Dillingham office, (907) 842-2427.

Facilities: No developed public facilities. Guide services and private lodging are available nearby at Grosvenor Camp or King Salmon.

Contact: For campground and general information, contact Superintendent, Katmai National Park and Preserve, P.O. Box 7, King Salmon, AK 99613; (907) 246-3305. For guide services and lodging for fishing American Creek, contact Katmailand, Inc., 4550 Aircraft Drive #2, Anchorage, AK 99502; (800) 544-0551 or (907) 243-5448. For guided float-fishing, contact Ouzel Expeditions, P.O. Box 935, Girdwood, AK 99587, (800) 825-8196. For an air taxi, contact Branch River Air Service, 4540 Edinburgh Drive, Anchorage, AK 99515; (907) 248-3539 (winter) or (907) 246-3437 (summer).

Fishing the American Creek: Along with Brooks and Kulik, the American has some of Katmai's better stream fishing for rainbows and charr. Short (40 miles long) and relatively small (about 15 yards wide), the stream flows swiftly from Hammersly and Murray Lakes into Coville Lake, about 45 miles east of King Salmon. Because of its rocky rapids and size, access to most of American Creek is restricted to the outlet and lower few miles of river at Coville Lake. It can be floated by raft or kayak, but fluctuating water levels make it extremely risky. With an average gradient of 30 to 60 feet per mile and two canyons, it has continuous rapids over much of the middle and lower river in normal or high-water conditions. The upper 10 miles below Hammersly, shallow and rocky, can be a nightmare to pull a boat through in low water.

Fly-fishing conditions are excellent—some of Katmai's best—particularly in early spring and fall when abundant lake-resident charr and rainbows feed heavily on the young and eggs of salmon. (Smolt-and-egg patterns and small spinners are deadly.) The creek is especially noted for its dry fly–fishing opportunities (in June and July) and heavy sockeye salmon runs (in August). Be prepared to share the river with an abundant bear population, however, particularly in mid- to late summer.

You can fly in from King Salmon to Hammersly Lake, camp and fish the outlet and few miles of stream below (for rainbows, charr, and lake trout), or obtain a boat and guide from the park concessionaire and fish the lower creek (for rainbows and charr). The upper creek can also be accessed via a small pothole lake and trail about five miles down from Hammersly. If you're planning a trip to fish Katmai, include American Creek in your itinerary. The best times to plan a trip are in late June and from late August through early September.

30 Coville-Grosvenor Lakes

Location: In Katmai National Park and Preserve, north Alaska Peninsula, 250 miles southwest of Anchorage; see map page 226.

USGS maps: Mount Katmai C-4, C-5, D-5, D-6.

How to get there: By floatplane from King Salmon.

Highlights: One of Katmai's best lake fishing locations, noted for lake trout, rainbow trout, and charr.

Species: Charr, grayling, lake trout, rainbow trout, red salmon.

Facilities: Grosvenor Lodge, a concessionaire-run lodge, is located on the lake narrows.

Regulations: Unbaited, artificial lures only from March 1 through November 14. For additional restrictions, consult the current Alaska Department of Fish and Game regulations or the ADF&G Dillingham office, (907) 842-2427.

Contact: For campground and general information, contact Superintendent, Katmai National Park and Preserve, P.O. Box 7, King Salmon, AK 99613; (907) 246-3305. For lodge-based fishing on Coville-Grosvenor, contact Katmailand, Inc., 4550 Aircraft Drive #2, Anchorage, AK 99502; (800) 544-0551 or (907) 243-5448.

Fishing Coville-Grosvenor Lakes: Among the more notable lake locales within Katmai (along with Kulik, Naknek, and Nonvianuk-Kukaklek), Coville-Grosvenor Lakes are the site of one of the original Peterson fish camps, Grosvenor. Part of a migration corridor for a substantial number of Naknek sockeyes, the two lakes are well known for their productive rainbow trout, charr, grayling, and lake trout fishing.

Rustic Grosvenor Lodge is situated at the narrows between the two lakes, a most advantageous fishing spot. Anglers take rainbows, charr, and lake trout there frequently, especially in the spring. Coville and Grosvenor both share a reputation for having the best of Katmai's lake trout fishing, with trophy fish (20 pounds plus) taken almost every season; this is one of the few Katmai areas where serious effort for lakers occurs. Nearby American Creek and the outlet to Savonoski provide additional opportunities for rainbows and charr. The Bay of Islands (Naknek Lake) can also be accessed by a one-mile trail from the southwest shore of Grosvenor.

In many ways, Grosvenor is the best of the three Katmai camps, as it escapes the crowds that flock to Brooks and is much more laid back than Kulik. It also has more fishing variety. If you're planning a Katmai trip, you might want to consider it over the others. The best times for fishing are in the spring (June) and late summer through early fall (mid-August through mid-September).

③ Naknek Lake

Location: In Katmai National Park and Preserve, 300 miles southwest of Anchorage; see map page 226.

USGS maps: Naknek C-1, C-2; Mount Katmai C-5, C-6.

How to get there: By plane from Anchorage to King Salmon via commercial flights, then floatplane to Brooks Camp or various spots along the lake. Boat access is possible from the Naknek River (King Salmon).

Highlights: One of Alaska's top lake fisheries for giant rainbows and charr; also good fishing for lake trout.

Species: Charr, chum salmon, grayling, lake trout, pink salmon, rainbow trout, red salmon, silver salmon.

Regulations: From March 1 through November 14, unbaited, artificial lures only; size restriction for rainbows. For additional restrictions, consult the current Alaska Department of Fish and Game regulations or contact the ADF&G Dillingham office, (907) 842-2427.

Facilities: A National Park Service campground and a concessionaire-operated lodge and cabins are available on the lake at the Brooks River. You'll find lodging, gas, groceries, and boat rentals in King Salmon.

Contact: For campground and general information, contact Superintendent, Katmai National Park and Preserve, P.O. Box 7, King Salmon, AK 99613; (907) 246-3305. For guide services, lodging and boat rentals on Naknek Lake, contact King Ko Inn, 3340 Arctic Boulevard #203, Anchorage, AK 99503, (907) 562-0648 (winter) or P.O. Box 346, King Salmon, AK 99613, (907) 246-3377 (summer); or Katmailand, Inc., 4550 Aircraft Drive #2, Anchorage, AK 99502, (800) 544-0551 or (907) 243-5448. For an air taxi, contact Branch River Air Service, 4540 Edinburgh Drive, Anchorage, AK 99515; (907) 248-3539 (winter) or (907) 246-3437 (summer).

Fishing Naknek Lake: The Naknek Lake system is one of Alaska's most productive fisheries for rainbow trout, charr, and sockeye salmon. Thousands of folks fish the numerous streams and lakes of this system each summer, yet few take the opportunity to see what Naknek Lake itself has to offer. Over the years, its deep emerald waters have provided some remarkable and consistent trophy fishing—big rainbows to 15 pounds or more, giant charr to 20 pounds, and lake trout to 30 pounds.

Not an easy lake to fish, Naknek is immense, deep, and subject to wild weather; the services of a seasoned area guide are requisite for first-time anglers. The most popular areas to fish are the Naknek River outlet, the Bay of Islands in the North Arm, and the coves and bays along the northwest shore. Anglers jet into King Salmon, then usually rent boats and/or guides there or fly over to Brooks Camp for some reasonably priced daily guided fishing excursions in the nearby Bay of Islands. If you're planning a vacation in Katmai, leave a day open to fish the lake; Naknek has been known to yield exciting treasure when the fishing in the streams has cooled down.

Guides' tip: Naknek Lake rainbows are the state's largest on average—more than 24 inches long. (A 23-pounder was taken from the Bay of Islands in 1991.) Trolling with big spoons and plugs or drift jigging is the ticket. Use big Krocodiles (chrome, silver prism, blue prism), Hot Shots (silver, silver-blue, fluorescent red) or Crippled Herrings (chrome, nickel/neon blue, fluorescent red/yellow).

32 Naknek River

Location: On eastern Bristol Bay, 300 miles southwest of Anchorage; see map page 226.

USGS maps: Naknek C-2, C-3.

How to get there: By plane from Anchorage to King Salmon via commercial flight, then boat and car to locations along the river.

Highlights: Southwest Alaska's most popular fishing location, with outstanding fishing for rainbow trout, king, and silver salmon.

Species: Charr, chum salmon, grayling, king salmon, lake trout, pink salmon, rainbow trout, red salmon, silver salmon.

Regulations: Fishing is open from June 8 through April 9 on most of the upper river; king salmon fishing is open from June 8 through July 31. Unbaited, single-hook, artificial lures only; size restriction for rainbows. For details and additional restrictions, consult the current Alaska Department of Fish and Game regulations or contact the ADF&G Dillingham office, (907) 842-2427.

Facilities: No developed public facilities. Lodges, hotels, guide services, and boat rentals are available in King Salmon.

Contact: For lodging and boat rentals on the Naknek River, contact King Ko Inn, 3340 Arctic Boulevard #203, Anchorage, AK 99503, (907) 562-0648 (winter); or P.O. Box 346, King Salmon, AK 99613, (907) 246-3377 (summer). For guided fishing, contact Mark Emery, Wet Waders, P.O. Box 516, Ocklawaha, FL 32183, (352) 288-3341.

Fishing the Naknek River: Draining the immense lake system of the same name in Katmai National Park, the Naknek empties into Kvichak Bay some 30 miles to the west. Since the 1950s, it has been popular as one of Alaska's premier locales for big rainbows (up to 10 pounds or more). The lakes' abundant food sources support a trout population that rivals that of the famed Iliamna for numbers and average size, and provides lively fishing in the river during spring and fall. The Naknek's easy access and availability of species other than trout—abundant king, silver, and sockeye salmon, plus charr and grayling—have made it the most popular river in Southwest Alaska. (Up to a fifth of the region's angling effort takes place here.)

Most folks fish rainbow, grayling, and sockeye at the lake outlet and along the river down to the Rapids Camp (about nine miles). Fly-fishing opportunities abound in the crystal blue waters. King and coho salmon are mostly drift fished from boats on the lower river, from the mouth of Big Creek to Pauls Creek. Many reputable lodges and guides service the area and its surroundings. The most productive times for jumbo trout and charr are spring (as early as April in portions of the river) and fall (September and October), but don't pass up the opportunity to visit this top-rated fishery for salmon either (kings in late June and early July, silvers in August). A short junket here combined with a trip to nearby Katmai and the Brooks River is easy to arrange and highly recommended.

For fly-fishing Naknek River rainbow and charr, use smolt and egg patterns, Sculpins, Woolly Buggers, Leeches, and attractors. Also try dry flies (on warm, sunny days) and deer hair mice.

33 Brooks River

Location: In Katmai National Park and Preserve, 275 miles southwest of Anchorage; see map page 226.

USGS map: Mount Katmai C-6.

How to get there: By plane from Anchorage to King Salmon via commercial flight, then floatplane to Brooks Camp on Naknek Lake or Brooks Lake. Boating is also possible from King Salmon.

Highlights: Katmai's most famous location, still producing great fishing for rainbow trout and sockeye salmon, with more bears than ever.

Species: Charr, chum salmon, grayling, lake trout, pink salmon, rainbow trout, red salmon.

Regulations: Fishing is open from June 8 through April 9; single-hook, unbaited, artificial lures only. Fly-fishing only from the bridge upriver (June 8 through October 31). For additional restrictions, consult the current Alaska Department of Fish and Game regulations or contact the ADF&G Dillingham office, (907) 842-2427.

Facilities: A National Park Service campground, concessionaire-run lodge, and rental cabins are available.

Contact: For campground and general information, contact Superintendent, Katmai National Park and Preserve, P.O. Box 7, King Salmon, AK 99613; (907) 246-3305. For lodging, cabin and boat rentals, and guided fishing, contact Katmailand, Inc., 4550 Aircraft Drive #2, Anchorage, AK 99502; (800) 544-0551 or (907) 243-5448. For an air taxi, contact Branch River Air Service, 4540 Edinburgh Drive, Anchorage, AK 99515; (907) 248-3539 (winter) or (907) 246-3437 (summer); or PenAir, P.O. Box 36, King Salmon, AK 99613, (907) 246-3372.

Fishing the Brooks River: For more than 40 years, Brooks Camp has been one of Alaska's most unique and alluring locations. As the quintessential Katmai attraction, Brooks features arm-long rainbow trout, smoldering volcanic valleys, 1,000-pound bears that fish for salmon, and a rustic "real Alaska" lodge in one of the world's prettiest lake and mountain settings.

The river itself is barely more than a mile long, connecting Naknek Lake with Brooks Lake. One of the major migration and spawning areas for the incredible, salmon-rich Naknek Lake system, it's amazingly productive for its size. Originally known solely for its outstanding rainbow trout fishing (in the early days, 30-inchers were quite common), Brooks has also achieved notoriety as one of the few places where anglers routinely coax strikes from the normally tight-lipped sockeye salmon.

This area is also well known for it brown bears, with some of Alaska's highest densities during the salmon season. On a typical day in July, a dozen or more of Katmai's famous cinnamon grizzlies can be seen from the observation platform at Brooks Falls, as they try their fishing skills on the milling, leaping salmon. It's quite a show, with scenes hilariously reminiscent of human streamside follies. Don't forget your camera if you go!

You can rent one of the lodge cabins or stay in the National Park Service campground, then get supplies, meals, canoes, and even daily guide service through the concessionaire. Although Brooks is showing strains of burgeoning visitor use and the fishing might not be all it used to be, the overall experience remains quite worthwhile—a glimpse of one of the more charming and rustic outpost camps in the Last Frontier.

Guides' tip: Brooks is a great river for dry fly–fishing, especially in early summer—try a Cahill, Adams, Caddis, Irresistible, or Wulff. The lagoon and lower river are the traditional angling locations, but some excellent fly-fishing water can also be found from the Brooks Lake outlet down to the falls, if you're willing to brave the prospect of meeting bears at close range along the brushy stream. Be cautious of your profile when working these crystal waters, as the rainbows are easily spooked.

Other popular flies for Brooks Camp include Sockeye John (rainbows, charr); Green Marvel (sockeye salmon); Montana Brassy (sockeye salmon); Orange and Chartreuse Comets (sockeye salmon); Muddler Minnow (rainbows, charr); Thunder Creek (rainbows, charr); and Katmai Smolt (rainbows, charr).

㉞ King Salmon River

Location: On the North Alaska Peninsula, 350 southwest of Anchorage; see map page 226.

USGS maps: Mount Katmai A-6; Naknek A-1, A-2, A-4, A-5, B-2, B-3, B-4.

How to get there: By plane from Anchorage to King Salmon via commercial flight, then floatplane to upper Gertrude Creek or wheelplane to gravel bars on upper Contact Creek. Camp, hike, and fish the surrounding area, or raft or kayak down to the Egegik River (a five-day trip) and the village of Egegik, which has scheduled wheelplane flights to King Salmon and connecting flights to Anchorage.

Highlights: An out-of-the-way Katmai river featuring rainbow trout in its clear tributaries with good charr, grayling, and seasonal salmon fishing.

Species: Charr, chum salmon, grayling, king salmon, pink salmon, rainbow trout, red salmon.

Regulations: Open year-round, all species. For details, consult the current Alaska Department of Fish and Game regulations or contact the ADF&G Dillingham office, (907) 842-2427.

Facilities: No developed public facilities.

Contact: For information on the lower river area, contact the Alaska Peninsula/Becharof National Wildlife Refuge, P.O. Box 277, King Salmon, AK 99613; (907) 246-3339. For an air taxi, contact Branch River Air Service, 4540 Edinburgh Drive, Anchorage, AK 99515; (907) 248-3539 (winter) or (907) 246-3437 (summer). For guided float-fishing, contact Eruk's Wilderness Tours, 12720 Lupine Road, Anchorage, AK 99516; (907) 345-7678.

Fishing the King Salmon River: Part of the Egegik River system (draining Becharof Lake), the King Salmon offers remote country to fish and explore as an alternative to the more accessible—and sometimes slightly crowded— rainbow trout locales of Katmai. The extreme southern occurrences for rainbow trout on the

Alaska Peninsula are in its headwaters, along with decent charr, grayling, and fair to good fishing for salmon in season.

Usually accessed by floatplane at the headwaters of Gertrude Creek, the 60-mile King Salmon for the most part is a silty, tundra river with good fishing only in its headwaters and some of the clear south side tributaries. It can be floated, but the weather is iffy and navigation along the flat lower sections are complicated by strong headwinds and tidal action. Wildlife, especially bears, is abundant, so care must be taken. It's an intriguing area, with some promising rainbow fishing possibilities, so it's worth checking out.

Alaska Peninsula

South of Katmai lies the Alaska Peninsula—a narrow strip of barren tundra, volcanic peaks, glaciers, and rugged coasts sprawling hundreds of miles out into the stormy North Pacific. A true no-man's-land, this area has some of the most remote and inhospitable terrain on the continent, routinely lashed by some of the world's worst weather. It's not a particularly attractive area for humans, of course, but its myriad clear streams, lakes, and abundant runoff make it perfectly suited for fish. Salmon and charr throng in nearly every drainage, including those in the Aleutians, and there are even steelhead trout in a handful of streams.

For years, the peninsula has been the almost exclusive domain of commercial anglers and hunters. But more and more, this area is opening up to sportfishing, with new lodges and outpost camps making it possible to sample waters that not too long ago were just points on the map of fishing dreams.

㉟ Becharof Lake

Location: On the north Alaska Peninsula, 325 miles southwest of Anchorage; see map page 226.

USGS maps: Naknek A-2, A-3; Karluk C-6, D-6; Ugashik C-1, D-1, D-3.

How to get there: By plane from Anchorage to King Salmon via commercial flight, then floatplane to various points on the lake.

Highlights: An underutilized giant fishery, with abundant sockeye salmon and giant grayling and charr; also good fishing for silver salmon and untapped possibilities for lake trout.

Species: Charr, chum salmon, grayling, lake trout, pink salmon, red salmon, silver salmon, *rainbow trout.*

Regulations: Open year-round, all species.

Facilities: No developed public facilities.

Contact: For public lands information, contact Alaska Peninsula/Becharof National Wildlife Refuge, P.O. Box 277, King Salmon, AK 99613, (907) 246-3339; or Aniakchak National Preserve, P.O. Box 7, King Salmon, AK 99613, (907) 246-3305. For guided fishing services, contact Gus Lamoureux, Ugashik Lakes Lodge, P.O. Box 90-444, Anchorage, AK 99502, (907) 248-3012; or Gary King's Alaskan Experience, 202 East Northern Lights Boulevard, Anchorage, AK 99502, (800) 777-7055. For an air taxi, contact Peninsula Airways, Inc., 4851 Aircraft Drive, Anchorage, AK 99502; (907) 243-2485 (in Alaska), (800) 448-4226 (outside Alaska), or (907) 243-6848 (fax).

Fishing Becharof Lake: The second largest lake in Alaska, Becharof Lake is an isolated, enormous body of water best known for its abundant sockeye salmon runs, wildlife (including brown bears, caribou, and waterfowl), and unforgiving weather. It's a sleeping giant as far as fishing goes, and nearly all who have sunk line in its vast waters have walked away impressed with its awesome potential. This lake and river system receives one of the most significant sockeye salmon runs in Alaska, with smaller numbers of silver, pink, chum, and even a few king salmon. Stories of monstrous charr and giant grayling and lake trout are substantiated by some remarkable catches from the few anglers intrepid enough to challenge these waters. (Some of the state's largest specimens for these species have been caught here.) When you consider the size, remoteness, and productivity of this drainage, there's no telling what this lake might hold.

But there's a catch: This part of Alaska is known for its wind tunnel weather—and on a lake of this size with no cover, that can make for some scary conditions. But if you can duck in on a nice day, all of the guides, anglers, and biologists familiar with Becharof say the outlet waters and numerous creek mouths around the lake offer truly remarkable fishing. Some of these drainages are even rumored to have rainbows, although you'll have a hard time prying any details from the folks who would know these things. For the adventuresome angler with time and money to burn, Becharof Lake is definitely on the list of Alaska's most promising untapped waters.

36 Ugashik Bay Streams

Location: On Ugashik Bay, Alaska Peninsula, 375 miles southwest of Anchorage; see map page 226.

USGS maps: Ugashik A-3, A-4, A-5, A-6, B-3, B-4, B-5, B-6; Bristol Bay B-1.

How to get there: By plane from Anchorage to King Salmon via commercial flight, then scheduled or chartered wheelplane to Pilot Point and boat or small plane (floats or wheels) to the streams.

Highlights: Ugashik Lake area drainages with good angling potential for all five species of salmon and charr.

Species: Charr, chum salmon, grayling, king salmon, northern pike, pink salmon, red salmon, silver salmon.

Regulations: Open year-round, all species.

Facilities: No developed public facilities. A few private hunting and fishing lodges serve the area, including one in Pilot Point.

Contact: For public lands information, contact Alaska Peninsula/Becharof National Wildlife Refuge, P.O. Box 277, King Salmon, AK 99613; (907) 246-3339. For lodge-based fishing, contact Painter Creek Lodge, 7111 Spruce Street, Anchorage, AK 99507, (907) 344-5181; or Gary King's Alaskan Experience, 202 East Northern Lights Boulevard, Anchorage, AK 99503, (800) 777-7055. For guided boat fishing, contact Tracy's Great Alaskan Outfitters, P.O. Box 433, Pilot Point, AK 99649, (907) 797-2246. For an air taxi, contact Peninsula Airways, Inc., 4851 Aircraft Drive, Anchorage, AK 99502; (907) 243-2485 (in Alaska), (800) 448-4226 (outside Alaska), or (907) 243-6848 (fax).

Fishing Ugashik Bay Streams: The Ugashik Lakes vicinity boasts several notable streams that area guides and lodges visit regularly for their fine runs of all five species of salmon, abundant charr, and even grayling and northern pike. They are accessed by small plane or boat from Pilot Point on lower Ugashik Bay.

The King Salmon River emptying into lower Ugashik Bay is perhaps the most popular of these, as it is easily accessed by floatplane at Mother Goose Lake and offers good fishing for (what else?) chinook salmon, as well as sockeye, coho, and charr in the river below the lake and in adjoining tributaries. (The well-known, private Painter Creek Lodge is in the area, along the creek of the same name.) Dog Salmon River, a few miles away, is turbid, with fishing limited to its clear feeders. Both streams have glacial sources, but the King Salmon benefits from the settling effect of Mother Goose Lake. Like its neighbor, Dog Salmon has all five species of salmon, plus northern pike and grayling. In fact, it's one of the southernmost spots to fish grayling on the peninsula.

The Cinder River, 12 miles south, is a small runoff stream originating from the cinder beds of nearby Aniakchak. Braided and clear, this black sand drainage is only rarely fished for its abundant silver salmon. A small hunting camp is located there, with access limited to small wheelplane landings on the beach or on cinder beds along the upper river.

③⑦ Ugashik Lake and River

Location: On the north Alaska Peninsula, 350 miles southwest of Anchorage; see map page 226.

USGS maps: Ugashik B-3, B-4, B-5, C-2, C-3, C-4, C-5, D-2.

How to get there: By plane from Anchorage to King Salmon via commercial flight, then floatplane to the lake or wheelplane to Pilot Point or Ugashik, with boat access to river.

Highlights: A legendary Southwest Alaska hot spot for charr; also receives strong runs of silver and sockeye salmon.

Species: Charr, chum salmon, grayling, lake trout, pink salmon, red salmon, silver salmon.

Regulations: The Ugashik River below the lake outlet is closed to grayling fishing, but the narrows and the remainder of the lake drainage is open to single-hook, artificial lure, catch-and-release fishing. The entire drainage is open year-round for all other species. For additional regulations, consult the current Alaska Department of Fish and Game regulations or contact the ADF&G Dillingham office, (907) 842-2427.

Facilities: Two private lodges are located in the area.

Contact: For public lands information, contact Alaska Peninsula/Becharof National Wildlife Refuge, P.O. Box 277, King Salmon, AK 99613, (907) 246-3339; or Aniakchak National Preserve, P.O. Box 7, King Salmon, AK 99613, (907) 246-3305. For lodge-based guided fishing, contact Gus Lamoureux, Ugashik Lakes Lodge, P.O. Box 90444, Anchorage, AK 99502, (907) 248-3012; or Gary King's Alaskan Experience, 202 East Northern Lights Boulevard, Anchorage, AK 99503, (800) 777-7055. For an air taxi, contact Peninsula Airways, Inc., 4851 Aircraft Drive, Anchorage, AK 99502; (907) 243-2485 (Alaska), (800) 448-4226 (outside Alaska), or (907) 243-6848 (fax).

Fishing the Ugashik Lake and River: For the longest time, the Ugashik Lakes were Alaska's top trophy grayling fishery. (The former IGFA world record, a four-pound, 13-ounce fish, was caught there in 1981.) In the glory days of the '60s and '70s, countless anglers from the world over made the long trip to the windblown, barren "narrows" or outlet below the lakes for an almost certain chance at a wall-hanging (19-inch or more) sailfin.

Heavy fishing pressure and other factors brought a noticeable decline in the quality of angling, so in the early 1990s the Alaska Department of Fish and Game enacted restrictive measures to preserve the quality of the fishery. Currently grayling fishing is closed in the river below the lakes, with single-hook, artificial lure, catch-and-release restrictions for the narrows and rest of the lake drainage.

Though most of the angling effort has targeted the short, but extremely productive, water connecting the lower and upper lakes (the narrows) and the Ugashik River outlet, the numerous creeks that flow into both lakes can be just as productive for the system's abundant charr and grayling. Salmon are also plentiful, with notable silver and sockeye runs, best fished in the outlet waters and river. The best times to hit the Ugashik are in early summer (June through mid-July) and fall (late August through early September).

③⑧ Meshik River

Location: On the central Alaska Peninsula, 400 miles southwest of Anchorage; see map page 226.

USGS maps: Sutwik Island D-6; Chignik C-1, C-2, D-1, D-2.

How to get there: By floatplane from King Salmon or Port Heiden (both are serviced by scheduled flights) to Meshik Lake or the lower river. Floating by raft or kayak is possible, with floatplane pickup at the mouth. The lower river also may be reached by boat from Port Heiden.

Highlights: One of the more remote Alaska Peninsula drainages, with untapped potential for salmon and charr fishing.

Species: Charr, chum salmon, king salmon, red salmon, silver salmon.

Regulations: Open year-round, all species.

Facilities: No developed public facilities. Lodge-based guided fishing is available from area lodges.

Contact: For public lands information, contact Alaska Peninsula/Becharof National Wildlife Refuge, P.O. Box 277, King Salmon, AK 99613, (907) 246-3339; or Aniakchak National Preserve, P.O. Box 7, King Salmon, AK 99613, (907) 246-3305. For lodge-based guided fishing, contact Gary King's Alaskan Experience, 202 East Northern Lights Boulevard, Anchorage, AK 99503, (800) 777-7055. For guided float-fishing, contact Eruk's Wilderness Tours, 12720 Lupine Road, Anchorage, AK 99516; (907) 345-7678. For an air taxi, contact Peninsula Airways, Inc., 4851 Aircraft Drive, Anchorage, AK 99502; (907) 243-2485 (Alaska), (800) 448-4226 (outside Alaska), or (907) 243-6848 (fax).

Fishing the Meshik River: Very little serious sportfishing effort occurs south of the Ugashik Lakes area, because of the expense of transportation, weather, lack of services, and other factors. Most of the better streams (quite a few have outstanding salmon and charr runs) receive only light pressure from locals or visiting hunters. The Meshik River of the Port Heiden area is worth mentioning because of its high potential, relatively easy access, and location (the upper river) within Aniakchak National Preserve. With more and more folks discovering the outstanding adventure recreation potential of this area, it's only a matter of time before the Meshik draws more visitors for its exciting fishing and floating possibilities.

Originating on steep mountain slopes southeast of the Aniakchak caldera, the Meshik flows west for about 50 miles before emptying into Port Heiden. It's known for strong runs of chinook and coho salmon, along with sockeyes, chums, and charr. A headwater lake 40 miles up from the mouth, and numerous smaller lakes along the lower river, provide access possibilities for floatplanes. The best way to fish the Meshik is to float down from the upper river by raft or kayak, or to access the lower river and tributaries (where the best silver, king, and charr fishing is) by boat or floatplane from Port Heiden.

With its many clear, shallow tributaries and wadable runs, the Meshik has considerable fly-fishing opportunities. Aside from the abundant bear population and unpredictable weather, there is nothing here to preclude productive and enjoyable fishing ventures along this remote and utterly pristine drainage.

③⑨ Peninsula Steelhead Streams

Location: On the lower Alaska Peninsula, Cape Seniavin to Cold Bay; see map page 226.

USGS maps: Chignik A-5, A-6, A-7, A-8; Port Moller C-4, C-5, C-6, D-4, D-5, D-6; Cold Bay A-2, A-3, B-2, B-3.

How to get there: By small wheelplane from Port Heiden or points north. Some primitive airstrips are available; floatplane landings are also possible in some areas.

Highlights: North America's last frontier for wild steelhead.

Species: Charr, chum salmon, king salmon, pink salmon, red salmon, silver salmon, steelhead.

Regulations: Open year-round, all species.

Facilities: Scattered outpost hunting camps, guided fishing, and lodging are available in the area.

Contact: For public lands information, contact Alaska Peninsula/Becharof National Wildlife Refuge, P.O. Box 277, King Salmon, AK 99613, (907) 246-3339; or Aniakchak National Preserve, P.O. Box 7, King Salmon, AK 99613, (907) 246-3305. For guided lodge-based fishing, contact Mel Gillis, Alaska Trophy Hunting and Fishing, P.O. Box 220247, Anchorage, AK 99522, (907) 344-8589; or Gary King's Alaskan Experience, 202 East Northern Lights Boulevard, Anchorage, AK 99503, (800) 777-7055. For an air taxi, contact Peninsula Airways, Inc., 4851 Aircraft Drive, Anchorage, AK 99502; (907) 243-2485 (Alaska), (800) 448-4226 (outside Alaska), or (907) 243-6848 (fax).

Fishing Peninsula Steelhead Streams: On the lower arc of the western extremes of the Alaska Peninsula lie the continent's last unexplored wild steelhead streams. At least a dozen small drainages from Chignik to Cold Bay are known to have spawning populations of the coveted sea-run rainbows, with the best occurring along Cape Seniavin, the Nelson Lagoon area, and Cold Bay. They are undoubtedly more widespread than this, judging from accounts of locals, hunters, commercial anglers, and others who have sampled the far-flung waters of Unimak and the rugged Pacific side of the lower peninsula.

The peninsula steelhead runs are all very small, most numbering in the hundreds. As with Kodiak Island, they occur predominantly during fall, with peaks from late September through October. (Some bright spring fish have been reported in certain areas during April and May, however.) The weight of the fish averages the same or slightly more than those on Kodiak, with fish in the low teens reported on some streams. A 16-pounder was taken recently from a stream along Cape Seniavin.

These remote, brushy streams are all difficult to access and fish. Most of them have only been worked by hunting guides during the fall season, with focused effort occurring only recently on a few of the better ones. All initial reports indicate outstanding possibilities for virgin fishing. Drawbacks are the notorious peninsula weather and the expense of getting in, factors that shouldn't stop hard-core adventure anglers from exploring this Last Frontier of wild steelhead fishing.

④⓪ Chignik River

Location: On the southern Alaska Peninsula, Pacific side, 175 miles southwest of Kodiak, 475 miles southwest of Anchorage; see map page 226.

USGS maps: Chignik A-3, B-3.

How to get there: By plane from Anchorage to King Salmon via commercial flight, charter, or scheduled plane service to the town of Chignik Lagoon or Chignik Lake, then river access by boat or raft. Access from Kodiak by the state ferry system or a charter plane is also possible.

Highlights: A remote, highly productive river system with untapped sportfishing potential for salmon (kings, reds, and silvers) and charr.

Species: Charr, chum salmon, king salmon, pink salmon, red salmon, silver salmon.

Regulations: Open year-round, all species.

Facilities: No developed public facilities. Bed-and-breakfast-style lodging and guide services are available in the town of Chignik Lake.

Contact: For public lands information, contact Alaska Peninsula/Becharof National Wildlife Refuge, P.O. Box 277, King Salmon, AK 99613, (907) 246-3339; or Aniakchak National Preserve, P.O. Box 7, King Salmon, AK 99613, (907) 246-3305. For lodging and guide service on the Chignik River, contact Johnny Lind, P.O. Box 4, Chignik Lake, AK 99548, (907) 845-2228; or Gary King's Alaskan Experience, 202 East Northern Lights Boulevard, Anchorage, AK 99503, (800) 777-7055. For an air taxi, contact Peninsula Airways, Inc., 4851 Aircraft Drive, Anchorage, AK 99502, (907) 243-2485 (Alaska), (800) 448-4226 (outside Alaska), or (907) 243-6848 (fax).

Fishing the Chignik River: Located 175 miles southwest of Kodiak, the Chignik is one of the most important salmon systems of the entire Alaska Peninsula, supporting extensive runs of sockeye, coho, pink, and chum salmon and the south side peninsula's only significant population of chinook. Because of its remoteness, it receives little outside angling pressure. Keep it in mind for future angling adventures, as more and more of the state's accessible waters become well visited.

This short river system connects two very productive sockeye salmon nurseries, Black and Chignik Lakes, to the Pacific coast. Most of the current sportfishing effort occurs from Chignik Lake to the lagoon, where boat anglers target the river's chinook, silver salmon, and abundant charr populations. The Chignik's substantial sockeye salmon runs (from early June through late July) receive almost no sportfishing pressure and there are even some rumors of steelhead spawning here. Access is by two gravel airstrips or by floatplane at the lake or lagoon. At present, visitor facilities are minimal, but the village native corporation plans to construct a lodge in the future. If you're looking for something different and have the time and resources to explore this unique fishery, give Johnny Lind a call at Chignik Lake.

Chapter 5

Southcentral Fishing

Southcentral Alaska

Alaska State Map .... *page* 8

204

1

Tonzona River

Susitna River

3

Susitna Lake

Lake Louise

2

49

1

Glennallen

McCarthy

S. Fork Kuskokwim

Yentna River

River

Talkeetna

3 4

Sheep R.

5

8

Tazlina Lake

48

47

Copper River

Chitina River

10

6 7

46

Chitina

45

Skwentna

Willow

9

Palmer

1

4

11

10

12

Valdez

38

15 14

13

ANCHORAGE

Prince William Sound

39 Cordova

16

17

32

37

Orca Bay

40 41 42

43 44

19 18

COOK INLET

29

Kenai

28

30

9

36

Cape Suckling

20

27

31

35 34

Lake Clark

26

1

Skilak Lake

Seward

33

Blying Sound

MONTAGUE ISLAND

21

25

Tustumena Lake

Homer

24

Lake Iliamna

23

Kamishak Bay

226

326

22

GULF OF ALASKA

AFOGNAK ISLAND

KODIAK ISLAND

For fishing in the Kodiak Island area, please see map on page 267

266

SHUYAK
ISLAND

50

Perenosa Bay

51

*SHELIKOF
STRAIT*

52

AFOGNAK
ISLAND

MARMOT
ISLAND

54

RASPBERRY
ISLAND

53

Marmot Bay

WHALE
ISLAND

UGANIK
ISLAND

*Kupreanof
Strait*

*Viekoda
Bay*

SPRUCE
ISLAND

*Uganik
Passage*

56

69 ○ Kodiak

*Chiniak
Bay*

*Uganik
Bay*

55

68

Uyak
○

Spiridon Bay

67

Karluk ○

57

*Zachar
Bay*

66

64

65

Karluk ○

KODIAK
ISLAND

63

*Ugak
Bay*

*Karluk
Lake*

*Uyak
Bay*

UGAK
ISLAND

58

62

*Killuda
Bay*

60

61

Sitkalidak Strait

Olga Bay

○ McCord

59

*Deadman
Bay*

*Kaiugnak
Bay*

SITKALIDAK
ISLAND

*Alitak
Bay*

○ Kaguyak

MIULIK
PENINSULA

TUGIDAK
ISLAND

GULF OF ALASKA

SITKINAK
ISLAND

Southcentral Hot Spots

Southcentral

On a clear bedrock creek above the silty tidewaters of Turnagain Arm, an interesting assortment of anglers shares a stretch of water and the warm August sunshine: some retired folks, a couple with two small children, a woman who looks like a schoolteacher, a few business types, and others crowd a piece of riverbank no bigger than your driveway, flipping lines and lures nonstop in all directions. The intensity and anticipation grow unbearable. Suddenly, a commotion erupts downstream as someone connects with a big, bright fish that catapults toward the Pacific Ocean. Seconds later, a lad in a designer sweatshirt screams as another salmon bursts through the rapids, threatening to yank his rod from his hands. The silvers are in! Pandemonium ensues. Like a chain reaction, the salmon surge spreads up the creek, wreaking havoc on rods and limbs. For the next hour, a wild melee of leaping fish, screaming reels, mad downriver dashes, and muddy smiles takes over as every man, woman, and child gets a taste of salmon fishing the way it was meant to be.

This scene would be remarkable enough just for its level of fishing excitement, but when you consider that these folks are a mere 20-minute drive from Alaska's largest city, Anchorage, in the heart of the state's most populous region, it's no less than astounding. Most states can't match this kind of angling in their wildest backcountry, yet Alaska's most "developed" region, Southcentral, provides an abundance of similar opportunities a short ride by car, plane, or boat from any of its major (and modern) towns and cities. And while it's true that the more accessible of these locations can be quite crowded by Alaska standards, Southcentral still offers plenty of quality fishing that's light years beyond anything available in the Lower 48.

Country, Climate, and Conditions

In many ways, Southcentral Alaska is the most well endowed of the state's geographic regions. Blessed with benign weather, majestic scenery, and abundant resources, the mainland area south and east of the Alaska Range understandably attracts the most residents and tourists. Dominated by a massive arc of mountains, its diverse and impressive geography includes Alaska's tallest peaks and largest glaciers (some the size of states), along with immense, sprawling rivers, tundra uplands, dense coastal forests, and rich marine environments.

Shielded from arctic blasts by the high and wide Alaska Range, Southcentral's weather is surprisingly mild, greatly influenced by the Gulf of Alaska and the warm, moist air from the Pacific—some of the rainiest and snowiest places in the world are found here. Ample sunshine makes for very pleasant summers, with temperatures usually ranging from the 60s to low 70s, with low 50s to high 80s possible. Winters vary with location but are generally mild with moderate snow loads (five to 10 feet total on average). Highs reach 40 degrees or more, while lows dip to 10 below, but rarely less. Breakup comes in mid- to late April (later at higher elevations), while the rivers and lakes usually freeze by late October or early November. The sunniest, driest months are April through July; the wettest time is August through October.

Southcentral Fishing Highlights

The region's fishing is as varied and impressive as its geography. Abundant runs of all five salmon species occur in countless coastal streams and lakes as well as in immense glacial systems such as the Susitna and Copper. These are major producers, even though their fishing potential is confined to clear-water tributaries. Look for world-class trophy king salmon and halibut in the fabulous fisheries of the lower Cook Inlet, along with some of Alaska's best rainbow trout, steelhead, and silver salmon fishing on the Kenai Peninsula and Kodiak Island. Cutthroat trout, grayling, trophy lake trout, and even some fine northern pike fishing round out the delightful variety of angling possible in the Southcentral region.

Access, Services, and Costs

Southcentral's network of access, services, and facilities allows visitors of any age, physical condition, or economic status to enjoy a measure of unbeatable fishing. There are four major highway systems, a state ferry, millions of acres of national forests, and scores of parks, campgrounds, and public use cabins, not to mention the hundreds of private lodges, guides, and outfitters eager to help make that dream vacation come true. From lonely lakes tucked high and far in the rugged mountain country to hatchery-enhanced creeks and ponds in the middle of Alaska's largest city, Southcentral Alaska can virtually guarantee everyone an angling adventure. Nowhere else in the world will you find wilderness splendors so seamlessly matched with the easy comfort and conveniences of civilization.

Four main highways—the Glenn, Parks, Seward, and Sterling—connect the major communities of Southcentral with each other and the outside world. A state-run railroad and ferry system provides additional access. Commercial airlines service the Anchorage, Kenai, Cordova, and Kodiak hubs with daily flights (some connecting) from the West Coast and points beyond, while numerous air taxis make regular connections to the more remote areas. Access to the best Southcentral fly-in fishing generally involves floatplanes. Costs vary with the distance and size of party, but typically run from $125 to $350 per person.

Southcentral Run Timing: Freshwater

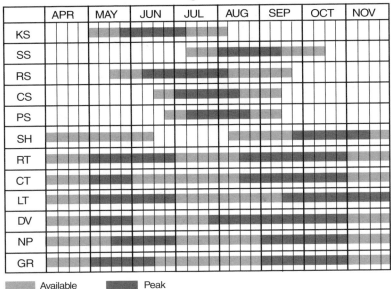

	APR	MAY	JUN	JUL	AUG	SEP	OCT	NOV
KS								
SS								
RS								
CS								
PS								
SH								
RT								
CT								
LT								
DV								
NP								
GR								

Available   Peak

KS=King Salmon, SS=Silver Salmon, RS=Red Salmon, CS=Chum Salmon, PS=Pink Salmon, SH=Sheefish, RT= Rainbow Trout, CT=Cutthroat Trout, LT=Lake Trout, DV=Dolly Varden, NP=Northern Pike, GR=Grayling

Southcentral Run Timing: Salt Water

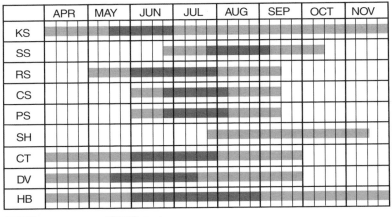

	APR	MAY	JUN	JUL	AUG	SEP	OCT	NOV
KS								
SS								
RS								
CS								
PS								
SH								
CT								
DV								
HB								

Available   Peak

KS=King Salmon, SS=Silver Salmon, RS=Red Salmon, CS=Chum Salmon, PS=Pink Salmon, SH=Sheefish, CT=Cutthroat Trout, DV=Dolly Varden, HB=Halibut

Note: Time periods are shown for bright fish, in the case of salmon entering rivers, or for general availability for resident species. Salmon are present in many systems after the period shown, but are usually in spawning/postspawning condition. Peak sportfishing periods for each species are highlighted. Run timing can vary somewhat from drainage to drainage and generally follows a later trend in waters to the west and north in Alaska. Check with local contacts listed for area run-timing specifics.

Mat-Su Valley/Upper Cook Inlet

The glacial Susitna, Southcentral Alaska's most significant river in terms of size and recreational use, offers quality sportfishing opportunities for salmon, trout, and grayling in its many outstanding clear-water tributaries. Adjacent drainages along the upper Cook Inlet enhance the sport fish potential. Access is almost entirely by boat, floatplane, or car via the George Parks Highway.

❶ Chulitna River System

Location: In the northeast Alaska Range drainage, 75 miles north of Anchorage; see map page 266.

USGS maps: Talkeetna B-1, C-1, D-1; Talkeetna Mountains D-6; Healy A-5, A-6, B-5, B-6.

How to get there: By car, plane, and boat. The Parks Highway between Anchorage and Fairbanks parallels the river system for most of its length, providing road access. The highway crosses the lower Chulitna main stem as well as a handful of its clear-water tributaries (also providing boat or raft launch). Small wheelplanes can land on gravel bars along the river.

Highlights: Good, easily accessible fishing for king salmon (from late June through early July), silver salmon (in the second half of August), rainbow trout (from August through September), and grayling (from June through September).

Species: Grayling, king salmon, lake trout, rainbow trout, red salmon, silver salmon, *chum salmon, Dolly Varden, pink salmon.*

Regulations: King salmon fishing is prohibited in all areas of the system, except on the East Fork of the Chulitna River. For additional restrictions, consult the current Alaska Department of Fish and Game sportfishing regulations or contact the ADF&G Palmer office, (907) 745-5016.

Facilities: Food and lodging are available nearby on the Parks Highway.

Contact: For lodging and guide information, contact the Chulitna River Lodge, P.O. Box 13282, Trapper Creek, AK 99688; (907) 733-2521.

Fishing the Chulitna River System: The Chulitna River headwaters drain off the towering slopes of the Alaska Range near Denali National Park. Heavily silted from melting glaciers, the main stem has noteworthy fishing conditions only in its clear-water tributaries (the middle and east forks both run clear). The surrounding scenery, with North America's tallest mountains nearby, is quite stirring. Although a major highway bisects the area, the wilderness and great fishing are only a short hike or float away.

Road anglers would do best to start from the highway access points at the major tributary creeks and hike upstream and downstream to find the fish. The mouths and lower reaches usually boast the best salmon fishing, with trout and grayling concentrated in upstream stretches during the summer months. You can fish the Chulitna from rafts or by boat, putting in and taking out at the highway bridges (either the Middle or East Fork, the Chulitna River bridge, or Talkeetna). Novices should not attempt the upper Chulitna above the bridge (milepost 135 of the Parks Highway), as it is very fast, with serious rapids and other hazards.

Some prime Chulitna angling spots include the Middle Fork (rainbow trout) and East Fork (king salmon, silver salmon, grayling) of the Chulitna River, Honolulu Creek (silver salmon, rainbow trout, grayling), Coal Creek (silver salmon, rainbow trout, grayling), Little Coal Creek (silver salmon, rainbow trout, grayling), Byers Creek (silver salmon, red salmon, rainbow trout, grayling), Spink Creek (silver salmon, red salmon, rainbow trout, grayling), Troublesome Creek (silver salmon, red salmon, rainbow trout, grayling), Horseshoe Creek (silver salmon, red salmon, rainbow trout, grayling), and Sunny Creek (silver salmon, red salmon, rainbow trout, grayling). King, silver, and red salmon are the most sought-after species of summer, while rainbow trout earn that title in the fall. Occasionally, anglers take lake trout from Byers, Summit, and Miami Lakes, although these waters have certainly seen their time.

❷ Tyone River System

Location: In the upper Susitna River drainage, 35 miles northwest of Glennallen, 140 miles northeast of Anchorage; see map page 266.

USGS maps: Gulkana B-6, C-6.

How to get there: By car, boat, and plane. Lake Louise Road, a gravel road heading north from the Glenn Highway between Anchorage and Glennallen, provides access to Lake Louise, the largest lake in the Tyone River drainage. Boat travel is possible from there to all points along the system. Floatplanes can land anywhere in the system, but there is a landing strip on the south shore of Lake Louise.

Highlights: Southcentral Alaska's best lake trout waters, with excellent fishing in June, September, and October, and abundant opportunities for grayling from June through October.

Species: Grayling, lake trout, northern pike.

Regulations: Lake Louise prohibits burbot fishing and imposes size restrictions on lake trout. For additional restrictions, consult the current Alaska Department of Fish and Game sportfishing regulations or contact the ADF&G Glennallen office, (907) 822-3309.

Facilities: Commercial lodging, a guide service, boat rentals and a launch, fuel, a campground, sporting goods, and groceries are available in the Lake Louise area.

Contact: For lodging and guide services, contact the Wolverine Lodge, HC 01, Box 1693, Glennallen, AK 99588; (907) 822-3988. For an air taxi, contact Lee's Air Taxi, HC 03, Box 8857, Palmer, AK 99645; (907) 822-3343.

Fishing the Tyone River System: The Tyone River system consists of an extensive complex of lakes and streams in the high plateau country of the upper Susitna, east of the Talkeetna Mountains. Sportfishing opportunities, mostly for grayling and lake trout, are significant, especially in the three largest and deepest lakes—Louise, Susitna, and Tyone. These waters lie fairly close to the Glenn Highway, a major road between Anchorage and Glennallen. Because of their location and relatively easy access, they see a large share of the state's urban lake fishing effort.

The slow, meandering Tyone connects the outlet of Tyone Lake to the silty Susitna River, a distance of about 30 miles. Boaters and anglers gravitate toward the clear lakes and associated streams—dozens of them. Motorboats, canoes, kayaks, and inflatables can all be used to access

and fish different parts of the system, putting in at the end of Lake Louise Road by car or anywhere between there and the outlet of Tyone Lake by floatplane. Arrange a pickup by plane at any of the lakes or the confluence of Tyone and Susitna Rivers.

Major species inhabiting the Tyone River system are grayling, lake trout, and burbot. (After years of overharvest, burbot are currently off-limits to anglers in Lake Louise.) Lake trout and grayling are still abundant. Despite growing pressure from the nearby urban populations, Lake Louise and Susitna, known for their trophy lake trout potential, still boot out a fair share of lakers—some up to 30 pounds each year. Like many deep, large lakes, they're best fished right after ice-out in spring (usually late May or early June) or later, in fall. Trolling big spoons, bait, and plugs is standard practice on these deep waters, but you can do well casting from shore or a skiff if you know what you're doing. (Check with the lodges on Lake Louise for the latest conditions before heading up for fishing.) You can find grayling in most of the system's lakes and streams, and locals contend that there are even a few good pike lakes and spots for rainbow trout fishing.

The air taxi services and lodges will gladly help you find the kind of fishing you're looking for. Since this is wild, big water country with rapidly changing weather and tricky conditions, it's probably best to enlist their services, at least for starters. They can fly or boat you to the best areas of the season and put you into some truly outstanding fishing for a reasonable price. Two of the best are Wolverine Lodge at Lake Louise, (907) 822-3988; and Lee's Air Taxi in Glennallen, (907) 822-3343.

❸ Upper Susitna River System

Location: In the northwest Talkeetna Mountains drainage, 80 miles north of Anchorage; see map page 266.

USGS maps: Talkeetna B-1, C-1; Talkeetna Mountains C-1, C-6, D-1, D-2, D-3, D-4, D-5, D-6; Healy A-1, A-2, B-1; Mount Hayes B-6.

How to get there: By boat from the Parks Highway bridge or the town of Talkeetna, or by train or plane. The Alaska Railroad offers regularly scheduled service between Anchorage and Fairbanks, and prearranged stops can be made at Chulitna (where a small gravel road leads to the upper Indian River and lower Portage Creek) or Gold Creek. Some rafters put in at tributary streams and float downstream to Talkeetna or the Parks Highway bridge.

Highlights: Excellent fishing for king salmon (in early July) and rainbow trout (from July through September). Good fishing for silver salmon (in late August) and grayling (from July through September).

Species: Grayling, king salmon, lake trout, rainbow trout, silver salmon, *chum salmon, Dolly Varden, pink salmon, red salmon.*

Regulations: King salmon fishing is closed from July 14 through December 31. The upper Susitna is designated as a Trophy Trout Area, and only single-hook artificial lures may be used. For additional restrictions, consult the current Alaska Department of Fish and Game sportfishing regulations or contact the ADF&G Palmer office, (907) 745-5016.

Facilities: No developed public facilities. Guide services are available in Talkeetna.

Contact: For guide services, contact Mahay's Riverboat Service, P.O. Box 705, Talkeetna, AK 99676, (907) 733-2223; or Tri River Charters, P.O. Box 312, Talkeetna, AK 99676, (907) 733-2400.

Fishing the Upper Susitna River System: The Susitna River, Southcentral Alaska's most significant fish producer, has its beginnings in the runoff of enormous glaciers in the eastern Alaska Range. From there, it flows swiftly south, then cuts west through the edge of the Talkeetnas before meandering south again down into the forested lowlands of upper Cook Inlet. Although anglers seldom venture into the upper part of this amazing system, it's worth pursuing. (Because of the heavy silt load, sportfishing is mostly limited to clearwater tributaries and sloughs.) The most visited part of the upper Susitna is the section between Devils Canyon—an unrunnable stretch of Class VI white water just north of the Talkeetna Mountains—and the confluence of the Chulitna and Talkeetna Rivers near the town of Talkeetna. North of Devils Canyon, the upper Susitna is a remote wilderness river, with white water, limited access, and few sportfishing opportunities. Although much tamer (mostly Class I), the heavily braided water below the canyon still has logjams and submerged hazards; boat it with caution. But the scenery is outstanding (great views of Mount McKinley), the crowds nonexistent, and the fishing quite impressive.

Most anglers who visit the upper Susitna do so by powerful jet boats, while a few opt to use the railway (with some hiking). With careful scouting, planes can access certain sections, but boaters undoubtedly have the best of all worlds, as the upper Susitna's small tributary streams and sloughs hold salmon and hungry rainbows and grayling.

Fishing for king and silver salmon can be superb, with the brighter fish available early in the season. Two major clear-water tributaries, the Indian River and Portage Creek, sustain the largest fish populations. Try Portage Creek (king salmon, silver salmon, grayling), Whiskers Creek (king salmon, silver salmon, grayling), Lane Creek (king salmon, silver salmon, rainbow trout), Fourth of July Creek (king salmon, silver salmon, rainbow trout), and Indian River (king salmon, silver salmon, rainbow trout).

For those with the yearning (and resources) for a real wilderness angling adventure, remote fly-in lakes off the upper river—such as Watana, Clarence, Deadman, and Big Lakes—see little pressure and have the potential for truly outstanding wilderness fishing for lake trout and grayling; the best times are late spring through early summer and fall. Check with air taxi services in Talkeetna for latest conditions.

❹ Talkeetna River System

Location: In the middle Susitna River drainage, 80 miles north of Anchorage; see map page 266.

USGS map: Talkeetna Mountains A-3, A-4, A-5, B-3, B-4, B-5, B-6, C-4, C-5, C-6.

How to get there: By car, plane, boat, and raft. The Talkeetna Spur Highway (from the Parks Highway) ends in the town of Talkeetna and the mouth of the river. Access to the mouths of clear-water tributary streams is by riverboat or raft, while float- and wheelplanes can land at several headwater locations. Check with air taxis in Talkeetna before flying in to float or camp along the river, as certain areas have been conveyed to native ownership.

Highlights: Excellent for king salmon (in early July), silver salmon (in mid-August), chum salmon (in early August), and pink salmon (in late July). Also good for red salmon (in late July), rainbow trout (in August and September), Dolly Varden (July through September), and grayling (June through September).

Species: Chum salmon, Dolly Varden, grayling, king salmon, pink salmon, rainbow trout, red salmon, silver salmon.

Regulations: King salmon fishing is closed from July 14 through December 31. For additional restrictions, consult the current Alaska Department of Fish and Game sportfishing regulations or contact the ADF&G Palmer office, (907) 745-5016.

Facilities: Groceries, sporting goods, gas, lodging, camping, boat launching, and air taxi and guide services are available in Talkeetna.

Contact: For guide services, contact Mahay's Riverboat Service, P.O. Box 705, Talkeetna, AK 99676, (907) 733-2223; or Tri River Charters, P.O. Box 312, Talkeetna, AK 99676, (907) 733-2400. For an air taxi, contact Talkeetna Air Taxi, P.O. Box 73, Talkeetna, AK 99676; (907) 733-2218.

Fishing the Talkeetna River System: A major tributary of the Susitna and one of the most significant fishing rivers in Southcentral Alaska, the Talkeetna is a large, glacial, swift wilderness river. The best fishing potential is concentrated in its clear-water tributary streams. Barring hot weather and heavy rains, however, the main stem is fishable. In spring and fall, the water usually takes on a greenish tint.

Due to the size and productivity of this system, the Talkeetna offers superb and varied fishing. All five salmon species fill the river from midsummer into fall, along with rainbow trout, charr, and grayling. The ultimate way to sample the hot salmon action—some of the best in the region for kings, chums, silvers, and reds—is by boat from the town of Talkeetna, accessing the mouths of some of the clear-water spawning tributaries upstream. This is definitely not a river for novice boaters, however, with its swift currents, rocky shoals, and hidden boulders. Jet boats can run way up Clear and Prairie Creeks and some of the tributaries for truly notable rainbow trout, charr, and grayling fishing. Avoid travel by boat on the main stem above Iron Creek.

The Talkeetna is also one of Alaska's premier white-water rivers, with two long canyons of rapids (Class III and IV) beginning below Prairie Creek. For floating, most folks put in by floatplane at Murder Lake (below Stephan Lake), or by wheelplane on gravel bars along the upper river (near Yellowjacket Creek), making for a five- to seven-day trip down to the mouth.

Some of the Talkeetna's best fishing spots include Clear Creek for rainbows, king salmon, silver salmon, red salmon, chum salmon, and pink salmon (also Dolly Varden and grayling); Larson Creek for red and silver salmon (also pink salmon, rainbow trout, Dolly Varden, and grayling); Disappointment Creek for chum salmon (also rainbow trout, Dolly Varden, and grayling); and Prairie Creek for silver and chum salmon (also red salmon, rainbow trout, Dolly Varden, and grayling).

Rainbow fishing in the main stem Talkeetna can be very productive in late September and early October for fish in the two- to three-pound range, with trout up to 10 pounds a possibility.

❺ Montana Creek

Location: In the middle Susitna River drainage, 60 miles north of Anchorage; see map page 266.

USGS maps: Talkeetna Mountains A-5, A-6, B-6; Talkeetna A-1.

How to get there: By car. The Parks Highway intersects the creek's lower portion, providing excellent access to the mouth as well as to trails leading upstream. A gravel road off the Talkeetna Spur Highway (which connects to the Parks Highway) will take you to the upper creek.

Highlights: Excellent road-accessible stream fishing for king salmon (from late June through early July), silver salmon (first half of August), and pink salmon (from late July through early August). Good fishing for chum salmon (from late July through early August), rainbow trout (in May and September), and grayling (from June through September).

Species: Chum salmon, Dolly Varden, grayling, king salmon, pink salmon, rainbow trout, silver salmon, *red salmon*.

Regulations: Unbaited, artificial lures only from September 1 through July 13. For additional restrictions, consult the current Alaska Department of Fish and Game sportfishing regulations or contact the ADF&G Anchorage office, (907) 267-2218.

Facilities: The state campground next to the Parks Highway bridge draws crowds during the height of salmon runs. Gas, groceries, sporting goods, and lodging are available a few miles north and south along the highway.

Contact: For fishing information, contact the Alaska Department of Fish and Game Regional Office, Sportfish Division, 333 Raspberry Road, Anchorage, AK 99518; (907) 267-2218. For camping information, contact the Public Lands Information Center, 605 West Fourth Avenue, Suite 105, Anchorage, AK 99501; (907) 271-2737.

Fishing Montana Creek: Gravel-bottom Montana Creek is an east-side Susitna tributary that comes off the western edge of the Talkeetnas north of Sheep Creek. With headwaters considerably less alpine and glacial than its neighbor (its three forks join about 10 miles east of the highway), the Montana generally runs quite clear. This, along with its ample productivity as a salmon stream, makes it one of the more popular of all Susitna road-fishing streams.

Most angling takes place at the mouth, within easy walking distance of the campground beside the Parks Highway bridge. Fish of all species migrating up Montana Creek or continuing up the Susitna to other spawning areas find sanctuary at the confluence. Anglers concentrating on salmon can also do well in the runs and holes upstream.

King salmon weighing in at 60 to 70 pounds, sometimes more, are possible, with a good number of fish in the 40-pound range. Silvers, chums, and pinks are also abundant from late summer into fall, while rainbows of eight to 10 pounds have been taken, mostly from the lower river in spring and fall. Grayling fishing isn't too bad on the upper river. Because of its size, the Montana is strictly a bank fishing stream, but you can launch a small raft from the upper access point and float to the mouth (just watch for shallow water and sweepers).

❻ Lake Creek

Location: In the Yentna River drainage, 65 miles northwest of Anchorage; see map page 266.

USGS maps: Talkeetna A-2, A-3, B-3, B-4, C-3, C-4; Tyonek D-3.

How to get there: By plane, boat, or raft. Floatplanes can land at the Chelatna Lake headwaters, at several other smaller lakes (such as Bulchatna Lake) along the Yentna, or at the mouth of the river; wheelplanes can utilize gravel bars. Boaters can access the mouth from the community of Skwentna, which has scheduled air services. Floaters usually put in at Chelatna, with takeout at the mouth.

Highlights: One of Southcentral's finest rivers, with excellent fishing for king salmon (from mid-June through early July) and good fishing for silver salmon (from mid-August through early September), rainbow trout, and grayling (in May, September, and October). Also fair to good fishing for red, chum, and pink salmon (from late July through early August) and northern pike (from June through September).

Species: Chum salmon, Dolly Varden, grayling, king salmon, northern pike, pink salmon, rainbow trout, red salmon, silver salmon.

Regulations: King salmon fishing is closed from July 14 through December 31. For additional restrictions, consult the current Alaska Department of Fish and Game sportfishing regulations or contact the ADF&G Palmer office, (907) 745-5016.

Facilities: Lodging, fuel, and water are available.

Contact: For lodging information, contact Riversong Lodge, 2463 Cottonwood Street, Anchorage, AK 99508, (907) 274-2710; or Wilderness Place Lodge, P.O. Box 190711, Anchorage, AK 99519, (907) 248-4337. For an air taxi, contact Ketchum Air Service, Pouch O, P.O. Box 190588, Anchorage, AK 99519, (907) 243-5525 or (800) 433-9114; Regal Air, P.O. Box 190702, Anchorage, AK 99579, (907) 243-8535; or Rusts Flying Service, P.O. Box 190325, Anchorage, AK 99519, (907) 243-1595 or (800) 544-2299.

Fishing Lake Creek: Beginning at Chelatna Lake near Kahiltna Glacier at the base of the Alaska Range, this fast, clear-water stream flows south through rocky rapids and canyons some 50 miles to its confluence with the glacial Yentna River. One of the most scenic sportfishing streams in the Susitna River basin, Lake Creek offers good to excellent angling for five species of salmon, rainbow trout, grayling, and even northern pike. But Lake Creek is not the easiest water to fish, what with its white water and boulders. The best angling opportunities lurk in the deep holes, slower runs, and mouths of tributary creeks above and below the canyon in the river's midsection.

Early in the season, look for bright king salmon holding from their journey upriver (to both Lake Creek and other clear tributaries of the Yentna) and resident rainbow trout and grayling at the confluence of Lake Creek and the Yentna. Later in the season, in the middle and upper sections, salmon fishing continues to be very good (Lake Creek kings are quite large, some exceeding 50 or even 60 pounds). August usually brings a fair run of silvers and some lively rainbow trout and grayling. Chelatna Lake at the headwaters has a good population of northern pike.

Perhaps the most exciting way to fish Lake Creek is to put in at Chelatna Lake and float the entire length by raft, down to the mouth at the Yentna. With white water varying from Class I to Class III, this is not a river that novice floaters should attempt.

❼ Deshka River

Location: In the lower Susitna River drainage, 35 miles northwest of Anchorage; see map page 266.

USGS maps: Talkeetna A-1, A-2, B-1, B-2; Tyonek C-1, D-1, D-2.

How to get there: Anglers have three access options. One is by floatplane to Neil Lake (just west of the river between Trapper Creek and the "Forks") or to the mouth of the river. Another is by boat from Deshka Landing south of Willow on the Parks Highway. The last option is the Petersville Road via the Parks Highway, which crosses Kroto and Moose Creeks, the two main forks of the Deshka. Many anglers float the river from Petersville Road down, mainly via Moose Creek, with take-out at the Susitna River confluence.

Highlights: Excellent fishing for silver salmon (in early August), rainbow trout (from June through September), and grayling (from May through September).

Species: Chum salmon, Dolly Varden, grayling, pink salmon, rainbow trout, red salmon, silver salmon, *king salmon, northern pike.*

Regulations: King salmon fishing is closed. For additional restrictions, consult the current Alaska Department of Fish and Game sportfishing regulations or contact the ADF&G Palmer office, (907) 745-5016.

Facilities: Lodging, fuel, water, and guide services are available.

Contact: For lodging information, contact Deshka River Lodge, P.O. Box 190355, Anchorage, AK 99519, (907) 243-6813; or Deshka Silver-King Lodge, P.O. Box 1037, Willow, AK 99688, (907) 733-2055. For an air taxi, contact Ketchum Air Service, Pouch O, P.O. Box 190588, Anchorage, AK 99519, (907) 243-5525 or (800) 433-9114; Regal Air, P.O. Box 190702, Anchorage, AK 99579, (907) 243-8535; or Rusts Flying Service, P.O. Box 190325, Anchorage, AK 99519, (907) 243-1595 or (800) 544-2299.

Fishing the Deshka River: The Deshka River, also known as Kroto Creek, is a major clear-water tributary of the Susitna and a highly productive fishing stream. Flowing approximately 90 miles from its origins south of the Alaska Range near Talkeetna, the slow-moving Deshka empties into the Susitna about eight miles southwest of Willow.

Abundant numbers of the other salmon, along with a healthy population of resident rainbow trout and grayling, contribute to its perennial popularity as one of Alaska's most heavily fished rivers. It can be reached and fished in several ways. Floatplanes carry anglers to the mouth or drop off rafting parties along the midsection. For those with jet boats, the river is navigable to the "Forks," where Kroto and Moose Creeks come together, about 30 miles upstream from the mouth. Shore fishing is mostly done on the upper and middle river sections, with the mouth and lower river better suited to fishing from a boat or raft.

The confluence of the Deshka and Susitna Rivers serves as a pit stop for vast schools of salmon migrating farther up the Susitna. Anglers can expect to tangle with all five species of salmon there, in season. Rainbow trout and grayling fill the upper Deshka River in late summer and early fall, where conditions are perfect for fly and ultralight spin casting. Parts of the river attract growing numbers of northern pike.

❽ Sheep Creek

Location: In the middle Susitna River drainage, 50 miles north of Anchorage; see map page 266.

USGS maps: Talkeetna Mountains A-5, A-6; Talkeetna A-1; Tyonek D-1.

How to get there: By car. The Parks Highway intersects the middle stretch of Sheep Creek north of Willow. Trails lead both upstream and downstream. To reach the confluence with the Susitna River, take the gravel road about one mile south of the bridge crossing.

Highlights: Good road-accessible fishing for king salmon (from mid-June through early July), silver salmon (in the first half of August), chum and pink salmon (from late July through early August), rainbow trout (in May and September), and grayling (from June through September).

Species: Chum salmon, Dolly Varden, grayling, king salmon, pink salmon, rainbow trout, silver salmon, *red salmon*.

Regulations: Unbaited, artificial lures only from September 1 through July 13. For additional restrictions, consult the current Alaska Department of Fish and Game sportfishing regulations or contact the ADF&G Anchorage office, (907) 267-2218.

Facilities: Lodging, camping, and gas are available at the Parks Highway crossing. Camping and a boat launch are available at the mouth. Look for groceries and sporting goods on the highway a few miles north of Sheep Creek.

Contact: For fishing information, contact the Alaska Department of Fish and Game Regional Office, Sportfish Division, 333 Raspberry Road, Anchorage, AK 99518; (907) 267-2218. For lodging information, contact the Sheep Creek Lodge, HC 89, Box 406, Willow, AK 99688; (907) 495-6227.

Fishing Sheep Creek: This small clear-water tributary of the Susitna issues from the western edge of the Talkeetna Mountains and flows 50 miles west before joining the big glacial stream at midriver. A well-used highway angling destination, Sheep Creek offers potentially good salmon fishing, especially for kings.

The creek is especially suited for bank fishing, which is the only real way to work the middle and upper river, but the mouth can also be fished from a boat. For an easy half-day trip down to the mouth, put in small rafts at the highway bridge—be wary of logjams and sweepers though.

Although fishing is good for four salmon species in season, kings draw the most anglers to the banks of Sheep Creek, as they tend to be slightly above average (up to 40 or 50 pounds, with rare specimens up to 80 pounds a possibility). In spring or late summer and fall, rainbow trout and grayling are best fished in the lower or upper river. Sheep has a tendency to become silty and run high during prolonged periods of hot weather or heavy rain.

❾ Willow Creek

Location: In the middle Susitna River drainage, 40 miles north of Anchorage; see map page 266.

USGS maps: Anchorage C-7, C-8, D-6, D-7, D-8; Tyonek D-1.

How to get there: By car. A four-mile gravel road from the town of Willow leads to the confluence of Willow Creek and the Susitna River. The Parks Highway in Willow intersects the middle river, parts of which can also be reached from the first few miles of Hatcher Pass Road. Hatcher Pass Road offers access to the upper stream section.

Highlights: Excellent fishing for king salmon (from mid-June through early July), silver salmon (first half of August), and pink salmon (from late July through early August). Good fishing for chum salmon (from late July through early August), rainbow trout (in May and September), and grayling (from June through September).

Species: Chum salmon, Dolly Varden, grayling, king salmon, pink salmon, rainbow trout, silver salmon, *red salmon*.

Regulations: Unbaited, artificial lures only from September 1 through July 13. For additional restrictions, consult the current Alaska Department of Fish and Game sportfishing regulations or contact the ADF&G Palmer office, (907) 745-5016.

Facilities: Camping, gas, groceries, a guide service, and a boat launch are available in Willow. Camping is also available at the mouth of the stream.

Contact: For lodging and guide services, contact the Willow Island Resort, P.O. Box 85, Willow, AK 99688; (907) 495-6343. For camping information, contact the Public Lands Information Center, 605 West Fourth Avenue, Suite 105, Anchorage, AK 99501; (907) 271-2737.

Fishing Willow Creek: Willow Creek, a rocky, clear-water stream, flows swiftly west off the edge of the southern Talkeetna Mountains onto the flatlands of the lower Susitna, near the town of Willow. It's one of the most popular fishing streams in the area, especially for bank fishing, with plenty of road-accessible holes, runs, and pools for decent salmon and trout fishing in season.

Most folks fish the Willow from the road, getting there from the Parks Highway or farther up from Hatcher Pass Road. Floating is another way to fish the creek. You can launch rafts, kayaks, and canoes for short trips from any of the road access points on the upper or middle river. But the Willow is a rapid runoff stream with sweepers, logjams, and a high gradient in its upper reaches, so floaters should use caution and stay within the middle and lower river sections.

Salmon is the top draw here, with four runs providing substantial action from early summer into fall. Kings are the most sought-after species and can reach a respectable size in the Willow. (Most fish caught here run between 15 and 30 pounds, but anglers have a good chance of hooking fish weighing as much as 65 pounds. Kings nudging the 80-pound mark have been taken.) The mouth of the Willow draws considerable crowds during the height of the runs, but anglers willing to hike a little can find good fishing for salmon, trout, and grayling on the river's middle and upper sections. Spring and fall are very popular and productive for trout on the Willow.

⑩ Alexander Creek

Location: In the lower Susitna River drainage, 25 miles northwest of Anchorage; see map page 266.

USGS maps: Tyonek B-2, C-2, C-3, D-3.

How to get there: By floatplane and jet boat. Planes use calm stretches of the river and lakes as landing sites. Boats can be launched from the Port of Anchorage or from Deshka Landing near Willow on the Parks Highway. Floating the river with rafts and canoes is very popular.

Highlights: One of Southcentral's best loved and most productive fisheries. Good fishing for king salmon (in early June), silver salmon (in early August), rainbow trout (from June through September), pink salmon (in late July), grayling (from May through September), and northern pike (May and June).

Species: Chum salmon, Dolly Varden, grayling, king salmon, northern pike, pink salmon, rainbow trout, red salmon, silver salmon.

Regulations: King salmon fishing is closed from July 14 through December 31. For additional restrictions, consult the current Alaska Department of Fish and Game sportfishing regulations or contact the ADF&G Palmer office, (907) 745-5016.

Facilities: Lodging, fuel, water, and a guide service are available.

Contact: For lodging and guide services, contact Gabbert's Fish Camp, P.O. Box ACR, Alexander Creek, AK 99695; (907) 733-2371. For an air taxi, contact Ketchum Air Service, Pouch O, P.O. Box 190588, Anchorage, AK 99519, (907) 243-5525 or (800) 433-9114; Regal Air, P.O. Box 190702, Anchorage, AK 99579, (907) 243-8535; or Rusts Flying Service, P.O. Box 190325,

Anchorage, AK 99519, (907) 243-1595 or (800) 544-2299.

Fishing Alexander Creek: Alexander Creek holds large runs of salmon throughout much of the summer and into fall. The creek drains a fairly significant area between the Yentna River and Mount Susitna, running south some 40 miles from its origin at Alexander Lake to join the glacial Susitna River near tidewater. The surrounding marshland contributes significantly to the iron-colored tint of this slow, meandering stream.

Access is relatively easy. Most anglers fly in to the lower river by floatplane, landing on the calm waters near the mouth or on Alexander Lake. Although bank fishing is popular on the upper and middle river, most angling on lower Alexander Creek is done from boats. Jet boats can run from the mouth upstream about 18 miles to the confluence with Sucker Creek, a major clear-water tributary, fishing good water along the way. One of the best ways to enjoy the Alexander is to float and fish down from the lake in rafts or canoes (an easy four- to five-day trip), with take-out at the mouth. Alexander Lake itself has a reputation for producing excellent northern pike catches, with trophies up to 30 pounds possible.

The creek mouth is the most productive fishing spot. Its confluence with the large glacial Susitna serves as a major holding area for a tremendous number of salmon heading upstream to spawn in the Susitna's other clear-water tributaries. But the Alexander itself boasts significant runs of king and silver salmon, along with good numbers of red, chum, and pink salmon; rainbow trout; Dolly Varden; and grayling—even a few northern pike.

⑪ Talachulitna River

Location: In the Yentna River drainage, 60 miles northwest of Anchorage; see map page 266.

USGS maps: Tyonek B-4, C-3, C-4, C-5, D-4, D-5.

How to get there: By floatplane to the headwaters at Judd Lake, near Hiline Lake at the river's midpoint, or the mouth at the Yentna. Boaters can reach the mouth from the community of Skwentna, which is serviced by air. Wheelplanes

can also land near the mouth. Floating the river gives anglers access to the best fishing.

Highlights: Southcentral's classic salmon and trout stream, excellent for king salmon (late June through early July), silver salmon (late August through early September), rainbow trout (June through September), and grayling (June through September). Also good for red and pink salmon (from late July through early August) and chum salmon (late June through early July).

Species: Chum salmon, Dolly Varden, grayling, king salmon, pink salmon, rainbow trout, red salmon, silver salmon.

Regulations: King salmon fishing is closed from July 14 through December 31; catch-and-release fishing only for rainbow trout. For additional restrictions, consult the current Alaska Department of Fish and Game sportfishing regulations or contact the ADF&G Palmer office, (907) 745-5016.

Facilities: Private lodges are available along the lower river.

Contact: For lodging and guide services, contact Skwentna Lodge, 8051 Rabbit Creek Road, Anchorage, AK 99516; (907) 345-1702 or (907) 733-2722. For an air taxi, contact Ketchum Air Service, Pouch O, P.O. Box 190588, Anchorage, AK 99519, (907) 243-5525 or (800) 433-9114; Regal Air, P.O. Box 190702, Anchorage, AK 99579, (907) 243-8535; or Rusts Flying Service, P.O. Box 190325, Anchorage, AK 99519, (907) 243-1595 or (800) 544-2299.

Fishing the Talachulitna River: One of Alaska's premier fishing locations, the Tal offers some of the finest stream fishing in all of Southcentral Alaska. Located about 60 miles west of Anchorage, the clear-water Talachulitna rises from several sources in the highlands above the lower Skwentna, then winds through birch and spruce forests and scenic gorges for some 50 miles before emptying into the Susitna's swift glacial tributary.

In addition to offering great fishing, seclusion, scenery, and exciting floating, the Talachulitna rates as one of Alaska's choicest rivers to enjoy by raft, kayak, or canoe. The upper section is fairly slow and quite shallow in spots (mostly Class I and II). An abrupt series of Class II and III rapids livens things up just below the Hiline Lake put in at midriver, and the lower river plunges through several high canyons (Class II and III) before reaching the Skwentna. Overall, the Tal is definitely not for the novice boater.

Despite the fishing pressure of recent years, the Talachulitna is holding up remarkably well, with strong runs of king and silver salmon, and fairly abundant rainbow trout fishing. In its heyday back in the '50s and '60s, the river was known for trophy trout, but nowadays you'll have to work the water pretty hard to turn up a fish of any size. (Rainbows average 12 to 16 inches and are among the prettiest strains found in Alaska.) The best chances for bigger trout are in the middle and upper river during late summer, where you'll find decent grayling fishing as well.

For salmon, the mouth of the river and confluences of the tributary creeks (such as Friday and Thursday Creeks) have traditionally been the most reliable, but the river has plenty of holding water—pools, riffles, and sloughs— for good fishing all the way down. The trip from Judd Lake to the Skwentna makes a perfect seven-day float with ample time to fish all the good water.

Guides' tip: The Tal has miles of perfect fly-fishing water, with some of Southcentral's best dry fly–fishing (grayling, rainbows, and even, although rarely, silver salmon), so bring proper gear.

⑫ Little Susitna River System

Location: In the upper Cook Inlet drainage, Susitna Flats, 15 miles west of Anchorage; see map page 266.

USGS maps: Anchorage C-6, C-7, C-8, D-6; Tyonek B-1, C-1.

How to get there: By car. For the middle river, access is from the town of Houston along the Parks Highway. For the lower river, access is from Knik—Goose Bay Road off the Parks Highway near Wasilla. Many anglers raft or canoe between access points. Another option is a 12-mile boat ride across upper Cook Inlet from the Port of Anchorage to the mouth of the river. Exercise extreme caution if you travel by boat.

Highlights: Excellent road-accessible fishing for silver salmon (in early August), chum salmon (from late July through early August), and pink salmon (in late July); good fishing for king salmon (in early June).

Species: Chum salmon, Dolly Varden, grayling, king salmon, pink salmon, rainbow trout, red salmon, silver salmon.

Regulations: King salmon fishing is closed from July 14 through December 31. For additional restrictions, consult the current Alaska Department of Fish and Game sportfishing regulations or contact the ADF&G Palmer office, (907) 745-5016.

Facilities: Lodging, guide services, groceries, sporting goods, gas, boat launching, and camping are available in Houston. Camping and boat launching are also available on the lower river.

Contact: For lodging information and guide services, contact Fishtale River Guides, HCO 2, Box 7383, Palmer, AK 99645, (907) 376-3687; or Trophy Catch Charters, P.O. Box 245, Palmer, AK 99645, (907) 745-4101.

Fishing the Little Susitna River System: The Little Susitna is a popular road-fishing stream that meanders through spruce and birch from its origins on the south slopes of the Talkeetna Mountains. It is a moody river. During summer hot spells or rainy periods, its clear waters can easily become high, muddy, and difficult to fish, especially on the swift upper and middle sections (beginning and intermediate boaters should stay on the wide lower river, where the current is slower). While the river has many sharp bends and twists with some sweepers, most of the Little Su is fairly tame. However, its upper reaches are rated Class II to Class III. Rafters can spend two or three days floating the river from the upper or middle access points down to the lower river and Burma Road.

All five salmon species migrate up the Little Susitna in good numbers and hold in the river's many holes, pools, and runs from Houston downstream. Boaters fishing the tides mostly work the lower river, although bank fishing is possible. Shore anglers prefer the Little Su's narrower middle and upper parts, which concentrate the fishing, while salmon anglers gravitate toward the confluence with Nancy Lake Creek.

The upper river also has fairly good rainbow trout, Dolly Varden, and grayling action during the summer and fall months when spawning salmon are present.

🔞 Ship Creek

Location: In the north Cook Inlet drainage, downtown Anchorage; see map page 266.

USGS map: Anchorage A-8.

How to get there: By car. Ship Creek is located off First Avenue and Loop Road near the Port of Anchorage. Both sides of the stream offer parking with foot access throughout. Respect private property and please be cautious around inlet mud.

Highlights: Salmon fishing in the heart of Alaska's biggest city, with good fishing for king salmon (throughout June) and silver salmon (from mid-August through early September).

Species: King salmon, pink salmon, silver salmon, *chum salmon, Dolly Varden, red salmon*.

Regulations: Portions are closed to fishing. King salmon fishing is open from January 1 through July 13. For the latest closures or restrictions, consult the current Alaska Department of Fish and Game sportfishing regulations or contact the ADF&G Anchorage office, (907) 267-2218.

Facilities: There is parking by the stream and hotels nearby. Groceries, sporting goods, and gas are available in Anchorage.

Contact: For fishing information, contact the Alaska Department of Fish and Game Regional Office, Sportfish Division, 333 Raspberry Road, Anchorage, AK 99518; (907) 267-2218. For lodging information, contact the Comfort Inn, 111 West Ship Creek Avenue, Anchorage, AK 99501; (907) 277-6887 or (800) 362-6887.

Fishing Ship Creek: Ship Creek originates high in the Chugach Mountains and flows west through the greater Anchorage area to Knik Arm. It typically runs clear, but may turn slightly glacial during heavy rains or hot weather. The wooded upper stream sections have little development, but that changes drastically as the stream nears its terminus in the Port of Anchorage near downtown Anchorage. Salmon fishing takes place in the tidal area of the stream below the Chugach Electric power plant. Although totally lacking the wilderness associated with Alaska, angling with the tide can be quite good during the height of salmon season, particularly in deep holes and runs near the road crossings.

Starting in late spring and continuing into mid-summer, a run of wild and hatchery king salmon returns to Ship Creek. Some years, the action heats up to provide even higher catch rates than in the better streams of the Kenai or Susitna. As the king is Alaska's number one game fish and this stream sits in the heart of the state's largest city, expect huge crowds. Anglers pay less attention, however, to an almost equally productive run of silver salmon that peaks in late summer and continues through most of fall. "Even" years also see a fair run of pink salmon, in addition to a few chums and Dolly Varden.

Ship Creek certainly can't compare to other streams in Alaska, but it makes a nice diversion if you happen to be in Anchorage with a few hours to kill. Many a visitor has walked from a hotel down to Ship Creek and come back toting a 20- to 50-pounder.

🔞 Theodore River

Location: In the west upper Cook Inlet drainage, 30 miles west of Anchorage; see map page 266.

USGS maps: Tyonek A-3, B-3, B-4.

How to get there: By floatplane, landing on ponds next to the lower river, or by wheelplane to two small runways west of the lower river. A road running parallel to the river upstream from one of the runways provides additional access.

Highlights: A great fly-in fishing spot, only 20 minutes from Anchorage. Good fishing for silver salmon (in early August), and rainbow trout (from June through September).

Species: Dolly Varden, pink salmon, rainbow trout, silver salmon, *chum salmon, grayling, king salmon, red salmon*.

Regulations: King salmon fishing is closed. For additional restrictions, consult the current Alaska Department of Fish and Game sportfishing regulations or contact the ADF&G Palmer office, (907) 745-5016.

Facilities: No developed public facilities.

Contact: For an air taxi, contact Ketchum Air Service, Pouch O, P.O. Box 190588, Anchorage, AK 99519, (907) 243-5525 or (800) 433-9114; Regal Air, P.O. Box 190702, Anchorage, AK 99579, (907) 243-8535; or Rusts Flying Service, P.O. Box 190325, Anchorage, AK 99519, (907) 243-1595 or (800) 544-2299.

Fishing the Theodore River: Originating near the west side of Little Mount Susitna, south of the Talachulitna River, this small, clear stream meanders through mixed forest and lowland brush for some 35 miles to the tidal flats of upper Cook Inlet. It's fairly productive for salmon (as well as trout and charr), with an abundance of holding water, and ideal for the angler who wants to fish apart from crowds but without the expense of a long fly-in.

Salmon fishing is best during and after high tide in the lower river. Later in the season, salmon congregate in dense schools near the spawning grounds on the middle and upper river. The upper stretches of the Theodore also offer decent trout and Dolly Varden charr action, especially in late summer and fall, when the salmon are well into their spawning. Grayling are an occasional bonus. Fly-fishing conditions on the upper river are quite good, with lots of rocky runs and cover.

Kenai Peninsula/ Cook Inlet

Encompassing the waters of the Kenai Peninsula and Cook Inlet, this area boasts some of the state's most notable marine and freshwater sportfisheries. Many characterize the Kenai Peninsula as a miniature Alaska, with its immense ice fields, turquoise glacial lakes, sparkling runoff streams, forests, fjords, and towering mountains. Even its wildlife—large moose, abundant waterfowl and marine mammals, bears, and caribou—mirrors the state's. What's more, the Kenai Peninsula and surrounding waters are amply blessed with an amazing fecundity, producing unique fishing opportunities, particularly for trophy king salmon and halibut. And best of all, nearly all of it lies within easy reach by boat, car, or a short plane ride.

⑮ Beluga River System

Location: In the northwest Cook Inlet drainage, 30 miles west of Anchorage; see map page 266.

USGS maps: Tyonek A-3, A-4, B-3, B-4, B-5, B-6, C-5, C-6.

How to get there: By air from Anchorage. Floatplanes touch down on Beluga and Lower Beluga Lakes and the lower river. Boat travel may be possible along sections of river.

Highlights: Good fishing for king salmon (in late June), silver salmon (in early August), and pink salmon (in late July); also rainbow trout (from June through September). Only a short flight from Anchorage.

Species: Dolly Varden, king salmon, pink salmon, rainbow trout, red salmon, silver salmon.

Regulations: King salmon fishing is closed from July 1 through December 31. For additional restrictions, consult the current Alaska Department of Fish and Game sportfishing regulations or contact the ADF&G Anchorage office, (907) 267-2218.

Facilities: No developed public facilities.

Contact: For fishing information, contact the Alaska Department of Fish and Game Regional Office, Sportfish Division, 333 Raspberry Road, Anchorage, AK 99518-1599; (907) 267-2218. For an air taxi, contact Alaska Helicopters, P.O. Box 190283, Anchorage, AK 99519, (907) 243-3404 or (907) 243-1466; Ketchum Air Service, P.O. Box 190588, Anchorage, AK 99519, (907) 243-5525 or (800) 433-9114; or Regal Air, P.O. Box 190702, Anchorage, AK 99519, (907) 243-8535.

Fishing the Beluga River System: Beluga Lake is a large, silty body of meltwater from two enormous glaciers pouring down the slopes of the Alaska Range north of Mount Spurr. The Beluga River issues from the lake, flowing rapidly through a canyon down to the mudflats of Cook Inlet 30 miles away. Though the lake and river are too silty for sportfishing, several clearwater tributary streams support moderate populations of salmon, trout, and charr, all a mere 20-minute flight from Anchorage.

While the Beluga's upper and lower sections

move slowly, the middle canyon sections are extremely difficult and dangerous to negotiate, even with a powerful boat. Anglers fishing the Beluga should probe the mouths of the clear-water streams for holding salmon (king, silver, and sockeye in season), with the best charr and rainbow trout water reached with a little hiking. Some of the best creeks are Pretty, Olsen (accessed at the mouth by small wheelplane), Drill, Scarp, and Coal. Coal Creek, which drains into the lower end of Beluga Lake, has the largest population of salmon and trout and is easily accessed by floatplane. The lake and upper river are among the most dramatically scenic locations in Cook Inlet.

⑯ Chakachatna-McArthur River System

Location: In the northwest Cook Inlet drainage, Trading Bay, 65 miles southwest of Anchorage; see map page 266.

USGS maps: Lime Hills A-1, B-1; Tyonek A-5, A-6, A-7, A-8, B-7, B-8; Kenai D-5.

How to get there: By helicopter or wheelplane from Anchorage or Kenai. The Chakachatna side of the system may be scouted for wheelplane landing areas—gravel bars—but the McArthur side is accessible only by helicopter.

Highlights: Good fly-in fishing for king salmon (in the last half of June) and silver salmon (in the first half August); just a short flight from Anchorage.

Species: Chum salmon, Dolly Varden, king salmon, pink salmon, red salmon, silver salmon.

Regulations: Consult the current Alaska Department of Fish and Game sportfishing regulations or contact the ADF&G Soldotna office, (907) 262-9368.

Facilities: No developed public facilities.

Contact: For fishing information, contact the Alaska Department of Fish and Game, Sportfish Division, P.O. Box 3150, Soldotna, AK 99669; (907) 262-9368. For an air taxi, contact Alaska Helicopters, P.O. Box 190283, Anchorage, AK 99519, (907) 243-3404 or (907) 243-1466; or Kenai Air, 155 Granite Point Court, Kenai, AK 99611, (907) 283-7561.

Fishing the Chakachatna-McArthur River System: This massive coastal system drains a sizable area of the Alaska Range within Lake Clark National Park. Of glacial origin with heavy silt loads, the rivers' sportfishing is limited to a handful of clear tributary streams that provide some concentrated fishing in season, with little pressure. Kings and silvers are the top draw, with fair to good angling for other salmon (reds, chums, and pinks) and Dolly Varden charr. Access is tricky.

The Chakachatna River is somewhat limited in suitable fishing locations. Try the clear north fork of Straight Creek for salmon. Small wheelplanes can land on gravel bars and ridges nearby. McArthur River has a few more streams to choose from, all of them unnamed. The better ones run through the flats between the two watersheds (west of Noaukta Slough). These clear streams, usually accessed by helicopter, are especially good for silver salmon during the peak of the runs.

⑰ Chuitna River

Location: In the northwest Cook Inlet drainage, 40 miles west of Anchorage; see map page 266.

USGS maps: Tyonek A-4, A-5, B-5.

How to get there: By plane or helicopter from Anchorage or Kenai. Most anglers get to the mouth of the Chuitna by wheelplane, landing on the north beach. A gravel road network runs along the coast to provide additional (albeit primitive) access to the lower river. The upper Chuitna can be reached by helicopter. Anglers may launch rafts from there and float down to the mouth.

Highlights: Excellent fly-in fishing for king salmon (in the first part of June), silver salmon (in the first part of August), and pink salmon (in the second half of July). Good fishing for rainbow trout (from June through September).

Species: Chum salmon, Dolly Varden, king salmon, pink salmon, rainbow trout, red salmon, silver salmon.

Regulations: King salmon fishing is closed from July 1 through December 31; bait restrictions may apply. For additional restrictions, consult the current Alaska Department of Fish and Game sportfishing regulations or contact the ADF&G Anchorage office, (907) 267-2218.

Facilities: A commercial lodge and guide services are available on the river.

Contact: For fishing information, contact the Alaska Department of Fish and Game Regional Office, Sportfish Division, 333 Raspberry Road, Anchorage, AK 99518-1599; (907) 267-2218. For lodging and guide services, contact the Chuitna River Guides, P.O. Box 82048, Tyonek, AK 99682; (907) 583-2282. For an air taxi, contact Alaska Helicopters, P.O. Box 190283, Anchorage, AK 99519, (907) 243-3404 or (907) 243-1466; or Ketchum Air Service, P.O. Box 190588, Anchorage, AK 99519, (907) 243-5525 or (800) 433-9114.

Fishing the Chuitna River: Draining a sizable, very pretty area of uplands between the Chakachatna and Beluga Rivers, the Chuitna is perhaps the most significant west-side Cook Inlet salmon and trout stream, known for outstanding king and silver salmon fishing. It is away from crowds, yet only a short distance from Anchorage by plane. Its clear water, deep holes, swift and rocky runs, and canyons offer ideal stream fishing conditions, as do several of its tributaries (such as Lone and Chuit Creeks).

The Tyonek Native Corporation owns Chuitna's south side, so obtain a permit before treading on this land. Most public use occurs on the north side. The mouth and lower river are the most popular spots for fishing, with the best action during and shortly after the incoming tides. Nearby Threemile Creek, accessible by gravel road, also offers outstanding salmon fishing. The middle and upper river contain an abundance of good holding and spawning water, along with decent populations of rainbow trout and Dolly Varden charr in late summer and fall. A gravel road that runs along the river a ways up from the mouth will get you to these sections, as will a boat or helicopter. (Some anglers even bring their own all-terrain vehicles or dirt bikes to navigate the gravel road.)

⑱ Kustatan River

Location: In west-side Cook Inlet, Redoubt Bay, 60 miles southwest of Anchorage; see map page 266.

USGS maps: Kenai C-5, D-6; Tyonek A-6.

How to get there: By floatplane from Anchorage or Kenai. Boat access is possible.

Highlights: A famous west-side Cook Inlet salmon stream, with excellent fishing for silver salmon (from August through early September).

Species: Dolly Varden, pink salmon, red salmon, silver salmon, *king salmon*.

Regulations: For bag limits and restrictions, consult the current Alaska Department of Fish and Game sportfishing regulations or contact the ADF&G Soldotna office, (907) 262-9368.

Facilities: Tent camps and guide services are available on the river.

Contact: For an air taxi and guide services, contact Ketchum Air Service, P.O. Box 190588, Anchorage, AK 99519, (907) 243-5525 or (800) 433-9114; Regal Air, P.O. Box 190702, Anchorage, AK 99519, (907) 243-8535; or Rusts Flying Service, P.O. Box 190325, Anchorage, AK 99519, (907) 243-1595.

Fishing the Kustatan River: Although it sees quite a bit of use during the season, the Kustatan River of Redoubt Bay is worth mentioning for its high quality of angling and close proximity to Anchorage. It garners recognition as one of the more productive silver salmon streams of Cook Inlet's west side.

Access is by small floatplane from Anchorage or Kenai to adjoining lakes along the middle section of river. Most anglers fish the river near the lakes, small tributary streams, or the mouth (an old gas field road provides access). The scenic upper river offers still more good fishing, accessed via a small floatplane landing on a few small lakes in the hills. Several guide services operate on the river, and recreational use is growing, so expect company when the action grows hot on the Kustatan.

⑲ Big River Lakes System

Location: In west-side Cook Inlet, 60 miles southwest of Anchorage; see map page 266.

USGS maps: Kenai C-6, C-7, D-6, D-7.

How to get there: By floatplane from Anchorage.

Highlights: A well-known west-side Cook Inlet salmon stream, with excellent fishing for red salmon (from mid-June through mid-July) and good fishing for silver salmon (in August).

Species: Dolly Varden, rainbow trout, red salmon, silver salmon.

Regulations: For bag limits and restrictions, consult the current Alaska Department of Fish and Game sportfishing regulations or contact the ADF&G Soldotna office, (907) 262-9368.

Facilities: A commercial lodge and guide services are available on one lake.

Contact: For lodging and guide services, contact Branham Adventures, P.O. Box 190184, Anchorage, AK 99519; (907) 243-4901. For an air taxi, contact Ketchum Air Service, P.O. Box 190588, Anchorage, AK 99519, (907) 243-5525 or (800) 433-9114; Regal Air, P.O. Box 190702, Anchorage, AK 99519, (907) 243-8535; or Rusts Flying Service, P.O. Box 190325, Anchorage, AK 99519, (907) 243-1595.

Fishing the Big River Lakes System: The lovely Big River Lakes area across the inlet from Nikiski on the Kenai has been a popular fly-in spot for years, thanks to its abundant salmon fishing in a magnificent, secluded setting. With four connected lakes, all of glacial origin, nestled above Redoubt Bay, this system forms a major habitat for salmon, particularly sockeye. In early summer, hundreds of thousands of feisty reds jam up into the lakes.

The lakes are easy to access and the fishing hard to beat, especially in and around the inlet/outlet streams, where sockeyes congregate and aggressively strike a variety of enticements. (Wolverine Creek is designated as fly-fishing only—check Alaska Department of Fish and Game regulations.) This is one of the few places in Alaska where bright red salmon can be caught consistently on Pixee spoons. You can find silver salmon later in summer in the mouths of clear-water tributaries along Bachatna Flats, but access is difficult. There are even Dolly Varden and a few rainbow trout. The lakes and adjoining streams are also exceedingly popular among brown bears during fishing season, so use caution.

⑳ Crescent River/Lake

Location: In west-side Cook Inlet, 75 miles southwest of Anchorage; see map page 266.

USGS maps: Kenai B-7, B-8; Lake Clark B-1.

How to get there: By floatplane from Anchorage. Boat access is possible to the lower river.

Highlights: Excellent fishing for red salmon (from late June through July) and good for silver salmon (in August).

Species: Dolly Varden, pink salmon, red salmon, lake trout, silver salmon.

Regulations: For bag limits and restrictions, consult the current Alaska Department of Fish and Game sportfishing regulations or contact the ADF&G Soldotna office, (907) 262-9368.

Facilities: No developed public facilities.

Contact: For an air taxi, contact Kenai Air, 155 Granite Point Court, Kenai, AK 99611, (907) 283-7561; or Ketchum Air Service, P.O. Box 190588, Anchorage, AK 99519, (907) 243-5525 or (800) 433-9114.

Fishing Crescent River/Lake: One of the more significant salmon systems for its size in Southcentral Alaska, and a popular fly-in location, Crescent River/Lake is tinted a glacial blue-green. It garners a run of reds starting in late June, and silvers later in the summer, with good fishing for Dolly Varden as well. Because it's close to Kenai and Anchorage, and has such great fishing for sockeye salmon, consider it as an inexpensive alternative to the crowded Russian River and other roadside fisheries.

The system's most heavily fished parts are the lake outlet (a great camping spot) and clearwater tributaries, where salmon hold in great concentrations during the peak of the runs. Spring and fall are the best times for Dolly Varden. (Keep in mind that the lake doesn't break up until the middle or last part of June.) Nearby Polly Creek offers good silver salmon fishing and outstanding razor clam digging at low tide. It can be accessed by wheelplane at its mouth.

㉑ Silver Salmon Creek

Location: In west-side Cook Inlet, 115 miles southwest of Anchorage; see map page 266.

USGS maps: Kenai A-8; Seldovia D-8.

How to get there: By small floatplane from Anchorage.

Highlights: Excellent fishing for silver salmon (in August).

Species: Dolly Varden, pink salmon, red salmon, silver salmon.

Regulations: For bag limits and restrictions, consult the current Alaska Department of Fish and Game sportfishing regulations or contact the ADF&G Soldotna office, (907) 262-9368.

Facilities: No developed public facilities.

Contact: For lodging information, contact the Silver Salmon Creek Lodge, P.O. Box 3234, Soldotna, AK 99669; (907) 262-4839. For an air taxi, contact Kenai Air, 155 Granite Point Court, Kenai, AK 99611, (907) 283-7561; or Ketchum Air Service, P.O. Box 190588, Anchorage, AK 99519, (907) 243-5525 or (800) 433-9114.

Fishing Silver Salmon Creek: Set along the lower west side of Cook Inlet, Silver Salmon Creek is a popular fly-in location for (what else?) silver salmon in season. Located almost directly across from Ninilchik on the Kenai, this short but extremely productive drainage is accessed by small floatplane, landing in either the Silver Salmon Lakes nearby or in the narrow tidal lagoon at the mouth (a very tricky landing). Fishing in August and early September can land you with bigger silvers than are generally encountered elsewhere. The deep blue waters of the Pacific absorb the inlet's gray, glacial silt.

㉒ Kamishak River

Location: In the southwest Cook Inlet, 210 miles southwest of Anchorage; see map page 266.

USGS maps: Afognak C-6; Mount Katmai C-1, C-2, D-1, D-2; Iliamna A-4.

How to get there: By plane from Homer, Kenai, or Anchorage, landing on gravel beaches at the mouth of the river.

Highlights: Excellent fishing for silver salmon (from September through early October). Good fishing for chum salmon (in July), pink salmon (in August), and Dolly Varden charr (from July through September).

Species: Chum salmon, Dolly Varden, king salmon, pink salmon, red salmon, silver salmon, *rainbow trout*.

Regulations: For restrictions, consult the current Alaska Department of Fish and Game sportfishing regulations or contact the ADF&G Soldotna office, (907) 262-9368.

Facilities: No developed public facilities.

Contact: For an air taxi, contact Homer Air, P.O. Box 302, Homer, AK 99603; (907) 235-8591.

Fishing the Kamishak River: On the west side of lower Cook Inlet across from Kachemak Bay lie less visited clear-water streams with good seasonal fishing for salmon and charr. The area is made more appealing thanks to the sweeping coastal scenery and abundant wildlife. The lodge crowd (particularly from the Iliamna area) regularly fishes the Kamishak River for silver salmon in late summer and fall.

The Kamishak rises in the coastal mountains of Katmai National Park near the headwaters of the Naknek and flows northeast through deep valleys, picking up water from several tributaries (such as the Little Kamishak and Strike Creek) to become a fair-size river before it spills out on the mudflats of Akumwarvik Bay. The snow-covered peaks of Mount Douglas and nearby volcanic Mount Augustine enhance the rugged splendor of the surroundings, and the world famous bear habitat of the McNeil River State Game Sanctuary is only eight miles away.

The trick to fishing the Kamishak, as with all of these short coastal drainages, is getting in. Floatplane landings are perilous with the tides, and wheelplane access is limited to short gravel bars and beaches. Most of the angling effort occurs on the lower river, fishing the incoming tides for fresh salmon and charr, but excellent fishing and some access can be found along the middle section. Since the Kamishak is in an area with dense concentrations of brown bears, anglers should use extreme caution when wading smaller channels and hiking through the brush.

Guides' tip: The Kamishak (and some nearby drainages) is rumored to have a small run of fall steelhead.

㉓ Rocky River

Location: In the northwest Gulf of Alaska drainage, Kenai Peninsula, 145 miles southwest of Anchorage; see map page 266.

USGS map: Seldovia B-4.

How to get there: By boat or floatplane to the mouth of the river from the towns of Homer and Seldovia. Hiking upriver is possible. Floatplanes access the middle river via adjoining Rocky Lake.

Highlights: Excellent fishing for silver salmon (in the first half of September), pink salmon (from late July through early August), and Dolly Varden charr (from July through September); good fishing for red salmon (in the first half of August).

Species: Chum salmon, Dolly Varden, pink salmon, red salmon, silver salmon.

Regulations: King salmon fishing is prohibited. For additional restrictions, consult the current Alaska Department of Fish and Game sportfishing regulations or contact the ADF&G Soldotna office, (907) 262-9368.

Facilities: No developed public facilities.

Contact: For fishing information, contact the Anchor Angler Tackle Store, P.O. Box 84, Anchor Point, AK 99536; (907) 235-8351. For an air taxi, contact Homer Air, P.O. Box 302, Homer, AK 99603; (907) 235-8591. Note: The river is on native lands; camping permits are required. For details, contact the Port Graham Native Corporation, P.O. Box 5569, Port Graham, AK 99603-5569; (907) 284-2212.

Fishing the Rocky River: A small, pristine watershed on the southern tip of the Kenai Peninsula, just south of Kachemak Bay, Rocky River drains out of the Red Mountain area and runs a short distance south to Rocky Bay and the Gulf of Alaska. It's beautifully endowed, with thick surrounding forests, abundant wildlife, and water that is remarkably clear and deep, creating superb habitat for salmon and charr.

The lower river is the most productive and popular area to fish, working the big schools of anadromous fish that incoming tides push into the mouth and deep holes. The river's middle and upper sections are difficult to reach, except by helicopter or hiking, but have great opportunities for anglers willing to prospect. A drop-off by floatplane on Big Rocky Lake and a hike up the washed-out logging road that parallels the river is another possibility.

One of the best times of the year to visit this river is autumn (especially September), when trophy-size sea-run Dolly Varden charr (up to eight pounds) and big silver salmon (more than 15 pounds) lurk at the mouth and in the deep holes.

Note: Since the river is on native lands, a permit is required for camping. For more information, contact the Port Graham Native Corporation at (907) 284-2212.

㉔ Kachemak Bay

Location: Near the southwest Kenai Peninsula, 115 miles southwest of Anchorage; see map page 266.

USGS maps: Seldovia B-4, B-5, C-3, C-4, C-5, D-3, D-4.

How to get there: By car and boat. The most common point of access is from the town of Homer at the end of the Sterling Highway. The Homer Harbor provides boat launching facilities for anglers wishing to target fisheries in the bay and adjacent coves. Shore fishing is also possible.

Highlights: Road-accessible marine fishing (some of Alaska's best); excellent for king salmon (from late May through early June), silver salmon (from late August through early September), pink salmon (in the second half of July), and halibut (from mid-June through mid-August). Good fishing for red salmon (in the second half of July) and Dolly Varden charr (in May and June).

Species: Chum salmon, Dolly Varden, halibut, king salmon, pink salmon, red salmon, silver salmon.

Regulations: Halibut fishing is closed from January 1 through January 31. For additional restrictions, consult the current Alaska Department of Fish and Game sportfishing regulations or contact the ADF&G Soldotna office, (907) 262-9368.

Facilities: Lodging, groceries, gas, a boat rental, a boat launch, and guide services are available in the towns of Homer and Seldovia.

Contact: For guide services, contact Central Charters Booking Agency, 4241 Homer Spit Road, Homer, AK 99603, (907) 235-7847; Ci-Jae Charters, P.O. Box 380, Homer, AK 99603, (907) 235-5587; or Inlet Charters, P.O. Box 2083,

Homer, AK 99603, (907) 235-6126 or (800) 770-6126. For lodging information, contact the Coastal Alaska Wilderness Lodge, P.O. Box 110, Seldovia, AK 99663, (907) 234-7858; or the Lands End Resort, 4786 Homer Spit Road, Homer, AK 99603, (907) 235-0400 or (800) 478-0400.

Fishing Kachemak Bay: Beautiful Kachemak Bay, situated on the southern end of the Kenai Peninsula, is known for its diverse natural setting. Grassy bluffs and long sand beaches dominate the north side of the bay, while mountains, glaciers, deep valleys, and hidden coves characterize the rugged south side. With its relatively easy access, renowned fishing, and superlative marine environment, Kachemak, along with Resurrection Bay, attracts more visitors than almost any Alaska coastal destination.

The clear-greenish waters are home to both natural and enhanced runs of salmon, in addition to a rich assemblage of shellfish and bottomfish. Well-known fishing spots to consider include Homer Spit (king salmon, silver salmon, pink salmon, Dolly Varden) and Bluff Point (king salmon, halibut) on the north side and Halibut Cove/Lagoon (king salmon), Seldovia Bay (king salmon, silver salmon, pink salmon), Tutka Bay/Lagoon (pink salmon), China Poot Bay (red salmon), and Glacier Spit and Gull Island (halibut) on the south side. However, one can do quite well for salmon and charr fishing in or near stream mouths nearly anywhere in the bay and for halibut and bottomfish on shoals and reefs in deeper water. Trolling for feeder king salmon is good year-round, with some of the better fishing occurring in spring and fall.

Kachemak Bay is ideal for open skiffs, kayaks, and other small craft as well as for larger sportfishing vessels. It's a short run, about three to four miles straight across from Homer Harbor to the south side, where the majority of good angling occurs. Shore fishing is also productive, particularly in areas where enhanced salmon runs occur; try Homer Spit.

🄬 Anchor River

Location: In the southeast Cook Inlet drainage, Kenai Peninsula, 115 miles southwest of Anchorage; see map page 266.

USGS maps: Seldovia C-4, C-5, D-4, D-5.

How to get there: By car. The Sterling Highway offers several access points to the lower and middle river just north of the town of Homer, the most popular being in the vicinity of the town of Anchor Point.

Highlights: Excellent fishing for king salmon (in the first half of June) and Dolly Varden (from July through October). Good fishing for silver salmon (in the second half of August), pink salmon (from late July through early August), steelhead (from late September through October), and rainbow trout (from July through October).

Species: Dolly Varden, king salmon, pink salmon, rainbow trout, silver salmon, steelhead, *chum salmon, red salmon.*

Regulations: Catch-and-release fishing only for steelhead and rainbow trout. For additional restrictions, consult the current Alaska Department of Fish and Game sportfishing regulations or contact the ADF&G Soldotna office, (907) 262-9368.

Facilities: A campground, lodging, gas, groceries, sporting goods, and guide services are available in Anchor Point on the lower river.

Contact: For fishing and guide services, contact the Anchor Angler Tackle Store, P.O. Box 84, Anchor Point, AK 99536; (907) 235-8351. For lodging information, contact the Anchor River Inn, P.O. Box 154, Anchor Point, AK 99556; (907) 235-8531.

Fishing Anchor River: This small clearwater stream is known for its runs of steelhead trout—some of the best in Southcentral Alaska—along with outstanding fishing for king and silver salmon. Just north of Kachemak Bay, its close proximity to Anchorage gives it a high amount of seasonal use.

The river begins in a broad valley north of Bald Mountain and flows approximately 34 miles before emptying into Cook Inlet 16 miles northwest of Homer. Shallow and rocky for most of its length, the typically clear Anchor turns a chocolaty brown after spells of rain.

The lower river is open to salmon fishing, and it is especially popular in early summer when the king salmon arrive. The mouth of the river also serves as a launch point for boaters seeking salmon and halibut in the adjoining marine waters. For fresh runs of salmon (as well as steelhead trout and Dolly Varden in season), fish the incoming tides. The Anchor's steelhead start to appear in late August most years, peaking in numbers by early October. Fishing stays good into November, provided the weather cooperates. The fish overwinter in the river, spawn in spring, and then return to sea. Recent years have seen a rebound of the Anchor's wild steelhead stocks and some excellent fall fishing.

During late summer and fall, the middle and upper river also support high numbers of Dolly Varden, along with resident rainbows. With a little hiking, anglers can enjoy a measure of solitude and classic stream fishing conditions.

㉖ Lower Cook Inlet

Location: Near the southwest Kenai Peninsula, 100 miles southwest of Anchorage; see map page 266.

USGS maps: Kenai A-4, A-5, B-4; Seldovia A-5, A-6, B-6, D-5.

How to get there: Mostly by boat, although it can be fished by surf casting. Several points along the Sterling Highway offer launches; check between Ninilchik Village and Anchor Point. The mouths of the Ninilchik and Anchor Rivers, Deep Creek, and surrounding beaches, including Whiskey Gulch, are the most popular locations.

Highlights: Excellent marine inshore fishing for king salmon (from mid-May through early June and in early July) and halibut (from June through August). Good fishing for silver salmon (in early August and early September), pink salmon (in late July), and Dolly Varden charr (from May through June).

Species: Dolly Varden, halibut, king salmon, pink salmon, red salmon, silver salmon, *chum salmon, steelhead*.

Regulations: Fishing for halibut is closed from January 1 through January 31; catch-and-release only for steelhead trout. For additional restrictions, consult the current Alaska Department of Fish and Game sportfishing regulations or contact the ADF&G Soldotna office, (907) 262-9368.

Facilities: Lodging, campgrounds, tackle, groceries, gas, and a guide service are available along the Sterling Highway.

Contact: For camping and fishing information, contact the Anchor Angler Tackle Store, P.O. Box 84, Anchor Point, AK 99536; (907) 235-8351. For guide services, contact Alasking Charters, 3507 Willow Place, Apartment C, Anchorage, AK 99517, (907) 243-0564; Central Charters Booking Agency, 4241 Homer Spit Road, Homer, AK 99603, (907) 235-7847; Reel 'Em Inn, Cook Inlet Charters, P.O. Box 39292, Ninilchik, AK 99603 (in summer), 13641 Venus Way, Anchorage, AK 99515 (in winter), (907) 345-3887; or R.W.'s Fishing, P.O. Box 3824, Soldotna, AK 99669, (907) 262-7888 or (800) 478-6900.

Fishing Lower Cook Inlet: Cook Inlet mixes chill gray glacier runoff with the clear-greenish Pacific Ocean, stirring in strong tides and unpredictable weather. Despite the daunting waters, fishing off the surf-swept beaches and bluffs along the western Kenai Peninsula can be outstanding. Besides, the setting is magnificent. On clear days, the inlet mirrors the snowcapped peaks of Mount Redoubt and Iliamna, two active volcanoes of Alaska's "Ring of Fire."

Lower Cook Inlet also serves as a migration corridor for countless fish bound for the Kenai Peninsula, streams on the west side of the inlet, and the immense Susitna River drainage to the north. Salmon fishing is often fast and furious during the peak of the runs, with most anglers opting to troll along the beaches and near stream mouths from Ninilchik south to Anchor Point.

This area is noted for its trophy king salmon and halibut fisheries, with record catches not uncommon. Halibut up to 300 or 350 pounds or more and kings of 70 to 80 pounds plus have been caught (commercial fishermen have even reported catching fish well over 100 pounds). There are two runs each of king salmon, silver salmon, and red salmon. Although the action is usually best during the early runs, the late runs have larger fish. Red salmon are the most abundant of the three, but due to their reluctance to strike hardware, fishing for them is seldom better than fair. Better locations for salmon in the lower Cook Inlet include areas near the Ninilchik

River, Deep Creek, Stariski Creek, Anchor Point/ River, The Falls, Whiskey Gulch, and Happy Valley.

Halibut fishing is outstanding in summer, with these gargantuan flatfish hitting best at slack high and low tide a few miles offshore on shoals and reefs just about anywhere along the coast of the Kenai Peninsula. Try the Barren and Chugach Islands around Kennedy Entrance at the mouth of the inlet in early season.

㉗ Kasilof River System

Location: In the east Cook Inlet drainage, Kenai Peninsula, 75 miles southwest of Anchorage; see map page 266.

USGS map: Kenai A-2, A-3, A-4, B-3, B-4.

How to get there: By car, from the Sterling Highway just south of Soldotna. Side roads access the lower river and its confluence with Crooked Creek and the upper river and the Tustumena Lake outlet.

Highlights: An immensely popular road-accessible stream fishery; excellent for king salmon (in the first half of June) and silver salmon (from mid-August through early September). Good fishing for Dolly Varden charr (from August through September).

Species: Dolly Varden, king salmon, lake trout, pink salmon, red salmon, silver salmon, steelhead, *chum salmon*.

Regulations: King salmon fishing is closed from August 1 through December 31. For additional restrictions, consult the current Alaska Department of Fish and Game sportfishing regulations or contact the ADF&G Soldotna office, (907) 262-9368.

Facilities: A campground and a boat launch are located on the river. Lodging, guide services, and a grocery store are available on the highway nearby.

Contact: For guide services, contact Alasking Charters, 3507 Willow Place, Apartment C, Anchorage, AK 99517, (907) 243-0564; R.W.'s Fishing, P.O. Box 3824, Soldotna, AK 99669, (907) 262-7888 or (800) 478-6900; the Timberline Guide Service, P.O. Box 32, Soldotna, AK 99669, (907) 262-4170 or (907) 561-3037. For lodging information, contact the Kenai River Lodge, 393 Riverside Drive, Soldotna, AK 99969; (907) 262-4292.

Fishing the Kasilof River System: The greenish-gray Kasilof River drains the glacially turbid waters of Tustumena Lake (the Kenai Peninsula's largest lake) at the base of the Kenai Mountains. It provides a fairly significant amount of sportfishing in its lower reaches and clear-water tributaries and is easily accessed from Anchorage. Most anglers fish from the Sterling Highway bridge downstream to the confluence with clear Crooked Creek, a major salmon spawning tributary. Fishing is equally productive from the bank or from a raft or driftboat.

During the month of June, when the kings are in heavy, the Kasilof becomes one of the most popular fisheries in all of Southcentral Alaska. Two runs enter the Kasilof, the first in May and June, the second in July and August. The first is comprised of both wild and hatchery fish and is by far the stronger of the two. The late run is much weaker in strength but produces larger fish—60 and 70 pounds or more. Silver salmon, which show in good numbers in late summer and fall, are targeted primarily at the mouth and lower sections of Crooked Creek. The Kasilof also has the distinction of sustaining the northernmost natural population of steelhead trout in Cook Inlet, as a small run of these flashy fighters returns every fall to spawn in Crooked Creek the following spring.

The Kasilof system, including Tustumena Lake and its tributaries, ranks among the leading producers of red salmon in Cook Inlet, but because of its milky nature, it does not have productive sportfishing. However, there's really fine fishing for Dolly Varden charr, which feed on the smolt and eggs (especially in the fall and spring) at the outlet and mouths of the clear-water tributaries along Tustumena Lake. (Accessing by boat is treacherous, due to potentially swamping winds and submerged rocks in the lake and river.) Fair to good lake trout fishing also occurs near the outlet in spring.

Guides' tip: The extremely turbid waters of the Tustumena and Kasilof River system call for maximum size, flash, and color in your lure presentations. Fishing bait, as a teaser or alone, will give you the needed edge in these conditions.

㉘ Lower Kenai River System

Location: In the east Cook Inlet drainage, Kenai Peninsula, 50 miles southwest of Anchorage; see map page 266.

USGS maps: Kenai A-1, B-1, B-2, B-3, B-4, C-1, C-2, C-3, C-4.

How to get there: By car and boat. The Sterling Highway (via Anchorage) more or less parallels the river from Skilak Lake down to the mouth, offering extensive access. Many pulloffs, gravel roads, and trails lead to viable waters in the system. Major access points include the towns of Sterling, Soldotna, and Kenai.

Highlights: Alaska's monster king fishery; excellent fishing for silver salmon (in the second half of August and from late September through early October), red salmon (in the second half of July), and Dolly Varden charr (from July through October). Good fishing for king salmon (in the first half of June and second half of July) and rainbow trout (from July through October).

Species: Dolly Varden, king salmon, lake trout, rainbow trout, red salmon, silver salmon, *chum salmon, northern pike*.

Regulations: King salmon fishing is closed from August 1 through December 31 unless otherwise noted. For additional restrictions, consult the current Alaska Department of Fish and Game sportfishing regulations or contact the ADF&G Soldotna office, (907) 262-9368.

Facilities: Lodging, gas, groceries, sporting goods, guide services, boat rentals and launching, and campgrounds are available in nearby towns.

Contact: For guide services, contact R.W.'s Fishing, P.O. Box 3824, Soldotna, AK 99669, (907) 262-7888 or (800) 478-6900; Salmon Chaser Charters, P.O. Box 654, Soldotna, AK 99669, (907) 262-9681; or Timberline Guide Service, P.O. Box 32, Soldotna, AK 99669, (907) 262-4170 or (907) 561-3037. For lodging information, contact the Great Alaska Fish Camp, HC 01, Box 218, Sterling, AK 99672, (907) 262-4515; or Kenai River Lodge, 393 Riverside Drive, Soldotna, AK 99969, (907) 262-4292.

Fishing the Lower Kenai River System: The most popular sportfishery in Alaska and perhaps the most famous salmon river in all the world, the bluish-green Kenai is the queen of Alaska's rivers. Easy access, incomparable trophy fishing, and abundant salmon runs are the main attractions, especially in the lower river, which begins at glacial Skilak Lake and flows 50 miles west to Cook Inlet, through spruce-cottonwood forests and rolling hills.

Unlike most of the state's rivers, the Kenai receives two distinct waves, or runs, of king, silver, and red salmon each year. Early run king and red salmon invade the river in May and June, with the first silver salmon run during July and August. The second run of kings and reds happens in July and August, while silver salmon numbers peak again in September and October.

Above all, the Kenai River is noted for its mammoth strain of king salmon. The current International Game Fish Association (IGFA) world record for a sport-caught fish—weighing more than 97 pounds—was taken near Soldotna in 1985, and larger kings of more than 100 pounds have been confirmed. The largest sport-caught fish each summer invariably go 80 to 95 pounds, with many weighing more than 60 and 70 pounds. The Kenai system has also produced numerous world records (IGFA "All Tackle," "line," and "fly rod tippet" classes) for red and pink salmon and Dolly Varden charr, as well as a good share of Alaska's largest trophy rainbows. (See the rainbow trout chapter on page 97.)

The lower Kenai remains partially ice-free in winter, with open-water angling possible from the outlet of Skilak Lake to a few miles downstream. A late run of silver salmon might yield bright fish beyond New Year's, and Dolly Varden are almost always present. The late-running salmon also lure many bald eagles to feed on carcasses, so bring binoculars. Several tributary streams and lakes along the lower river are also worth fishing.

Prime local fishing spots include the Moose River (king salmon, silver salmon, red salmon, pink salmon, rainbow trout, Dolly Varden), East Fork of the Moose River (rainbow trout), Killey River (silver salmon, pink salmon, rainbow trout, Dolly Varden), Funny River (silver salmon, pink salmon, rainbow trout, Dolly Varden), Beaver Creek (rainbow trout, Dolly Varden), King County Creek (silver salmon, red salmon, rainbow trout,

Dolly Varden), Kelly Lake (rainbow trout), Peterson Lake (rainbow trout), Egumen Lake (rainbow trout), Watson Lake (rainbow trout), Afonas Lake (rainbow trout), Loon Lake (rainbow trout), Grebe Lake (rainbow trout), Longmere Lake (rainbow trout), Scout Lake (landlocked salmon), Sport Lake (rainbow trout), Union Lake (rainbow trout, landlocked salmon), and Arc Lake (landlocked salmon).

Guides' tip: The majority of angling for king and silver salmon takes place on the far lower river below the Soldotna bridge. Both private and guide boats, as well as a few bank fishermen, actively fish the area on the incoming tides using attractor lures with or without salmon roe. Back trolling and drifting are the most popular methods for kings, while anchoring up and still fishing is best for silvers, especially when soaking salmon eggs. The red salmon hug the riverbanks and are particularly susceptible in the stretch of water from Soldotna bridge upstream to the Killey River. Good numbers of trophy rainbow trout and sea-run Dolly Varden are taken in the first few miles of river from the Skilak Lake outlet to the mouth of the Funny River.

㉙ Swanson River System

Location: In the northeast Cook Inlet drainage, Kenai Peninsula, 40 miles southwest of Anchorage; see map page 266.

USGS maps: Kenai C-2, C-3, D-2, D-3.

How to get there: By car. One of the two major points of access is on the middle river, off Swanson River Road from the Sterling Highway, especially among anglers putting in with canoes to reach the upper river or connecting lakes. The second, on the lower river where the Swanson dumps into Cook Inlet, can be reached via the Kenai Spur and Sterling Highways.

Highlights: Excellent fishing for silver salmon (from mid-August through early September); good fishing for rainbow trout (from June through October) and Dolly Varden charr (from July through October).

Species: Dolly Varden, lake trout, pink salmon, rainbow trout, red salmon, silver salmon, *king salmon*.

Regulations: King salmon fishing is prohibited. For additional restrictions, consult the cur-

rent Alaska Department of Fish and Game sportfishing regulations or contact the ADF&G Soldotna office, (907) 262-9368.

Facilities: A campground sits at the mouth of the river. Lodging, gas, groceries, and sporting goods are available on the road system nearby.

Contact: For fishing information, contact the Alaska Department of Fish and Game, Sportfish Division, P.O. Box 3150, Soldotna, AK 99669; (907) 262-9368. For camping information, contact the Public Lands Information Center, 605 West Fourth Avenue, Suite 105, Anchorage, AK 99501; (907) 271-2737.

Fishing the Swanson River System: Although fairly small and slow moving, the Swanson River drains a large area of lowland lakes and swamps in the northern Kenai Peninsula. More than 35 lakes connect to the Swanson system through tiny streams or short portages, many of them with good fishing for rainbow trout, Dolly Varden charr, and landlocked silver salmon.

Canoeists trying to reach the Swanson River Canoe Route can do so easily from Swan Lake Road via the Swanson River Road (put in at Paddle Lake). A canoe trip can last anywhere from several days to one week. The Swanson can also be accessed at midriver from the end of Swanson River Road; from there down to the mouth, it's an easy two-day float and fish trip. Except for some slight rapids near the mouth, most of the water is flat. Takeout is at the Captain Cook Recreation Area, about 36 miles north of the town of Kenai.

Several salmon species spawn in the drainage, but the silvers provide more fishing action on the Swanson. You may encounter large schools of these fine fighters throughout the river (especially around the confluences of streams and adjoining lakes) from late summer into fall, but your best bet is to fish the lower river during incoming tides.

㉚ Upper Kenai River System

Location: In the east Cook Inlet drainage, Kenai Peninsula, 50 miles south of Anchorage; see map page 266.

USGS maps: Seward B-6, B-7, B-8, C-6, C-7, C-8; Kenai B-1.

How to get there: By car and boat. From Anchorage, take the Sterling and Seward Highways to the upper section of the Kenai River and its tributaries. The Sterling Highway parallels the river's main stem most of its length and crosses it twice. Boats or rafts may be launched from several places to reach the river's more inaccessible areas; from the road you'll see numerous pull-offs and trails.

Highlights: Alaska's number one salmon/trout river fishery; excellent for red salmon (in the second half of June and late July through early August). Good fishing for silver salmon (from late August through early September and in the first half of October), rainbow trout (from July through October), and Dolly Varden charr (from July through October).

Species: Dolly Varden, grayling, kokanee, lake trout, pink salmon, rainbow trout, red salmon, silver salmon, *chum salmon.*

Regulations: King salmon fishing is prohibited. For additional restrictions, consult the current Alaska Department of Fish and Game sportfishing regulations or contact the ADF&G Soldotna office, (907) 262-9368.

Facilities: Lodging, gas, groceries, sporting goods, guide services, campgrounds, and boat launching are available along the highway in the Cooper Landing area.

Contact: For guide services, contact the Alaska River Company, P.O. Box 827, Cooper Landing, AK 99572, (907) 595-1226; or the Alaska Trout Fitters, Mile 50 Sterling Highway, Cooper Landing, AK 99572, (907) 595-1557. For lodging information, contact the Kenai Lake Lodge, P.O. Box 828, Cooper Landing, AK 99572; (907) 595-1590.

Fishing the Upper Kenai River System: The lovely upper Kenai River, with its emerald waters, scenic mountains, and forests, has a phenomenally productive fishery and a real wilderness character that, despite high use, continues to thrill and amaze newcomers and seasoned Alaskans alike.

Rising from runoff streams and creeks in the Kenai Mountains, the river issues from the outlet of Kenai Lake and flows swiftly west toward Cook Inlet. Most of the river from the lake down is Class I water perfectly suited for drift fishing in boats or rafts. In the last few miles before Skilak Lake, the river enters a canyon with Class III water, which experienced boaters only should negotiate.

Like the lower Kenai, the upper river gets two distinct runs of king salmon, silver salmon, and red salmon but is currently closed for king salmon fishing. Silvers are available in August through September and again in October through November. Red salmon appear in abundance during June and again in July and August, creating some of Alaska's best fishing for the species (especially at Russian River—see the description on page 295). Another feature unique to the upper Kenai is that it remains ice-free throughout winter—even during temperatures of 20 below or colder—thus creating a small fishery for charr and a winter run of silver salmon.

The upper Kenai also boasts some of Alaska's best trophy water for rainbow trout and Dolly Varden charr, especially during September and October. Other angling opportunities in the system include Trail Lake (rainbow trout, lake trout, Dolly Varden), Hidden Lake (kokanee, rainbow trout, lake trout, Dolly Varden), Cooper Lake (rainbow trout, Dolly Varden), Vagt Lake (rainbow trout), Grant Lake (rainbow trout), Jean Lake (rainbow trout), Daves Creek (rainbow trout, Dolly Varden), Quartz Creek (Dolly Varden), Hidden Creek (red salmon, rainbow trout, Dolly Varden), Crescent Lake (grayling), Ptarmigan Creek (rainbow trout, Dolly Varden), Grant Creek (Dolly Varden, silver salmon), and Trail River (rainbow trout, Dolly Varden).

Guides' tip: The upper Kenai has some of the best fly-fishing opportunities for trophy rainbow trout and Dolly Varden in Southcentral. The main river between Kenai and Skilak Lakes is designated a Trophy Trout and Charr Area, with catches up to 10 or 12 pounds not unusual. Autumn is the best time using egg-imitations, flesh flies, and attractors, but dry fly–fishing is gaining more recognition with excellent results during certain parts of the season.

㉛ Russian River System

Location: In the east Cook Inlet drainage, Kenai Peninsula, 50 miles south of Anchorage; see map page 266.

USGS map: Seward B-8.

How to get there: By car and floatplane. A trail system allows anglers to access any part of the Russian River from its headwaters at Upper Russian Lake down to the mouth on the Kenai, but it is most commonly accessed from the Sterling Highway at Cooper Landing.

Highlights: World famous road-accessible salmon locale; excellent for red salmon (in late June and from late July through early August). Good fishing for silver salmon (from late August through early September), rainbow trout (from June through September), and Dolly Varden charr (from August through September).

Species: Dolly Varden, king salmon, pink salmon, rainbow trout, red salmon, silver salmon, *grayling*.

Regulations: King salmon fishing is prohibited; catch-and-release fishing only for rainbow trout. For additional restrictions, carefully consult the current Alaska Department of Fish and Game sportfishing regulations or contact the ADF&G Soldotna office, (907) 262-9368.

Facilities: A Forest Service campground is located close to the mouth of the river. The nearby community of Cooper Landing has lodging, gas, groceries, and sporting goods stores. Forest Service cabins are available on Upper and Lower Russian Lakes and on the section of river between the two lakes.

Contact: For lodging information, contact the Kenai Lake Lodge, P.O. Box 828, Cooper Landing, AK 99572; (907) 595-1590. For more information on Forest Service cabins and campgrounds, contact Chugach National Forest, 201 East Ninth Avenue, Anchorage, AK 99501-3698; (907) 271-2500.

Fishing the Russian River System: The Russian River, a major clear-water tributary of the upper Kenai River, provides a readily accessible stream fishery for salmon in Southcentral Alaska. From its headwaters high in the Kenai Mountains, it flows swift and shallow through a narrow valley lined with spruce and cottonwood, forming two major lakes along the way—the Upper and Lower Russian. Trails follow the river's entire length (12 miles), from the upper lake to the Kenai confluence, providing for superlative hiking and access to remote stretches of water.

The Russian draws anglers with a combination of clear-water sight-fishing, easy access, and huge schools of salmon (sockeye and silver) that invade every summer. The first of two large runs of red salmon enters the river in June, the second in July and August, followed by a smaller and much less fished run of silver salmon in August and September. It's total carnival-style fishing (at the river mouth) during the peak of the sockeye run, but perfect conditions for taking the normally tight-lipped salmon on a fly, so most folks get their limit (three fish).

In late summer and fall, rainbow trout and charr fishing heats up in the lower sections of the Russian near spawning salmon, but it can be good as well in the upper river (from the Upper Russian Lake outlet down, for example). Anglers seldom try the lakes' small tributary streams, but they can also provide good fishing for trout and charr in early summer and fall. Since the Russian River sees an enormous amount of spawning activity in August and September, watch for brown and black bears, particularly along the upper river and near the campground. Use caution when fishing and tramping through the brush along the banks, especially in early morning and late evening.

Note: The Russian was one of the first Alaska streams to see successful techniques for fly-fishing sockeyes. See the chapter on red salmon on page 51 for details on methods, gear, and flies.

㉜ Portage Area River Systems

Location: In the northeast Cook Inlet drainages, Turnagain Arm, 45 miles southeast of Anchorage; see map page 266.

USGS map: Seward D-6.

How to get there: By car. From Anchorage, the Seward Highway crosses the lower river systems near tidewater. Most upstream access is by boat, equipped with a jet unit, although canoeists can paddle to nearby tributaries and sloughs. Dense vegetation makes hiking difficult. Rafting is possible on Portage Creek from Portage Lake down to the Seward Highway bridge, a four-hour trip.

Highlights: Excellent fishing for silver salmon (from mid-August through mid-September); good fishing for pink salmon (from late July through early August) and Dolly Varden (from July through October).

Species: Chum salmon, Dolly Varden, pink salmon, red salmon, silver salmon, *king salmon*.

Regulations: King salmon fishing is prohibited. For additional restrictions, consult the current Alaska Department of Fish and Game sportfishing regulations or contact the ADF&G Anchorage office, (907) 267-2218.

Facilities: Primitive boat launches are available on the Twentymile and Placer Rivers.

Contact: For fishing information, contact the Alaska Department of Fish and Game Regional Office, Sportfish Division, 333 Raspberry Road, Anchorage, AK 99518-1599; (907) 267-2218.

Fishing the Portage Area River Systems: The Portage area at the head of Turnagain Arm has three drainages of glacial origin—the Twentymile, Portage, and Placer Rivers—all within Chugach National Forest. The lower river sections are in open country, where the gray stems of dead spruce trees serve as stark reminders of the 1964 earthquake. (The once flourishing forest subsided during the quake and flooded with salt water, killing much of the vegetation.) The setting is spectacular, especially on sunny days, as surrounding mountain peaks showcase greenish-blue glaciers, while a thick spruce forest covers the slopes.

The Twentymile River, the larger of the three systems, originates from ice fields around Twentymile Glacier in the Chugach Mountains, running southward to Turnagain Arm. The lower section near the Seward Highway is wide and slow but becomes quite swift, shallow, and braided six to seven miles upstream. The main species in the Twentymile are silver, red, and chum salmon and Dolly Varden charr.

Draining out of Portage Lake at the base of world famous Portage Glacier, Portage Creek flows east to silty Turnagain Arm, fairly fast through most of its length, but particularly so on the upper end. Good runs of silver, red, chum, and pink salmon mark this drainage, along with some Dolly Varden.

The Placer River originates from the Spencer Glacier and flows north. The slow moving lower river becomes shallow, fast, and braided about two and a half miles upstream from the highway bridge. Placer is known for its strong late run of silver salmon, some of which weigh up to 18 pounds. Other interesting species include red salmon and Dolly Varden.

On all three systems, look for clear-water sloughs and stream mouths to target schools of migrating salmon and hungry charr. Keep in mind that many of these spots do not have names, but are nonetheless very productive.

Chugach Mountains/ Prince William Sound

The Chugach area, for our purposes, includes the drainages and marine waters along the Gulf of Alaska from the Copper River Delta area to western Prince William Sound. A rich and unexploited coastal paradise, this region has tremendous potential, from some of the mainland's best halibut and silver salmon to cutthroat trout.

㉝ Resurrection Bay

Location: Off the North Gulf Coast, 75 miles south of Anchorage; see map page 266.

USGS maps: Seward A-7; Blying Sound C-7, D-7.

How to get there: By car. The Seward Highway connects Anchorage to the coastal community of Seward, terminating at the head of Resurrection Bay. Shore fishing is popular around Seward, with the greater fishery occurring in the boat-accessible outer waters of the bay.

Highlights: One of the best road-accessible marine fishing locations in Alaska. Excellent fishing for silver salmon (from mid- through late

August), pink salmon (from late July through early August), and halibut (from June through August); also good fishing for king salmon (in the first half of June and early August) and Dolly Varden (from June through July).

Species: Chum salmon, Dolly Varden, halibut, king salmon, pink salmon, red salmon, silver salmon.

Regulations: Lingcod fishing is prohibited. For additional restrictions, consult the current Alaska Department of Fish and Game sportfishing regulations or contact the ADF&G Soldotna office, (907) 262-9368.

Facilities: Lodging, motels, gas, guide services, boat rentals and a launch, groceries, and sporting goods are available in Seward.

Contact: For guide services, contact Excellent Adventures, P.O. Box 467, Seward, AK 99664, (907) 224-2030; Mariah Charters and Tours, 3812 Katmai Circle, Anchorage, AK 99517-1024, (907) 224-8623 (in summer) or (907) 243-1238 (in winter); Sablefish Charters, P.O. Box 1588, Seward, AK 99664, (907) 224-3283; or Saltwater Safari Company, P.O. Box 241225, Anchorage, AK 99524, (907) 277-3223 or (800) 382-1564. For lodging, contact The Breeze Inn, P.O. Box 2147, Seward, AK 99664; (907) 224-5237.

Fishing Resurrection Bay: Located at the north end of Blying Sound along coastal Kenai Peninsula, Resurrection Bay is a greenish-clear fjord with several glacial and clear-water streams emptying into it. Although the area receives its share of bad weather from the Gulf of Alaska, the surrounding mountain ridges keep the bay fairly protected. Thick forests, mountains, snowfields, and glaciers make it particularly scenic. Sea otters, whales, waterfowl, eagles, and even an occasional bear or moose enhance the overall experience for anglers.

Excellent fishing for salmon and Dolly Varden charr and halibut, plus easy access and a world famous silver salmon derby in August, make Seward one of Alaska's most visited destinations. Fishing from shore—docks, beaches, points, and stream mouths—is popular and productive, especially during the peak of the runs. (Occasionally, anglers fishing from deepwater docks in front of town take halibut up to 85 pounds or more.)

Boaters definitely have the edge for accessing the best fishing. During the early part of the season, the outer bay is most productive for salmon, with the rest of the area's waters competing as summer progresses. Feeder kings and large halibut are taken only in the outer bay area. Trolling bait is the preferred method for kings and silvers, with some mooching, jigging, and casting done at times when feeding is concentrated. Look for jumpers and feeding seabirds for sure signs of fish.

Some proven angling spots include: the Seward Harbor area (king salmon, silver salmon, pink salmon), the mouths of Lowell Creek (king salmon, pink salmon) and Fourth of July Creek (silver salmon, chum salmon, pink salmon); Lowell Point (silver salmon, pink salmon, Dolly Varden) and Tonsina Point (chum salmon, pink salmon, Dolly Varden); Caines and Callisto Heads (silver salmon); Thumb Cove (pink salmon, silver salmon), Humpy Cove (silver salmon, pink salmon), Pony Cove (silver salmon), Agnes Cove (silver salmon), Porcupine Cove (silver salmon), and Bulldog Cove (silver salmon); Aialik Cape (king salmon, halibut), Granite Cape (halibut), and Resurrection Cape (halibut); Eldorado Narrows (king salmon, silver salmon); and Rugged Island (king salmon, silver salmon) and Chiswell Island (halibut).

㉞ Nellie Martin/ Patton Rivers

Location: In the southeast Montague Island drainage, 120 miles southeast of Anchorage; see map page 266.

USGS maps: Blying Sound D-1, D-2.

How to get there: By wheelplane from Seward or Cordova. Land on the beach area around the mouth of the river or along Patton Bay at low tide. Although the river is within reasonable boating distance, the weather can be hazardous for small craft.

Highlights: Excellent fishing for silver salmon (from late August through early September) and pink salmon (in the second half of July); also good fishing for Dolly Varden charr (in July and August).

Species: Dolly Varden, pink salmon, silver salmon, *cutthroat trout, red salmon.*

Regulations: Open year-round, all species.

Facilities: A Forest Service cabin is available on the river.

Contact: For an air taxi, contact Ketchum Air Service, P.O. Box 190588, Anchorage, AK 99519, (907) 243-5525 or (800) 433-9114. For cabin rentals, contact Chugach National Forest, 201 East Ninth Avenue, Suite 206, Anchorage, AK 99501; (907) 271-2500.

Fishing Nellie Martin/Patton Rivers: The Nellie Martin/Patton Rivers of southern Montague Island are popular destinations for fly-in anglers, with some of the best silver salmon fishing in Prince William Sound (abundant runs, with fish up to 18 pounds), along with large numbers of pink salmon and Dolly Varden charr. Crystal clear, with gravel and sand bottoms, long runs, and deep pools, the rivers offer great fly- and spin casting possibilities.

The mouth and lower sections of both rivers are the most popular and productive areas to fish, especially on the rising tide, but Patton Bay offers good skiff fishing for silver and pink salmon as well as halibut. Anglers planning a trip to these rivers should allow several days in their schedule for the possibility of bad weather and travel delays. A 12-foot-by-14-foot Forest Service cabin is available for public use half a mile from the beach.

㉟ Montague Strait

Location: In south Prince William Sound, 100 miles southeast of Anchorage; see map page 266.

USGS maps: Seward A-1, A-2, A-3, B-1, B-2, B-3, C-2; Blying Sound D-1, D-2, D-3, D-4.

How to get there: By boat or floatplane from Anchorage, Whittier, Seward, or Cordova. (Boats are recommended since the majority of sportfishing in this area is done offshore.) Wheelplane access is possible along beaches.

Highlights: One of the best marine locations in Prince William Sound; excellent fishing for silver salmon (in the second half of August), pink salmon (in the second half of July), and halibut (from June through August).

Species: Cutthroat trout, Dolly Varden, halibut, pink salmon, silver salmon, *chum salmon*.

Regulations: Halibut fishing is prohibited from January 1 through 31. For additional restrictions, consult the current Alaska Department of Fish and Game sportfishing regulations or contact the ADF&G Anchorage office, (907) 267-2218.

Facilities: Cabins are available on Montague and Green Islands.

Contact: For guide services, contact the Saltwater Safari Company, P.O. Box 241225, Anchorage, AK 99524; (907) 277-3223 or (800) 382-1564. For an air taxi, contact Ketchum Air Service, P.O. Box 190588, Anchorage, AK 99519, (907) 243-5525 or (800) 433-9114; or Rusts Flying Service, P.O. Box 190325, Anchorage, AK 99519, (907) 243-1595 or (800) 544-2299. For cabin rentals, contact Chugach National Forest, 201 East Ninth Avenue, Suite 206, Anchorage, AK 99501; (907) 271-2500.

Fishing Montague Strait: Montague Strait is a long, wide passage on the southern end of Prince William Sound, between Montague, Knight, and Latouche Islands. Along with Hinchinbrook Entrance, Montague serves as a major migration corridor for salmon bound for streams deep inside the sound. There are several major bays, ports, and harbors, but the strait lacks the abundance of cutting fjords and islands that characterize most of western Prince William Sound, and is more open and susceptible to bad weather.

Montague Strait has long been known for some of the best halibut action in Prince William Sound. The fish here are much larger than those inside the sound, with trophies up to 250 pounds or more not uncommon. Waters near bays containing salmon streams, or around small islands, points, and sandy shoals, are favorable locations to find these behemoths, along with other bottomfish species such as rockfish and lingcod.

Although large numbers of salmon pass through the strait, relatively few streams in the area contain substantial runs. Creeks here are typically shallow, short, and clear, with small numbers of pink and silver salmon and some Dolly Varden. Fair action for cutthroat trout may be had in a few streams on Montague Island.

Green and Montague Islands both have 12-foot-by-14-foot Forest Service cabins available for public use. A boat or some type of watercraft is almost a necessity to access the best fishing, but surf casting is fairly productive near the mouths of salmon spawning streams, particularly those on the southern half of Montague Island.

Good angling spots to explore include: Knight Island/Bay of Isles (silver salmon, halibut); Green Island (Dolly Varden, halibut); and Port Chalmers (silver salmon, pink salmon, cutthroat trout, Dolly Varden), Montague Point (halibut), Hanning Bay (Dolly Varden, pink salmon), MacLeod Harbor (pink salmon, Dolly Varden), Cape Cleare (halibut), and San Juan Bay (silver salmon, pink salmon, Dolly Varden) on Montague Island.

36 Knight Island Passage

Location: In west Prince William Sound, 90 miles southeast of Anchorage; see map page 266.

USGS maps: Seward A-3, A-4, B-3, B-4, C-2, C-3.

How to get there: By floatplane or boat from Anchorage, Seward, Whittier, or Valdez, to various lagoons, coves, beaches, and bays. (Small crafts such as pleasure boats and kayaks can be used in these sheltered waters.)

Highlights: Excellent fishing for pink salmon (in July) and halibut (from June through August); good fishing for silver and red salmon (in the first half of August), chum salmon (in the second half of July), and Dolly Varden (in May and June).

Species: Chum salmon, cutthroat trout, Dolly Varden, halibut, pink salmon, red salmon, silver salmon.

Regulations: Halibut fishing is prohibited from January 1 through 31. For additional restrictions, consult the current Alaska Department of Fish and Game sportfishing regulations or contact the ADF&G Anchorage office, (907) 267-2218.

Facilities: No developed public facilities.

Contact: For an air taxi, contact Ketchum Air Service, P.O. Box 190588, Anchorage, AK 99519, (907) 243-5525 or (800) 433-9114; or Rusts Flying Service, P.O. Box 190325, Anchorage, AK 99519, (907) 243-1595 or (800) 544-2299.

Fishing Knight Island Passage: Located on the west side of Prince William Sound between the eastern Kenai Peninsula and Knight, Chenega, Bainbridge, Evans, and Latouche Islands, the passage has dozens of bays, coves, clear-water streams, and lakes. It offers a variety of fishing, including four species of salmon, charr, and bottomfish, and plenty of opportunities to set out pots for crab and shrimp. Thick spruce forests and an amazing variety of marine animals enhance the overall experience. Protected from strong winds and high seas, the area is ideal for small crafts such as pleasure boats and kayaks.

Although surf casting can be highly productive, mooching or trolling for salmon or jigging for halibut from boats are the preferred ways of fishing most of the passage. Though not as big as fish taken from other parts of the state—they average only 15 to 20 pounds—the plentiful halibut of western Prince William Sound are nonetheless worth a try, especially on light tackle. Salmon, although present throughout the passage, are more commonly encountered near spawning streams, so anglers should wisely select bays and coves with streams to maximize their chances for success.

Top Knight Island Passage angling spots include: Main Bay (chum salmon, pink salmon, Dolly Varden, halibut), Ewan Bay (chum salmon, pink salmon, Dolly Varden, halibut), Jackpot Bay (silver salmon, pink salmon, cutthroat trout, Dolly Varden, halibut), Eshamy Bay (silver salmon, chum salmon, pink salmon, Dolly Varden, halibut), and Eshamy Lagoon (silver salmon, red salmon, chum salmon, pink salmon, cutthroat trout, Dolly Varden). Anglers who explore a bit can find many locations that offer great fishing with virtually no pressure.

37 Wells Passage Area

Location: In northwest Prince William Sound, 65 miles east of Anchorage; see map page 266.

USGS maps: Anchorage A-2, A-3, A-4, B-2; Seward C-3, C-4, C-5, D-3, D-4, D-5.

How to get there: By boat or kayak from the town of Whittier through Passage Canal or by floatplane from Anchorage.

Highlights: Excellent fishing for silver salmon (in the second half of August) and pink and chum salmon (in the second half of July). Also good fishing for Dolly Varden (in May and June) and halibut (in June and August).

Species: Chum salmon, Dolly Varden, halibut, king salmon, pink salmon, red salmon, silver salmon.

Regulations: Halibut fishing is prohibited from January 1 through 31. For additional restrictions, consult the current Alaska Department of Fish and Game sportfishing regulations or contact the ADF&G Anchorage office, (907) 267-2218.

Facilities: Gas, a boat launch, and guide services are available in the town of Whittier. Several Forest Service cabins are located in the area.

Contact: For lodging information, contact the Sportsman Inn, P.O. Box 688, Whittier, AK 99693; (907) 472-2352. For an air taxi, contact Ketchum Air Service, P.O. Box 190588, Anchorage, AK 99519, (907) 243-5525 or (800) 433-9114; or Rusts Flying Service, P.O. Box 190325, Anchorage, AK 99519, (907) 243-1595 or (800) 544-2299. For cabin rentals, contact Chugach National Forest, 201 East Ninth Avenue, Suite 206, Anchorage, AK 99501; (907) 271-2500.

Fishing the Wells Passage Area: For the angler hoping to experience something out of the ordinary, Wells Passage in the heart of Prince William Sound has icy blue bays, secluded coves, deserted islands, and crystal clear streams with abundant fishing for salmon, charr, and bottomfish, as well as rich ocean fauna and picturesque scenery.

Located in northwest Prince William Sound within Chugach National Forest (there are several public-use cabins in the vicinity, at Shrode Lake and Pigot and Paulson Bays), the Passage is most quickly and conveniently accessed by floatplane. But to truly savor the essence of this special area, travel by boat, taking time to explore and fish the countless bays, coves, and stream mouths. (Streams are typically short, shallow, and clear. Many drain narrow, jutting peninsulas and islands.)

Pink salmon are by far the most common species. In season, they swarm through the sound in huge schools, invading almost any flowing body of water. Look for schools of bright fish early on in the season to enjoy the best angling

for this species. Silver salmon arrive sometime after the pinks and provide superb action when concentrated in bays and coves near their streams of birth, while red salmon and good numbers of chums and Dolly Varden charr are present in some locations. A hatchery run of king salmon returns to the Esther Island area. Halibut, although usually not of any great size, are also abundant throughout most of the area.

Top angling spots include: Pigot Bay (chum salmon, pink salmon, halibut), Cochrane Bay (chum salmon, pink salmon, Dolly Varden, halibut), and Long Bay (silver salmon, pink salmon, Dolly Varden); Passage Canal Lagoon (silver salmon, pink salmon), Harrison Lagoon (chum salmon, pink salmon), and Coghill Lagoon (silver salmon, pink salmon, Dolly Varden); and Culross Passage (silver salmon, pink salmon, Dolly Varden) and Esther Passage (king salmon, silver salmon, chum salmon, pink salmon, Dolly Varden).

38 Valdez Arm

Location: In north Prince William Sound, 105 miles east of Anchorage; see map page 266.

USGS maps: Valdez A-7, A-8; Cordova D-8; Seward D-1.

How to get there: By car, plane, or boat. The town of Valdez is at the head of Port Valdez and linked to the rest of the state through the Richardson Highway. The outer bay area is reached by plane or boat, while anglers can fish the inner waters from the road system and boats.

Highlights: Excellent fishing for silver salmon (from late August through early September), pink salmon (in the first half of July), and halibut (from July through September); good fishing for chum salmon (from mid-July through late August) and Dolly Varden charr (from June through July).

Species: Chum salmon, Dolly Varden, halibut, king salmon, pink salmon, silver salmon, *red salmon*.

Regulations: Halibut fishing is prohibited from January 1 through 31. For additional restrictions, consult the current Alaska Department of Fish and Game sportfishing regulations or contact the ADF&G Glennallen office, (907) 822-3309.

Facilities: Lodging, motel, gas, boat rentals, a boat launch, sporting goods, groceries, and guide services are available in Valdez.

Contact: For guide services, contact Coho Charters, P.O. Box 2198, Valdez, AK 99686, (907) 835-4675; or Seaview Charters, P.O. Box 331, Valdez, AK 99686, (907) 835-5115. For lodging, contact Totem Inn, P.O. Box 648, Valdez, AK 99686, (907) 835-4443; or Village Inn, P.O. Box 365, Valdez, AK 99686, (907) 835-4445.

Fishing Valdez Arm: Valdez Arm is a long, curved inlet in northern Prince William Sound. Numerous clear-water and glacial streams draining from the Chugach Mountains influence its physical character and angling. In the greenish-gray, cold waters, all five species of salmon, charr, and bottomfish can be taken, but the lure-snapping silver and pink salmon and good-size halibut draw anglers' attention most. (Valdez is known as the "Pink Salmon Capital of the World" and has three salmon derbies each summer.) The presence of the Solomon Creek Hatchery across the bay from Valdez considerably enhances the salmon fishing, in some years producing thick concentrations of returning fish and wild action at the head of the bay. (Silvers have been known to jump into boats and up on docks here.)

Excellent shore fishing for pinks and silvers can be had from beaches, points, docks, and creek mouths during the peak of salmon season (in July and August), but the most consistent action is found in areas reached by boats or plane. Halibut fishing is great in the deep waters of the outer bay, particularly in late summer and fall. Feeder king salmon are present in small numbers in spring and early summer, while Dolly Varden charr are usually taken near the mouths of clear rivers and creeks.

Some worthwhile angling spots include: Valdez Harbor (silver salmon, pink salmon), Allison Point (silver salmon, chum salmon, pink salmon), the mouth of Gold Creek (silver salmon, pink salmon), Glacier Island (halibut), Port Fidalgo (halibut, silver salmon, chum salmon, pink salmon), Anderson Bay (silver salmon, chum salmon, pink salmon), Jack Bay (halibut, silver salmon, chum salmon, pink salmon, Dolly Varden), Sawmill Bay (chum salmon, pink salmon, Dolly Varden), and Galena Bay (silver salmon, chum salmon, pink salmon, Dolly Varden, halibut).

39 Orca Bay/Inlet

Location: In east Prince William Sound, 135 miles southeast of Anchorage; see map page 266.

USGS maps: Cordova B-5, B-6, B-7; C-5, C-6, C-7, C-8.

How to get there: By boat (there are hundreds of miles of sheltered coastline) or wheel- or floatplane (landing in bays or on long gravel beaches near salmon streams) from the town of Cordova. There are also some limited shore fishing opportunities.

Highlights: Excellent fishing for king salmon (in the first half of June), silver salmon (in the second half of August), pink salmon (in the second half of July), and halibut (from June through August); good fishing for Dolly Varden (in May and June).

Species: Chum salmon, Dolly Varden, halibut, king salmon, pink salmon, red salmon, silver salmon.

Regulations: Halibut fishing is prohibited from January 1 through 31. For additional restrictions, consult the current Alaska Department of Fish and Game sportfishing regulations or contact the ADF&G Anchorage office, (907) 267-2218.

Facilities: Lodging, gas, boat rentals, a boat launch, guide services, sporting goods, and groceries are available in the town of Cordova. A 12-foot-by-14-foot Forest Service cabin is available on Double Bay, Hinchinbrook Island.

Contact: For guide services, contact the Alaska Wilderness Outfitting Company, P.O. Box 1516, Cordova, AK 99574, (907) 424-5552; or Winter King Charters, P.O. Box 14, Cordova, AK 99574, (907) 424-7170. For an air taxi, contact Cordova Air Service, P.O. Box 528, Cordova, AK 99574, (907) 424-7611; or Fishing and Flying, P.O. Box 2349, Cordova, AK 99574, (907) 424-3324. For lodging, contact the Cordova Rose Lodge, P.O. Box 1494, Cordova, AK 99574, (907) 424-7673; or Reluctant Fisherman Inn, P.O. Box 150, Cordova, AK 99574, (907) 424-3272. For cabin rentals, contact Chugach National Forest, 201 East Ninth Avenue, Suite 206, Anchorage, AK 99501; (907) 271-2500.

Fishing Orca Bay/Inlet: Orca Bay and its inlet, which are in eastern Prince William Sound, encompass a number of smaller bays, coves, Hawkins Island, and the northeastern corner of Hinchinbrook Island. A multitude of stream and bays, splendid scenery, wildlife, and relatively easy access make it one of the more popular coastal fishing areas of Southcentral Alaska.

The major species of fish that anglers target are silver and pink salmon, Dolly Varden charr, and halibut, though feeder king salmon are becoming increasingly popular in late winter and spring. Several area streams support small populations of cutthroat trout. The better salmon action occurs at the head of bays near spawning streams, the best of them around Hinchinbrook and Hawkins Islands and the northern section of Orca Bay.

The small clear-water streams offer outstanding spin and fly casting opportunities for salmon, trout, and Dolly Varden charr. Halibut are taken in shallow waters during the spring, moving deeper as the season progresses. (They may also be taken in the fall off the mouths of salmon streams in certain areas.) Casting from shore is most frequently done near the town of Cordova, as enhanced runs of king and silver salmon return to locations nearby, but it also works well anywhere concentrations of fish hold close to shore—in the intertidal areas of streams, near points, and at the heads of bays.

The best fishing locations in the Orca Bay area include: Orca Inlet (king salmon, silver salmon, pink salmon, halibut), Hartney Bay (king salmon, silver salmon, pink salmon), Flemming Spit (king salmon, silver salmon), and the mouth of Humpback Creek (pink salmon), outside the town of Cordova; Simpson Bay (pink salmon, silver salmon, halibut), Sheep Bay (silver salmon, pink salmon, halibut), and Port Gravina (silver salmon, pink salmon, halibut), on the northern half of Orca; stream mouths on Hawkins Island-Hawkins Creek (pink salmon, cutthroat trout, Dolly Varden) and Canoe Passage (pink salmon, cutthroat trout, Dolly Varden); and Anderson Bay (pink salmon, cutthroat trout, Dolly Varden),

Double Bay (pink salmon, cutthroat trout, Dolly Varden, halibut), and Boswell Bay (pink salmon, Dolly Varden) on Hinchinbrook Island.

⓵ Eyak River/Lake

Location: In the Copper River Delta drainage, 150 miles southeast of Anchorage; see map page 266.

USGS maps: Cordova B-5, C-5.

How to get there: By car. The main river and lake are accessible from the town of Cordova, while small boats may be launched to fish more remote areas. A well-developed trail system provides foot access to the middle river section as well as to Power Creek, a major tributary emptying into Eyak Lake.

Highlights: Good fishing for silver salmon (in the second half of August), red salmon (from late June through early July), cutthroat trout (in May), and Dolly Varden charr (in May and August).

Species: Cutthroat trout, Dolly Varden, red salmon, silver salmon.

Regulations: For restrictions, consult the current Alaska Department of Fish and Game sportfishing regulations or contact the ADF&G Anchorage office, (907) 267-2218.

Facilities: Lodgings, hotel, gas, boat rentals and launch, groceries, and sporting goods are available in Cordova. A Forest Service cabin is located on Power Creek.

Contact: For general, lodging, and cabin rental information, contact the Cordova Ranger District, 612 Second Street, Cordova, AK 99574; (907) 424-7661.

Fishing Eyak River/Lake: The Eyak River is a semiglacial stream originating from Shephard Glacier in the Chugach Mountains above Cordova. Power Creek drains the valleys of the Heney Range before emptying into Eyak Lake, from which the smooth-flowing river begins. The Eyak flows wide and deep for a short distance before fanning out onto the flats of the muddy Copper River Delta and then into the Gulf of Alaska.

Due to its easy access (it can be reached via the Copper Highway from Cordova) and good fishing, the Eyak River is one of the more popular and productive locations in the entire Copper

River system, with good runs of silver and red salmon. Since it is fairly glacial, anglers do best working the river with extremely bright lures or bait. Although red salmon show up in large numbers in early summer, they can be finicky about lure selection, with best results occurring in areas with large fish concentrations and currents. (For more details, see the sockeye chapter on page 51.) Silvers are much more responsive and provide good action in late summer and fall, while trout and charr make themselves known during their annual migrations to and from the sea.

The lake itself offers limited possibilities. The outlet is perhaps the best location for fishing on the entire river, but the remainder of the lake is fairly shallow, with deeper channels toward the middle, following the pattern of the Eyak River. Power Creek is also semiglacial and is the major spawning ground for the Eyak River fish stocks. Salmon fishing is prohibited here, but anglers do very well with Dolly Varden, with catches of up to four or five pounds. Some cutthroat trout are also taken. The best time to fish is during August and September, when the salmon are on the spawning beds.

㊶ Alaganik Slough System

Location: In the Copper River Delta drainage, 165 miles southeast of Anchorage; see map page 266.

USGS maps: Cordova B-3, B-4.

How to get there: By car, via the Copper River Highway from the town of Cordova. The main road parallels the slough for a few miles, crossing tributary streams in places, while side roads and trails access other parts of the system, including McKinley Lake. Boat launching is possible to reach more remote sections, while floatplanes can be used to reach the main lake.

Highlights: Excellent fishing for silver salmon (from late August through early September); good fishing for red salmon (from late July through early August), cutthroat trout (from June through September), and Dolly Varden (from July through September).

Species: Cutthroat trout, Dolly Varden, red salmon, silver salmon.

Regulations: King salmon fishing is prohibited. For additional restrictions, consult the current Alaska Department of Fish and Game sportfishing regulations or contact the ADF&G Anchorage office, (907) 267-2218.

Facilities: Forest Service cabins are available on the slough and lake.

Contact: For general and cabin information, contact the Cordova Ranger District, 612 Second Street, Cordova, AK 99574; (907) 424-7661.

Fishing the Alaganik Slough System: The Alaganik Slough system consists of an extensive drainage of lakes, clear-water streams, and glacial sloughs in the Copper River Delta. Much of the lower system consists of open marshland with slow-moving, semiglacial water best accessed by boat. The upper system, however, has several small, clear creeks and the main channel is fairly wide with thick vegetation around the bank. Glacial meltwater from area mountains and the silty Copper River influences the Alaganik.

The majority of sportfishing takes place on Alaganik Slough near the highway and in McKinley Lake and surrounding streams. A 14-foot-by-20-foot Forest Service cabin is on the lake, tied into an extensive and popular trail system connecting a series of small lakes and the highway (the cabin is two miles from the road). Since Alaganik Slough is so slow, even canoeists can thoroughly enjoy the area by putting in at the highway and paddling upstream to McKinley Lake and the upper system.

The system receives good runs of silver and red salmon, with the best fishing in the middle and upper sections of the slough itself, the outlet of McKinley Lake and the mouths of inlet streams. While silvers can be taken throughout the system, red salmon usually congregate in areas with at least some current. Cutthroat trout and Dolly Varden are also present, mostly in McKinley Lake and tributary streams. Lake fishing is most productive early in the season. Locations holding concentrations of spawning salmon are the best bets for larger fish in late summer and fall.

For the angler looking to hike or canoe along with his favorite sport, the Alaganik Slough system is one of the best options around, with miles of trails, abundant easy water, scenery, wildlife, and great fishing.

㊷ Martin River System

Location: In the Copper River Delta drainage, 180 miles southeast of Anchorage; see map page 266.

USGS maps: Cordova B-1, B-2, B-3.

How to get there: By plane from the town of Cordova. Floatplanes land on area lakes; wheelplanes use the open country along the main stem Martin River.

Highlights: Excellent fishing for silver salmon (in the last half of August); good fishing for red salmon (from late June through early July), Dolly Varden (from July through September), and lake trout (from May through October).

Species: Dolly Varden, lake trout, red salmon, silver salmon, *cutthroat trout, steelhead.*

Regulations: Open year-round, all species.

Facilities: A Forest Service cabin is available at Martin Lake.

Contact: For general and cabin rental information, contact the Cordova Ranger District, 612 Second Street, Cordova, AK 99574; (907) 424-7661. For an air taxi, contact the Cordova Air Service, P.O. Box 528, Cordova, AK 99574, (907) 424-7611; or Fishing and Flying, P.O. Box 2349, Cordova, AK 99574, (907) 424-3324.

Fishing the Martin River System: The Martin River system drains a heavily glaciated area of the coastal Chugach Range and empties into the eastern Copper River Delta. The main river is silty, originating from the Martin River Glacier, while the tributary streams and lakes run clear and are ideal for sportfishing. Splendid scenery, abundant wildlife, and exciting fishing make it a popular destination.

Considering its size, the system does not support very large numbers of sport fish. Still, the fish usually concentrate in only a few locations, making for fast action. Most visiting anglers stay at the Forest Service cabin at the outlet of Martin Lake, as this location has prime fishing, but the lower reaches of streams draining into the southern half of the lake are certainly worth a try. Other good fishing spots include the outlet of Little Martin Lake, Tokun Lake, and the mouths of clear-water streams and sloughs off the Martin River.

The most sought-after species is the silver salmon. These flashy fighters are present from late summer through early fall, and can be caught with regularity throughout much of the system. The best location is probably the confluence of the Martin River and the small stream draining Martin Lake. The fish school here and yield superb action, with good conditions for easy spin casting and fly-fishing. Red salmon, difficult to catch, reside in good numbers in some of the tributary streams.

Other species, such as Dolly Varden and lake trout, are likewise present in fishable numbers, along with a few cutthroat trout. Large Dollies are taken during the peak of the salmon runs in Martin Lake and its tributaries, while lake trout are taken out of deeper sections of Martin and Tokun Lakes. (These lake trout are some of the farthest south- and east-ranging populations of the species in Alaska.)

㊸ Katalla River

Location: In the north Gulf Coast drainage, 190 miles southeast of Anchorage; see map page 266.

USGS maps: Cordova A-2, B-2.

How to get there: By small wheelplane from the town of Cordova. There is a rough, short landing strip on the lower river near the mouth with a few trails providing access to other sections of the Katalla.

Highlights: A promising out-of-the-way salmon and trout stream, with excellent fishing for silver salmon (from late August through early September), pink salmon (from late July through early August), and cutthroat trout (from August through September); good fishing for Dolly Varden (from July through September).

Species: Chum salmon, cutthroat trout, Dolly Varden, pink salmon, silver salmon, *king salmon, red salmon.*

Regulations: Unbaited, artificial lures only from April 15 through June 14. For additional restrictions, consult the current Alaska Department of Fish and Game sportfishing regulations or contact the ADF&G Anchorage office, (907) 267-2218.

Facilities: No developed public facilities.

Contact: For an air taxi, contact Cordova Air Service, P.O. Box 528, Cordova, AK 99574, (907) 424-7611; or Fishing and Flying, P.O. Box 2349, Cordova, AK 99574, (907) 424-3324.

Fishing the Katalla River: The Katalla River is perhaps the best prospect of several lesser visited coastal streams found just east of the Copper River Delta. Gathering water from several sources draining the uplands between Bering Lake and the Ragged Mountains, the clear Katalla meanders down through a brushy, wet valley into the gulf at Katalla Bay. The few (mostly hunters) who have fished and explored its reaches report abundant silver salmon, cutthroat trout, and Dolly Varden in a totally wild setting.

To fish the Katalla, one must fly by small plane from Cordova, landing on floats in the slough or bay, or by wheelplane to a rough strip along the beach. Fishing spinners and spoons in the mouth and lower river with the tides is certainly one of the better ways to connect with bright salmon, but a hike upstream to check out the pools and small side creeks can yield delightful fly-fishing, especially for Dollies and cutthroats. The best time to fish is in late summer and fall (from late August through September). Watch out for bears, which are numerous.

The Katalla is definitely worth investigating as one of the more promising gateway streams to the vast unexplored North Gulf Coast beyond the Copper River Delta.

🕸 Bering River System

Location: In the North Gulf Coast drainage, Controller Bay, 205 miles southeast of Anchorage; see map page 266.

USGS maps: Cordova A-1, B-1; Bering Glacier B-8.

How to get there: By plane from Cordova. Floatplanes can land on area lakes (Bering, Charlotte, and Kushtaka) or wide, deep sloughs along the river; wheelplane landings are possible on gravel bars. Some hiking is required to reach choice fishing spots.

Highlights: A little visited salmon system with great potential. Good fishing for silver salmon (from mid-August through early September),

red salmon (from late June through early July), and Dolly Varden charr (from July through September).

Species: Chum salmon, Dolly Varden, pink salmon, red salmon, silver salmon.

Regulations: Unbaited, artificial lures only from April 15 through June 14. For additional restrictions, consult the current Alaska Department of Fish and Game sportfishing regulations or contact the ADF&G Anchorage office, (907) 267-2218.

Facilities: No developed public facilities.

Contact: For an air taxi, contact Cordova Air Service, P.O. Box 528, Cordova, AK 99574, (907) 424-7611; or Fishing and Flying, P.O. Box 2349, Cordova, AK 99574, (907) 424-3324.

Fishing the Bering River System: Bering River is a fair-size glacial system lying east of the Copper River Delta that, like the Katalla, gets little attention. Originating from the edge of the huge Saint Elias ice fields, the silty Bering flows south to Controller Bay and the Gulf of Alaska. A few of the large lakes have clear-water streams with habitat for salmon and charr. Along with a number of small holding sloughs and creeks on the east side of the lower river, they hold most of the Bering's sport fish potential.

Anglers flying in to the area from Cordova can land on beaches, lakes, and sloughs near holding fish (spotted from the air). Most folks look for red and silver salmon and Dolly Varden. More promising drainages to scout include Dick Creek (Bering Lake), Shepherd Creek, and Stillwater Creek (Kushtaka Lake), although just about any clear-water slough will have salmon potential during the peak of the runs. Bears are quite common, so use caution. The Bering system is perfect for anglers with a spirit of adventure and a yearning for truly unexploited, exciting fishing.

Wrangell Mountains/ Copper River

In the early 1980s, reports of 20-pound-plus rainbow trout from a remote location in the rugged Wrangell Mountains focused attention on the vastly underrated sportfishing potential of this scenic corner of the state. Dominated by the huge, glacial Copper River and towering, icy mountains, the Wrangell subregion has much to offer fishermen in its clearer-flowing tributary streams and associated lakes. King and red salmon, grayling, lake trout, some rainbow, and even a few steelhead trout are the species highlights for this area.

45 Tebay River System

Location: Wrangell Mountains, 200 miles east of Anchorage; see map page 266.

USGS maps: Valdez A-1, A-2, B-1; McCarthy A-7, A-8.

How to get there: By floatplane to lakes (Hanagita, Tebay, Summit) from Tolsona or Cordova.

Highlights: Remote, wild watershed with high-quality rainbow trout, grayling, and lake trout, along with spectacular scenery and abundant wildlife.

Species: Grayling, king salmon, lake trout, rainbow trout, red salmon, steelhead.

Regulations: Seasonal closures, gear and size restrictions on rainbow trout in parts of watershed. For restrictions, consult the current Alaska Department of Fish and Game sportfishing regulations or contact the ADF&G Glennallen office, (907) 822-3309.

Facilities: No developed public facilities.

Contact: For air taxi and guide services, contact the Alaska Air Ventures, P.O. Box 8758, Palmer, AK 99645, (907) 822-3905; or Alaska Wilderness Outfitting Company, P.O. Box 7516, Cordova, AK 99574, (907) 424-5552.

Fishing the Tebay River System: The Tebay River system, in the heart of the Wrangell–Saint Elias Wilderness, is a little visited but no less esteemed drainage comprised of several high mountain lakes and streams that empty into the silty Chitina River, a major tributary of the Copper. With the area's isolation, magnificent surroundings, and wild populations of rainbows, grayling, and lake trout, it offers the potential for some of the best angling in Southcentral Alaska.

The river heads at the Tebay Lakes, a fine spot for a fly-in fish camp, with abundant fishing (es-

pecially at the connecting outlets) for small to medium rainbows. Six miles below the lower lake outlet, the Tebay joins its major tributary, the Hanagita River, which drains a series of small lakes to the east. Rainbows and grayling can be found in the Hanagita and its tributaries, as well as a few lake trout in the lakes. (A small fall run of steelhead also spawns in the river below the lakes, but they can be elusive.) The Summit Lake and Bridge Creek drainage, which joins the Tebay from the west about a mile above the Hanagita, also has rainbows and a very interesting history. Originally thought to be barren, Summit Lake produced phenomenal catches of trophy rainbows in the early 1980s, with quite a few fish in the 20-pound (and over) range. Crowds of fly-in anglers plundered the lake in subsequent years. The Alaska Department of Fish and Game imposed restrictive measures, but apparently too late to save the trophy fishery. The rainbow fishing here is still good, though few fish reach any semblance of the size of yesteryear. The best time to fish Summit and the rest of Tebay is in early July or from late August through late September.

46 Tonsina River System

Location: In the Copper River drainage, 150 miles east of Anchorage; see map page 266.

USGS maps: Valdez B-3, B-4, B-5, C-2, C-3, C-4, C-5.

How to get there: By car, plane, and boat. The Richardson and Edgerton Highways cross the middle and lower river respectively. (Several trails and dirt roads lead away from the roads to points along the river.) More remote locations can be fished by jet boats, rafts, or floatplanes (via Tolsona).

Highlights: Good fishing for king salmon (in the first half of July), silver salmon (in September), red salmon (in the second half of July), Dolly Varden charr (in September and October), and grayling (from June through September).

Species: Dolly Varden, grayling, king salmon, lake trout, rainbow trout, red salmon, silver salmon, *steelhead*.

Regulations: King salmon fishing is prohibited from July 20 through December 31. For additional restrictions, consult the current Alaska Department of Fish and Game sportfishing regulations or contact the ADF&G Glennallen office, (907) 822-3309.

Facilities: Guide services and lodging are available along the road system.

Contact: For guide services and lodging information, contact the Upper Tonsina Lodge, P.O. Box 143003, Anchorage, AK 99514; (907) 337-1281, (907) 822-5557, or (800) 822-5584.

Fishing the Tonsina River System: The Tonsina drainage is a fairly small system that heads in Tonsina Glacier on the north slope of the Chugach Mountains and flows north and east 60 miles or so before emptying into the lower Copper River. A challenging white-water river (mostly Class II), the greenish-gray Tonsina offers good fishing for salmon, charr, and grayling in the slower upper section below the lake and mouths of its clear-water tributary streams.

Although fished primarily by locals, this river shouldn't be overlooked. A few faint trails exist for hiking in to the river and tributaries, but probably the most convenient way to access the Tonsina is by jet boat or raft from the highway crossings. You can also fly in to Tonsina Lake and float down, but be advised that high water can make the river, particularly the lower sections, unnavigable and dangerous. Anglers would be wise to search for slower water or places where clear-water tributaries join the milky Tonsina; it is here that the schools of salmon, charr, and grayling tend to congregate.

Some of the best fishing for king salmon, red salmon, and grayling occurs at the mouths of streams draining into Tonsina Lake and in the first few miles of river below the outlet, though these species may be taken anywhere on the river in certain holes and runs. One roadside tributary, the Little Tonsina River, has productive angling for a small fall run of silver salmon, as well as Dolly Varden and grayling. Another good spot for salmon is at the mouth of the Tonsina, which may be reached by boat or raft from the Edgerton Highway. Here the river runs slower and wider, ideal holding water for migrating fish. Rumor has it that a few steelhead spawn in the Tonsina system.

⑰ Klutina River System

Location: In the Copper River drainage, 140 miles east of Anchorage; see map page 266.

USGS maps: Valdez B-6, C-5, C-6, C-7, D-4, D-5, D-6.

How to get there: By car and plane. The major point of access is where the Richardson Highway crosses the lower river near the town of Copper Center, just south of Glennallen. Floatplanes and jet boats are often used to reach more remote fishing areas.

Highlights: A very popular road-accessible salmon and trout stream. Good fishing for king salmon (in early July and late July), red salmon (from late June through late July), and Dolly Varden (from July through October).

Species: Dolly Varden, grayling, king salmon, lake trout, red salmon, rainbow trout, *silver salmon, steelhead.*

Regulations: King salmon fishing is prohibited from August 11 through December 31. For additional restrictions, consult the current Alaska Department of Fish and Game sportfishing regulations or contact the ADF&G Glennallen office, (907) 822-3309.

Facilities: Guide services, camping, gas, lodging, and groceries are available in Copper Center.

Contact: For guide services, contact Grove's Klutina River King Salmon Charters, P.O. Box 236, Copper Center, AK 99573, (907) 822-5822; or Ruffitters, P.O. Box 397, Gakona, AK 99586, (907) 822-3168.

Fishing the Klutina River System: The Klutina, a glacial river, originates from Klutina Lake at the base of the Chugach Range. This greenish-gray river flows northeast 30 miles through rugged and scenic highlands to its confluence with the Copper River. Swift (Class III) and cold, the Klutina offers good to excellent fishing for king and red salmon, Dolly Varden, and grayling.

One of the three ways to fish the Klutina drainage is by road, where the Richardson Highway intersects the lower river. Fishing here is mainly from the bank, with a limited trail system along the river. The dirt road that leads from the highway to the outlet of Klutina Lake makes for a long, rough ride in a four-wheeler. Another option is to launch a jet boat and fish the slower sections of the river, but this is not recommended for novice or intermediate boaters—the strong current is further complicated by numerous hidden rocks and boulders. The third access option is a floatplane to the lake and mouths of clear-water streams.

Shore fishing can be very productive along most of the river, particularly for red salmon. (King salmon and Dolly Varden are often taken, too.) Boaters have the most success fishing for kings, as the choice locations are more remote. (The Klutina kings are among the largest in the region, with fish weighing more than 50 pounds not uncommon.) There are two runs of these monarchs, one in June and July, another in July and August, but not always distinct. Most Dolly Varden encounters occur on the upper river and at the outlet of Klutina Lake, with specimens up to six or seven pounds possible. Red salmon run continuously from June through September, with a prolonged peak lasting four or five weeks.

Other less significant species, such as grayling and lake trout, are taken near the mouths of clear-water streams at times. Spots to try for these, as well as the more abundant species, include Manker and St. Anne Creeks and the Mahlo River.

48 Tazlina River System

Location: In the Copper River drainage, 110 miles east of Anchorage; see map page 266.

USGS maps: Anchorage D-1; Valdez C-6, C-7, C-8, D-6, D-7, D-8; Talkeetna Mountains A-1, A-2; Gulkana A-3, A-4, A-5, A-6.

How to get there: By car or plane. The Richardson Highway intersects the lower part of the Tazlina River, and the Glenn Highway provides access to clear-water tributaries. Launch boats and rafts from the highway crossings. Floatplanes (via Tolsona or Anchorage) access more remote fishing areas.

Highlights: Excellent fishing for grayling (from May to October). Good fishing for king and red salmon (in early July) and rainbow trout (from June through September).

Species: Grayling, king salmon, rainbow trout, red salmon, *lake trout, steelhead*.

Regulations: King salmon fishing is prohibited from July 20 through December 31. For additional restrictions, consult the current Alaska Department of Fish and Game sportfishing regulations or contact the ADF&G Glennallen office, (907) 822-3309.

Facilities: Camping, boat launching, lodging, gas, groceries, and guide services are available in Glennallen and surrounding areas.

Contact: For an air taxi and guide services, contact Alaska Air Ventures, P.O. Box 8758, Palmer, AK 99645; (907) 822-3905.

Fishing the Tazlina River System: The Tazlina Glacier spills down the northeast slope of the central Chugaches to form Tazlina Lake, a large, deep body of water. From its outlet, the Tazlina River flows east about 60 miles to join the huge Copper River. Although the river and lake are for the most part too silty for sportfishing, the clear tributary lakes and streams offer good to excellent fishing for lake trout, Dolly Varden, grayling, and two species of salmon.

Floatplanes offer the quickest and easiest way to reach various choice locations; however, it is possible to launch jet boats from the Richardson Highway bridge and run up the Tazlina River. A few tributary lakes and streams may be accessed by car from the Glenn Highway. Another option is by raft, putting in at the little Nelchina River on the Glenn Highway and then floating down to Tazlina Lake. You can camp and fish at the inlet and fly back, or cross the lake and continue down the Tazlina River to the Richardson Highway bridge. (Be wary of strong winds that blow off the glacier—take a small outboard along just in case.) Since the Nelchina and Tazlina Rivers are fast, white-water rivers (possible Class III to IV rapids during high-water conditions) and very cold, only experienced river runners should attempt them, and only during low water conditions.

Some of the best spots to try on the Tazlina system include Kaina Lake (rainbow trout), High Lake (rainbow trout, lake trout, grayling), Moose Lake (rainbow trout, grayling), Tolsona Lake (rainbow trout, grayling), Mendeltna Creek (grayling), Moose Creek (grayling), Tolsona Creek (grayling), and Kaina Creek (king salmon, red salmon, rainbow trout). The stream mouths are best for salmon in summer. In spring and fall, try for trout and grayling. Some of these streams are major grayling producers and can be phenomenal during the annual spawning migrations in May; use flies and small spinners. A small steelhead population reportedly spawns on the Tazlina River and a few tributaries.

㊾ Gulkana River System

Location: In the Copper River drainage, 165 miles northeast of Anchorage; see map page 266.

USGS maps: Mount Hayes A-3, A-4; Gulkana A-3, A-5, B-3, B-4, B-5, C-4, C-5, C-6, D-4, D-5, D-6.

How to get there: By car, plane, and boat. The Richardson Highway parallels the river more or less from the headwaters down to near the mouth, offering access to the main stem and clear-water tributaries. Use floatplanes to reach more remote parts of the drainage. Boats, rafts, and other craft can be launched from various locations.

Highlights: One of Alaska's premier recreational waters, with excellent fishing for grayling (from May through October). Good fishing for king salmon (from late June through early July), red salmon (from late June through mid-August), rainbow trout (from July through September), and lake trout (in June and from September through October).

Species: Grayling, king salmon, lake trout, rainbow trout, red salmon, *steelhead*.

Regulations: King salmon fishing is closed from July 20 through December 31; catch-and-release fishing only for rainbow and steelhead trout. For additional restrictions, consult the current Alaska Department of Fish and Game sportfishing regulations or contact the ADF&G Glennallen office, (907) 822-3309.

Facilities: Lodging, camping, gas, groceries, boat launching, sporting goods, cabins, and guide services are available in many locations along the road.

Contact: For guide services, contact the Alaska Wilderness Outfitting Company, P.O. Box 1516, Cordova, AK 99574, (907) 424-5552; or Ruffitters, P.O. Box 397, Gakona, AK 99586, (907) 822-3168. For lodging information, contact Paxson Lodge, P.O. Box 3001, Paxson, AK 99737; (907) 822-3330. For an air taxi, contact Gulkana Air Service, P.O. Box 342, Anchorage, AK 99588, (907) 822-5532; or Lee's Air Taxi Service, Glennallen, AK 99585, (907) 822-3343.

Fishing the Gulkana River System: An immense clear-water drainage of lakes and streams, the Gulkana River system rises at the base of the Alaska Range near the headwaters of the Susitna, then flows south and east approximately 100 miles to join the Copper River. Its two major tributaries, the Middle Fork and the West Fork, begin in a series of lakes and uplands west of the main stem. The most significant sportfishing tributary of the entire Copper River, the Gulkana has been designated a National Wild and Scenic River.

The river has one of Alaska's most productive grayling fisheries, particularly on the main stem between Paxson Lake and the West Fork confluence, but also in tributary lakes (Dickey Lake) and streams (Tangle River). Although fishing pressure has affected their average size, grayling are still quite abundant and easy to catch. The Gulkana is also known for its king salmon fishing (from the Middle Fork confluence down) and a prolonged run of red salmon (they're hard to catch, however). Lake trout lurk in the large, deep lakes, such as Summit, Paxson, and Swede, and the fishing ranges from quite good to outstanding, with some catches of these large lake charr exceeding 30 pounds. The Gulkana also has a few rainbows and some of the northernmost runs of steelhead trout in North America. The best times to fish these elusive fish are in spring and fall in tributaries of the upper Middle Fork and in the main stem above the West Fork confluence.

Perhaps the most exciting way to fish the Gulkana is by raft, canoe, or kayak, putting in at either Paxson Lake, Tangle River at milepost 22 of the Denali Highway (with a portage into Dickey Lake), or flying in to one of the headwater lakes of the West Fork. The most popular take-out point is Sourdough Campground, at milepost 147.5 of the Richardson Highway. (Almost all powerboat users put in here and fish the stretch upriver to the West Fork confluence.) You can fish farther down and take out where the Richardson Highway intersects the river near Gakona Junction if you like. The only serious hazards to boaters and floaters are boulders and swift currents (mostly Class II, with short stretches of Class III to IV at the Canyon Rapids on the main stem and below Dickey Lake on the Middle Fork). For the hiker-angler, the following cross-country trails offer access to strategic points along the river system: the Swede Lake Trail, beginning at milepost 16 of the Denali Highway; the Meiers Lake Trail, beginning at milepost 169 of the Richardson Highway; and the Haggard Creek Trail, beginning at milepost 161 of the Richardson Highway.

Guides' tip: The hot lure for grayling on the Gulkana is a no. 2 silver Vibrax spinner. If the grayling act finicky, try a wet fly on the end of the spinner.

Kodiak-Afognak Islands

Kodiak Island and its associated archipelago (including Afognak, Shuyak, and Raspberry Islands) is a world unto itself. Most geographers group it with Southwest Alaska, but it really stands apart from the rest of the state, a unique island complex—the second largest in the U.S. at 3,950 square miles—with its own special character. At the same latitude as Scotland, the big island has similar maritime climate, but lusher vegetation and more mountainous terrain. Most people know it for its giant bears, but Kodiak also has one of the richest marine environments on earth, with abundant wildlife along its coasts and an incredibly prolific fishery. Some of the most productive salmon streams in Alaska are here, along with Southcentral's best steelhead fishing. A short road system that extends from the town of Kodiak out along Chiniak Bay provides road-fishing opportunities, but for the most part, Kodiak's rugged and remote terrain is accessible by floatplane or boat only.

50 Shuyak Island

Location: North of Afognak Island, 50 miles north of Kodiak, 200 miles southwest of Anchorage; see map page 267.

USGS maps: Afognak B-2, C-1, C-2, C-3.

How to get there: Primarily by floatplane, landing in protected bays and coves of the island such as Big and Neketa Bays and Carry Inlet. Inflatable rafts and the like are ideal for fishing the smaller bays, while hiking along the beach to stream mouths may be better in others.

Highlights: Excellent fishing for silver salmon (in the second half of August), pink salmon (from late July through early August), and halibut (from May through September).

Species: Dolly Varden, halibut, king salmon, pink salmon, silver salmon, *red salmon, steelhead*.

Regulations: Halibut fishing is closed from January 1 through 31. For additional regulations, consult the current Alaska Department of Fish and Game sportfishing regulations or contact the ADF&G Kodiak office, (907) 486-4791.

Facilities: Shuyak Island State Park cabins, commercial lodging, and guide services are available.

Contact: For lodging and guide services, contact the Port William Wilderness Lodge, P.O. Box 670556, Chugiak, AK 99567; phone or fax (907) 688-2253. For more information, contact the Alaska State Parks, S.R. Box 3800, Kodiak, AK 99615, (907) 486-6339; or the Public Lands Information Center, 605 West Fourth Avenue, Suite 105, Anchorage, AK 99501, (907) 271-2737. For an air taxi, contact Sea Hawk Air, P.O. Box 3561, Kodiak, AK 99615, (907) 486-8282 or (800) 770-HAWK.

Fishing Shuyak Island: A rich endowment of marine and animal life inhabit the many bays, coves, islands, and small lakes and streams of this small landmass just north of Afognak. The island's entire coastline has excellent angling potential for salmon, charr, and bottomfish, particularly the northwest shore's archipelago of reefs, protruding rocks, and inlets. Angling activity for salmon and sea-run charr is concentrated in bays and inlets with streams. Although the numbers of fish are usually quite small, fishing can be outstanding near the mouths of these spawning streams when the runs peak.

Since much of the best fishing takes place in tidal water, small skiffs, rafts, or even kayaks provide the best access. Surf casting is possible at stream mouths, from points, and along beaches. Salmon is the top draw around Shuyak, with the choice locations including Neketa, Big and Shangin Bays, and Carry Inlet. All of these have spawning systems at their heads with small but highly concentrated runs of silver and pink salmon, as well as fair numbers of Dolly Varden and a sprinkling of reds.

A few feeder king salmon may be available in outlying waters, but anglers are most likely to encounter halibut there. These popular flatfish appear wherever there is open water with sufficient reef and shoal structure. One of the more promising locations for this species is Shuyak Strait between Shuyak and Afognak Islands.

Shuyak Island, without a doubt, remains one of the most promising destinations in the entire Kodiak area, with its scenic marine setting and excellent fishing potential.

51 Pauls Creek System

Location: In the north Afognak Island drainage, Perenosa Bay area, 40 miles north of Kodiak, 210 miles southwest of Anchorage; see map page 267.

USGS maps: Afognak B-1, B-2.

How to get there: By floatplane to the head of Pauls Bay, a small inlet on the east side of Perenosa Bay on Afognak Island. Hike from the landing site along the beach to the stream mouth and lower sections. Outlets of Pauls and Laura Lakes provide viable access to more remote parts of the system.

Highlights: Some of Afognak's most outstanding stream fishing for silver salmon (from mid-August through early September); also excellent red salmon fishing (in the second half of June) and good pink salmon fishing (from late July through early August).

Species: Dolly Varden, pink salmon, red salmon, silver salmon, steelhead.

Regulations: Spring closure on rainbow and steelhead trout fishing from April 1 through June 14. For additional restrictions, consult the current Alaska Department of Fish and Game sportfishing regulations or contact the ADF&G Kodiak office, (907) 486-4791.

Facilities: No developed public facilities.

Contact: For an air taxi, contact Sea Hawk Air, P.O. Box 3561, Kodiak, AK 99615, (907) 486-8282 or (800) 770-HAWK.

Fishing the Pauls Creek System: Like Portage Creek to the south, Pauls Creek is rather small, shallow, and clear. Part of a system of several lakes (including Pauls, Laura, and Gretchen), Pauls Creek begins at the Gretchen Lake outlet and runs several miles northwest to Laura Lake, then continues about a mile to Pauls Lake. From there, it empties into Pauls Bay, a short distance away.

The Pauls Creek system supports only moderate populations of salmon and charr, so it does not receive much angling effort. Fishing, however, can be excellent at the mouth and surrounding bay area or in the lake inlets and outlets during the height of the runs, when fish school up and move into the system on incoming tides. Silver salmon fishing is particularly noteworthy in the lower river and outlet of Laura Lake, while reds are best fished in the shallow runs of the creek below Pauls Lake. You'll find hordes of fat sea-run Dollies in the upper parts of the system late in the season. Since the creek system also has a little-fished fall run of steelhead, it's hard to beat overall for varied stream fishing in a remote setting.

52 Portage Creek

Location: In the north Afognak Island drainage, Perenosa Bay area, 30 miles north of Kodiak, 215 miles southwest of Anchorage; see map page 267.

USGS map: Afognak B-2.

How to get there: By floatplane to the head of Discoverer Bay, a small inlet on the southern end of Perenosa Bay. From there, hike along the beach to the mouth and lower sections of the stream. Another access option is from Portage Lake, fishing the outlet and hiking downstream.

Highlights: Excellent fishing for silver salmon (from mid-August through early September) and red salmon (second half of June); good fishing for pink salmon (from late July through early August) and Dolly Varden (from June through August).

Species: Dolly Varden, pink salmon, red salmon, silver salmon, steelhead.

Regulations: Spring closure on rainbow and steelhead trout from April 1 through June 14. For additional restrictions, consult the current Alaska Department of Fish and Game sportfishing regulations or contact the ADF&G Kodiak office, (907) 486-4791.

Facilities: No developed public facilities.

Contact: For an air taxi, contact Sea Hawk Air, P.O. Box 3561, Kodiak, AK 99615, (907) 486-8282 or (800) 770-HAWK.

Fishing Portage Creek: Portage Creek is a shallow clear-water stream that flows from Portage Lake on northern Afognak Island to Discoverer Bay, two miles away. Since the drainage is quite small, salmon and charr populations are not very large. However, stream conditions are perfect for concentrating fish in shallow runs and pools, while the clear waters make for easy sight-fishing. Fly-fishing for silver and red salmon in this creek can be as good as it gets.

The best fishing locations on Portage Creek are the mouth on Discoverer Bay and the lake outlet, where schools tend to herd up. Fish the incoming tides for best results on the lower river, especially for silvers and Dolly Varden. The sockeyes seem more prone to hit once they are concentrated within the confines of the creek. (Sparse flies like a chartreuse Comet or Brassie work well on them.) The creek also has a small fall run of steelhead that begin showing up in September. Check with the Alaska Department of Fish and Game for the latest run conditions before heading down. As quite a few brown bears patrol this area during the height of the runs, caution is advised for anglers.

(53) Afognak (Litnik) River/Lagoon

Location: In the southwest Afognak Island drainage, 25 miles northwest of Kodiak, 235 miles southwest of Anchorage; see map page 267.

USGS map: Afognak A-3.

How to get there: By boat or floatplane from Anton Larsen Bay or Kodiak Island to the river mouth. The Afognak Lake outlet is also a popular gateway to the drainage via floatplanes. The main stretch of the river is accessible by four-wheeler road running between the river mouth at the head of Afognak Bay and the Afognak Lake outlet.

Highlights: One of Kodiak-Afognak's most popular fishing locations. Good fishing for silver salmon (from mid-August through early September), red salmon (in mid-June and the second half of July), and pink salmon (from late July through early August).

Species: Dolly Varden, pink salmon, rainbow trout, red salmon, silver salmon, steelhead.

Regulations: Spring closure on rainbow and steelhead trout fishing from April 1 through June 14. For additional restrictions, consult the current Alaska Department of Fish and Game sportfishing regulations or contact the ADF&G Kodiak office, (907) 486-4791.

Facilities: Commercial lodging and guide services are available.

Contact: For lodging and guide services, contact Afognak Adventures, P.O. Box 1277, Kodiak, AK 99615, (907) 486-6014 or (800) 770-6014; or Afognak Wilderness Lodge, Seal Bay, AK 99697, (907) 486-6442. For an air taxi, contact Sea Hawk Air, P.O. Box 3561, Kodiak, AK 99615, (907) 486-8282 or (800) 770-HAWK.

Fishing Afognak (Litnik) River/Lagoon: The Afognak or Litnik River is on the south end of Afognak Island at Marmot Bay, approximately 25 air miles northwest of the town of Kodiak. Draining the largest body of water on the island—long and narrow Afognak Lake—the river runs east a few miles and forms a long lagoon at Afognak Bay. The good fishing in the crystal clear waters of the river and lagoon combines with the magnificent setting and relatively easy access to make this location one of the most popular on the island.

The Afognak's width, depth, and good pools and runs make it especially suitable for fly-fishing. Most of the angling for silver salmon occurs in the lagoon and lake outlet, where coho tend to school, especially during periods of low water. A small road that parallels the river from the mouth to the lake outlet simplifies access upstream. The best bet would be to work the lagoon and lower river with the tide, then move upstream. The Afognak receives two runs of red salmon, the first during the month of June and the second in July. The lake outlet is a popular area to try (for silvers, as well). The Afognak also has abundant Dolly Varden charr (best fished in spring and late summer), small rainbow trout, and even a small fall run of steelhead that enter the river from September through November. As this is also world-class brown bear country, extreme caution is advised.

54 Malina Creek System

Location: In the southwest Afognak Island drainage, 35 miles northwest of Kodiak, 235 miles southwest of Anchorage; see map page 267.

USGS map: Afognak A-4.

How to get there: By small plane to the stream mouth at Shelikof Strait or outlets of Upper and Lower Malina Lakes. Hike from landing areas to access all stream sections. Boating to the area is not recommended for small craft since the waters of Shelikof Strait can be turbulent and unpredictable.

Highlights: Good to excellent fishing for silver salmon (from mid-August through early September), red salmon (in the second half of June), and Dolly Varden charr (from June through August); good fishing for pink salmon (from late July through early August) and fair angling for steelhead trout (from October through November).

Species: Dolly Varden, pink salmon, red salmon, silver salmon, steelhead.

Regulations: Spring closure on rainbow and steelhead trout fishing from April 1 through June 14. For additional restrictions, consult the current Alaska Department of Fish and Game sportfishing regulations or contact the ADF&G Kodiak office, (907) 486-4791.

Facilities: Various air taxi operators use a small, abandoned cabin on Upper Malina Lake.

Contact: For an air taxi, contact Sea Hawk Air,

P.O. Box 3561, Kodiak, AK 99615, (907) 486-8282 or (800) 770-HAWK. For lodge-based fishing, contact Tom Stick, Kodiak Discoveries, P.O. Box 8972, Kodiak, AK 99615, (907) 486-8972.

Fishing the Malina Creek System: Malina Creek and its associated lakes drain the hills just west of Afognak Lake and flow west to Shelikof Strait on the southwest side of the island. A small clear-water system, the Malina gets only moderate runs of salmon, trout, and charr, but fish tend to concentrate in a few choice locations. At present, fishing pressure is light.

Anglers arrive by floatplane to Lower Malina Lake and hike along the creek, scouting for schools of fish. During incoming tides, the mouth is one of the best places to fish, as is the outlet and inlet of Lower Malina during the peak of the runs. Charr are abundant during summer and most often caught while fishing for other species. Some steelhead trout run the lower creek in late fall, but tend to receive very little attention. The surrounding scenery is outstanding and wildlife is abundant. Brown bears and elk are commonly spotted near the lakes (hunters use the area in fall).

55 Uganik River System

Location: In the northwest Kodiak Island drainage, 35 miles west of Kodiak, 270 miles southwest of Anchorage; see map page 267.

USGS maps: Kodiak C-4, C-5.

How to get there: By floatplane from Kodiak. Drop-off at the outlet of Uganik Lake, raft to the mouth of the river, and pick up in the tidal area at the head of the east arm of the Uganik Bay.

Highlights: Excellent for red salmon (from late June through early July), silver salmon (from late August through mid-September), pink salmon (from late July through early August), and Dolly Varden charr (year-round).

Species: Chum salmon, Dolly Varden, pink salmon, rainbow trout, red salmon, silver salmon.

Regulations: Spring closure on rainbow and steelhead trout fishing from April 1 through June 14. For additional restrictions, consult the current Alaska Department of Fish and Game sportfishing regulations or contact the ADF&G Kodiak office, (907) 486-4791.

Facilities: A Forest Service cabin is available on Uganik Lake.

Contact: For an air taxi, contact Sea Hawk Air, P.O. Box 3561, Kodiak, AK 99615, (907) 486-8282 or (800) 770-HAWK; or Wilderness Air, P.O. Box 768, Kodiak, AK 99615, (907) 486-8101. For general and cabin rental information, contact the Kodiak National Wildlife Refuge, 1390 Buskin River Road, Kodiak, AK 99615; (907) 487-2600.

Fishing the Uganik River System: The Uganik River gathers water from some of the highest peaks on the central part of Kodiak Island, its several arms emptying into Uganik Lake, from which the river then flows northwest to the east arm of Uganik Bay. The fishing is superb—some of Kodiak's finest—with huge silver salmon and incredible numbers of Dolly Varden. Some of the largest silvers on Kodiak originate here, with fish regularly caught in the middle and upper teens. There is even potential for cohos weighing more than 20 pounds.

The majority of anglers who fish the Uganik system target the lower river between Uganik Lake and Uganik Bay, generally with a raft. It's about a two-hour straight float, but can be extended easily to two days, allowing time to work all of the productive stretches of the river. The upper river above Uganik Lake, with its tributaries, is also productive, but it's more difficult to access. Aside from floating the river, some anglers choose to fish only the lake outlet or the mouth.

The Uganik supports one of the healthiest populations of Dolly Varden charr on Kodiak, along with substantial runs of red and pink salmon. (Fishing for pinks is better on the lower Uganik, while reds and charr can be taken throughout the system.) Fair rainbow trout fishing is also available in the lake and upper river.

56 Little River Lakes

Location: In the northwest Kodiak Island drainage, 50 miles west of Kodiak, 270 miles southwest of Anchorage; see map page 267.

USGS maps: Kodiak D-5, D-6.

How to get there: By floatplane from Kodiak or area lodges. Little River Lake is the usual gateway to the drainage.

Highlights: Good fishing for silver salmon (throughout September) and red salmon (throughout June); also steelhead trout (from October through November) and Dolly Varden (from May through October).

Species: Dolly Varden, red salmon, silver salmon, steelhead.

Regulations: Spring closures on rainbow and steelhead trout fishing from April 1 through June 14. For additional restrictions, consult the current Alaska Department of Fish and Game sportfishing regulations or contact the ADF&G Kodiak office, (907) 486-4791.

Facilities: A Forest Service cabin is available nearby.

Contact: For an air taxi, contact Cub Air, P.O. Box 1616, Kodiak, AK 99615, (907) 486-5851. For general and cabin rental information, contact the Kodiak National Wildlife Refuge, 1390 Buskin River Road, Kodiak, AK 99615; (907) 487-2600.

Fishing Little River Lakes: The Little River Lakes (actually just one large lake with a small extension) is on a peninsula on the northwest side of Kodiak Island, between Spiridon and Uganik Bays. Little River, the outlet stream, is fairly small, clear, and fast, with several tributary creeks and forks. Access can be a problem due to the steep and difficult terrain. For starters, try the lake outlet and the first few miles of river below the lake. Look for schools of silver and red salmon (in season) stacked in the deeper holes and runs. Dolly Varden are abundant on the upper river and the outlet early and late in the season, while steelhead trout can be found during the fall months. Watch for brown bears.

57 Karluk River System

Location: In the west Kodiak Island drainage, 75 miles southwest of Kodiak, 290 miles southwest of Anchorage; see map page 267.

USGS maps: Karluk B-1, C-1, C-2; Kodiak B-6.

How to get there: By floatplane, with three options for fishing access. One is to fly to the mouth of the river at Karluk Lagoon (a run upstream with a jet boat is possible). Another is to land in Larsen Bay and make a two-mile portage to the midsection of the river (aptly named "Portage") and then raft to the mouth. The last is to fly to the Karluk Lake outlet and float downstream to the Karluk Lagoon or Portage.

Highlights: Kodiak's ultimate fishing. Excellent for king salmon (from mid-June through early July), silver salmon (in the second half of September), red salmon (in mid-June and the second half of July), pink salmon (from late July through early August), steelhead trout (from late September through November), and Dolly Varden charr (from May through November).

Species: Dolly Varden, king salmon, pink salmon, red salmon, silver salmon, steelhead, *chum salmon.*

Regulations: Spring closures for rainbow and steelhead trout fishing from April 1 through June 14. For additional restrictions, consult the current Alaska Department of Fish and Game sportfishing regulations or contact the ADF&G Kodiak office, (907) 486-4791.

Facilities: Commercial lodging, guide services, and two public cabins are available.

Contact: For lodging and guide service, contact the Karluk Lodge, P.O. Box 3, Karluk, AK 99608; (907) 241-2229 or (907) 241-2205. For an air taxi, contact Sea Hawk Air, P.O. Box 3561, Kodiak, AK 99615, (907) 486-8282 or (800) 770-HAWK. For more information, contact the Kodiak National Wildlife Refuge, 1390 Buskin River Road, Kodiak, AK 99615; (907) 487-2600.

Fishing the Karluk River System: The Karluk River is Kodiak's largest and most productive drainage. Located about 75 miles southwest of the town of Kodiak, the 22-mile river is the island's most popular fly-in location, world famous for its salmon and steelhead runs. It ranks among the finest fishing streams in Alaska.

The Karluk's extensive mountain headwaters gather at Karluk Lake, from which the main river flows north to Shelikof Strait. It is clear, fairly good-sized, with moderate depth and flow—generally rated Class I water for rafting and kayaking. The upper and middle river sections run through marshlands and open country in the Kodiak National Wildlife Refuge, while the lower river cuts a narrow canyon and eventually widens into Karluk Lagoon. Karluk Lake is situated in a beautiful mountain setting, with nearly a dozen clear-water tributaries draining deep-cut valleys.

The Karluk is one of the most productive fish systems of its size in the world, with prolific runs of all five salmon species, particularly sockeye, pink, and coho, in addition to Alaska's most significant runs of steelhead north of Yakutat. The Karluk sportfishing season starts in June with the return of the first kings and the beginning of the first of two heavy sockeye runs (the other run starts in July). By late July, pink salmon are well into the lower river, and shortly after, silvers and the first of the fall steelhead show up.

The lagoon and lower river are the most popular areas to target bright salmon early in the season. Later, anglers will usually fly into midriver, or the Portage area, or float down from the lake to intercept migrating fish. Steelhead fishing is done mostly in late September and October from midriver, where the fish tend to congregate, or the lagoon. The Karluk's abundant Dolly Varden charr provide mostly incidental fishing excitement throughout the season, but they can be targeted in spring, late summer, and fall at the lagoon and in tributaries around the lake (like the Thumb River).

The river lends itself perfectly to a leisurely raft trip of two to five days (depending on the put in). Most of the river is wide and fairly shallow (one to four feet), with good holding areas noticeably scarce on sections (especially below Portage). Good campsites and firewood are even harder to find. All in all, however, the Karluk is rated extremely high for its stream conditions, abundant runs, and ease of fishing. It definitely ranks among Alaska's top 10 fishing rivers.

Note: A land-use permit may be required to fish the Karluk. Check with Koniag Inc., 210 Kashevarof, Suite 6, Kodiak, AK 99615, (907) 486-4147, for details.

58 Ayakulik River System

Location: In the southwest Kodiak Island drainage, 85 miles southwest of Kodiak, 315 miles southwest of Anchorage; see map page 267.

USGS maps: Karluk A-1, A-2, B-1, B-2.

How to get there: By floatplane from Kodiak. Points of entry are limited to the outlet of Red Lake, Red River, and the Bear Creek vicinity. Take-outs are normally arranged at the mouth of the river. A few trails are present, particularly around the cabin on Red Lake.

Highlights: Kodiak's best king salmon fishing (in the first half of June). Excellent for silver salmon (throughout September), red salmon (in mid-June and mid-July), pink salmon (from mid-July through early August), and steelhead trout (from October through November); good fishing for Dolly Varden (from June through August).

Species: Chum salmon, Dolly Varden, king salmon, pink salmon, rainbow trout, red salmon, silver salmon, steelhead.

Regulations: Spring closures on rainbow and steelhead trout fishing from April 1 through June 14. For additional restrictions, consult the current Alaska Department of Fish and Game sportfishing regulations or contact the ADF&G Kodiak office, (907) 486-4791.

Facilities: A Forest Service cabin is located at the outlet of Red Lake. Guide services are available.

Contact: For guide services, contact Ayakulik Camp, P.O. Box 670071, Chugiak, AK 99567, (907) 696-2484; or Kodiak Adventures, P.O. Box 1403, Seward, AK 99664, (907) 373-2285. For an air taxi, contact Sea Hawk Air, P.O. Box 3561, Kodiak, AK 99615, (907) 486-8282 or (800) 770-HAWK. For more information, contact the Kodiak National Wildlife Refuge, 1390 Buskin River Road, Kodiak, AK 99615; (907) 487-2600.

Fishing the Ayakulik River System: The Ayakulik River (also known as the Red River) on the southwest corner of the island has the second best fishing on Kodiak, which says quite a bit, considering the amazing field of rivers it's rated among. Like its exalted neighbor, the Karluk, the Ayakulik is blessed with a proliferation of salmon—all five species—as well as charr and steelhead. Considerably smaller than the Karluk, it has much better stream conditions, and it doesn't get anywhere near as many visitors.

The Ayakulik meanders through a shallow valley above Olga Bay, surrounded by rolling green hills, tiny lakes, and marshlands. A series of small tributary streams draining the slopes of nearby mountains help shape the river's character, especially Red River, flowing out of Red Lake, which contributes significantly to the Ayakulik sportfishery.

Salmon fishing kicks off on the lower river (below the Red River confluence, near Bear Creek) in early June, starting with king salmon. It trails off in the fall with deep-bodied silvers and steelhead, with nonstop action for red and pink salmon in between. The Ayakulik is especially noted for its king salmon fishing, which in many ways outclasses the Karluk's (more fish, better fly-fishing conditions, and fewer people). The red run has two components, just like on the Karluk; one occurs in June, the other in July. Pink salmon, as most everywhere else on the island, swarm the lower part of Ayakulik in midsummer alongside less numerous chums. Dolly Varden fill in the brief gaps between salmon runs. The Ayakulik fall steelhead run is about half the size of the Karluk's, but is more spread out along the river. That diffusion, plus the river's size, makes for challenging fishing. A small population of rainbow trout resides in Red Lake.

Most folks fish the Ayakulik just below the Red River confluence, near Bear Creek, which is accessible by floatplane. The river makes an excellent float trip of three to five days, from the Red Lake or the Red River put in.

59 Olga Lake System

Location: In the south Kodiak Island drainage, 90 miles southwest of Kodiak, 325 miles southwest of Anchorage; see map page 267.

USGS maps: Karluk A-1, A-2.

How to get there: By floatplane from Kodiak or area lodges. Points of access include the outlet of Upper and Lower Olga Lakes as well as the mouth of Olga Creek on Olga Bay.

Highlights: Excellent fishing for silver salmon (in September), red salmon (from late June through early July and in early September), and pink salmon (in the second half of July); good fishing for Dolly Varden (from June through August).

Species: Dolly Varden, pink salmon, rainbow trout, red salmon, silver salmon, *steelhead*.

Regulations: Spring closures for rainbow and steelhead trout fishing from April 1 through June 14. For additional restrictions, consult the current Alaska Department of Fish and Game sportfishing regulations or contact the ADF&G Kodiak office, (907) 486-4791.

Facilities: Commercial lodging and a cabin are available.

Contact: For lodging information, contact the Olga Bay Lodge, 321 Maple Street, Kodiak, AK 99615; (907) 486-5373. For an air taxi, contact Sea Hawk Air, P.O. Box 3561, Kodiak, AK 99615, (907) 486-8282 or (800) 770-HAWK. For general and cabin rental information, contact the Kodiak National Wildlife Refuge, 1390 Buskin River Road, Kodiak, AK 99615; (907) 487-2600.

Fishing the Olga Lake System: The Olga Lakes are on lower Olga Bay, about 85 miles southwest of Kodiak. A short, wide channel connects South Olga Lakes (also known as Upper and Lower Olga Lakes) with Olga Creek, a narrow and slow stream, as the primary outlet to salt water. Though small, the Olga Lakes system offers a variety of superb fishing experiences—lake, small stream, and tidal water—in salmon-rich Olga Bay.

At the mouth, huge schools of red salmon throng beginning in late June and continuing into July, followed by vast numbers of pinks, then silvers later in fall. (There is another red run in September.)

Each tide brings in more fresh, bright salmon, creating opportunities for fishing equal to the best anywhere on the island. Anglers take sea-run Dollies in the salt off the creek mouth all season and in the river from midsummer on. The outlet of Lower Olga Lake is another prime fishing location for salmon, Dolly Varden charr, and even a few rainbows.

Note: Visiting anglers should be aware that area land is privately owned and a land-use permit is required to fish the stream and lakes. Contact Koniag Inc., 210 Kashevarof, Suite 6, Kodiak, AK 99615, (907) 486-4147, for a use permit. A fee, which varies with length of stay, is required.

60 Akalura Lake/Creek

Location: In the south Kodiak Island drainage, 80 miles southwest of Kodiak, 315 miles southwest of Anchorage; see map page 267.

USGS map: Karluk A-1.

How to get there: By floatplane from Kodiak or nearby lodges, landing at the outlet of Akalura Lake or near the creek mouth at Cannery Cove.

Highlights: Excellent fishing for silver salmon (throughout September) and pink salmon (in the second half of July); good fishing for Dolly Varden charr (from June through August).

Species: Dolly Varden, pink salmon, rainbow trout, red salmon, silver salmon.

Regulations: Spring closures for rainbow and steelhead trout fishing from April 1 through June 14. For additional restrictions, consult the current Alaska Department of Fish and Game sportfishing regulations or contact the ADF&G Kodiak office, (907) 486-4791.

Facilities: No developed public facilities.

Contact: For an air taxi, contact Sea Hawk Air, P.O. Box 3561, Kodiak, AK 99615, (907) 486-8282 or (800) 770-HAWK.

Fishing Akalura Lake/Creek: Located on Olga Bay, just south of Red Lake, Akalura Lake is only two and a half miles wide and shaped like a triangle. The brushy outlet stream is swift and clear, and empties into Cannery Cove two miles away.

Although not much in size, the Akalura drainage has concentrated fishing. Silver salmon are thick around the creek mouth during incoming tides in fall, as are pink salmon and Dolly Varden earlier in the season. A smaller run of red salmon also move into the area in early summer, translating into good fly-fishing at the mouth and lake outlet. The lake's native rainbow trout provide fair fishing in the spring and fall, but the real show at Akalura is the silver salmon fishing. It's popular with the fly-in lodge crowd, who often stop to check the fishing on their way to the Karluk or Ayakulik.

61 Dog Salmon (Frazer) River System

Location: In the south Kodiak Island drainage, 80 miles southwest of Kodiak, 315 miles southwest of Anchorage; see map page 267.

USGS maps: Karluk A-1, B-1.

How to get there: By floatplane from Kodiak or any of the area lodges. Access is through the Frazer Lake outlet or the flats at the mouth of the river. Trails lead along upper stretches of Dog Salmon River from the outlet. As this is private land, a permit is required to fish here.

Highlights: Kodiak's best chum salmon fishing (from July through early August). Also excellent fishing for red salmon (in the first half of July) and pink salmon (in the second half of July); good silver salmon fishing (in September).

Species: Chum salmon, Dolly Varden, king salmon, pink salmon, red salmon, silver salmon, steelhead.

Regulations: King salmon fishing is prohibited; spring closures for rainbow and steelhead trout fishing from April 1 through June 14. For additional restrictions, consult the current Alaska Department of Fish and Game sportfishing regulations or contact the ADF&G Kodiak office, (907) 486-4791.

Facilities: Forest Service cabins are available in the Frazer Lake vicinity.

Contact: For an air taxi, contact Sea Hawk Air, P.O. Box 3561, Kodiak, AK 99615, (907) 486-8282 or (800) 770-HAWK. For general and cabin rental information, contact the Kodiak National Wildlife Refuge, 1390 Buskin River Road, Kodiak, AK 99615; (907) 487-2600.

Fishing the Dog Salmon (Frazer) River System: Dog Salmon River, also known as Frazer River, drains the second largest lake on the island, Frazer, which lies between Karluk and Red Lakes in the southwest corner of Kodiak. Along with its fabulous neighbor rivers (the Karluk and Ayakulik), the Frazer is one of the island's most productive salmon systems, particularly for sockeye and chum.

The fast and rocky river flows about 11 miles from the lake to the east end of Olga Bay, with a set of falls roughly a mile below the outlet. On the lower reaches near the mouth, the river slows in an area known as Dog Salmon Flats and the main channel splits. A handful of tributaries, many of them with small lakes at their headwaters, drain into Frazer Lake and the Dog Salmon River. Wildlife, especially bears, is abundant.

True to its name, Dog Salmon River has Kodiak's prime chum salmon fishing. In July, incoming tides push huge numbers of the sea-bright calicos into the river mouth, creating exceptional angling opportunities. Red and pink salmon also return in great numbers to spawn in the drainage, along with a notable silver run. And like so many other productive island streams, the Dog Salmon has a super abundance of Dolly Varden charr—to the point of being a nuisance at times. There are also small numbers of king salmon and steelhead trout, but not enough to support a sportfishery. (Fishing for king salmon is prohibited.)

Many anglers fish the system through Frazer Lake, working the section of river above the falls for silvers and reds. Forest Service cabins are available on the north end of the lake and on a small tributary lake west of the outlet.

Note: The land along the creek is private. If you decide to fish there, contact Koniag Inc., 210 Kashevarof, Suite 6, Kodiak, AK 99615, (907) 486-4147, for a use permit.

(62) Uyak Bay

Location: Off west Kodiak Island, 60 miles west of Kodiak, 285 miles southwest of Anchorage; see map page 267.

USGS maps: Kodiak B-5, B-6, C-6; Karluk C-1.

How to get there: By plane from Kodiak or area lodges. Traditional points of access have been Larsen Bay and Amook Bay in the central portion of Uyak Bay. Some lodge operators provide skiffs to fish the better locations around the bay.

Highlights: Excellent fishing for silver salmon (in the second half of August), pink salmon (from late July through early August), and halibut (from June through August); good fishing for king salmon (from July through August) and Dolly Varden (from May through June).

Species: Dolly Varden, halibut, king salmon, pink salmon, silver salmon, *chum salmon, red salmon.*

Regulations: Halibut fishing is closed from January 1 through 31. For additional restrictions, consult the current Alaska Department of Fish and Game sportfishing regulations or contact the ADF&G Kodiak office, (907) 486-4791.

Facilities: Commercial lodging, a cabin, and guide services are available.

Contact: For lodging and guide services, contact Amook Lodge, P.O. Box 111, Larsen Bay, AK 96624, (907) 847-2312; The Cannery at Zachar Bay, P.O. Box 2609, Kodiak, AK 99615, (907) 486-4120; Zachar Bay Camp, P.O. Box 3911, Kodiak, AK 99615, (907) 486-3008; or Zachar Bay Lodge, P.O. Box 2609, Kodiak, AK 99615, (907) 486-4120. For general information, contact the Kodiak National Wildlife Refuge, 1390 Buskin River Road, Kodiak, AK 99615; (907) 487-2600. For an air taxi, contact Sea Hawk Air, P.O. Box 3561, Kodiak, AK 99615, (907) 486-8282 or (800) 770-HAWK.

Fishing Uyak Bay: On the west side of Kodiak Island by Shelikof Strait, this long, clear fjord penetrates the heart of the island. Surrounded by the steep mountain slopes and evergreen forests of the Kodiak National Wildlife Refuge, Uyak is home to abundant marine life—such as fish, waterfowl, seals, and whales—and a healthy brown bear population that stalks its beaches and streams in search of food. Some of Kodiak's largest river systems are found in the area, assuring anglers of excellent salmon fishing. Part of Uyak Bay, Larsen Bay has traditionally served as an access point to the ever-popular Karluk River drainage.

The greater bay area between Rocky Point and Cape Kuliuk encompasses 34 streams and rivers—some small and crystal clear, others vast, glacial, and turbid. Almost without exception, these systems support fish runs to varying degrees. The best way to explore these numerous prospects is by boat. Surf casting can be quite productive around the better stream locations, but a boat allows easy access and enables one to probe the deeper water for bottomfish. Salmon, especially silvers and pinks, are abundant throughout much of Uyak, along with good numbers of feeder king salmon and Dolly Varden charr. Look for halibut and king salmon around reefs, shoals, points, and islands in the outer bay, in moderately deep water. For charr and pinks, target areas around the mouths of clear-water streams. Silver salmon, depending on the time, are best encountered in deeper outer waters or in the smaller bays near stream mouths. Spiridon and Zachar Bays receive heavy runs, but for anglers in search of varied saltwater fishing in an area yet to be fully discovered by the public, Uyak Bay is it.

(63) Ugak Bay

Location: Off northeast Kodiak Island, 25 miles south of Kodiak, 280 miles southwest of Anchorage; see map page 267.

USGS maps: Kodiak B-1, B-2, B-3, B-4, C-3.

How to get there: By plane or car from Kodiak. Float- and wheelplanes can land in coves and on beaches around the bay. Two road-accessible locations are Saltery Cove via Saltery Cove Road and Pasagshak Bay via Pasagshak Bay Road through Rezanof Drive West. The road to Saltery Cove is very rough and recommended for four-wheel-drive vehicles only, but the road to Pasagshak is open to all traffic.

Highlights: Good, easily accessible Kodiak fishing for king salmon (from July through August), silver salmon (from late August through early September), pink salmon (from late July through early August), Dolly Varden charr (from May through June), and halibut (from June through August).

Species: Chum salmon, Dolly Varden, halibut, king salmon, pink salmon, silver salmon, *red salmon, steelhead.*

Regulations: Halibut fishing is closed from January 1 through 31. For additional restrictions, consult the current Alaska Department of Fish and Game sportfishing regulations or contact the ADF&G Kodiak office, (907) 486-4791.

Facilities: Commercial lodging, a campground, and guide services are available.

Contact: For lodging and guide services, contact the R&R Lodge, P.O. Box 1272, Kodiak, AK 99615, (907) 486-3704; or Saltery Lake Lodge, 1516 Larch Street, Suite One, Kodiak, AK 99615, (907) 486-5037. For general information, contact the Kodiak National Wildlife Refuge, 1390 Buskin River Road, Kodiak, AK 99615; (907) 487-2600. For an air taxi, contact Sea Hawk Air, P.O. Box 3561, Kodiak, AK 99615, (907) 486-8282 or (800) 770-HAWK.

Fishing Ugak Bay: Ugak Bay is a pristine outlet to the Gulf of Alaska, its shores contained within the Kodiak National Wildlife Refuge. A fairly deep, clear bay with a diverse bottom structure accommodating a variety of fish species, Ugak is a popular angling and recreation destination for locals and visitors alike, easily accessible by road or air. Forested mountains and hills surround the outer bay, while the inner bay features deep-cutting valleys and snow-covered peaks that make for a beautiful setting.

A handful of clear-water streams empty into Ugak, providing good salmon and charr fishing for boaters and surf casters alike. Recreational craft like skiffs and kayaks can be launched from beaches or river mouths in Saltery Cove and Pasagshak Bay. (Be aware that strong east winds from the Gulf of Alaska can turn outer Ugak into a whirlpool of white water, although its more protected bays and coves are a pleasure to fish on good weather days.) Large schools of silver and pink salmon traveling close to shore can be seen and targeted, and halibut tend to be on the aggressive side. There is also a developing feeder king salmon fishery in the outer bay. Dolly Varden action is best during late spring and again in late summer, when these sea-run charr forage the points, beaches, and stream mouths in search of prey or spawning salmon.

Suggested areas for boaters include Saltery Cove, Portage Bay, Pasagshak Bay, and Eagle Harbor for salmon and charr, and the reefs and shoals of their moderately deep waters for bottomfish. Surf casters do well at the mouths of the Saltery and Pasagshak Rivers and the mouths of streams draining into Portage Cove and Eagle Harbor.

(64) Saltery River

Location: In the northeast Kodiak Island drainage, 25 miles southwest of Kodiak, 275 miles southwest of Anchorage; see map page 267.

USGS map: Kodiak C-3.

How to get there: By car via Rezanof Drive West and Saltery Cove Road, from the town of Kodiak; also by plane from Kodiak, landing at Saltery Cove. Saltery Cove Road is very rough—a four-wheel-drive vehicle is recommended.

Highlights: Excellent fishing for silver salmon (in the second half of September), red salmon (in the first half of July), pink salmon (from late July through early August), and Dolly Varden charr (in May and from July through October).

Species: Dolly Varden, pink salmon, rainbow trout, red salmon, silver salmon, *chum salmon, steelhead*.

Regulations: Spring closures for rainbow and steelhead trout fishing from April 1 through June 14. For additional restrictions, consult the current Alaska Department of Fish and Game sportfishing regulations or contact the ADF&G Kodiak office, (907) 486-4791.

Facilities: Commercial lodging is available.

Contact: For lodging and guide services, contact the Saltery Lake Lodge. 1516 Larch Street, Suite One, Kodiak, AK 99615; (907) 486-5037 or (800) 770-5037. For an air taxi, contact Sea Hawk Air, P.O. Box 3561, Kodiak, AK 99615, (907) 486-8282 or (800) 770-HAWK.

Fishing the Saltery River: The Saltery River begins on the south slopes of Center Mountain and flows into Ugak Bay, 25 miles southwest of Kodiak. Accessed via the rough Saltery Cove Road, it's noted for superb silver and red salmon fishing and abundant Dolly Varden charr.

The river above Saltery Lake runs swift and straight, but slows considerably and meanders through a flat valley before reaching Saltery Cove. The water is crystal clear, with many deep holes, riffles, and runs, and a bottom of fine gravel. Wildlife is abundant in the area and the scenery pleasing. It's fairly remote, even though it lies along the road system, and is highly recommended for first-time Kodiak anglers.

The majority of anglers fish the river's silver and red salmon runs. The reds are the first to arrive in early July and spice up the action for fly fishers until August. Next come the hefty silvers, many weighing into the teens, which can be caught from tidewater all the way up to the lake outlet. Along with the Buskin and Pasagshak, the Saltery also provides some of the best spring Dolly Varden action along the Kodiak road system, as thousands of fish move out of Saltery Lake on their way to the ocean. This fishery turns on again later in the season (from late summer through fall), as fat Dollies return to the river to feed on salmon eggs and prepare for spawning and overwintering. The upper river, just above the lake, is a major salmon spawning area and one of the best places to find thick schools of voracious charr. Fair to good Dolly fishing can also be enjoyed all summer long in the cove, using narrow silver spoons, herring strips, or small diving plugs.

⑥⑤ Pasagshak River System

Location: In the northeast Kodiak Island drainage, 25 miles south of Kodiak, 275 miles southwest of Anchorage; see map page 267.

USGS map: Kodiak B-1.

How to get there: From the town of Kodiak, by car via Rezanof Drive West and Pasagshak Bay Road. Pasagshak Bay Road briefly parallels a small tributary creek en route to Lake Rose Tead and Pasagshak State Recreation Site near the river's mouth. Several trails along the river provide additional access.

Highlights: Kodiak's best road-accessible coho fishing (in September). Also excellent fishing for pink salmon (from late July through early August); good fishing for red salmon (from late June through early July) and Dolly Varden charr (in May and from July through October).

Species: Dolly Varden, pink salmon, red salmon, silver salmon, *chum salmon, king salmon*.

Regulations: King salmon fishing is prohibited. For additional restrictions, consult the current Alaska Department of Fish and Game sportfishing regulations or contact the ADF&G Kodiak office, (907) 486-4791.

Facilities: A campground is available at the Pasagshak State Recreation Site.

Contact: For fishing information, contact the Alaska Department of Fish and Game, Kodiak Office, 211 Mission Road, Kodiak, AK 99615; (907) 486-1880. For lodging information, contact the Northland Ranch Resort, P.O. Box 2376, Kodiak, AK 99615; (907) 486-5578. For campground information, contact Alaska State Parks, Kodiak District, S.S.R. Box 3800, Kodiak, AK 99615; (907) 486-6339.

Fishing the Pasagshak River System: The Pasagshak is one of the most famous and visited streams on the Kodiak road system. With clear, wide waters that are easy to fish, it's one of the most productive systems of its size on the island, with abundant salmon and Dolly Varden charr.

Originating from the south slopes of Marin Range, the headwaters drain into Lake Rose Tead. From there, the river flows only two miles to Ugak Bay. The beach area around the mouth is the hot spot on the Pasagshak, and, as is common on most coastal streams, incoming tides usually bring the best fishing for snappy, bright schools of salmon and charr. Of particular note is the river's trophy silver salmon fishery. Thousands of above-average-size coho invade the Pasagshak every fall, with ample opportunities for fish weighing in the midteens and occasional specimens to 18 and 20 pounds or more. Many diehard anglers still use salmon roe clusters with predictable results, but flies and hardware take a good share of these big Pasagshak silvers.

A strong red salmon run usually occurs in early to midsummer; they're best taken in the shallow, faster sections. Pink salmon usually follow the reds, but they can be caught anywhere, although the mouth is probably the most popular area. Dolly Varden are another Pasagshak highlight. The prime times are during the spring out-migration from Lake Rose Tead right after breakup and again in late summer and fall as the fish return fat, bright, and full of fight from the salt of Pasagshak and Ugak Bays.

⑥⑥ Olds River System

Location: In the northeast Kodiak Island drainage, 25 miles south of Kodiak, 265 miles southwest of Anchorage; see map page 267.

USGS map: Kodiak C-2.

How to get there: By car via Rezanof Drive West, from the town of Kodiak. The road crosses the lower river and two tributaries, with limited trail access to the river mouth and upstream areas.

Highlights: Excellent fishing for silver salmon (in the second half of September), pink salmon (from late July through early August), and Dolly Varden (from September through October).

Species: Chum salmon, Dolly Varden, pink salmon, silver salmon, *red salmon*.

Regulations: King salmon fishing is prohibited; closed to salmon fishing upstream of the road crossing from August 1 through September 11. For additional restrictions, consult the current Alaska Department of Fish and Game sportfishing regulations or contact the ADF&G Kodiak office, (907) 486-4791.

Facilities: Commercial lodging, gas, and a campground are available.

Contact: For fishing information, contact the Alaska Department of Fish and Game, Kodiak Office, 211 Mission Road, Kodiak, AK 99615; (907) 486-1880. For lodging information, contact the Kalsin Inn Ranch, P.O. Box 1696, Kodiak, AK 99615; (907) 486-2659. For campground information, contact the Alaska State Parks, Kodiak District, S.S.R. Box 3800, Kodiak, AK 99615; (907) 486-6339.

Fishing the Olds River System: Olds River is a road-accessible, clear-water stream draining from near Marin Range into Kalsin Bay, on the south side of Chiniak, approximately 14 air miles south and slightly west of Kodiak. A few small lakes are connected to the system. Like other productive road streams of Chiniak Bay, the Olds receives moderate pressure from local and visiting anglers, but holds up well, with especially good fishing for pink and silver salmon, as well as Dolly Varden charr.

Winding through a narrow valley covered with dense forests, the upper and middle sections of the Olds flow fairly fast, while the wider lower river moves more slowly, especially in its last mile, where Kalsin Creek joins in from the south. Most people fish salmon in the mouth and lower river, working the incoming tides. During low water, conditions are good for sight-fishing.

In addition to great silver and pink salmon runs, the Olds gets a healthy run of spawning Dolly Varden in autumn. These colorful charr brighten up the fishing along the entire river. Like the American, the Olds makes a popular one-day destination for anyone sampling the fishing along the Kodiak road system, with adjacent Kalsin Bay holding some of the more popular and productive salmon and halibut waters in Chiniak Bay.

57 American River

Location: In the northeast Kodiak Island drainage, 12 miles southwest of Kodiak, 260 miles southwest of Anchorage; see map page 267.

USGS map: Kodiak C-2.

How to get there: By car via Rezanof Drive West, from the town of Kodiak. The road crosses the lower stream with trails leading upstream to productive holes or downstream to the mouth. Just south of the stream crossing, the rough Saltery Cove Road begins and more or less follows the middle and upper river for several miles, crossing in two places.

Highlights: Excellent fishing for silver salmon (in the second half of September), pink salmon (from late July through early August), and Dolly Varden charr (from September through October); good fishing for chum salmon (from late July through early August).

Species: Chum salmon, Dolly Varden, pink salmon, silver salmon.

Regulations: King salmon fishing is prohibited; closed to salmon fishing upstream of the road crossing from August 1 through September 10. For additional restrictions, consult the current Alaska Department of Fish and Game sportfishing regulations or contact the ADF&G Kodiak office, (907) 486-4791.

Facilities: Commercial lodging, gas, and a campground are available.

Contact: For fishing information, contact the Alaska Department of Fish and Game, Kodiak Office, 211 Mission Road, Kodiak, AK 99615; (907) 486-1880. For lodging information, contact the Kalsin Inn Ranch, P.O. Box 1696, Kodiak, AK 99615; (907) 486-2659. For campground information, contact Alaska State Parks, Kodiak District, S.S.R. Box 3800, Kodiak, AK 99615; (907) 486-6339.

Fishing the American River: The clear American River originates near Center Mountain and runs east through a forested valley to Middle Bay, a small inlet connected to Chiniak Bay. Moderately fast, with good stream fishing conditions, the American has several small tributary creeks and lakes and provides one of the most extensive and popular salmon/charr fisheries on the Kodiak road system.

From midsummer through late fall, the American hosts large runs of silver, chum, and pink salmon. The abundance of the smallish humpbacked salmon can be staggering, so much so

322   **Alaska State Map—page 8**

that anglers wishing to target the flashy silvers sometimes delay their fishing until late in the season, when the pinks thin out. The American is also a major spawning ground for sea-run Dollies. Although the fish are not very large, typically about 10 to 15 inches, their concentrations make for top-notch action. The American is definitely worth checking out if you're fishing the Kodiak road system in late summer or fall.

68 Chiniak Bay

Location: Off northeast Kodiak Island, southeast of Kodiak, 250 miles southwest of Anchorage; see map page 267.

USGS maps: Kodiak C-1, D-1, D-2.

How to get there: By boat from the town of Kodiak. All parts of the bay are easily accessible by almost any size craft, although outlying areas require larger boats due to rough seas. An extensive road network spans the bay from Spruce Cape to Cape Chiniak, with ample locations for launching skiffs, rafts, or kayaks.

Highlights: Good fishing for king salmon (in May and from August through September), silver salmon (from late August through early September), pink salmon (in the first half of August), and halibut (from June through August).

Species: Dolly Varden, halibut, king salmon, pink salmon, silver salmon, *chum salmon, red salmon, steelhead.*

Regulations: Halibut fishing is closed from January 1 through 31. For additional restrictions, consult the current Alaska Department of Fish and Game sportfishing regulations or contact the ADF&G Kodiak office, (907) 486-4791.

Facilities: Hotels, gas, lodging, boat rentals and launches, guide services, sporting goods, and groceries are available in Kodiak.

Contact: For guide services, contact the Kodiak Island Charters, P.O. Box 3750, Kodiak, AK 99615; (907) 486-5380. For lodging information, contact Shelikof Lodge, 211 Thorsheim, Kodiak, AK 99615, (907) 486-5657; or Westmark Kodiak, 236 Rezanof Drive West, Kodiak, AK 99615, (907) 486-5712.

Fishing Chiniak Bay: Chiniak Bay, near the town of Kodiak and the island's only highway system, is the most popular recreational marine fishery on Kodiak Island. Its numerous islands and lesser bays contain important salmon- and charr-producing streams. Lush, green mountain slopes drop dramatically into the bay's clear blue waters, making for an idyllic Alaska setting.

Despite its easy access and high use, Chiniak Bay manages to hold its own, producing good catches of salmon, charr, and bottomfish. Large runs of acrobatic silvers invade the bay every fall, and halibut lurk on reefs and shoals in the deeper waters. Both natural and enhanced populations of king salmon are present, along with sea-run Dolly Varden charr. Fishing from a boat is the best way to enjoy the action, but angling from shore near the mouths of spawning streams can also be productive for salmon and charr. The bay has long been a year-round feeding ground for king salmon, but a new fishery now makes it possible to catch these dime-bright brutes in their prime. Although not particularly large, about 12 to 20 pounds on average, they're plentiful in the middle and outer parts of Chiniak. Cape Chiniak and Buoy Four are two of the more popular locations. An early summer return of hatchery kings to Mill Bay, just north of Chiniak Bay, provides good action. Pink salmon flood the area in late summer, with the best fishing occurring in bays near the mouths of rivers and creeks. (A few weeks later, schools of silvers pour into the same areas.) Halibut are abundant during the summer months and can be best taken from outer bay areas, which have the proper depth and structure.

The best angling locations around Chiniak Bay include Monashka Bay (pink salmon, Dolly Varden), Mill Bay (king salmon, silver salmon), Womens Bay (silver salmon, pink salmon, Dolly Varden), Middle Bay (silver salmon, pink salmon, Dolly Varden), Kalsin Bay (silver salmon, pink salmon, Dolly Varden), Isthmus Bay (pink salmon, Dolly Varden), Long and Woody Islands (king salmon, halibut), Pinnacle Rock (king salmon, halibut), Cape Chiniak (king salmon, halibut), Williams Reef (halibut), and Buoy Four (king salmon, halibut).

69 Buskin River

Location: In the northeast Kodiak Island drainage, five miles southwest of Kodiak, 250 miles southwest of Anchorage; see map page 267.

USGS map: Kodiak D-2.

How to get there: By car, there are several access points from the town of Kodiak.

Highlights: One of Kodiak's best road-accessible fisheries. Excellent fishing for pink salmon (from late July through early August) and Dolly Varden charr (in May and from July through October); good fishing for silver salmon (in the second half of September) and red salmon (from late June through mid-July).

Species: Chum salmon, Dolly Varden, king salmon, pink salmon, red salmon, silver salmon, *rainbow trout, steelhead.*

Regulations: King salmon fishing is prohibited, except by emergency order; steelhead trout fishing is also prohibited. Portions of the river below the first bridge are closed to salmon fishing from August 1 through September 11. For additional fishing restrictions, consult the current Alaska Department of Fish and Game sportfishing regulations or contact the ADF&G Kodiak office, (907) 486-4791.

Facilities: Commercial lodging, gas, and a campground are available.

Contact: For fishing information, contact the Alaska Department of Fish and Game, Kodiak Office, 211 Mission Road, Kodiak, AK 99615; (907) 486-1880. For lodging and camping information, contact Alaska State Parks, Kodiak District, S.S.R. Box 3800, Kodiak, AK 99615, (907) 486-6339; or Buskin River Inn, 1395 Airport Road, Kodiak, AK 99615, (907) 487-2700.

Fishing Buskin River: The clear-flowing Buskin, on Chiniak Bay just southwest of the town of Kodiak, is the most popular fishery on the island (supporting nearly half of Kodiak's total sportfishing effort), with easy access and abundant salmon and Dolly Varden charr.

The Buskin system drains a fairly small valley between Pyramid and Erskine Mountains and contains a small lake of the same name a few miles above Chiniak Bay. The medium-size river is gravel-bottomed and brushy, with plenty of holding water and good sight-fishing possibilities. Since the Buskin is along the road system so close to town, it receives its fair share of angling pressure from locals, as well as from outside anglers with limited time or funds to enjoy the Kodiak area.

The Buskin is perhaps best known for its amazing Dolly Varden fishing. Scads of out-migrating fish are typically caught right after breakup (in April and May) on small silver spinners and spoons, while fattened, prime fish that enter the river from midsummer through fall are taken mostly on bright flies and spinners. Very nice runs of red salmon flood the Buskin in June and July, creating one of Kodiak's most significant, easily accessed sockeye fisheries. Next to the sea-run Dollies, however, silvers are the most sought-after fish, entering the Buskin in mid-August and continuing into September. Because of regulations, the early part of this fishery is restricted to the mouth and lagoon, while later on (in mid-September) it opens up to include the entire river.

In some years, small numbers of king salmon move into the Buskin. These are not native fish but hatchery kings from Mill Bay (on the northeast side of Kodiak) that have strayed from the release site and are in search of a suitable rearing habitat. Most of these kings are taken near the river mouth on incoming tides.

Chapter 6

Southeast Fishing

Southeast Alaska

204

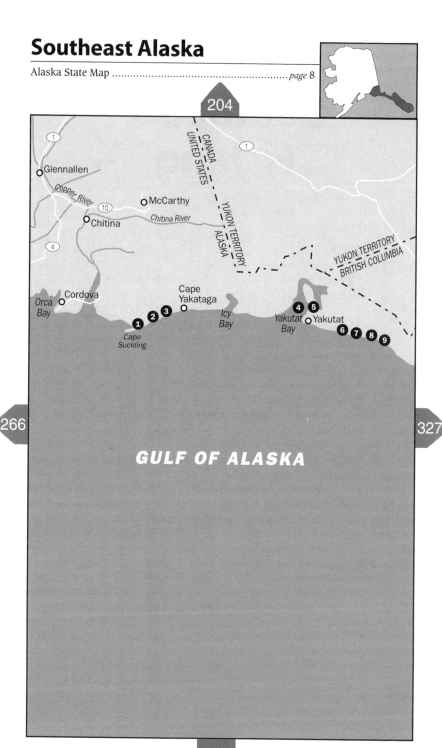

Glennallen

Copper River

McCarthy

Chitina River

Chitina

CANADA
UNITED STATES

YUKON TERRITORY
ALASKA

YUKON TERRITORY
BRITISH COLUMBIA

Cordova

Orca
Bay

Cape
Yakataga

Icy
Bay

Yakutat
Bay

Yakutat

Cape
Suckling

266

327

GULF OF ALASKA

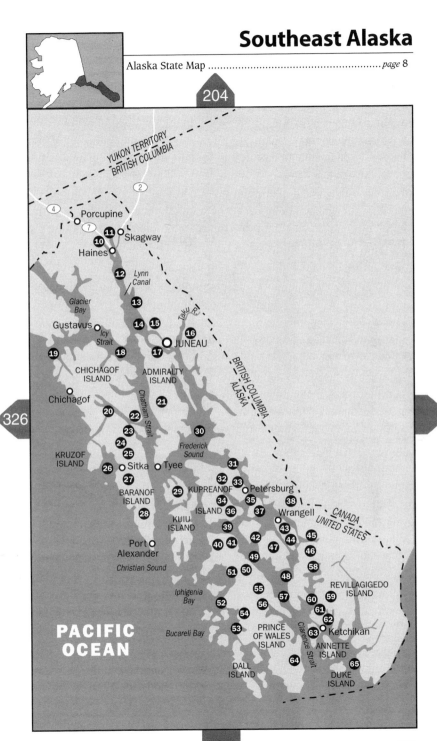

326

YUKON TERRITORY
BRITISH COLUMBIA

② 2

④ 4
Porcupine
⑦ 7
⑪ 11
⑩ 10   Skagway
Haines

⑫ 12   *Lynn Canal*

⑬ 13

Glacier Bay

Gustavus   *Icy Strait*
⑭ 14 ⑮ 15

Taku R.

⑲ 19   ⑱ 18   ⑰ 17   ⑯ 16 JUNEAU

CHICHAGOF ISLAND

ADMIRALTY ISLAND

BRITISH COLUMBIA
ALASKA

Chichagof

⑳ 20   ㉑ 21

KRUZOF ISLAND

㉒ 22
㉓ 23   *Chatham Strait*
㉔ 24
㉕ 25
㉖ 26 Sitka   Tyee
㉗ 27

㉚ 30

Frederick Sound

㉛ 31

㉜ 32 ㉝ 33
㉞ 34   ㉟ 35   Petersburg
㊱ 36   ㊲ 37   Wrangell
KUPREANOF ISLAND
㉙ 29
㊳ 38
CANADA
UNITED STATES

BARANOF ISLAND

㉘ 28

KUIU ISLAND

㊴ 39

㊵ 40 ㊶ 41   ㊷ 42   ㊸ 43
㊹ 44   ㊺ 45
㊻ 46
㊼ 47
㊾ 49   ㊽ 48   ㊿ 58

Port Alexander

Christian Sound

㊿ 51 50
㊼ 48

REVILLAGIGEDO ISLAND

Iphigenia Bay

55   56   57
52
54   60 59
53   61
62
PRINCE OF WALES ISLAND
63 Ketchikan

Bucareli Bay

Clarence Strait

ANNETTE ISLAND

64

DALL ISLAND

65

DUKE ISLAND

PACIFIC OCEAN

Southeast Hot Spots

Southeast

Imagine a vacation destination where you spend quiet mornings stalking wild steelhead on small, secluded streams, then, after lunch, boat out to scenic bays and fjords, clip on downriggers and hunt fat feeder kings, or jig for big halibut. At day's end, arms weary, you feast on a cornucopia of delights you've harvested—chunks of batter-dipped halibut, grilled salmon, rockfish, and succulent shrimp and crab pulled fresh from the pot. Later on, around the fire, the next day's anticipation is stoked with talk of exciting adventure, like flights to nearby mountain lakes, where the cutthroat trout and Dolly Varden run thick and hungry, furious to the fly.

Believe it or not, such a place does exist, beyond the realm of anglers' dreams—along the magnificent coastline, islands, and sheltered passages that make up the Southeast Panhandle of Alaska. This narrow, 120-mile-wide strip of land wedged between the Pacific and the coast of British Columbia contains some of the most fabulous country anywhere for sport anglers. Nowhere else in the world can you find such a variety and abundance of world-class opportunities—for steelhead and cutthroat trout, saltwater salmon, halibut, Dolly Varden, and others—all within easy reach by boat or plane from a half dozen communities scattered along the coast.

Country, Climate, and Conditions

The Southeast region is set apart from the rest of the state in its geography, climate, and character. From Dixon Entrance, which divides Canada's Queen Charlotte Islands from their neighboring American counterparts, north in an enormous arc to Icy Cape, the panhandle stretches nearly 600 miles. Within this region lies an impressive and dynamic landscape, shaped by the powerful force of glacial action and uplift of mountains, and nurtured by a benign climate and rich marine environment.

This is the land of temperate rain forests, with most of its coast cloaked in dense stands of hemlock and spruce, including 17-million-acre Tongass National Forest, the largest in the nation. Islands abound, hundreds of them, in a maze that includes some of the largest in the U.S., among them Prince of Wales, which ranks third in size behind Kodiak and Hawaii. Even more significant are the countless straits, channels, sounds, narrows, bays, and fjords contained within this vast archipelago, which create a haven for a diverse array of marine wildlife, from seabirds to whales and salmon. With its glaciers and abundant rainfall, this coastal paradise is further enhanced with thousands of lakes and streams, most of them containing sport fish of some kind. Much of this area is spectacular wilderness that is protected in national forests, parks, monuments, and preserves.

Southeast's climate is mild in comparison with the rest of Alaska. Warmed in winter and cooled in summer by the maritime influence of the North Pacific, conditions can be surprisingly more favorable to outdoor activities than in some locations in the lower 48 states. (Compare the January or July average temperature here with that of Chicago, for instance.) Visitors should come prepared for mild but moist weather, with temperatures in summer ranging from the mid-50s to the upper 60s (with highs in the upper 70s possible) and from the teens to the lower 40s in winter. Areas near large glaciers are subject to strong, cold winds that can sweep down at any time of year. Precipitation is extremely varied within the region (from 30 to more than 200 inches a year), but follows the same trend prevalent most elsewhere in Alaska. Late spring and early summer (from May to July) are the driest, sunniest parts of the year, while fall and early winter (from October to January) are the cloudiest and stormiest.

Southeast Fishing Highlights

As an angling destination, Southeast Alaska has so much to offer that one can only wonder why folks would want to fish anywhere else. For one thing, it has far and away Alaska's most abundant and varied inshore opportunities, with quite a few world famous salmon and halibut locations. (Communities here actively compete for the "world's best fishing" distinction.) It's also the state's wild steelhead mecca, with hundreds of identified streams containing the species, quite a few of them enjoying world-class distinction. Cutthroat trout and Dolly Varden are found throughout the region in hundreds of streams, lakes, and ponds. Trophy anglers should take special note of the fact that most of the state's largest specimens of silver, chum, steelhead, cutthroat, and halibut come from Southeast's waters.

Thanks to the region's mild climate, the fishing season typically begins earlier and continues later than elsewhere in Alaska, with an extended open water period that allows for fishing in some areas 12 months of the year. (Higher elevation lakes and some locations in northern Southeast ice over much the same as Alaska waters do elsewhere, however.)

Access, Services, and Costs

The region's close proximity to the outside world and its well-developed network of transportation and services adds immeasurably to its appeal as a vacation destination. Daily commercial jetliners link the major hubs of Juneau, Ketchikan, and Sitka with West Coast cities. With a limited local road network, access to the better fishing locations is primarily by boat or small plane, with a well-established state ferry route linking many communities. Numerous hiking trails in the region provide access to prime fishing waters. A very well-known and extensive system of public-use cabins is maintained by the U.S. Forest Service, many of them in popular lake and stream locations, with some skiffs available for fishing. And you'll find a burgeoning visitor services industry to help you make it all happen, with a bewildering array of wilderness lodges, family-style fishing camps, bed-and-breakfasts, fishing charters, guides, air taxis, boat rentals, and even floating hotels offering a world of options for every whim and price range (from $75 to several hundred for a day of fishing).

Southeast Run Timing: Freshwater

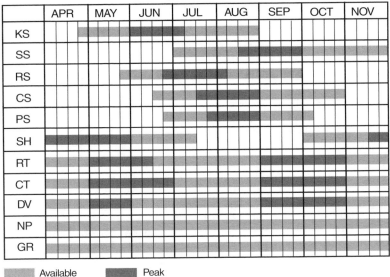

Available   Peak

KS=King Salmon, SS=Silver Salmon, RS=Red Salmon, CS=Chum Salmon, PS=Pink Salmon, SH=Sheefish, RT=Rainbow Trout, CT=Cutthroat Trout, LT=Lake Trout, DV=Dolly Varden, NP=Northern Pike, GR=Grayling

Southeast Run Timing: Salt Water

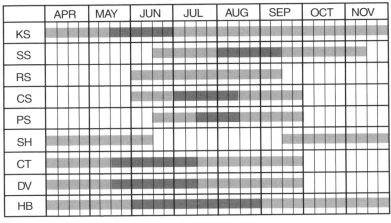

Available   Peak

KS=King Salmon, SS=Silver Salmon, RS=Red Salmon, CS=Chum Salmon, PS=Pink Salmon, SH=Sheefish, RT=Rainbow Trout, CT=Cutthroat Trout, LT=Lake Trout, DV=Dolly Varden, NP=Northern Pike, GR=Grayling

Note: Time periods are shown for bright fish, in the case of salmon entering rivers, or for general availability for resident species. Salmon are present in many systems after the period shown, but are usually in spawning/postspawning condition. Peak sportfishing periods for each species are highlighted. Run timing can vary somewhat from drainage to drainage and generally follows a later trend in waters to the west and north in Alaska. Check with local contacts listed for area run-timing specifics.

Yakutat and North Gulf Coast

West of Glacier Bay and Cape Spencer, the wild and stormy North Gulf Coast beckons with some fabulous fishing possibilities. A remote expanse with enormous glaciers and towering mountains (the Saint Elias Range, with peaks up to 19,850 feet) that drop abruptly to coastal flatlands and deserted beaches, this area, with its short, meandering streams, surprisingly holds some of Alaska's finest steelhead and silver salmon fishing. Except for the area surrounding Yakutat, it receives little visitation, despite its awesome sport fish potential. Access can be difficult and expensive, usually by small plane or boat from Yakutat or Cordova, and the weather can be extremely unpredictable and potentially violent. But the species available include abundant steelhead, trophy silver salmon, cutthroat and rainbow trout, sockeyes, Dolly Varden, and even some king salmon and halibut. This is truly an unspoiled, unexplored paradise for the adventure angler.

❶ Kiklukh River

Location:: In the north Gulf of Alaska drainage, 145 miles northwest of Yakutat, 220 miles southeast of Anchorage; see map page 326.

USGS maps: Bering Glacier A-7, A-8.

How to get there: By wheelplane from Cordova or Yakutat. Gravel bars next to the river are prime locations to land on the lower sections, but they can be tricky.

Highlights: One of the Gulf Coast's finest, unexploited stream fishing locations for trophy silver salmon (in September) and cutthroat trout (from June through August).

Species: Cutthroat trout, silver salmon, red salmon, Dolly Varden.

Regulations: Unbaited, artificial lures only from November 16 through September 14. For additional restrictions, consult the current Alaska Department of Fish and Game regulations or contact the ADF&G Yakutat office, (907) 784-3222.

Facilities: Lodging and guide services are available on the river.

Contact: For lodging and guide services, contact Alaska Gulf Coast Adventures, P.O. Box 1849, Cordova, AK 99574; (907) 784-3703 (spring through fall). For an air taxi, contact Fishing and Flying, P.O. Box 2349, Cordova, AK 99574; (907) 424-3324.

Fishing the Kiklukh River: Known also as Eightmile Creek, the Kiklukh drains a small glacial moraine just northeast of Cape Suckling near Suckling Hills. Meandering through extensive marshland in the upper sections, the lower river area is wooded with gravel beaches at its mouth. The Kiklukh is not large as rivers go, or particularly long, but it has some noteworthy possibilities for salmon and trout for anyone willing to brave the elements and explore a rarely visited area.

Every fall, strong runs of silver salmon enter the Kiklukh from the Gulf Coast. The river's clear, rushing waters and long runs provide perfect conditions for stalking and battling these sea-bright brutes. The last few miles above the mouth are especially noted for ideal fly-fishing for coho, with many fish being taken on dry flies. Earlier in the season, the Kiklukh River has a good showing of sea-run cutthroat trout in the 10- to 20-inch range.

For a long time, the Kiklukh has been known only to a few locals and serious outsiders. Even today, it remains virtually hidden from most of the angling public. But with its amazing potential, this short river on the edge of the Bering Glacier promises to get the renown it deserves.

❷ Tsiu River

Location: In the north Gulf of Alaska drainage, 125 miles northwest of Yakutat, 235 miles southeast of Anchorage; see map page 326.

USGS map: Bering Glacier A-6.

How to get there: By plane from Cordova or Yakutat. Wheelplanes can land on gravel beaches and sand dunes next to the river. Charter flights into the area regularly use a landing strip on the lower river.

Highlights: A premier Gulf Coast silver salmon stream (from late August through mid-September), with good fishing for red salmon (from late June through early July) and other species.

Species: Red salmon, silver salmon, steelhead, *Dolly Varden, pink salmon.*

Regulations: Unbaited, artificial lures only from November 16 through September 14. For additional restrictions, consult the current Alaska Department of Fish and Game regulations or contact the ADF&G Yakutat office, (907) 784-3222.

Facilities: Lodging and guide services are available on the river.

Contact: For lodging and guide services, contact the Alaska Wilderness Outfitting Company, P.O. Box 1516, Cordova, AK 99574; (907) 424-5552. For an air taxi, contact Totem Air, P.O. Box 51, Yakutat, AK 99689, (907) 784-3563; or Gulf Air, P.O. Box 37, Yakutat, AK 99689, (907) 784-3240.

Fishing the Tsiu River: The Tsiu is a very small clear-water river in the heart of Yakataga State Game Refuge, just south of the Bering Glacier. It's part of an extensive, braided, gravelly drainage that includes the Tsivat River and at least a dozen tributaries and numerous small ponds, creating perfect spawning habitat for major runs of silver salmon. Phenomenally productive for its size, the Tsiu has been called the "best coho stream in all of Alaska" by both area fishing guides and biologists.

About two feet deep, the river rushes from upwellings at the headwaters through an area resembling the Sahara Desert, complete with sand dunes and very scant vegetation—ideal for fly-fishing, yet certainly not your typical Alaskan stream surroundings. The river slows the last two or three miles and widens considerably as it joins the Tsivat system and the terrain becomes vegetated. Most anglers concentrate on this lower section but access and fishing are good throughout.

The Tsiu River system produces more salmon for its size than perhaps any other stream in the world—almost 200,000 silvers in a good year. The run traditionally begins in August, peaks during September, and tapers off in October. At the peak of the influx, these waters boil with bright, aggressive coho.

Although much smaller, a run of red salmon earlier in the season provides good action for anglers in the know. Bright yarn and sparse bucktail flies are the most productive enticements.

While salmon most occupy the thoughts and energy of anglers visiting the Tsiu, the drainage is host to an as yet undiscovered fall run of steelhead trout. Few have had the chance to participate in this fishery, largely because of the area's unpredictable, and notoriously raw, autumn weather. But fish up to at least 20 pounds or more are present, presenting a tantalizing challenge for those willing to brave the uncertainties of weather and the area's remoteness.

❸ Kaliakh River System

Location: In the north Gulf of Alaska drainage, 115 miles northwest of Yakutat, 245 miles southeast of Anchorage; see map page 326.

USGS maps: Bering Glacier A-5, A-6.

How to get there: By plane from Cordova or Yakutat. Wheelplanes can land on gravel bars along or near clear-water streams. A road leads from Cape Yakataga, crosses the main stem Kaliakh River, and runs up into the foothills with access to a few smaller tributaries.

Highlights: An undiscovered Gulf Coast drainage with outstanding possibilities for silver salmon (in September) and cutthroat trout (from June through August).

Species: Cutthroat trout, silver salmon, *red salmon.*

Regulations: Only unbaited, artificial lures from November 16 through September 14. For additional restrictions, consult the current Alaska Department of Fish and Game regulations or contact the ADF&G Yakutat office, (907) 784-3222.

Facilities: No developed public facilities.

Contact: For an air taxi, contact Totem Air, P.O. Box 51, Yakutat, AK 99689, (907) 784-3563; or Gulf Air, P.O. Box 37, Yakutat, AK 99689, (907) 784-3240.

Fishing the Kaliakh River System: The Kaliakh is a fairly large, silt-laden river system originating from the Robinson Mountains and the vast Bering Glacier, east of Cape Suckling.

Numerous clear-water tributaries drain into it, providing ideal habitat for sport fish, particularly silver salmon. Of all the watersheds in the Yakutat area, the Kaliakh is probably one of the least fished, due to its remoteness and notorious weather, but it is potentially one of the finest streams around.

Anglers with the time and resources to venture to this isolated drainage will discover fishing for awesome silver salmon and sea-run cutthroat trout. Both species are found throughout the Kaliakh and are encountered in the clearer sloughs, backwaters, and streams. The Kulthieth River flowing into the midsection of the main river is a particularly good spot for silvers and is often jammed with these sleek fighters during the peak of the run. (The lower Kulthieth is somewhat glacial, but the middle and upper sections usually run clear and are very fishable.) Cohos arrive here in full force towards the latter half of September, bringing dynamite action.

Another major tributary, the clear Chiuki River, or Stink Creek, is best known for its trophy-sized cutthroat trout. In summer and fall, it is possible to hook cuts weighing four and five pounds or more, with silver salmon fishing unparalleled at the mouth during the first part of September.

The Kaliakh River is a true wilderness system, with all the qualities associated with a premier Alaska fishing stream—abundant angling, very little or nonexistent pressure, classic scenery, and undisturbed wildlife. Enjoy it while it's still unspoiled and leave it the way you found it.

❹ Yakutat Bay

Location: In the north Gulf of Alaska, Yakutat area, 350 miles southeast of Anchorage; see map page 326.

USGS maps: Mount Saint Elias A-4, A-5, C-4, C-5, C-6, C-7, D-4, D-5, D-6.

How to get there: By boat or car. Boats may be launched from the Yakutat Harbor or the mouth of the Situk River. Forest Road 9962 provides vehicle access to the Ocean Cape area.

Highlights: Excellent marine fishing for halibut (from June through August); good fishing for king salmon (in the first half of June), silver salmon (from mid-August through early Sep-

tember), and pink salmon (in the second half of July).

Species: Dolly Varden, halibut, king salmon, pink salmon, silver salmon, *chum salmon, red salmon.*

Regulations: Closed to halibut fishing in the month of January; closed to lingcod fishing from December 1 through April 30. For additional restrictions, consult the current Alaska Department of Fish and Game regulations or contact the ADF&G Yakutat office, (907) 784-3222.

Facilities: Lodging, a boat launch, water, fuel, and guide services are available in Yakutat.

Contact: For guide services, contact Yakutat Bay and River Charters, P.O. Box 7, Yakutat, AK 99689; (907) 784-3415. For lodging information, contact Blue Heron Inn, P.O. Box 254, Yakutat, AK 99689, (907) 784-3287; or Harlequin Lodge, P.O. Box 162, Yakutat, AK 99689, (907) 784-3341.

Fishing Yakutat Bay: Just north of Cape Fairweather, Yakutat Bay lies in a spectacular setting. On the west, colossal glaciers (Malaspina, Hubbard, and others) spill down from the Saint Elias Mountains, emptying their silty load into the waters of the bay. The east side, however, has small islands, bays, and coves and a few streams flowing clear into the green of Yakutat Bay. Bottom fishing is the most popular angling activity here, but in the outer bay and beaches along the coast, you'll find some very productive but underutilized salmon fishing. In years past, Yakutat was mostly a local fishery, but its appeal is broadening as anglers familiar with the region's salmon and trout streams discover more variety and excitement in nearby marine waters.

Halibut are very plentiful in the Yakutat area; some of the best fishing occurs in the deeper parts of the bay and all along the Gulf Coast from Ocean Cape southward. The shoals and reefs found off points and beaches offer perfect habitat for these huge flatfish, and locals haul in many fish in the 20- to 60-pound range, with occasional catches up to 300 pounds.

Although there is good salmon fishing on the east side of the bay and off the mouths of rivers draining into the gulf, this fishery remains underused. Some feeder kings are available year-round in area waters, with mature kings taken in early summer prior to entering major spawning systems such as the Situk and Alsek Rivers. Yakutat area streams have some of the finest sportfishing for silver salmon in all Alaska; large schools of these tackle-busters cruise the shorelines near town awaiting the heavy fall rains that push them into freshwater. Pink salmon, cutthroat trout, and Dolly Varden also inhabit the marine waters of Yakutat and offer fair to good fishing during summer. While enjoying the world-class stream fisheries for salmon and trout, you might want to give Yakutat Bay a try for some great halibut jigging and salmon trolling.

❺ Situk River System

Location: In the north Gulf of Alaska drainage, five miles east of Yakutat, 375 miles southeast of Anchorage; see map page 326.

USGS maps: Yakutat B-5, C-4, C-5.

How to get there: By car or floatplane from Yakutat. Forest Road 10 crosses the midsection of the river; hiking and tractor trails provide additional access downstream. Gravel roads along the Gulf Coast lead to flats near the mouth of river. Floatplanes can be used for the short hop to Situk, Mountain, and Redfield Lakes.

Highlights: Northern Southeast's number one stream fishing location, world famous for steelhead. Excellent angling for king salmon (from mid-June through early July), silver salmon (in the first half of September), red salmon (in the first half of July), pink salmon (from late July through early August), and steelhead trout (from late March through mid-May and October through early December).

Species: Chum salmon, cutthroat trout, Dolly Varden, king salmon, pink salmon, rainbow trout, red salmon, silver salmon, steelhead.

Regulations: Unbaited, artificial lures only; for additional restrictions, consult the current Alaska Department of Fish and Game regulations or contact the ADF&G Yakutat office, (907) 784-3222.

Facilities: Commercial lodging and a boat launch are available. The town of Yakutat, a few miles away, has sporting goods, groceries, guide services, fuel, water, and hotels. Forest Service cabins are available on Situk Lake and Situk River.

Contact: For lodging and guide services, contact Glacier Bear Lodge, P.O. Box 303, Yakutat, AK 99689, (907) 784-3202; Yakutat Bay and River Charters, P.O. Box 7, Yakutat, AK 99689, (907) 784-3415; Yakutat Lodge, P.O. Box 287, Yakutat, AK 99689, (907) 784-3232; or Blue Heron Inn, P.O. Box 254, Yakutat, AK 99689, (907) 784-3287. For cabin rentals, contact Yakutat Ranger District, P.O. Box 327, Yakutat, AK 99689; (907) 784-3359.

Fishing the Situk River System: Yakutat's Situk River certainly isn't lacking notoriety among the world angling fraternity. Small in size, it's a giant of unbelievably productive fishing for a variety of prized sport species, particularly steelhead and salmon. With its easy access, it has been an extremely popular destination for years. Draining three headwater lakes near Russell Fjord in Tongass National Forest, the Situk runs clear through the wooded Yakutat Forelands into the Gulf of Alaska, some 18 miles away. Small and brushy, it has some excellent stretches for fly and spin casting, particularly at the lower end and outlets of the lakes.

The Situk's abundant spring and fall runs of steelhead trout are the stuff of legend. These stocks are wild, native fish that offer some of the most exciting fishing available for the species, with runs in good years that jam in like cordwood in some of the better holes. The river receives a major influx of sea-run rainbow in September and October, but the more abundant and spunky spring steelhead (in April and May) give the Situk its claim to fame.

Quite a few salmon are also present in the Situk from May into October, providing some of Southeast's best stream fishing. Kings averaging 25 pounds mix with flotillas of red salmon and completely pack certain stretches of the system. Pinks jam in later on, followed by a run of silver salmon that produces some of the highest catch rates in Alaska. Some trophy cohos (20 to 23 pounds) wrestled out of the river from time to time add yet more appeal to this sizzling hot fishery. Cutthroat, rainbow trout, and Dolly Varden can be taken incidentally, with the best areas to target being the adjoining Situk, Redfield, and Mountain Lakes.

There are several ways to sample the superb Situk. Most anglers begin by fishing either the mouth or the sections of river up and downstream from the bridge (nine miles out from town). Both areas are easily accessible by road, and have well-used trails for hiking along the river. A popular option is to rent a boat in town and float and fish down from the bridge, a one- to three-day trip. Yet another possibility is to fly to one of the lakes and camp and fish or float down. (It's very brushy, so be sure to bring a saw and ax.) No matter how you decide to fish it, the Situk is a must-fish river for anyone aspiring to sample some of the very best of Alaska's stream angling.

❻ Italio River System

Location: In the north Gulf of Alaska drainage, 25 miles southeast of Yakutat, 380 miles southeast of Anchorage; see map page 326.

USGS maps: Yakutat B-3, B-4.

How to get there: By plane from Yakutat. Wheelplanes are traditionally used to access the river, landing on the tidal flats near the mouth. At high tide, boats may enter the mouth. Trails lead upstream. It's also possible to float the river to reach remote areas.

Highlights: Another phenomenal Yakutat area stream, world famous for its silver salmon (from late August through mid-September). Also good fishing for cutthroat (in May and September) and Dolly Varden (from July through September).

Species: Cutthroat trout, Dolly Varden, rainbow trout, silver salmon, *chum salmon, king salmon, pink salmon, red salmon, steelhead.*

Regulations: Unbaited, artificial lures only from November 16 through September 14. For additional restrictions, consult the current Alaska Department of Fish and Game regulations or contact the ADF&G Yakutat office, (907) 784-3222.

Facilities: A Forest Service cabin is available a few miles from the main river.

Contact: For cabin rentals, contact the Yakutat Ranger District, P.O. Box 327, Yakutat, AK 99689; (907) 784-3359. For an air taxi, contact Totem Air, P.O. Box 51, Yakutat, AK 99689, (907) 784-

3563; or Gulf Air, P.O. Box 37, Yakutat, AK 99689, (907) 784-3240.

Fishing the Italio River System: Draining several lakes at the foot of the Brabazon Range in Tongass National Forest east of Yakutat, the clear-flowing Italio is one of the premier silver salmon streams in Southeast Alaska, consistently yielding trophy fish. Comprised of several branches and tributaries, the river changed its main channel during the giant 1964 earthquake, though little changed in the way of the great fishing. (The Forest Service cabin once sat at the river's edge, but since the quake shifted the river's course, a 3.5-mile hike is required to reach the main stem.)

The Italio has three main branches, which are popularly referred to as the "Middle," the "Old," and the "Little." Sharing much the same headwaters, the Middle and Old Branches flow out into the Dangerous River Delta, while Little Italio drains into the lower portion of the Akwe River. Silver salmon is the most sought after and abundant fish species in the system, and runs begin ascending from the Gulf of Alaska in August. The fishing doesn't peak until September, however, when thousands of these powerful salmonids move in following the heavy fall rains. Lasting well into October, the Italio's famous silver run typically yields catches weighing in the mid- to upper teens, with some 20- to 23-pound fish not uncommon.

Dolly Varden are not particularly abundant in the Yakutat subregion, although they're present in good numbers in the Italio, along with some cutthroat trout and even a few rainbow. (Rumor has it you'll encounter some steelhead, as well.) The best spots are the upper reaches of the system and in the lakes, with good fishing possible. Next to the Situk River, the Italio is the most popular destination in the Yakutat area. Fish it for its trophy cohos someday and you'll understand why.

❼ Akwe River System

Location: In the north Gulf of Alaska drainage, 32 miles southeast of Yakutat, 400 miles southeast of Anchorage; see map page 326.

USGS maps: Yakutat A-3, B-3.

How to get there: By plane from Yakutat. Wheelplanes often access the river by landing on gravel bars near the mouth or at the confluences with clear-water tributaries. Boats may enter the mouth and run some nine miles upstream through the slough.

Highlights: A lesser-known Gulf Coast stream with good chances for silver salmon (from late August through mid-September) and cutthroat trout (from June through August).

Species: Cutthroat trout, Dolly Varden, red salmon, silver salmon, *chum salmon, king salmon*.

Regulations: Unbaited, artificial lures only from November 16 through September 14. For additional restrictions, consult the current Alaska Department of Fish and Game regulations or contact the ADF&G Yakutat office, (907) 784-3222.

Facilities: A Forest Service cabin is located on nearby Square Lake, a tributary lake to the Ustay River.

Contact: For cabin rentals, contact the Yakutat Ranger District, P.O. Box 327, Yakutat, AK 99689; (907) 784-3359. For an air taxi, contact Totem Air, P.O. Box 51, Yakutat, AK 99689, (907) 784-3563; or Gulf Air, P.O. Box 37, Yakutat, AK 99689, (907) 784-3240.

Fishing the Akwe River System: The glacial, green waters of the Akwe originate from Akwe Lake at the base of the Brabazon Range, east of Yakutat. Since glaciers and snow fields dominate the mountainous terrain at the headwaters, there is a fair amount of silt in the river during the summer months. However, anglers can explore several clear-water tributaries for terrific salmon and trout fishing.

Meandering through forests and marshlands toward the coast, the last nine miles of the Akwe widen into a long stillwater slough as it meets the Ustay River, a large glacial tributary. Salmon, trout, and charr often use this slough as a feeding and staging area prior to moving upstream, but because of the glacial silt in the water, relatively few anglers fish this section.

A large run of silver salmon is available every fall, along with a sizable population of cutthroat trout and fair numbers of reds (from June through July) and Dolly Varden charr. Fishing for both cohos and cutthroats is considered excellent, but experienced anglers concentrate on the mouths of clear streams and sloughs for the best action. Near the first of June, before the river begins shedding a lot of silt, a few king salmon can even be picked up on the lower few miles of river.

The Akwe does not produce the number of salmon and other species that neighboring systems do, but it receives much less angling pressure. It can offer outstanding fishing during the height of the season, usually in late summer and fall.

❽ East Alsek River

Location: In the north Gulf of Alaska drainage, 60 miles southeast of Yakutat, 420 miles southeast of Anchorage; see map page 326.

USGS maps: Yakutat A-1, A-2.

How to get there: By wheelplane from Yakutat. There is an airstrip at midriver near the Forest Service cabin. Also, the lower river near the mouth has gravel beaches ideal for landings. Hiking and tractor trails lead along the river.

Highlights: A developing, productive Yakutat area stream, with good fishing for king salmon (in the first half of June), silver salmon (from late August through mid-September), red salmon (from late July through early August), and chum salmon (in early August).

Species: Chum salmon, king salmon, red salmon, silver salmon, *pink salmon*.

Regulations: Unbaited, artificial lures only from November 16 through September 14. For additional restrictions, consult the current Alaska Department of Fish and Game regulations or contact the ADF&G Yakutat office, (907) 784-3222.

Facilities: A Forest Service cabin is available.

Contact: For cabin rentals, contact the Yakutat Ranger District, P.O. Box 327, Yakutat, AK 99689; (907) 784-3359. For an air taxi, contact Totem Air, P.O. Box 51, Yakutat, AK 99689, (907) 784-3563; or Gulf Air, P.O. Box 37, Yakutat, AK 99689, (907) 784-3240.

Fishing the East Alsek River: Flowing through Glacier Bay National Preserve, the East Alsek River, or East River, is a short coastal drainage just a few miles south of the vast Alsek River system. Draining into Dry Bay, East Alsek shares a common mouth with the larger Alsek and the clear Doame River. Although it looks like nothing more than a flat, unexciting stream, the East Alsek contains tremendously productive fish habitat.

Although merely an upwelling of groundwater from the glacial Alsek River, the ice-cold East Alsek pumps out astonishing numbers of red salmon for its size. Only about eight miles long, the river sees returns of some 200,000 of these feisty fighters in an average year. The run arrives much later—three to four weeks—than usual for the species in the Yakutat area, with above-average-sized fish (seven pounds) available to fly fishermen. If conditions are perfect and anglers hit it just right, they'll also catch a small run of kings entering the mouth of the river in early summer, which can provide some good, even excellent, action for a very brief period before moving up to the glacial Alsek River. The only substantial run of chum salmon around Yakutat is found here as well, with this species particularly abundant on the lower river in late summer. Later in fall, a good run of cohos puts on a finale for this amazing fishery.

A Forest Service cabin on the west side of East Alsek provides access to the middle and upper sections of the river, and to two smaller tributaries. This is a developing fishery with high potential, especially for fly-fishing. With relatively easy and inexpensive access, it's destined to become one of the new hot spots in the Yakutat subregion.

⑨ Doame River System

Location: In the north Gulf of Alaska drainage, 65 miles southeast of Yakutat, 425 miles southeast of Anchorage; see map page 326.

USGS map: Yakutat A-1.

How to get there: By plane from Yakutat. Wheelplanes can use gravel bars along the river and beaches near the mouth as landing sites. Upper Doame Lake is suitable for smaller floatplanes, but caution is advised.

Highlights: One of the prettiest rivers in the Yakutat area, with excellent fishing for silver sal-

mon (from late August through mid-September), and good fishing for red salmon (from late June through early July) and cutthroat and rainbow trout (from August through September).

Species: Cutthroat trout, rainbow trout, red salmon, silver salmon, king salmon, *chum salmon*.

Regulations: Unbaited, artificial lures only from November 16 through September 14. For additional restrictions, consult the current Alaska Department of Fish and Game regulations or contact the ADF&G Yakutat office, (907) 784-3222.

Facilities: No developed public facilities.

Contact: For an air taxi, contact Totem Air, P.O. Box 51, Yakutat, AK 99689, (907) 784-3563; or Gulf Air, P.O. Box 37, Yakutat, AK 99689, (907) 784-3240.

Fishing the Doame River System: Only a few miles south of glacial Alsek River, the Doame River system consists of a series of small lakes and streams originating from the Deception Hills in Glacier Bay National Park and Preserve. Meandering through a densely wooded region containing seven lakes, its crystal blue waters are perfectly suited for angling, especially sight-fishing the river's large schools of salmon as they move upstream from hole to hole. Virtually an untapped fishery, the Doame is destined to become a classic.

Sharing a common outlet with both the East Alsek and Alsek Rivers, the Doame receives strong runs of silver and red salmon, along with a few chums. The Doame's sockeyes arrive about a month earlier than those of the East Alsek, and average less in weight. While they're not quite as plentiful, they still present a delightful challenge. Silver salmon fishing on the Doame is much better, with substantial runs. Like the reds, they're available throughout the length of the river from mouth to headwater lakes, and are most abundant during late summer and fall. Some worthwhile fishing for cutthroat and rainbow trout is also reported from the system, primarily in the lakes of the upper drainage, but there have been a few reports of action in the lower river sections as well.

In years past, the Doame has been overshadowed by the spectacular Situk and Italio fisher-

338   **Alaska State Map—page 8**

ies nearby. But as more people search out new, uncrowded territory, this sleeper, like the East Alsek, should gain increasing fame for high-quality stream fishing in a remote, very scenic setting.

Juneau—North Tongass

The Juneau area encompasses the portion of the Panhandle from Cape Fairweather to Upper Stephens Passage and includes the northern tip of Chichagof and north Admiralty Islands, Glacier Bay, Icy Strait, and Lynn Canal. Here you'll find all five species of salmon, some limited steelhead, cutthroat trout, Dolly Varden charr, kokanee, and even some rare brook trout and grayling.

Along with the Ketchikan area, this is one of the major saltwater angling hubs for Southeast, with some of the finest marine fisheries for salmon and halibut in all of Alaska. Most of the effort for salmon occurs as an inside terminal fishery targeting fish bound for important spawning systems like the Taku and Chilkat Rivers. Sport anglers do well fishing familiar trolling drags in waters nearby: northern Gastineau Channel along Shelter Island; the "Breadline" from Bridget Cove to Tee Harbor; Berner's Bay in southern Lynn Canal; Auke Bay/Fritz Cove; Taku Inlet and the northern end of Douglas and Admiralty Islands. Occasionally, ventures as far as Icy Strait and Cross Sound are made, often with spectacular results. The productive outer waters of Cross Sound, Chichagof, and Glacier Bay are more effectively accessed from local towns like Elfin Cove, Gustavus, and Hoonah.

With the most extensive roadside access of any city in Southeast, Juneau has numerous opportunities for both freshwater and saltwater shoreline day fishing, although some locations can be crowded during peak season. Some of the more popular locations and species are: Cowee, Montana, and Auke Creeks and surrounding bays for salmon (silver, chum, and pink) and Dolly Varden; Gastineau Channel near the Gastineau Hatchery for king and coho salmon (a considerable amount of new fishing has been created by hatchery releases); Picnic Cove on north Douglas Island; and Eagle River Beach for Dolly Varden. The area's most significant freshwater fisheries occur at nearby Turner Lake and in the rivers around Haines (such as Chilkat and Chilkoot).

⑩ Chilkat River System

Location: In the north Lynn Canal drainage, 85 miles northwest of Juneau, 500 miles southeast of Anchorage; see map page 327.

USGS maps: Skagway A-2, A-3, B-2, B-3, B-4, C-3, C-4.

How to get there: By car from Haines or Canada. The Haines Highway parallels much of the middle and lower Chilkat, crossing the river near Wells, and heads up a major tributary, the Klehini River, to the Canadian border. A few side roads lead to tributary streams and lakes, such as Mosquito Lake. Chilkat Lake can be accessed by floatplane from Haines.

Highlights: One of Alaska's special places, noted for fine fall fishing for silver and chum salmon (in the first half of October), spring Dolly Varden (in March and April), and unique, world famous bald eagle viewing.

Species: Chum salmon, cutthroat trout, Dolly Varden, halibut, pink salmon, red salmon, silver salmon, *king salmon, steelhead.*

Regulations: Unbaited, artificial lures only from November 16 through September 14; king salmon fishing is prohibited. For additional restrictions, consult the current Alaska Department of Fish and Game regulations or contact the ADF&G Juneau office, (907) 465-4180.

Facilities: Hotels, lodging, gas, groceries, sporting goods, and guide services are available in Haines and at points along the Haines Highway.

Contact: For guide services, contact Don's Fishing, P.O. Box 74, Haines, AK 99827; (907) 766-2272. For lodging information, contact the Captain's Choice Motel, P.O. Box 392, Haines, AK 99827; (907) 766-3111.

Fishing the Chilkat River System: Originating high in the Coast Mountains in Canada and flowing south to Chilkat Inlet and Lynn Canal, the very braided Chilkat River cuts a valley between the Takshanuk and Takhinsha Mountains. Along the way, it's joined by several major glacial tributaries including the Klehini and Tsirku Rivers. Since the river is glacially fed, the Chilkat runs heavy with silt in the warm summer months, limiting angling to clear-water tributary lakes and streams. However, during the cooler months of the year, from about mid-September to mid-April, the river runs clear and is very fishable due to the lack of meltwater from the mountains. A large section of the Chilkat River Valley has been designated the Alaska Chilkat Bald Eagle Preserve. Thousands of these majestic birds gather each fall along the river to feed on a late run of chum and silver salmon.

The prime time to fish the main stem Chilkat is late fall, particularly in October, as the silt settles and the river clears, revealing a heavy run of chum salmon. Many anglers prefer to target this species near tidewater on the lower river as chances of catching brighter fish are better. An area along the highway by the airport is a favored chum spot, but the fish may be taken just about anywhere, upstream to the Tsirku River confluence. Big, bright silvers can be caught at the same time, and remain in small numbers into February. In late winter and early spring, angling for Dolly Varden is a favorite local pastime as overwintering fish begin to actively feed. A very small winter run of steelhead trout spawn in the Chilkat as well.

The outlets of Chilkat and Mosquito Lakes are good for fall silvers and fair for reds. Cutthroat trout fishing is great in the lakes, especially after breakup and before freeze-up, but fish are present year-round. Pink salmon run in small, clear-water streams of the Chilkat in late summer. Stocked grayling may be found in Herman Lake by Klehini River.

For anglers wanting an experience that is out of the ordinary, the Chilkat comes highly recommended. Its great late autumn fishing, easy access, and splendid bald eagle viewing in a magnificent Alaska setting make this location one of a kind.

⑪ Chilkoot River System

Location: In the north Lynn Canal drainage, 85 miles northwest of Juneau, 500 miles southeast of Anchorage; see map page 327.

USGS maps: Skagway B-2, B-3, C-3.

How to get there: By car, a few miles from Haines. The road parallels the entire lower river and ends at the outlet of Chilkoot Lake. There are pull-offs along the road, with several trails leading to various sections of the river and lake.

Highlights: The most popular river in the Haines area. Good fall fishing for silver salmon (in the first half of October), late summer pink salmon, and spring Dolly Varden (in April and May).

Species: Dolly Varden, pink salmon, red salmon, silver salmon, *chum salmon, cutthroat trout, king salmon, steelhead.*

Regulations: Unbaited, artificial lures only from November 16 through September 14; king salmon fishing is prohibited. For additional restrictions, consult the current Alaska Department of Fish and Game regulations or contact the ADF&G Juneau office, (907) 465-4180.

Facilities: Commercial lodging and a campground are available by the river and lake outlet. A few miles away, the town of Haines has sporting goods, groceries, a motel, and gas.

Contact: For lodging and camping information, contact Captain's Choice Motel, P.O. Box 392, Haines, AK 99827, (907) 766-3111; or Haines Visitor Bureau, P.O. Box 530, Haines, AK 99827; (800) 458-3579 or (907) 766-2234.

Fishing the Chilkoot River System: The semiglacial Chilkoot emerges from a series of ice fields high in the Coast Mountains above Haines and flows south to Chilkoot Lake, continuing to Lutak Inlet. Above Chilkoot Lake, the river is fairly fast and narrow with several tributaries entering the main stem from the surrounding mountains. The lower river, however, is wider and slower, with plenty of deep holes and runs. From the lake down to tidewater, the river is only a little more than a mile long; most of the sportfishing takes place there. Boulders and rocks are scattered throughout the Chilkoot, providing excellent fish habitat. A state recreation site lies near the outlet of Chilkoot Lake. The area receives a lot of pressure during the height of the salmon and charr migrations.

Like the neighboring Chilkat River, the emerald Chilkoot draws considerable attention from northern Southeast Alaskan and Canadian anglers. The fishing is often very good, with silver and red salmon and Dolly Varden the main targets. Silver salmon can be taken along the lower river from the mouth upstream to and including the outlet of Chilkoot Lake. This late run of coho (in the first half of October) consists of large fish, with many taken in the midteens and some specimens of 18 pounds or more. Good numbers of red salmon enter the river in two separate runs, one in June and July, another in August. Action for reds is said to be only fair, as the fish are usually finicky about anglers' offerings, but they've been known to strike red or orange flies and sponge balls. Pink salmon also fill the river in late summer (in the second half of August), and are much easier to catch. Dolly Varden are available year-round, but the best fishing for them occurs in spring (April and May) at the lake outlet as the fish gather in large schools preparing for the annual downstream migration to salt water. Many charr are caught in late summer and fall after returning from the ocean. Every year, a few stray king salmon show up in the Chilkoot from nearby hatchery release sites.

⑫ Upper Lynn Canal

Location: In the Haines/Skagway area, 25 miles northwest of Juneau, 515 miles southeast of Anchorage; see map page 327.

USGS maps: Skagway A-1, A-2, B-1, B-2.

How to get there: Primarily by boat from Haines, Skagway, or Juneau. Anglers fish the Chilkat and Chilkoot Inlets and area waters by boat out of Haines and Skagway, while the southern canal around Berner's Bay is nearer Juneau and also boat accessible. Shore fishing is possible from the road system in Haines (Mud Bay Road) and Juneau (Juneau Veterans Memorial/Glacier Highway).

Highlights: A very scenic Alaska marine setting, with good fishing for king salmon, silver salmon, pink salmon, Dolly Varden, and halibut.

Species: Dolly Varden, halibut, king salmon, pink salmon, silver salmon, *chum salmon, cutthroat trout, red salmon, steelhead.*

Regulations: For details on halibut and lingcod seasons, and special restrictions for Chilkat Inlet king salmon, consult the current Alaska Department of Fish and Game regulations or contact the ADF&G Juneau office, (907) 465-4180.

Facilities: Hotels, gas, lodging, campgrounds, groceries, sporting goods, boat rental and launching, and guide services are available in Haines, Skagway, and Juneau.

Contact: For guide services, contact Auke Bay Sportfishing Charters, P.O. Box 32744, Juneau, AK 99803, (907) 789-2562 or (907) 789-9783; Islander Charters, P.O. Box 20927, Juneau, AK 99802, (907) 780-4419; or Puffin Charters, 4418 Mint Way, Juneau, AK 99801, (907) 789-0001. For lodging information, contact Captain's Choice Motel, P.O. Box 392, Haines, AK 99827, (800) 247-7153 or (907) 766-3111; or Adlersheim Lodge, P.O. Box 210447, Auke Bay, AK 99821, (907) 780-4778. For an air taxi, contact Ward Air, 8991 Yandukin Drive, Juneau, AK 99801; (800) 478-9150 or (907) 789-9150.

Fishing Upper Lynn Canal: You couldn't ask for a more picturesque area of northern Southeast Alaska. Bordered by the snow-clad Chilkat Range in the west, the Takshanuk Mountains in the north, and the Chilkoot Range and Coast Mountains in the east, the upper Lynn Canal area encompasses Chilkat, Chilkoot, Lutak, and Taiya Inlets—four significant fjords within Tongass National Forest—and the coastline south to Berner's Bay. The many glacial rivers and creeks pouring into the north end of Lynn Canal give its water a greenish-gray tint. Numerous clear-water streams along upper Lynn Canal, however, receive strong runs of salmon and charr.

Though not as productive as waters to the west or south, upper Lynn Canal holds some great fishing. There are some year-round feeder kings as well as mature prespawners. Early summer (the first half of June) is the best time to visit as moderate numbers of these popular sport fish migrate through on their way to local rivers. Later in the season, about midsummer (from late July through early August), a strong run of pink salmon arrives and keeps anglers busy. Chilkat Inlet and Berner's Bay are the best places to catch these ocean-fresh pinks. Silvers show up in fall (from late August through late September) and remain until the snow flies. Berner's Bay and Lutak Inlet are the best spots to intercept fish bound for area waters. Although present year-round, halibut are at their best in late summer, with the better catches made in the outer areas of Chilkat Inlet and south along the coast to William Henry and Berner's Bays. Sea-run Dolly Varden offer good action in early summer (in June and July) along beaches and points of the Chilkat Peninsula and Berner's Bay.

The upper Lynn Canal is perfect for day trips out of Haines, Skagway, or Juneau for the angler short on time or just wanting to sample a little bit of Alaska's renowned fishing.

Hot spots in the canal include Chilkat Inlet: Letnikof Cove, Glacier, and Anchorage Points; Chilkoot Inlet: Taiya and Lutak Inlets, Skagway Harbor, Portage, and Carr's Coves; Sullivan Island; Point Sherman; William Henry Bay; and Berner's Bay: Point Saint Mary, Echo Cove, and Point Bridget.

⑬ Cowee Creek

Location: In the southeast Lynn Canal drainage, 35 miles northwest of Juneau, 550 miles southeast of Anchorage; see map page 327.

USGS map: Juneau C-3.

How to get there: By car from Juneau. The Glacier Highway crosses the lower section of Glacier Creek. Trails lead to upstream and downstream areas.

Highlights: The best fishing stream on Juneau's road system, known for salmon and Dolly Varden.

Species: Chum salmon, cutthroat trout, Dolly Varden, pink salmon, silver salmon, steelhead.

Regulations: Unbaited, artificial lures only from November 16 through September 14; king salmon fishing is prohibited. For additional restrictions, consult the current Alaska Department of Fish and Game regulations or contact the ADF&G Douglas office, (907) 465-4320.

Facilities: No developed public facilities.

Contact: For fishing information, contact the Alaska Department of Fish and Game, Sportfish Division, P.O. Box 240020, Douglas, AK 99824; (907) 465-4320.

Fishing Cowee Creek: Situated close to Juneau, Alaska's capital, and offering consistent fishing with easy access, Cowee Creek is one of

the favorite locations among the local angling community. Healthy runs of three species of salmon and charr are present at various times from early summer to late fall. Anglers primarily target areas close to the highway in the last few miles of water above the ocean. Those in the know hit the holes and runs near the mouth during incoming and high tides, and areas farther upstream a few hours after the tide. Big schools of fresh salmon can be intercepted at these locations on their way to the spawning grounds higher up in the valley.

A very heavy run of pink salmon (in the second half of July) always draws crowds to this popular stream, but early summer chums (from late June through early July) and fall silvers (in mid-September) are also big draws. Dolly Varden move into the stream during the early part of summer (in June and July) and yield fast action on light tackle. A small spring run of steelhead trout spawns in the creek as well, and a few pan-sized cutthroat trout occasionally add to the creel.

⑭ Favorite/ Saginaw Channels

Location: North of Admiralty Island, 25 miles west of Juneau, 550 miles southeast of Anchorage; see map page 327.

USGS maps: Juneau B-3, C-3.

How to get there: Primarily by boat from the Juneau area to Shelter Island and the "Breadline." Boat launches are located in several spots between Juneau and Berner's Bay on the Glacier Highway with easy access to both channels. Surf casting is also possible from locations along the highway system.

Highlights: An all-time local favorite, with good fishing for king salmon (in the second half of May), silver salmon (in mid-August), and halibut (from June through August).

Species: Chum salmon, cutthroat trout, Dolly Varden, halibut, king salmon, pink salmon, silver salmon.

Regulations: For details on halibut and lingcod seasons, consult the current Alaska Department of Fish and Game regulations or contact the ADF&G Juneau office, (907) 465-4180.

Facilities: Boat rentals and launching, gas, sporting goods, lodges, hotels, groceries, and guide services are available in Juneau, Auke Bay, and Dotsons Landing.

Contact: For guide services, contact Auke Bay Sportfishing Charters, P.O. Box 32744, Juneau, AK 99803, (907) 789-2562 or (907) 789-9783; Islander Charters, P.O. Box 20927, Juneau, AK 99802, (907) 780-4419; or Puffin Charters, 4418 Mint Way, Juneau, AK 99801, (907) 789-0001. For lodging information, contact Adlersheim Lodge, P.O. Box 210447, Auke Bay, AK 99821, (907) 780-4778; or Best Western Country Lane Inn, 9300 Glacier Highway, Juneau, AK 99801, (800) 528-1234 or (907) 789-5005.

Fishing Favorite/Saginaw Channels: For several decades, the clear blue waters of Favorite and Saginaw Channels have been a major attraction for Juneau area anglers. Between the mainland and Mansfield Peninsula just west of Juneau, nine-mile-long Shelter Island creates the two channels that connect Lynn Canal and Stephens Passage. Untold numbers of migrating and feeding salmon and bottomfish move through every season and are traditionally harvested by both commercial and sportfishing fleets.

The best way to enjoy this fishery is by boat. The west side and south end of Shelter Island and all along the mainland coast of Favorite Channel are top locations for king and silver salmon, while midchannel islands and reefs are great for halibut. The "Breadline," stretching from Tee Harbor to Benjamin Island along the mainland, is a longtime favorite trolling drag. Feeder kings are available year-round, with the best action occurring in late spring and early summer when mature fish arrive. Silvers are abundant in late summer throughout the area. You'll discover some of the best fishing around Shelter Island, where coho in excess of 20 pounds are taken quite regularly. Fair numbers of chum and pink salmon and Dolly Varden are present, as well as a few cutthroat trout. The trout and charr are most often encountered near the mouth of Peterson Creek and at various points and narrows in Favorite and Saginaw Channels, while both natural and hatchery enhanced runs of pinks and chums pass through on their way to Gastineau Channel outside Juneau. Decent numbers of halibut are taken from deeper parts of the channels, with most averaging 15 to 20 pounds and occasional catches over 100 pounds.

Favorite and Saginaw Channels are perfect for day fishing excursions out of Juneau. Top locations to try are Favorite Channel: Benjamin, Gull, and Aaron Islands, Poundstone Rock, Eagle Reef, the "Breadline," Tee Harbor, and Point Lena; Lincoln Island: Lincoln Anchorage; North Pass; Shelter Island: Handtrollers Cove, South Shelter, and Favorite Reef; Saginaw Channel: Point Retreat, Barlow Point, and Barlow Islands.

🅱 Montana Creek

Location: In the mainland drainage, Juneau area, 590 miles southeast of Anchorage; see map page 327.

USGS maps: Juneau B-2, B-3.

How to get there: By car from Juneau. Mendenhall Loop Road crosses the lower stream section with trails leading upstream and downstream. Also, Montana Creek Road provides access to reaches of the upper river. From the end of the latter road, a developed trail continues to the headwaters of Montana Creek.

Highlights: A favorite spot for local anglers, with good fishing for silver salmon (in the second half of September), chum salmon (in the first half of July), pink salmon (in the second half of July), and Dolly Varden (in July).

Species: Chum salmon, Dolly Varden, pink salmon, silver salmon, *cutthroat trout, king salmon, red salmon, steelhead.*

Regulations: Unbaited, artificial lures only; king salmon fishing is prohibited. For additional restrictions, consult the current Alaska Department of Fish and Game regulations or contact the ADF&G Juneau office, (907) 465-4180.

Facilities: No developed public facilities by stream crossings, but nearby areas have lodging, hotels, sporting goods, groceries, and gas.

Contact: For lodging information, contact the Adlersheim Lodge, P.O. Box 210447, Auke Bay, AK 99821, (907) 780-4778; or Best Western Country Lane Inn, 9300 Glacier Highway, Juneau, AK 99801, (800) 528-1234 or (907) 789-5005.

Fishing Montana Creek: Not far from Juneau, Montana Creek is a small clear-water stream draining out of valleys near Mount Stroller White and McGinnis Mountain. It's short, only about 10 miles long, with many riffles and some deep holes and runs. Approximately two miles downstream from the lower access point (Mendenhall Loop Road), the Montana joins the silty Mendenhall River originating from its namesake lake and glacier.

Due to its close proximity to Juneau, the Montana is a popular stream with local anglers. Its clear waters support healthy fish populations, and angling opportunities for salmon and charr are excellent. Pink salmon and Dolly Varden are plentiful throughout most of the stream, and you'll encounter small schools of silver and chum salmon in the deeper parts of the lower Montana. For brighter salmon, try the last few miles of water above the mouth. A few king salmon run the creek in midsummer along with fall steelhead and cutthroat trout.

The Montana is great for anglers who enjoy sight-fishing, as you can easily spot and cast to schools of salmon. For the best action, hike in from the road crossings and explore the more remote stream areas. From the upper access point (Montana Creek Road), anglers can scout the shallows for charr among the spawning salmon. For those having some spare time in or around Juneau, Montana Creek makes a good half-day or day trip.

⑯ Turner Lake

Location: On the east side of Taku Inlet, 22 miles east of Juneau, 585 miles southeast of Anchorage; see map page 327.

USGS map: Taku River B-6.

How to get there: Primarily by a short floatplane hop from Juneau. Most visitors land near the lake outlet or one of the two cabins on the lakeshore. Some anglers choose to access the lake by boat via Taku Inlet, where a trail leads to Turner Lake along the outlet stream.

Highlights: One of northern Southeast's prime trophy cutthroat waters, with good fishing for kokanee (from May through August), pink salmon (in early August), and Dolly Varden (from July through October).

Species: Cutthroat trout, Dolly Varden, kokanee salmon, pink salmon, silver salmon.

Regulations: Unbaited, artificial lures only; catch-and-release only for cutthroat trout. For additional restrictions, consult the current Alaska Department of Fish and Game regulations or contact the ADF&G Juneau office, (907) 465-4180.

Facilities: Forest Service cabins are located at the west and east ends of the lake.

Contact: For cabin rentals, contact the Juneau Ranger District, Tongass National Forest, 8465 Old Dairy Road, Juneau, AK 99803; (907) 586-8800. For an air taxi, contact Ward Air, 8991 Yandukin Drive, Juneau, AK 99801; (800) 478-9150 or (907) 789-9150.

Fishing Turner Lake: A deep, clear blue body of water, Turner Lake is beautifully situated among tall, snow-capped peaks in Tongass National Forest, 22 miles east of Juneau. Bound by steep cliffs with cascading waterfalls, and surrounded with thick stands of spruce, the lake is one of the most scenic angling locations in all of Southeast Alaska.

Turner Lake has long been regarded as one of the premier trophy cutthroat trout waters in the state. Rich in food sources, the lake supports a sizable population of cutthroat trout. Many of Turner's cuts reach three to four pounds, and you may find a few five-pounders (or even more). (The largest recorded fish from Turner was a six-pound, seven-ounce cutthroat.) Most of them are in the 12- to 16-inch range, with enough large fish present to make a trip to these waters worthwhile. To preserve this remarkable fishing (a three-pound cutthroat may be 12 years old), Turner Lake has been designated a special trophy cutthroat trout water, with only catch-and-release fishing and the use of bait prohibited.

Kokanee, the pan-sized, landlocked sockeye salmon that provide the main forage for the big cutthroats, are abundant in Turner and pursued as sport fish year-round, although the best action occurs in late spring and summer. Dolly Varden provide additional excitement.

Fishing for all species in the lake is still quite good overall, but at certain times and places the action is nothing less than red hot. Just after breakup and before freeze-up, the salmon and trout bite really peaks, particularly at the lake outlet and near any of the waterfalls. The outlet stream below the falls is another famous Turner fishing location for good catches of trout, charr, and pink and coho salmon. The best times to hit it are from about midsummer until October, with small spinners and bright attractor flies the best enticements. Some good fishing can be had on the lower stream sections near Taku Inlet.

It's a good idea for anglers to bring along a small inflatable raft to access the deeper parts of the lake for the best trophy fishing, as trolling is the proven method for the big ones; small skiffs are available for use at the Forest Service cabins. (See the cutthroat chapter on page 118 for more details on angling techniques.) Plenty of folks, however, do just fine with the smaller fish casting from the shore, with an occasional lunker taken near the lake outlet or stream inlets with spinning gear.

⑰ Upper Stephens Passage

Location: North of Admiralty Island, 10 miles south of Juneau, 565 miles southeast of Anchorage; see map page 327.

USGS maps: Juneau A-1, A-2, A-3, B-1, B-2, B-3; Taku River A-6; Sitka C-1, D-1; Sumdum C-5, C-6, D-5, D-6.

How to get there: By boat and car to the Douglas Island, Auke Bay, and Gastineau Channel area in upper Stephens Passage. Locations along the shores of Admiralty Island and the eastern mainland are strictly for boaters. Several roads extending from Juneau can be used to reach good surf casting spots, chief among them Glacier, North Douglas, and Douglas Highways, Egan Drive, and Thane Road.

Highlights: The perfect location for overnight boat trips. Great silver salmon fishing (from late August through late September), with good fishing for king salmon (from late May through mid-July), pink salmon (from mid- through late July), Dolly Varden (in May), and halibut (from mid-June through late August).

Species: Chum salmon, cutthroat trout, Dolly Varden, halibut, king salmon, pink salmon, silver salmon, *red salmon, steelhead.*

Regulations: For details on halibut and lingcod seasons, and special restrictions on Auke Bay Dolly Varden, consult the current Alaska Department of Fish and Game regulations or contact the ADF&G Juneau office, (907) 465-4180.

Facilities: Hotels, lodges, sporting goods, groceries, gas, boat launches and rentals, and guide services are available in and around the greater Juneau area.

Contact: For guide services, contact Auke Bay Sportfishing Charters, P.O. Box 32744, Juneau, AK 99803, (907) 789-2562 or (907) 789-9783; Islander Charters, P.O. Box 20927, Juneau, AK 99802, (907) 780-4419; or Puffin Charters, 4418 Mint Way, Juneau, AK 99801, (907) 789-0001. For lodging information, contact Blueberry Lodge, 9436 North Douglas Highway, Juneau, AK 99801, (907) 463-5886; or Westmark Juneau, 51 West Egan Drive, Juneau, AK 99801, (907) 586-6900 or (800) 544-0970. For an air taxi, contact Ward Air, 8991 Yandukin Drive, Juneau, AK 99801; (907) 789-9150 or (800) 478-9150. For more information, contact Admiralty Island National Monument, P.O. Box 2097, Juneau, AK 99803; (907) 586-8790.

Fishing Upper Stephens Passage: This is a fairly narrow body of water extending from Shelter Island and Favorite and Saginaw Channels in the north to the mouth of Seymour Canal and Windham Bay in the south. The passage parts Admiralty Island from the mainland within Tongass National Forest. It has several large fjords within its domain—Taku Inlet, Port Snettisham, and Tracy and Endicott Arms, along with Seymour Canal and several smaller bays and coves. The rugged Coast Mountains are seen clearly in the north, and large glacial rivers pour into the passage from the mainland.

Fish populations are healthy and strong in Upper Stephens Passage with a mix of natural and hatchery enhanced runs of salmon returning to semiglacial waters. Feeder kings (10 to 15 pounds) are available throughout the year with peak abundance in midsummer, while mature fish (20 to 25 pounds) are at their best in late spring and early summer. The prespawning, wild kings make for Taku River at the head of Taku Inlet; adult hatchery fish are primarily destined for Juneau area release sites. Large hatchery enhanced runs of silver, chum, and pink salmon also flood the upper passage from July until October. Waters adjacent to the Gastineau Hatchery are prime locations to scout for big schools of salmon. Boaters and surf casters both enjoy these artificial runs, with offshore areas producing best early in the season and near-shore locations proving better later on. Although chum salmon are only caught incidentally out in the open sea, action can be quite good at the terminal fisheries.

Other species popular with local anglers include Dolly Varden and halibut. Sea-run Dollies are present along beaches and stream mouths through much of spring and summer, and halibut and other bottomfish are taken in deeper parts of the passage all summer long. Anglers usually take a few cutthroat trout while fishing for charr.

If you're looking for fast action on a short trip, head into the fisheries of Upper Stephens Passage around Douglas Island outside Juneau. For longer excursions, however, the main passage beyond Taku Inlet is great for wild runs of salmon. There's an abundance of great spots in this area, including Mansfield Peninsula: Piling Point and Colt and Horse Islands; Point Louisa; Portland Island; Auke Bay; Cothlan Island; Spuhn Island; Gibby Rock; Douglas Island: Outer, False Outer, Middle, and Inner Points, Icy Point, White Marker, Marmion Island, and Point Hilda; Scull Island; North Admiralty Island: Young Bay, Admiralty, and Green Coves, Point Young, Stink Creek, Outer Oliver Inlet, False Point Arden, and Point Arden; Gastineau Channel: Salmon and Sheep Creeks, Dupont, and Point Salisbury; Taku Inlet: Point Bishop, Cooper and Greely Points/ Falls; East Admiralty Island: Cove and Station Points, Doty Cove, and South Island; Circle Point; Slocum Inlet; Grand Island; Suicide Cove; Grave Point; Taku Harbor; Stockade Point; Midway Island; Holkham Bay: Round Islets, Wood Spit; Point Hugh; Seymour Canal: Flaw Point/Mole Harbor and Swan Island; and Windham Bay.

⑱ Icy Strait

Location: North of Chichagof Island, 35 miles west of Juneau, 525 miles southeast of Anchorage; see map page 327.

USGS maps: Mount Fairweather A-1, B-1, B-2; Juneau A-3, A-4, A-5, A-6, B-4, B-5, B-6.

How to get there: By boat and plane. Most anglers access Icy Strait from Juneau by boat, but some use planes, landing at the towns of Gustavus or Hoonah and traveling by boat from there. Surf casting is possible, but to reach the better fishing, a boat is recommended.

Highlights: Alaska's number one marine fishing location, with excellent fishing for king salmon (from mid-May through late June), silver salmon (in the second half of August), pink salmon (in the second half of July), and halibut (from May through September); good fishing for chum salmon (in the first half of July).

Species: Chum salmon, Dolly Varden, halibut, king salmon, pink salmon, silver salmon, *cutthroat trout, red salmon, steelhead.*

Regulations: For details on halibut and lingcod seasons, consult the current Alaska Department of Fish and Game regulations or contact the ADF&G Douglas office, (907) 465-4320.

Facilities: Commercial lodging and guide services are available.

Contact: For lodging and guide services, contact the W.T. Fugarwe Lodge, P.O. Box 27, Gustavus, AK 99826, (907) 697-3262; Gustavus Marine Charters, P.O. Box 81, Gustavus, AK 99826, (907) 697-2233; Glacier Bay Lodge, 1500 Metropolitan Park Building, Olive Way at Boren Avenue, Seattle, WA 98101, (907) 697-3221 (summer) or (206) 624-8551 (winter); or Hoonah Charters, P.O. Box 384, Hoonah, AK 99829, (907) 945-3334. For an air taxi, contact Ward Air, 8991 Yandukin Drive, Juneau, AK 99801, (800) 478-9150 or (907) 789-9150; or Glacier Bay Airways, P.O. Box 1, Gustavus, AK 99826, (907) 697-2249.

Fishing Icy Strait: Bordering world famous Glacier Bay National Park, Icy Strait's cold, blue waters split Chichagof Island from the mainland and the Chilkat Range. The strait is 10 to 15 miles wide and 55 miles long, connecting Cross Sound with Chatham Strait. It serves as the largest migrational corridor for mainland-bound salmon in northern Southeast, and is an active feeding ground for halibut and other bottomfish. Area waters teem with a variety of marine animals, particularly whales, birds, and seals, drawing substantial numbers of visitors to view and photograph them.

The productivity of these waters is nothing less than phenomenal, and many anglers, guides, and biologists regard Icy Strait as the top saltwater fishing destination in all of Alaska. Millions of salmon pour through the strait bound for inland spawning streams starting in April and continuing to October, with untold numbers of halibut scattered throughout. Most anglers arrive by boats, guided or private, from the Juneau area or the local towns of Hoonah and Gustavus. King and silver salmon and halibut are undoubtedly the favorite target species, with excellent action almost guaranteed. Smaller feeder kings are available year-round, but the larger mainland spawners show up later in the spring and entertain anglers until midsummer. The late summer silver salmon fishing is especially noteworthy, with considerable trophy potential. (The current state record fish of 26 pounds was taken from Icy Strait and several silvers over 20 pounds are caught there every season.)

Halibut are plentiful and better fishing for this species would be hard to find anywhere in the world. Although present year-round, most effort for these behemoths occurs from late spring to early fall when larger fish can be found in moderately shallow water. The former state record, a fish of some 440 pounds, was pulled from the bottom here, and flatties weighing more than 300 pounds are caught regularly. It's not uncommon to catch 40 to 50 halibut a day from some of the better locations in Icy Strait.

Other species not to be ignored are the chum and pink salmon. A flood of ocean-bright pinks comes through in midsummer and can be caught on virtually every cast. Just before the pinks peak in area waters, huge runs of chums arrive. Saltwater chums have never been known to hit anglers' offerings with any vigor, but with the fish streaming through in concentrated schools the action can be quite hot.

Top locations around Icy Strait are Chichagof Island: Idaho Inlet, Spasski, and Mud Bays, Point Adolphus, Burger, Neck, and Eagle Points, Flynn Cove, Harry Island, Hoonah Island/Gedney Channel, and Whitestone Harbor; Point Dundas; South Passage; Lemesurier Island: Willoughby Cove and North Passage; Point Carolus; Glacier Bay: Bartlett Cove, Young Island, and Beardslee Entrance; Point Gustavus; Icy Passage; Pleasant Island Reef; Port Frederick: Halibut Island, Crist Point, Point Sophia, and the Narrows; Excursion Inlet: Sawmill Bay; Porpoise Islands; Sisters Reef; the Sisters; Spasski Island; Homeshore; Couverden Island/Swanson Harbor; Rocky Island; and Hanus Reef.

⑲ Cross Sound

Location: North of Chichagof Island, 75 miles west of Juneau, 510 miles southeast of Anchorage; see map page 327.

USGS maps: Mount Fairweather A-1, A-2, A-3, B-2, B-3.

How to get there: By boat or floatplane. Boat traffic comes mainly from area communities and sportfishing lodges in Hoonah, Gustavus, and Elfin Cove. Floatplanes are used to access these communities and lodges from Juneau and other major population centers in Southeast.

Highlights: An angler's mecca with great marine wildlife viewing, known for its excellent salmon and halibut fisheries.

Species: Chum salmon, Dolly Varden, halibut, king salmon, pink salmon, silver salmon, *cutthroat trout, red salmon, steelhead*.

Regulations: For details on halibut and lingcod seasons, consult the current Alaska Department of Fish and Game regulations or contact the ADF&G Douglas office, (907) 465-4320.

Facilities: Commercial lodging and guide services are available.

Contact: For lodging and guide services, contact Elfin Cove Sportfishing Lodge, Glacier View, Elfin Cove, AK 99825, (907) 697-3131 (summer) or (206) 228-7092 (winter); Elfin Cove Charters, P.O. Box 69, Elfin Cove, AK 99825, (800) 323-5346; Tanaku Lodge, General Delivery, Elfin Cove, AK 99825, (907) 239-2205; or Cross Sound Lodge, P.O. Box 85, Elfin Cove, AK 99825, (800) 323-5346. For an air taxi, contact Ward Air, 8991 Yandukin Drive, Juneau, AK 99801, (800) 478-9150 or (907) 789-9150; or Glacier Bay Airways, P.O. Box 1, Gustavus, AK 99826, (907) 697-2249.

Fishing Cross Sound: Set largely within the boundaries of Tongass National Forest, Cross

Sound is a fairly wide passage between Chichagof Island, Yakobi Island, and the Glacier Bay National Park mainland. Several large bays adjoin the sound, and islands of all sizes are scattered along its edges. Brady Glacier, a huge mass of ice dropping into Taylor Bay in the northern part of Cross Sound, contributes to the water's greenish hue.

The sound is home to incredible numbers of marine wildlife and fish. Along with Icy Strait to the east, Cross Sound serves as a major migration corridor for the millions of salmon bound for spawning streams throughout northern Southeast Alaska, thus attracting predators such as seals, sea lions, whales, birds, and, of course, sport anglers.

Situated on the Alaska Gulf Coast, the area's weather often can be unpredictable and anglers venturing into the sound must be prepared for difficult conditions. Aside from that, the fishing in Cross Sound is fantastic for salmon and bottomfish; the sound has been said to host some of the best saltwater fisheries in the state. Anglers fish the area mainly by boat, concentrating their efforts on obvious lies and feeding grounds, such as points, tidal rips, and narrow passages for salmon, and shoals and reefs for halibut.

Anglers come mostly from local communities such as Gustavus and Hoonah, a few from as far away as Juneau, and some from as near as shoreline lodges in Elfin Cove. As is common throughout most of Southeast, the main species targeted are king and silver salmon and halibut. Visitors can expect superb action for these and other salmon and bottomfish species. Feeder kings and halibut are present year-round, but more frequently caught from spring to fall. Mature, prespawning kings arrive in late spring and early summer (from May through June), offering some of the best action in the region, while larger-than-average silvers (in the second half of August), healthy numbers of ocean-bright chum (in the first half of July), and pink salmon (in the second half of July) provide excitement in late summer. "Barn door" halibut are active in the sound from spring into fall (from May through September) as concentrations of these flatfish move into shallow water to feed. Fish-

ing is outstanding, with many trophy fish taken and record-size catches possible.

Some of the more popular and proven locations to try in the sound include Graves Harbor; Yakobi Island: Cape Bingham, Surge Bay; Lisianski Inlet; Port Althorp: Point Lucan, Threemile Island, Elfin Cove; and North Indian Pass: Point Wimbledon.

Sitka—West Tongass

The Sitka area is home to significant freshwater and marine locations on and around Baranof, Yakobi, western Chichagof, and south Admiralty Islands. Species include king, silver and red salmon, halibut, steelhead and cutthroat trout, and Dolly Varden charr.

Most of the serious salmon effort occurs in salt water, along the productive outer coast, where big king (some of the largest in Southeast) and coho are intercepted on their way to spawning destinations in Alaska, Canada, and beyond. Anglers target Sitka, Salisbury, and Nakwasina Sounds and Katlian Bay for salmon and halibut.

Roads leading north and south of town provide access to some seasonally productive shore fishing (Starrigavan Bay) and a few popular roadside streams (such as Starrigavan Creek and Indian River). Species most often taken are Dolly Varden and silver and pink salmon. Area lakes (Blue, Beaver, and Thimbleberry) offer fair to good fishing for rainbow trout, Dollies, and even rare brook trout and grayling. More remote and productive are the prestigious locations of the Sitkoh and Lake Eva, Port Banks, and Mitchell Bay systems.

20 Salisbury Sound/ Peril Strait

Location: Northwest Baranof Island, 25 miles from Sitka, 570 miles from Anchorage; see map page 327.

USGS maps: Sitka B-3, B-4, B-5, B-6, C-3, C-4, C-5, C-6.

How to get there: By boat and floatplane to Salisbury Sound and Peril Strait; access by boat is the more popular and practical method. Anglers arrive in the area through the protected waters of upper Sitka Sound and Olga and Neva Straits from Sitka, or by crossing Chatham Strait into Peril Strait from Angoon on Admiralty Island.

Highlights: A favorite location of Sitka's charter fleet, excellent for king salmon (from mid-May through mid-July), silver salmon (in the second half of August), and halibut (from June through August); good fishing for pink salmon (from late July through early August), cutthroat trout, and Dolly Varden (from May through July).

Species: Chum salmon, cutthroat trout, Dolly Varden, halibut, king salmon, pink salmon, silver salmon, *red salmon, steelhead.*

Regulations: For details on the open season and bag limits for bottomfish, consult the current Alaska Department of Fish and Game regulations or contact the ADF&G Sitka office, (907) 747-5355.

Facilities: No developed public facilities, although some lakes in the immediate area have Forest Service cabins.

Contact: For guide services, contact Sportsman Charters, 821 Charles Street, Sitka, AK 99835, (907) 747-8756. For lodging information, contact Whalers Cove Lodge, P.O. Box 101, Angoon, AK 99820; (800) 423-3123 or (907) 788-3123. For cabin rentals, contact Tongass National Forest, 204 Siginaka Way, Sitka, AK 99835; (907) 747-6671.

Fishing Salisbury Sound/Peril Strait: Separating the large islands of Chichagof and Baranof is the narrow Peril Strait. Less than a mile wide in places, the strait is an active feeding and migration route for fish bound for Chatham Strait. On the west end is Salisbury Sound, a tremendously productive area between Kruzof and Chichagof Islands that offers some of the best saltwater angling in the Sitka area.

The sound features a number of deep bays, tiny islands, clear-water streams, and jutting peninsulas, which are ideal for concentrating anadromous species and bottomfish. On the west side of the strait, in Salisbury Sound, the most sought-after sport fish include king and silver salmon and halibut. These attract considerable

attention from local and visiting anglers out of Sitka. The landscape is wild, unruly, and very breathtaking; along with the abundant marine wildlife and superb fishing, it makes for a very memorable experience.

King salmon up to 60 or 70 pounds are possible in early summer, while feeder fish are available any time of the year. Behemoth halibut to 300 pounds are present in almost untapped numbers throughout the summer months. In late summer and fall, anglers are busy with the huge coho destined for nearby streams and lakes.

Peril Strait always seems to offer some kind of fishing action. Although the big, mature kings are not particularly abundant (like those found in Salisbury Sound), feeders weighing 10 to 25 pounds are common. They are targeted by anglers in the narrower sections, in Hoonah Sound, and on the outer edge at Chatham Strait. Two major fish-producing waters drain into Peril Strait: Lake Eva and Sitkoh Creek. Both have good populations of silver, chum, and pink salmon, sea-run cutthroat trout, Dolly Varden, and other game species. Sitkoh Bay is especially favored for mixed creel catches.

Salisbury Sound and Peril Strait are perfect marine locations for boating. Their diverse, highly scenic waters and good fishing truly capture the essence of Southeast Alaska.

Top locations for salmon, trout, charr, and halibut include Fortuna Strait/Klokachef Island; Kruzof Island: Point Kruzof and Kalinin Point; Sinitsin Island; Scraggy Island; Kakul Narrows; Big Island; Baranof Island: Point Kakul, Saint John Baptist Bay, Fish Bay, Pogibishi and Elizabeth Points, Outer Rodman Bay, and Saook Point/Bay; Povorotni Island; and Chichagof Island: Poison Cove, Sitkoh and Florence Bays, Point Craven, and Morris Reef.

㉑ Mitchell Bay System

Location: Central Admiralty Island drainage, 50 miles northeast of Sitka, 600 miles southeast of Anchorage; see map page 327.

USGS maps: Sitka B-1, B-2, C-1, C-2, D-1, D-2.

How to get there: By floatplane from Sitka or Juneau; by boat from Angoon. Planes can land on any of the lakes in the system or at one of the three canoe portage/trail access sites: Mitchell Bay, Mole Harbor, and Windfall Harbor. An extensive canoe route/trail network (part of the Cross Admiralty Canoe Route) connects the system, providing access to almost all lakes and streams in the drainage.

Highlights: The most popular recreation area on Admiralty Island, with excellent fishing for cutthroat trout and good salmon angling.

Species: Chum salmon, cutthroat trout, Dolly Varden, pink salmon, red salmon, silver salmon, *steelhead*.

Regulations: Unbaited, artificial lures only from November 16 through September 14; king salmon fishing is prohibited. For additional restrictions, consult the current Alaska Department of Fish and Game regulations or contact the ADF&G Juneau office, (907) 465-4180.

Facilities: Six Forest Service cabins and 10 public shelters are available within and around the Mitchell Bay system.

Contact: For lodging information, contact Thayer Lake Lodge, P.O. Box 211614, Auke Bay, AK 99821; (907) 789-5646. For cabin rentals, contact Admiralty Island National Monument, P.O. Box 2097, Juneau, AK 99803; (907) 586-8790. For an air taxi, contact Ward Air, 8991 Yandukin Drive, Juneau, AK 99801; (907) 789-9150 or (800) 478-9150.

Fishing the Mitchell Bay System: Admiralty Island's Mitchell Bay system is comprised of a series of beautiful lakes of varying sizes connected by small streams. Ten major lakes, and several smaller ones, offer outstanding cutthroat trout fishing and excellent hiking and canoeing, making the system one of the more attractive recreational destinations in Southeast Alaska.

The more popular locations include Hasselborg Lake, the largest lake in the system, and Distin, Davidsons, Jims, Guerin, Beaver, and Alexander Lakes, all of which produce exceptional numbers of trout (from May to September), along with some kokanee and charr. Hasselborg Lake contains trophy fish of four to five pounds or heavier, with a few taken out of Jims, Guerin, and Distin Lakes as well. (See the chapter on cutthroat on page 118 for details on trophy fishing in Southeast lakes.) Fishing can be worthwhile

in the small streams during the summer months. Hasselborg Creek, draining out of Hasselborg Lake, ties the system to the salt water of Mitchell Bay, and has the most angling potential, with sea-run trout and charr. From July to October, silver, red, chum, and pink salmon move into the stream, with good action reported for all species.

Hasselborg Creek empties into Salt Lake, a brackish body of water separated from the head of Mitchell Bay only by the Falls, a narrow chute of water, which is impassable to boaters on low tide. Salmon school in this area before entering the spawning stream. Mitchell Bay itself is a very protected part of Chatham Strait, with its many nooks offering good action for salmon and small halibut. Feeder king salmon are available in the outer bay near Angoon. (It has some very tricky and dangerous tides, so extreme caution is advised if traversing these waters by kayak or small powerboat.)

In addition to a true variety of fishing—lake, stream, and saltwater—the Mitchell Bay system offers canoeing and hiking via the popular, island-traversing Mole Harbor Trail. It's highly recommended for anyone who wants to experience world famous Admiralty Island in Tongass National Forest.

22 Sitkoh Creek/Lake

Location: Southeast Chichagof Island drainage, 35 miles northeast of Sitka, 580 miles southeast of Anchorage; see map page 327.

USGS maps: Sitka B-3, B-4, C-3.

How to get there: By plane or boat from Sitka or area lodges. Floatplanes can land on Sitkoh Lake or use the Chatham Seaplane Base in Sitkoh Bay. From the seaplane base, a rough forest road network provides access to the lake. For those arriving through Sitkoh Bay by boat via Peril Strait, a trail begins at the mouth of Sitkoh Creek and leads 4.3 miles along the north side of the stream to a cabin at the Sitkoh Lake outlet.

Highlights: One of northern Southeast's premier steelhead streams, with excellent fishing for pink salmon (from late July through mid-August). Also good fishing for silver salmon (from late August through mid-September), cutthroat trout (from May through June), and Dolly Varden (from July through October).

Species: Chum salmon, cutthroat trout, Dolly Varden, pink salmon, rainbow trout, silver salmon, steelhead, *red salmon*.

Regulations: Unbaited, artificial lures only from November 16 through September 14; king and red salmon fishing is prohibited. For additional restrictions, consult the current Alaska Department of Fish and Game regulations or contact the ADF&G Sitka office, (907) 747-5355.

Facilities: Two Forest Service cabins are available, one on the west end of Sitkoh Lake, another on the lake's east end.

Contact: For cabin rentals, contact Tongass National Forest, 204 Siginaka Way, Sitka, AK 99835; (907) 747-6671. For an air taxi, contact Ward Air, 8991 Yandukin Drive, Juneau, AK 99801, (907) 789-9150 or (800) 478-9150; Bellair, P.O. Box 371, Sitka, AK 99835, (907) 747-8636; or Mountain Aviation, P.O. Box 875, Sitka, AK 99835, (907) 966-2288.

Fishing Sitkoh Creek/Lake: Sitkoh Lake is nestled in a picturesque valley in the Moore Mountains of Chichagof Island. It's small—only about 2.5 miles long—and drains into Sitkoh Bay through Sitkoh Creek. Thick, rain forest vegetation dominates the landscape with 2,500-foot-high mountains towering over the lake. The clear and highly productive waters of the drainage have long been a major attraction for salmon and trout enthusiasts, with good chances to spot bears feeding on fish in the stream during late summer and fall.

Sitkoh is among the top producers of sport fish in the Sitka area. Known throughout Southeast for its outstanding steelhead fishing, this drainage has plenty of windfall, and is quite deep in places, but still offers some classic fly-fishing. From late April through late May, the spring run of these large sea-run rainbows (averaging nine to 11 pounds) receives the most attention, although there is a much smaller late autumn run as well. Silver and pink salmon are thick in late summer and fall, attracting a fair number of anglers, both humans and bears.

Anglers looking for less robust sport can find an abundance of cutthroat trout and Dolly Varden from the stream mouth at Sitkoh Bay all the way up into the lake. (The area around the mouth of Sitkoh Creek in the bay also has great fishing for bright silvers, pinks, and even a few chums. Halibut are taken in deeper waters farther out.) Spring, late summer, and fall are particularly good times to try for these species during their annual migrations to and from salt water. The trail from Sitkoh Bay to Sitkoh Lake parallels the whole length of the creek, opening up miles of small stream angling opportunities.

㉓ Lake Eva

Location: North Baranof Island drainage, 20 miles northeast of Sitka, 580 miles southeast of Anchorage; see map page 327.

USGS map: Sitka B-4.

How to get there: By floatplane or boat from Sitka and Angoon. Marine travelers from Sitka must traverse upper Sitka Sound and upper Salisbury Sound into and through Peril Strait, and from Angoon, cross the Chatham Strait into Peril Strait. Drop-offs are usually made by plane near the lake outlet, while boaters moor in Hanus Bay and hike Hanus Bay Trail about a mile to Lake Eva.

Highlights: A well-known, remote Sitka area lake, with a reputation for good spring and fall cutthroat trout and Dolly Varden (from May through June and September through October). Also good salmon fishing for silvers, reds, and pinks.

Species: Chum salmon, cutthroat trout, Dolly Varden, pink salmon, red salmon, silver salmon, steelhead.

Regulations: Unbaited, artificial lures only in the lake; king salmon fishing is prohibited. For additional restrictions, consult the current Alaska Department of Fish and Game regulations or contact the ADF&G Sitka office, (907) 747-5355.

Facilities: A Forest Service cabin is available on the north shore of Lake Eva. It is wheelchair accessible, with railings and ramps present. Also, a public shelter is found on the southwest shore.

Contact: For cabin rentals, contact Tongass National Forest, 204 Siginaka Way, Sitka, AK 99835; (907) 747-6671. For an air taxi, contact Ward Air,

8991 Yandukin Drive, Juneau, AK 99801; (907) 789-9150.

Fishing Lake Eva: Only about two miles long, Lake Eva offers good angling for cutthroat trout and Dolly Varden, and has a small spring run of steelhead trout as well. The lake is situated in a particularly scenic part of Baranof Island. Snow-capped mountains loom to the southwest and the blue waters of narrow Peril Strait lie just a few miles to the north. A small stream drains the lake and pours into Hanus Bay, providing passage for salmon, trout, and charr. Although the drainage is not large, it's a very appealing destination due to its pretty location and productive fisheries.

The mouths of inlet streams are concentration areas in fall, as is the lake outlet in spring and early summer. The outlet stream is good during the annual migrational periods and its mouth at Hanus Bay can be productive all summer. Though not of trophy proportions, the fish are nonetheless plentiful and aggressive.

Salmon are popular with anglers visiting the area and can be caught from midsummer on into fall almost anywhere in the drainage. The lake outlet, the outlet stream, and the mouth of the stream at Hanus Bay are all recommended locations for Lake Eva silvers, reds, and pinks. Generally, pink salmon are most abundant, but the other salmon species can be found in high numbers. A few chum salmon are always mixed in with the crowd.

The Forest Service cabin is popular among a wide range of recreational users. Built for the physically challenged, many elderly and wheelchair-restricted visitors make use of its unique facilities to enjoy the great outdoors. A fishing platform is available, and a public shelter is located at the lake inlet where the Hanus Bay Trail ends.

24 Nakwasina River

Location: North Baranof Island drainage, 15 miles north of Sitka, 580 miles southeast of Anchorage; see map page 327.

USGS maps: Sitka A-4, B-4.

How to get there: By boat from Sitka. Crossing upper Sitka Sound and passing through Nakwasina Sound, marine travelers usually anchor off the river mouth or beach their boats and approach the river on foot.

Highlights: One of Southeast's premier locations for stream Dolly Varden fishing (from July through August), with good fishing for pink salmon (in early August) and silver salmon (from late September through early October).

Species: Chum salmon, Dolly Varden, pink salmon, silver salmon.

Regulations: Unbaited, artificial lures only from November 16 through September 14; king salmon fishing is prohibited. For additional restrictions, consult the current Alaska Department of Fish and Game regulations or contact the ADF&G Sitka office, (907) 747-5355.

Facilities: No developed public facilities.

Contact: For fishing information, contact the Alaska Department of Fish and Game, 304 Lake Street, Room 103, Sitka, AK 99835; (907) 747-5355.

Fishing Nakwasina River: The Nakwasina flows into Nakwasina Sound on the upper part of Sitka Sound. Although the upper river sections are fast and rocky, extending high into the surrounding mountains (well over 2,000 feet), the lower section is ideal for angling. A fairly small river, shallow in many places, the Nakwasina is a prime spawning ground for salmon, but most anglers come to this clear-water stream for its healthy run of large sea-run Dolly Varden charr.

Any angler hiking along the river soon discovers why this stream is so popular for Dolly Varden. These bright fish, some as large as eight pounds, enter Nakwasina starting in early summer and remain until fall, offering exceptional fly-fishing and spin casting. The best fishing traditionally coincides with the large return of chum and pink salmon, as Dollies feed heavily on eggs. (Egg pattern flies, attracts, and bright spoons and spinners work best, obviously.) A late run of silver salmon, peaking in late October, enters the river, but in the Nakwasina, these fish begin their spawning soon after entering freshwater. Near tide water or at the river mouth early on in the run is best for some fair to good fishing.

The river's banks are ideal for walking and casting. You can spot-cast toward schools of salmon and pick up the Dolly Varden stacked up behind them, especially in the deep holes on the lower river near salt water. (This is particularly effective on the Nakwasina, with many big fish taken this way.) Anglers focusing on Nakwasina Sound off the river mouth will find superb silver and pink salmon and Dolly Varden fishing. The variety here is nothing to write home about, but the top-notch Dolly fishing—some of the best in all of Southeast—more than makes up for it.

25 Katlian River

Location: North Baranof Island drainage, 11 miles northeast of Sitka, 585 miles southeast of Anchorage; see map page 327.

USGS map: Sitka A-4.

How to get there: By boat from Sitka. Crossing upper Sitka Sound into Katlian Bay, marine travelers can access the mouth of the Katlian River at high tide. Mooring off the mouth or beaching the boat, the lower river is easily accessible.

Highlights: Another excellent Sitka area stream for big Dolly Varden (from July through August); also good fishing for pink salmon (in early August) and silver salmon (from late September through early October).

Species: Chum salmon, Dolly Varden, pink salmon, silver salmon.

Regulations: Unbaited, artificial lures only from November 16 through September 14; king salmon fishing is prohibited. For additional restrictions, consult the current Alaska Department of Fish and Game regulations or contact the ADF&G Sitka office, (907) 747-5355.

Facilities: No developed public facilities.

Contact: For fishing information, contact the Alaska Department of Fish and Game, 304 Lake Street, Room 103, Sitka, AK 99835; (907) 747-5355.

Fishing the Katlian River: Located at the head of Katlian Bay in upper Sitka Sound, the Katlian River drains a mountainous, heavily forested region of central Baranof Island. In the east, mountain peaks can be seen towering over 4,600 feet high, bearing ice and snow fields. Although it's not a particularly large river, the Katlian supports good runs of salmon and, one of the main local attractions, a population of trophy sea-run Dolly Varden charr.

Fairly shallow, with lots of riffles and some deeper pools, the Katlian has perfect spawning habitat for salmon. It receives substantial numbers of chums and pinks in August and a smaller showing of silvers peaking in late October. It's common for these fish to stage off the mouth of the river for several days to a couple of weeks before moving into freshwater; they are often in or near spawning condition shortly after entering the river. However, early in the season it's possible to get fairly bright salmon, especially at or near the mouth. Expect fair to good action for silvers and chums, but hot action for pinks.

Most anglers fish for salmon at the head of Katlian Bay, focusing their attention on the river when Dolly Varden begin entering in fishable numbers around the first of July. It's a popular fishery since many of these charr tend to be on the heavy side; two- to four-pound fish are fairly common, with occasional lunkers up to eight pounds. Look for trophy charr in holes, sloughs, or tailouts near spawning salmon on the lower river for best results. Fly-fishing conditions on the Katlian are excellent.

26 Sitka Sound

Location: West of Baranof Island, Sitka area, 580 miles southeast of Anchorage; see map page 327.

USGS maps: Sitka A-4, A-5, A-6, B-5, B-6; Port Alexander D-4, D-5.

How to get there: By boat or car from Sitka. The best way to reach the more productive fishing areas around the sound is by boat, although surf casting is possible along Sitka's road system, particularly Halibut Point and Sawmill Creek Roads. When the weather cooperates, kayaking is an option for access to the inner areas of Sitka Sound.

Highlights: The number one marine fishery on Baranof Island, one of the best in Southeast. Excellent fishing for king salmon (from mid-May through mid-June), silver salmon (from mid-August through early September), pink salmon (from late July through early August), Dolly Varden (from May through July), and halibut (from June through August); good fishing for chum salmon (from early to mid-August).

Species: Chum salmon, cutthroat trout, Dolly Varden, halibut, king salmon, pink salmon, silver salmon, *red salmon*.

Regulations: For details on the open season and bag limits for bottomfish, consult the current Alaska Department of Fish and Game regulations or contact the ADF&G Sitka office, (907) 747-5355.

Facilities: Commercial lodging, hotels, gas, boat rental and launching, campgrounds, sporting goods, groceries, and guide services are available in Sitka.

Contact: For guide services, contact Sportsman Charters, 821 Charles Street, Sitka, AK 99835, (907) 747-8756. For lodging information, contact Baranof Sportsman's Vacations, 325 Seward Street, Sitka, AK 99835; (907) 747-4937. For cabin rentals, contact Tongass National Forest, 204 Siginaka Way, Sitka, AK 99835; (907) 747-6671.

Fishing Sitka Sound: Located on the west side of Baranof Island, Sitka Sound has perhaps the most prolific saltwater sportfishery in the area. The sound leads directly to the Pacific Ocean, and boasts one major island, Kruzof, and many smaller islands scattered throughout its waters. Westerly winds can whip the waters into a froth, but on calm days it's one of the most scenic, peaceful bays in Southeast Alaska. Smaller, semiprotected bays adjoin the sound, and Mount Edgecumbe, a 3,200-foot volcano on Kruzof Island, adorns the west side across from the town of Sitka. Boating and kayaking are extremely popular with locals and visitors alike. There is prime bottomfish angling in the middle and outer bay areas and unsurpassed action for anadromous species near islands and river mouths closer to Sitka.

The sound's myriad aquatic life attracts feeding fish. Halibut are present year-round, but are larger in size and more numerous during the warmer months. Early and late in the season the outer waters of the sound produce the best halibut catches, while late summer and early fall see these giants closer to town and in shallower wa-

ter. Hungry salmon and charr cruise the blue depths of the sound from May until October. All five salmon species are present; king, silver, pink, and chum salmon are the most frequently caught.

Immature king salmon weighing 15 to 20 pounds are available any day of the year, but appear to be more numerous from May to September. In early summer anglers frequently intercept mature prespawners bound for mainland rivers and streams, some up to a hefty 70 pounds or more. Trophy coho are another possibility, with some specimens reaching 20 pounds. Dolly Varden charr are taken off beaches and points around town, with major populations inhabiting areas in the northern part of Sitka Sound, such as Nakwasina Sound and Katlian Bay.

Good locations for salmon, charr, and halibut in the sound include Necker Islands: Biorka Channel and Biorka, Legma, Elovoi, and Golf Islands; Saint Lazaria Island; Vitskari Rocks/Island; Eastern Channel; Sheldon Jackson Hatchery; Silver Bay; Kasiana Island/Western Channel; Middle/Crow Island; Inner Point; Hayward Strait; Magoun Island; Olga Strait; Lisianski Point; Starrigavan Bay; Katlian Bay; Krestof Sound: Halleck, Neva, and Whitestone Points; and Nakwasina Sound.

27 Redoubt Lake

Location: Central Baranof Island drainage, 10 miles south of Sitka, 600 miles southeast of Anchorage; see map page 327.

USGS map: Port Alexander D-4.

How to get there: There are three access options. One is by floatplane from Sitka, a short hop lasting only a few minutes. (Drop-off is usually near the channel connecting the lake to salt water or at a cabin near the lake inlet.) Another way is to hike in via the Redoubt Lake Trail from Silver Bay. The third is by small boat or kayak from Redoubt Bay through the channel into the west end of the lake. Some portaging is required for the latter option; a set of falls must be crossed prior to reaching the lake.

Highlights: A very popular Sitka area lake and stream fishing location, with excellent fishing for silver salmon (in the second half of September); also good fishing for sockeye salmon (in the second half of July) and rainbow and cutthroat trout (in May and from September through October).

Species: Chum salmon, Dolly Varden, pink salmon, red salmon, silver salmon, *king salmon*.

Regulations: Unbaited, artificial lures only from November 16 through September 14; king salmon fishing is prohibited. For additional restrictions, consult the current Alaska Department of Fish and Game regulations or contact the ADF&G Sitka office, (907) 747-5355.

Facilities: A Forest Service cabin is located at the northeastern end of the lake.

Contact: For cabin rentals, contact Tongass National Forest, 204 Siginaka Way, Sitka, AK 99835; (907) 747-6671. For an air taxi, contact Bellair, P.O. Box 371, Sitka, AK 99835, (907) 747-8636; or Mountain Aviation, P.O. Box 875, Sitka, AK 99835, (907) 966-2288.

Fishing Redoubt Lake: This is a clear, narrow, 10-mile-long lake in the heart of Baranof Island. Mountains rising to 3,500 feet, topped with snow fields, hem the north and south shores, with their steep cliffs dropping almost vertically into the lake. Small streams pour off the forest-clad slopes, creating magnificent waterfalls. This area, considered one of the better spots around Sitka for salmon and trout, receives a fair amount of angling pressure.

Healthy runs of silver and red salmon arrive in the drainage in midsummer and last well into fall. Successful anglers concentrate their efforts in three specific areas: the falls below Redoubt Lake—a temporary barrier for migrating fish, it creates a haven for spin and fly-casting, particularly for tackle-busting coho and sockeye salmon; the lake outlet—a very good location, especially for schooling silvers; and the mouth of Redoubt Creek near the Forest Service cabin.

Resident species, such as rainbow and cutthroat trout, offer very good action, particularly in spring and fall, but can be taken quite readily through the summer in deeper parts of the lake near the inlet and outlet. When the salmon spawn in autumn, target these magnificent game fish near the inlet stream.

For a combination salmon/trout excursion with a variety of water (intertidal, stream, and lake) in the most scenic part of Baranof Island, Redoubt Lake is the top choice of locals and visitors alike.

28 Port Banks System

Location: Southwest Baranof Island drainage, 35 miles southeast of Sitka, 625 miles southeast of Anchorage; see map page 327.

USGS map: Port Alexander C-3.

How to get there: By plane or boat. Floatplanes traditionally access the area from Sitka by landing either at Port Banks near the mouth of the stream draining Plotnikof Lake, the outlet or inlet of Plotnikof Lake, or the upper end of Davidof Lake. Boaters can reach the system from Sitka via Whale Bay and moor at Port Banks.

Highlights: A famous Sitka area angling spot, with excellent fishing for silver salmon (from late July through late August); good fishing for steelhead (from late April through late May) and rainbow trout (in May and from September through October).

Species: Rainbow trout, silver salmon, steelhead, *chum salmon, pink salmon*.

Regulations: Unbaited, artificial lures only from November 16 through September 14; king salmon fishing is prohibited. For additional restrictions, consult the current Alaska Department of Fish and Game regulations or contact the ADF&G Sitka office, (907) 747-5355.

Facilities: Two Forest Service cabins are available, one at the inlet of Plotnikof Lake, the other at the inlet of Davidof Lake.

Contact: For cabin rentals, contact Tongass National Forest, 204 Siginaka Way, Sitka, AK 99835; (907) 747-6671. For an air taxi, contact Bellair, P.O. Box 371, Sitka, AK 99835, (907) 747-8636; or Mountain Aviation, P.O. Box 875, Sitka, AK 99835, (907) 966-2288.

Fishing the Port Banks System: Situated within the South Baranof Wilderness, the Port Banks system is indeed one of the more scenic fishing locations on the island. High mountain ridges and snow-covered peaks (some reaching 4,000 feet or higher) surround two larger drainage lakes, Plotnikof and Davidof, providing spectacular views on clear days. This clear-water system is endowed with healthy populations of salmon and trout and draws many an angler during spring and summer.

Quite unique for Southeast sport fisheries, the Port Banks drainage lakes and streams receive a summer run of silver salmon and an extended run of steelhead trout. Starting as early as the Fourth of July and continuing into September, bright cohos enter the system in large numbers, providing outstanding action for anglers taking the time to fish and explore its waters. Although most salmon fishing takes place at the mouth of the stream draining Plotnikof Lake, silvers may be taken just about anywhere within the Port Banks system.

Steelhead are another popular species that receive a fair amount of attention. Considered a spring run, these silvery torpedoes filter into Port Banks beginning in April, with a few ocean-fresh fish still arriving into July. Early in the season, anglers seem to do best near tide water at Port Banks, while later on (in May and June) action peaks at the outlets of Plotnikof and Davidof Lakes.

The third major species in the system is rainbow trout. These fine sport fish may be taken from drainage lakes throughout the season, with some of the best angling occurring in spring and fall. Autumn months are particularly good as cool temperatures and spawning salmon create perfect feeding (and fishing) conditions.

Petersburg/Wrangell

The Petersburg/Wrangell area, from Cape Fenshaw to the Cleveland Peninsula, encompasses numerous islands—including Kupreanof, Kuiu, Etolin, Wrangell, and Zarembo—along with the Stikine Wilderness on the mainland and many straits, channels, sounds, and bays. With its abundance of rugged coastline, sheltered waters, and dozens of small lakes and streams, this area has significant opportunities for high-quality marine and freshwater fishing, which are probably unequaled for variety anywhere in the Southeast region.

All five species of salmon occur here. As elsewhere, most of the effort for king and coho takes place primarily in salt water as an intercept fishery, with trolling, mooching, and jigging the predominant methods. (The giant Stikine River is far and away the largest spawning destination in the area.) Frederick Sound and Wrangell Narrows, Eastern Passage, and Zimovia and Stikine Straits are the most frequently fished marine areas. Local hatcheries have created substantial new opportunities for both king and coho. Some of the better locations to target these hatchery (and wild stock) fisheries are Blind Slough, Earl West Cove, lower Duncan Canal, and the mouths of Petersburg and Falls Creeks.

A fairly developed road system allows access to many quality locations—both fresh- and salt water—within a short hike from the road. Some of the more outstanding spots are the Thoms Lake and Creek system, 39 miles south of Wrangell (steelhead, red salmon, cutthroat trout, Dolly Varden, silver salmon); Blind River and Blind Slough, 15 miles southeast of Petersburg (king salmon, silver salmon, cutthroat trout, Dolly Varden); Pat Creek and Pat Lake, 11 miles south of Wrangell (king salmon, silver salmon, pink salmon, cutthroat trout, Dolly Varden); the Zimovia and Mitkof Highway shorelines (silver salmon, pink salmon, Dolly Varden, cutthroat trout); and Falls and Ohmer Creeks, south of Petersburg (steelhead, king salmon, silver salmon, Dolly Varden, cutthroat trout).

Many secluded stream and lake locations within easy reach of a boat or small plane offer outstanding fishing. Steelhead, cutthroat trout, and Dolly Varden are the main attractions, with some high-quality fishing for salmon (silver, pink, chum) and even rainbow trout in some locations. Petersburg and Kadake Creeks, and the Anan, Marten, Swan, Virginia, and Eagle Lake systems are a few of the more noteworthy ones.

The U.S. Forest Service maintains 42 public-use cabins in the area, many of them remote. Each accommodates four to six people, and some even come equipped with skiffs. Reservations at some of the more popular locations should be made at least six months in advance.

㉙ Kadake Creek

Location: North Kuiu Island drainage, 45 miles west of Petersburg, 635 miles southeast of Anchorage; see map page 327.

USGS maps: Petersburg D-6; Port Alexander C-1.

How to get there: By plane or boat from Petersburg, Wrangell, or other area towns. Boaters from Petersburg must go through Frederick Sound and Keku Strait to reach Kadake Bay. From there, access to the mouth of Kadake Creek requires an 18-foot tide. A limited network of forest roads crisscross the northern part of Kuiu Island, providing access to the upper drainage.

Highlights: Good fishing for silver salmon (in the first half of September), chum and pink salmon (from late July through early August), steelhead (from late April through mid-May), cutthroat trout (in May and June), and Dolly Varden (in May and from August through September).

Species: Chum salmon, cutthroat trout, Dolly Varden, pink salmon, rainbow trout, silver salmon, steelhead.

Regulations: Unbaited, artificial lures only from November 16 through September 14; king salmon fishing is prohibited. For additional restrictions, consult the current Alaska Department of Fish and Game regulations or contact the ADF&G Ketchikan office, (907) 225-2859.

Facilities: A Forest Service cabin is located at Kadake Bay at the mouth of Kadake Creek.

Contact: For cabin rentals, contact Tongass National Forest, 204 Siginaka Way, Sitka, AK 99835; (907) 747-6671. For an air taxi, contact Kupreanof Flying Service, P.O. Box 768, Petersburg, AK 99833; (907) 772-3396.

Fishing Kadake Creek: Situated on the northern end of Kuiu Island, Kadake Creek is a fairly small drainage flowing into Kadake Bay and Keku Strait. Due to muskeg in the area, it runs slightly brown in color. The four lakes connected to the stream are small and of little significance to the fishery. The most sought-after species include silver salmon, steelhead, and cutthroat trout, which are present in abundance.

Most angling effort occurs on the lower creek sections near the Forest Service cabin. Visiting fishers usually work the tides at the mouth at Kadake Bay, moving upstream to search for holding fish after the crest of the tide. A big spring run of steelhead and hungry cutthroat trout open the season every year, especially for fly-fishing. July and August bring chum and pink salmon into the system. Fishing the tides at the mouth usually produces the most and brightest fish.

Coho invade Kadake beginning in late summer and continuing into October. (Look for in-migrating cutthroats and Dollies along with the salmon, especially around spawning beds.) Some resident rainbow trout can be found in the upper and middle sections of Kadake Creek, but they're seldom targeted. Also, a very small run of fall steelhead may be present in the latter part of November.

30 Lower Stephens Passage

Location: Southeast of Admiralty Island, 40 miles from Petersburg, 625 miles southeast of Anchorage; see map page 327.

USGS maps: Sitka A-1, B-1; Sumdum A-5, A-6, B-4, B-5, B-6, C-5, C-6.

How to get there: The lower passage is accessible by boat from Petersburg (via Frederick Sound), Juneau, or area lodges. Floatplanes often land in protected bays and coves, especially near Forest Service cabins.

Highlights: A remote marine fishery with little angling pressure but great action. Good fishing for king salmon (from late May through late June), silver salmon (from mid-August through mid-September), pink salmon (from mid-July through mid-August), and halibut (from mid-June through mid-July).

Species: Chum salmon, cutthroat trout, Dolly Varden, halibut, king salmon, pink salmon, silver salmon, *red salmon*.

Regulations: For details on the open season for halibut and lingcod, consult the current Alaska Department of Fish and Game regulations or contact the ADF&G Juneau office, (907) 465-4180.

Facilities: Two Forest Service cabins are available, one at Church Bite in Gambier Bay, the other at Donkey Bay in Pybus Bay.

Contact: For guide services, contact Real Alaska Adventures, P.O. Box 1124, Petersburg, AK 99833; (907) 772-4121. For cabin rentals, contact Admiralty Island National Monument, P.O. Box 2097, Juneau, AK 99803; (907) 586-8790. For an air taxi, contact Kupreanof Flying Service, P.O. Box 768, Petersburg, AK 99833; (907) 772-3396.

Fishing Lower Stephens Passage: Set between Admiralty Island and the mainland, Lower Stephens Passage includes all waters from Gambier Bay and Hobart Bay south to Frederick Strait. Dense rain forests dominate the lower elevations, while snow-capped mountain peaks and glacial valleys adorn the horizon to the east. Although very remote from most recreational boat traffic, the few anglers who target the area with overnight trips often find themselves richly rewarded.

The clear blue waters of Stephens Passage are a major migration corridor and feeding ground for many anadromous and resident species. Many small rivers and streams drain into the passage and adjoining waters, adding excitement to the fishery. Salmon bound for spawning in these and other drainages nearby are effectively intercepted by trolling and mooching along shorelines and small islands. Bottomfish are very abundant during the summer months and most frequently caught by jigging in moderately deep water.

King and silver salmon and halibut are the most sought-after species, with outstanding possibilities for all three in some locations. Feeder kings are available year-round, with the addition of larger, mature fish in late spring and early summer. (Pybus and Gambier Bays are exceptional locations for these monarchs.) When the kings wane in midsummer, the smallest members of the salmon clan, pinks, appear. They're easily taken near the mouths of clear-water streams where they congregate in huge schools. Husky chum salmon are mixed in with the pinks, but expect only fair fishing for them. In late summer, silvers heat up the action in many of the same areas that were most productive for kings. They peak in numbers in fall, and, like the pinks, are taken near or in the mouths of spawning streams.

Sea-run cutthroat trout and Dolly Varden are not abundant here, although some fish may be picked up in small bays and coves with sizable streams at the head of them. The passage is known for its great halibut fishing, however, with the action much more consistent than for salmon. While they are present in great numbers from spring to fall, early summer usually is the best time to catch large fish to 200 pounds or more.

Top locations for salmon, charr, and halibut include Admiralty Island; Point Pybus, Gambier, Price, and Elliott Islands, and Gambier, Pybus, and Little Pybus Bays; Hobart Bay/Entrance Island; Point Hobart; Whitney Island; and Cape Fanshaw.

㉛ Eastern Frederick Sound

Location: Northeast of Kupreanof Island, Petersburg area, 650 miles southeast of Anchorage; see map page 327.

USGS maps: Sumdum A-3, A-4, A-5, A-6; Petersburg C-2, C-3, D-2, D-3, D-4.

How to get there: Primarily by boat from Petersburg or area lodges. It's possible to land floatplanes in parts of the sound, such as its protected bays and coves. Boat access from Wrangell is via Sumner Strait and Wrangell Narrows, or, if tides permit, Dry Strait on the Stikine River Flats.

Highlights: A traditional local hot spot, with good fishing for king salmon (from late May through late June), silver salmon (from mid-August through mid-September), pink salmon (from late July through early August), and halibut (from June through August).

Species: Chum salmon, cutthroat trout, Dolly Varden, halibut, king salmon, pink salmon, silver salmon, *red salmon, steelhead.*

Regulations: For details on the open season for halibut and lingcod, consult the current Alaska Department of Fish and Game regulations or contact the ADF&G Ketchikan office, (907) 225-2859.

Facilities: Lodging, groceries, sporting goods, boat rentals and launching, fuel, and water are available in Petersburg. Two Forest Service cabins are located in the area, one on Cascade Creek, the other on Spurt Cove in Thomas Bay.

Contact: For guide services, contact Real Alaska Adventures, P.O. Box 1124, Petersburg, AK

99833; (907) 772-4121. For lodging information, contact the Petersburg Chamber of Commerce, P.O. Box 649, Petersburg, AK 99833; (907) 772-3646. For cabin rentals, contact Tongass National Forest, 204 Siginaka Way, Sitka, AK 99835; (907) 747-6671. For an air taxi, contact Kupreanof Flying Service, P.O. Box 768, Petersburg, AK 99833; (907) 772-3396.

Fishing Eastern Frederick Sound: Separating Kupreanof and Mitkof Islands from the mainland, eastern Frederick Sound includes all waters from Cape Fanshaw and Pinta Point in the west to Stikine River Flats in the southeast. A breathtaking area of dense coastal forests, deeply incised valleys, and enormous tidewater glaciers, it's blessed with an abundance of fish and marine life.

Seasoned marine boaters, primarily from Petersburg, enjoy a fishery that has been producing good catches of salmon and bottomfish for decades. Today it's still one of the leading sport fish locations in the entire region. King and silver salmon and halibut are the most popular species and subject to intense harvest efforts during the summer and fall months.

King salmon, although present year-round, are far more numerous in late spring and early summer as wild runs bound for spawning areas up the Stikine River and hatchery fish returning to release sites in Wrangell Narrows pass through these waters in full force. While they average 15 to 25 pounds, larger fish to 50 or 60 pounds, sometimes more, are frequently taken. By July, as the best king fishing declines, things start to get hot with returning pink salmon. These scrappy fighters are taken in inshore waters everywhere, particularly near and in the mouths of clear-water streams. (Look for numbers of chum salmon, cutthroat trout, and Dolly Varden at this time.) Silvers are the last of the salmon to show and continue to arrive through most of autumn. Many fish are of wild stock origin, with a significant portion being returning hatchery releases.

Halibut fishing is good, with huge flatfish abundant throughout Frederick Sound. Jigging is the most popular angling method, but a fair number are taken incidentally while fishing other species, especially salmon. It's worthwhile to note that the lower southeast section of Frederick Sound may get cloudy with glacial silt in summer. This is due to the heavy discharge from the nearby Stikine River. When the weather cools, the runoff generally subsides and the sound becomes clear blue again. Frederick Sound is regarded by most folks as a day-trip fishery, but longer stays are possible by mooring off beaches and stream mouths in protected bays and coves.

Some of the proven locations in this area for salmon and halibut include Kupreanof Island; Pinta, Boulder, West, East, and Beacon Points; Schooner and Portage Islands; Cape Strait; and Big Creek.

㉜ Duncan Saltchuck Creek

Location: Central Kupreanof Island drainage, 15 miles west of Petersburg, 660 miles southeast of Anchorage; see map page 327.

USGS maps: Petersburg D-4, D-5.

How to get there: By plane and boat from Petersburg or Wrangell. From Petersburg, access is via Wrangell Narrows up into Duncan Canal and Saltchuck. (Boaters can access the Saltchuck area and the mouth of the creek only on high tides of at least 17 feet.)

Highlights: Good fishing for silver salmon (in September), steelhead (from late April through mid-May), cutthroat trout (from May through June), and Dolly Varden (in May and from August through September).

Species: Chum salmon, cutthroat trout, Dolly Varden, pink salmon, rainbow trout, silver salmon, steelhead.

Regulations: Unbaited, artificial lures only from November 16 through September 14; king salmon fishing is prohibited. For additional restrictions, consult the current Alaska Department of Fish and Game regulations or contact the ADF&G Ketchikan office, (907) 225-2859.

Facilities: Two Forest Service cabins are located at the saltchuck at the head of Duncan Canal.

Contact: For cabin rentals, contact Tongass National Forest, P.O. Box 309, Petersburg, AK 99833; (907) 772-3871. For an air taxi, contact Kupreanof Flying Service, P.O. Box 768, Petersburg, AK 99833; (907) 772-3396.

Fishing Duncan Saltchuck Creek: The creek lies at the head of Duncan Canal in the central part of Kupreanof Island. Draining areas of muskeg around the Bohemian Range, it usually has a tannic-brown color, especially after heavy fall rains, but it offers productive fishing for salmon, trout, and charr in a small stream setting.

Long known for its cutthroat trout, the saltchuck hosts above average numbers of these fine game fish in late spring to early summer and again in fall. The last few miles above Duncan Canal is the most popular stretch, and anglers frequently fish it with light spinning and fly-fishing gear. Sea-run Dolly Varden are available during the same times; substantial catches have been made on egg and attractor pattern flies in the creek and flashy spoons off the mouth.

Steelhead trout bust into the drainage in spring, offering a few weeks of top-notch fly-fishing. Most successful anglers fish the tides on the lower creek sections, intercepting these robust sea-run rainbows on their way upstream to spawning areas. Other important species in Duncan Saltchuck include silver salmon and rainbow trout; the lower river and mouth are best for coho, while the upper sections harbor the most rainbow. Additionally, some chum and pink salmon can be enticed into striking flashy hardware right above the mouth in late summer.

The two Forest Service cabins on the shore of the saltchuck make perfect points for staging boat excursions into Duncan Canal or for fishing the lower reaches of the creek.

㉝ Petersburg Creek

Location: Southeast Kupreanof Island drainage, five miles west of Petersburg, 670 miles southeast of Anchorage; see map page 327.

USGS map: Petersburg D-4.

How to get there: Primarily by floatplane or boat from Petersburg or Wrangell. Planes traditionally land on Petersburg Lake. Boaters from nearby Petersburg have two options to access the stream and lake: If tides are higher than 15 feet, boats can reach the creek mouth via Wrangell Narrows, where a trail leads 6.5 miles to Petersburg Lake. Or, if tides don't allow, boaters can moor at a state dock on Wrangell Narrows and take a trail 11.5 miles to lake.

Highlights: A tremendously popular and productive Southeast steelhead and salmon stream, with good fishing for silver salmon (in the second half of September), red salmon (in late July), chum and pink salmon (from late July through early August), steelhead (in May), rainbow and cutthroat trout (in May and June), and Dolly Varden (in May and from August through September).

Species: Chum salmon, cutthroat trout, Dolly Varden, pink salmon, rainbow trout, red salmon, silver salmon, steelhead.

Regulations: Unbaited, artificial lures only from November 16 through September 14; king salmon fishing is prohibited. For additional restrictions, consult the current Alaska Department of Fish and Game regulations or contact the ADF&G Petersburg office, (907) 772-3801.

Facilities: A Forest Service cabin is located at Petersburg Lake.

Contact: For fishing information, contact the Alaska Department of Fish and Game, Sportfish Division, P.O. Box 667, Petersburg, AK 99833; (907) 772-3801. For cabin rentals, contact Tongass National Forest, P.O. Box 309, Petersburg, AK 99833; (907) 772-3871.

Fishing Petersburg Creek: Located on the Lindberg Peninsula of Kupreanof Island, Petersburg Lake and Creek draw a great many local recreationists, who heavily fish these waters during the height of the salmon and steelhead runs. The lower stream is lined by the crests of Petersburg Mountain and Del Monte Peak, adding considerable scenic appeal. Flowing clear and fairly fast west to Wrangell Narrows across from the town of Petersburg, the creek is perfect for one- or two-day outings to sample some of the area's better stream fishing.

As part of the Petersburg Creek–Duncan Saltchuck Wilderness, this area offers some fairly high-quality lake and stream fishing in combination with short trail excursions. Silver salmon and steelhead trout receive most of the attention on the lower section of the creek, while sea-run cutthroats, Dollies, and resident rainbows are taken usually in Petersburg Lake, particularly during the spring and fall months.

Starting in late summer and continuing until late fall, spin and fly-casters pursue the silvers with vigor, while spring-run steelhead grab anglers' attention earlier in the season. Petersburg Creek steelies tend to be some of the largest in Southeast, with a few exceptional fish up to 20 pounds or more.

Sockeye salmon briefly appear during the midsummer lull; fish for them from the lake and below. During the same period, but running slightly later, the creek often sees good numbers of chum and pink salmon.

It's a rare delight to find such a productive stream close to a major town. If you have some time to kill in Petersburg, head over and enjoy some of the good fishing close at hand.

34 Castle River

Location: South Kupreanof Island drainage, 20 miles southwest of Petersburg, 670 miles southeast of Anchorage; see map page 327.

USGS maps: Petersburg C-4, C-5.

How to get there: By floatplane or boat from Petersburg or Wrangell. Boaters from Petersburg arrive via Wrangell Narrows and Duncan Canal, and from Wrangell via Sumner Strait and Duncan Canal. A tide of at least 15 feet is required for floatplanes and 13 feet for boats to access the mouth of river.

Highlights: An important area steelhead and silver salmon stream; good fishing for silver salmon (in the first half of September), chum and pink salmon (from late July through early August), steelhead (from late April through mid-May), rainbow and cutthroat trout (in May and June), and Dolly Varden (in May and from August through September).

Species: Chum salmon, cutthroat trout, Dolly Varden, pink salmon, rainbow trout, silver salmon, steelhead.

Regulations: Unbaited, artificial lures only from November 16 through September 14; king salmon fishing is prohibited. For additional restrictions, consult the current Alaska Department of Fish and Game regulations or contact the ADF&G Ketchikan office, (907) 225-2859.

Facilities: Two Forest Service cabins are located near the mouth.

Contact: For cabin rentals, contact Tongass National Forest, P.O. Box 309, Petersburg, AK 99833; (907) 772-3871. For an air taxi, contact Kupreanof Flying Service, P.O. Box 768, Petersburg, AK 99833; (907) 772-3396.

Fishing the Castle River: Flowing into west Duncan Canal on Kupreanof Island, the Castle River is a tannic-brown stream surrounded by muskeg, rain forests, and rolling hills. Small in size, the river is nonetheless one of the most productive streams of the area, known best for silver salmon and steelhead trout.

Most anglers access the drainage at the mouth, then fish and hike upstream. The first major game fish of the season are spring-run steelhead trout. They are best intercepted early on in the first few miles of the river, fishing the tides. Later on, anglers do better by hiking to holes and runs on the middle Castle. Resident rainbows, as well as sea-run cutthroat trout and Dolly Varden, are also available from spring through fall.

Silver salmon begin running in August and remain until October, inspiring a fair amount of angling effort in the Castle. Chum and pink salmon also show in large numbers, but a little earlier than the coho. Brighter fish are generally taken at the mouth or in the lower river.

Two Forest Service cabins with boats are ideally situated for anglers who want to fish Castle River and perhaps even do some trolling or jigging in the salt water of Duncan Canal. (Trips to Duncan Saltchuck Creek to the north or the Kah Sheets River to the south are possible by boat.) Because of their popularity, reservations for these cabins should be made well in advance.

35 Wrangell Narrows/ Duncan Canal

Location: Southeast of Kupreanof Island, Petersburg area, 675 miles southeast of Anchorage; see map page 327.

USGS maps: Petersburg C-3, C-4, D-3, D-4, D-5.

How to get there: By boat and floatplane from Petersburg. Boating is by far the most popular method, while floatplanes are able to use protected waters, such as bays and coves, for access. Marine travelers from Wrangell can access the narrows and canal via Sumner Strait.

Highlights: One of the best marine fisheries in the Petersburg area, with excellent fishing for king salmon (from late May through late June) and silver salmon (from mid-August through mid-September); also good fishing for chum and pink salmon (from late July through early August) and halibut (from mid-June through mid-July).

Species: Chum salmon, cutthroat trout, Dolly Varden, halibut, king salmon, pink salmon, silver salmon, *red salmon, steelhead.*

Regulations: For details on the open season for halibut and lingcod, consult the current Alaska Department of Fish and Game regulations or contact the ADF&G Ketchikan office, (907) 225-2859.

Facilities: Lodging, sporting goods, guide service, boat rentals and launching, fuel, and water are available in the town of Petersburg. Nine Forest Service cabins are located in the Duncan Canal area: Kah Sheets Bay (one), Bains Cove (one), Beecher Pass (one), Harvey Lake (one), Breiland Slough (one), Castle River/Flats (two), and Saltchuck (two).

Contact: For guide services, contact Real Alaska Adventures, P.O. Box 1124, Petersburg, AK 99833; (907) 772-4121. For lodging information, contact the Petersburg Chamber of Commerce, P.O. Box 649, Petersburg, AK 99833; (907) 772-3646. For cabin rentals, contact Tongass National Forest, 204 Siginaka Way, Sitka, AK 99835; (907) 747-6671. For an air taxi, contact Kupreanof Flying Service, P.O. Box 768, Petersburg, AK 99833; (907) 772-3396.

Fishing Wrangell Narrows/Duncan Canal: Separating Mitkof Island from the larger Kupreanof Island, Wrangell Narrows is known as one of the most intense marine sportfisheries in southern Southeast. Stretching from Frederick Sound in the north to Sumner Strait in the south, the narrows average only about a mile in width. Cutting deep into the center of Kupreanof Island is Duncan Canal, a fairly long, wide fjord that connects with Wrangell Narrows at Woewodski Island near Sumner Strait. Both serve as major recreational waters for boaters

and anglers and also provide access to streams and cabins in the area.

Petersburg anglers most often target king salmon. Feeders can be taken consistently at the outer ends of Wrangell Narrows and a large hatchery run of these fish returns every season to Blind Slough on Mitkof Island a few miles south of town. An enhanced run of silvers mixed in with wild stocks offers fast action in late summer and fall in the slough and adjoining Blind River, and in varying amounts, throughout the narrows and Duncan Canal. Although primarily a boat fishery early in the season, it can be fished with good results by shore anglers later on. Chum and pink salmon are usually caught in areas where large concentrations of these fish occur, such as near the mouths of rivers and streams.

Sea-run cutthroat trout and Dolly Varden are spread throughout the narrows and canal in fair numbers and are usually caught at the mouths of Petersburg, Falls, and Duncan Saltchuck Creeks, as well as along points and beaches in the vicinity. Halibut fishing predominantly takes place at the north and south ends of the narrows; some smaller fish may be hauled out of deeper parts of Duncan Canal in midseason.

Visiting anglers are by no means restricted to the Petersburg area for accommodations, as there are quite a few Forest Service cabins along Duncan Canal.

The main fishing areas for salmon and halibut in Wrangell Narrows and Duncan Canal include Kupreanof Island: Prolewy, Mountain, Finger, and North Points; Mitkof Island: Petersburg Harbor, Scow Bay, Danger, Blind, and December Points, Blind Slough, and Point Alexander; Duncan Canal: Whiskey Pass/Butterworth Island, Castle Islands, and Saltchuck; and Woody Island.

③⑥ Kah Sheets River

Location: South Kupreanof Island drainage, 25 miles southwest of Petersburg, 670 miles southeast of Anchorage; see map page 327.

USGS maps: Petersburg C-4, C-5.

How to get there: By boat or floatplane from Petersburg or Wrangell. Boaters from Petersburg go through Wrangell Narrows and lower Duncan

Canal to Kah Sheets Bay; those from Wrangell follow Sumner Strait to the bay. (To reach the trailhead at Kah Sheets Bay by boat, a 14-foot tide is required.) The trail leads 2.75 miles to the outlet of Kah Sheets Lake, where floatplane access is possible.

Highlights: One of Southeast's better steelhead and salmon streams; good fishing for silver salmon (in the first half of September), chum and pink salmon (from late July through early August), steelhead (from late April through mid-May), rainbow and cutthroat trout (in May and June), and Dolly Varden (in May and from August through September).

Species: Chum salmon, cutthroat trout, Dolly Varden, pink salmon, rainbow trout, red salmon, silver salmon, steelhead.

Regulations: Unbaited, artificial lures only from November 16 through September 14; king salmon fishing is prohibited. For additional restrictions, consult the current Alaska Department of Fish and Game regulations or contact the ADF&G Ketchikan office, (907) 225-2859.

Facilities: Two Forest Service cabins are available, one at the head of Kah Sheets Bay near the mouth of the river, the other at the outlet of Kah Sheets Lake.

Contact: For cabin rentals, contact Tongass National Forest, P.O. Box 309, Petersburg, AK 99833; (907) 772-3871. For an air taxi, contact Kupreanof Flying Service, P.O. Box 768, Petersburg, AK 99833; (907) 772-3396.

Fishing the Kah Sheets River: The Kah Sheets is a lightly tannic-stained stream draining into Kah Sheets Bay and upper Sumner Strait. Only about two miles long, the river is easily fished along its entire length from tidewater to the outlet of Kah Sheets Lake via a well-marked trail. Anglers come from near and far to experience one of the best streams in southern Southeast for silver salmon and steelhead trout.

Like other drainages on Kupreanof Island, Kah Sheets has a vibrant run of spring steelhead trout. Steelhead can be taken anywhere on the river, with the best success reported on incoming tides near the mouth early in the run and in the upper river just below the lake later on. Resident rainbows are found in the lake, giving anglers with canoes or inflatables some action

during spring and fall months. Some sea-run cutthroat trout and Dolly Varden are also present throughout the season.

The Kah Sheets has a reputation for its ballistic coho. Large schools of these fighters enter the river in August and stay into October. They can be taken from Kah Sheets Bay right up into the lake. Trips early in midsummer can be productive for hefty chum salmon and spunky pinks. (A small run of reds also occurs, with the best opportunities found in the river's faster flowing stretches.)

Both of the two Forest Service cabins are ideally situated for excellent access to the best of Kupreanof Island fishing—whether casting for salmon and steelhead in the river, jigging for halibut in the bay, or fly-fishing trout and Dollies in the lake.

37 Ohmer Creek

Location: South Mitkof Island drainage, 20 miles south of Petersburg, 680 miles southeast of Anchorage; see map page 327.

USGS map: Petersburg C-3.

How to get there: By car from Petersburg. The Mitkof Highway out of town leads along Wrangell Narrows and Blind Slough to a stream crossing and parallels Ohmer Creek for about one mile. Roads can take anglers to other stream sections.

Highlights: Petersburg's top roadside stream, with good fishing for king salmon (from late June through mid-July), silver salmon (in the first half of September), chum and pink salmon (in early August), cutthroat trout (from May through June), and Dolly Varden (in May and from August through September).

Species: Chum salmon, cutthroat trout, Dolly Varden, king salmon, pink salmon, rainbow trout, silver salmon, steelhead.

Regulations: Unbaited, artificial lures only from November 16 through September 14. For additional restrictions, consult the current Alaska Department of Fish and Game regulations or contact the ADF&G Petersburg office, (907) 772-3801.

Facilities: A campground is located next to the Mitkof Highway, near the mouth of the stream.

Contact: For fishing information, contact the Alaska Department of Fish and Game, Sportfish Division, P.O. Box 667, Petersburg, AK 99833; (907) 772-3801. For camping information, contact the Petersburg Chamber of Commerce, P.O. Box 649, Petersburg, AK 99833; (907) 772-3646.

Fishing Ohmer Creek: Like the Petersburg Creek drainage, Ohmer Creek is a heavily fished clear-water stream with easy access and good overall fishing. Situated on the mountainous southern end of Mitkof Island, it's a relatively small drainage containing both wild and hatchery stocks of salmon and healthy populations of trout and charr.

One of the creek's more unique features is its run of big king salmon. Although it's hatchery maintained, the fishery is one of few stream locations in Southeast where anglers can legally fish these great sport fish. Present in early and midsummer, the kings add welcome variety to the creek's angling prospects. Silver salmon are popular in fall when a natural run of these spectacular battlers enters the stream in fairly large schools. For both species, local anglers tend to favor the river's lower section, including the mouth.

Other fine species to consider are sea-run cutthroat trout and Dolly Varden, as they can offer steady action near the road crossing and other spots. Additionally, late summer runs of chums and pinks add some excitement between the king and silver salmon runs. A small run of native steelhead trout shows up in spring, with fair fishing to be expected during the peak in May. If you're ever passing through Petersburg and have a few hours to spare, this creek makes a fine possibility.

➌➑ Stikine River System

Location: Mainland drainage east of Mitkof Island, 30 miles southeast of Petersburg, 690 miles southeast of Anchorage; see map page 327.

USGS maps: Bradfield Canal C-6, D-6; Petersburg C-1, C-2, D-1.

How to get there: By boat or plane from Petersburg and Wrangell. From Petersburg, access is via Frederick and Dry Straits; from Wrangell, access is via Eastern Passage. (To successfully reach the main stem Stikine River and its clearwater tributaries, you must have a tide of at least 14 feet to cross the Stikine River Flats.) Small planes are capable of landing in a few locations, if conditions permit.

Highlights: Outstanding angling options on Southeast's largest river, the mile-wide Stikine, with good fishing for silver salmon (in September), chum and pink salmon (late July through early August), steelhead (from late April through mid-May), rainbow and cutthroat trout (from May through June), and Dolly Varden (in May and from August through September).

Species: Chum salmon, cutthroat trout, Dolly Varden, pink salmon, rainbow trout, red salmon, silver salmon, *king salmon, steelhead*.

Regulations: Unbaited, artificial lures only from November 16 through September 14; king salmon fishing is prohibited. For additional restrictions, consult the current Alaska Department of Fish and Game regulations or contact the ADF&G Ketchikan office, (907) 225-2859.

Facilities: Five Forest Service cabins are available in the Stikine River drainage: Red Slough (one), Shakes Slough (two), Figure Eight Lake (one), and Andrew Creek (one).

Contact: For guide services, contact Ellis Inc., P.O. Box 1068, Petersburg, AK 99833; (907) 772-3039. For cabin rentals, contact Tongass National Forest, P.O. Box 309, Petersburg, AK 99833; (907) 772-3871. For an air taxi, contact Kupreanof Flying Service, P.O. Box 768, Petersburg, AK 99833; (907) 772-3396.

Fishing the Stikine River System: The very large, glacial Stikine River system originates in the snow- and ice-bound Cassiar Mountains in British Columbia, Canada. The largest transboundary system in Southeast, only the last 30 to 35 miles of the river lies within Alaska, fanning out into a huge, sandy delta at the head of Sumner Strait and Frederick Sound just east of Mitkof Island. With a vast number of tributary lakes and clearwater streams, it supports fairly large populations of salmon, charr, and trout, and has quite a bit of sport fish potential for anglers who have the time to explore its many productive waters.

Since the Stikine is heavily laden with fine silt, most sportfishing takes place at the confluences of clear-water streams and sloughs. The largest and most popular tributary among local anglers is Andrew Creek, on the south bank only a few miles from tidewater. Another slightly smaller stream is nearby Government Creek, situated near the mouth. Both receive a fair amount of angling pressure during the height of salmon runs in summer and fall.

Although it has a substantial run of large king salmon (from May through July), the Stikine is currently closed to fishing for the species, with most fish heading unimpeded into major spawning streams in Canada. Many silvers, chums, and pinks, along with smaller numbers of reds, are present throughout the lower drainage and provide the bulk of angling activity. Dolly Varden are available and seasonally abundant (best in late summer to fall), and occasionally you can even take cutthroat and rainbow trout. (Some may be found in the main stem from late fall to early spring, when the river clears for lack of meltwater.) The best areas to fish in the summer are clear-water sloughs and creek mouths. Steelhead are rumored to be available, but elusive; apparently they're concentrated in tributaries farther upriver.

Sport anglers have quite a few options in this impressive drainage. You can float the river by kayak, raft, or canoe, with a put in usually at Telegraph Creek (150 miles above tidewater), which can be accessed via the Cassiar Highway, or at other points along the river by small float or wheelplane. This is ideal as it allows anglers to sample good angling in tributary creeks, streams, lakes, and sloughs on the way down. It's also possible to jet boat upriver from Wrangell and camp and fish or float down. Public-use cabins are available, and you'll even discover some hot springs along the river.

Part of the Stikine-Leconte Wilderness, the river is dramatically scenic, with ice-capped mountain peaks soaring above 4,000 feet, steep gorges, forested valleys, and tidewater glaciers. Wildlife is abundant. Anyone willing to explore this huge drainage will not be disappointed by the wild, impressive surroundings and the fishing. Since this is a true wilderness river with volatile nature and tidal flats, sandbars, and extreme tides on the lower end, the services of a local guide are highly recommended, unless you're a seasoned wilderness traveler.

39 Upper Sumner Strait

Location: North of Prince of Wales and Zarembo Islands, south of Kupreanof and Mitkof Islands, 25 miles south of Petersburg, 675 miles southeast of Anchorage; see map page 327.

USGS maps: Petersburg B-2, B-3, B-4, B-5, C-2, C-3, C-4.

How to get there: By boat from Petersburg (via Wrangell Narrows) and Wrangell. Protected bays and coves in the area provide access opportunities for floatplanes.

Highlights: A longtime favorite spot for salmon and bottomfish, with good fishing for king salmon (from mid-May through mid-June), silver salmon (from early August through early September), pink salmon (from mid-July through early August), and halibut (from June through August).

Species: Chum salmon, cutthroat trout, Dolly Varden, halibut, king salmon, pink salmon, silver salmon, *red salmon, steelhead.*

Regulations: For details on the open season for salmon, halibut, and lingcod, consult the current Alaska Department of Fish and Game regulations or contact the ADF&G Ketchikan office, (907) 225-2859.

Facilities: A Forest Service cabin is available at the head of Kah Sheets Bay.

Contact: For guide services, contact Real Alaska Adventures, P.O. Box 1124, Petersburg, AK 99833; (907) 772-4121. For cabin rentals, contact Tongass National Forest, 204 Siginaka Way, Sitka, AK 99835; (907) 747-6671. For an air taxi, contact Kupreanof Flying Service, P.O. Box 768, Petersburg, AK 99833; (907) 772-3396.

Fishing Upper Sumner Strait: Running from Stikine River Flats to Point Baker on Prince of Wales Island and Point Barrie on Kupreanof Island, Sumner Strait is a major migration channel for salmon bound for spawning systems on area islands and the mainland. (The Stikine River is one of the major contributing systems.) In summer, bottomfish use the strait as an active feeding ground. It's common knowledge that some of the best marine sportfishing in the southern Southeast region may be found off the strait's beaches, points, reefs, shoals, and stream mouths.

Most king salmon are caught in spring and early summer when mature fish bound for their streams of birth arrive, but persevering anglers can catch smaller, feeder kings on a year-round basis. The waters near Petersburg and Wrangell in particular receive quite a bit of attention from charter fleets. Silver salmon are present in late summer and fall, and can be caught just about anywhere along the shoreline during the height of the run. Pinks, usually not targeted specifically, are fairly abundant. They are most often encountered in mid- to late summer in the vicinity of spawning streams. Some sea-run cutthroat trout and Dolly Varden may be picked up in late spring and summer off the mouths of clear-water streams and adjoining points and beaches.

Bottomfishing is popular during the warmer months, with halibut the obvious favorite. Although they're available throughout the year (except in January, during the statewide closure), early summer is the preferred time to go after huge flatties up to 200 pounds or more. Areas near the eastern end of Sumner Strait are most productive, yielding fish averaging between 20 and 75 pounds.

Like other straits and passages around the mouth of the glacial Stikine River, the eastern end of Sumner can get silty at times, especially during the warm summer months when runoff peaks. From late fall into spring, however, the strait is usually clear blue.

Hot spots for salmon, charr, and halibut include Prince of Wales Island: Point Baker, Merryfield and Red Bays, and Point Colpoys; the Eye Opener; McArthur Reef; Level Islands; White Rock; Zarembo Island: Vichnefski Rock, Saint John and Baht Harbors, and Low and Craig Points; Kupreanof Island: Outer Kah Sheets Bay/ Lung Island; Mitkof Island: Midway, Wilson, and Station Islands, Point Alexander, Banana Point, Outer Blind Slough, and Point Howe; Vank Island; Two Tree Island; Sokolof Island; Greys Island/Pass; Rynda Island; Kadin Island; and Liesnoi Island.

40 Red Lake

Location: North Prince of Wales Island drainage, 40 miles southwest of Petersburg, 675 miles southeast of Anchorage; see map page 327.

USGS maps: Petersburg A-4, B-4.

How to get there: By floatplane from Petersburg, Wrangell, Klawock, Craig, or other area towns, landing at the outlet of Red Lake. Also, there is limited road access by Prince of Wales Forest Road 5600, from Klawock or Craig via Big Salt Road; Thorne Bay Road, from Thorne Bay, crosses the outlet stream and provides access to the lake.

Highlights: Exceptional scenery and outstanding stream and lake angling possibilities, with good fishing for silver salmon (in the first half of September), red salmon (in late July), chum and pink salmon (from late July through early August), rainbow and cutthroat trout (in June and September), and Dolly Varden (in May and from August through September).

Species: Chum salmon, cutthroat trout, Dolly Varden, pink salmon, rainbow trout, red salmon, silver salmon, steelhead.

Regulations: Unbaited, artificial lures only from November 16 through September 14; king salmon fishing is prohibited. For additional restrictions, consult the current Alaska Department of Fish and Game regulations or contact the ADF&G Ketchikan office, (907) 225-2859.

Facilities: A Forest Service cabin is located at Red Lake.

Contact: For cabin rentals, contact Thorne Bay Ranger District, Tongass National Forest, P.O. Box 1, Ketchikan, AK 99919; (907) 828-3304. For an air taxi, contact Kupreanof Flying Service, P.O. Box 768, Petersburg, AK 99833, (907) 772-3396; or Taquan Air, 1007 Water Street, Ketchikan, AK 99901, (907) 225-8800 or (800) 770-8800.

Fishing Red Lake: Situated on the northern tip of Prince of Wales Island, Red Lake is fairly small—only two miles long and about a half mile wide—with a small outlet stream connecting it to Red Bay and Sumner Strait. It has a good variety of sport fish, with outstanding fishing at times.

Starting in spring, out-migrating cutthroat trout and Dolly Varden are taken from the lake outlet area and head of Red Bay. Fishing with ultralight gear is best as these fish can weigh up to two or three pounds. Resident rainbows running about the same size are active in all areas of the lake. Additionally, a small spring run of steelhead trout is available, with fair to good fishing in the outlet stream.

After a short break in the spring fishery, decent runs of red, chum, and pink salmon begin in mid- to late summer and provide variety and excitement from the lake outlet to tidewater. (Reds are the most sought-after, and may be pursued effectively with sparse bucktail flies in faster flowing, shallow stream sections.) A few weeks later, silver salmon jam the small outlet stream all the way up into the lake, sustaining the fishing action into the fall. As the salmon are running, cutthroat trout and Dolly Varden move into the drainage from the salt water and begin feeding actively.

Although the drainage is accessible by road, many anglers choose to experience Red Lake by flying or boating in to the mouth of the outlet stream.

㊶ Salmon Bay Lake

Location: North Prince of Wales Island drainage, 40 miles south of Petersburg, 680 miles southeast of Anchorage; see map page 327.

USGS maps: Petersburg A-4, B-4.

How to get there: Primarily by floatplane from Petersburg, Wrangell, Klawock, Craig, or other area towns, landing on Salmon Bay Lake. Boat access is possible to the stream outlet, but is not recommended, since only very high tides can allow clear passage through the shallow intertidal areas of Salmon Bay. Once there, a trail leads 1.8 miles to the lake outlet.

Highlights: One of the top area locations for spring and fall angling, with good fishing for silver salmon (in the first half of September), red salmon (in late July), steelhead (in late November and from late April through mid-May), rainbow trout (in June and September), cutthroat trout (from May through June), and Dolly Varden (in May and from August through September).

Species: Cutthroat trout, Dolly Varden, rainbow trout, red salmon, silver salmon, steelhead.

Regulations: Unbaited, artificial lures only from November 16 through September 14; king salmon fishing is prohibited. For additional restrictions, consult the current Alaska Department of Fish and Game regulations or contact the ADF&G Ketchikan office, (907) 225-2859.

Facilities: A Forest Service cabin is located at Salmon Bay Lake.

Contact: For cabin rentals, contact Thorne Bay Ranger District, Tongass National Forest, P.O. Box 1, Ketchikan, AK 99919; (907) 828-3304. For an air taxi, contact Kupreanof Flying Service, P.O. Box 768, Petersburg, AK 99833, (907) 772-3396; or Taquan Air, 1007 Water Street, Ketchikan, AK 99901, (907) 225-8800 or (800) 770-8800.

Fishing Salmon Bay Lake: Draining into upper Clarence Strait through Salmon Bay, Salmon Bay Lake is well known for its lively mix of sportfishing options. The majority of anglers visiting this drainage do so through Salmon Bay Lake, a body of water about one mile wide and four miles long. There is a Forest Service cabin at the lake for public use. A trail leads from the lake outlet along the stream towards Salmon Bay.

Red salmon enter the stream and Salmon Bay Lake in midsummer, with most successful anglers concentrating efforts in areas with moderately fast current and shallow depth. Later on, bright coho show up and continue running through most of the fall; along with the red salmon, they're the most sought-after species in the drainage. The Salmon Bay Lake outlet, the deeper holes below in the outlet stream, and the mouth are the best spots to fish this punchy fighter.

Steelhead trout enter the drainage in two distinct runs, one in late fall, another in spring. Both can produce some good fishing action, especially for fly-casters, with the spring run probably receiving the most attention. The entire length of the outlet stream offers good fishing during the peak of the runs. Sea-run cutthroat trout and Dolly Varden are also available throughout the drainage. Resident rainbow trout are mostly confined to Salmon Bay Lake, and are best fished in early summer and fall.

As a focal point for fishing and hunting excursions, Salmon Bay Lake is very popular with locals from nearby Petersburg and Wrangell. If you're interested in using the Forest Service cabin, reserve space well ahead of time.

42 Stikine Strait

Location: Northeast of Etolin Island, 35 miles south of Petersburg, 700 miles southeast of Anchorage; see map page 327.

USGS maps: Petersburg A-2, A-3, B-2, B-3.

How to get there: Primarily by boat from Wrangell, with some traffic also from Petersburg via Wrangell Narrows and Sumner Strait, or, if tides are high enough, through Dry Strait at Stikine River Flats. Floatplanes are used only to access the Forest Service cabin at Steamer Bay.

Highlights: Good fishing for king salmon (from mid-May through mid-June), silver salmon (from early August through early September), and halibut (from June through August).

Species: Dolly Varden, halibut, king salmon, pink salmon, silver salmon, *chum salmon, cutthroat trout, red salmon, steelhead.*

Regulations: For details on the open season for halibut and lingcod, consult the current Alaska Department of Fish and Game regulations or contact the ADF&G Ketchikan office, (907) 225-2859.

Facilities: A Forest Service cabin is located at Steamer Bay on Etolin Island.

Contact: For guide services, contact Real Alaska Adventures, P.O. Box 1124, Petersburg, AK 99833, (907) 772-4121; or Alaskan Star Charters, P.O. Box 2027, Wrangell, AK 99929, (907) 874-3084. For cabin rentals, contact Wrangell Ranger District, Tongass National Forest, P.O. Box 51, Wrangell, AK 99929; (907) 874-2323. For an air taxi, contact Kupreanof Flying Service, P.O. Box 768, Petersburg, AK 99833; (907) 772-3396.

Fishing Stikine Strait: One of the main pathways for returning salmon and other species bound for the glacial Stikine River (and other streams), Stikine Strait is one of the most productive Southeast fishing locations, especially for king and silver salmon and halibut. The strait separates Zarembo Island from the larger Etolin Island, connecting Sumner and Clarence Straits near Wrangell.

Despite the fact that the northern part of the strait may at times carry a silt load from the nearby Stikine River (particularly during hot summer months), the fishery yields consistent catches throughout the season. King salmon, present year-round, are taken primarily in late spring and early summer when large pre-spawners cruise through the area. Following these salmon monarchs, silvers begin to show up in July and remain into October. Pinks and sea-run Dollies are not particularly abundant in these waters, but they offer fair action at times when encountered in concentrations near stream mouths.

Halibut fishing is good, with the best catches coming from the north section of Stikine bordering Sumner Strait. Good anglers can find flatties any day of the year (except during the January closure), but most success occurs in early summer when fish are in shallower water. Various other species of bottomfish are available, as well as outstanding crab, clams, and abalone in near-shore waters (which are said to be some of the best for the Wrangell and Petersburg area).

The best spots for salmon and halibut include Etolin Island: Point Harrington/Steamer Bay, the Bend, Chichagof Pass, Steamer Point, and Quiet Harbor; Zarembo Island: Point Nesbitt, Meter Bight, Fritter Cove, South Point, and Roosevelt Harbor; Vank Island: Mud Bay and Neal Point; and Woronkofski Island: Elephants Nose, Woronkofski, and Reef Points, Sunrise Creek, Point Ancon, and Drag Island.

43 Eastern Passage

Location: Northeast of Wrangell Island, 35 miles southeast of Petersburg, 700 miles southeast of Anchorage; see map page 327.

USGS maps: Petersburg B-1, B-2, C-1, C-2; Bradfield Canal A-6, B-6.

How to get there: Primarily by boat from Wrangell, but also from Petersburg via Wrangell Narrows and Sumner Strait, or, if tides permit, through Dry Strait at Stikine River Flats.

Highlights: Good fishing for king salmon

(from mid-May through mid-June), silver salmon (from mid-August through mid-September), pink salmon (from late July through early August), Dolly Varden (from June through August), and halibut (from June through early July).

Species: Chum salmon, Dolly Varden, halibut, king salmon, pink salmon, silver salmon, *steelhead*.

Regulations: For details on the open season for salmon, halibut, and lingcod, consult the current Alaska Department of Fish and Game regulations or contact the ADF&G Ketchikan office, (907) 225-2859.

Facilities: A Forest Service cabin is located on the mainland at Berg Bay.

Contact: For guide services, contact Real Alaska Adventures, P.O. Box 1124, Petersburg, AK 99833, (907) 772-4121; or Alaskan Star Charters, P.O. Box 2027, Wrangell, AK 99929, (907) 874-3084. For cabin rentals, contact Wrangell Ranger District, Tongass National Forest, P.O. Box 51, Wrangell, AK 99929; (907) 874-2323. For an air taxi, contact Kupreanof Flying Service, P.O. Box 768, Petersburg, AK 99833; (907) 772-3396.

Fishing Eastern Passage: Separating Wrangell Island from the mainland, long and narrow Eastern Passage stretches from Stikine River Flats to Ernest Sound and Bradfield Canal. Part of Tongass National Forest, the passage boasts great fishing potential and highly scenic surroundings, with evergreens, lush valleys, and snow-capped mountains, some of which rise to 5,300 feet. Along with Stikine and Zimovia Straits, the passage is one of the prime Wrangell destinations for salmon.

Eastern Passage receives substantial numbers of hatchery salmon, as well as wild fish, especially feeder kings. The northern section yields native salmon bound for the glacial Stikine River, while the central portion is more famous for its enhanced runs of king, silver, and chum returning to the Earl West Cove Hatchery. Around the southern end, at outer Blake Channel, anglers do well intercepting schools of fish heading for Bradfield Canal drainages.

Mature, prespawning kings are abundant in late spring and early summer, with immature fish scattered throughout year-round. The Narrows, a half-mile-wide chute separating the passage from Blake Channel, is a major feeder king attraction from November to April, but also holds hatchery salmon later in the season. (A Forest Service cabin in Berg Bay, only a few miles away, makes a fine point of access.) Large spawner kings up to 40 or 50 pounds are taken in June and July at the south end. In late summer, anglers begin taking more silver salmon as the smaller pinks peak in area waters. Running into October and even November in some locations, these fall coho closely follow the kings in popularity and attract considerable angling attention. Dolly Varden provide fair angling for anyone with patience. Halibut are most predictably hooked in moderately deep water around the north and south ends of Eastern Passage and range between 15 and 60 pounds with occasional larger catches.

Favorite spots include Babbler Point; the Narrows; Wrangell Island: Point Highfield and Earl West Cove; and Blake Channel: Blake (Ham) Island.

44 Thoms Creek System

Location: South Wrangell Island drainage, 55 miles southeast of Petersburg, 720 miles southeast of Anchorage; see map page 327.

USGS map: Petersburg A-1.

How to get there: There are three ways to access this drainage. The first is by floatplane, landing on Thoms Lake. The second is by car from Wrangell, crossing Thoms Creek and hiking one mile to Thoms Place at the mouth of the stream. The third is by boat from Wrangell, with the option of using a trail from Zimovia Strait to Thoms Lake, or continuing down to Thoms Place and the mouth of Thoms Creek.

Highlights: Wrangell's most productive, road-accessible stream, with good fishing for silver salmon (in the second half of September), red salmon (from late July through early August), chum and pink salmon (from late July through early August), rainbow trout (in May and September), cutthroat trout (from May through June), and Dolly Varden (in May and from August through September).

Species: Chum salmon, cutthroat trout, Dolly Varden, pink salmon, rainbow trout, red salmon, silver salmon, steelhead.

Regulations: Unbaited, artificial lures only from November 16 through September 14; king salmon fishing is prohibited. For additional restrictions, consult the current Alaska Department of Fish and Game regulations or contact the ADF&G Ketchikan office, (907) 225-2859.

Facilities: A Forest Service cabin is located on Thoms Lake.

Contact: For cabin rentals, contact Wrangell Ranger District, Tongass National Forest, P.O. Box 51, Wrangell, AK 99929; (907) 874-2323.

Fishing the Thoms Creek System: Emptying into Zimovia Strait, the Thoms Creek drainage is a small road-accessible system located on the southern end of Wrangell Island. Three lakes comprise the heart of the drainage, with Thoms Lake being the largest and most visited. As a fair amount of muskeg is present, the water color is slightly tannic-stained. Easily reached by road from the town of Wrangell, it's a favorite destination among locals, known for its surprisingly good catches of some of the region's more sought-after game fish.

Thoms Creek has a reputation for some of the best red salmon fishing opportunities in the Petersburg/Wrangell area. Although they don't really return in a very large run, the sockeyes concentrate in dense schools, making for good fly-fishing conditions. The action is usually best on the lower stream near the road crossing and at the mouth (especially during the height of the run). Chums and pinks are also present in fishable numbers and provide some excitement just as the sockeyes begin tapering off. In fall, a strong showing of chunky silver salmon caps the salmon season, with good fishing to be expected from tidewater up to the lakes well into November.

Some sea-run cutthroat trout and Dolly Varden can be taken, and they're best fished in spring and fall in Thoms Lake and the lower stream sections. The mouth of Thoms Creek at Thoms Place can yield fairly good results during the summer months. Also, resident rainbow trout are available in Thoms Lake and the upper stream.

Many visiting anglers fish the system from the road crossing, but in recent years it has become popular to moor a boat at Thoms Place State Marine Park at the mouth of Thoms Creek, then fish the intertidal area for schools of salmon. If you want to steer clear of roadside and marine traffic, a stay at the Forest Service cabin on Thoms Lake is highly recommended.

㊺ Harding River

Location: North Bradfield Canal drainage, 70 miles southeast of Petersburg, 730 miles southeast of Anchorage; see map page 327.

USGS maps: Bradfield Canal A-5, B-5, B-6.

How to get there: By boat or floatplane, usually from Wrangell, but also as far away as Petersburg and Ketchikan. From Wrangell, boaters reach the Harding River via Eastern Passage and Blake Channel. Boats and planes access the river through its mouth at Bradfield Canal.

Highlights: One of Alaska's best locations for trophy freshwater chum salmon (from late July through early August), with good fishing for silver salmon (in the second half of September), cutthroat trout (in May and June), and Dolly Varden (in May and from August through September).

Species: Chum salmon, cutthroat trout, Dolly Varden, pink salmon, rainbow trout, silver salmon, steelhead, *king salmon*.

Regulations: Unbaited, artificial lures only from November 16 through September 14; king salmon fishing is prohibited. For additional restrictions, consult the current Alaska Department of Fish and Game regulations or contact the ADF&G Ketchikan office, (907) 225-2859.

Facilities: A Forest Service cabin is located near the mouth of the river.

Contact: For cabin rentals, contact Tongass National Forest, P.O. Box 309, Petersburg, AK 99833; (907) 772-3871. For an air taxi, contact Kupreanof Flying Service, P.O. Box 768, Petersburg, AK 99833; (907) 772-3396.

Fishing the Harding River: This fairly remote river, located on the north mainland of Bradfield Canal, cuts through a forested valley surrounded by 3,000-foot snow-capped mountain ridges within Tongass National Forest. Its clear waters support strong runs of salmon and healthy populations of trout and charr. Best of all, the area gets only moderate pressure from anglers.

Most visitors arrive at the mouth of the river (where a Forest Service cabin is available). There's a small lake, Fall Lake, several miles upstream, but due to its size (just over one mile long), it can be risky for floatplane landings. The lower Harding is where the best fishing takes place, with anglers concentrating efforts around the tides for best results.

A fall run of silver salmon attracts some attention, but it is the midsummer run of above-average-sized chums for which the Harding is really noted. Although perhaps not equal to the fish taken from the Keta River of Revillagigedo Channel, the Harding does have some trophy fish that weigh as much as 20 pounds or more. A small run of king salmon also enters the river in early summer, but they're currently off-limits to anglers. Pinks are not abundant in this drainage. A resident population of rainbows and a spring run of steelhead trout are available, usually offering fair fishing, but better numbers of sea-run cutthroat trout and Dolly Varden are present in early spring and again during the salmon spawning runs in late summer and fall.

㊻ Anan Creek System

Location: South Bradfield Canal drainage, 60 miles southeast of Petersburg, 730 miles southeast of Anchorage; see map page 327.

USGS maps: Bradfield Canal A-5, A-6.

How to get there: By boat and floatplane, primarily from Wrangell, but also from Petersburg and Ketchikan. For boaters, Wrangell is the closest port, and offers access to Anan Bay via Eastern Passage and Blake Channel, crossing Bradfield Canal. Trails lead from Anan Bay to the Anan Lake outlet. Floatplanes regularly fly to area lakes, such as Anan and Boulder Lakes.

Highlights: An outstanding recreational area with excellent fishing for pink salmon (from late July through early August) and good action for silver salmon (in September), steelhead (in the second half of May), rainbow trout (in May and September), cutthroat trout (from May through

June), and Dolly Varden (in May and from August through September).

Species: Chum salmon, cutthroat trout, Dolly Varden, pink salmon, rainbow trout, silver salmon, steelhead, *king salmon*.

Regulations: Unbaited, artificial lures only from November 16 through September 14; king salmon fishing is prohibited. For additional restrictions, consult the current Alaska Department of Fish and Game regulations or contact the ADF&G Ketchikan office, (907) 225-2859.

Facilities: A Forest Service cabin is located at the mouth of Anan Creek in Anan Bay; there is also a public shelter on Anan Creek.

Contact: For cabin rentals, contact Tongass National Forest, P.O. Box 309, Petersburg, AK 99833, (907) 772-3871; or Tongass National Forest, Federal Building, Ketchikan, AK 99901, (907) 225-3101. For an air taxi, contact Kupreanof Flying Service, P.O. Box 768, Petersburg, AK 99833, (907) 772-3396; or Taquan Air, 1007 Water Street, Ketchikan, AK 99901, (907) 225-8800 or (800) 770-8800.

Fishing the Anan Creek System: Best known for its dense bear population, Anan Creek also is an excellent stream for sportfishing. Its clear waters offer a wide variety of species in pleasant forest surroundings, and are fairly accessible by trails from Anan Bay. There are two major lakes in the system—Anan and Boulder—with a dozen smaller lakes spread throughout the drainage. Salmon, trout, and charr are relatively abundant, providing anglers with exciting fishing in a small stream setting.

Emptying into Bradfield Canal, the Anan receives a good number of visitors, primarily outdoor enthusiasts and photographers hoping to catch a glimpse of the area's famous bear population. A platform has been built expressly for the purpose of watching the bears in their natural environment.

The fishing on the Anan is great. A big run of pink salmon enters the creek in late summer, along with a fair showing of chums. "Fish on every cast" action is common during the peak of the runs, with the brightest fish taken near salt water. In fall, a run of silvers arrives and remains through October into November. For this species, the lower portion of Anan Creek and the mouth is best, but fish may also be taken out of the Anan and Boulder Lake inlets and outlets, as well as the connecting stream.

Little effort is directed toward the spring run of steelhead trout in the system, though fishing can be quite good during some years. Resident rainbow also are found in Anan and Boulder Lakes and inlet streams, while sea-run cutthroat trout and Dolly Varden can be found throughout the system.

47 Zimovia Strait

Location: Southwest of Wrangell Island, northeast of Etolin Island, 35 miles southeast of Petersburg, 700 miles southeast of Anchorage; see map page 327.

USGS maps: Petersburg A-1, A-2, B-1, B-2.

How to get there: Primarily by boat from Wrangell Harbor, but also from Petersburg via Wrangell Narrows and Sumner Strait, or, if tides permit, through Dry Strait at Stikine River Flats. The Zimovia Highway out of Wrangell is used by boaters and shore casters to fish areas south of town. Floatplanes can land in the strait's protected waters.

Highlights: Good fishing for king salmon (from mid-May through mid-June), silver salmon (from early August through early September), red salmon (from mid- through late July), pink salmon (from late July through early August), cutthroat trout and Dolly Varden (from June through August), and halibut (from June through July).

Species: Chum salmon, cutthroat trout, Dolly Varden, halibut, king salmon, pink salmon, red salmon, silver salmon, *steelhead*.

Regulations: For details on the open season for halibut and lingcod, consult the current Alaska Department of Fish and Game regulations or contact the ADF&G Ketchikan office, (907) 225-2859.

Facilities: Commercial lodging, sporting goods, groceries, boat rentals and a boat launch, fuel, water, and guide services are available in Wrangell.

Contact: For guide services, contact Real Alaska Adventures, P.O. Box 1124, Petersburg, AK

99833, (907) 772-4121; or Alaskan Star Charters, P.O. Box 2027, Wrangell, AK 99929, (907) 874-3084. For lodging information, contact the City of Wrangell, 205 Brueger Street, Wrangell, AK 99929; (907) 874-2381. For cabin rentals, contact Wrangell Ranger District, Tongass National Forest, P.O. Box 51, Wrangell, AK 99929; (907) 874-2323.

Fishing Zimovia Strait: With great fishing and abundant marine wildlife, Zimovia Strait is an attractive and very popular recreation area within easy reach of the town of Wrangell. South of town, it lies between the islands of Etolin and Wrangell. Rolling green hills and occasional peaks surround the strait, lending scenic contrast to its deep blue waters.

Zimovia is slightly narrower and longer than Stikine Strait. Like Stikine, it can get cloudy in its upper end during summer hot spells, due to glacial outwash from the giant Stikine River, but generally it's clear most of the year. King salmon are the most sought-after species here. Feeders can be caught year-round, with the best action from October into May or June, when the big spawners heading for the mainland take over. (Most of the salmon that pass through the strait are headed for clear-water tributaries of the Stikine, with some bound for smaller local streams like Thoms and Pat Creeks.) Silver salmon arrive soon after and stay from late summer into fall, with a few fish available into November at the south end of the strait. Very good fishing for pink and red salmon, cutthroat trout, and Dolly Varden is possible at times at the mouth of Thoms Creek in Thoms Place. Halibut are primarily caught at the outer ends of Zimovia Strait in deeper water, with the best action in early summer.

For easily accessed angling excursions of a few hours up to a day, Zimovia Strait is highly recommended for anyone planning to be in the Wrangell area. Since the strait is fairly protected from most severe weather, kayak and even canoe trips are a possibility.

Good locations for salmon, charr, and halibut include Wrangell Island: Thoms Place, Nemo and Cemetery Points, Pat Creek Landing, Bluffs/ Shoemaker Bay, and Wrangell Harbor; Etolin Island: Olive Cove, Anita Point, Anita Bay, and

Chichagof Pass; Woronkofski Island: Elephants Nose/Woronkofski Point; and Young Rock.

48 Ernest Sound

Location: East of Etolin Island and southeast of Wrangell Island, 65 miles southeast of Petersburg, 730 miles southeast of Anchorage; see map page 327.

USGS maps: Bradfield Canal A-5, A-6; Petersburg A-1; Ketchikan D-6; Craig C-1, D-1, D-2.

How to get there: By boat from Wrangell via Zimovia Strait or from Ketchikan via Tongass Narrows and Clarence Strait. Some boaters head through Eastern Passage and Blake Channel to access Bradfield Canal on the upper sound. Floatplane access is also possible in protected waters, such as small bays and coves.

Highlights: Excellent fishing for pink salmon (from mid-July through mid-August); good fishing for king salmon (in June), silver salmon (from late August through mid-September), and halibut (from June through August).

Species: Chum salmon, cutthroat trout, Dolly Varden, halibut, king salmon, pink salmon, silver salmon, *red salmon, steelhead*.

Regulations: For details on the open season for halibut and lingcod, consult the current Alaska Department of Fish and Game regulations or contact the ADF&G Ketchikan office, (907) 225-2859.

Facilities: Two Forest Service cabins are located in Bradfield Canal, one at the mouth of Harding River, the other at Anan Bay.

Contact: For guide services, contact Alaskan Star Charters, P.O. Box 2027, Wrangell, AK 99929; (907) 874-3084. For cabin rentals, contact Wrangell Ranger District, Tongass National Forest, P.O. Box 51, Wrangell, AK 99929, (907) 874-2323; or Tongass National Forest, Federal Building, Ketchikan, AK 99901, (907) 225-3101. For an air taxi, contact Kupreanof Flying Service, P.O. Box 768, Petersburg, AK 99833; (907) 772-3396.

Fishing Ernest Sound: Although fished mostly by Petersburg locals, Ernest Sound has great angling potential for a variety of game species. The sound is bordered by the Cleveland Peninsula and the mainland in the east and Etolin and Wrangell Islands in the west, and includes Bradfield Canal. Situated within Tongass National Forest, it's quite scenic, with a multitude of bays, coves, and jutting points set among snow-clad mountains and forested valleys.

The central and outer areas of Ernest Sound are regarded as a highly productive marine fishery for salmon and halibut. Trolling or mooching for king salmon is done year-round, but success rates are much higher in early summer as mature prespawners enter the waters. Some of these monarchs eventually head up a few of the rivers draining into Bradfield Canal, but most continue onto other areas farther north.

With a great number of clear rivers and streams flowing into Ernest Sound and connecting waters, angling for the other salmon species is highly productive. Well-known drainages like the Harding and Eagle Rivers and Anan Creek top the list. In midsummer, look for schools of dime-bright chum and pink salmon, especially in Bradfield Canal. (Anan Bay receives a tremendous run of pinks, and is regarded as one of the best locations in Southeast for the species. It also has trophy chum salmon up to 20 pounds or more.)

Silver salmon are present from late summer through fall, with a few fresh fish remaining in November. The sound is a good area to intercept these battlers, but Bradfield Canal is better, with larger concentrations of fish near the mouths of spawning streams. Halibut can be found in deeper parts of the sound, and fair numbers of cutthroat trout and Dolly Varden cruise the shorelines near salmon streams in late spring and early summer.

Some proven locations around Ernest Sound for salmon, charr, and halibut include Peterson Island; Westerly Island; Easterly Island; Deer Island/Point Peters; Found Island; Wrangell Island: Fools Inlet and Southeast Cove/Thoms Point; and Cleveland Peninsula: Lemesurier, Magnetic, Eaton, and Watkins Points, Anan Bay, Point Warde, Lemly Rocks, Union and Emerald Bays, and Cannery Creek.

49 Upper Clarence Strait

Location: East of Prince of Wales Island, southwest of Etolin Island, 50 miles south of Petersburg, 685 miles southeast of Anchorage; see map page 327.

USGS maps: Petersburg A-2, A-3, A-4, B-3, B-4; Craig D-1, D-2, D-3.

How to get there: By boat from Wrangell and Petersburg via Wrangell Narrows and Sumner Strait (from Petersburg) or Stikine Strait (Wrangell). Protected bays and coves are sometimes used by floatplanes to access various parts of the strait.

Highlights: Good fishing for king salmon (from mid-May through mid-June), silver salmon (from early August through early September), and halibut (from June through August).

Species: Chum salmon, Dolly Varden, halibut, king salmon, pink salmon, silver salmon, *cutthroat trout, red salmon, steelhead.*

Regulations: For details on the open season for halibut and lingcod, consult the current Alaska Department of Fish and Game regulations or contact the ADF&G Ketchikan office, (907) 225-2859.

Facilities: Two Forest Service cabins are located in the immediate area, at Steamer Bay on Etolin Island and Barnes Lake on Prince of Wales Island.

Contact: For lodging and guide services, contact Real Alaska Adventures, P.O. Box 1124, Petersburg, AK 99833, (907) 772-4121; Last Frontier Charters, P.O. Box 19443, Thorne Bay, AK 99919, (907) 828-3989; or the Boardwalk Wilderness Lodge, P.O. Box 19121-BW, Thorne Bay, AK 99919, (907) 828-3918 or (800) 764-3918. For cabin rentals, contact Wrangell Ranger District, Tongass National Forest, P.O. Box 51, Wrangell, AK 99929, (907) 874-2323; or Thorne Bay Ranger District, Tongass National Forest, P.O. Box 1, Ketchikan, AK 99919, (907) 828-3304. For an air taxi, contact Kupreanof Flying Service, P.O. Box 768, Petersburg, AK 99833; (907) 772-3396.

Fishing Upper Clarence Strait: A wonderland of islands, reefs, hidden bays, and coves, upper Clarence Strait includes all waters north of a line extending between Narrow Point on Prince of Wales Island and Lemesurier Point on the Cleveland Peninsula. Surrounding land is covered by dense rain forest, inhabited by a multitude of wildlife. Frequented by boaters from the Ketchikan, Petersburg, and Wrangell areas, the strait is one of the better marine fisheries in Alaska as it serves as a major migration and feeding corridor for salmon and bottomfish.

The strait's clear-water streams hold substantial numbers of anadromous fish species. Two of the more important drainages include Salmon Bay Lake and Sweetwater Lake in the Kashevarof Passage area, but fish destined for spawning rivers in Ernest Sound, Sumner Strait, and even the vast Stikine River system flood upper Clarence Strait.

King salmon, always a favorite and present year-round in the form of immature feeders, are at their best in late spring and early summer, when the large prespawners move to their spawning destinations. Silver salmon is the next most sought-after species, and are usually taken during late summer and fall by trolling and casting in the strait's bays. Schools of pink salmon may be encountered at times near the mouths of spawning streams as well. You may encounter some sea-run cutthroat trout and Dolly Varden when fishing these areas for salmon.

Halibut are common, and are mainly targeted in waters of moderate depth during the summer months, though some fish are present in deeper parts of the strait year-round. Lingcod and rockfish are abundant in areas with appropriate bottom structure.

Frequented spots for salmon, charr, and halibut include Prince of Wales Island: Point Colpoys, Bay, Ratz, and Narrow Points, Outer Salmon Bay, Exchange Cove/Island, Thorne Island/Whale Passage, Stevenson Island, Coffman Cove/Island, and Ratz Harbor; Rookery Island; Tide Island; Zarembo Island: McNamara Point, Snow Passage, and Point Nesbitt; Kashevarof Islands: Bushy, Shrubby, and Blashke Islands; Rose Rock; Rose Island; Seal Rock; and Key Reef.

50 Sweetwater Lake System

Location: Northeast Prince of Wales Island drainage, 50 miles southwest of Petersburg, 705 miles southeast of Anchorage; see map page 327.

USGS maps: Craig D-3, D-4; Petersburg A-4.

How to get there: By floatplane from Petersburg, Wrangell, Klawock, Craig, or other area towns and communities, landing on Sweetwater and Galea Lakes. A limited forest road system from Klawock, Craig, and Thorne Bay provides access to the lake, tributaries, and a Forest Service cabin.

Highlights: An extensive Prince of Wales drainage, known for good fishing for silver salmon (from late July through early August and in the second half of September), red salmon (in late July), steelhead (from late April through mid-May), rainbow trout (in May and September), cutthroat trout (from May through June), and Dolly Varden (in May and from August through September).

Species: Chum salmon, cutthroat trout, Dolly Varden, pink salmon, rainbow trout, red salmon, silver salmon, steelhead.

Regulations: Unbaited, artificial lures only from November 16 through September 14; king salmon fishing is prohibited. For additional restrictions, consult the current Alaska Department of Fish and Game regulations or contact the ADF&G Ketchikan office, (907) 225-2859.

Facilities: Three Forest Service cabins are located within the system, at Sweetwater Lake, Galea Lake, and Barnes Lake.

Contact: For cabin rentals, contact Thorne Bay Ranger District, Tongass National Forest, P.O. Box 1, Ketchikan, AK 99919; (907) 828-3304. For an air taxi, contact Kupreanof Flying Service, P.O. Box 768, Petersburg, AK 99833, (907) 772-3396; or Taquan Air, 1007 Water Street, Ketchikan, AK 99901, (907) 225-8800 or (800) 770-8800.

Fishing the Sweetwater Lake System: Draining into northern Clarence Strait, the Sweetwater Lake system consists of dozens of lakes and ponds connected by small streams in the interior of Prince of Wales Island. Due to heavy muskeg surrounding much of the drainage, Sweetwater is largely tannic brown. Angling is very good overall, with a satisfying variety of species available. With all the good water in this drainage, a visitor can spend weeks exploring and fishing different areas, from headwaters down to the tidal zone. A well-established canoe route makes the going easy.

The first important game fish to invade Sweetwater are some spring-run steelhead trout. These flashy fighters are at their best in the outlet stream of Sweetwater Lake—Indian Creek—but can also be encountered in many other flowing waters of the system, including Hatchery and Logjam Creeks. Resident rainbow trout are present in the main lake and in its tributaries, along with sea-run cutthroats and Dolly Varden. Traditionally they have been taken at the lower end of the lakes and inlet streams, particularly in spring and fall.

Later on in the season, silver and red salmon begin to show in large numbers. Sweetwater has perfect conditions for taking these fine sport fish; anglers do well for them in Indian Creek and the lower sections and the mouths of other large tributaries. While the sockeyes come through in one big push, there are two distinct runs of coho in the system. The first occurs primarily during July and August, while the second hits its peak in September and continues into October. Only small numbers of chum and pink salmon show every year, in late summer, with fishing action reported fair for pinks at times.

Ketchikan—South Tongass

The Ketchikan area, from Dixon Entrance to Ernest Sound, includes the Revillagigedo, Annette, Gravina, and Prince of Wales Island complexes, along with part of the Cleveland Peninsula, Behm Canal, Clarence Strait, and Misty Fjords National Monument. It has some of Alaska's most significant marine and freshwater fisheries, particularly for salmon, steelhead, and cutthroat trout.

This is famous saltwater trolling country—the Salmon Capital of the World—with a major charter fleet working the waters of West Behm Canal, Tongass Narrows, and Clarence Strait for king and coho salmon. The extremely productive outside waters are usually targeted for salmon and halibut by area lodges and guides from Prince of Wales (Klawock, Waterfall, Craig, Thorne Bay). Most of the recreational effort, however, occurs near town, from Clover Pass to Mountain Point.

Ketchikan's surrounding area is also known for its unique and outstanding freshwater angling. Southeast's finest lakes (including Naha, Wilson, Humpback, and Manzanita) are located here, with Alaska's best trophy cutthroat and kokanee possibilities. Prince of Wales Island, the largest island in Southeast, has abundant, high-quality stream fishing—some of the best in Alaska, including world famous steelhead rivers like the Karta, Klawock, and Thorne. An extensive logging road network (more than 700 miles) compromises the wilderness somewhat, but also provides access to dozens of remote spots. Anglers can drive or hike in practically any direction and reach superb fishing for steelhead, cutthroat and rainbow trout, Dolly Varden, and silver and red salmon.

The U.S. Forest Service maintains numerous cabins, shelters, and some campgrounds in the Ketchikan area, many in remote areas. They're available by advance registration for a reasonable fee. Alaska State Parks also maintains picnic sites and campgrounds along Ketchikan's road system.

(51) Sarkar River System

Location: Northwest Prince of Wales Island drainage, 75 miles northwest of Ketchikan, 695 miles southeast of Anchorage; see map page 327.

USGS map: Craig D-4.

How to get there: By plane, car, and boat. Floatplanes land on Sarkar Lake, providing access to the public cabin on the north end of the lake, the lake outlet, and tributary streams. Boaters arrive at the mouth of the river from Craig or Klawock via Cristoval Channel, Gulf of Esquibel, and Tuxekan Passage. Prince of Wales Island Road from Klawock crosses the Sarkar River, as well as a tributary stream, near the outlet of Sarkar Lake.

Highlights: A great getaway location, offering a variety of angling, including good fishing for silver salmon (in September), sockeye salmon (in June and July), chum salmon (from late August through early September), pink salmon (in the first half of August), steelhead (from early April through mid-May and late November through late December), and cutthroat and Dolly Varden (from May through June and September through October).

Species: Chum salmon, cutthroat trout, Dolly Varden, pink salmon, red salmon, silver salmon, steelhead, *rainbow trout*.

Regulations: Unbaited, artificial lures only from November 16 through September 14; king salmon fishing is prohibited. For additional restrictions, consult the current Alaska Department of Fish and Game regulations or contact the ADF&G Ketchikan office, (907) 225-2859.

Facilities: A Forest Service cabin is located at Sarkar Lake.

Contact: For cabin rentals, contact Craig Ranger District, Tongass National Forest, P.O. Box 500, Craig, AK 99921; (907) 826-3271. For an air taxi, contact Taquan Air, 1007 Water Street, Ketchikan, AK 99901; (907) 225-8800 or (800) 770-8800.

Fishing the Sarkar River System: Sarkar Lake, the largest lake in the Sarkar River drainage, serves as the gateway to area fishing and anglers will find a public-use Forest Service cabin on the north shore. Beyond the lake, the Sarkar River system encompasses 18 more lakes and ponds of varying sizes and two major tributary streams that drain into El Capitan Passage and Sea Otter Sound. Despite the somewhat brown water, salmon, trout, and charr are abundant in the main river and lake, and offer outstanding action from late spring through fall.

Only about 2.5 miles long, the Sarkar River is tidally influenced. The mouth and lower river are more of a lagoon or cove, and serve as a staging area for anadromous species. Some of the better action generally occurs at the road crossing just upstream from the tidal section or in the lake itself, particularly near the mouth of tributary streams. Anglers wise enough to bring a canoe along can navigate throughout much of the system and enjoy some outstanding fishing.

The Sarkar and its tributaries receive sizable runs of silver, chum, and pink salmon, along with fair numbers of reds. Sea-run cutthroat trout and Dolly Varden overwinter in Sarkar Lake and outmigrate in late spring. Fly-fishing can be superb at times. Both spring and fall runs of steelhead trout occur in the Sarkar, with some good fishing possible during the height of the runs. In spring, look for these large, ocean-going trout in the deeper holes of tributary streams.

(52) Gulf of Esquibel

Location: On west Prince of Wales Island, 75 miles west of Ketchikan, 700 miles southeast of Anchorage; see map page 327.

USGS maps: Craig B-5, B-6, C-4, C-5, C-6, D-4, D-5, D-6.

How to get there: By boat from Klawock, Craig, or area lodges via the San Cristoval Channel north of San Fernando Island or Portilla Channel east of Lulu Island, a 15- to 20-mile run. Floatplanes can access the gulf by landing in protected bays and coves, such as the Steamboat Bay Seaplane Base on Noyes Island.

Highlights: A traditional local favorite, among the best in Southeast, with excellent fishing for silver salmon (from late July through mid-September) and halibut (from July through September), and good fishing for king salmon (from mid-May through early July) and pink salmon (from mid-July through late August).

Species: Dolly Varden, halibut, king salmon, pink salmon, silver salmon, *chum salmon, cutthroat trout, red salmon, steelhead.*

Regulations: For details on the open season for halibut and lingcod, consult the current Alaska Department of Fish and Game regulations or contact the ADF&G Ketchikan office, (907) 225-2859.

Facilities: Commercial lodging, fuel, water, and guide services are available on area islands.

Contact: For guide services, contact Klawock Bay Charters, P.O. Box 145, Klawock, AK 99925; (907) 755-2329. For cabin rentals, contact Craig Ranger District, Tongass National Forest, P.O. Box 500, Craig, AK 99921; (907) 826-3271.

Fishing the Gulf of Esquibel: Located on the west side of Prince of Wales Island, the scenic Gulf of Esquibel area features heavily wooded isles (the Maurelle Islands Wilderness) and an abundance of marine life. It has long been regarded as a top marine fishing location for salmon and halibut, and the area's natural beauty is truly breathtaking.

Part of Tongass National Forest, the Gulf of Esquibel is an active summer feeding ground for fish bound for watersheds on Prince of Wales Island and the mainland. Very little shore fishing takes place in this area, with most effort expended by boaters from Craig and Klawock. Points of interest include the Heceta and Maurelle Islands and, of course, Noyes Island for big feeder kings (50 to 70 pounds possible) and silver and pink salmon.

You can catch halibut year-round, although the action is generally better during the summer months in the shallower water surrounding islands and around certain points that have suitable bottom structure. Trophy catches weighing up to 350 pounds or more are possible. Other game fish worth considering include rockfish, lingcod, and a multitude of other cod and flounder species. Fair numbers of Dolly Varden can be found off mouths of clear-water streams. For anglers wanting to spice up their visit, area waters also teem with shrimp and crab, so come prepared to set pots for these tasty shellfish prior to going salmon and halibut fishing.

Some of the more productive locations in the gulf for salmon and halibut include Noyes Island: Saint Nicholas Point/Channel, Cape Addington, Shaft Rock, Roller Bay, and Cape Ulitka; Saint Joseph Island; Sonora Passage; Maurelle Islands: San Lorenzo, Turtle, Sonora, Flotilla, Esquibel, and Hendida/Pesquera Islands, Hole-In-The-Wall, Anguilla Bay; Saint Phillip Island; Heceta Island: Point Desconocida, Warm Chuck Inlet, Cape Lynch, Gull and Camp Islands, and Port Alice; Portilla Channel; Point Station Gertrudis; and San Fernando Island: Point Garcia, Hermagos Island, and San Cristoval Channel.

(53) Bucareli Bay

Location: Along west Prince of Wales Island, 65 miles west of Ketchikan, 720 miles southeast of Anchorage; see map page 327.

USGS maps: Craig A-5, B-3, B-4, B-5, B-6, C-3, C-4.

How to get there: By boat from Klawock, Craig, or area lodges. Floatplanes reach the area by landing in protected bays and coves, such as the privately operated Waterfall Seaplane Base at Point Antonio in Ulloa Channel east of Suemez Island.

Highlights: A favorite saltwater destination of area fishing guides, with excellent fishing for silver salmon (from late June through late August) and halibut (from July through September), and good fishing for king salmon (from mid-May through July) and pink salmon (from mid-July through late August).

Species: Dolly Varden, halibut, king salmon, pink salmon, silver salmon, *chum salmon, cutthroat trout, red salmon, steelhead*.

Regulations: For details on the open season for halibut and lingcod, consult the current Alaska Department of Fish and Game regulations or contact the ADF&G Ketchikan office, (907) 225-2859.

Facilities: Commercial lodging, sporting goods, groceries, boat rentals and launching, guide services, gas, and water are available in the island towns of Klawock and Craig. A Forest Service cabin is located at Point Amargura on the southern tip of San Fernando Island.

Contact: For guide services, contact Klawock Bay Charters, P.O. Box 145, Klawock, AK 99925; (907) 755-2329. For cabin rentals, contact Craig Ranger District, Tongass National Forest, P.O. Box 500, Craig, AK 99921; (907) 826-3271. For an air taxi, contact Taquan Air, 1007 Water Street, Ketchikan, AK 99901; (907) 225-8800 or (800) 770-8800.

Fishing Bucareli Bay: Without a doubt, Bucareli Bay is one of the more scenic and productive saltwater fishing spots on Prince of Wales Island. The bay area includes the ever popular San Alberto Bay just outside Klawock and Craig and, of course, some of the larger islands, such as Suemez, Baker, Lulu, and San Fernando. Some fantastic salmon and halibut angling can be had off points and in bays, passages, and channels throughout Bucareli, as area lodges and guides will attest.

Residents from nearby communities report year-round catches of feeder king salmon and some outstanding action for mature prespawners up to 70 pounds in late spring and early summer. There are virtually no king salmon spawning streams on the island; the vast majority of fish are actually heading for mainland locations, and are caught when feeding heavily along the surf-swept coast.

The salmon delivering the hottest action around

Bucareli Bay is actually the spunky silver. From late summer into fall, anglers target these flashy fighters as they feed heavily and prepare to enter the area and more distant streams. The best fishing occurs right outside the towns of Klawock and Craig. In between the king and silver runs, good numbers of pink salmon and halibut are up for grabs. Although they're present all year in the outer bay, midsummer is the best time to target huge flatties up to 200 pounds or more.

For a true ocean safari complete with great fishing, lots of marine animals and spectacular coastal scenery, Bucareli Bay delivers. Proven spots for salmon and halibut include Baker Island: Veta and Fortaleza Bays, Cape Bartolome, Point Fortaleza, Port San Antonio, Point San Roque, Port Asuncion, Veta/Outer and Granite Points, Cape Chirikof and Point Maria; Saint Ignace Island; Port Real Marina; Suemez Island: Cape Felix, Point Rosary, Port Santa Cruz, Cabras and Ridge Islands, Port Dolores, and Point Verde; Ulloa Channel; Point San Antonio; Joe Island/ Cape Flores; Port Estrella; Point Providence; Point Lomas; Port Caldera; San Juan Bautista Island: Diamond Point, Balandra Island, and Point Eugenia; Trocadero Bay; Doyle Bay/Culebrina Island; Coronados Island; Port Saint Nicholas; Cape Suspiro; Ursua Channel; San Fernando Island: Point Colocano, Cruz Pass, Point Amargura, Fern Point, and Point Cuerbo; and San Alberto Bay: Fish Egg, Sombrero, Abbess, and Ballena Islands, San Cristoval Channel, Klawock Inlet, and Crab Bay.

54 Klawock River

Location: West Prince of Wales Island drainage, 55 miles west of Ketchikan, 725 miles southeast of Anchorage; see map page 327.

USGS maps: Craig B-3, C-3, C-4.

How to get there: Floatplanes from Ketchikan can access Klawock Lake or the Klawock Seaplane Base near the mouth of the river. The most popular road access is from Klawock or Craig. The Craig-Klawock-Hollis Road crosses over a narrow portion of Klawock Lagoon and parallels the river more or less from its mouth upstream to the lake outlet and the north shore of the lake.

Highlights: One of the more famous Prince of Wales streams, known for winter steelhead (from late February through early April) and silver salmon (in September); also good fishing for sockeye salmon (in the second half of August), spring and fall Dolly Varden and cutthroat trout (in May, June, September, and October).

Species: Chum salmon, cutthroat trout, Dolly Varden, pink salmon, rainbow trout, red salmon, silver salmon, steelhead, *king salmon*.

Regulations: Unbaited, artificial lures only from November 16 through September 14. King salmon fishing is prohibited; catch-and-release only for red salmon. For additional restrictions, consult the current Alaska Department of Fish and Game regulations or contact the ADF&G Ketchikan office, (907) 225-2859.

Facilities: Commercial lodging, gas, water, groceries, sporting goods, boat rentals and a boat launch, and guide services are available in the towns of Klawock and Craig, which are a few miles away.

Contact: For lodging information, contact the City of Klawock, P.O. Box 113, Klawock, AK 99925, (907) 755-2261; or the City of Craig, P.O. Box 23, Craig, AK 99921, (907) 826-3275. For cabin rentals, contact Craig Ranger District, Tongass National Forest, P.O. Box 500, Craig, AK 99921; (907) 826-3271. For an air taxi, contact Taquan Air, 1007 Water Street, Ketchikan, AK 99901, (907) 225-8800 or (800) 770-8800; or Kupreanof Flying Service, P.O. Box 768, Petersburg, AK 99833, (907) 772-3396.

Fishing the Klawock River: Beautiful, seven-mile-long Klawock Lake sits in a valley between Sunny Hay Mountain and Pin Peak near the town of Klawock. The Klawock River heads at the lake and runs approximately two miles west to Klawock Inlet and San Alberto Bay. The light brown waters are considered to be some of the top salmon and steelhead producers on Prince of Wales Island and receive quite a bit of angling attention during the peak of the runs.

The most sought-after game fish in the Klawock are silvers and steelhead trout. Silvers run heavy in fall, with some specimens weighing up to 18 pounds, followed by a smaller run of steelhead trout. The sea-run rainbows continue to trickle in throughout the winter months before a sizable showing of spring-run fish arrives sometime around the first of April. A late summer run of red and pink salmon and a fall run of chums also grab anglers' interest. Good trout action may be had in the lake and at the mouth of inlet streams.

The Klawock is very accessible, which makes it even more attractive to anglers looking to save money. The main road in the area provides plenty of parking with an extensive trail system covering the entire north side of the river. Several step falls are present in this short river; successful anglers concentrate their efforts in the areas of lesser gradient between the falls.

As in many streams in the Southeast region, the Klawock's salmon and trout seem to be quite sensitive to water levels and often time their entrance into the river accordingly. During much of the summer the Klawock typically runs slow and clear, but once the late summer and fall rains begin and the water rises, fishing really heats up. Look for major influxes of fresh fish after periods of heavy precipitation.

55 Thorne River System

Location: East Prince of Wales Island drainage, 45 miles northwest of Ketchikan, 725 miles southeast of Anchorage; see map page 327.

USGS maps: Craig C-2, C-3, D-2, D-3.

How to get there: By floatplane, car, and boat. Thorne Bay Road, which runs between Thorne Bay and Klawock, crosses the lower river two miles from its mouth and parallels the drainage for several miles; it also intersects tributary streams. Floatplanes can access the upper drainage through Thorne Lake, while the mouth of the Thorne can be reached by boat from Ketchikan.

Highlights: A world famous Prince of Wales location, noted for outstanding salmon and steelhead, especially silver salmon (from mid-August through early September) and pink salmon (in the first half of August); also good fishing for steelhead trout (from late March through mid-May and late November through late December) and cutthroat trout and Dolly Varden (in May, June, September, and October). Also good saltwater fishing.

Species: Cutthroat trout, Dolly Varden, pink salmon, rainbow trout, red salmon, silver salmon, steelhead, *chum salmon.*

Regulations: Unbaited, artificial lures only from November 16 through September 14; king salmon fishing is prohibited. For additional restrictions, consult the current Alaska Department of Fish and Game regulations or contact the ADF&G Ketchikan office, (907) 225-2859.

Facilities: Commercial lodging and a boat launch are available in the Thorne Bay area. A Forest Service cabin is located at Control Lake on the upper Thorne.

Contact: For lodging and guide services, contact Boardwalk Wilderness Lodge, P.O. Box 19121-BW, Thorne Bay, AK 99919; (907) 828-3918 or (800) 764-3918. For cabin rentals, contact Thorne Bay Ranger District, Tongass National Forest, P.O. Box 1, Ketchikan, AK 99919; (907) 828-3304. For an air taxi, contact Taquan Air, 1007 Water Street, Ketchikan, AK 99901, (907) 225-8800 or (800) 770-8800; or Kupreanof Flying Service, P.O. Box 768, Petersburg, AK 99833; (907) 772-3396.

Fishing the Thorne River System: The largest river system on Prince of Wales Island and a world famous steelhead location, the Thorne River drains some 28 lakes and ponds of varying size, covering a substantial part of the central island. It's also one of the most accessible prime fishing locations in the Ketchikan area, since a good part of it can be reached by plane, boat, car, and foot. It's also one of the few rivers on the island that can be floated.

Draining into Thorne Arm and Clarence Strait on the east side of Prince of Wales, the main stem and North Fork total about 30 miles in length, and support spring and fall runs of wild steelhead, salmon, cutthroat and rainbow trout, and Dolly Varden charr. The fishing season usually kicks off in late March, with the arrival of the first spring steelies, followed by out-migrating schools of cutthroat trout and Dolly Varden in April and May. Summer first brings sockeye, pink, and chum, then later silver salmon, which enter the river in early fall. In late September and October, the action picks up with in-migrating sea-run cuts, Dollies, and a well-known run of fall steelhead that continues into early winter.

As some anglers have discovered, the Thorne can be float-fished for most its length. Put in by floatplane is done at Thorne Lake, with a take-out at the road crossing or the boat launch near Thorne Bay. The run is approximately eight river miles, or a good one- to two-day float. This is a superb option, allowing anglers to sample sections of the Thorne that receive little pressure. A canoe route also covers a substantial part of the drainage with a few portages. The trip takes about three days.

Lakes and streams of the upper drainage have poor to fair trout and charr fishing, with good numbers of spawning salmon; for this reason, most anglers concentrate their efforts from Thorne Lake down the main stem to Thorne Bay. For additional variety, try the marine fisheries for salmon and halibut in adjacent Thorne Bay and Clarence Strait.

56 Karta River System

Location: East Prince of Wales Island drainage, 45 miles west of Ketchikan, 730 miles southeast of Anchorage; see map page 327.

USGS maps: Craig C-2, C-3.

How to get there: By floatplane or boat from Ketchikan or area lodges. Planes frequently land on Salmon and Karta Lakes and in Karta Bay. Boat access from Ketchikan is lengthy, crossing Clarence Strait, up Kasaan Bay to Karta Bay and the mouth of Karta River. A trail leads from the mouth upstream to the lakes.

Highlights: A world famous steelhead fishery in spring and late fall (from late March through early May and late November through late December), with excellent fishing for sockeyes (in the second half of July) and spring and fall Dolly Varden and cutthroat trout, and good fishing for silver salmon (from mid-August through late September) and fall rainbow trout (in September and October).

Species: Chum salmon, cutthroat trout, Dolly Varden, pink salmon, rainbow trout, red salmon, silver salmon, steelhead.

Regulations: Unbaited, artificial lures only from November 16 through September 14; king salmon fishing is prohibited. For additional restrictions, consult the current Alaska Department of Fish and Game regulations or contact the ADF&G Ketchikan office, (907) 225-2859.

Facilities: Four Forest Service cabins for public use are located along the Karta River system.

Contact: For cabin rentals, contact Thorne Bay Ranger District, Tongass National Forest, P.O. Box 1, Ketchikan, AK 99919; (907) 828-3304. For an air taxi, contact Taquan Air, 1007 Water Street, Ketchikan, AK 99901; (907) 225-8800 or (800) 770-8800.

Fishing the Karta River System: The Karta River drainage is one of the most productive systems in southern Southeast Alaska, well known for its abundant steelhead and salmon. Situated 35 miles west of Ketchikan at the head of Kasaan Bay in the central portion of Prince of Wales Island, the 10-mile system drains two major lakes (Karta and Salmon) and several smaller ones. Salmon Lake is the largest and has two Forest Service cabins (one at McGilvery Creek), while Karta Lake (Little Salmon Lake) has only one cabin. Another cabin is located at the mouth of the river. Part of the Karta River Wilderness, the area boasts an excellent network of Forest Service trails that accesses its world-class fishery.

Beginning in early spring and continuing into late fall, the Karta offers consistent, outstanding stream fishing for trout, charr, and salmon, especially steelhead and sockeyes. Tens of thousands of bright reds migrate into the system in most years, providing some of Southeast's best fly-fishing opportunities for the species. The Karta's steelies come in a spring and fall run. On average, they're larger (10 to 12 pounds) than elsewhere in Southeast, with fair numbers in the mid- to upper teens, and potential for specimens up to 20 pounds or more. Spin fishing (with Spin-N-Glos, Okie Drifters, and Li'l Corkies, among others) and flies (attractors, egg and forage patterns) are most popular. April, May, and October are the best times. Karta anglers also target fairly abundant silver and pink salmon, rainbows, and fall and spring runs of sea-run Dolly Varden and cutthroat trout.

Trails begin at Karta Bay, where boaters can moor their boat at the beach near the first Forest Service cabin, and extend upstream along the tea-colored river to Karta Lake and the sec-ond public-use cabin. From there, a trail leads to the north shore of Salmon Lake and the third Forest Service cabin, then continues along the lake and up Andersen Creek, a major tributary. The fourth Forest Service cabin is located at the mouth of McGilvery Creek in the southwest corner of Salmon Lake.

For anglers wishing to sample some of the best freshwater fishing in Southeast Alaska, particularly for steelhead, the Karta River must be given serious consideration. If you're planning on staying in one of the Forest Service cabins, keep in mind that reservations are at a premium due to the river's growing popularity. Drawings are held in late winter and early spring for reservation dates in the coming summer and fall seasons. (Reserve through the Thorne Bay Ranger District at the address and phone number listed above.)

57 Lower Clarence Strait

Location: Along east Prince of Wales Island, west of Etolin Island, 20 miles west of Ketchikan, 735 miles southeast of Anchorage; see map page 327.

USGS maps: Craig A-1, A-2, B-1, B-2, B-3, C-1, C-2, D-1, D-2; Ketchikan A-5, A-6, B-6, C-6; Dixon Entrance C-1, D-1; Prince Rupert D-5, D-6.

How to get there: By boat or floatplane from Ketchikan, Wrangell, and area lodges and towns. Boats run to the specific fishing areas, while floatplanes usually land in protected coves and bays near the mouths of salmon spawning streams.

Highlights: One of Southeast's better marine fishing locations for salmon and bottomfish, with excellent fishing for silver salmon (August and September), pink salmon (from mid-July through early August), and halibut (from June through August), and good trolling and mooching for king salmon (in June).

Species: Chum salmon, Dolly Varden, halibut, king salmon, pink salmon, silver salmon, *cutthroat trout, red salmon, steelhead.*

Regulations: For restrictions on bottomfish, consult the current Alaska Department of Fish and Game regulations or contact the ADF&G Ketchikan office, (907) 225-2859.

Facilities: Commercial lodging and guide services are available in the towns along the strait. Forest Service cabins are available at Karta Bay and Trollers Cove (Kasaan Bay), Phocena Rocks (Gravina Island), and Kegan Cove (Moira Sound).

Contact: For guide services, contact Classic Alaska Charters, P.O. Box 6117, Ketchikan, AK 99901, (907) 225-0608; Rock 'N' Rollin' Charter Boat, 11380 Alderwood Street North, Ketchikan, AK 99901, (907) 225-6919 or (800) 876-0925; or Last Frontier Charters, P.O. Box 19443, Thorne Bay, AK 99919, (907) 828-3989. For lodging information, contact Boardwalk Wilderness Lodge, P.O. Box 19121-BW, Thorne Bay, AK 99919, (907) 828-3918 or (800) 764-3918. For cabin rentals, contact Thorne Bay Ranger District, Tongass National Forest, P.O. Box 1, Ketchikan, AK 99919, (907) 828-3304; or Tongass National Forest, Federal Building, Ketchikan, AK 99901, (907) 225-3101. For an air taxi, contact Taquan Air, 1007 Water Street, Ketchikan, AK 99901; (907) 225-8800 or (800) 770-8800.

Fishing Lower Clarence Strait: Like Icy Strait in the Juneau region, Clarence Strait is a major migration channel and feeding ground for salmon, trout, charr, and halibut bound for other locations (the west coast of Prince of Wales Island, Behm Canal, Revillagigedo Island, and Ernest Sound). The strait includes all waters south of Thorne Bay and the north tip of the Cleveland Peninsula. A gorgeous marine haven of islands, reefs, and steep, forest-clad slopes dropping into crystal clear waters, Clarence is a favorite playground for anglers from Ketchikan and beyond, world famous for having some of the best fishing in Alaska.

Most angling effort is aimed at the more popular sport species, such as king and silver salmon and halibut, but the strait has good numbers of other salmon and bottomfish species as well. Feeder king salmon are available all year, as they are most everywhere in Southeast. The better fishing action takes place in early summer when big concentrations of prespawners invade the cool, blue waters of lower Clarence on their way to the mainland. Occasional catches up to 60 and 70 pounds or more have been recorded, with the typical king averaging 15 to 25 pounds. Silver salmon run the strait throughout late summer and into fall, with specimens up to 20 pounds possible. Early in the season, when they're feeding heavily, boaters target them around the traditional holding locations such as point and breakwater beaches. Later, bays, narrows, and shorelines in the vicinity of clearwater rivers and streams produce good catches.

Although not the most valued salmon, chums and pinks are the most numerous species here. Ocean-bright pinks, a few of trophy size, provide excellent action on light tackle all along the coast, but primarily near spawning streams. Anglers have hoisted record-size chums—some between 20 and 30 pounds—from locations near Gravina Island and the mouth of Behm Canal during the months of June and July.

Lower Clarence Strait also offers some of Ketchikan's best action for bottomfish throughout the summer, including some flatties that occasionally exceed 300 pounds, as well as rockfish and lingcod.

The best locations to target salmon and halibut are Thorne Bay; Tolstoi Point; Tolstoi Bay; Cleveland Peninsula: Lemesurier, Niblack, and Caamano Points, Meyers Chuck, and Ship Island; Grindall Passage; Grindall Island/Approach Point; Kasaan Bay: Patterson/High Islands, Island, Skowl, Baker, and Outer Points, Skowl and Twelvemile Arms, Saltery Cove, and Mills and Karta Bays; Twenty-Fathom Bank; Clover Point; Skin Island; West/South Arms; Cholmondeley Sound; Outer Cholmondeley Sound; Trollers Cove; Chasina Point; South Chasina Point; Windy Point; Guard Islands; Wedge Islands; Outer Moira Sound: Moira Rock, Moira Island, and Rip Point; Polk Island; Outer Kendrick Bay; Outer McLean Arm/McLean Point; Stone Rock; Cape Chacon; Percy Island; Bee Rocks; Hassler Reef; West Rock; and Club Rocks.

58 McDonald Lake System

Location: West Behm Canal drainage, 45 miles north of Ketchikan, 740 miles southeast of Anchorage; see map page 327.

USGS maps: Ketchikan D-6; Bradfield Canal A-6.

How to get there: By floatplane or boat from Ketchikan or area lodges. Planes land on

McDonald Lake or in Yes Bay at the mouth of Wolverine Creek. Boats arrive via Behm Canal and Yes Bay to the outlet stream. Foot trails lead from there to McDonald Lake.

Highlights: A famous southern Southeast fishing spot, especially noted for sockeye salmon (from August through early September), with excellent fishing for silver salmon (from mid-September through mid-October), Dolly Varden charr (in May, June, September, and October); good fishing for pink salmon (from mid-August through early September), steelhead (from mid-April through late May), rainbow trout (in September and October), and cutthroat trout (in May, June, September, and October).

Species: Chum salmon, cutthroat trout, Dolly Varden, pink salmon, rainbow trout, red salmon, silver salmon, steelhead.

Regulations: Unbaited, artificial lures only from November 16 through September 14; king salmon fishing is prohibited. For additional restrictions, consult the current Alaska Department of Fish and Game regulations or contact the ADF&G Ketchikan office, (907) 225-2859.

Facilities: Commercial lodging and a Forest Service cabin are available at Wolverine Creek and McDonald Lake.

Contact: For lodging information, contact the Yes Bay Lodge, P.O. Box 6440, Ketchikan, AK 99901; (907) 225-7906 or (800) 999-0784. For cabin rentals, contact Tongass National Forest, Federal Building, Ketchikan, AK 99909; (907) 225-3101. For an air taxi, contact Taquan Air, 1007 Water Street, Ketchikan, AK 99901; (907) 225-8800 or (800) 770-8800.

Fishing the McDonald Lake System: One of the richest freshwater fisheries in the Ketchikan area, the McDonald Lake system attracts considerable attention from anglers near and far. Situated on the scenic Cleveland Peninsula, the system consists of eight lakes, of which McDonald is the largest. You can expect good to excellent angling for all of the region's popular game species in McDonald's lakes and streams.

The tinted waters of this drainage are home to distinctive stocks of sockeye salmon, which usually enter Wolverine Creek and McDonald Lake

two weeks to a month later than in most other area waters. The area also has a population of trophy pink salmon that commonly weigh six to eight pounds, with specimens up to 10 pounds possible.

A healthy run of bright spring steelhead kicks off the fishing season in April, closely followed by an outward migration of sea-run cutthroat and Dolly Varden, in addition to good spring fishing for resident rainbow trout. Summer brings returning hordes of red, pink, and chum salmon. The sockeye run is made up of both wild and hatchery fish. Their sheer numbers often flood Wolverine Creek, creating some of Southeast's best fly-fishing for the species. Later in the fall, a late run of large silver salmon keep the action hopping.

The Forest Service cabin at McDonald Lake (reservations by lottery only) provides anglers with access to the lake outlet and all of Wolverine Creek via the trail network that extends to Yes Bay. A canoe or inflatable is a definite plus on McDonald Lake, but you can do fairly well just wading and hiking. Wolverine Creek flows rather fast and is quite brushy, making for some challenging fly-fishing. From the northern end of McDonald Lake, a trail leads upstream from an abandoned fish hatchery along Walker Creek, a major system tributary.

59 Naha River System

Location: West Revillagigedo Island drainage, 20 miles northwest of Ketchikan, 765 miles southeast of Anchorage; see map page 327.

USGS map: Ketchikan C-5.

How to get there: By floatplane from Ketchikan or area lodges to Heckman and Patching Lakes or the mouth at Roosevelt Lagoon. Boats can access Naha Bay and Roosevelt Lagoon from Ketchikan. Trails lead from Roosevelt Lagoon to the river and upstream into the system.

Highlights: One of the region's premier sportfishing systems, known for its outstanding salmon and trout fishing and unique opportunities for grayling. Excellent angling for pink salmon (in the first half of August) and steelhead trout (from early April through mid-May and late

November through late December); good fishing for silver salmon (from mid-August through late September), sockeye salmon (in the second half of July), cutthroat trout (in May, June, September, and October), and grayling (from May through October).

Species: Chum salmon, cutthroat trout, Dolly Varden, grayling, pink salmon, rainbow trout, red salmon, silver salmon, steelhead.

Regulations: Unbaited, artificial lures only from November 16 through September 14; king salmon fishing is prohibited. For additional restrictions, consult the current Alaska Department of Fish and Game regulations or contact the ADF&G Ketchikan office, (907) 225-2859.

Facilities: Four Forest Service cabins are located in the system at Jordan (one), Heckman (two), and Patching (one) Lakes.

Contact: For cabin rentals, contact Tongass National Forest, Federal Building, Ketchikan, AK 99909; (907) 225-3101. For an air taxi, contact Taquan Air, 1007 Water Street, Ketchikan, AK 99901; (907) 225-8800 or (800) 770-8800.

Fishing the Naha River System: Like the Karta River, the Naha River and its environs are a significant sportfishing area in southern Southeast Alaska. Flowing out of Orton Lake in the central part of Revillagigedo Island, 25 miles northeast of Ketchikan, the Naha is more than 17 miles long and annexes eight small but deep lakes along its way to Naha Bay and Behm Canal. Fishing is good to excellent in both the river and lakes. Silver and red salmon, steelhead, and cutthroat trout are the top draws.

The Naha has a variety of waters for anglers to test their skills on. Tidally influenced Roosevelt Lagoon is a major holding area for silver and pink salmon. From the lagoon, a well-developed and popular trail (the Naha River Trail) leads to the river and adjoining lakes. Jordan Lake, the first lake in the system, has a Forest Service cabin along with some of the Naha's best fishing (for cutthroat trout, steelhead, rainbow, Dollies, and coho). Try the outlet, the mouths of tributary creeks (Emma or others that are unnamed), and the river above and below the lake (for steelhead). Next is Heckman Lake, with two Forest Service cabins and great trout fishing; try the outlet and river below the lake. Beyond

Heckman is Patching Lake, the largest, deepest lake in the system, with two cabins. Salmon can't make it up this far because of a barrier waterfall, but cutthroat trout do very well, with trophy fish up to six pounds available in the lake's deep waters. Try the outlet above the falls for small trout. Bigger fish are best pursued from a boat or raft. The lake also has a few kokanee and arctic grayling. Farther on are Chamberlain, Snow, and Orton Lakes, all mountain headwater lakes beautifully situated, and offering some of Southeast's rare opportunities for arctic grayling (from stocking done in the 1960s).

Chum and pink are more prevalent in the lower system, while silvers and reds are scattered throughout the drainage. The best fishing can be found below the lake outlets, near inlet streams, and in holding areas of the main stem between lakes.

⑥⓪ West Behm Canal

Location: Along west Revillagigedo Island, 20 miles north of Ketchikan, 750 miles southeast of Anchorage; see map page 327.

USGS maps: Ketchikan B-6, C-5, C-6, D-5, D-6; Craig C-1.

How to get there: By boat or floatplane from Ketchikan or area lodges. The western canal can be reached via Tongass Narrows, and the eastern through the upper sections of Revillagigedo Channel.

Highlights: One of Alaska's premier saltwater fishing locations, renowned for king salmon (in June), silver salmon (from late August to late September), and chum salmon (in the first half of July and the first half of September). Also, good fishing for halibut (from June through August), pink salmon (from mid-July through mid-August), and spring Dolly Varden (in May and June).

Species: Chum salmon, cutthroat trout, Dolly Varden, halibut, king salmon, pink salmon, silver salmon, *red salmon, steelhead.*

Regulations: For restrictions on salmon and bottomfish, consult the current Alaska Department of Fish and Game regulations or contact the ADF&G Ketchikan office, (907) 225-2859.

Facilities: Commercial lodging, campgrounds,

boat launching, and guide services are available, primarily in the west canal area. Forest Service cabins are located at Helm Bay, Blind Pass, and Anchor Pass.

Contact: For guide services, contact Classic Alaska Charters, P.O. Box 6117, Ketchikan, AK 99901, (907) 225-0608; Rock 'N' Rollin' Charter Boat, 11380 Alderwood Street North, Ketchikan, AK 99901, (907) 225-6919 or (800) 876-0925; Anderson Charters, P.O. Box 7118, Ketchikan, AK 99901, (907) 225-2456; or Ketchikan Sportfishing, P.O. Box 3212, Ketchikan, AK 99901, (907) 225-7526. For lodging information, contact Yes Bay Lodge, 1515 Tongass Avenue, Ketchikan, AK 99901, (907) 225-7906 or (800) 999-0784; or Salmon Falls Resort, P.O. Box 5420-B, Ketchikan, AK 99901, (907) 225-2752 or (800) 247-9059. For cabin rentals, contact Tongass National Forest, Federal Building, Ketchikan, AK 99901, (907) 225-3101. For an air taxi, contact Taquan Air, 1007 Water Street, Ketchikan, AK 99901; (907) 225-8800 or (800) 770-8800.

Fishing West Behm Canal: World famous Behm Canal separates Revillagigedo Island from the mainland. It serves as a conduit for fish bound for numerous area lakes and streams, which include some of Southeast Alaska's most significant spawning systems (such as the Naha River, Wolverine Creek, McDonald Lake, and the Chickamin and Unuk Rivers). Sportfishing, rated among the best in Southeast, is concentrated in the fjords, bays, and coves of the outer and upper areas of West Behm Canal (around the southern tip of the Cleveland Peninsula and Bell Island).

Silver salmon regularly grab the limelight as huge (up to 20 pounds or more), aggressive fish make their way through the clear waters of the canal for island and mainland spawning grounds. In some years, the fish are so plentiful that anglers can hook dozens in a single day. King salmon fishing is also very productive with the bulk of the catch hauled out of the outer canal near Clarence Strait. Although feeders can be taken year-round, mature prespawners become available during early summer.

If you're looking for a trophy, West Behm Canal is definitely the place to go. Consistent catches of chums between 18 and 25 pounds are reported from the outer and upper canal, with the current state and world record fish (32 pounds) taken from Caamano Point on the Cleveland Peninsula in 1985. July is the best month. You'll find trophy pinks as well, with typical catches of five or six pounds and up to 10 pounds or more possible.

Halibut fishing is good in the deeper parts of Behm throughout the season, and in a few of the bays near salmon spawning streams in late summer and fall. Rockfish, Dolly Varden, other bottomfish species, and even crab are also available.

The best spots for salmon and halibut in West Behm are Cleveland Peninsula: Caamano Point, Bond, Outer Smuggler, Helm, Spacious, and Yes Bays, Helm Point, Wadding Cove, and Point Francis; Revillagigedo Island: Point Higgins, Survey, Indian, and Chin/Nose/Brow Points, Betton Island/Clover Passage, Tatoosh, Back, Grant, and Stack Islands, Bushy Point/Cove, and Naha and Neets Bays; Gedney Island; Hassler Island/Pass; Black Island; and Bell Island/Behm Narrows.

Note: The world record steelhead (42 pounds, three ounces) was caught in West Behm near Bell Island in 1970, by an eight-year-old boy fishing for salmon.

(61) Ward Lake System

Location: Southwest Revillagigedo Island drainage, five miles northwest of Ketchikan, 770 miles southeast of Anchorage; see map page 327.

USGS maps: Ketchikan B-5, B-6.

How to get there: By car. The North Tongass Highway crosses Ward Creek just above Ward Cove. Also, Ward Lake Road provides access to Ward Lake, with trails continuing to the upper drainage.

Highlights: A great do-it-yourself excursion, with easy access and potentially good fishing for silver salmon (from mid-July through early August), pink salmon (in the first half of August), steelhead trout (from early April through mid-May), and Dolly Varden (in May, June, September, and October).

Species: Chum salmon, cutthroat trout, Dolly Varden, pink salmon, rainbow trout, red salmon, silver salmon, steelhead.

Regulations: Unbaited, single-hook, artificial lures only from November 16 through September 14; king salmon fishing is prohibited. For additional restrictions, consult the current Alaska Department of Fish and Game regulations or contact the ADF&G Ketchikan office, (907) 225-2859.

Facilities: Commercial lodging, fuel, water, and a campground are available. The nearby towns of Ward Cove and Ketchikan have additional services, supplies, and facilities.

Contact: For lodging information, contact the Ketchikan Chamber of Commerce, P.O. Box 5957, Ketchikan, AK 99901; (907) 225-3185.

Fishing the Ward Lake System: Originating on the north side of Slide Ridge and running south to Ward Cove and Tongass Narrows, the Ward Lake system is comprised of four lakes—Ward, Connell, Talbot, and Perseverance. All are popular with anglers and other recreationists in the Ketchikan area. It's a scenic, heavily forested area, and trails allow for good combined hiking and fishing trips. Muskeg-stained Ward Creek is host to significant numbers of salmon, trout, and charr, offering good to excellent fishing within a few minutes drive of Ketchikan.

The most abundant and sought-after species are silver and pink salmon, steelhead trout, and Dolly Varden charr. Targeted mostly between April and October, they provide a high-yield fishery of natural and hatchery fish. In April and May, the creek's sizable spring run of steelhead migrate in from the salt at the same time that overwintering Dollies move out of the system, providing some exciting fishing. In July, a strong run of coho enters the creek, followed by a much smaller fall run in September and October. (The summer fish are primarily hatchery stock and contribute significantly to area marine fisheries.) A small run of red salmon destined for Ward Lake also offers fair fly-fishing.

The better salmon and steelhead fishing is found at the Ward Lake inlet and in the creek above the lake. Since the drainage is in a fairly developed area of the region, access is no problem, with ample parking and hiking trails. In the upper system, Connell and Talbot Lakes are also road and trail accessible, with good opportunities for Dolly Varden and fair numbers

of cutthroat trout. Perseverance Lake has a population of stocked brook trout. For an angler with a day or two to spare in the Ketchikan area, the Ward Lake system is highly recommended.

62 Ketchikan Creek System

Location: Southwest Revillagigedo Island drainage, Ketchikan area, 775 miles southeast of Anchorage; see map page 327.

USGS map: Ketchikan B-5.

How to get there: By car from downtown Ketchikan. The South Tongass Highway crosses the stream, with trail access to upper stream sections and Ketchikan Lakes.

Highlights: The best city angling in all of Southeast Alaska. Excellent for pink salmon (in the first half of August), with good fishing for king salmon (in July), silver salmon (from mid-August through late September), and some steelhead (from early April through mid-May and late November through late December).

Species: Chum salmon, cutthroat trout, Dolly Varden, king salmon, pink salmon, rainbow trout, red salmon, silver salmon, steelhead.

Regulations: Closed to fishing from May 16 through September 14, except by emergency order. This is a heavily regulated urban fishery. For details on restrictions, consult the current Alaska Department of Fish and Game regulations or contact the ADF&G Ketchikan office, (907) 225-2859.

Facilities: Hotels, commercial lodging, gas, boat rentals and a boat launch, sporting goods, groceries, and water are available in Ketchikan.

Contact: For fishing information, contact the Alaska Department of Fish and Game, Sportfish Division, 2030 Sea Level Drive, Suite 205, Ketchikan, AK 99901; (907) 225-2859. For lodging information, contact the Ketchikan Chamber of Commerce, P.O. Box 5957, Ketchikan, AK 99901; (907) 225-3185.

Fishing the Ketchikan Creek System: Swift Ketchikan Creek originates from several mountain lakes just north of the town of Ketchikan. (There are four lakes, of which Ketchikan Lake is the largest.) Surrounded by picturesque mountain scenery, with trail access, this extremely popular recreation area at times has impressive fishing for salmon and steelhead, and is worth investigating if you're in the area.

Most of the fishing effort occurs on lower Ketchikan Creek from the mouth at Tongass Narrows upstream a mile. Here, every season local anglers intercept runs of mixed hatchery and wild stock salmon and trout. Although these waters are heavily regulated and open to angling only by emergency order, when fishing occurs, it can be quite outstanding.

A hatchery run of king salmon returns to the stream in midsummer, giving anglers a unique freshwater sportfishery for these 15- to 25-pound brutes. The best time is July and early August. A summer run of silvers is also available; later on, a fall run of wild fish keeps the action going strong until October. Pink salmon, the most abundant species in Ketchikan Creek, are available in August. For variety, anglers can try their fly-fishing skills on the creek's steelhead trout in spring and fall (a smaller run). Dolly Varden show up at roughly the same times.

Many other Southeast locations provide far better fishing than Ketchikan Creek; few, however, can match the easy accessibility of the stream that runs through the middle of Ketchikan. If you've only got a few hours in this Southeast waterfront town, give Ketchikan Creek a try.

(63) Gravina Island/ Tongass Narrows

Location: Southwest of Revillagigedo Island, Ketchikan area, 765 miles southeast of Anchorage; see map page 327.

USGS maps: Ketchikan A-6, B-5, B-6.

How to get there: By boat from Ketchikan. Gravina Island is located about one mile across Tongass Narrows from Ketchikan. Kayaking out to and around the island is possible on calm days. Floatplanes can land in more protected waters on the south/southeast side of Gravina.

Highlights: An all-time local favorite, with easy access—only minutes away from Ketchikan—and excellent fishing for silver salmon (from late August through September) and pink salmon (from early July through early August). Also, good fishing for king salmon (from late May through early July), chum salmon (throughout July), and halibut (from June through August).

Species: Chum salmon, Dolly Varden, halibut, king salmon, pink salmon, silver salmon, *cutthroat trout, red salmon, steelhead.*

Regulations: For restrictions on bottomfish, consult the current Alaska Department of Fish and Game regulations or contact the ADF&G Ketchikan office, (907) 225-2859.

Facilities: Ketchikan and other nearby towns have hotels, commercial lodging, sporting goods, groceries, guide services, gas, boat rentals and launching, and water. A Forest Service cabin is located at Phocena Bay on the southern end of Gravina Island.

Contact: For guide services, contact Classic Alaska Charters, P.O. Box 6117, Ketchikan, AK 99901, (907) 225-0608; Rock 'N' Rollin' Charter Boat, 11380 Alderwood Street North, Ketchikan, AK 99901, (907) 225-6919 or (800) 876-0925; Anderson Charters, P.O. Box 7118, Ketchikan, AK 99901, (907) 225-2456; Ken's Charters, P.O. Box 9609, Ketchikan, AK 99901, (907) 225-7290; or Ketchikan Sportfishing, P.O. Box 3212, Ketchikan, AK 99901, (907) 225-7526. For cabin rentals, contact Tongass National Forest, Federal Building, Ketchikan, AK 99901; (907) 225-3101.

Fishing Gravina Island/Tongass Narrows: Gravina Island lies to the south and west of giant Revillagigedo Island, along fish-rich Clarence Strait. Part of Tongass National Forest, it is heavily wooded with 17 small creeks streaming down its green slopes, most of them with at least one or more sport fish species present. The island isn't simply noted for its stream fishing opportunities, but also for its remarkable marine fishery. Gravina's western coastline lies along the path of tens of thousands of salmon bound for rivers, streams, and lakes in the region, with good numbers of halibut actively feeding just offshore. Tongass Narrows, along the island's other side, supports both natural and hatchery runs of all five salmon species, as well as Dolly Varden and bottomfish.

Trophy-size silver salmon abound in late summer and early fall, with fish in the upper teens not unusual and a 20-pounder always a possibility. Equally large chum salmon also cruise the island's beaches, particularly on the west side. Pinks are found all around the island, but are more noticeable in Tongass Narrows, where spawning runs headed for the Ward Lake system and Ketchikan Creek school up in shallow, near-shore areas. King salmon are available as feeder and mature fish, with locals reporting catches throughout the year. (Prespawners dominate in late spring and early summer.)

Anglers who want more variety can try for sea-run Dolly Varden along the east side of the island or in Tongass Narrows (Ward Cove), or anywhere a clear-water stream flows into salt water. For bottomfish, the west side of Gravina is a traditional halibut hole, with fish weighing more than 100 pounds caught on occasion, along with a healthy mix of lingcod, rockfish, and other bottomfish species. Set pots for crab and shrimp in Nichols Passage.

One of the most attractive features about the marine waters around Gravina is the accessibility. Only minutes from the town of Ketchikan, anglers can easily reach productive salmon fishing sites for trolling, mooching, and even surf casting along Tongass Narrows (especially from the shores of Revillagigedo Island).

The best spots around the island for salmon, charr, and halibut include Clarence Strait: Vallenar and South Vallenar Points, Grant and Nelson Coves, Phocena Rocks, and Vallenar Bay; Nichols Passage: Gravina, Blank, and Bostwick Points, Blank and Bostwick Inlets, Stomach Bay, Dall Head, Bronaugh and Blank Islands, and Point McCartey; and Tongass Narrows: Pennock Island, Point Higgins, Mud Bay, and Ward Cove.

64 Kegan Creek

Location: South Prince of Wales Island drainage, 25 miles southwest of Ketchikan, 765 miles southeast of Anchorage; see map page 327.

USGS map: Craig A-1.

How to get there: From Ketchikan by floatplane or boat. Floatplanes routinely land on Kegan Lake while anglers arrive by boat via Nichols Passage, crossing Clarence Strait into Moira Sound, then Kegan Cove, and finally the mouth of the Kegan River. A trail leads from Kegan Cove upstream along the river to the outlet of Kegan Lake, about a half-mile hike.

Highlights: A well-known Prince of Wales stream, with good fishing for salmon and steelhead—silver salmon (from mid-August through late September), red salmon (in the second half of July), pink salmon (in the first half of August), steelhead trout (from early April through mid-May), rainbow trout, cutthroat trout, and Dolly Varden (from May through June and September through October).

Species: Chum salmon, cutthroat trout, Dolly Varden, pink salmon, rainbow trout, red salmon, silver salmon, steelhead.

Regulations: Unbaited, artificial lures only from November 16 through September 14; king salmon fishing is prohibited. For additional restrictions, consult the current Alaska Department of Fish and Game regulations or contact the ADF&G Ketchikan office, (907) 225-2859.

Facilities: Two Forest Service cabins are available, one at Kegan Cove, another 200 yards downstream from Kegan Lake.

Contact: For cabin rentals, contact Thorne Bay Ranger District, Tongass National Forest, P.O. Box 1, Ketchikan, AK 99919; (907) 828-3304. For an air taxi, contact Taquan Air, 1007 Water Street, Ketchikan, AK 99901; (907) 225-8800 or (800) 770-8800.

Fishing the Kegan River System: Situated within Tongass National Forest on south Prince of Wales Island, the Kegan River area has long been a popular recreation destination. The stream itself is short—less than a mile long—and runs from Kegan Lake to Kegan Cove and salt water on Moira Sound. All of the areas are accessible by foot; a well-developed trail parallels the drainage through an old-growth forest. Since this is a particularly attractive destination known for good fishing for a variety of game species, the area's public-use cabins are reserved by lottery drawings from June through September.

The tea-colored waters of the creek and Kegan Lake host healthy numbers of wild salmon, trout, and charr, as well as salmon and halibut just off the mouth of Kegan Cove. During the height of the river's runs, anglers can fish the entire length from the outlet of Kegan Lake downstream to Kegan Cove, often with very good results. (Schools of fish often stage in the cove and lake outlet and are very susceptible at these times.)

Good fishing begins in July with reds and pinks, and continues into October with silvers, cutthroats, and rainbows. Visitors from nearby towns and from around the country come to experience the first-class fishing, with a stay in a comfortable cabin only yards away from the action. A spring run of bright steelhead trout also enters the river, peaking in April and May and drawing considerable attention.

Kegan Lake offers good opportunities for cutthroat and charr, with excellent fishing for rainbow trout reported at times. A lightweight canoe comes in handy to reach the more inaccessible parts of the drainage and can be carried from nearby cabins to the lake. On the lake's northeast shore, a tributary stream draining four other lakes in the system serves as a holding and feeding area; it's a good spot to try.

65 Revillagigedo Channel

Location: Along south Revillagigedo Island, 10 miles southeast of Ketchikan, 775 miles southeast of Anchorage; see map page 327.

USGS maps: Ketchikan A-2, A-3, A-4, A-5, B-2, B-3, B-4, B-5; Prince Rupert D-3, D-4.

How to get there: By boat from Ketchikan or area lodges. Floatplanes can land in protected bays and coves in the area. Revillagigedo Channel also provides boat access to George and Carroll Inlets, Thorne Arm, East Behm Canal, Duke Island, and Boca de Quadra.

Highlights: A highly productive intercept fishery, one of the best in the southern Southeast region, known for silver salmon (from late August through late September), pink salmon (from mid-July through mid-August), king salmon (in June), and halibut (from June through August).

Species: Dolly Varden, halibut, king salmon, pink salmon, silver salmon, *chum salmon, cutthroat trout, red salmon, steelhead.*

Regulations: For restrictions on bottomfish, consult the current Alaska Department of Fish and Game regulations or contact the ADF&G Ketchikan office, (907) 225-2859. Also, observe private property around Annette Island Indian Reservation.

Facilities: Commercial lodging, a boat launch, fuel, and water are available at Mountain Point on Revillagigedo Island.

Contact: For guide services, contact Classic Alaska Charters, P.O. Box 6117, Ketchikan, AK 99901, (907) 225-0608; Rock 'N' Rollin' Charter Boat, 11380 Alderwood Street North, Ketchikan, AK 99901, (907) 225-6919 or (800) 876-0925; Anderson Charters, P.O. Box 7118, Ketchikan, AK 99901, (907) 225-2456; Ken's Charters, P.O. Box 9609, Ketchikan, AK 99901, (907) 225-7290; Ketchikan Sportfishing, P.O. Box 3212, Ketchikan, AK 99901, (907) 225-7526. For lodging information, contact Mink Bay Lodge, 1515 Tongass Avenue, Ketchikan, AK 99901; (907) 225-7906 or (800) 999-0784. For cabin rentals, contact Tongass National Forest, Federal Building, Ketchikan, AK 99901; (907) 225-3101. For an air taxi, contact Taquan Air, 1007 Water Street, Ketchikan, AK 99901; (907) 225-8800 or (800) 770-8800.

Fishing Revillagigedo Channel: Set between Annette Island and the mainland, Revillagigedo Channel is an important salmon feeding and migration route south of Revillagigedo Island. The outer channel borders Dixon Entrance near Canada. Anadromous fish heading for mainland rivers and island streams pass through the channel in substantial numbers and are mainly targeted by sportfishing fleets out of Ketchikan.

Salmon and halibut dominate the fishery. Feeder kings weighing between 10 and 40 pounds can be taken year-round in the channel's clear waters, while larger, mature specimens up to 60 or 70 pounds are taken in early summer. (Many of these mature kings are bound for the glacial Chickamin River in East Behm Canal, a major spawning system for the Southeast region.)

Silver and pink salmon are the most prolific species in Revillagigedo Channel. These fish can be particularly abundant in late summer and fall, and are best targeted fairly close to shore near bays or coastlines with spawning streams. Cohos weighing in the teens are not unusual. Reds and chums run heavy at times, but sport anglers take them much less frequently than they take silvers and pinks. As with many other major saltwater locations in Southeast, Revillagigedo Channel produces some decent halibut fishing at times, with additional opportunities for rockfish, lingcod, and even shellfish.

The scenery is fantastic, with an abundance of marine wildlife and inlets cutting far into mainland mountain ranges and islands. (The eastern half of Revillagigedo Channel is part of Misty Fjords National Monument.) Although not as popular with recreational users as nearby Clarence Strait or West Behm Canal, the channel offers some fabulous sportfishing potential for anglers willing to take the time to explore, particularly the outer Revillagigedo for bottomfish and the mainland bays for salmon. Favorite areas are Mountain Point near Ketchikan and outer East Behm Canal.

Known hot spots for salmon and halibut in Revillagigedo Channel include Revillagigedo Island: Mountain Point, Lucky Cove, Cone Island/Point, Herring Bay, California Head, Carroll Point/Ice House Cove, and Thorne Arm; Behm Canal: Point Alava, Alava Bay, and Point Sykes; Black Island; Slate Island; Quadra Point; White Reef; Kah Shakes Point; Snail Rock; Black Rock; House Rock; Foggy Bay; Foggy Point; Lakekta Point; Humpy Point; Tree Point; Cape Fox/Fox Island; Mary Island; and Duke Island: Duke Point, Kelp Island, and East Island.

Appendices

Species Quick Reference

Arctic/Dolly Varden Charr
Salvelinus alpinus/malma

Alaska common names: Charr, arctic charr, Dolly Varden, Dolly, trout, salmon-trout, blue or golden fin trout, western brook trout/charr.

Description: Small to moderately large salmonid. Appearance variable; generally silvery/bluish, gray or brown back and sides; distinct red, pink, or orange spots; whitish underbelly. Ventral fins are yellow to carmine with white edges. The sexually mature fish is dark olive to brown in color, with orange-red shading on undersides, and vivid spots. Males have pronounced jaw kypes. Flesh is white, pink, or orange.

Size: Average weight in Alaska is one to two pounds; in western Alaska and especially the northwest part of the state, up to 12 pounds or more.

Meristics: Gill rakers variable 11–32; vertebrae 57–71; pyloric cacae 13–75; lateral line scales 105–152; branchiostegal rays 10–15; dorsal fin 12–16 rays; anal fin 8–15 rays; pelvic fin 8–11 rays.

Range: Coastal, Southeast to Arctic Ocean; inland along major rivers and scattered isolated river and lake dwelling forms across the state.

Best times: Available year-round; peak spring (April–June) and late summer and fall (late August–October).

State record: 19 pounds, 12.5 ounces, Kelly River (Northwest), Ken Ubben, 1991.

Best lures: Spinners—nos. 1 to 6 silver Vibrax, Mepps nos. 0 to 5 (Aglia fluorescent), Black Fury, Comet. Spoons—Krocodile, Dardevle, Fjord, Crippled Herring, Hot Rod, Pixee. Plugs—Tadpolly (chrome-blue and fluorescent orange), Hot Shot, silver Kwikfish. Other—Spin-N-Glo (red/orange/pink). Flies—Polar Shrimp, Two-Egg Marabou, smolt and fry imitations, Marabou Muddler, Egg-Sucking Leech.

Best waters: Major coastal salmon streams and adjacent salt water, Southeast to Arctic. Southeast: Nakwasina, Katlian, Chilkoot, and Chilkat Rivers. Southcentral: Kenai rivers and Kodiak Island. Southwest: Ugashik, Becharof, Iliamna, Naknek Lake systems; Togiak and Nushagak Rivers and Kuskokwim Bay streams. Northwest: Noatak and Wulik Rivers. Interior: Chena and Harding Lakes. Arctic: Sagavanirktok, Canning, and Kongakut Rivers.

Arctic Grayling
Thymallus arcticus

Alaska common names: Grayling, sailfin.

Description: Slender, whitefish-like salmonid. Males characterized by huge dorsal fin. Coloration varied; from silvery gray to dirty brown to almost black, with spawning individuals darker. Black, gold, and purple spots decorate the sides of the fish. The belly is yellowish white. Red and pink markings on dorsal fin are common during spawning period. Flesh is white.

Size: Average length eight to 14 inches; up to 23 inches and five pounds.

Meristics: Gill rakers 16–23; vertebrae 58–62; pyloric cacae 14–21; lateral line scales 75–103; branchiostegal rays 7–9; dorsal fin 17–25 rays; tail fin 11–15 rays; pelvic fin 10–11 rays; pectoral fin 14–16 rays.

Range: Revillagigedo Island (Southeast) to North Slope (Arctic).

Best times: Available year-round; peak May to September.

State record: Four pounds, 13 ounces, Ugashik Narrows (Southwest), Paul Kanitz, 1981.

Best lures: Small spinners (Mepps, Panther Martin, Vibrax) in silver, yellow, gold, blue, and black, and dry and wet flies and nymphs.

Best waters: Clear-water highland lakes and streams, in Southcentral, Southwest, Northwest, Arctic, and Interior. Southcentral: Gulkana and Upper Susitna Rivers. Southwest: Becharof River, Tikchik Lakes, and Kuskokwim headwaters. Northwest: Pilgrim, Snake, and Sinuk Rivers. Arctic: Sagavanirktok, Kuparuk, and Canning Rivers. Interior: Tangle Lakes and Goodpaster River.

Chum Salmon

Oncorhynchus keta

Alaska common names: Chum, chum salmon, dog, calico, silver salmon (bright fish in some locations in the Interior), silver bright.

Description: A medium-sized salmon with dark metallic-blue back, silvery sides, silver-white on the belly. Minute spotting on the back and dorsal fin. Spawning individuals display vertical bars of red, yellow, and black on the sides. Females may have a dark lateral band on the sides. Some fins have whitish tips. Males develop a hooked jaw with several protruding canine teeth. Flesh is orange.

Size: Average weight is six to 10 pounds, up to 20 pounds.

Meristics: Short, smooth gill rakers 16–28; vertebrae 59–71; pyloric cacae 140–249; lateral line scales 124–153; branchiostegal rays 12–16; dorsal fin 10–14 rays; tail fin 13–17 rays; pectoral fin 13–16 rays; pelvic fins 10–11.

Range: Cape Muzon (Southeast) to Point Hope (Northwest).

Run timing: Available May through December; peak July through September.

State record: 32 pounds, Caamano Point (Southeast), Fredrick Thynes, 1985.

Best lures: Flashy spoons—Pixee, Dardevle, Krocodile, Little Cleo. Spinners—Mepps, Vibrax, etc. Bright, attractor pattern flies in silver, gold, green, chartreuse, orange, and red.

Best waters: Coastal clear-water rivers and adjacent saltwater in Southeast, Southcentral, Southwest, Northwest, and Interior. Southeast: Behm Canal and Chilkat River. Southcentral: Susitna and Dog Salmon Rivers. Southwest: Nushagak, Alagnak, Lower Kuskokwim Bay tributaries, Anvik River. Northwest: Unalakleet, Noatak, and Kobuk Rivers. Interior: Tanana River tributaries, Salcha and Delta Rivers.

Cutthroat Trout

Oncorhynchus clarkii

Alaska common names: Coastal cutthroat, cutthroat trout, cut.

Description: True trout appearance. Sea-run forms have bright silver sides with steel-blue/green back, turning darker, more bronze in fresh water. Spotting is sparse and concentrated on the upper body. Residents range from silver to gold with olive backs and profuse spotting on the body and fins. Colors darken when spawning and some take on a violet hue. Both forms have characteristic blood red marking on inner folds of lower jaw, with upper jaw extending well beyond the posterior edge of the eye and small basibranchial teeth at the base of the tongue. Flesh is white to orange.

Size: Average length is 10 to 14 inches, up to 26 inches.

Meristics: Gill rakers 14–22; vertebrae 60–64; pyloric cacae 28–56; lateral line scales 115–235; branchiostegal rays 10–12; dorsal fin 8–13; anal fin

11–13 rays; pectoral fin 12–15 rays; pelvic fin 9–11 rays.

Range: Coastal rain forest from the Southern Alaskan border to Prince William Sound.

Run timing: Residents are available all year; sea-run cutthroat leave fresh water in spring and return in summer through fall. May and September are best.

State record: Eight pounds, six ounces, Wilson Lake (Southeast), Robert Denison, 1977.

Best lures: Red and yellow with gold blade Roostertail spinner (1/16 to one-quarter ounce); silver and gold Kastmaster spoon (1/12 to one-quarter ounce); chartreuse fleck, pumpkin seed, smoke (body colors) Foxee jigs (1/16 to one-quarter ounce); red or pink Pixee spoon (one-eighth ounce); flies: olive and brown leeches or Woolly Buggers (nos. 6 to 10), smolt patterns and Muddler minnows (nos. 6 to 8); haystack (nos. 10 to 12) Hare's Ear Nymph (nos. 10 to 12); Glo Bugs (nos. 6 to 8).

Best waters: Coastal streams, lakes, and ponds from Ketchikan to eastern Prince William Sound, especially lakes in southern Southeast. Southeast: Florence, Orchard, Wilson, Turner, and Hasselborg Lakes, and Naha, Karta, Kiklukh, and Kaliakh Rivers. Southcentral: Katalla and Martin River systems and Hawkins Island streams.

King Salmon

Oncorhynchus tshawytscha

Alaska common names: King, king salmon, chinook, chinook salmon, feeders (Southeast—immature salt water).

Description: The largest Pacific salmon. Purple-blue to black topsides, silver sides, silver-white belly. Irregular black markings on back and dorsal fins, and on entire caudal fins. Black gum line in lower jaw. Breeding males are dusky red, copper, or brown, with blackish shading, jaw elongated, teeth enlarged. Spawning females are less dramatic. Flesh is bright reddish-orange.

Size: Average weight is 18 pounds, to about 50 to 60 pounds or more. Length is 30 to 36 inches.

Meristics: Gill rakers 16–30; vertebrae 67–75; pyloric cacae 90–240; lateral line scales 130–165; branchiostegals 13–19; dorsal fin 10–14 rays; anal fin 13–19 rays; pectoral fin 14–17 rays; pelvic fin 10–11 rays.

Range: Coastal Southeast to Point Hope (Northwest); inland along major rivers—Yukon, Kuskokwim.

Run timing: Available May through July, with run peaks late June to mid-July, later to the north of the range; some systems into August. Immature fish (feeders) available year-round in salt water.

State/world record: 97 pounds, 4 ounces, Kenai River (Southcentral), 1985, Les Anderson.

Best lures: Large Spin-N-Glo, Vibrax, and Tee-spoon spinners; Magnum Tadpolly; no. 3/0 Flashabou, Alaskabou, or Fat Freddy streamer flies; also cut or whole herring and salmon eggs.

Best waters: Large coastal river systems and saltwater bays, straits, channels, and canals. Southeast: Situk River, Behm Canal, Icy/Clarence Straits, Favorite Channel, and Bucareli Bay. Southcentral: Kenai, Susitna, and Karluk Rivers. Southwest: Nushagak, Naknek, and Alagnak Rivers; Kuskokwim Bay streams. Northwest: Unalakleet, Shaktoolik, and Kwiniuk Rivers.

Lake Trout

Salvelinus namaycush

Alaska common names: Lake trout, laker.

Description: Large lake-dwelling charr.

Trout-like, with silver gray or brown back and sides and gold, yellow, or white oval spots and vermiculations. Bellies are cream-colored, with lower fins milky, yellow, or orange with white borders. Tail fins are deeply forked. Flesh is yellowish orange.

Size: Average weight is three to five pounds, up to 30 pounds or more.

Meristics: Gill rakers 16–26; vertebrae 61–69; pyloric cacae 92–210; lateral line scales 116–138; branchiostegal rays 10–14; dorsal fin 8–10 rays; anal fin 8–10 rays; pelvic fin 8–11 rays; pectoral fin 12–17 rays.

Range: Interior highland lakes, Chugach coastal range to the Arctic coastal plain.

Best times: Available year-round, with the peak in spring (May to June) and fall (August through September).

State record: 47 pounds, Clarence Lake (Southcentral), Daniel Thorsness, 1970.

Best lures: Spoons and spinners (Vibrax, Mepps, Krokodile, Dardevle, Hot Rod); also smolt, muddler, leech, and attractor pattern streamers.

Best waters: Deep, clear mountain lakes, especially in the Alaska and Brooks Ranges, Southcentral to Arctic. Southcentral: Lake Louise/Susitna and Crosswind and Paxson Lakes. Southwest: Lake Clark, Tikchik Lakes, and Lakes Colville-Grosvenor. Northwest: Walker, Feniak, and Selby-Narvak Lakes. Arctic: Schrader-Peter, Elusive, and Chandler Lakes. Interior: Tangle Lakes and Glacier Lake.

Northern Pike

Esox lucius (linnaeus)

Alaska common names: Pike, northern pike, jackfish, pickerel.

Description: A long, predatory salmonid, with elongated snout and prominent teeth. Green to greenish-gray or brown back and sides, with numerous white or yellow oval markings and yellow or white belly. Flesh is white.

Size: Average four to seven pounds, up to 30 pounds and 50 inches or more.

Meristics: Vertebrae 57–65; no pyloric cacae; lateral line scales 105–150; branchiostegal rays 14–16 each side; dorsal fin 15–25 rays; anal fin 12–22 rays; pectoral fin 14–17 rays; pelvic fin 10–11 rays.

Range: Northern Southeast to the Arctic Slope.

Best times: Available year-round, with the peak from spring (May to June) through fall (October).

State record: 38 pounds, Innoko River (Southwest), Jack Wagner, 1991.

Best lures: Krocodile, Dardevle, Silver Minnow, Red-Eye spoons; Marabou jigs, soft baits, plugs, and crankbaits—Mr. Twister, Rapala, Flatfish, Jensen minnow, etc.; also large, bushy bait and attractor pattern streamers. Effective bait: whole or strip herring and whitefish.

Best waters: Flatland sloughs and lakes, especially in Interior, Southwest, and Northwest. Southwest: Lower Innoko and Holitna River systems. Northwest: Lower Selawik, Noatak, and Kobuk Rivers, and Imuruk basin drainages in the Seward Peninsula. Interior: Minto and Yukon Flats, lower Koyukuk, Tanana, and Nowitna River drainages. Southcentral: Susitna River Valley lakes.

Pacific Halibut

Hippoglossus stenolepis

Alaska common names: Halibut, flattie.

Description: Large flatfish; dark or dirty brown, with irregular blotches on topside; white or yellowish white on bottom. Somewhat elongated body and small scales. The lateral line extends from head to tail, curving over the pectoral fin. Teeth on both sides of the jaw. Flesh is white.

Size: Average 15 to 60 pounds, up to 550 pounds and 100 inches.

Meristics: Vertebrae 49–51; scales cycloid, about 150 along lateral line; dorsal fin 90–106 rays; anal fin 69–80 rays; pectoral fin 19 rays; pelvic fin six rays.

Range: Cape Muzon (Southeast) to Bering Strait (Northwest).

Run timing: Available year-round; peak May to September.

State record: 459 pounds, Unalaska Bay (Southwest), 1996.

Best lures: Bait—herring, smelt, salmon head. Large jigs (Krocodile, Sebastes, Vi-Ke, Yohoho), preferably fish imitations.

Best waters: Gravel or sand bottom structure off beaches, around points and islands, and shoals in 30 to 150 feet of water, in Southeast, Southcentral, Southwest, and Northwest. Southeast: Icy/Clarence Strait, Sitka Sound, Gulf of Esquibel, and Yakutat Bay. Southcentral: Lower Cook Inlet, Resurrection Bay, Montague Island, Valdez Arm, and Chiniak Bay. Southwest: Dutch Harbor.

Pink Salmon
Oncorhynchus gorbuscha

Alaska common names: Pink, pink salmon, humpy, humpback salmon.

Description: A small salmon with steel-blue to bluish-green head and back, iridescent silver sides, and whitish belly when sea-bright, and oval black markings on back and tail fin. Spawning individuals are dirty brown on back; sides yellowish-green with slight vertical markings. Males develop distinctive humped back, jaw kype, and prominent teeth. Flesh is pink.

Size: Average weight two to five pounds, up to 10 pounds or more; length is 16 to 22 inches.

Meristics: Gill rakers 24–35; vertebrae 63–72; pyloric cacae 95–224; lateral line scales 145–208; branchiostegal rays 9–15; dorsal fin 10–15 rays; tail fin 13–20 rays; pectoral fin 14–17 rays; anal fin 13–19 rays; pelvic fin 9–11 rays.

Range: Cape Muzon (Southeast) to Point Hope (Northwest).

Run timing: Available June through October; peak July through August.

State record: 12 pounds, 9 ounces, Moose River (Southcentral), Steven Lee, 1974.

Best lures: Small spinners (Mepps, Vibrax, Panther Martin) and spoons (Pixee, Krocodile, Little Cleo) in red, orange, green, chartreuse, and silver; also small attractor or egg pattern flies.

Best waters: Lower sections of clearwater coastal rivers and streams, also adjacent salt water. Southeast to Northwest. Southeast: Wolverine, Anan, and Cowee Creeks and Situk River. Southcentral: Kenai, Karluk, and Susitna (tributary) Rivers. Southwest: Alagnak, Nushagak, and Anvik Rivers. Northwest: Unalakleet and Noatak Rivers. Arctic: Colville River system.

Rainbow/Steelhead Trout
Oncorhynchus mykiss

Alaska common names: Rainbow trout, rainbow, 'bow, 'rainer, steelhead, steelie, metalhead.

Description: A sleek, small to medium-sized salmonid; with greenish or gray topsides in resident forms, silver-gray to steel-blue in lake resident and sea-run fish. Silvery sides with trademark pink or scarlet band along the lateral line in river resident forms, faint or missing in lake resident and sea-run rainbows. Spotted top, sides, and tail fin with whitish belly. Tail is slightly forked or square in large individuals. Flesh is pink.

Size: Average two to three pounds for river resident fish; three to five or more for lake resident and sea-run forms; up to 15 pounds or more.

Meristics: Gill rakers long 15–22; vertebrae 60–66; pyloric cacae 27–80; lateral line scales 100–155; branchiostegal rays 8–13; dorsal fin 10–12 rays; tail fin 8–12 rays; anal fin 8–2 rays; pectoral fin 11–17 rays.

Range: Coastal Southeast to Kuskokwim Bay (Southwest).

Run timing: Resident forms are available year-round; the peak for both sea-run and resident is in spring (April to June) and fall (September to November).

State/world record: 42 pounds, 3 ounces, Bell Island (Behm Canal—Southeast), David White, 1970.

Best lures: Vibrax and Mepps spinners; Pixee and Hot Rod spoons; Spin-N-Glo and Li'l Corkie drift bobbers; Hot Shot and Tadpolly plugs; smolt, leech, sculpin, egg/flesh, and attractor pattern flies and streamers.

Best waters: Clear, swift coastal streams and lake and river systems, especially Southeast and Southwest. Southeast: Situk, Karta, Klawock, and Thorne Rivers. Southcentral: Kenai, Anchor, and Karluk Rivers. Southwest: Naknek, Iliamna, and Tikchik Lake systems. Interior: Quartz and Birch Lakes and Piledriver Slough.

Sheefish
Stenodus leucichthys

Alaska common names: Sheefish, shee, inconnu, cony, Eskimo tarpon, Arctic tarpon.

Description: A large, slender, silvery whitefish with a strong projecting lower jaw. Dorsal body surface is a darker color—metallic-green, blue, or light brown. Dorsal and tail fins are dusky; other fins are clear. No spots are present. Both sexes are alike, but larger sized fish are always female. No coloration differences exist and tubercles are not present at spawning time. Mouths are toothless and fin rays do not possess spines. Flesh is white.

Size: Up to 12 pounds for nonanadromous populations; up to 25 pounds or more for anadromous populations.

Meristics: Gill rakers 17–24; vertebrae 63–69; lateral line scales 90–115; dorsal fin 11–19 rays; pectoral fin 14–17 rays; anal fin 14–19 rays; pelvic fin 11–12 rays; head length is 30 percent of body length.

Range: Only in Yukon and Kuskokwim Rivers and their tributaries and Kobuk and Selawik Rivers. Introduced into lakes in Interior Alaska. Not found south of the Alaska Range or 60 degrees north latitude.

Best times: Available year-round with peak from breakup to freeze-up (May to October) throughout most of its range.

State record: 53 pounds, Pah River (Northwest), Lawrence Hudnall, 1986.

Best lures: Pixee, Dardevle, Krocodile, Doctor spoons. Flies—large smolt and other forage imitation streamers, attractors, saltwater patterns (Deceiver, Clouser Minnow, etc.), large tube flies.

Best waters: Kobuk and Selawik Rivers, Selawik Lake, and Hotham Inlet; and Yukon River tributaries including the Rodo, Innoko, Yuki, Melozitna, Nowitna, Koyukuk, Dall, Ray, Porcupine, Kandik, Nation, Seventymile, Chena, Tolovana, and Chatanika Rivers and Hess and Goldstream Creeks. Also Kuskokwim River tributaries including the Aniak, George, Holitna, Tatlawiksuk, Takotna, and Middle Fork Rivers.

Silver Salmon
Oncorhynchus kisutch

Alaska common names: Silver, silver salmon, coho, coho salmon.

Description: A medium-sized to large salmon, with steel-blue/green back, brilliant silver sides, and white belly in sea-bright individuals. Similar in appearance to small king salmon, but less robust, with irregular black spots across the back and the upper lobe of the caudal fin (none on the lower lobe) and no dark pigment along the gum line of the lower jaw. Breeding fish are duskier, with green on backs, blackish heads, and red/maroon sides. Males have prominent curved jaw kype. Flesh is reddish orange.

Size: Average six to eight pounds, up to 20 pounds or more.

Meristics: Gill rakers 18–25; vertebrae 61–69; pyloric cacae 45–114; lateral line scales 112–148; branchiostegal rays 11–15; dorsal fin 9–13 rays; tail fin 12–17 rays; pectoral fin 13–16 rays; pelvic fin 9–11 rays.

Range: Coastal Southeast to Point Hope (Northwest, intermittent in northern end of range). Also Yukon and Kuskokwim River drainages in Interior.

Run timing: Available late July through November; peak months are August to October throughout most of range.

State record: 26 pounds, Icy Strait (Southeast), Andrew Robbins, 1976.

Best lures: Nos. 4 to 6 Vibrax spinners; seven-eighths-ounce Pixee spoon; Hot Shot plugs; Spin-N-Glo; flies—Flash fly, Coho fly, Egg-Sucking Leech; bait—salmon eggs, plug-cut or whole herring.

Best waters: Coastal streams and adjacent salt water, especially northern Southeast, Kodiak, Alaska Peninsula and Kuskokwim Bay. Southeast: Klawock, Thorne, Situk, Italio Rivers and McDonald Lake system, Icy Strait, Bucareli Bay, and Behm Canal/Clarence Strait. Southcentral: Pasagshak, Karluk, Susitna, and Kenai Rivers; Resurrection Bay. Southwest: Naknek, Togiak, and Nushagak River systems; Kuskokwim Bay streams. Northwest: Unalakleet, Shaktoolik, and Fish-Niukluk Rivers. Interior: Tanana and Nenana Rivers and clear-water tributaries (such as Delta Clearwater River and Clear Creek).

Sockeye Salmon
Oncorhynchus nerka

Alaska common names: Red, red salmon, sockeye, sockeye salmon.

Description: A medium-sized salmon with a steel-blue/green back and top of head, iridescent silver sides, and whitish belly when fresh from the sea. No prominent markings on the back or tailfins. Spawning individuals turn bright red with greenish black heads, jaw kype, and humped backs in males. Females are smaller and less brilliant. Flesh is bright red.

Size: Average weight five to six pounds, up to 12 pounds or more; length is 22 to 28 inches.

Meristics: Gill rakers 30–40 long, serrated first arch; vertebrae 56–67; pyloric caeca 45–115; lateral line scales 120–150; branchiostegals 11–16; dorsal fin 11–16 rays; anal fin 13–18 rays; pectoral fin 11–21 rays; pelvic fin 9–11 rays.

Range: Southeast to Point Hope (Northwest) coastal streams.

Run timing: Available June through August throughout most of range; peak late June to mid-July.

State record: 16 pounds, Kenai River (Southcentral), Chuck Leach, 1974.

Best lures: Sparse bucktail streamers—Russian River Fly, Comet, Brassie, etc.; Yarn Fly, Sockeye Willie.

Best waters: Coastal freshwater lake and river systems, especially Southwest to Southeast; in Southeast, also in adjacent salt water. Southcentral: Russian, Kenai, and Karluk Rivers. Southwest: Kvichak, Brooks, and Alagnak Rivers. Southeast: Thoms Creek, McDonald Lake, and Karta and Situk Rivers.

Fly Patterns For Alaska

by Steve Wottlin, René Limeres, Bob Maker, Matt Potter,
Gunnar Pederson, and others
Illustrations by Mark Whitfield and William Hickman

A dozen basic patterns take approximately 90 percent of the fish caught on flies in Alaska. No rules exist as far as how these individual patterns should be tied as the design, materials, colors, hooks, and other factors vary among different anglers and locations. It's far better to understand the generic groups these patterns belong to—what they represent (more or less), why they are effective, and when and how to use them—than to try and memorize the bewildering number and variety of flies used in Alaska.

Forage imitations are the most effective patterns over a wide range of conditions because they mimic important prey species, such as sculpins, smolts, and leeches. In a strict sense, this group also includes nymphs, egg patterns, and dry flies. Fish these patterns deep— cross current, up or downstream, with a lively strip.

Egg/flesh patterns are flies and streamers tied in colors and shapes to imitate salmon roe on flesh. They're extremely effective in Alaska, especially late in the season when the rivers are pumped full of spawning salmon, and all resident species (such as trout, charr, and grayling) are keyed into feeding on loose, drifting roe and the flesh of spawned-out fish. They're best fished on a deep drift or with a very slight strip.

Attractors are a broad, catch-all group of flies that trigger instinctual, aggressive responses in salmon and trout with their bright colors and tantalizing action. Like forage imitations, they can be effective nearly any time and place, and should be fished similarly—deep, with lively action.

Dry flies should be included in every Alaska angler's fly box, and their appeal is well known and obvious. Though most of the fishing done for the important sport species in Alaska involves sinking presentations, certain conditions call for dry flies; these are outlined in the species chapters in the beginning of this book. (In particular, see the silver salmon, rainbow trout, and grayling chapters beginning on pages 39, 97, and 127 respectively.) All dry flies should be fished with floating line and long leaders, although the techniques used for Alaska can depart considerably from classic trout tactics elsewhere.

"Specialty patterns" is an arbitrary grouping used to describe patterns created for a unique set of conditions or species. These can include streamers and flies that work with either forage, egg, or attractor appeal or a combination of all three. (The Alaskabou is a perfect example.) Many are gaudy and overstated but extremely potent in stimulating a strike response.

Use the patterns listed below only as guidelines. Learn the feeding habits and behavior of your favorite species, then experiment and create your own "classics" that are just as effective, less expensive, and infinitely more satisfying to use. We've included some specialty patterns and even a few proven favorites of our own. What follows are the basics—don't leave home without 'em:

(Unless otherwise noted, thread color is black.)

Forage Imitations

MUDDLER MINNOW

Species: Charr, chum salmon, cutthroat trout, king salmon, lake trout, rainbow trout, sheefish, silver salmon

Hook: Size 2–8 Streamer

Body: Flat gold tinsel

Tail: Mottle brown turkey quill strip

Head: Spun deer hair, some left unclipped to form hackle

Wing: Brown turkey quill sections over gray squirrel tail

Description: A North American classic, effective in Alaska for rainbows, charr, grayling, and salmon. Olive, black, brown, and yellow are the most popular colors used. Many variations are possible: marabou, especially white or yellow, can be used as a wing before spinning deer hair (for the famous Marabou Muddler); gold tinsel chenille or other colors can be used on the body, and the tail can be dressed up with bright red hackle.

KATMAI SMOLT

Species: Charr, cutthroat trout, lake trout, rainbow trout, sheefish

Hook: Size 2–8 Streamer or Salmon/Steelhead Wet

Body: Light green floss

Butt: Peacock herl

Rib: Peacock herl

Tail: Green hackle or floss

Wing: Green over white bucktail

Throat: Mixed red and blue hackle

Cheeks: Jungle cock or imitation

Description: One of the more complicated smolt patterns, but very effective, developed especially for Alaska by Dan Flanders. A fantastic, early season fly for rainbows and charr during smolt outmigrations.

WOOLLY BUGGER

Species: Charr, cutthroat trout, grayling, king salmon, lake trout, northern pike, rainbow trout, sheefish, silver salmon

Hook: Size 2–8 Streamer, long shank

Body: Chenille, with palmered hackle

Tail: Marabou

Wing: None

Description: A very versatile and popular pattern in Alaska, used mainly for rainbow/steelhead, but also for charr and salmon. The palmered hackle and marabou give it irresistible action, mimicking the movement of a leech, a universal forage species. This fly can be tied in a variety of colors, but purple, black, brown, and olive are used most often in Alaska. Tail, body, and hackle colors can be mixed.

BUNNY FLY

Species: Charr, chum salmon, cutthroat trout, king salmon, lake trout, northern pike, rainbow trout, sheefish, silver salmon

Hook: Size 1/0–6 Streamer, long shank

Body: Rabbit fur strip in ginger, gray, purple, brown, black

Tail: Rabbit fur strip tied long enough to wrap body

Wing: None

Description: A classic Alaskan pattern used heavily for rainbows as a flesh pattern, tied in gray or ginger; or in darker colors, as a forage imitation, mimicking a leech or sculpin to attract a variety of species.

ALEVIN/FRY

Species: Charr, cutthroat trout, grayling, lake trout, rainbow trout

Hook: Size 2–10 Nymph/Streamer Hook, long

Body: Flat tinsel, tinsel chenille, or mylar

Tail: Sparse black hackle

Wing: None

Throat: Red marabou, sparse

Eyes: Small silver bead or painted

Description: A very effective spring and early summer pattern, when rainbows, charr, and cutthroat are feeding on young salmon. Tie it small and sparse for alevin (newly hatched salmon) imitations, larger and dressier for a fry pattern.

EGG-SUCKING LEECH

Species: Charr, cutthroat trout, king salmon, lake trout, northern pike, rainbow trout, sheefish, silver salmon

Hook: Size 2–8 Streamer or Salmon/Steelhead Wet

Body: Purple chenille, with palmered purple hackle

Tail: Purple marabou

Head: Pink chenille tied to resemble egg

Description: Along with Polar Shrimp and Marabou Muddler, one of the all-purpose patterns that should be part of every fly fisher's Alaska survival kit. It's hard to categorize its appeal—is it a forage, egg pattern, or attractor? Whatever it is, all Alaskan fish, from pike to rainbows, find it irresistible. Other popular variations use sparkle chenille in the body and Krystal Flash in the tail, or black marabou and bright red chenille in the body and head.

Egg/Flesh Patterns

GLO BUG

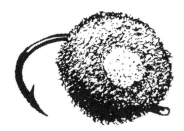

Species: Charr, cutthroat trout, grayling, rainbow trout, sheefish

Hook: Size 2–10 Egg or Glo-Bug Hook

Body: Glo Bug yarn in peach, orange, red, pink

Tail: None

Wing: None

Description: One of the most-fished flies in Alaska, the Glo Bug can be tied in a variety of colors. Because of the food source it so closely imitates, it is extremely effective for rainbow trout and charr, when fished on a dead drift, just like loose spawn.

TWO-EGG SPERM FLY

Species: Charr, cutthroat trout, grayling, rainbow trout, sheefish

Hook: Size 2–8 Salmon Steelhead Wet or Streamer

Body: Tinsel rib over orange or pink chenille (or yarn)

Tail: White bucktail or hackle

Wing: Orange hackle wrapped over white marabou

Description: A very popular and effective egg/flesh fly for rainbow trout and charr, best fished on a dead drift.

Attractors

POLAR SHRIMP

Species: Charr, chum salmon, cutthroat trout, king salmon, pink salmon, rainbow trout, sheefish, silver salmon

Hook: Size 1/0–8 Salmon/Steelhead Wet

Body: Fluorescent orange chenille

Tail: Orange or red hackle

Wing: White bucktail, calf, or fishhair

Description: The standard Northwest steelhead pattern for many years, and an excellent all-around fly for Alaska's rainbow/steelhead, charr, and salmon. Try a larger version (up to 3/0) for king salmon.

COHO (Russian River)

Species: Charr, red salmon, sheefish, silver salmon

Hook: Size 4 Streamer, long shank

Body: None

Tail: None

Wing: Sparse, bright bucktail, two or more colors

Description: A sparsely tied streamer fly that has become the standard for sockeye salmon on the Kenai River and elsewhere. Red over white is the most common combination, but only one of many possibilities. Try others, such as red over orange, red over yellow, green over yellow, and purple over pink. Fishair can be substituted for bucktail.

COHO

Species: King, silver, chum salmon; charr, rainbow trout/steelhead

Hook: Size 2–4, Mustad 36890 or 9672

Body: Silver mylar tubing

Tail: Unwound tubing from body

Wing: Bucktail, three colors (i.e., red, orange, white) wound over

Many variations of this classic streamer

are used to take salmon. In its simplest form, it's the classic bucktail wing streamer, useful for nearly all Alaskan game species. Try different colors—purple/pink/white; pink/black/white; red/orange/yellow; chartreuse/green/yellow; etc.

COMET

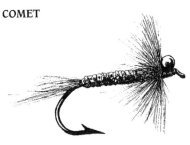

Species: Charr, chum salmon, cutthroat trout, king salmon, pink salmon, rainbow trout, red salmon, sheefish, silver salmon

Hook: Size 1/0–8 Streamer and Wet Fly

Body: Gold tinsel (oval) or gold mylar

Tail: Orange hackle or bucktail

Wing: Hackle, orange and yellow mixed

Eyes: Gold bead chain

Description: Another classic pattern that works well for all species of salmon in Alaska, especially sockeye. It's got good attractor color and a design that allows it to sink and stay deep where the fish are. Try different colors like chartreuse and pink.

FLASH FLY

Species: Charr, chum salmon, cutthroat trout, king salmon, lake trout, northern pike, pink salmon, rainbow trout, red salmon, sheefish, silver salmon

Hook: Size 1/0–8 Steelhead/Salmon

Body: Wrapped silver tinsel or mylar

Tail: Silver tinsel

Wing: Bright hackle (red, orange, purple) over tinsel

Description: Another classic Alaska attractor pattern for salmon, particularly silvers, which combines a heavy dose of flash and bright color for broad appeal.

ALASKABOU

Species: Charr, chum salmon, king salmon, lake trout, northern pike, rainbow trout, sheefish, silver salmon

Hook: Size: 3/0–6 Salmon/Steelhead Wet or Streamer, forged

Body: None

Tail: None

Thread: Fluorescent orange

Wing: Hackle over dense layers of bright marabou, Flashabou, or Krystal Flash in colors of pink, chartreuse, purple, or cerise, with optional strands of tinsel or peacock herl

Description: A popular, gaudy pattern that's deadly on Alaska's salmon, particularly kings and silvers. It's usually tied in colors of red, purple, pink, and white, but many effective variations are possible. Smaller sizes are good for rainbows, charr, and other salmon.

Nymphs and Dry Flies

GOLD-RIBBED HARE'S EAR

Species: Charr, cutthroat trout, grayling, rainbow trout

Hook: Size 10–16 Wet Fly and Nymph Hook

Body: Hare's mask fur, dubbed with guard hairs included

Rib: Gold wire

Thorax: Dubbed fur including guard hairs

Tail: Guard hairs from hare's mask

Wing case: Mottle brown turkey feather tied in over thorax

Description: A versatile nymph pattern for Alaska, good in a variety of conditions for trout, charr, and grayling.

ELK HAIR CADDIS

Species: Charr, cutthroat trout, grayling, rainbow trout, silver salmon

Hook: Size 10–16 Dry Fly

Body: Dubbed olive poly yarn, with brown palmered hackle

Tail: Elk body hair

Wing: Elk body hair

Description: One of Alaska's most versatile, all-purpose dries, good for rainbows, charr, cutthroat, grayling, and even (occasionally) salmon.

BLACK GNAT

Species: Cutthroat trout, grayling, rainbow trout

Hook: Size 10–18 Dry Fly

Body: Black fur, chenille, or floss

Wing: Barred black mallard or similar

Hackle: Black

Description: The Black Gnat is another classic dry fly pattern that is useful for a wide variety of surface-feeding conditions. Keep some in your fly box—always!

ADAMS

Species: Charr, grayling, rainbow trout

Hook: Size 10–18 Dry Fly

Body: Dubbed fur

Tail: Mixed gray hackle

Wing: Grizzled hackle tips

Hackle: Mixed gray and brown hackle

Description: A standard dry fly pattern used throughout the world, and a popular fly in Alaska for grayling and rainbows.

Specialty Flies, Saltwater Patterns, and Others

MOUSE

Species: Charr, lake trout, northern pike, rainbow trout, sheefish, silver salmon

Hook: Size 2–4 Dry Fly long or Nymph/Streamer

Body: Spun deer hair trimmed to shape of mouse

Tail: Deer hair or leather

Description: Alaska's most famous dry fly for rainbows and charr, the Mouse is most effective when fished along stream margins, lake shores, and under cutbanks, especially where vole and shrew populations are abundant.

THE GAY BLADE, A.K.A. "THE ALMIGHTY ONE"

Species: Salmon, rainbow trout, charr

Hook: Size 2/0–4, Daichi 2441

Tail: No. 1 Colorado Spinner blade and split ring on twisted stainless wire

Wing: Cerise Marabou, Krystal Flash, and Flashabou over Orange Marabou

Hackle: Purple Schlappen heavy

Thread: Orange Danville Plus

Description: The quintessential "spinner fly" created by Matt Potter of the Kingfisher Fly Shop, Missoula, Montana (see address in the Resource appendix on page 409). Deadly trolled or fished with a fast strip, the Gay Blade will enrage salmon, trout, and charr like nothing else, especially in late summer.

PINK POLLYWOG

Species: Silver and chum salmon, charr, rainbow trout, northern pike

Hook: Nos. 2/0–3/0 Mustad 3369 or W3369A

Body: Spun pink or cerise deer hair, trimmed to shape

Tail: Cerise or pink marabou with like color crystal flash

Description: The pollywog is a great top-water pattern for eliciting smashing strikes from salmon, trout, and charr. Fish it fast and erratically for best results.

SOCKEYE WILLIE

Species: Charr, chum salmon, cutthroat trout, rainbow trout, red salmon, silver salmon

Hook: Size 2–4 Streamer Fly

Body: Pearl mylar over fluorescent chartreuse or orange yarn

Wing: Two colors bucktail, chartreuse/white (blue), orange/white

Tail: Fluorescent yarn with unraveled strands of mylar

Thread: Fluorescent orange

Description: A specialty pattern created by Willie Morris for (what else?) the notoriously tight-lipped sockeye salmon of Bristol Bay. It's fast becoming one of the standards for the Kvichak drainage (including Alagnak) and elsewhere. Tie it weighted with lead wire for best results fishing deep.

GREEN BUTT SKUNK

Species: Charr, cutthroat trout, rainbow trout, sheefish

Hook: Size 2–6 Wet Fly or Salmon/Steelhead

Body: Black chenille with fluorescent green or chartreuse butt section

Tail: Red hackle

Ribbing: Flat silver tinsel

Wing: White bucktail

Hackle: Black

Description: One of the standard Northwest steelhead patterns, equally effective on Alaska's wild, sea-run rainbows.

FAT FREDDY

Species: Charr, king salmon, rainbow trout, silver salmon

Hook: 1/0 Mustad 36890 Salmon Fly

Body: Glo Bug yarn wrapped abundantly—orange, pink, peach, or chartreuse

Wing: White marabou, strands of silver tinsel/Flashabou

Description: A standard king salmon fly that imitates a giant glob of roe. Fished on a dead drift, the Fat Freddy will also take silver salmon, charr, and rainbows.

OUTRAGEOUS

Species: Charr, chum salmon, king salmon, northern pike, rainbow trout, sheefish, silver salmon

Hook: Size 1/0–4 Mustad 3407 or Tiemco 800S

Body: None

Tail: Paired saddle hackles (red, orange or pink) extending well beyond bend of hook

Wing: Hackle wound over abundant marabou (pink, red, purple, or yellow), tied a half hook down from eye; a few strands of tinsel, Flashabou (blue or purple), or peacock herl optional

Thread: Red or hot orange nylon wound down throat, Tarpon-fly style

Description: The Outrageous is another "super attractor" designed to spark a strike response in salmon, trout, and other species when all else fails. This Tarpon fly variation can be tied in a wide range of colors and materials, and is very effective on king and silver salmon and rainbow trout, especially in turbid conditions. Fish it deep, with a lively strip.

MATUKA

Species: Charr, cutthroat trout, rainbow trout, sheefish, silver salmon

Hook: Size 2–8 Salmon/Steelhead Wet or Streamer

Body: Black, brown, or purple wool

Wing: Hackle, tied "fixed wing" style

Ribbing: Flat, silver, or gold tinsel

Hackle: Neck hackle in black, brown, or purple

Description: The classic New Zealand trout pattern, proven on North America's waters under all conditions, and a standard for Alaska rainbows. Fish it deep, like you would a leech or sculpin pattern, with lively but varied strips. It can be tied weighted to improve sinking characteristics.

HERRING FLY

Species: Chum salmon, king salmon, northern pike, sheefish, silver salmon

Hook: Double tie, size 5/0 and 4/0 Bait Hook (Gamakatsu or Mustad)

Body: White Pearlescent Krystal or cactus chenille

Throat: Red hackle

Wing: Silver Krystal Flash over layers of green, blue then white bucktail, topped with five strands peacock herl; all wing and tail materials tied to just past trailing hook

Tail: Silver Krystal Flash

Head: Optional, painted white or red eye with black pupil

Description: A very important fly for saltwater salmon fishing, also effective in tidal waters and lower river mouths. It can be tied in a variety of color combinations (such as purple/pink/white and red/orange/white).

CLOUSER MINNOW

Hook: Nos. 3/0–2, Mustad 3407 or 34007

Eyes: Large, nickel plated lead

Wing: Long white/chartreuse bucktail over sparse, silver Flashabou strands

Thread: Heavy wrapped white Danville

Description: A very versatile, popular saltwater streamer that has made its way into Alaska anglers' fly boxes for its surefire results on all salmon species, rainbows, and charr. Hottest colors for Alaska include white/chartreuse, white/red, red/orange, and purple/cerise.

ALASKA CANDLEFISH

Hook: Nos. 1/0–2, Mustad 34007

Body: Flat silver tinsel

Ribbing: Oval silver tinsel

Wing: Blue over chartreuse and white bucktail with sparse red bucktail for sides

Thread: Black Danville

Description: A good salmon pattern for salt water, estuaries, and lower rivers. Try the Candlefish on rainbows and charr as well.

D.P. KINGILLER

Species: Charr, chum salmon, king salmon, lake trout, rainbow trout, silver salmon

Hook: Size 1/0–3/0 English Bait Hook or Eagle Claw Kahle Horizontal (with upturned eye)

Body: Sparkle Chenille

Tail/Back Overlay: Pearlescent Flashabou

Wing: None

Eyes: Plastic beads extended from a half inch of 30-pound mono

Description: A sparkle shrimp with a twist, the D.P. Kingiller effectively mimics an important forage species for salmon, with proven results in the lower rivers and tidal waters of Southcentral Alaska. The most popular colors are chartreuse, cerise, and pink. Here's the procedure: Tie the tail and body material in, wrap the body, then bring the excess tail material forward and wrap it with thread as ribbing. Tie in a piece of mono, thread the bead, and then melt the protruding end down to the bead and snub.

MAKER'S ROGUE

Species: Charr, chum salmon, king salmon, rainbow trout, silver salmon

Hook: Size 1/0 Mustad 36890 (Streamer Fly)

Body: Pink Flash Chenille with palmered red hackle

Tail: Abundant white marabou

Wing: Gold or orange Krystal Flash

Description: This is a very successful fly for all salmon, especially kings, but it will also take rainbows and charr. Fish it on a drift, with sinking line and short leaders.

BLACK FURY

Species: Charr, grayling, rainbow trout

Hook: Size 1/0–8 Salmon/Steelhead Wet or Streamer Fly

Body: Black silk floss with flat silver tinsel ribbing

Tail: Red hackle

Wing: Bright red bucktail over black marabou

Throat: Red hackle

Description: A "most killing fly" for trophy charr and rainbow, proven on the incomparable rivers of western Alaska.

Resources

Statewide Information

For information on sportfishing resources in Alaska:

Alaska Department of Fish and Game
P.O. Box 25526
Juneau, AK 99802-5526
(907) 465-4112,
(907) 465-3088 (fax)

For information on state and national parks, refuges, and forests:

Alaska Public Lands
Information Center
605 West Fourth Avenue, Suite 105
Anchorage, AK 99501-5162
(907) 271-2737

For information on fisheries on undesignated federal land and Wild and Scenic Rivers, and cabin rentals:

Bureau of Land Management
222 West Seventh Avenue, Box 13
Anchorage, AK 99513
(907) 271-5960

For specific information on Alaska's national forests, including fishing resources and cabin rentals:

U.S. Forest Service
Information Center
Centennial Hall
101 Egan Drive
Juneau, AK 99801
(907) 586-8751

Maps

For a reference map with all Alaska state record fish locations, best rivers, species, Alaska fish facts, state/world records list (all tackle and line class):

RJ Publishing
5140 East 104th Avenue
Anchorage, AK 99516
(907) 346-2193
(Include $5)

For "Alaska Atlas and Gazetteer," a handy atlas of topographic maps and information on the entire state:

DeLorme Maps
P.O. Box 298-7000
Freeport, ME 04032
(800) 227-1656, ext. 7000
(Include $19.95 and $5 postage/handling)

For Alaska maps (including USGS and NOAA Nautical and Aeronautical):

The Maps Place
113 West Northern Lights Boulevard
Anchorage, AK 99503-2601
(907) 243-6277

For U.S. Geological Survey maps of Alaska by mail:

USGS Map Distribution
P.O. Box 25286, Building 810
Federal Center
Denver, CO 80255

or

USGS Earth Science
Information Center
101 12th Avenue, Box 12
Fairbanks, AK 99701

For over-the-counter purchase of U.S. Geological Survey maps:

U.S. Geological Survey
4230 University Drive, Room 101
Anchorage, AK

or

U.S. Geological Survey
New Federal Building
101 12th Avenue
Fairbanks, AK

Organizations

For an international organization devoted to promoting the sport of gamefishing, knowledge of species and preservation, and maintaining information on record fish:

International Game Fish Association
1301 East Atlantic Boulevard
Pompano Beach, FL 33060
(305)941-3474,
(305) 941-5868 (fax)

For America's leading nonprofit cold-water fisheries conservation organization, with more than 400 local chapters:

Trout Unlimited
Membership Department
800 Follin Lane Southeast, Suite 250
Vienna, VA 22180
(703) 281-1100
($25 annual membership, includes a one-year subscription to *Trout Magazine*)

Publications

For useful trip planning information, with local information and addresses, send for the free "Alaska Vacation Planner" from:

Alaska Division of Tourism
P.O. Box E, Juneau, AK 99811-0800
(907) 465-2010

For The Highway Angler, *the most comprehensive guide to fishing Alaska's roadside waters, with information on more than 460 locations:*

Alaska Viking Press
P.O. Box 90557
Anchorage, AK 99509
(Include $19.95 and $4 postage/handling)

For "Fly Patterns of Alaska," a color desktop reference of Alaska fly patterns:

Frank Amato Publications
P.O. Box 82112
Portland, Oregon 97282
(503) 653-8108
(Include $19.95 and $3 postage/handling)

For The Milepost, *a useful guidebook and trip planner (updated annually) listing all roadside attractions along roads and ferries within, to, and from Alaska, including fishing:*

Vernon Publications, Inc.
3000 Northup Way #200
Bellevue, WA, 98004-1446
(800) 726-4707
(Include $21.95 and $6 first-class postage/handling)

Services

For statewide rentals of rafts, catamarans, and kayaks:

"SOTAR" Boats: Alaska Wildwater
P.O. Box 110615
Anchorage, AK 99511
(907) 344-8005

or

"AIRE" Boats: Wild Alaska Rivers
1840 International Airport Road
Anchorage, AK 99502
(907) 344-9453

For a complete catalog of Alaskan fly patterns available through mail order:

The Kingfisher
P.O. Box 3627
Missoula, MT 59802
(406) 542-3347,
(406) 543-6232 (fax)

For Alaska's premier fly shop:

Rod and Reel
701 West 36th Avenue
Anchorage, AK 99503
(907) 561-0662

Salmon-Steelhead Life Cycle Glossary

Alevin: newly hatched fish with yolk sac still attached

Fry: juvenile fish about one inch long

Parr: juvenile fish larger than fry but smaller than smolt

Smolt: fish preparing to migrate to sea, usually two to five inches long

Buck/Cock: a sexually mature male fish

Hen: a sexually mature female fish

Jack: precocious, sexually mature male fish

Kelt: steelhead that has spawned and is out-migrating

Milt: salmon sperm

Redd: large nest excavated in gravel by female

Roe: salmon eggs

Guides' Tips for Salmon Fishing

As high-seas predators, adult salmon spend most of their lives responding to stimuli associated with the all-powerful drive to track down and consume prey (small fish, crustaceans, squid, and other marine life). Among these, the most important are movement, color, scent/taste, and vibration. Successful angling strategies in salt water and to a lesser extent freshwater, exploit one or more of these cues to prompt a strike response. Here are suggestions for fishing all salmon species:

- **Get Them While They're Fresh and Bright:** All Pacific salmon undergo rapid physical changes once they enter freshwater. Their bright silver flanks fade, they lose their hard fighting edge, and their behavior becomes unpredictable after only a short time in rivers; because of this, it's advantageous to fish them as close to the salt as possible (ideally within 30 miles or so).

- **Use Sturdy Gear:** All salmon fight unbelievably hard, unlike any other fish. Use only the highest-quality heavy duty tackle you can find and never rig light for them, no matter how strong the temptation.

- **Fish Slow, Deep, and With Care:** It's common knowledge that when salmon enter freshwater, they begin fasting as part of the complex body changes they undergo prior to spawning. This doesn't mean that you can't get them to strike out of a reflexive feeding response, however. Careful presentations, fished slow and deep, are the rule, for salmon usually won't stray very far to pursue a lure, fly, or bait.

- **Use Super Sharp and Strong Hooks:** To varying degrees, the mouths of all salmon harden considerably once they enter freshwater; in chinook, coho, and chum species, mouths become hard as bone. For this reason, you must fish hooks that are especially sharp and strong.

- **Keep a Tight Line:** The "take" of a salmon is often little more than a tap or a slight tug; avoid slack line at all times.

- **Set the Hook Hard:** At the slightest indication of a pickup by a fish, drive your hook home, then hang on tight! A salmon's initial runs and jumps will be the most explosive and difficult to contain.

- **Play the Fish Smart:** Once you've hooked a salmon, keep your line and drag tight and try to maintain a downstream position so that the fish must fight both you and the river current. If a powerful fish should make it out more than 50 yards into the main current, you have four options: pursue it along the banks or by boat; continue pressure to try and turn it; break it off by tightening the drag all the way and pointing the rod at the fish; or ease off the pressure totally to try and coax it back in. Your experience, river conditions, type of gear, and the individual fish will determine the best strategy.

- **Draw the Fish Into Battle:** If a big fish sits and sulks in a pool, resisting all of the pressure you can muster, try one or more of these strategies: change position to gain better leverage; throw rocks to scare him into moving; release all pressure on the line to make him think he's free; or pound the palm of your hand into the butt of your rod to send vibrations through the line to scare the fish into moving.
- **Use a Landing Net:** When fishing from a boat or shore, a landing net can make things much easier when it's time to bring the fish in. Make sure the fish is ready—it should be resting on its side or finning slowly from exhaustion before you attempt to scoop it up. Have a fishing buddy ready with the net in the water and lead the fish gently into it while he scoops forward and upward. As soon as the fish is entirely within the bag, seal the mouth of the net with a quick turn of the wrist and pull it two-thirds out of the water and into hand. If you're planning on releasing the fish, keep some of the net—and the fish—in the water if possible (alongside the boat or in the shallows by shore).

- **If Releasing the Fish, Do It Gently:** Use stout needlenose pliers to release the hook. Don't attempt it by hand! When releasing the fish back into the water, if the salmon is totally exhausted and turns up on its side, gently cradle it in your hands (one hand gripping the "wrist" of the tail and the other supporting it beneath the belly) and rock it back and forth slightly to help it revive. Release it into the shallows or a slow current area when it is ready to swim away.
- **If Keeping the Fish for Food, Kill It Quickly:** If you plan on keeping the fish to eat, kill it right away. First stun it with a sharp blow to the top of the head (behind the eyes) with a blunt object, then take a sharp knife and sever the spine in back of the head. Clean the fish as soon as possible, throwing all offal into the water, then store in a cool, dry place.

About Catch-and-Release

As Alaska's population continues to grow, increasing numbers of people are fishing the state's accessible waters as well as its remote areas. Many sportfishers practice catch-and-release, taking only what they need for food while releasing undersized or over-limit fish. Whether or not Alaska remains a high-quality sportfishing destination depends on how many anglers choose to employ this practice. What follows is a guide to catch-and-release.

Tackle
- Use strong line to bring your catch in quickly.
- Fish caught with flies or lures survive more often than fish caught with bait.
- Overly large hooks can damage mouth parts or eyes.
- Small hooks may be taken deeply by fish.
- Use pliers to pinch barbs down.

Landing Your Catch
- Land your fish as carefully and quickly as possible.
- Avoid removing the fish from the water.
- Do not let fish flop in shallow water, over rocks, or on dry land.
- Use nets made with soft or knotless mesh.

Handling Your Catch
- Keep the fish in the water.
- Cradle the fish gently with both hands, one under its belly, one near its tail.
- Keep your fingers out of and away from the gills.
- Use wet cloth gloves or wet your hands when handling the fish.
- Never squeeze the fish.
- If someone is taking a photo of you with the fish, support the fish in the water.

Removing the Hook
- Remove the hook quickly and gently, keeping the fish underwater.
- Use long-nosed pliers or a hemostat to back the hook out.
- When a fish is hooked deeply, cut the line near the hook.
- Use steel hooks that will rust out quickly: *Avoid using stainless steel hooks.*
- Cut your line rather than injure an active fish.

Reviving Your Catch
- Point your fish into a slow current or gently move it back and forth until its gills are working properly and the fish can maintain its balance. Large fish may take some time to revive.

Releasing Your Catch
- When the fish recovers and attempts to swim out of your hands, let go.

Summary
- Land the fish quickly.
- Keep the fish in the water.
- Keep hands away from gills.
- Handle the fish gently.
- Back the hook out.
- Cut your line if the fish is hooked deeply.
- Support the fish facing into the current until it swims away.
- *Keep only the fish you need.*

Alaska Fishing Records

Alaska State Record fish and IGFA-certified All-Tackle,
Line, and Tippet Class Records

DOLLY VARDEN

Alaska State Record

| 19 lbs, 12.5 oz | Kelly River | 1991 | Ken Ubben |

All-Tackle

| 18 lbs, 9 oz | Mashutuk River | July 13, 1993 | Richard B. Evans |

Line   01 kg (2 lb)

| 7 lbs, 3 oz | Noatak River | July 8, 1988 | Kenneth T. Alt |

Line   02 kg (4 lb)

| 12 lbs, 1 oz | Sagavanirktok R. | July 8, 1991 | George William West |

Line   03 kg (6 lb)

| 16 lbs, 4 oz | Noatak River | July 30, 1994 | John L. Nicholson |

Line   04 kg (8 lb)

| 17 lbs, 9 oz | Wulik River | September 14, 1995 | Robert H. Mace |

Line   06 kg (12 lb)

| 18 lbs, 9 oz | Kivalina River | July 13, 1993 | Richard B. Evans |

Tippet 01 kg (2 lb)

| 7 lbs, 1 oz | Ugashik Narrows | October 4, 1995 | Gen. Norman Schwarzkopf |

Tippet 02 kg (4 lb)

| 5 lbs, 8 oz | Karluk River | September 5, 1993 | Norman S. Cohen, M.D. |

Tippet 03 kg (6 lb)

| 5 lbs | Kvichak River | October 10, 1995 | George Hapler Jr. |

Tippet 04 kg (8 lb)

| 12 lbs, 2 oz | Wulik River | July 18, 1992 | John A. Holland |

Tippet 06 kg (12 lb)

| 12 lbs, 12 oz | Wulik River | July 17, 1992 | Philip E. Driver |

Tippet 08 kg (16 lb)

| 12 lbs | Wulik River | July 9, 1990 | Col. Reeves Lippincott |

GRAYLING, ARCTIC

Alaska State Record

| 4 lbs, 13 oz | Ugashik Narrows | 1981 | Paul Kanitz |

Tippet 08 kg (16 lb)

| 3 lbs | Niukluk River | August 12, 1993 | Mo Tidemanis |

Tippet 10 kg (20 lb)

| 3 lbs, 3 oz | Niukluk River | August 7, 1993 | Mo Tidemanis |

HALIBUT, PACIFIC

All-Tackle

| 459 lbs | Unalaska Bay | 1996 | unknown |

Line   Women's-01 kg (2 lb)

| 26 lbs | Cape Muzon | May 26, 1990 | Marjorie Cushman |

Line   Men's-01 kg (2 lb)
25 lbs, 12 oz   Cook Inlet   August 2, 1986   Rick Townsend

Line   W-02 kg (4 lb)
70 lbs   Yasha Island   July 25, 1991   Dorothy A. Loros

Line   M-02 kg (4 lb)
44 lbs   Elfin Cove   September 8, 1989   Paul Leader

Line   W-04 kg (8 lb)
123 lbs   Basket Bay   August 12, 1988   Susan McCarty Grimes

Line   M-04 kg (8 lb)
244 lbs   Basket Bay   August 18, 1988   Gene Grimes

Line   W-06 kg (12 lb)
149 lbs, 8 oz   Cook Inlet   June 26, 1989   Jocelyn J. Everette

Line   W-08 kg (16 lb)
131 lbs   Douglas   September 13, 1986   Marsha L. Montag

Line   M-08 kg (16 lb)
165 lbs   Resurrection Bay   May 28, 1989   Earl D. Cagle

Line   M-10 kg (20 lb)
242 lbs, 6 oz   Funter Bay   July 27, 1988   Greg Anderson

Line   W-15 kg (30 lb)
214 lbs, 4 oz   Gustavus   August 24, 1987   Roxanna M. Andrews

Line   M-15 kg (30 lb)
356 lbs, 8 oz   Gastineau Chnl   Nov.r 8, 1986   Gregory C. Olsen

Line   W-24 kg (50 lb)
264 lbs   St. Lazaria Islan   August 24, 1986   Elaine M. Loopstra

Line   M-24 kg (50 lb)
344 lbs   Thomas Bay   September 13, 1986   Gordon S. Newhouse

Line   W-37 kg (80 lb)
368 lbs   Gustavus   July 5, 1991   Celia H. Dueitt

Line   M-37 kg (80 lb)
284 lbs, 6 oz   Gustavus   June 5, 1987   Anthony C. Manguso

Line   W-60 kg (130 lb)
237 lbs   Flat Island   August 19, 1988   Brenda K. Hearnsberger

Line   M-60 kg (130 lb)
350 lbs   Homer   June 30, 1982   Vern S. Foster

Tippet 02 kg (4 lb)
3 lbs, 12 oz   Chugach Island   September 7, 1988   E. Z. Marchant

Tippet 04 kg (8 lb)
74 lbs   Port Armstrong   July 19, 1990   Dick DeMars

Tippet 06 kg (12 lb)
51 lbs, 6 oz   Chrome Point   June 19, 1993   Lance P. Anderson

Tippet 08 kg (16 lb)
59 lbs   Port Armstrong   August 27, 1986   Tim Dunnagan

Tippet 10 kg (20 lb)
70 lbs, 8 oz   Chrome Point   June 18, 1993   Lindy Keirn

INCONNU

All-Tackle

53 lbs	Pah River	August 20, 1986	Lawrence E. Hudnall

Line   01 kg (2 lb)

41 lbs, 4 oz	Kobuk River	August 10, 1987	Lawrence E. Hudnall

Line   02 kg (4 lb)

38 lbs, 12 oz	Kobuk River	August 8, 1987	Lawrence E. Hudnall

Line   04 kg (8 lb)

39 lbs	Kobuk River	August 20, 1986	Daniel J. Hudnall

Line   06 kg (12 lb)

35 lbs	Kobuk River	August 7, 1987	Daniel J. Hudnall

Line   08 kg (16 lb)

36 lbs	Kobuk River	August 7, 1987	Lawrence E. Hudnall

Line   10 kg (20 lb)

53 lbs	Pah River	August 20, 1986	Lawrence E. Hudnall

Line   15 kg (30 lb)

34 lbs	Kobuk River	August 10, 1987	Daniel J. Hudnall

Line   24 kg (50 lb)

32 lbs	Kobuk River	August 12, 1987	Daniel J. Hudnall

Tippet 01 kg (2 lb)

21 lbs	Kobuk River	August 12, 1987	Lawrence E. Hudnall

Tippet 02 kg (4 lb)

27 lbs, 8 oz	Kobuk River	August 14, 1987	Lawrence E. Hudnall

Tippet 04 kg (8 lb)

33 lbs, 4 oz	Kobuk River	August 13, 1987	Lawrence E. Hudnall

Tippet 06 kg (12 lb)

18 lbs	Pah River	August 19, 1986	Lawrence E. Hudnall

Tippet 08 kg (16 lb)

30 lbs	Kobuk River	August 11, 1987	Daniel J. Hudnall

Tippet 10 kg (20 lb)

13 lbs	Holitna River	June 12, 1995	Jim Seegraves

PIKE, NORTHERN

Alaska State Record

38 lbs	Innoko River	1991	Jack Wagner

Line   01 kg (2 lb)

23 lbs, 15 oz	Innoko River	August 10, 1990	Rick Townsend

Line   02 kg (4 lb)

25 lbs, 8 oz	Yukon River	August 14, 1991	Dr. Craig Johnston

Line   03 kg (6 lb)

25 lbs, 4 oz	Hill Lake	August 9, 1994	Dr. Craig Johnston

Line   15 kg (30 lb)

34 lbs, 8 oz	Yukon	August 10, 1991	Bill Tenney

Tippet 02 kg (4 lb)

24 lbs, 12 oz	Gator Lake	August 17, 1992	Dr. Craig Johnston

Tippet 04 kg (8 lb)

25 lbs, 8 oz	Gator Lake	August 10, 1994	Dr. Craig Johnston

Tippet 10 kg (20 lb)

23 lbs, 8 oz	Yukon River	August 2, 1994	Lori Townsend

SALMON, CHINOOK

All-Tackle

97 lbs, 4 oz	Kenai River	May 17, 1985	Les Anderson

Line   01 kg (2 lb)

44 lbs, 12 oz	Kenai River	July 1, 1995	Raleigh Werking

Line   06 kg (12 lb)

67 lbs, 4 oz	Kenai River	July 31, 1986	Michael J. Fenton

Line   08 kg (16 lb)

77 lbs, 8 oz	Kenai River	July 18, 1985	Jerry Downey

Line   15 kg (30 lb)

97 lbs, 4 oz	Kenai River	May 17, 1985	Les Anderson

Line   24 kg (50 lb)

81 lbs, 4 oz	Cook Inlet	July 15, 1985	Dale C. Anderson

Line   37 kg (80 lb)

71 lbs, 4 oz	Kenai River	June 30, 1988	Nathaniel J. Anderson

Line   60 kg (130 lb)

63 lbs, 1 oz	Kenai River	July 2, 1994	Raleigh Werking

Tippet 02 kg (4 lb)

29 lbs	Karluk River	July 11, 1984	Rod Neubert

Tippet 06 kg (12 lb)

56 lbs, 14 oz	Kenai River	July 19, 1989	Walter E. Bottelsen

Tippet 10 kg (20 lb)

48 lbs	Kenai River	June 3, 1992	Guido Rahr III

SALMON, CHUM

All-Tackle

32 lbs	Behm Canal	June 7, 1985	Fredrick E. Thynes

Line   01 kg (2 lb)

15 lbs, 7 oz	Fish Creek	August 1, 1986	Jeff Trom

Line   02 kg (4 lb)

17 lbs, 5 oz	Fish Creek	August 1, 1986	Martin Vanderploeg

Line   06 kg (12 lb)

19 lbs	Ketchikan	July 18, 1987	Lee W. Putman

Tippet 01 kg (2 lb)

13 lbs	Pah River	August 18, 1986	Lawrence E. Hudnall

Tippet 02 kg (4 lb)

13 lbs, 9 oz	Baranof Island	July 28, 1988	Lawrence E. Hudnall

SALMON, COHO

Alaska State Record

26 lbs	Icy Strait	1976	Andrew Robbins

Line 01 kg (2 lb)

16 lbs, 1 oz	Kenai River	October 9, 1988	Pat K. Johnson

Line 02 kg (4 lb)

18 lbs, 1 oz	Karluk River	September 15, 1990	Burton R. Leed

Line 03 kg (6 lb)

18 lbs, 7 oz	Kiklukh River	October 10, 1995	George R. Davis

Line 04 kg (8 lb)

19 lbs, 8 oz	Situk River	September 20, 1984	Melvin E. Snook

Line 06 kg (12 lb)

22 lbs	Kiklukh River	September 22, 1995	Harold F. Baritell Sr.

Line 24 kg (50 lb)

17 lbs, 4 oz	Kenai River	September 14, 1984	Paul W. Pearson

Tippet 01 kg (2 lb)

15 lbs, 2 oz	Kenai River	January 23, 1991	Don A. Middleton

Tippet 02 kg (4 lb)

17 lbs, 13 oz	Karluk River	September 15, 1990	Burton R. Leed

Tippet 03 kg (6 lb)

18 lbs, 8 oz	Kiklukh River	Nov. 30, 1994	Alex Brant

Tippet 04 kg (8 lb)

19 lbs, 9 oz	Kodiak Island	September 23, 1992	Paul Leader

Tippet 06 kg (12 lb)

21 lbs	Karluk River	September 6, 1988	Gary R. Dubiel

Tippet 08 kg (16 lb)

18 lbs, 2 oz	Kiklukh River	October 12, 1994	George R. Davis

Tippet 10 kg (20 lb)

19 lbs, 4 oz	Karluk River	September 4, 1992	Burton R. Leed

SALMON, PINK

Alaska State Record

12 lbs, 9 oz	Moose River	1974	Steven Lee

Line 01 kg (2 lb)

10 lbs, 4 oz	Karluk River	July 13, 1984	Rod Neubert

Line 02 kg (4 lb)

8 lbs, 9 oz	Kenai River	August 20, 1988	Pat K. Johnson

Line 03 kg (6 lb)

11 lbs, 8 oz	Karluk River	July 13, 1984	Rod Neubert

Line 06 kg (12 lb)

12 lbs, 9 oz	Moose River	August 17, 1974	Steven Alan Lee

Tippet 01 kg (2 lb)

10 lbs	Karluk River	July 13, 1984	Rod Neubert

Tippet 02 kg (4 lb)
11 lbs, 8 oz	Karluk River	July 10, 1984	Rod Neubert

Tippet 03 kg (6 lb)
6 lbs, 8 oz	Alagnak River	August 6, 1994	Terry Gun

Tippet 03 kg (6 lb) Tie
6 lbs, 8 oz	Ungalikthluk R.	August 14, 1994	Robert M. Nutting
6 lbs, 8 oz	American River	August 21, 1994	Jonathan J. Wexler

Tippet 04 kg (8 lb)
6 lbs, 12 oz	Douglas Island	July 23, 1989	Andrea U. Warner

Tippet 06 kg (12 lb)
6 lbs, 13 oz	Salmon Creeek	July 31, 1985	Bob Garfield

Tippet 08 kg (16 lb)
5 lbs, 15 oz	Wolverine Creek	July 27, 1990	Lawrence E. Hudnall

Tippet 10 kg (20 lb)
4 lbs, 4 oz	Togiak River	August 15, 1994	Robert M. Nutting

SALMON, SOCKEYE

Alaska State Record
16 lbs	Kenai River	1974	Chuck Leach

All-Tackle
15 lbs, 3 oz	Kenai River	August 9, 1987	Stan Roach

Line 01 kg (2 lb)
12 lbs, 5 oz	Russian River	August 20, 1987	Martin Vanderploeg

Line 02 kg (4 lb)
10 lbs, 15 oz	Russian River	August 14, 1984	Martin Vanderploeg

Line 03 kg (6 lb)
12 lbs, 2 oz	Russian River	August 20, 1987	Dale Hallman

Line 06 kg (12 lb)
14 lbs, 12 oz	Koktuli River	July 17, 1993	Warren J. Redmond

Line 08 kg (16 lb)
14 lbs, 8 oz	Kenai River	August 2, 1994	Archer J. Richardson

Line 10 kg (20 lb)
13 lbs	Kenai River	July 3, 1990	Jesse J. Zalonis

Line 15 kg (30 lb)
15 lbs, 3 oz	Kenai River	August 9, 1987	Stan Roach

Tippet 01 kg (2 lb)
11 lbs, 5 oz	Baranof Island	July 29, 1988	Lawrence E. Hudnall

Tippet 02 kg (4 lb)
11 lbs, 8 oz	Prince of Wales Island	August 3, 1989	Lawrence E. Hudnall

Tippet 03 kg (6 lb)
11 lbs, 8 oz	Kulik River	August 10, 1994	Robert M. Nutting

Tippet 04 kg (8 lb)
11 lbs, 12 oz	Kenai River	September 6, 1987	Galen (Skip) Perry

Tippet 06 kg (12 lb)

14 lbs, 3 oz   Russian River   August 16, 1987   Marcy Yentzer

Tippet 08 kg (16 lb)

14 lbs, 8 oz   Mulchatna River   July 16, 1993   Alan Haynes

Tippet 10 kg (20 lb)

11 lbs, 8 oz   Ugashik River   July 17, 1992   Ted Hartley

TROUT, RAINBOW

All-Tackle

42 lbs, 2 oz   Bell Island   June 22, 1970   David Robert White

Tippet 10 kg (20 lb)

15 lbs, 7 oz   Kvichak River   October 9, 1995   George Halper Jr.

Index

BOLD PAGE NUMBERS INDICATE MAIN LISTINGS

About the Authors

René Limeres

Wilderness guide and outdoors writer/ photographer René Limeres spends busy summers leading remote fishing expeditions in Alaska and Russia. René is the creator and publisher of the award-winning *Alaska Hunting and Fishing Calendar,* and former staff editor of *Alaska Outdoors Magazine.* His articles and photographs have appeared in *Alaska Magazine, Alaska Outdoors Magazine, Alaska Roadside Salmon Angler's Guide, Alaska Angling Guide, Salmon-Trout Steelheader Magazine, Flyfisherman Magazine,* and the *Alaska Professional Hunter.* René lives in Anchorage.

Gunnar Pedersen

Growing up in Trondheim, Norway, Gunnar Pedersen developed his passion for fishing along the rugged coast, and fly-fished for trout and salmon on the country's many pristine rivers and lakes. Gunnar is a professional wilderness guide, author of *The Highway Angler,* and a frequent writer for local sporting magazines and newspapers. He has lived in Alaska since 1979.

About the Contributors

Ken Alt

Ken Alt has been involved with the fisheries of western and northern Alaska for nearly 30 years. As a research biologist for the Alaska Department of Fish and Game in the 1960s, Ken conducted most of the original fish surveys and stream cataloging for a major portion of the state, in addition to pioneering studies of the life history and movements of Alaska sheefish. Retired and living in Fairbanks, Ken now works as a fisheries consultant and still spends considerable time in the field.

Thomas Cappiello

Born in Santa Barbara, California, Thomas Cappiello is a lifelong fisherman. He attended Humboldt State University for a B.S in fisheries and while in school worked in Alaska as a seasonal aid for the U.S. Forest Service. Since graduating, he has worked for the Alaska Department of Fish and Game and the

Prince William Sound Aquaculture Corporation. Cappiello recently completed his master's degree in fisheries at the University of Alaska, Fairbanks.

Robert Farmer

Lifelong Alaskan Bob Farmer grew up the son of a popular river lodge owner and spent his youth sampling the still-unexploited angling treasures of the Susitna Valley. Later forays as a surveyor into remote western and arctic regions provided a broad perspective on the state's vast angling potential. Today he maintains a world-class heli-fishing operation out of his Deshka River Lodge and is a respected authority on sportfishing in the state.

Pete Hardy

Born in Oregon to a U.S. Forest Service family, Pete Hardy moved to Alaska while still a lad, getting his first taste of great fishing at an early age. His family relocated to the Lower 48 when he was 14, and Pete continued to fish warmwater species through his teens. At age 26, he returned to Alaska as a volunteer worker in the village of Grayling on the Yukon River (one can only guess what kind of fish Pete caught there). In 1974, Pete moved to Anchorage, where he developed an interest in halibut fishing. He has served on the board of directors of the Alaska Sportfishing Association and leads "Halibut Basics" seminars for the group, the Great Alaskan Sportsman Show, local retailers, and at a variety of private venues.

Bill Hickman

As an artist, Bill Hickman is remarkably versatile—able to move freely and proficiently through a variety of mediums, from wood carving to computer graphics. His illustrations and designs have enhanced many publications for business, government, and the public. Raised in Iowa, Bill came to Alaska more than 25 years ago, built a cabin in the woods, raised a family, then surrendered to the easy city life in Anchorage. His illustration talents can be tapped at Last Minute Publishing, 2221 Muldoon Road, Anchorage, AK 99504, (907) 337-0482.

Gary Souza

A confirmed Northwest steelhead addict for years, Gary Souza was raised in California. He "apprenticed" on the coastal streams of his home state and other big rivers of the Northwest and British Co-

lumbia before making his pilgrimage to Alaska 13 years ago. Since then, he has spent the better part of every year fishing for trout and salmon in Southeast waters. Gary has conducted steelhead seminars and served as chairman and vice-chair of the Tongass Sportfishing Association chapter of Trout Unlimited for the past five years. He holds bachelor's and master's degrees in theology from Abilene Christian University.

Mark Whitfield

Mark Whitfield's pen and ink talent is a throwback to the great heyday of outdoor literature illustration. His distinct style has been seen in sporting publications such as the nationally acclaimed *Alaska Hunting and Fishing Calendar* and *Alaska Outdoors Magazine,* as well as dozens of newsletters, brochures, and business logos.

Steve Wottlin

Steve Wottlin hails from the Pacific Northwest, where he spent a considerable part of his formative years chasing steelhead and salmon in the region's bays and big rivers. His deep love of fishing and the outdoors prompted a move to Alaska and a stint as a professional wilderness fishing guide. His expertise is vast and respected; he has authored fishing articles for many outdoors publications and is consulted regularly for his knowledge of adventure recreation and fly-fishing in Alaska. He currently lives in Anchorage with his wife and works as a teacher.

FOGHORN ⛛ OUTDOORS

Founded in 1985, Foghorn Press has quickly become one of the country's premier publishers of outdoor recreation guidebooks. Through its unique Books Building Community program, Foghorn Press supports community environmental issues, such as park, trail, and water ecosystem preservation.

Foghorn Press books are available throughout the United States in bookstores and some outdoor retailers. If you cannot find the title you are looking for, visit Foghorn's Web site at http://www.foghorn.com or call 1-800-FOGHORN.

The Complete Guide Series

- *New England Hiking* (416 pp) $18.95
- *New England Camping* (520 pp) $19.95
- *Utah and Nevada Camping* (384 pp) $18.95
- *Southwest Camping* (544 pp) $17.95
- *Baja Camping* (294 pp) $12.95
- *California Camping* (848 pp) $19.95
- *California Hiking* (688 pp) $20.95—New 3rd edition
- *California Waterfalls* (408 pp) $17.95
- *California Fishing* (768 pp) $20.95—New 4th edition
- *California Golf* (864 pp) $20.95—New 7th edition
- *California Beaches* (640 pp) $19.95
- *California Boating and Water Sports* (608 pp) $19.95
- *California In-Line Skating* (480 pp) $19.95
- *Tahoe* (678 pp) $20.95
- *Pacific Northwest Camping* (720 pp) $19.95
- *Pacific Northwest Hiking* (648 pp) $20.95—New 2nd edition
- *Washington Fishing* (528 pp) $19.95

The National Outdoors Series

- *America's Secret Recreation Areas—Your Recreation Guide to the Bureau of Land Management's Wild Lands of the West* (640 pp) $17.95
- *America's Wilderness—The Complete Guide to More Than 600 National Wilderness Areas* (592 pp) $19.95
- *The Camper's Companion—The Pack-Along Guide for Better Outdoor Trips* (464 pp) $15.95
- *Wild Places: 20 Journeys Into the North American Outdoors* (305 pp) $15.95

A book's page length and availability are subject to change.

For more information, call 1-800-FOGHORN,
e-mail: foghorn@well.com, or write to:
Foghorn Press
340 Bodega Avenue
Petaluma, CA 94952

Alaska Overview Map

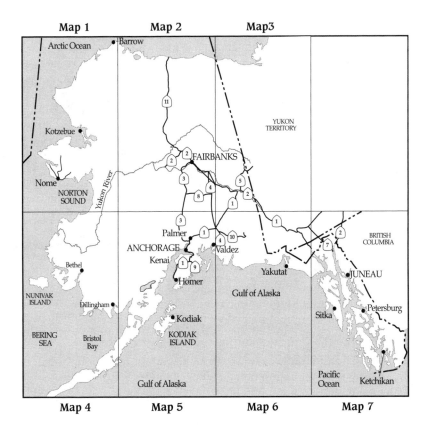

Map 1   Map 2   Map3

Arctic Ocean   Barrow

Kotzebue

YUKON
TERRITORY

FAIRBANKS

Nome

Yukon River

NORTON
SOUND

BRITISH
COLUMBIA

Palmer

ANCHORAGE

Kenai   Valdez

Bethel

Yakutat

JUNEAU

NUNIVAK
ISLAND

Homer

Gulf of Alaska

Dillingham

Petersburg

BERING
SEA

Bristol
Bay

Kodiak

Sitka

KODIAK
ISLAND

Pacific
Ocean   Ketchikan

Gulf of Alaska

Map 4   Map 5   Map 6   Map 7

Looking for a HOT Fishing Spot?

These Alaska Road & Recreation Maps are a COOL Deal!

Kenai River

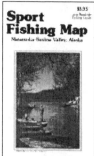

Matanuska-Susitna Valley

U.S. Geologic Survey topographic maps with added local details showing buildings and the best spots to fish.

Be sure to check out our other Alaska Road & Recreation Maps. They'll lead you to all the spectacular roadside scenery plus some of the best fishing spots in the state. Each one will take you on a new Alaska adventure.

Title	Price	Quantity	Total
Kenai River	4.95		
Sport Fishing Map – Mat-Su Valley	3.95		
Anchorage & Vicinity	4.95		
Big Lake & Pt. MacKenzie	4.95		
Kachemak Bay	4.95		
Kenai Lake & Vicinity	2.95		
Kenai Peninsula	2.95		
Matanuska Valley	4.95		
Parks Highway	4.95		
	Shipping & Handling	$1.50 first map .50 each add'l	
To order:		Total	

To order:

Todd Communications
203 W. 15th Ave., Suite 102AF
Anchorage, AK 99501
(907) 274-8633 **Fax (907) 276-6858**
e-mail: fishalaska@toddcom.com

Send check or credit card number (VISA or MC) - sorry, no AMEX
Please include expiration date.
fax or e-mail to:
fishalaska@toddcom.com